THE SLAVIC LANGUAGES

The Slavic group of languages – the fourth largest Indo-European sub-group – is one of the major language families of the modern world. With 297 million speakers, Slavic comprises 13 languages split into three groups: South Slavic, which includes Bosnian, Serbian and Croatian; East Slavic, which includes Russian and Ukrainian; and West Slavic, which includes Polish, Czech and Slovak. This book, written by two leading scholars in Slavic linguistics, presents a survey of all aspects of the linguistic structure of the Slavic languages, considering in particular those languages that enjoy official status. As well as covering the central issues of phonology, morphology, syntax, word-formation, lexicology and typology, the authors discuss Slavic dialects, sociolinguistic issues and the socio-historical evolution of the Slavic languages.

Accessibly written and comprehensive in its coverage, this book will be welcomed by scholars and students of Slavic languages, as well as by linguists across the many branches of the discipline.

ROLAND SUSSEX is Professor of Applied Language Studies at the University of Queensland, and formerly Professor of Russian at the University of Melbourne. He has taught a wide variety of courses in linguistics and applied language studies, including the linguistic description of the Slavic languages. He has previously published *A Bibliography of Computer-Aided Language Learning* (with David Bradley and Graham Scott, 1986), and *Computers, Language Learning and Language Teaching* (with Khurshid Ahmad, Margaret Rogers and Greville Corbett, Cambridge University Press, 1985).

PAUL CUBBERLEY was Senior Research Fellow in Linguistics at the University of Melbourne until 2001, and was previously Head of Russian there. He has also taught Czech, Polish, Old Church Slavonic, comparative Slavonic linguistics and the history of the Russian language. His previous publications include *The Suprasegmental Features in Slavonic Phonetic Typology* (1980), and most recently *Russian: a Linguistic Introduction* (Cambridge University Press, 2002).

CAMBRIDGE LANGUAGE SURVEYS

General editors
P. Austin (*University of London*)
J. Bresnan (*Stanford University*)
B. Comrie (*Max Planck Institute for Evolutionary Anthropology, Leipzig*)
S. Crain (*University of Maryland*)
W. Dressler (*University of Vienna*)
C. Ewen (*University of Leiden*)
R. Lass (*University of Cape Town*)
D. Lightfoot (*University of Maryland*)
K. Rice (*University of Toronto*)
I. Roberts (*University of Cambridge*)
S. Romaine (*University of Oxford*)
N. V. Smith (*University College, London*)

This series offers general accounts of the major language families of the world, with volumes organized either on a purely genetic basis or on a geographical basis, whichever yields the most convenient and intelligible grouping in each case. Each volume compares and contrasts the typological features of the languages it deals with. It also treats the relevant genetic relationships, historical development and sociolinguistic issues arising from their role and use in the world today. The books are intended for linguists from undergraduate level upwards, but no special knowledge of the languages under consideration is assumed. Volumes such as those on Australia and the Amazon Basin are also of wider relevance, as the future of the languages and their speakers raises important social and political issues.

Volumes already published include
Chinese *Jerry Norman*
The languages of Japan *Masayoshi Shibatani*
Pidgins and Creoles (Volume I: Theory and structure; Volume II: Reference survey) *John A. Holm*
The Indo-Aryan languages *Colin Masica*
The Celtic languages *edited by Donald MacAulay*
The Romance languages *Rebecca Posner*
The Amazonian languages *edited by R. M. W. Dixon and Alexandra Y. Aikhenvald*
The languages of Native North America *Marianne Mithun*
The Korean language *Ho-Him Sohn*
Australian languages *R. M. W. Dixon*
The Dravidian languages *Bhadriraju Krishnamurti*
The languages of the Andes *Willem Adelaar with Pieter Muysken*
The Slavic languages *Roland Sussex and Paul Cubberley*

THE SLAVIC LANGUAGES

ROLAND SUSSEX

PAUL CUBBERLEY

 CAMBRIDGE
UNIVERSITY PRESS

CAMBRIDGE UNIVERSITY PRESS
Cambridge, New York, Melbourne, Madrid, Cape Town,
Singapore, São Paulo, Delhi, Tokyo, Mexico City

Cambridge University Press
The Edinburgh Building, Cambridge CB2 8RU, UK

Published in the United States of America by Cambridge University Press, New York

www.cambridge.org
Information on this title: www.cambridge.org/9780521294485

First published 2006
First paperback edition 2011

A catalogue record for this publication is available from the British Library

ISBN 978-0-521-22315-7 Hardback
ISBN 978-0-521-29448-5 Paperback

For Bogusia and Gladys
Matthew and Joanna
Nadine and Michelle

CONTENTS

PREFACE

Like Rebecca Posner, whose *The Romance languages* in this series was published in 1996, we have often been daunted by the size and complexity of the task. Slavic is not only a large group of languages but it is also the most written-about (see the Introduction).

Over the last decade Slavic has also been arguably the most externally unstable of the Indo-European language families. The fall of Euro-Communism was marked most dramatically by the tearing down of the Berlin Wall in 1989 and the subsequent dissolution of the USSR, the Warsaw Pact, COMECON and the structures and infrastructures of what US President Ronald Reagan called the "evil empire". What emerged from the political rebirth of the Slavic lands has turned out to be a linguistic landscape where some stable and persisting features have found themselves side-by-side with a dynamic, unstable and volatile cultural context. The Slavic languages are living in more than just interesting times. It has been our task to try and seize them in motion. We have spent most of our academic lives working in these languages, and this book is partly by way of thanks to the stimulus that working in and on Slavic has given us, and to our colleagues in Slavic around the world who have contributed to the discipline.

A book like this has a dual audience. On the one hand we are addressing Slavists who need to widen their knowledge about other Slavic languages – scholars who know some Russian, say, and are curious about the other Slavic languages. On the other hand are students and scholars of languages and linguistics with no particular knowledge of a Slavic language. This double focus makes for difficulties of selection and presentation. We have tried to write to, and for, both audiences.

We have also tried to meet the needs of both the consecutive reader and the reference reader, who needs to find how, say, questions are formed in East Slavic. We do tell a story of Slavic, but the text and index are structured so as to make it possible to locate specific issues, and cross-references allow navigation through such issues.

The survey is a relentless genre. In a hugely documented language family like Slavic, survey authors are constantly faced with major decisions of omission, inclusion and angle of view. We have had to weigh our favorite crannies of a language, and cherished idiosyncrasies of this corner of phonology, or that lexical oddity, against the big picture, but at the same time a big picture with enough detail to give a true feel for what snaps into focus when the camera zooms in, as well as a valid panorama when it zooms out again.

We have culled the examples for what we analyze as the eleven Slavic languages from many sources, published, web-based, oral and personal, and we are sometimes not sure where some of them originated. We apologize to previous authors if we have borrowed their examples without acknowledgment, and invite colleagues to use ours freely in the same spirit of scholarly investigation.

ACKNOWLEDGMENTS

Among the many friends and colleagues who have contributed to the preparation of this book, we would like to extend particular thanks to Ian Press, who read the manuscript for the Press and made many invaluable suggestions; to Bernard Comrie, Grev Corbett, Roger Lass, John Lyons and Ron Sussex; to Judith Ayling, Kate Brett and Helen Barton at Cambridge University Press; and, most of all to our families, who have patiently supported this complex project over many reefs and through many mountain passes.

Czech

Slovak

Slovenian

Bosnian/
Serbian/
Croatian

Macedonian

Bulgarian

Russian

Ukrainian

Belarusian

Polish

Sorbian   Upper
          Lower

NORWAY

FINLAND

NORWAY

SWEDEN

DENMARK

R U S S I A

GERMANY

Lower

Upper

POLAND

BELARUS

CZECH
REP.

SLOVAKIA

UKRAINE

AUSTRIA

HUNGARY

ITALY

ROMANIA

BLACK SEA

BULGARIA

ALBANIA

GREECE

TURKEY

0

Introduction

0.1 Survey

This book presents a survey of the modern Slavic languages – known as "Slavonic" languages in Britain and some of the Commonwealth countries[1] – seen from the point of view of their genetic and typological properties, their emergence and standing as national languages and selected sociolinguistic characteristics.

The language survey as a genre, and as defined in the description of this series, is not the same as a comprehensive comparative grammar. The survey does require breadth, to cover the full range of languages; and selective depth, to identify and highlight the specific properties of the language family as a whole, and the properties of sub-families and languages within the family. Our treatment is deliberately selective, and we concentrate on topics and features which contribute to the typology of the members of the Slavic language family.

We have tried to achieve this balance with two goals in view: to present an overview of the Slavic languages, combined with sufficient detail and examples to form a sound empirical basis; and to provide an entry point into the field for linguistically informed and interested readers who do not already command a Slavic language.

0.2 The Slavic languages in the world

The Slavic languages are one of the major language families of the modern world. In the current world population of over 6 billion the most populous language family is Indo-European, with over 40 percent. Within Indo-European Slavic

---

[1] North America favors "Slavic", while (British) Commonwealth countries prefer "Slavonic". North Americans usually pronounce "Slavic" and "Slavist" with the vowel [a], corresponding to [æ] in British English. This dual nomenclature is not found in other major languages of scholarship: French *slave*, German *slawisch*, Russian *slavjánskij*.

is the fourth largest sub-family, with around 300 million speakers, after Indic, Romance and Germanic, and ahead of Iranian, Greek, Albanian and Baltic.

0.3   Languages, variants and nomenclature

Modern Slavic falls into three major groups, according to linguistic and historical factors (table 0.1). We shall concentrate on the Slavic languages which enjoy official status in modern times, and have an accepted cultural and functional standing: Slovenian; Croatian, Bosnian and Serbian; Bulgarian and Macedonian in South Slavic (2.2); Russian, Belarusian and Ukrainian in East Slavic (2.3); and Upper and Lower Sorbian, Polish, Czech and Slovak, in West Slavic (2.4). The status of Bosnian, Croatian and Serbian is explained in more detail below. In listing Montenegrin as a "sub-national variety" we simply assert that it is not the language of an independent state, nor an officially designated language.

We shall also make considerable reference to Proto-Slavic, the Slavic dialect which emerged from Indo-European as the parent language of Slavic; and to Old Church Slavonic, originally a South Slavic liturgical and literary language now extinct except in church use, which is of major importance as a cultural, linguistic and sociolinguistic model. Both Proto-Slavic and Old Church Slavonic are fundamental to an understanding of the modern languages, especially in the chapters

Table 0.1. *Modern Slavic families and sub-families*

	National languages	Sub-national varieties	Extinct languages
South Slavic	Slovenian Croatian Bosnian Serbian Bulgarian Macedonian	Montenegrin	Old Church Slavonic
East Slavic	Russian Belarusian Ukrainian	Rusyn (Rusnak) Ruthenian	
West Slavic	Sorbian (Upper and Lower) Polish Czech Slovak	Kashubian Lachian	Polabian Slovincian

on phonology and morphology. Other Slavic languages/dialects will be used as relevant for illustration and contrast.

The modern Slavic languages exhibit a moderate degree of mutual comprehensibility, at least at the conversational level. The ability of Slavs to communicate with other Slavs across language boundaries is closely related to linguistic and geographical distance. East Slavs can communicate with each other quite well. So can Czechs and Slovaks, Poles and Sorbs, and indeed all West Slavs to some extent. Among the South Slavs, Bulgarian and Macedonian are inter-communicable, as are Bosnian, Croatian and Serbian, to varying degrees (2.2.4).

The Slavic languages and variants discussed in this book are listed in table 0.1. We adopt the convention of listing the three major families in the order South, East, West, which allows for a convenient discussion of historical events. Within each family we follow the order north to south, and within that west to east; languages in columns 2 and 3 are related to those within the same sub-family in column 1. The geographical distribution of the national languages is shown in the map on page xx.

There are also some important issues of nomenclature. The names of the languages and countries in English can vary according to convention and, to some extent, according to personal preference. We use the most neutral current terms in English. A useful distinction is sometimes made in English between the nominal ethnonym and the general adjective, e.g. "Serb", "Slovene", "Croat", for the ethnonym *vs* "-ian" for the adjective: "Serbian", "Slovenian", "Croatian"; "Slav" is also used as an ethnonym. We have used "-ian" for the languages, following common practice.

The word "language" has a major symbolic significance among the Slavs. A variety which warrants the label "language" powerfully reinforces the ethnic sense of identity. Conversely, "variants" look sub-national and so lack status and prestige. A typical case is Croatian: under Tito's Republic of Yugoslavia, Croatian was one of the two national variants of Serbo-Croatian. But the Croats fought vigorously from the 1960s for the recognition of Croatian as a "language", for instance in the constitution of the Republic of Croatia (Naylor, 1980), a battle which they won with the establishment of the independent Republic of Croatia in 1991.

The criteria relevant to language-hood also vary. For any two variants, the factors which will tend to class them as languages include mutual unintelligibility, formal differentiation, separate ethnic identity and separate political status. Sometimes politics and ethnicity win over intelligibility, as happened with Croatian and Serbian, and now with the recently created Bosnian: Bosnia entered the United Nations in 1992, accompanied by the emergence of the Bosnian language. Sorbian presents a very different profile: numerically small in population terms, and with no political autonomy, Upper and Lower Sorbian show significant formal differences, though they are mutually intelligible to a substantial degree. We have classed them as variants of a single language, Sorbian. The reasons for such classifications for different languages and varieties are given in chapter 3. We aim broadly, where the linguistic data warrant it, to respect the declared identity and linguistic allegiance of the different Slavic speakers. In using the term "language" we mean a defined variety with formal coherence and standardization, and some cultural and political status.

0.3.1   South Slavic

"Yugoslavia" is also written "Jugoslavia", or "Jugoslavija", following Croatian usage. The name means "south Slavdom". We favor "Yugoslavia" as being more common in English usage. Until 2003 Serbia, including Montenegro, continued to use the name Yugoslavia/Jugoslavia. The Federal Republic of Yugoslavia (commonly abbreviated as "FRY") was admitted to the United Nations in 2000. In early 2003 legislation paved the way for the separation of Montenegro and Serbia within three years.

"Slovenian" is also known as "Slovene", especially in British usage. We prefer the former, bringing it into line with the other South Slavic languages Bosnian, Croatian (also "Croat"), Serbian, Macedonian and Bulgarian.

"Croatian", "Bosnian" and "Serbian" merit special comment, and the relation of Croatian and Serbian to each other and to "Serbo-Croatian" (also "Serbo-Croat") is culturally, ethnically and linguistically highly sensitive (2.2.4). Serbo-Croatian was negotiated in 1850 as a supra-ethnic national language to link the Serbs and Croats. It survived with some rough periods until the 1980s, when it was effectively dissolved by the secession of the Croats as they established an independent Croatia. Bosnia then separated from Serbia in 1992. "Serbo-Croatian" is consequently now an anachronism from the political point of view, but there is still an important linguistic sense in which Croatian, Bosnian and Serbian belong to a common language grouping. For this reason we use the abbreviation "B/C/S" to cover phenomena which are common to these three languages. We shall use "Serbo-Croatian" in relation to scholarship specifically referring to it (or to common elements of the former standard, now the three modern standards). "Bosnian" was generally assumed to be included under "Serbo-Croatian" before the creation of the state of Bosnia. Bosnian, Croatian and Serbian will be relevant to such scholarship in differing degrees.

Montenegrin, a western variety of Serbian, has also been proposed for language-hood by Montenegrin nationalists. However, Montenegrin is not fully standardized, and is properly considered at this stage as a sub-national western variety of Serbian.

"Bulgarian", though the name originally belonged to a non-Slavic invader (2.2.2), is an uncontroversial name for the language and inhabitants of contemporary Bulgaria, reinforced by more than a millennium of literacy.

The new name of the former Yugoslav Republic of Macedonia (also "FYROM") is currently unresolved, with the Greek government claiming prior historical rights to the name "Macedonia". In this book we shall use "FYR Macedonia", the common current political compromise for the "Former Yugoslav Republic of Macedonia". The name of the Macedonian language is also disputed by the Greeks and Bulgarians, but we shall follow the established Slavists' convention and use "Macedonian", since there is no other language competing for this name (2.2.3).

0.3.2 East Slavic

"Russian" was also known as "Great Russian", a term dating from the days of Imperial Russia (–1917), though it was also used in the Russian-language imperialist policies of the USSR, especially in the 1930s and 1940s. "Great Russian" is now of historical interest only. "Russia" was sometimes loosely used in English during the time of the USSR to refer to the USSR itself.

"Ukrainian" was formerly known as "Little Russian", as distinct from "Great Russian", and thought by some to imply that Ukrainian was a subordinate variety. This term has now been erased by nationalistic pressures in Ukraine. Ukrainian has sometimes also been misnamed "Ruthenian", a name used especially before 1945, when much of this area became part of Soviet Ukraine, to designate the Transcarpathian dialects around Prešov in Slovakia. Nowadays "Ruthenian" is used mainly for immigrants from this area in the USA and in the Vojvodina area of former Yugoslavia (Shevelov, 1993: 996).

Ukrainians prefer English "Ukraine" to "The Ukraine" and Russian "*v Ukraine*" to "*na Ukraine*" for 'in Ukraine'. In each case the second form suggests a region rather than a country. We shall follow their English preference.

"Belarusian" was known as "Belorussian" before independence in 1991, reflecting the Russian spelling of the language. Belarusians have always used (and still use) *belarúskij*. After the dissolution of the USSR, national sentiment moved the Belarusians to differentiate their language from Russian. Belarusian was also known in English as "White Russian" (the root *bel-* means 'white'). The official name of the modern country is *Belarus* (Belarusian *Belarús'*), not the former *Belorussia*, hence "Belarusian" is the most suitable English form; some also call it

"Belarusan". These names have no specific connection with the anti-Communist White Russians of the years following the Russian Revolution.

The name "Rusyn" (or "Rusnak") has been used in various senses, sometimes overlapping with Ukrainian. There is disagreement over whether Rusyn is a dialect of Ukrainian or independent. One contemporary designation is for a group of about 25,000–50,000 speakers of an East Slovak dialect who now live in the Vojvodina area of Yugoslavia. Magocsi (1992) marks the proclamation of a new Slavic literary language in East Slovakia, the west of Ukraine and south-east Poland around Lemko. They claim 800,000–1,000,000 speakers for Rusyn. This declaration has not so far been matched by wider recognition outside the Rusyn area. Shevelov calls Rusyn 'an independent standard micro-language' (1993: 996).

0.3.3   West Slavic

"Czechoslovak", sometimes used for the language of the former Czechoslovak Republic, is a misnomer. Czech and Slovak are distinct languages, and the official languages of the modern Czech and Slovak Republics, respectively.

"Sorb" and "Sorbian" are equivalent, but this language is also sometimes known as "Wendish", a term which now can have pejorative connotations in German, and which must also be distinguished from "Windish" or "Windisch", the name normally given to a group of Slovenian dialects in Austria. "Lusatian", another name used for the language (e.g. by de Bray, 1980c), properly refers to any inhabitant of Lusatia, the homeland of the Sorbs in modern Germany, irrespective of race or language. The language is also sometimes known as "Saxon Lusatian" and "Sorabe" (the regular French term). We shall use "Sorbian", following Stone, (1972, 1993a), leaving "Sorb" as the ethnonym.

Polish is one of the least controversial ethnonyms and linguanyms among the Slavs. Although the political status of Poland has varied widely across the centuries, the area of the Poles and the Polish language, centred approximately around Warsaw, have been relatively more stable.

Rusyn, which overlaps between the West and East Slavic areas, is discussed above under "East Slavic".

Kashubian (Polish *kaszubski*) is also known as "Cassubian" (Stone, 1993b). Although it is variously reported as numbering around 300,000 speakers, Ethnologue (see table 0.2) has it at only 3,000, with most of the speakers using dialectal Polish. Kashubian lacks most of the linguistic and social determinants of language-hood, and we will treat it as a north-western variety of Polish.

In this book we regard Lachian, a numerically small variety of Czech, as a dialect.

Table 0.2. *Slavic languages: numbers of speakers following Ethnologue (www.sil.org)*

Language	Total speakers	Homeland speakers	Country
South Slavic			
Serbo-Croatian	21 million	10.2 million	Bosnia, Croatia, Serbia
Bulgarian	9 million	8 million	Bulgaria
Slovenian	2 million	1.7 million	Slovenia
Macedonian	2 million	1.4 million	FYR Macedonia
East Slavic			
Russian	167 million	153.7 million	Russia
Ukrainian	47 million	31.1 million	Ukraine
Belarusian	10.2 million	7.9 million	Belarus
West Slavic			
Polish	44 million	36.6 million	Poland
Czech	12 million	10 million	Czech Republic
Slovak	5.6 million	4.9 million	Slovak Republic
Kashubian	3,000	3,000	Poland
Sorbian	69,000	69,000	Germany
Total (millions)	319.8 +	265.5 +	

Note: The figures for Sorbian are Ethnologue's estimate for total speakers, but many are Sorbian ~ German bilinguals, and the total figure for primary users is probably under 30,000.

A common feature of the modern Slavic "literary" languages – the Slavs use this term for the written standard – is a strong regard for the integrity of the national language as a kind of symbolic monument. There is strong centralized regulation of the language, and highly developed "corpus planning" to establish and maintain the languages' identity and purity. While regional variation is acknowledged and encouraged, social variation and sub-"literary" use are treated with some caution. This care for managing the languages is one of the strongest continuities between pre-Communist and Communist conceptions of language. It has begun to break down in the post-Communist era, when the concept of "literary" language has been broadened to allow much more slang, vernacular usage and creativity, including borrowing from Western languages, especially English.

Since the fall of Communism there has also been a growing pressure to ethnic self-determination, which has resulted in the emergence of national language movements in several areas of the Slavic world. We shall discuss the re-differentiation of Belarusian and Ukrainian from Russian in chapters 2 and 11. Most of the tension in this area has been between Russian and the non-Slavic members of the Confederation of Independent States. For South Slavic, the main issue is that of B/C/S, but Montenegrin is another potential candidate for language-hood. All these tensions involve a complex mixture of political autonomy and language politics.

0.4   Languages, polities and speakers

The territorial adjustments following the Second World War made the political boundaries of the modern Slavic nations coincide to a larger extent than before with major linguistic and ethnic boundaries, though they were still far from being a perfect match, as can be seen from the sad violence in Yugoslavia over the past decade.

After the fall of Euro-Communism in 1989–1991 there were additional geopolitical changes. The Czechs and Slovaks separated smoothly into the Czech Republic and the Slovak Republic in the "Velvet Divorce" of 1992. Elsewhere the changes were more violent. The USSR fell apart. Ukraine and Belarus emerged as sovereign states, and as Russia lost its dominant position numerous states became autonomous: the Baltic states of Latvia, Lithuania and Estonia, the Caucasus states of Armenia and Georgia, and Central Asian states like Uzbekistan and Turkmenistan. This struggle is continuing along ethnic, political, linguistic and religious (Islamic/non-Islamic) lines, most notably in Chechnya.

The situation was especially unstable in Yugoslavia, where the federation had been held together mainly by Tito's ability as president. After his death in 1980 the components soon separated along ethnic-linguistic lines into Slovenia, Croatia, Serbia (incorporating Montenegro, Vojvodina and Kosovo, the last under UN protection since 1999), Bosnia (independent from 1992) and FYR Macedonia. The supra-ethnic national language Serbo-Croatian came to an effective end as a political and national force.

There is also a substantial Slavic diaspora. Most of the Slavic languages are spoken by significant émigré groups, especially in North America, Western Europe and Australasia, which places different geographical and cultural pressures on the languages (chapter 11). However, migration from the Slavic lands for ideological and economic reasons has now slowed, and a number of former émigré refugees are now returning home.

Table 0.2 summarizes the total numbers of homeland speakers, and the totals including speakers in émigré communities. The data for émigré speakers are not wholly reliable or comparable, since censuses in different countries have counted language ability and identity in different ways. And the total figures for homeland speakers may include minority ethnic groups: for Russian, for instance, the figure of 153.7 million includes about 16 million ethnic non-Russians. It is also important to remember that the status of Russian was considerably enhanced by its widespread use as a second "native" language in the former USSR, and as a major foreign language of education, administration, defence, culture and trade in the other Slavic and East European countries before the disintegration of the Soviet Bloc (see chapter 11). Including speakers of Russian as a second language, the total figure for Russian was 270 million in the USSR. Since 1990 the second-language status of Russian is being replaced by other languages, especially English.

0.5 Genetic classification and typology

Slavic provides us with many examples like (1), a characteristic instance of genetic differentiation. Here the East Slavic languages have an extra syllable, a phenomenon known as "pleophony", Russian *polnoglásie* (for transcription conventions and diacritics, see below and appendix B):

(1) 'milk', 'road'

South Slavic		West Slavic		East Slavic	
Slovenian:	*mléko*	Russian:	*molokó*	Sorbian:	*mloko*
	drága		*doróga*		*droga*
B/C/S:	*mléko*	Belarusian:	*malakó*	Polish:	*mléko*
	drăga		*daróha*		*droga*
Macedonian:	*mleko*	Ukrainian:	*molokó*	Czech:	*mléko*
			doróha		*dráha*
Bulgarian:	*mljáko*			Slovak:	*mlieko*
					dráha

There are other phenomena which distinguish West Slavic from East and South Slavic, or South Slavic from East and West Slavic, or Slavic sub-families from each other. In chapters 1 and 3–9 we shall show historically based patterns which support: a West *vs* East + South divide; a South *vs* West + East divide; a North *vs* South divide (Polish and Sorbian + East Slavic *vs* Czech, Slovak + South Slavic); and sub-patterns within the three major Slavic sub-families, with Polish and Sorbian contrasted to Czech and Slovak in West Slavic; and Bosnian, Croatian and Serbian contrasted to Bulgarian and Macedonian in South Slavic. Some features cut across internal Slavonic boundaries. The fixed-stress languages, for instance, are West Slavic and Macedonian. And there are religiously based typological features, as when Orthodox countries write in the Cyrillic script (appendix B) and tend to favour Greek-based lexis; while the non-Orthodox write in Roman and often show a greater preference for indigenous or Western lexis (chapter 9).

Moreover, not all the properties of the languages form such intra-Slavic genetic groupings. Balkan languages like Bulgarian and Macedonian (Slavic), Romanian (Romance) and Albanian (an Indo-European language-isolate), in a geographically coherent area, are genetically part of different sub-branches of Indo-European, but show similar post-posed article forms. These typological features cut across the underlying genetic classification, and since Trubetzkoy they have been covered by the term *Sprachbund* 'language union'. Balkan languages are one of the standard examples:

(2)   'city'   'the city'
   Bulgarian: *grad*   *gradắt*
   Romanian: *oraş*   *oraşul*
   Albanian: *qytét*   *qytéti*

Macedonian shares this feature with Bulgarian, and they stand apart from the rest of South Slavic and other standard Slavic languages, though there are some dialects, for instance in Russia, where post-posed articles are also found. They also occur in Scandinavian languages.

Other *Sprachbund* features are not far to seek. Greek, Romanian, Albanian, Bulgarian and Macedonian, for instance, all lack an infinitive, and express 'I want to go' as 'I want that I may go' (Joseph, 1983). And the imperfect and aorist tenses have now effectively disappeared from all the Slavic languages except two in South Slavic (Bulgarian and Macedonian) and two in West Slavic (Upper and Lower Sorbian: 5.5.5.4). In Serbian and Croatian they are archaic or restricted to formal/literary style.

Slavic, then, exhibits both strong internal cohesion and some distinctive features which link it to adjacent language families and groups within Indo-European, especially Baltic (chapter 1). These properties form many intersecting groupings, which can lead to highly complex and articulated typologies. Our goal is not a formal typology or taxonomy in the sense of Greenberg (1978), but rather a broader and less formal, as well as less theoretically driven, treatment. This approach will be closely linked to the requirements of a linguistic survey.

0.6   The linguistics of Slavic: empirical and theoretical characteristics

The systematic comparative study of Slavic, in the opinion of many Slavists, dates from the *Vergleichende Grammatik der slavischen Sprachen* (1875–1883) by Miklosich (1825–1874), which has been to Slavic what Grimm has been to Germanic. A great deal of the comparative work on Slavic since Miklosich has followed his example in concentrating on the diachronic study of the languages.

The bulk of this work until the last few decades has been written in the Slavic languages, and in German and French.

The only four extended studies of Slavic available in English are Entwistle and Morison's *Russian and the Slavonic languages* (1964), a diachronic analysis with a bias towards Russian data, which is now dated; de Bray's *Guide to the Slavonic languages* (1980a–1980c), which is synchronic but not contrastive, since it treats each language separately; Horálek's *An introduction to the study of the Slavonic languages* (Horálek, 1992), a translation and amending by Peter Herrity of the original *Úvod do studia slovanských jazyků*, first published in Czech in 1955 and with a strong historical bias; and *The Slavonic languages*, edited by Comrie and Corbett (1993), a more structured, synchronic and theoretically oriented treatment on a language-by-language basis. Two recent cross-Slavic studies are by Dalewska-Greń (1997), a comparative study mainly concerned with phonology, morphophonology, morphology and syntax; and Panzer (1991a), which combines single-language summaries with a short treatment of Slavic typology and a historical treatment of phonology and morphology. The present book differs from its predecessors in approaching Slavic from both a synchronic and a contrastive-typological point of view, following the model of the other books in this series. We also incorporate a deliberate diachronic perspective through much of the book, in the spirit of Townsend and Janda (1996; and see the end of this section).

Modern Slavic linguistics has now happily moved beyond the interference of political ideology which was typical of much of the twentieth century (L'Hermitte, 1987), and the artificial opposition of "Western" and "non-Western" models. The Russian Revolution forced the emigration of Slavists like Trubetzkoy and Jakobson, to the advantage of the Prague Linguistic Circle. After the Second World War Jakobson's further relocation to the USA helped to establish the strong North American tradition of Slavic linguistics. Under Communism in the Soviet Union from the late 1920s into the 1950s linguistics in general, and Slavic linguistics in particular, were hindered by an anti-Western and often xenophobic ideology which eschewed "empty formalism" (i.e. structuralism and "Western", "bourgeois" models, including much of diachronic linguistics). The thaw *vis-à-vis* Western linguistics dates from 20 June 1950, when an article under Stalin's name in *Pravda* opened the way for the judicious incorporation of Western linguistics, including philological and structuralist frameworks and methodologies. But for much of the century Slavic linguistics was a matter of the West and the rest. In the West there were continuations of the powerful Moscow and Prague traditions; Jakobson's school at Harvard and the dominant effect of his students; and theory-based approaches deriving from current advances, especially in generative and later functional grammar. The reintegration of non-Western and Western Slavic linguistics – though this happened more rapidly in Yugoslavia, Poland, the then Czechoslovakia and the DDR – took much of the rest of the century.

Soviet and East European Slavic linguistics under Communism made solid contributions to the empirical collection, analysis and description of the languages, particularly national Slavic languages, and the establishment of authoritative norms and reference materials. So too has research into the history of the national languages, albeit often from a single-sided historical-ideological perspective. This has been particularly important for more recent literary languages like Macedonian, which lacked both historical validation and contemporary authentication in dictionaries, grammars and a stable written language. Dialectology has been strongly supported, with publications in the form of dialect atlases, partly in the context of the drive to reaffirm the national languages and their regional varieties. The same cannot be said for most of the rest of sociolinguistics, since it was difficult to synchronize socially determined language variation with an ideology which promoted a classless society. The first Soviet books on sociolinguistics were published only in the late seventies (Nikol'skij, 1976), though the Prague School tradition of integrated linguistics, culture and sociolinguistics fared rather better. Lexicology and lexicography, however, have been more intensively studied in both the standard languages and regional variants than in the West, where these areas rather languished in the face of the dominance of syntax between 1957 and the 1980s. In the core of Slavic linguistics, however, there was a backing-away from structural descriptive methods, particularly those which evoked models currently fashionable in the West. Outside the Soviet Union the hand of Moscow was less oppressive, at least from the late 1950s, which helped – for instance – the continuation of the existing traditions in research on historical linguistics and Indo-European in the work of linguists like Bednarczuk (1968–1988) and Kuryłowicz (1964) in Poland, Gamkrelidze (Gamkrelidze and Ivanov, 1991) in Georgia, and Georgiev (1981) in Bulgaria. There has also been the controversial Nostratic theory, which attempts to prove that Indo-European belongs to a more widely based proto-language (Illič-Svityč, 1971–1976, 1979).

In order to strike a reasonable balance between Soviet, post-Soviet and Western sources, the theoretical orientation of this book will be as neutral as possible within the major trends in each of the linguistic disciplines. In phonology, morphophonology and morphology we have tended to follow the approach of Comrie and Corbett (1993) (chapters 3–5). The syntactic approach will also be fairly theory-neutral. In the former Soviet Union this discipline has been influenced by the Russian classification of construction-types known as *slovosočetanija* ('word-combinations'), which has been taxonomic rather than theoretical in orientation, and by the Prague School's conception of Functional Sentence Perspective (7.5).

A characteristic feature of modern Slavic linguistics is the extent to which the field, both in this book and more generally, is closely tied to the historical study of the languages. This is no accident. Nineteenth-century Slavic linguistics, like Germanic and Romance linguistics of the period, had a strongly diachronic bias. What distinguishes Slavic is the continuation of the diachronic tradition into modern mainstream Slavic linguistics. In Germanic and Romance linguistics there was a reorientation to a more synchronic emphasis in the years following the publication of de Saussure's *Cours de linguistique générale* (1916). Matters never went so far in Slavic linguistics. The new interest in synchrony, which had been anticipated about twenty years before Saussure by Baudouin de Courtenay, a Polish linguist who spent much of his working life in Russia, was well established in major centers of linguistic research in Kazan, Moscow and St. Petersburg (Stankiewicz, 1972). And when the Saussurean ideas were transmitted to Slavic linguistics, they were absorbed into a fairly balanced discipline in which the synchronic and diachronic approaches complemented, rather than excluded, each other. This tradition continues today. The outstanding Slavists of the twentieth century, scholars like Trubetzkoj, Jakobson and Isačenko, have viewed synchronic processes not only in their own right but also in the context of the nature of historical processes which have formed Slavic. Thanks to them, and to the traditions which they helped to establish, the analysis of the modern Slavic languages is more consistent with the historical perspective. Particularly in phonology and morphology, the historical approach helps to explain much about the structure of the modern languages. It is the historical viewpoint, in short, which provides a key to what Stankiewicz (1986) calls the "unity in diversity" of modern Slavic.

0.7 Organization

This book is designed principally for English readers with some competence in descriptive linguistics. It does not assume a knowledge of the Slavic languages, nor of modern theoretical linguistics. We present a typology of the Slavic languages – what makes them a language family, and how they differ from one another – using conventional linguistic notions and terms. Our approach is oriented not towards theoretical problems of linguistics or typology, but rather towards describing and contrasting the modern Slavic languages and their linguistic properties: to show the characteristics of each of the languages in itself, and in its relations to other Slavic languages. The map on p. xx shows the geographical location of the modern Slavic languages.

The selection of data from the Slavic languages presents special problems. Slavic is the most studied language family in the world. In the *Bibliographie linguistique de l'année* for 1998 a raw count of entries shows that out of the 20,743 listings, Indo-European accounts for 53 percent or 11,066 items, and nearly half of Indo-European – 5,370 items, for 25.9 percent of all listings, or 48.5 percent of Indo-European – relates to Slavic. The next most studied language families in order are Germanic (10.8 percent) and Romance (with Italic; 10.1 percent). In the listings for Indo-European, Polish is the most studied language, with 11.4 percent, and on this count is the most studied language in the world. It is followed by Russian with 10.3 percent and – remarkably – English with 8.4 percent, German with 6.3 percent and French with 6 percent. These figures certainly underestimate the position of English in particular, since so much of the material indexed under "General Linguistics" deals directly or indirectly with English. Nonetheless, the domination of Slavic in the world's linguistic research output is evident, although the Slavs account for barely 6 percent of the world's population. Within Slavic linguistics work on Polish accounts for 23.6 percent, and Russian 21.1 percent, a significant fall from the 26–28 percent of a decade ago: apparently the non-Russian members of the former Eastern Bloc are not researching Russian as intensively as they used to. In terms of numbers of native speakers and socio-political position Russian is under-represented, and Polish over-represented. But these are the languages about which most is written, and the selection of material and references in this book often tends to reflect this fact. A typological study, however, has to be sensitive to qualitative as well as quantitative data, and for this reason the presence in the literature of the "larger" languages will be counter-balanced by a special focus on the less represented languages like Sorbian, which present features of inherent typological interest. Many students of the Slavic languages get only a short distance past the large languages, and many no further than Russian. In a survey like this there is also a temptation to spread the examples widely throughout the rich material and literature. We have tried to clump the examples together, so as to avoid buckshot exemplification. Readers will find blocks of examples on Sorbian, say, which serve to emphasize not only individual points of the language's characteristics but also their coherence within the language. There are substantial numbers of Russian examples, since readers are most likely to know Russian if they know a Slavic language; since it is often useful to have a point of reference and comparison in a known language; and since Russian not only outnumbers the speakers of all the other Slavic languages together, but has also had a larger historical, ideological and cultural influence on the other Slavic languages.

0.7.1   Transcription and transliteration

(The orthography and transliteration of all languages is given in appendix B.) Roman-script Slavic languages (Czech, Slovak, Polish, Upper and Lower Sorbian in West Slavic; Slovenian, Bosnian and Croatian in South Slavic) are given in the standard orthography, with the standard linguistic diacritics for tone and length in Bosnian, Croatian, Serbian, and for length and tone or quality in Slovenian, where we need to highlight phonological properties, even though these diacritics belong to dictionaries and specialized use rather than to regular orthography: see 0.7.2.

Languages written in the Cyrillic script (Russian, Ukrainian and Belarusian in East Slavic; Serbian, Bulgarian and Macedonian in South Slavic) are given in Roman transliteration. For Serbian the Roman version of the standard ekavian variant is used throughout, as was standard in the Roman-script version of Serbo-Croatian (2.2.4, 10.2.2, appendix B). For the other languages the transliteration follows the widely accepted "American–European" Slavic linguists' model, which is close to a letter-by-letter transliteration with the exception of the "yotated" vowels (pronounced with a preceding /j/ element) and compound consonant letters like *šč* (see (3b) and appendix B). In (3a) both *ë* and *ja* contain two elements: a vowel nucleus; and a preceding "j" sound which is realized as [j] syllable-initially and after vowels, and as a softening (palatalization) of preceding consonants (here [tʲ]). The Cyrillic "soft sign" (ь), which marks palatalization of preceding consonants, is marked with a following prime accent in the transliteration, and corresponding to the current IPA (International Phonetic Association) convention, the superscript "j" [ʲ] is used in phonetic transcription:

(3a)		Cyrillic	Transliteration	Phonetics	Translation
	Rus	тётя	tëtja	[ˈtʲötʲə]	'aunt'
		яйцо	jajcó	[jɪjˈt͡sɔ]	'egg'
(3b)	Rus	женщина	žénščina	[ˈʒɛnʃʲʃʲɪnə]	'woman'
(3c)	Rus	быть	byt′	[bɪtʲ]	'to be'

0.7.2   Accent and stress

The three East Slavic languages (Russian, Ukrainian and Belarusian), as well as Bulgarian, are Cyrillic script and have a word accent which is free (it can occur on any syllable in the word) and mobile (it can move between syllables within paradigms). Macedonian, also written in Cyrillic, normally has antepenultimate stress.

In our orthographic transliteraton word accent is marked with an acute accent on the accented syllable in examples (but not usually in proper names or in the titles of books or articles, unless their phonetic properties are relevant). In phonetic represent-ations – using IPA – we use the conventional vertical bar before the accented syllable:

(4a)	Rus	*ruká*	'hand'	[NomSg]	[rʊ'ka]
(4b)	Rus	*rúku*	'hand'	[AccSg]	['rukʊ]

All West Slavic languages are written in the Roman script and have fixed stress. Polish has penultimate stress, and the others have initial stress. None of these languages marks word-stress orthographically. Diacritics are part of the standard orthographies of these languages, as described in appendix B, and indicate modi-fications of quality in consonants (5a), or quality and/or length in vowels (5b):

(5a)	Cz	*mazat* ['mazat] 'to smear'	*mažu* ['maʒu] 'I smear'
(5b)	Cz	*dům* [duːm] 'house'	*domu* ['dɔmu] [GenSg]

Occasionally, however, even these languages exhibit unusual stress patterns, like Polish *czterysta* '400', which is stressed, abnormally for Polish, on the antepenulti-mate syllable instead of the expected penultimate. In such cases we shall mark stress in the IPA style, with a preceding prime:

(6)	Pol	*'czterysta* '400'	['tʃterɫsta]

Slovenian, Bosnian, Croatian and Serbian have – at least in some variants of the standard – preserved word-tone and vowel length, the former on the accented syllable only, which can be marked in their orthography, but is printed only in dictionaries and pedagogical texts. For Slovenian the default variant will be the non-tonal one, showing only length and vowel quality (3.5). We follow these conventions:

(7a)	Sln	*séstra* 'sister' [NomSg]
		(tonal variant: long rising tone on tonic)
		sêstra
		(non-tonal variant: long low- mid [ɛ])
(7b)	B/C/S	*sèstrē* 'sister' [GenSg]
		(short rising tone on tonic + post-tonic long vowel, here final)
(7c)	B/C/S	*sȅstro* 'sister' [VocSg]
		(short falling tone on tonic)
(7d)	B/C/S	*séstrā* 'sister' [GenPl]
		(long rising tone on tonic + post-tonic long)

0.7.3 Structure of the examples

The examples are selected to illustrate specific points, and to provide comparisons with other relevant data in other Slavic languages. Examples are numbered, with a new numerical sequence in each chapter. If the example deals only with one language, that language is identified immediately after the example number, so that "Sln" stands for "Slovenian" in (8a). If the example covers more than one language, the language of each is identified immediately before each data item, so that (8b) refers to examples from Russian and Slovenian. Translations are provided in single quotation marks. Grammatical information is given in square brackets (8c). Phonetic representations are also in square brackets, and follow the principles of the IPA. Phonetic representations are as narrow as is appropriate for each example (8d). Glosses are given where appropriate, and where the translation does not provide enough guidance to the structure of each word and phrase. Hyphens within a word indicate a morpheme boundary, and are given only where the internal structure of the word is under discussion (8e).

(8a) Sln   *séstra* 'sister' (long rising tone)

(8b)   'sister': Rus *sestrá*   Sln *séstra*

(8c)   'sister': Rus *sestrá* [NomSg]

(8d) Rus   *sestrá* [sɪˈstra] [NomSg] 'sister'

(8e) Rus   *sestr-á*   *čitá-et*
                  sister-[NomSg]   reads-[3Sg NonPast]
                  '(my) sister is reading'

0.7.4 Abbreviations

Language-name abbreviations and abbreviations of linguistic terms are given in appendix A.

0.8   **Outline**

The book begins with the linguistic evolution, genetic affiliation and classification of the Slavic languages – their relation to the Indo-European parent language, and particularly to Baltic, the closest of the language families to modern Slavic (chapter 1). We then turn to the "external history" of Slavic, covering the early history of the Slavic tribes, the emergence of Slavic from the Indo-European language family, and the national, cultural and linguistic formation of the modern languages (chapter 2). This initial survey takes a more language-by-language approach, in order to highlight the essential characteristics of the three groups of Slavic (South, East and West) and of the languages which they include. The following nine chapters take a more topic-based cross-language perspective, and are concerned with phonology and phonetics (chapter 3), morphophonology (chapter 4), inflexional morphology (chapter 5), morphosyntax (chapter 6), sentence structure (chapter 7), word formation (chapter 8), lexis (chapter 9), dialectology (chapter 10) and selected key sociolinguistic issues (chapter 11). Appendix A covers abbreviations of language names and linguistic terms. Appendix B deals with transliteration and orthography. And appendix C establishes an entry-point into Slavic linguistics for those approaching it from the viewpoint of a non-Slavic training. The bibliography is designed to guide the reader in exploring the wider literature. There is an emphasis on English-language sources, followed by French, German and Russian. Anyone seriously interested in Slavic linguistics will have to learn at least Russian in order to gain access to the very large literature. But there is more than enough material in English to provide the linguist with a sound starting-point, and in some areas (like syntactic and phonological theory applied to Slavic) much of the key literature is written in any case in English, which is becoming, in Slavic linguistics as elsewhere, the default language of international scholarship, especially since the end of Euro-Communism.

1

Linguistic evolution, genetic affiliation and classification

1.1 The Slavs: prehistory

The Slavs, according to archaeological and linguistic evidence, can be traced back to around 4000 BC. At this time the Great Eurasian Plain was inhabited by the people (or peoples) whom we now know by the name "Indo-Europeans". Our factual knowledge of this distant period of European pre-history is sketchy and partly conjectural. Although we can only guess how far their territory extended, it is possible that at least the European center of the Indo-European homeland – if not the original homeland itself (on one widely held view) – was in what is now Western Ukraine, and that they spoke a fairly homogeneous language.

By about 3000 BC the Indo-Europeans had occupied most of Europe. What had previously been local dialect variations in the Indo-European language would have begun to diverge in the direction of separate languages (based on linguistic difference), which led ultimately to the now familiar Indo-European language families.

The emergence of Proto-Slavic occurred around 2000–1500 BC. This is the period of Proto-Slavic unity, when the Slavs inhabited a broadly coherent land area, though its exact location remains a matter of some controversy. According to Birnbaum's (1979: ch. 1) summary of the then current state of play, the Slavs' first homeland was north of the Carpathian Mountains, and possibly to the east of the Carpathians' westernmost extremity in the Sudeten Mountains, both of which approximately mark the border between present-day Poland and the Czech and Slovak Republics. An alternative, and perhaps more popular, view favors a location further east, on the middle Dnieper (Schenker 1995: 7 – who offers a good discussion of the various theories). By the fourth century AD the Slav area stretched from the Oder (Pol *Odra*) River in the west to the Dnieper (Rus *Dnepr*, Ukr *Dnipró*) in the east. I. the north they had reached the Masurian Lakes in central Poland, the Baltic Sea and the Pripet (Pol *Prypeć*; also Eng *Pripyat*, from Ukr *Prýp'jat'*) Marshes. During this period the Slavs would have spoken a fairly uniform language. Although dialect differences soon began to appear, resulting *inter alia* in the division into Baltic, Slavic or an intermediate Balto-Slavic, the pace of linguistic change was relatively slow.

The Slavs' original language is called both "Common Slavic" (Rus *obščeslav-jánskij jazýk*, Ger *Gemeinslavisch*, Fr *slave commun*) and "Proto-Slavic" (Rus *praslavjánskij jazýk*, Ger *Urslavisch*, Fr *protoslave*). The difference is partly a matter of national convention and preference, and partly a matter of definition: some scholars assign the name "Proto-Slavic" to the earlier period, and "Common Slavic" to the period preceding the breakup of Slavic unity in the first millennium AD. As Birnbaum notes (1979: ch. 1), it is not possible to determine a clear separation between these periods, so that one might as well use a single term to cover the whole period, with the additional labels "early" and "late" where needed. While Birnbaum opts for "Common Slavic", we shall follow Comrie and Corbett (1993) in opting for "Proto-Slavic" (abbreviated as 'PSl').

According to general consensus in what is still a controversial area, the real break-up of Proto-Slavic unity began about the fifth century AD. There seems to have been a steady expansion to the north and east by the Eastern Slavs. For the others there is evidence that their migrations were related partly to the disintegration of the Roman and Hun empires and the ensuing vacuum in Central Europe. One group of Slavs moved westwards, reaching what is now western Poland and the Czech Republic, and the eastern and north-eastern part of modern Germany. A second wave broke away to the south towards the Balkan Peninsula, where they became the dominant ethnic group in the seventh century, some (in the east) in turn being conquered by the Bulgars, a non-Slavic people of Turkic Avar origin. Of the original Bulgars we have only a few loan-words as monuments, since they were linguistically and culturally assimilated to the Slavs. This group of Slavs – the future Bulgarians and Macedonians – would most likely have moved south via the Black Sea coast, to the east of the Carpathians, meaning that they were in origin Eastern Slavs; this may account for certain typological similarities between Bulgarian and East Slavic (see 1.4).

The Slavs, however, were not politically unified or well organized, and elected a joint leader (or "great prince", using a word [Rus *knjaz'*] derived from the Germanic form of 'king') only when external danger forced them to. This lack of a centralized power structure was to cause serious problems for all the Slavs in their new homelands. It also contributed to the regionalization and differentiation of the emerging Slavic dialects, which by about the tenth century AD had divided into the three major sub-groups of modern Slavic: the South Slavs, East Slavs and West Slavs.

We shall concentrate on three points in the evolution of Slavic: the status of Slavic within the Indo-European group (1.2); the relative standing of Slavic and Baltic in the context of the groups which derived from Proto-Indo-European (abbreviated 'PIE': 1.2.1); and the conventional three sub-groups of the Slavic languages mentioned above (1.3–1.4), which then formed the basis of the further diversification in the evolution of the modern languages (1.5–1.7).

This chapter will set out the genetic linguistic map of Slavic. It will also be our last major excursion outside Slavic in this book. The following chapters (2–11) will concentrate on the unity of Slavic, and the diversity which we find in its individual languages, both with respect to Slavic as a whole, and with respect to the major sub-groupings of languages within it.

1.2   Slavic in Indo-European

The Slavic languages belong to the "satem" group of Indo-European languages, which also includes the Baltic, Indic and Iranian languages. This well-known classification derives from the way each language treats the PIE initial palatal *k'-* of the word *k'm̥tom* '100'.

We shall follow the convention of using asterisks for unattested forms within the text, but not in tables, which they tend to clutter. All Proto-Indo-European and early Proto-Slavic forms are unattested. Where late Proto-Slavic forms are attested in Old Church Slavonic (1.5.1, 2.2.1) they are not marked with an asterisk.

The "satem" languages (named after the Avestan word for '100') all have a fricative or affricate sibilant for the original *k'* (1a). In contrast, the "centum" languages, which take their name from the Latin for '100', preserve an initial velar stop or its later reflexes (1b):

(1a) 'hundred'
       PIE   *k'm̥tom*
       Avestan (Old Persian)   *satəm*
       PSl   *sŭto (sъto)*

(1b)   Lat   *centum*
       Gk   *(he)katón*
       Germanic/Gothic   *hund(ert)*

1.2.1   Slavic and Baltic

One of the more contentious issues in the early history of Slavic concerns the nature of the relation between Slavic and Baltic. Clearly, both had a common ancestor in Proto-Indo-European. Equally clearly, the Baltic languages (Latvian, Lithuanian and the now extinct Old Prussian) form a later group which is distinct from Slavic. But did the Baltic and Slavic languages break away from Proto-Indo-European as a single conjoint group, which later divided into Slavic and Baltic?

Or did they break away from it in two separate groups at roughly the same time, and then develop further similarities through geographical contiguity, parallel development and interaction, rather than by being part of a single joint proto-language?

The idea that Baltic and Slavic did indeed share a common ancestor language after the breakaway from Indo-European is called the "Balto-Slavic Hypothesis". One of its originators was Brugmann, in his *Grundriß der vergleichenden Grammatik der indogermanischen Sprachen* (Vol. 1) of 1886. And among its best known critics was Meillet, whose *Les dialectes indo-européens* was published in 1908. There is certainly strong evidence to link Slavic more closely to Baltic than to any other Indo-European language family. Whether, however, this is enough to justify the analysis of a Balto-Slavic period of unity is still controversial.

Many of the commonly accepted features which mark the Slavic-Baltic parallelisms are shared, at least in part, with other IE languages. They include the following (with indicative examples).

1.2.1.1   Phonology

For the meaning of all symbols and abbreviations, see appendix A.

1.   PIE palatal stops become sibilants (part of the *satem* development, see above), probably via affricates:

	PIE	OCS (Late PSl)	Lith
$k' > (t)\check{s} >$ PSl s, Balt $\check{s}$	$k'\underset{\circ}{m}tom$ 'hundred'	*sъto*	*šimtas*

2.   Deaspiration of aspirated voiced stops (also Germanic):

$d^h > d$	*dhūm-* 'smoke'	*dymъ*	*dumai*
$g^h > g$	*gʰord-* 'town'	*gradъ*	*gardas*

3.   Delabialization of labialized velars:

$k^w > k$	$k^w\ŏ$	'what'	*kъto*	*kas*
g^{wh} (via g^w) $> g$	$snoig^{wh}$- 'snow'		*sněgъ*	*sniegas*

4.   PIE vocalic $\underset{\circ}{r}$ / $\underset{\circ}{l}$ / $\underset{\circ}{n}$ / $\underset{\circ}{m}$ yield *ir/ur, il/ul, in/un, im/um*

$\underset{\circ}{l} > il\ ul$	$(u)\underset{\circ}{l}k$- 'wolf'	*vьlkъ*	*vilkas*
$\underset{\circ}{m} > im\ um$	$dek'\underset{\circ}{m}$ 'ten' (*-ĭmt->*)	*desętь*	*dešimt*

5. $tt/dt > st$ (see 1.3.1.1–1.3.1.2, under simplification of clusters and opening of syllables):

$tt > st$	*met-ti* 'throw'	*mesti*	*mesti*
$dt > st$	*ved-ti* 'lead'	*vesti*	*vesti*

6. Changes to /s/: different results, appearance of /x/ in PSl (also Iranian
    and Indic languages, e.g. Sanskrit, also with different results):

    s > *x* (PSl) or *š* (Balt) between *k-, r-* and V:

aksi 'axle'	(*oks-* >) *osь*	(*akš-* >) *ašis*
u̯r̥s- 'top'	*vьrxъ*	*viršus*

    PSl only, not Balt:
    s > *x* between *i-, u-* and V:

ōu̯s- 'ear'	*uxo*	*ausis*
ōi̯su̯ LocPl ending	*-ěxъ*	*-uose/-yse*

7. Fusion of /a/ and /o/ (also Germanic):
    Short /ă/ and /ŏ/ merged into /ₒă/ (or /ă/) in both, long /ō/ and /ā/
    merged into /ₒā/ (or /ā/) in PSl only (later PSl /ₒă/ > /o/, /ₒā// > /a/):

/ă/	*ăk'si-* 'axle'	*osь*	*ašis*
/ŏ/	*ŏk-* 'eye'	*oko*	*akis*
/ā/	*bʰrātr-* 'brother'	*bratъ*	*broter-elis*
/ō/	*dō-* 'give'	*dati*	*duoti*

In levels other than phonology, rather than produce examples involving Baltic, we
refer simply to the relevant chapters containing the Proto-Slavic forms.

1.2.1.2 *Morphology and morphophonology*

1. Use of the original PIE ablative for the genitive singular in *o*-stem
    nouns (5.5.1.1)
2. Declension of active participles (present and past), and extension of their
    stems by /j/, giving *-Vnt-* > *-ǫ /ę-t'-* for the present and *-u̯s-* > *-vš-* for the
    past (5.5.5.10)
3. Parallelisms in the formation of some 1 Person singular pronouns
    without gender (oblique cases) (5.5.3)
4. Shifting the *consonant*-stems into the *ĭ*-stems (5.5.1.6)
5. Separation of the present-tense and infinitive stems as the basis for
    conjugation (5.5.5.2)

1.2.1.3 *Word formation*

1. Formation of collective numerals with the suffix *-er/-or* (5.5.4.3, 8.6.1)
2. Formation of "definite" long-form adjectives by adding a pronoun to
    an adjective stem (5.5.2.1)
3. Parallel adjectival suffixes, e.g. *-ĭn-, -ĭsk-* (though the latter is general
    PIE, cf. Eng. *-sh*) (8.4.3)

1.2.1.4   *Syntax*

1.   The use of the genitive for the accusative in negated direct objects (6.2.3–6.2.4).

2.   The use of the instrumental in the predicate of copulative sentences (*ibid.*, 7.2.2.2)

1.2.1.5   *Lexis*

Uniquely shared lexical items (Trautmann, 1923):

(2)		PSl	OCS	Lit	B/C/S	Rus	Pol
	'head':	golva	glava	galvà	gláva	golová	głowa
	'linden':	lipa	lipa	líepa	lȋpa	lípa	lipa
	'horn':	rogŭ	rogъ	rãgas	rȏg	rog	róg
	'hand, arm':	ronka	rǫka	rankà	rúka	ruká	ręka

Many Slavists (e.g. Horálek, 1955: 71; Shevelov, 1964: 613) have taken the line that one does not need to take a strong position on the Balto-Slavic Hypothesis in order to do viable Slavic linguistics, and we shall follow their example.

1.2.2   Slavic and other Indo-European language families

1.2.2.1   *Slavic and Iranian*

The Slavs were in direct contact with the Iranians in the south from about the seventh century BC to the second century AD. Not enough is known of the phonology of Scythian or Sarmatian, the Iranian languages in closest contact with the Slavs, but some broad-scale phonological correspondences between Slavic and Iranian (and often with Baltic as well) can be established.

A phonological feature which may stem from this contact is the change of /s/ to /x/ in certain contexts (between /i, u, r, k/ and V; also known as the *ruki* rule). We have seen above (1.2.1) that Baltic (and also Iranian and Indic) apparently shared part of this change (Baltic after /u, k/ only), and also that the Baltic result was /š/, not /x/. It could well be that the frequency of /x/ in Iranian languages contributed at least to the last step in Proto-Slavic, as it provided other sources of /x/ also, e.g. Rus *xoroš-* 'nice', possibly from the Iranian root *xors-* 'Sun God' (but refuted by Vasmer, 1964–1973, s.v. *xorošij*).

1.2.2.2   *Slavic and Germanic*

The Slavs were in contact with the Goths from the second to fourth centuries AD during the 'wanderings' of the latter as far as the Black Sea. Later the West Slavs were to have close contacts with the Germans, but that was to be at the time of the Proto-Slavic break-up, so that the effects are local, and reflected only in some Slavic areas, notably Sorbian, but also Czech, Slovak and Slovenian.

1.3   Proto-Slavic

"Proto-Slavic" (see above) is the name given to Slavic after its separation from Indo-European and Baltic, but before the partition of Slavic into its three main sub-families. This period lasted probably for more than 2,000 years, and the features listed below belong to what is assumed to be the core of the common language.

The earliest phonological developments, centered on suprasegmental features, were:

1. tone ceased to be phonemic, becoming a concomitant of length: long vowels and diphthongs had rising pitch (known as "acute"), and short vowels had falling (non-rising) pitch (known as "circumflex");
2. then the nuclear vowels of diphthongs were shortened, but the tone distinctions remained, so that tone again became phonemic, but only on diphthongs;
3. still later, word-stress arose from tonal features: an acute (or the first acute in a word) became the stressed vowel. If there was no acute, the word was stressless, and initial stress developed on such words in most areas. The pitch on endings thus accounts for the mobile patterns which developed. Inflexions or suffixes with acute following circum-flex stems account for fixed-end patterns.

The probable shape of the early Proto-Slavic phonological system is shown in table 1.1. Bracketed forms joined by a vertical line are likely regional variants; the vowel symbols ₑ̄ etc. represent notional intermediate phonemes. These reflect partly the dual origin of these phonemes, especially the back set, but mainly point to their future development at the time when length was replaced by quality (1.3.1.6). The use of the term 'diphthong' to cover sequences which are structurally 'vowel + sonorant' in pre-consonantal position, a much broader application than is normal elsewhere, is common within Slavic linguistic usage. In particular, it facili-tates the description of the development of such sequences.

Developments within Proto-Slavic   The following discussion is topic-based rather than chronological, though as far as possible chronological order is followed. For clarity of exposition the vowel symbols used from here on are those of later Proto-Slavic. The equivalences are shown in table 1.1 and discussed in 1.3.1.6.

Table 1.1. *Early Proto-Slavic phonological system*

Consonants

	Labial	Dental	Palatal	Velar
Stop	p	t		k
	b	d		(g) ⊣
Nasal	m	n		
Fricative		s		x
	(v) ⊣	z	j	(ɣ) ⊣
	(w) ⊣			
Liquid		r		
		l		

Vowels (in brackets are given the later Proto-Slavic symbols used from 1.3.1 on)

	Front	Central	Back
High	ĭ ī (ь i)		ŭ ū (ъ u)
Low	ₑă ₑā (e ě)		ₒă ₒā (o a)

Diphthongs (pre-consonantal VOWEL + SONORANT)

Low short vowels plus i̯, u̯: ₑăi̯ ₒăi̯ ₑău̯ ₒău̯(ei̯, oi̯, eu̯, ou̯)
All short vowels plus, r, l, m, n, e.g. ĭr ₑăr (ьr, er)

Suprasegmental

	Stress	Free
	Quantity	On all monophthongs (not on the above diphthongs)
	Tone	Automatic acute on long vowels; diphthongs may have acute or circumflex

1.3.1 Phonology

1.3.1.1 *Syllable*

In the following discussion of syllable structure we interpret the 'boundary' empirically, that is, as reconstructed on the basis of known developments and not on any abstract theoretical notion.

A generalization which may be made about almost all developments – and certainly all the major ones – within Proto-Slavic is that the syllable boundaries and relations within the syllable altered: the unit of the syllable became more discrete, the boundary was marked by a drop in sonority. This is the so-called 'Law of Rising Sonority' (within the syllable), which led to the 'Open Syllable Law', that is, syllables became 'open', always ending in a vowel (see below on word-final consonant loss). Initial consonant clusters were acceptable to the extent that they conformed to this rule (e.g. fricative + stop + glide, as *str-*, *zgl-*). Further, all the elements within the syllable would have been closely bound and able to influence one another, for instance to cause assimilation.

The first implementation of this syllable restructure, the 'opening of syllables', had major consequences for all aspects of the phonological system. We shall see the main effects below, but probably one of the earliest was the dropping of word-final consonants (e.g. PIE NomSg endings *-ŭs/ŭm* etc. > PSl *-ŭ/-ŏ*). Also early was the simplification or reorganization of unacceptable consonant clusters (usually of falling sonority, see 1.3.1.2).

1.3.1.2   *Simplification of clusters*

The opening of syllables in Proto-Slavic by elision (i.e. deletion) of syllable-final consonants was an effect of the more general principle of 'rising sonority': in accordance with this principle inherited consonant clusters remained acceptable only if they conformed to it. Otherwise some sort of simplification took place: elision, dissimilation or metathesis. Thus geminate clusters were always simplified. This is probably the earliest such simplification, as it is shared by Baltic (see above), and similar effects are observed in Greek and Iranian, either by elision (e.g. fricatives, as in NomSg final *-s*) or by dissimilation (e.g. stops: *tt > st*: PSl **plet-ti* 'braid, plait' Inf > *plesti*, *dt > st*: *ved-ti* 'lead' Inf > *vesti*). Clusters of 'stop + any consonant' usually involved the elision of the stop, e.g. PIE **wapsa* 'wasp' > PSl **osa* (Lith *vepsva*); **greb-ti* 'row, rake' Inf > *greti*; **greb-s-* (the aorist of the same verb) > *grěs-* (with lengthened root vowel). However, clusters of fricative + stop (e.g. *st*, *zg*) were accepted (and were indeed used as solutions to 'stop + stop', see *plesti* above) even though the stop was less sonorous, which indicates that ease of articulation within the overall open syllable structure was sometimes in conflict with rising sonority.

When a non-sonorant was followed by a sonorant, the first of the two consonants was usually kept, since such a cluster did comply with rising sonority (e.g. *tri* 'three'). Clusters of 'fricative + sonorant' were always accepted, on the same grounds as 'fricative + stop', cf. word-initial *sn-* (*sněg* 'snow'), *zn-* (*zna* 'know'), *sl-* (*slov* 'word'), *zv-* (*zvon* 'ring'). While 'stop + sonorant' clusters were also normally accepted (*tri*), the clusters *tl* and *dl* show hesitation by area, producing one of the distinguishing features of West Slavic, which alone retained them (1.7.1).

1.3.1.3   *Syllabic harmony*

Within the new syllabic structure (C(C)V) the relationship between the consonant and the following vowel would have become very close, such that each influenced the other. This general feature is known as 'syllabic harmony' (sometimes 'synharmony', Rus *singarmónija*). The features affected are centered on front/back tongue position, which for vowels means indeed front/back, and for consonants means the raising of the tongue at the front or back. Thus we have effects like the following: (1) a front vowel caused raising of the tongue at the front during the consonant articulation, producing a 'palatalizing' effect, and so-called 'palatalized' or 'soft(ened)' (or 'sharp') consonants; (2) in the case of the velars, the result was their conversion to full palatal consonants, that is, ones articulated in the high front tongue position (a shift from soft to hard palate location); (3) where palatal consonants had arisen as a result of the effect of [j] (see below), and where the following vowel had been a back one (say, /o/), this back vowel was fronted by the influence of the consonant. In the case of short /o/ and /ъ/ the fronted versions were, in fact, the front partners /e/ and /ь/ (e.g. PSl *měst-o̱* 'place' ~ *pol-e̱* 'field', *rab-ъ̱* 'slave' ~ *kon-ь̱* 'horse'), suggesting that any rounding was not strong in these short vowels. On the other hand, for the long /u/ (< ū) and nasal /ǫ/ (< 'back vowel + nasal consonant' before a consonant, see 1.3.1.7) the result was at most a fronted [ü] or nasal [ö̃], that is, they did not lose their rounding and merge with their front 'partners' (/i/, /ę/). Most interesting is the long /a/ (< ₒā), whose formal front partner was /ě/ (< ₑā) (e.g. PSl *ča̱ša̱* 'cup'): it seems that a fronted [ä] was the most common result, and since this is what we believe the pronunciation of /ě/ itself was in most areas, this result reflects normal fronting. However, the ultimate result in all areas was a reflex of /a/, and not of /ě/ (e.g. not **češe*), and moreover, the reflex of /ě/ itself preceded by a palatal was also /a/ (!) (e.g. PSl **ležěti* 'lie' > *leža̱ti*). Further, in those areas where /ě/ in other contexts shifted to another position (higher, e.g. in East Slavic) it was not joined by the vowels after palatals (e.g. PSl *lěto* > Rus *lé̱to*, but Rus *ležát'*), that is, the [ä] of these areas (*leža̱ti*) was not identical to /ě/. Incidentally, no area has retained the three fronted articulations (*ä, ü, ö̧*), which were only allophones, and which ceased to function after the syllable was again restructured – at which stage the sequence 'palatal consonant + back vowel' again became acceptable (see 3.2.1).

   The extent to which these shifts are reflected in the modern languages varies: for some (e.g. Russian, Polish) the "soft" articulation of consonants – and not just before front vowels – has become an inherent feature; and for all languages the fronting of vowels is reflected in morphophonological alternations, in particular in the opposition between hard and soft declension types (e.g. Russian neuter nouns, hard *mést-o* 'place' *vs* soft *pól-e* 'field', see 4.3).

1.3.1.4   *Palatalization by [j]*

An early consonant change which was to be a major feature of Slavic was the production of palatal consonants by 'fusion' with a following [j] (in reality palatalization by [j] followed by loss of the [j]). Sequences of 'consonant + *j*' would always have been acceptable within the new syllable unit, so this change is not tied to the syllable structure. But it does seem probable that it is a manifestation of an early (regressive) assimilative tendency which could be the precursor of the opening of syllables.

There are discrete stages in this development. Most subsequent results are common to the whole group, but some are not. In order better to observe the process, it is useful to see the first stage as fused consonants which are simply palatalized, or jotated, versions of the base consonant, e.g. stops like *p'*, *t'*, *k'*, fricatives like *s'*, *x'* and sonorants like *r'*, *l'*, *n'*.

In a few cases consonant clusters were affected as a unit, for example the clusters *kt* and *gt* jointly became *t'* at this first stage.

The final stage, producing consonants like the palatals or post-alveolars, is late, occurring after the syllable opening. Some of the results are phonetically "natural", and occur in many languages, if only in allegro speech, e.g. *s'* > *š'*, *z'* > *ž'* (cf. Eng *sure, pleasure*), common to all the group. Others are less so, for example the labials become clusters of labial plus *l'* – that is, the palatal element is realized as a palatal lateral [ʎ]. There is no agreement about whether this *l'* element was initially common or not. The western group (e.g. Polish, Czech) do not show it except in a few odd cases, so it is possible either that they never developed it and borrowed those few cases, or that they subsequently lost it and these cases are remnants (see 3.2.2). For the sonorants *r, l, n* there is no special further development until after the break-up into East, West and South Slavic. The velars show mostly common results: all languages have *k'* > *č'* and *x'* > *š'*:

(3a) 'I cry': PSl **plak-j-om* > *plačǫ*: all except Sln have the stem *plač-* (Sln *plakam* by analogy with Inf)

(3b) 'soul', PSl **dux-j-a* > *duša*: Cz *duše*, all others (including OCz) *duša*

The results of *g'* may have depended on the stop or fricative nature of this sound, the stop [gʲ] giving *dž'* (locally later simplified to *ž'*), and the fricative [ɣʲ] giving *ž'*. If the fricativization of /g/ is placed later – which is the traditional view – it would be accompanied at that later time by the deaffrication of *dž'* to *ž'*. Positing the early local occurrence of fricative /ɣ/ thus would seem reasonable.

1.3.1.5 *Velars and their palatalization*

A change which seems plausibly to predate the syllable opening is the fronting of the velars in the vicinity (on either side) of a front vowel, e.g. BSl **k'etūr-* 'four' > PSl **k'etyr-*; **-īkŭ* 'agent suffix' > **-ьk'ъ*. Within the revised (open) structure mutual effects across a sonority boundary should be minimal (and those within the unit maximal), so that the influence of a vowel on the following consonant is less likely. The second example (*-ьk'ъ*) might well therefore have been in place before the restructuring. We shall see below that this particular development of the velars has caused problems of chronology, and the positing of an early stage of fronting across the syllable boundary while it was still weak can help with this problem.

The above results of the effect of [j] on consonants may now be expanded to the specific context of the new open-syllable structure. Vowel articulation may now influence the articulation of preceding consonants: in particular, we would expect the typical palatalizing effect of a front vowel, producing fronted allophones. This is effectively the result for dentals and labials. However, for velars the result was much more drastic, matching the effect of /j/ noted above: again, in Proto-Slavic all areas have *k' > č'*, *x' > š'* and *g'/γ' > ž'* (possibly via *dž'*). These changes are traditionally called the '1st Palatalization of the Velars' (PV1), and the context is: before any of the front vowels existing at that time, namely high /i/ and low /e/, which may both be long or short (these are the vowels which became /i ь ě e/).

(4a)   1st Palatalization of the Velars (PV1)

PSl	B/C/S	Rus	Cz
(**kětūre >*) **k'etyre > četyre* 'four':	*četiri*	*četýre*	*čtyři*
(**gīv- >*) **g'iv- > živ-* '(a)live':	*žîv*	*živój*	*živý*
*strax'-ьn- > strašьn- 'terrible':	*stráš(a)n*	*strášnyj*	*strašný*

This change occurred in important inflexions, like the present tense of verbs, with the thematic vowels *e* and *i*:

(4b)

PSl	B/C/S	Rus	Cz
*pek'-e-tь > pečetь 'he bakes':	*pèčē*	*pečët*	*peče*
*mog'-e-tь > možetь 'he can':	*mòžē*	*móžet*	*může*
*dyx'-e-tь > dyšetь 'he breathes':	*dȋšē*	*dýšit*	(arch.) *dýše*

After this palatalization of the velars, producing post-alveolar consonants (/č/, /š/, /ž/), there occurred a second fronting process affecting the velars, producing probably first (alveolo-)palatal sounds like those in modern Polish and B/C/S, which by the time of the break-up had become soft dentals or alveolars. This is the reverse of the actual Polish and B/C/S cases, where these palatals were derived from soft dentals:

/k/ > /c'/, /g/ > /dz'/ or /z'/, /x/ > /s'/ or /š'/ (examples in (5)).

The variants for /g/ may have been parallel to those for the first set, that is, they may have related initially to the stop *vs* fricative nature of /g/. However, subsequently, in the same way, even areas with stop /g/ converted /dz'/ to /z'/. The variants for /x/, on the other hand, are geographically based, the post-alveolar /š/ occurring in the West only.

The context for this set of velar frontings is twofold. One is the expected following front vowel, specifically the two new front vowels /ě₂/ and /i₂/. They had not been present at the time of the first change, but had arisen later from the (monophthongized) diphthong /oï/ (see 1.3.1.7), and had merged with existing /ě/ and /i/. This set of changes is referred to as the '2nd Palatalization of the Velars' (PV2):

(5a)   2nd Palatalization of the Velars (PV2)

PSl	B/C/S	Rus	Cz
(*$koina$ >) *$k'ěna$ > $c'ena$ 'price':	céna	cená	cena
*$goilo$ > *$g'ělo$ > zělo: 'very'	Sln zeló	RChSl zeló	OCz zielo
*$xoid$- > *$x'ěd$- > sěd/šěd- 'grey (haired)'	sěd	sedój	šedý

This change, too, occurred in important inflexions, e.g. the locative singular and nominative plural of nouns, and the imperative of verbs (though most often this alternation has not survived analogical levelling):

(5b)   PSl

	B/C/S	ORus	Cz
(*$ronk$-oi >) *$rǫkě$ > $rǫcě$ 'hand' LocSg	rúci	rucě	ruce
(*nog-oi >) *$nogě$ > $nodzě$ 'foot' LocSg	(nòge)	nozě	noze
(*$doux$-oi >) *$duxě$ > $dusě/dušě$ 'spirit' LocSg	dùsi	dusě	duše

The second context in which this same set of changes occurred is more complex. It appears to be caused by a *preceding* high front simple or nuclear vowel (that is, mainly long and short /i/) (examples in (6)). This makes it a progressive assimilation, which in itself suggests rather the period *before* the opening of the syllables, since after that there was a clearer boundary between a vowel and a following consonant. On the other hand, the fact that only one diphthong with nuclear [i] – '*i* + nasal sonorant' (but not '*i* + liquid sonorant') – provokes the change means that it almost certainly occurred after the quantity changes (1.3.1.6) and monophthongization (1.3.1.7). (The *i* + N diphthong would have become first a nasalized [ĩ], then merged with the lower nasalized /ę/ [ẽ].) The identical results to the 2nd Palatalization also suggest a similar late period.) These conflicting facts have led to a range of interpretations about this set of velar changes. Traditionally it has been called the '3rd Palatalization of the Velars' (PV3), suggesting a late chronology, but it is now more commonly called the 'Progressive Palatalization of the Velars', and many scholars place it as the earliest of the three. A compromise position, which attempts to accommodate the contradictions, sees it as having occurred in two stages: the first is early, and produced simply fronted velars; and the second is simultaneous with PV2, taking these sounds along with those in the new front vowel context (PV2) forward to the palatal area. This is why we favor the view suggested above of the early appearance of fronted velars when adjacent to front vowels.

There are also several other complications with this set of changes. One is that certain following vowels (high and/or rounded) seem to have prevented it, which fits with the later (open) syllable situation. Second, there must have been some analogical levelling, for example in a paradigm where the following vowel was sometimes a preventer, sometimes a supporter (mainly /a/), and analogy would be particularly strong in this type, where the motive force was never an inflection, but always a stem vowel. These last facts account for the absence of alternations arising from this set:

(6)   3rd (Progressive) Palatalization of the Velars (PV3)

PSl		B/C/S	Rus	Cz	Pol
(*ot-ĭkŭ >) *ot-ьk'ъ > ot-ьc'ь 'father'		òt(a)c	ot(é)c	ot(e)c	ojciec
(*kŭnĭngŭ >) *kъnęg'ъ > kъnędz'ь 'prince'		knêz	knjaz′	OCz knĕz	ksiądz
(*vĭxŭ) > *vьx'ъ > vьs'ь 'all'		Sln v(è)s	v(e)s′	OCz v(e)š	OP wszy
suffix *-īkā > *-ik'a > -ic'a	-ica	-ica	-ica	-ica

Note that the former following back vowels which did not prevent the change were then fronted by the rules of syllabic harmony (1.3.1.3), as in the final vowel of the first three examples of (6).

1.3.1.6   *Vowel quantity > quality*

The system of four pure vowels with long and short versions was replaced by a system in which quantity ceased to be distinctive and was replaced by qualitative distinctions. Length was probably preserved phonetically for some time and was automatic, or residual, in the new vowels. We state the starting and finishing-points ('Early' and 'Late') in table 1.2:

On the quality of the new vowels, we can see that:

    a.   rounding has become distinctive in the low vowels. But for the high vowels, on the contrary, rounding was weak and was to be lost from

Table 1.2. *Vowel quantity > quality in PSl*

Early PSl	Late PSl			B/C/S	Rus	Cz
$_o\breve{a}$	*$n_o\acute{a}kt\breve{\imath}$	o	*not'ь* 'night'	*nôć*	*noč'*	*noc*
$_o\bar{a}$	*$d_o\bar{a}$-$t\breve{\imath}$	a	*da-ti* 'give'(Inf.)	*dȁti*	*dat'*	*dát*
$_e\breve{a}$	*$m_e\breve{a}d\breve{u}$	e	*medъ* 'honey'	*mêd*	*mëd*	*med*
$_e\bar{a}$	*$s_e\bar{a}d$-	ě ([ä])	*sěd-* 'sit'	*sed-*	*sed-*	*sed-*
ĭ	*$v\breve{\imath}x'\breve{u}$	ь ([ĭ])	*vьs'ь* 'village'	Sln *vâs*	*ves'*	*ves*
ī	*$gx'\bar{\imath}v\breve{u}$	i	*živъ* 'alive'	*živ*	*živój*	*živý*
ŭ	*$d\breve{u}kt(er)\bar{\imath}$	ъ ([ŭ] or [ə])	*dъt'(er)i* 'daughter'	*kćî/kćêr*	*doč'(-er)-*	*dcera*
ū	*$d\bar{u}m\breve{u}$	y ([ɨ])	*dymъ* 'smoke'	*d'ìm*	*dym*	*dým*

     the long /u/, and by inference also from the short. The subsequent development of /ь/ leaves its rounding status at this stage unclear. Since strong rounding of the high vowels appeared only with the monophthongization of diphthongs, i.e. when /oy/ > /u/ (1.3.1.7), it is also possible that it was only then that rounding was removed from the original long and short /u/.

b.   the short high vowels are assumed to have lowered to high-mid and more centered. In other words their quality may be said to have been 'reduced' (from periphery to center), so that they are frequently referred to as the 'reduced vowels' (Rus *reducírovannye*). Their symbols are the Cyrillic letters used for these vowels in OCS – ъ (back) and ь (front); see also (d) below on their length.

c.   the quality of /ě/ is also a matter of disputation, again because of the variety of later reflexes. Most popular is the view that at this stage it was a low front unrounded vowel ([ä] or [æ]). For others it was a rising diphthong of the [ịa]/[ịä] type. And for still others, it had already shifted to a higher position ([e] or [i]) in some areas, namely East Slavic. This last position is intended to account mainly for local reflexes, see 3.2.1.3, but the evidence from borrowings from East Slavic, e.g. into Finnish, suggests a change of quality in the East: *měra* 'measure' is borrowed early as Finn *määrä*, while *věstь* 'news' is borrowed later as Finn *viesti*. Its symbol is the Czech letter *ě*, representing its common reflex in Czech.

d.   the quantity of the old vowels continued to reside in the new vowels, so that /a/, /ě/, /i/ and /y/ were residually long, and the other four short. The subsequent developments of /ъ/ and /ь/ suggest that they were even shorter than /o/ and /e/. But this remains a hypothesis, related presumably to their higher position; the further shortening may have occurred later. The loss of rounding of /ъ/ causes it to tend towards *schwa* ([ə]), which it becomes in many areas (3.2.1.1).

1.3.1.7   *Monophthongization*

Diphthongs (as defined above, 1.3) were prime casualties of the principle of rising sonority, since in principle the semivowel or sonorant second part of a falling diphthong represents a drop in sonority and hence means a closed syllable – at least when followed by a consonant or word boundary. Virtually all such tauto-syllabic diphthongs were "monophthongized" in Proto-Slavic. We say 'virtually', because it appears that the final stages of this process were overtaken by other changes which reversed the syllabic structure and reinstated closed syllables within the system. The diphthongs which failed to complete the process were some of those in which the closing element was one of the sonorants *r, l*, while the rest changed consistently. The results are shown in (7a–c). Note that the vowel nucleus of the diphthong is always short, but the new pure vowel is (phonetically) long:

Diphthongs ending in a semivowel (i̯, u̯)

(7a)	monophthongization of diphthongs ending in a semivowel (i̯, u̯):				
	PSl	OCS	B/C/S	Rus	Cz
	oi̯ > ě, i	*berěte, beri* 'take' Imper. 2p, 2s	*bèri(te)*	*berí(te)*	*ber(te)*
	ei̯ > i	*iti, idǫ* 'go' Inf., 1SgPres	*ići, ìdēm*	*idtí, idú*	*jít, jdu*
	ou̯ > u	*uxo* 'ear' NomSg	*ȕho/ȕvo*	*úxo*	*ucho*
	eu̯ > (j)u	*l'ud-ъ, -ьje* 'people' NomSg, Pl	Sln *ljûd-i*	*ljúd-i*	*lid-é*

In the vowel system, the new /ě/ and /i/ merge with the existing ones from long front vowels (table 1.2) (though often they are marked for etymological purposes as /ě$_2$/ and /i$_2$/). The new /u/ occupies the place of the /u/ lost by unrounding to /y/ (and may have given the final push to its unrounding). The front /e/ of *eu̯* is reduced to [j], with its usual effect of fusing with the preceding consonant to make a new palatal consonant.

Diphthongs ending in a nasal sonorant (m, n)

(7b)	monophthongization of diphthongs ending in a nasal sonorant (*m, n*):			
	(F = Front, B = Back, N = Nasal, V = Vowel)			
		PSl	OCS	(Other PIE)
FV (e, ь) + m/n > FNV	ę	**pentĭ*	*pętь* 'five'	(Gk *pente*)
		*děsemtĭ	*desętь* 'ten'	(Lat *decem*)

BV (o, ъ) + m/n > BNVǪ   *pontĭ*   *pǫtь* 'way'   (Lat *pont-*)

                        domti   *dǫti* 'blow' Inf.   (Lith *dumti*)

As expected, the reflex of these is a nasal vowel, with the front or back quality of the nuclear vowel retained. The traditional marker of nasality in Slavic linguistic usage is the subscript hook, taken from the Polish alphabet. The underlying symbols are those of the basic (new) mid vowels *e* and *o* (while modern Polish uses underlying *a* for the back nasal – *ǫ*). Since the further development of the nasal vowels varies by area, modern examples are not given here, but in chapter 3 (3.2.1.2).

The quality of the underlying vowel may be taken initially to be low-mid *e, o*. The former height of the nuclear vowel is irrelevant, that is, height is irrelevant for the new nasals. The front/back opposition is reinforced within the system, as also is the feature [Round].

Diphthongs ending in a liquid sonorant (r, l)   This set of diphthongs is reflected in various distinct ways over the whole group, indicating that it had its final realization after the beginning of the break-up of the group. The motive force of syllable opening belongs to the unified period (before the sixth century, since the period of break-up is roughly sixth to ninth century), and so we treat it in this chapter. Its relative lateness may be related to the phonetic nature of the liquid sonorants, which are particularly able to function as vocalic nuclei themselves – witness the many languages, especially Slavic ones, in which both /r/ and /l/, or at least /r/, may be nuclei: Czech, Slovak, B/C/S, Slovenian, Macedonian.

The process here is not always strictly "monophthongization", but, rather, restructuring of the diphthong. In this set, the height of the nuclear vowel *is* relevant. Perhaps the lateness of the results means that the new vowel system was well in place by then, so that the different height of the former high vowels – that is, the height difference between the new /u/, /i/, on the one hand, and /ъ/, /ь/, on the other – is well established. This means that these latter vowels would not be fused with the low /e/, /o/ as happened with the nasals. Or perhaps it is simply that the combination of high(er) and/or short(er) /ъ/ and /ь/ with / r/, /l/ led more easily to a syllabic sonorant.

Thus we see in principle different results for *ъ/ь* + *r/l* and *o/e* + *r/l*. But in addition we see different results for each set across the dialectal spectrum. The most common way of formulating this structure is to use 'C' (some use 't') for any consonant and 'R' for *r/l*. So we are dealing with the late Proto-Slavic structures *CoRC* and *CeRC* (7c), *#oRC* (that is, where /o/ is word-initial) (7d), and *CъRC*, *CьRC* (7e). In some cases *r* and *l* behave differently. We treat the forms with /o/ and /e/ first, since they all result in an open syllable, and are thus relatively early. The forms with /ъ/ and /ь/ may not have reached the open-syllable stage throughout the area, and so may be relatively late.

CoRC, CeRC   For this structure we have three distinct groups, though initially there may only have been two types. There are really only two possibilities for resolution of the problem where the nuclear vowel is not of the reduced sort: (1) insertion of a new vowel (epenthesis), thereby creating an extra syllable ('type 1'); or (2) metathesis (inversion) of the vowel/sonorant sequence ('type 2'). Solution (1) is realized in East Slavic, and solution (2) in the Lekhitic area (north-west: Polish and Sorbian). A third type ('type 3') is a variant of metathesis, in which the vowel has additionally been lengthened (*o > a, e > ě*), and is found in the 'southern' area (South Slavic, Czech and Slovak, see 1.4.1). A common interpretation of type 2 is that it actually began as type 1, with epenthesis. Then the original vowel was lost and the epenthetic one remained, an analysis for which there is some circumstantial evidence. It is conceivable that type 3 also began as epenthesis, rather than metathesis, but there is no attested evidence of this. The three types, based on the modern situation, are shown in (7c):

(7c)   restructuring of diphthongs of '*o/e* + liquid sonorant'

    a East: CoRC (?via CoRəC) > CoRoC;

                                         CeRC (?via CeRıC) > CeReC

    b Pol/Sorb: CorC (?via CoRəC > CoRoC) > CRoC

                                         CeRC (?via CeRıC > CeReC) > CReC

    c South +

        Cz/Slk ('southern'):   CoRC (?via CoRəC > CoRoC) >

                                     CRōC > CRaC

                                       CeRC (?via CeRıC > CeReC) >

                                       CRēC > CRěC

(Late) PSl		B/C/S	Rus	Cz	Pol
*kórva	'cow'	krȁva	koróva	kráva	krowa
*bêrgъ	'bank'	brêg	béreg	břeh	brzeg
*zôlto	'gold'	zlȃto	zóloto	zlato	złoto
*mél-ti	'grind'	mlȅ̃-ti	molót′	mlét	mleć
*žêlbъ	'gutter'	žlȇb	žólob	žleb	žłób
*želzá	'gland'	žlézda	železá	žláza	zołza

The Eastern result is referred to in Russian as "*polnoglasie*", in English as "pleophony" or "full vocalization". As suggested in the bracketed forms, it is possible that the Lekhitic group went through this step also, but then removed the first vowel. The point-to-point statement could equally well be simply metathesis, as is accepted to be the case for the south, which then lengthened the one vowel, possibly in compensation.

At the suprasegmental level, the above picture is somewhat more complicated, since the stress in East Slavic may land on either the old or the new (inserted) vowel, and in the other languages the new vowel may be accompanied by different quantity or pitch. The cause of these variations is the nature of the pitch (rising or not) on the original diphthong (as marked on the examples in (7c) by ´, ˆ respectively).

#oRC   In theory we should also find the structure *#erC*. But there are no reliable examples, so it is normally excluded from consideration, though of course one can say how it might have developed. We have here two results, both described as metathesis, one with lengthening of the vowel in some forms. The inserted-vowel approach is, in theory, a possible intermediate step, as suggested for the Lekhitic group (type 2) above. But in this case there is no secondary evidence which might support it. Moreover, the isoglosses are different, since all of East and West Slavic have the same result – simple metathesis in some forms, metathesis plus lengthening in others – while the South always has metathesis plus lengthening. Thus, the South is consistent in its reflexes of the initial and medial contexts, but the East and the West are not. It is presumed that the initial position presented other factors, which caused either an earlier or later shift. Such factors include the vulnerablility of the absolute initial vowel position in a language shifting towards open syllables, since the preceding sound, that is, the end of the preceding word, would now be ending in a vowel. This produced undesirable hiatus (e.g. *ne orvьn-*'not (un-)even'). In other contexts the typical solution taken by Proto-Slavic was to insert a prothetic glide (*u̯* or *i̯*) which later became a consonant (*w*/*v* or *j*) (see further 3.2.1.4). In this particular context metathesis may have been seen as a more attractive solution:

(7d)   restructuring of diphthongs of 'initial *o* + liquid sonorant'
     a East/West: oRC > RoC/R$\bar{\text{o}}$C > RoC/RaC
     b South: oRC > R$\bar{\text{o}}$C > RaC

(Late) PSl	B/C/S	Rus	Cz	Pol
*ôrvьn- 'even'	ráv(a)n-	róv(e)n-	rovn-	równ-
*órdlo 'plough'	ra̋lo	rálo	rádlo	radło
*ôlkotь 'elbow'	la̋k(a)t	lók(o)t′	lok(e)t	łok(ie)ć
*ólk-om- 'hungry'	la̋kom-	lákom-	lakom-	łakom-

The two results in East/West are again caused by pitch differences in the underlying diphthong. A rising pitch was responsible for the lengthened form ($> \bar{o} > a$) of the new vowel.

As for the potential #*eRC*, it "should" therefore have become *ReC/RěC* in the East and West, and *RěC* in the South. One frequently produced example matching the criteria is **érdъk-* 'rare': B/C/S *réd(a)k-/rijèd(a)k-*, Rus *réd(o)k-*, Cz *řídk-*, Pol *rzadk-*; this etymology, based on the Lithuanian form *erdvas* 'spacious' (alongside *retas* 'rare'), is, however, challenged by Vasmer (1964–1973, vol. 3), for whom the Proto-Slavic form is **rědъk-*.

CъRC, CьRC   There are two views on the behavior of these diphthongs. One view (e.g. Schenker, 1993) holds that they were the first to become restructured with the opening of the syllable, facilitated by the ability of the liquids to function as vocalic nuclei, which allowed the conversion of the group to syllabic /r̥/ and /l̥/. The second (e.g. Carlton, 1990) claims that they were actually the last to change, as evidenced by their failure to open in some areas. The second view has the problem of explaining why just this type failed to open, especially given the inherent vocality of the liquids. The first has the problem of accepting a see-sawing effect of syllabicity. But this is not difficult, since it is clear that there were several episodes of this effect between PIE and modern Slavic. However, it has the more important problem of accepting that the syllabic segments retained the opposition of hard/soft (±Palatalized) in some form.

The tendency for the two *jers* (the name given to the vowels ъ and ь from the old name for these Cyrillic letters) to be reduced, and in many areas to end up as *schwa* ([ə]) (1.3.1.6), would easily have allowed these sequences to become syllabic sonorants. In order to account for the results, we must assume that the back/front quality of the vowel was at least initially preserved in the hard/soft varieties of the new syllabic sonorant. In this view, the syllabic sonorants are early Proto-Slavic, while the second stage, after the break-up, involves their retention in some areas, and their restructuring – once again – as sequences of 'vowel + liquid'. In this restructuring, the vowel is often "correctly" reconstituted as the back or front reflex of the *jer*, which can only occur if there remained a distinction in the syllabic versions. So long as one accepts this possibility, this view has the merit of conforming to the other structural developments of Proto-Slavic. But the view which accounts for the "correct" vowel reflexes through the failure to develop syllabic versions has the structural problem of accounting for the retention of closed syllables. We prefer the first view, and so shall assume the development of hard/soft syllabic liquids in Proto-Slavic and offer in (7e) only Proto-Slavic examples (roots), leaving the details of their further development to chapter 3 (3.2.1):

(7e)   restructuring of diphthongs of *jer* + liquid sonorant in Proto-Slavic

 CьrC > Cr̥C: *tъrg-* 'trade' > *tr̥g-*;   *gъrdl-* 'throat' > *gr̥dl-*

 CьrC > Cr'C: *pьrv-* 'first' > *pr̥'v-*;   *vьrxъ* 'summit' > *vr̥'x-*

(*kъrn-* >) *čьrn-* 'black' > *čr̥'n-*

CьlC > Cl̥C: *dъlg-* 'debt' > *dl̥g-*;   *tъlstъ(jь)* 'fat' > *tl̥st-*

CьlC > Cl'C: *dьlg-* 'long' > *dl̥'g-*;   *vьlkъ* 'wolf' > *vl̥'k-*

(*gъlt-* >) *žьlt-* 'yellow' > *žl̥'t-*

In all the above cases of diphthongs, wherever the diphthong was followed by a vowel, the solution to the open syllable impetus was simply to shift the new boundary to after the nuclear vowel. The former semivowel or sonorant became a syllable-initial consonant: *i̯ > j*, *u̯ > w* (> *v*), *m, n, r, l*. This is an important source of often quite complex morphophonological alternations, based on whether inflections began with a vowel or a consonant (4.4).

1.3.1.8 *Suprasegmental*

The following late changes occurred affecting all areas: (1) tone became restricted to stressed position; (2) all vowels which had rising pitch (automatic on the old long pure vowels, phonemic on those derived from diphthongs) were shortened, meaning that these vowels now had phonemic quantity under stress, since it was no longer predictable from quality. Furthermore, inasmuch as the new short vowels retained their rising pitch, tone was no longer limited to long vowels (and former diphthongs); (3) final long vowels were shortened, but pretonic length was preserved. Both quantity and tone were thus phonemic in a wide range of vowels, the latter only in stressed position.

1.3.1.9 *The Late Proto-Slavic phonological system*

We may now consider the system which has arisen by the end of the common period of development, just before the break-up in the sixth century, where we see different results for jointly motivated changes and the start of locally motivated changes. Table 1.3 may be compared with that of early Proto-Slavic (table 1.1). Brackets indicate regional or temporary variants. The combination of 'labial + *l*' (as the 'jotated' version) probably did not arise in the West. Of the soft dentals (from PV2/3) only /c'/ (from /k/) was general. The palatal stops are conveniently described as still general in this form throughout the area; /g/ and /v/ have alternative articulations by region, as stop *vs* fricative for the first, as labio-dental *vs* bilabial for the second. The apostrophe is used to distinguish palatal sounds from simply palatalized ones (marked with acute).

Table 1.3. *Late Proto-Slavic phonological system*

Consonants

	Labial	Dental	Palatal	Velar
Stop	p (pl')	t	t'	k
	b (bl')	d	d'	(g)
Nasal	m (ml')	n	n'	
Fricative		s (s')	š'	x
	(v) (vl') (w)	z (z')	ž'	(γ)
		j		
Affricate		c'	č'	
		(dz')	(dž')	
Liquid		r	r'	
		l	l'	

Vowels

	Front	Central	Back
High	i	y	u
High-mid	ь		ъ
Low-mid	e ę		o ǫ
Low	ě		a

Syllabic Sonorants

r̥, r̥' l̥, l̥'

Suprasegmental

Stress	Free
Quantity	On many vowels under stress or in pretonic position
Tone	On many vowels under stress

Note: there were also three fronted allophones after palatal consonants: ü, ǫ̈, ä.

1.3.2   Morphology

1.3.2.1   *Nominal*

The following are the features and categories of the late PIE nominal system and how they were treated in Proto-Slavic (discussion of the actual forms will be taken up in later chapters and sections as appropriate, especially chapter 5):

Case: the seven cases of PIE – nominative, accusative, genitive, dative, instrumental, locative, ablative, plus the vocative – were reduced to six plus vocative in Proto-Slavic (and Baltic) by the conflation of the ablative and genitive (into genitive);

Number: of the three numbers – singular, dual, plural – the dual was already losing ground in Proto-Slavic, having its range of cases reduced to three by the syncretization of NOMINATIVE + ACCUSATIVE, GENITIVE + LOCATIVE and DATIVE + INSTRUMENTAL. Subsequently it was completely lost except in Slovenian and Sorbian, but it was still functioning in at least OCS and Russian Church Slavonic in the "Old Russian" period (2.3.1, 5.4.1);

Gender: the three genders (masculine, feminine, neuter) were retained, inherent (syntactic) in substantives and agreeing (morphological) in adjectives (including participles), pronouns and some numerals (1–4);

Proto-Slavic refined the masculine group with sub-categories of ±Personal and ±Animate (5.4.4);

Adjectives: no change in gradation – positive, comparative and superlative; an added feature of ±Definite in most (non-possessive) adjectives (5.4.3);

Pronouns: no change to the general range and type.

1.3.2.2   *Verbal*

Tense: the six tenses of late PIE (present, future, aorist, imperfect, perfect, pluperfect) were all retained in Proto-Slavic. But their formation in many cases was different: the future, perfect and pluperfect were re-formed analytically with auxiliary verbs and either the infinitive or a past participle;

Mood: the four-way system of PIE (indicative, subjunctive, optative, imperative) became a three-way one in Proto-Slavic, with the replacement of the imperative forms by those of the optative and the functional loss of the latter; the subjunctive forms became primarily conditional, again analytic in form;

Voice: PIE active and middle were redefined in Proto-Slavic as ±Reflexive, and a new passive was added, a participial form like that of English *-en*;

Aspect: the most important development in Proto-Slavic was the gradual shift in the relative importance of aspect over tense. The feature ±Complete (perfective/ imperfective), while already present in PIE's past tenses, became more important than that of time. A further development was the splitting of imperfective motion verbs into ±Determinate (or ±Continuous).

Person: no difference, the three persons – 1st, 2nd, 3rd – were retained.

Two new, non-finite, verbal categories in Proto-Slavic were the infinitive and the supine, both derived from PIE deverbal nouns with an added *-t* suffix and an inflexion, frozen into indeclinable forms.

1.3.3   Syntax

Little more can be said about the details of syntax of either PIE or Proto-Slavic than follows from the morphological changes noted above. Given the continued high degree of inflection in Proto-Slavic, little would have had to change in terms of word order, and the overall categories able to appear in a given syntactic position would likewise have been the same in principle.

1.4   The sub-division of Slavic

The standard classification of Slavic involves a three-way grouping:

a.   East Slavic: Russia, Ukraine and Belarus, including Siberia and the Far East through the extension of Russian into Asia;

b.   West Slavic: to the west of East Slavic within northern Europe;

c.   South Slavic: the Balkans, from Slovenia south and east to Macedonia and Bulgaria.

These three groups reflect the three major dialects of Slavic after the break-up of Proto-Slavic unity. The modern Slavic languages then further sub-divided from these three main groups. However, there are numerous features which cut across this underlying classification between individual languages, or, in some cases, groups of languages. The future South Slavs would have entered the Balkan Peninsula via both the west and east of the Carpathian Mountains. Those to the west (the future Serbs, Croats and Slovenes) came from the earlier "south-west Slavic" group, while those to the east (the Bulgarians and Macedonians), followed the same way later by the non-Slavic Bulgarians, were from the "south-east Slavic" group. From this scenario follows the linguistic grouping observed in modern times, including parallels between, say, Slovak and Slovenian/Croatian, on the one hand, and Russian and Bulgarian, on the other (see chapter 10).

In the sections which follow, we present a hierarchical discussion of the characteristics of the Slavic languages. We begin with the macro-features which define the three major groups (which we shall call 'Stage 1 features'), then with sub-groups within the three major groups ('Stage 2 features') and, finally, with the individual languages ('Stage 3 features') (1.5–1.7). Unless otherwise specified, any language can be taken to have not only the Stage 3 features listed with it, but also the Stage 1 and Stage 2 features which belong further up its tree. Polish, for instance, also shares the features for Lekhitic (2) and West Slavic (1). We include not only features unique to a language group or language but also features which are commonly regarded as being among the typical characteristics: for instance, *akan'e* (the loss of distinction of low and low-mid vowels, especially /o/ and /a/), is found in both Russian and Belarusian (3.2.1.5).

Most of the features which we discuss involve phonology, morphophonology and morphology, together with some broad-scale lexical features. This reflects not only the traditional orientation of Slavic genetic linguistics but also the fact that the syntax of Slavic is less differentiated than these other levels of language. To facilitate comparison and consultation, the data are arranged in this order: phonology (vocalic system, consonantal system, suprasegmentals); morpho-phonology; morphology; syntax; lexis. This order also reflects the order of the chapters in this book. As far as possible in the following we avoid repetition of examples by cross-referring to other locations of relevant discussion and examples.

1.5 South Slavic

South Slavic covers Slovenian, B/C/S (including Serbo-Croatian, see 2.2.4), Macedonian and Bulgarian. Old Church Slavonic, the earliest Slavic liturgical and written language, also belongs to South Slavic (2.2.1). The South Slavs inhabit a geographically coherent area, and are now separated from West and East Slavic by Austria, Hungary and Romania.

1.5.1 Stage 1 features of South Slavic

The phonological grouping of South Slavic is more clear-cut than its morphological (chapter 5) or syntactic (chapter 7) grouping, where the eastern South Slavic languages (Bulgarian and Macedonian) are distinct not only from the other South Slavic languages but also from other non-South Slavic languages. However, there are few features which have united the whole group in the past, and even fewer in modern times:

1. The strong *jers* probably merged into *schwa* ([ə]), but this later shifted to [a] (B/C/S) or split according to the retained hard/ soft quality of the preceding consonant into /o e/ (Mac), /ə e/ (Blg) (3.2.1.1, table 3.1)
2. The front nasal ę > /e/ (3.2.1.2, table 3.2)
3. Loss of /y/, fused with and into /i/ (3.2.1.5, 3.3.1) (PSl *syn-* 'son' *vs* *sin-* 'blue': Rus *syn-, sin'-*; all South Slavic has *sin-* for both)
4. Syllabic liquids were initially retained, but /ḷ/ was then lost everywhere (> 'vowel + /l/' or '/l/ + vowel' in Bulgarian, Macedonian and Slovenian, > /u/ in B/C/S) and /ṛ/ became [ər/rə] in Bulgarian. A lost *jer* after a liquid produced the same results (3.2.1.1, 3.2.2.6 (42a–b))
5. Hardening of palatals and dental affricates (that is, lowering of the tongue blade), e.g. š' > š, č' > č, c' > c.

6. *tl dl > l*
7. *CoRC* etc. > *CRaC* (1.3.1.7 (7c–d) above)

1.5.2   Stage 2 features of South Slavic

The major sub-groups are "western": B/C/S and Slovenian, and "eastern": Bulgarian and Macedonian (and OCS). They derived from different origins and routes into the Balkans and/or different contacts once in the Balkans, for example the closer contacts of the eastern group with the Turks (the Bulgarians and Macedonians were under the domination of the Ottoman Empire from 1396 to 1897). This may account for their greater "Balkanization" – see the morphological features marked "Balkan" below.

1.5.2.1   *Features in support of the traditional Stage 2 grouping*
      a.   Phonology
          1.   Initial *je- > e* in the east, not in the west (3.2.1.4 (7)):

            (8) 'lake': B/C/S *jèzero*   Sln *jézero*   Blg, Mac *ézero*

          2.   Strong *ʙ > e* in the east, not the west (3.2.1.1, table 3.1)
          3.   Vocalic quantity/tone in the west, not the east (3.5)
      b.   Morphology and word formation
Eastern:
          1.   The loss of most of the case forms of the declensions (Balkan) (5.4.2, 5.5.1)
          2.   The 3 Person pronoun is *toj* 'he', related to the masculine singular nominative of 'that' (B *tója*, M *toj*), where the rest of Slavic has forms related to *on* (5.5.2.3)
          3.   Post-posed definite article (Balkan) (5.4.3, 5.5.1, 8.1.1)
          4.   The 3 Person plural present of all verbs ends in *-at* (the reflex of the back nasal *-*ǫ-t*); in the west this ending is *-e-* class only) (5.5.5.4)
          5.   The loss of the infinitive, which is replaced by subordinate clauses introduced by *da* 'in order to' (Balkan). Serbian has both, but prefers the latter, while Croatian is the reverse (5.5.5.3)
          6.   Bulgarian and Macedonian have taken over from Turkish the concept of "renarrative" verb forms, in which a separate set of inflexional forms of the verb are used to mark events which the speaker is unable to vouch for as fact. This has resulted in totally new paradigms of renarrative verb forms (Balkan) (5.5.5.8).

7. The formation of comparative adjectives and adverbs with the prefix *po-* (8.4.4)

Western:

1. In feminine *a*-stem nouns the *-e* and *-i* inflexions have "changed places" (in fact these are the former *ja-* stem endings) (5.5.1):

   (9) 'woman': PSl   *ženy* GenSg, *ženě* DatSg
                 B/C/S *žènē, žèni* Sln *žené, žéni*

2. In the plural of masculine *o*-stem nouns the nominative in *-i* is consistently distinguished from the accusative in *-e* (5.5.1.1):

   (10) 'town, castle' NomPl ∼ AccPl:
        B/C/S *grȁdovi* ∼ *grȁdove* Sln *gradôvi* ∼ *gradôve*

1.5.2.2   *Features not in support of the traditional Stage 2 grouping*

The features in 1.5.2.1 separate the "more Balkan" from "less Balkan" languages, but two features pair the languages differently:

1. Phonemic schwa in Bulgarian and Slovenian (3.3.1)
2. *x* > *v* in B/C/S (as a variant) and Mac:

   (11) 'ear': B/C/S *ȕho/ȕvo* Mac *uvo* Sln *uhó* Blg *uxó*

1.5.3   Stage 3 features (individual South Slavic languages)

a. *B/C/S*
   1. The failure to devoice final obstruents (3.4.3.2)
   2. *t' d'* (from *tj dj*) > *ć dź* (3.2.2.1)
b. *Slovenian*
   1. The back nasal *ǫ* > /o/ (3.2.1.2)
   2. High-mid ([e] [o]) and low-mid ([ɛ] [ɔ]) vowel phonemes
   3. *t' d'* > *č ž* (3.2.2.1)
c. *Bulgarian*
   1. Reduction of unstressed vowels (3.3.2.5)
   2. *ě* > *ja* (in certain contexts) in Eastern and Standard Bulgarian (3.2.1.3; 10.2.4)
   3. *t' d'* > *št žd* (3.2.2.1)
d. *Macedonian*
   1. *t' d'* > *ḱ ǵ* (3.2.2.1) (the dialectal phonetic range includes *t' d'* (c [ɟ]), 10.2.3)

2. The loss of /x/, although this is found also in some Croatian dialects (10.2.2):

    (12)   'bread': Mac *leb*, B/C/S *hlȇb*

3. Fixation of stress (3.5.1)

These features put Bulgarian at the most remote typological point of the South Slavic language sub-family (matching its geographical position). However, there are some features, particularly the presence of free and mobile stress (3.5.1) which relate Bulgarian more closely to East Slavic.

1.6   East Slavic

The modern East Slavic languages (Belarusian, Russian and Ukrainian) were all located within the former Soviet Union. They share a number of linguistic features – in addition to the features shared with West and South Slavic discussed in 1.4 – which distinguish them as a group from the other Slavic languages.

1.6.1   Stage 1 features of East Slavic

a.   Phonology
1. Pleophony (Rus *polnoglásie*, Ukr *povnoholóssja*) (1.3.1.7 (7c))
2. Proto-Slavic initial *je-* > *o-*
    The Proto-Slavic initial *je-* loses the *j* and changes *e* into *o* (unstressed *a*, stressed *vo-* in Belarusian). West Slavic and western South Slavic keep the initial *je-*, while Eastern South Slavic loses the *j* but retains the *e* (1.5.2.1):

    (13)   'lake': PSl *jezero*:
                        Rus, Ukr *ózero*, Bel *vózera* (with prothetic /v/)
                        Pol *jezioro* Cz *jezero* Slk *jazero* Sorb *jězor/jazor*

3. The strong *jers* > /o/, /e/ (3.2.1.1)

    (14a)   'sleep': PSl *sъnъ, sъna* NomSg ~ Gen Sg
                           Rus *son* ~ *sna* Ukr, Bel *son* ~ *snu*
    (14b)   'day':   PSl *dьnь, dьne* NomSg ~ Gen Sg
                           Rus, Ukr *den'* ~ *dnja* Bel *dzen'* ~ *dnja*

4. The nasal vowels > /u/, /a/ (3.2.1.2)

    (15a)   'tooth': PSl *zǫbъ*
                          Rus, Ukr, Bel *zub*

(15b)   'five':   PSl *pętь*
              Rus *pjat'*   Ukr *p'jat'*   Bel *pjac'*

5. The tendency to change /e/ into /o/ (3.2.1.5)

All three languages show this tendency, though the contexts are not identical and analogy confuses the issue. For Russian and Belarusian the context is: under stress and *not before* a consonant which was soft at the time of the change. The (then) hard consonants which allowed the change include some palatals for Russian, but none for Belarusian. For Ukrainian the context is *after* a palatal (Rus, Bel *ë* represents /o/ after a soft consonant, /jo/ after a vowel):

(16)   'green':   Rus *zelënyj* Bel *zjalëny* Ukr *zelényj*
      'you [Sg] carry':   Rus *nesëš'* Bel *njaséš* Ukr *neséš*
      'my' [NomSgNeut]: Rus *moë* Bel *maë* Ukr *mojé*
      'man':   Rus *čelovék* Bel *čalavék* Ukr *čolovík*

6. *t' d'* > *č ž* (3.2.2.1)
7. Syllabic /r̥/ and /l̥/ > 'vowel + liquid' (1.3.1.7):

(17)   'trade':   PSl *tr̥g-*:
              Rus *torg*   Bel, Ukr *torh*
      'first':   PSl *pr̥'v-*
              Rus, Ukr *pérvyj*   Bel *péršy*

8. Word accent: strong, free and mobile (3.5.1)

The strength of the accent leads to a reduction in length and quality of unstressed vowels, more in Russian and Belarusian, and less in Ukrainian, where there is a lower degree of contrast between the energy of stressed and unstressed vowels.

b.   Morphology

East Slavic has kept the dental ending of the inflexion of the 3 Person singular and plural: Russian (standard and most dialects) *-t*, Ukrainian (all reflexives, all plural, most singular) *-t'*, Belarusian (the same) *-c'* (cf. Bulgarian and Macedonian have *-t* in the plural, but never the singular):

		Rus	Ukr	Bel
(18a)	'he knows':	*zná-et*	*zná-je*	*zná-e*
	'they know':	*zná-jut*	*zná-jut'*	*zná-juc'*
	'he washes himself'	*mó-etsja*	*mý-jet'sja*	*mý-ecca*
(18b)	'he says':	*govor-í-t*	*hovór-yt'*	*havór-y-c'*
	'they say'	*govor-ját*	*hovór-jat'*	*havór-ac'*
	'they wash themselves'	*mó-jutsja*	*mý-jut'sja*	*mý-jucca*

c.   Lexis

Within East Slavic there are features which are either unique to East Slavic or link individual East Slavic languages to other non-East Slavic languages. Most of these words do not form particular groups, and are typical rather than systematic. Part of the reason for the special Eastern forms is contact with non-Slavs to the north (Finnic) and east and south (Turkic and Iranian). We give Russian, Polish and Bulgarian equivalents as examples of the three language groups:

(19)		East Slavic (Russian)	West Slavic (Polish)	South Slavic (Bulgarian)
	'40'	*sórok*	*czterdzieści*	*četírideset*
	'90'	*devjanósto*	*dziewięćdziesiąt*	*devetdesét*
	'good'	*xoróšij*	*dobry*	*dobắr*
	'wait'	*ždat'*	*czekać*	*čákam*
	'dog'	*sobáka, pës*	*pies*	*pes*

Some East Slavic lexis is shared with West Slavic, but not with South Slavic:

(20)		Rus	Pol	Blg	B/C/S
	'right' (side)	*právyj*	*prawy*	*dés(e)n*	*dèsnī*
	'spring' (season)	*vesná*	*wiosna*	*prólet*	*pròleće*

as is the common use of the verbal prefix *vy-*:

(21)	'choose'	*výbrat'*	*wybrać*	*izberá*	*izàbrati*

1.6.2   Stage 2 features of East Slavic

In overview, East Slavic consists of two poles – Russian and Ukrainian – with Belarusian as a typologically intermediate step. Virtually the only phonological feature from this set which unites Russian and Ukrainian is the preservation of soft /r'/, and even that is lost word-finally in Ukrainian. Elsewhere we find Belarusian sharing features with Ukrainian, and to a lesser extent with Russian, reflecting the early north-east/south-west division formed by the intrusion of Lithuania and Poland into the East Slavic area in the fourteenth-seventeenth centuries (Stage 2) (2.3).

1.6.2.1   *Features in support of the traditional Stage 2 grouping*
(south-western (SW) – Belarusian and Ukrainian *vs* north-eastern (NE) – Russian)

a.   Phonology (SW first)
1.   Initial i > [i̯] and /u/ > [u̯] if unstressed, if the previous word ends in a vowel, and if a single consonant follows (4.4.2)

2. 'Tense *jers*' (before /j/) > *y*/*i* (Rus *o*/*e*) (3.2.1.1)
3. *g* > fricative (ɦ/ɣ) (also South Russian) (3.2.2.3, 10.3.3)
4. *d'* (*dj*) > *dž* in verbal system only (alternation *d* ∼ *dž*) (Rus *d* ∼ *ž*) (4.3.1.2)
5. /v/ > /w/[w/u̯] in specific environments, including final (3.2.2.4) (Rus [v] or [f]): Ukr: prevocalic (except before [i]) > [w], before [i] > [v]; Ukr and Bel: post-vocalic and pre-consonantal or pre-pausal > [u̯]
6. Similarly post-vocalic, pre-consonantal or pre-pausal /l/ > [u̯], indicating the "darkness" of /l/ (3.2.2.5) (Rus [ł])
7. Loss of soft labials word-finally and before consonants (3.4.3) (Russian still soft finally)
8. Gemination of consonants before -(ь)j-: C'jV > CC'V (loss of /j/ and compensatory consonant length) (3.2.3, 3.4.3) (Russian still C'jV)
9. *CrъC CrьC ClъC ClьC* > *CryC ClyC* in unstressed syllables (probably via syllabic /r̩/ and /l̩/) (3.2.1.1, 3.2.2.6) (Rus *CroC, CloC*)
10. Stress location more often parallel in Belarusian and Ukrainian than in either with Russian (4.5)

b. Morphology
1. Some Russian adjectives have stressed *-oj* in NomSgMasc (actually the result of the Stage 2 NE phonetic change to the tense *jers*, see a. 2 above and 3.2.1.1) (5.5.2.1)
2. Russian adjectives and pronouns have a GenSgMasc/Neut written (and originally pronounced) '-ogo' which in the modern language is pronounced with a [-v-] (in dialects also [g], [ɣ] or ø) (5.5.2.1, 10.3.3)

c. Lexis
Specifically Russian is the presence of a large number of words and expressions which originated in Church Slavonic (9.2.2.1), and which have remained in the language in spite of various movements in favor of the vernacular. Many of these words can be identified by their phonological characteristics, particularly where they exhibit combinations not found in modern standard Russian. Belarusian, and even more Ukrainian, have gone much further towards adapting these words to native phonological patterns, which differentiates their lexis from both the Church Slavonic and the Russian models (contrasting features are bolded):

(22)   Church Slavonic (South Slavic) features in Russian

(22a)   Non-pleophonic forms:

'reward':	Rus *nagráda*	Ukr *nahoróda*
'return' [Noun]:	Rus *vozvrát*	Ukr *póvorot*
'main':	Rus *glávnyj*	Ukr *holóvnyj*
'Wednesday':	Rus *sredá*	Ukr *seredá*
'forewarning':	Rus *predvéstie*	Ukr *peredvístja* (prefix)

(22b)   Church Slavonic /žd/ for ESl /ž/:

'clothes':   Rus *odéžda* Ukr *odéža* (Rus, Ukr coll. *odëža*)

(22c)   Church Slavonic /šč/ for ESl /č/:

'illumination':   Rus *prosveščénie*   Ukr *osvíčennja*

(22d)   Church Slavonic /ra-/ (usually) for /ro/:

'equal':	Rus *rávnyj*	Ukr *rívnyj* (< *rov-*)
prefix 'apart':	Rus *raz-*	Ukr *roz-*

(22e)   Church Slavonic prefix forms {so-}, {voz-} for {s-}, {vz-}
(/uz/, /z/):

'gather':	Rus *sobirát'*	Ukr *zbiráty* (< *s-b-*)
'arouse'	Rus *vozbudít'*	Bel *uzbudzíc'*, Ukr *zbudýty*

(22f)   Church Slavonic prefix {iz-} for {vy-}:

'exile'   Rus *izgonját'*   Ukr *vyhanjáty*

1.6.2.2   *Features not in support of the traditional Stage 2 grouping*

Belarusian shows its intermediate nature in a number of parameters on which it is
closer to Russian than Ukrainian:

1. *akańe*: confusion of unstressed vowels, shared with Standard, Central
    and Southern Russian (3.2.1.5, 3.5.1, 10.3) (not Ukr and N-Rus)
2. *ě* > /e/ *vs* Ukr > /i/ (3.2.1.3)
3. The distinction of *i* and *y* is retained; Ukr *i* > *y* (with new *i* later, 3.2.1.5)
4. The palatalization opposition is more developed than in Ukrainian
    (3.2.2.2)

1.6.3   Stage 3 features (individual East Slavic languages)

1.6.3.1   *Russian*

The phonological and morphological features of Russian are those which were
discussed under 1.6.2.1 as Stage 2 NE features.

1.6.3.2   *Ukrainian*

a.   Phonology

1.   Unstressed /o/

The Ukrainian vocalic system shows free and mobile stress, but with less strength, and less contrast of quality and length between stressed and unstressed syllables. A corollary is that Ukrainian does not show *akan'e*, the pronunciation in particular of unstressed /o/ as [a] (3.2.1.5, 10.3).

2.   The most typical feature of the Ukrainian morphophonological system is the alternation resulting from the development of /e/ and /o/ in closed syllables – into /i/: /i/ before zero-desinence or some consonant clusters (especially geminate), /e/ or /o/ otherwise:

(23a)   'table':   PSl *stolъ* ~ *stol-a* NomSg ~ GenSg

[NomSg]   Rus *stol*   Ukr *stil* [sʲtʲil]   (Pol *stół*)

[GenSg]   Rus *stolá*   Ukr *stolá*   (Pol *stołu*)

(23b)   'honey': PSl *medъ* ~ *medu* NomSg ~ GenSg

[NomSg]   Rus *mëd*   Ukr *mid* [mʲid]   (Pol *miód*)

[GenSg]   Rus *mëdu/a*   Ukr *médu*   (Pol *miodu*)

(23c)   'night':   PSl *nočь* ~ *nočьjǫ* NomSg ~ InstrSg

[NomSg]   Rus *noč'*   Ukr *nič* [nʲitʃ]   (Pol *noc*)

[InstrSg]   Rus *nóč'ju*   Ukr *níčču*   (Pol *noca*)

3.   /ě/ > /i/ without any contextual constraint, thus with no alternation of vowels in open and closed syllables (3.2.1.3):

(24)   'snow':   PSl *sněgъ* ~ *sněga* NomSg ~ GenSg

[NomSg]   Rus *sneg*   Ukr *snih*   (Pol *śnieg*)

[GenSg]   Rus *snéga*   Ukr *sníha*   (Pol *śniegu*)

The new Ukrainian /i/ would have come into conflict with former /i/ if the latter had not been lowered and backed to /y/ as the consonants hardened (see below):

(25)   'blue':   PSl *sin-ьjь*   > Ukr *sýn-ij*
          cf. PSl *synъ* 'son'   > Ukr *syn*

4.   Ukrainian /c/ can be hard (mainly foreign source) or soft (native source – PSl /c'/), whereas in Russian it is always hard. (In Belarusian it can also be hard or soft, but the latter is from /t'/, see below and 3.2.2.2.)

    5. Consonants are hard before /e/ (*vs* soft in Russian and Belarusian) (3.2.2.2)

    6. Final obstruents do not devoice, a feature found only in B/C/S among the other Slavic literary languages (3.2.3, 3.4.3.6), though some dialects of Belarusian and Russian share this feature (10.3)

b. Morphology

    1. Retention of the old *-ovi* dative ending of the *u*-stem Masculine nouns (expanded to soft *-evi*) (5.5.1.1–5.5.1.2):

       (26) 'brother' [DatSg]   Ukr *brát-ovi* Rus, Bel *brát-u*

    2. Normal ("long") adjectives show a "short" ending (in fact, contracted) for the nominative and accusative singular (feminine and neuter), and the nominative plural (all genders). Belarusian has a "short" form only in the masculine singular, and Russian not at all in the normal adjective (5.5.2.1):

       (27) 'new':

          Ukr: *nov-ýj* [MascSg] *nov-á* [FemSg] *nov-é* [NeutSg] *nov-í* [Pl]
          Bel: *nóv-y*   *nóv-aja*   *nóv-ae*   *nóv-yja*

    3. The locative singular of adjectives and pronouns in the masculine/ neuter has two possible inflexional forms, one of which is identical to the dative singular (see 5.4.2 and 5.5.1 on the larger topic of the loss of locative):

       (28) 'green field'   Ukr *zeléne póle*   Rus *zelënoe póle*
            'in the green field' Ukr *u zelénomu/zelénim pólju* Rus *v zelënom póle*

    4. In the present tense of Class I verbs (5.5.5.2) with velar stems, which in Russian and Belarusian preserve the final velar in the 1 Person singular and 3 person plural, Ukrainian has normalized the stem to the palatalized consonant (that is, removed the alternation):

       (29) 'I can'   Rus *mog-ú*   Bel *mah-ú*   Ukr *móž-u*
            'you [Sg] can   Rus *móž-eš'* Bel *móž-aš* Ukr *móž-eš*
            'they can'   Rus *móg-ut*   Bel *móh-uc'* Ukr *móž-ut'*

c. Lexis

Ukrainian has applied native phonological processes to Church Slavonic borrowings, so that pleophony occurs regularly in words which in Russian preserve Church Slavonic phonology (1.6.2.1 above).

Ukrainian has a number of lexical Polonisms, dating from the period between the sixteenth and eighteenth centuries when Polish was the dominant cultural force. Most are shared with Belarusian, but there are some differences:

(30) 'town': Ukr *místo*   Pol *miasto*
              Rus *górod*   Bel *hórad*

1.6.3.3 *Belarusian*
  a. Phonology
    1. The Belarusian orthographic norm is more phonetic than that of Russian, in that the quality of unstressed vowels is expressly indicated. The *akan'e* system, where /o/ – as well as /a/ – is pronounced [a] *and* written with *a* in Belarusian, is said to be "strong(er)" and more active than in Russian: after hard consonants it has (for both) a vowel quality closer to [a] (= lower) in all positions than Russian, which has [ʌ] in absolute word-initial and first pre-tonic syllables, and [ə] elsewhere. And [a] occurs also after soft consonants (*ja-kan'e*), where Russian has [ı] (*i-kan'e*, 3.2.1.5, 10.3).
    2. Most typical of the Belarusian consonant system are *cekanne*, or the reflex /c'/ for Old Russian /t'/, and *dzekanne*, that is /dz'/ for Old Russian /d'/ (this affrication is a process typical also of Polish and Sorbian, where the reflexes are alveolo-palatal (*ć dź*) – see 1.7.1 below):

       (31) 'shadow': Bel *cen'* ([t͡sʲenʲ]) Rus *ten'* ([tʲenʲ]) Ukr *tin'* ([tʲinʲ])
            'day':   Bel *dzen'* ([d͡zʲenʲ]) Rus *den'* ([dʲenʲ]) Ukr *den'* ([dɛnʲ])

    3. All the palatals have hardened, that is, have low tongue positions, compared to Russian, where only some have hardened, and Ukrainian, where hard and soft appear as allophones (3.2.2.1, 3.4.1):

       (32) 'what' GenSg: Bel *čaho* ([tʃaˈhɔ]) Ukr *čoho* ([tʃɔˈhɔ])
                          Rus *čegó* ([tʃʲıˈvɔ])
            'six':   Bel *šèsc'* ([ʃesʲt͡sʲ]) Rus *šest'* ([ʃesʲtʲ])
                          Ukr *šist'* ([ʃʲisʲtʲ])

    4. /r'/ has also hardened, while remaining a soft phoneme in Russian and a soft allophone in Ukrainian (3.2.2.1):

       (33) 'river' Bel *raká* (/ra/-[ra]) Rus *reká* (/rʲe/-[rʲı]) Ukr *riká* (/ri/-[rʲı])

b.   Morphology

1. Belarusian has retained the old locative inflexion in *-i* (*-y*) after the hardened consonants /r c č ž š/) of soft-stem (*jo-*) masculine and neuter nouns:

(34) 'knife' LocSg: Bel *nažý*   Rus *nožé*   Ukr *noží* (*i < ě*)
      'beast' LocSg: Bel *zvéry*   Rus *zvére*   Ukr *zvíri* (*i < ě*)

2. Retention of the old dative and locative of feminine soft-stem (*ja-*) nouns:

(35) 'earth' DatLocSg: Bel *zjamlí*   Rus *zemlé*   Ukr *zemlí* (*i < ě*)

3. The nominative/accusative of neuters has acquired the masculine ending:

(36) 'village' Nom/AccPl: Bel *sëly*   Rus *sëla*   Ukr *séla*

1.7   West Slavic

The West Slavic languages cover modern Poland, the Czech and Slovak Republics, and a small area in the east of Germany.

The Northern branch of West Slavic consists of Polish, which with 35 million speakers is in no danger; Kashubian, spoken in northern Poland by perhaps only 3,000 people (see Introduction 1.3, 1.4, table 0.3), but without the status of a full literary language; and Upper and Lower Sorbian, spoken by perhaps 70,000 people in the eastern part of Germany around Bautzen and Cottbus, respectively. The Slavs on the Baltic originally covered a much larger area, including two now extinct languages, Polabian and Slovincian (10.4.2.1).

The Czecho-Slovak, or Southern, branch of West Slavic comprises two major modern Slavic languages, Czech and Slovak.

1.7.1   Stage 1 features of West Slavic

1. The *jers* merge into *e* (probably via *schwa*) (3.2.1.1, Table 3.1)
2. *t' d' > c' dz'*, then *> c dz*; the latter then changes at Stage 2 (1.7.2, 3.2.2.1 (36))
3. Extensive contraction through loss of intervocalic /j/; this then contributes to (5)
4. Stress is fixed on the initial syllable (3.2.4) until Stage 3 (Polish) (1.7.3.1)
5. Quantity is developed strongly until Stage 2.

1.7.2   Stage 2 features of West Slavic

The principal genetic treatment of West Slavic involves either two or three groups: Lekhitic, or Northern, includes at least Polish and Kashubian, but for some also Upper and Lower Sorbian, while for others Sorbian counts as a separate group; and Czecho-Slovak, or Southern. For discussion of the various attempts at subdivision see 2.4.2–2.4.3.

In some respects the Sorbian group represents a transition between the two other groups (Upper Sorbian being linguistically closer to Southern, Lower Sorbian to Northern). The Sorbian dialects are extremely diverse, and there are virtually no linguistic features common to all Sorbian dialects which distinguish them as a group from the other Slavic languages (10.4.1). There are also major dialect chains within West Slavic (10.4.5), and between West Slavic (especially Polish) and East Slavic (especially Belarusian and Ukrainian) (10.4.6).

The primary division is between Czecho-Slovak and the rest, Polish and Sorbian being much further apart than Czech and Slovak. Some of the features of Czecho-Slovak (especially Slovak) are also found in other Slavic languages, especially South Slavic, and especially Western South Slavic (Slovenian and B/C/S). From a typological viewpoint, the two Sorbian varieties present some features which cut across the underlying Lekhitic grouping (see 1.7.2.2). We shall treat Stage 2 as opposing Northern (N) to Southern (S).

1.7.2.1   *Features in support of the traditional Stage 2 grouping*
1.   The phonetic distinction between /i/ and /y/ is retained in N, lost in S (though with some retention of the effect on preceding consonants). The orthography does not indicate the phonetic fusion in S:

(37)   'to be':   PSl *byti*:   Pol, Sorb *być* ([bɨt͡ɕ])   Cz *být* ([biːt])
                                                 Slk *byt'* ([bɨc])
            'to beat':   PSl *biti*:   Pol, Sorb *bić* ([bʲit͡ɕ])   Cz *bít* ([biːt])
                                                 Slk *bit'* ([bɨc])

2.   /e/ > /o/ in some contexts in N, similar to East Slavic, especially Ukrainian:

(38)   'woman':   Cz, Slk *žena*   Pol *żona*   Sorb *žona*

3.   A highly developed hard ~ soft opposition in N, very restricted in S (3.2.2.2, 3.4.1)
4.   Syllabic liquids are retained in S, but become 'vowel + liquid' in N (3.2.2.6)
5.   /l/ > /w/ in N (3.2.2.5)

6. *t' d' > ć dź* in N (except LSorb, below), *> t' d'* (palatal stops) in S:

    (39) 'calf': Cz *tele* ([tɛ-]) Slk *tel'a* ([cɛ-]) Pol *cielę* ([t͡ɕɛ-])
          USorb *ćelo*
          'day': Cz *den* ([dɛ-]) Slk *deň* ([ɟɛ-]) Pol *dzień* ([d͡ʑe-]) USorb *dźeń*

7. *CoRC* etc. *> CRaC* etc. in S, *CroC* etc. in N (1.3.1.7)
8. Distinctive vowel length in S, lost in N (3.2.4, 3.5.3)

1.7.2.2   *Features not in support of the traditional Stage 2 grouping*

Beyond these features, at least in phonology, the languages show few features which group them differently:

1. *d' (dj)* (via *dz'* and *dz) > z* in Polish and Slovak, *dz* in Czech and Sorbian (3.2.2.1)
2. *v > v/f* in Polish and Czech, *>v/u̯* in Slovak, *>w* in Sorbian (3.2.2.4)

1.7.3   Stage 3 features (individual West Slavic languages)

One feature has different reflexes in each of the languages:

1. *r'* (or Palatal *r') > ř/ř̥* (devoiced) (Czech), *> ž/š* (orthographic *rz*) (Polish), *> r/š/s'* (Sorb), *> r* (Slovak):

    (40) 'river' (PSl *rěka*): Cz *řeka* Pol *rzeka* Sorb *rěka*   Slk *rieka*
          'a shout' (PSl *krikъ*): Cz *křik* (devoiced) Pol *krzyk* ([kʃɨ-]) Slk *krik*
          USorb *křik* ([kʃi-]) LSorb *kśik*

1.7.3.1   *Polish*

1. Retention of nasal vowels (3.2.1.2)
2. *ě* > /a/ or /e/ (depending on the following consonant) (3.2.1.3)
3. *g* remains a stop [g] (also LSorb), but becomes [ɦ] in Cz, Slk, USorb (3.2.2.3)
4. Stress is fixed on the penultimate syllable, on the initial in the rest of West Slavic (3.5.1)

1.7.3.2   *Sorbian*

a. Both Upper and Lower
    1. Prothetic consonants are attached to all initial vowels (elsewhere to some vowels or in some dialects only) (3.2.1.4)
    2. Retention of the dual (5.4.1)
    3. Retention of the aorist and imperfect (5.5.5.6)

b. Upper Sorbian
  1. *o/a > e* before soft consonants (*a* also in Polish, cf. Czech *after* palatal consonants):

> (41)   'salt' (PSl *solь*):   USorb *sel*   LSorb *sol*   Cz *sůl* (< *ō*)
>   Slk *sol'*   Pol *sól*
>   'to run' (PSl *běžati*): USorb *běžeć* LSorb *běžaś* Cz *běžet*
>   Slk *bežat'*   Pol *bieżeć*

  2. *ę > o* in final position:

> (42)   'calf' (see (39) PSl *telę*):   USorb *ćelo*

  3. *ě > y* after (hard only) *s z c*:

> (43)   'hay' (PSl *sěno*): Cz, Slk, LSorb *seno* Pol *siano* USorb *syno*

c. Lower Sorbian
  1. *ь* (*> e*) *>* a before hard consonants:

> (44)   'dog' (PSl *pьsъ*):   Cz, Slk *pes* Pol *pies* USorb *pos* LSorb *pjas*

  2. *ę > ě/e* (others *a/e*):

> (45)   'meat' (PSl *męso*):   Cz   *maso*   Slk   *mäso*   Pol *mięso*
>   USorb *mjaso*   LSorb *měso*

  3. *t' d' > ś ź* (see (39) also):

> (46)   'calf':   USorb *ćelo*   LSorb *śele*
>   'day':   USorb *dźeń*   LSorb *źeń*

  4. *r > ř > š* after /p t k/:

> (47)   'right' (PSl *prav-*):   USorb, Pol *prawy*   LSorb *pšawy*

  5. /g/ = stop (as Polish) (3.2.2.3)

1.7.3.3   *Czech*
  a. Phonology
  1. *přehláska*: the Czech "umlaut": back vowels are fronted *after* palatal consonants (3.2.1.5)
  2. Prothetic glottal stop before all initial vowels (a feature of literary Czech now breaking down) (3.2.1.4, 11.3.2)
  3. Loss of the hard/soft opposition, retained functionally only in /t d n/ before /i/, where the distinction is actually hard/palatal (see examples of /e/ in (39)) (3.2.2.2, 3.4.3)

b.   Morphology
1. Generally Czech has a relatively archaic nominal system, with less regularization of paradigms (5.5)
2. Secondary gender distinguishes only ±Animate, as in East and South Slavic, but unlike the rest of West Slavic, which has ±Personal (5.4.4)

1.7.3.4   *Slovak*
a.   Phonology
1. Long vowels have mostly become diphthongs *ia, ie, iu, ô* ([u̯ɔ]) (3.3.2.2)
2. Rhythmic Law: the avoidance of two consecutive long vowels or diphthongs (3.5.3)
3. *x > s* in the 2nd and 3rd Palatalization of the Velars (cf. *> š* in the rest of West Slavic) (1.3.1.7, examples (5) and (6))
b.   Morphology
1. Loss of the vocative (cf. retention in the rest of West Slavic) (5.4.2, 5.5.1)

1.8   **Overview**

In spite of the considerable divergence since the break-up of Proto-Slavic unity between the sixth and tenth centuries AD, the Slavic languages have remained both genetically and typologically coherent. There is nothing like the controversy over the genetic origins of Japanese (Shibatani, 1990: Ch. 5). And while foreign influences on Slavic have contributed a great deal in the area of lexis (chapter 9), and to a lesser extent to verb morphology (chapter 5) and syntax (chapter 7), the Slavic languages remain clearly Slavic in character, and Indo-European in inheritance.

They are also, to different extents, mutually intelligible. Speakers of the three languages within East Slavic – Russian, Ukrainian and Belarusian – communicate with reasonable ease. So, too, do speakers of Czech and Slovak; Serbian, Croatian and Bosnian; Bulgarian and Macedonian; and to some extent Polish and Kashubian. All of these sets of languages also show dialect continua which act as transitional variants between the standard languages (10.5). Communication between Polish and Sorbian, and B/C/S and Slovenian, is more difficult, given the typological differentiation of the languages. That said, however, it is also true that sentiments of ethnic identity, and from 1991 pressures of nationalism and separatism, are encouraging the speakers of the "smaller" languages to emphasize and develop the distinctiveness of their languages vis-à-vis the "larger" (first-cousin) language. There is also a universal turning-away from Russian influences, which have been dominant in lexis and style in political and economic language, in favor of western European and indigenous models. The break-up of the Eastern European block, while certain to have no underlying effect on the genetic cohesion of Slavic, may well lead, in a more superficial and less systematic way, to a certain emphasis on nationally distinctive characteristics, and an increase in variety between the languages.

Such issues, together with the historical events within which they belong, form the socio-cultural history of the Slavic languages, which is the topic of chapter 2.

2

Socio-historical evolution

2.1   The socio-historical context

The traditional classification of Slavic into West, East and South results not in three wholly distinct groups, but rather in three overlapping clusters of linguistic, religious, ethnic and cultural features (Birnbaum, 1966).

The South Slavs are less homogeneous. The Slovenes and Croats, as a result of their Catholic faith, use the Roman script, and have had long-standing traditional ties with the Austro-Hungarian empire. The Serbs and Macedonians, together with the Bulgarians, have been allied with the Orthodox Church and use the Cyrillic script. There are also considerable numbers of Muslims in former Yugoslavia, especially in Bosnia and Kosovo. The South Slavs have Albanian and Greek to the south, Turkish to the south-east and Italian to the west, and are separated geographically and linguistically from the West and East Slavs by a belt of Germanic (German), Romance (Romanian) and Finno-Ugrian (Hungarian) languages. This underlying religious–cultural diversity has contributed to the long history of instability in the Balkans.

The East Slavic languages have traditionally been mainly Orthodox in religious orientation, and use the Cyrillic script. Their cultural focus has been within European Russia, first in Kiev, and later in Moscow and St. Petersburg. They coexist with a considerable number of non-Slavic (e.g. Baltic), and also non-Indo-European, languages, both within European Russia and Ukraine, and especially in Asia, as a result of the colonial expansion of Imperial Russia to the east and south, notably in the nineteenth century (Comrie, 1981).

In contrast, the West Slavs have consistently been largely Catholic or Protestant. They use the Roman script and, like the South Slavs, were included in the Communist Eastern Bloc only after the Second World War. The West Slavs have had direct contact with East Slavic (Belarusian, Ukrainian) and Baltic (Lithuanian and the extinct Old Prussian) in the east and north, with German in the west and south, and with Hungarian in the south-east.

Most of the Slavic languages and cultures are now in a stronger position than in the past. Since about the eighth century AD the Slavs have had a growing influence in Europe and Asia, and more recently on the transported European cultures of the Americas and Australasia. Until the collapse of European Communism in 1989–1991, Russian in particular enjoyed a period of wide influence, not only as the main language of administration, politics, learning and the arts in Imperial Russia and then in the USSR, but also as an important linguistic, political and cultural force in Eastern Europe as well as on the international scene.

The Slavs refer to their standard languages as "literary languages", and regard them as bearers of their cultural traditions, closely bound up with their national and ethnic identity. The survival and establishment of the Slavs, their languages and their cultures, constitute the "external" history of the Slavic languages (Bidwell, 1970). We shall consider the languages individually, in order to establish the characteristics of each in terms of their social and cultural history. The order South Slavic–East Slavic–West Slavic roughly follows the chronology of major cultural development. We shall then survey the key features of this evolution in a cross-language perspective (2.5).

2.1.1   The external history of the Slavic languages

The "external" history of a language begins with factors of physical geography. The flat lands of Poland and European Russia facilitate migration or invasion, while inaccessible mountainous country can provide refuge, as in Slovenia and Montenegro in the former Yugoslavia. Equally important is political geography, as in the periods of Slavic history when the languages have been subject either to occupation by foreign powers or to pressures of political, cultural or religious conformity. In the Slavic world language has a particularly intimate link with the ethnic concept of nation ("natio") and the geographical–political notion of home-land ("patria": Walicki, 1982). Religion has also played a major role, both in terms of faith and as spiritual politics, either Christian *vs* non-Christian, or Catholic *vs* Orthodox, or Catholic *vs* Protestant. Here again the fusion of language and nation-alism is often crucial, as we find in Reformation Czechoslovakia and Slovenia. Other "external" factors which have influenced the evolution of the Slavic languages are more generally found in other language groups, and include social stability, military security, material prosperity, historical self-confidence and self-awareness, continu-ous historical continuity ("historicity"), ethnicity and national consciousness (11.2).

All three major Slavic language groups enjoyed an early period of power and prosperity – for example, during the flowering of the empires of Bulgaria and Serbia in the south, Kiev in the east, and Bohemia and Poland–Lithuania in the

west. They all subsequently underwent invasion, occupation and foreign domination from the early Middle Ages: by the Tartars in the east, the Ottoman Turks in
the south, and the Hapsburgs and Germanic states, together with the Russians, in
the West Slavic area. Some languages, like Polabian and Slovincian, died out.
Some, like Macedonian and Bosnian, have only recently achieved official status,
while other varieties, like Kashubian and Montenegrin, still lack that standing.
Unlike the Germans, the Slavs have tended to move towards a multiplicity of
languages, and of political and ethnic groupings:

> The Germanic group has been throughout history increasingly homo-
> geneous, and the Slavic group in some measure increasingly hetero-
> geneous. The tendency of German history has been towards
> consolidation – the concept of Grossdeutschtum has dominated
> directly or indirectly almost all Germanic political thought. The ten-
> dency of Slavic history on the other hand, in spite of sporadic efforts
> towards Pan-Slavism, has been in the direction of the formation of
> distinct branches of the larger group.   (Thomson, 1953: 131)

2.2   South Slavic

The modern South Slavic languages comprise two major sub-groups: North-west
South Slavic, consisting of Slovenian and B/C/S (Bosnian, Croatian and Serbian);
and South-east South Slavic, comprising Bulgarian and Macedonian. The Slavic
countries occupy an area bounded by the Adriatic in the west; the Black Sea in the
east; Italy, Austria, Hungary and Romania in the North; and Albania, Greece and
Turkey in the south. Slavic-speaking minorities are found in some of these adjacent
non-Slavic countries (0.4, 11.6). All these languages except Bulgarian were part of
the People's Republic of Yugoslavia until its recent disintegration, and are now
located in independent states.

The history of the South Slavic languages has been fundamentally shaped by
religious, mercantile and military conflicts. In comparison with the East and West
Slavs, the South Slavs have had to survive more foreign masters, more ideological
conflicts, more fluid political boundaries and more ethnic diversity. In place of
the Catholic *vs* Protestant conflict of the West Slavs, or the Catholic *vs* Orthodox
confrontation among the East Slavs, the South Slavs have had Catholicism,
Orthodoxy and Islam. Foreign masters, including the Turks, Germans,
Hungarians and Italians, have retarded the development of Slavic ethnic identity
and culture. This underlying heterogeneous character of the South Slavic states
remains to the present day.

The early history of the Balkans is known from Greek and Roman historians. The Balkan Peninsula passed from the Hellenic to the Roman sphere of influence about the third century BC, and remained under Roman control until the break-up of the Roman empire in the fifth century AD. By this time the Balkan area was Christian, but not Slavic. Its ethnic composition was hybrid, and it was only in the fifth century that the disintegration of the Roman empire contributed, directly or indirectly, to the arrival of the Slavs in the Balkans. The Slavs were known as the Antae or Wends. About the seventh century they may have been driven southwards from the Slavic homeland by the Avars, who also pillaged the Balkans from their base in the Danube Basin. The Slavs were pagan. The Balkans, after their arrival, were lost for Christianity from the sixth to the ninth centuries. But, unlike the other raiders, the Slavs were settlers, and by 750 they had spread through former Yugoslavia, Bulgaria and Greece. The indigenous populations were assimilated progressively and apparently fairly peacefully.

While Bulgaria and Bulgarian have a clearer identity, the history of the languages of former Yugoslavia (*jug-* = 'south'; *Jugoslavia* = 'south Slavdom') is very diverse. Macedonian (2.2.3) and Slovenian (2.2.5) are independent languages, with some complications vis-à-vis Bulgarian in the case of Macedonian. The other Slavs in the Serbian–Croatian area of former Yugoslavia fall into three main groups: Catholic Croatia and Dalmatia, where the Roman alphabet is used; Orthodox Serbia and Montenegro, as well as Republika Srpska, which use the Cyrillic alphabet; and Bosnia-Hercegovina, now Roman-script, where there are substantial numbers of Muslims in addition to Orthodox (Serbian) and Catholic (Croat) Christians. The religious and ethnic diversity of these groups has played an important role in the development of their languages. For much of their existence these languages have not had official national status. This is why political guarantees of the languages' standing and security have been so important, and why language policy and language rights play such a vital role among the Adriatic Slavs.

We address Old Church Slavonic first, with its historical origins and continuation in Bulgarian and Macedonian; then the three components of B/C/S, divided by religion and history; and finally Slovenian, which stands substantially apart from the other South Slav languages in terms of history until the establishment of Yugoslavia in 1945.

2.2.1   Old Church Slavonic and Church Slavonic

Old Church Slavonic ("OCS") is a special case among the Slavic languages. It is not identified with any one nation, and in modern times is largely a dead language, except in conservative ecclesiastical use. On the other hand, it played a pivotal role in the formation of the Slavic literary languages, particularly in the Orthodox world, and to a lesser extent in the development of Croatian. Old Church Slavonic has a supra-national character among the Orthodox Slavs.

The terms "Old Church Slavonic" and "Church Slavonic" ("ChSl") themselves present problems of usage. They are sometimes used interchangeably, which obscures several important factors. Old Church Slavonic was created in the ninth century as a religious language. It was based on the South Slavic of the Bulgarian–Macedonian area, though Old Church Slavonic would have been intelligible throughout the Slavic world at this time. It is not certain who "created" Old Church Slavonic, though credit is commonly given to Constantine (later St. Cyril) and Methodius, the two monks who converted the Slavs of Moravia to Orthodoxy in 863 (2.4.5). When Orthodoxy was expelled from Moravia in 870 the focus of the Orthodox movement moved to Bulgaria (Preslav) and Macedonia (Ohrid). At the end of the ninth century Old Church Slavonic was written in two distinct scripts, Glagolitic and Cyrillic (Appendix B), but within a century the more Greek-like Cyrillic had triumphed, although Glagolitic was used in parts of the South Slavic world into the eighteenth century. Unfortunately no manuscripts survive from the first century of Slavic literacy, but the later extant manuscripts show a rich literature, particularly during the Second Bulgarian Empire (2.2.2).

Old Church Slavonic was a liturgical and ecclesiastic language, and developed into a full written language used for doctrine, religious writings, translations of the Bible and for the celebration of church services. Strictly speaking, "Old Church Slavonic" refers only to the language of the early period, and to later writings which deliberately imitated it. Old Church Slavonic was initially maintained close to its original form for all the Slavic converts, and evidence of the early forms of the Slavic languages are known to us mainly through errors on the part of the monk-copyists, errors which reveal regional and individual variations in speech. Although it was South Slavic in phonology and morphology, Old Church Slavonic was influenced by Byzantine Greek in syntax and style, and was characterized by complex subordinate sentence structures and participial constructions. A significant part of its lexis, especially abstract and religious terms, was borrowed or calqued from Greek.

Nonetheless, over time accommodations took place between Old Church Slavonic and certain of the Slavic vernaculars. There were five major such versions ("recensions") of Old Church Slavonic, and these constitute Church Slavonic. The five were: the Czech-Moravian recension, deriving from the remains of the ninth-century Cyril-Methodius mission in Moravia; the Bulgarian recension, revived several times, for instance in the Euthymian revision of the fifteenth century, which was actively pursued in Ukraine; the Croatian recension, associated with the continued use of the Glagolitic alphabet; the Serbian recension, which developed in the eighteenth century into the hybrid Slavic-Serbian written medium; and, most importantly, the Russian recension (Mathiesen, 1984). Each recension had specific properties of spelling, phonology and morphology, colored by the local vernaculars. The first to exert major influence was the Bulgarian recension, which had the authority of the early church writings. The Russian recension took over the mantle of Old Church Slavonic when Moscow became perceived as the "Third Rome" after the fall of Constantinople in 1453. The Russian Church declared itself independent of Constantinople in 1448, and the patriarchate of Moscow was established in 1589.

The development of the regional recensions of Church Slavonic in the Orthodox countries provoked serious controversy, both within the church, and later in the debates over the developing Slavic national languages. The situation in the Catholic Slavic lands, with Latin as the liturgical language, was quite different. The status of Old Church Slavonic as a single, unified language of revealed Christian truth was one of the bases of the early Orthodox Church, and led to later attempts to "clean up" and regularize the other Church Slavonic recensions in the name of the purity of the scriptures. On the other hand, Old Church Slavonic was not used for administrative purposes – this role was fulfilled by variants of the so-called Chancery language, which was closer to the vernaculars, and played an important role in the emergence of Russian. Church Slavonic was important for all the Orthodox national revivals in the eighteenth–twentieth centuries, and for the evolution of Croatian. But Old Church Slavonic was not used as a model for these language revivals. Instead it acted as a kind of counterweight to balance the emerging vernacular literary languages against the proven models of established works in Church Slavonic. The Orthodox Slavs were in a typical diglossic situation, where they used one Slavic language for church affairs, and another for everyday business. The resolution of this bilingual or diglossic situation is one of the key issues for understanding the relation of Old Church Slavonic and Church Slavonic to the modern Slavic literary languages, and in particular those of the Orthodox world (Hüttl-Worth, 1978; Isačenko, 1958; Keipert, 1985; Thomas, 1989; Worth, 1975).

Church Slavonic is currently enjoying a revival with the resurgence of Orthodox religious faith in the post-Communist world of the old Soviet Union and the Balkans. It is still impossible to say whether it will withstand vernacularization in the years to come, or whether it will follow Mathiesen's prediction, made without foreknowledge of the fall of European Communism:

> It is not unlikely that the long history of Church Slavonic is finally drawing to its close, and that by its twelve hundredth anniversary in 2063 it will remain in use only marginally, if at all.   (Mathiesen, 1984: 64)

2.2.2   Bulgarian

After their arrival in the Balkans (2.2) the stabilizing effect of the Slavs' agricultural and non-nomadic village culture was counterbalanced by their loose political organization, and their lack of centralized authority, which made them vulnerable to organized opposition from a group like the Bulgars. This war-like Turkic tribe arrived in the Balkans from north of the Black Sea in AD 679 under the command of Asparukh, and had subdued the Slavs of modern Bulgaria and southern Serbia by AD 681. The Bulgars spoke an East Turkic language, and possessed a system of government and social organization superior to that of the Slavs, but their linguistic and cultural heritage was less solid. Within two centuries Bulgaria was speaking Slavic. The principal remains of the original Bulgarian Turkic language – apart from the ethnonym – are some common nouns and place-names.

The First Bulgarian Empire lasted until 1018, when Bulgaria and the whole Balkan Peninsula became part of the Byzantine empire. Byzantium was the most important political, spiritual and cultural influence on Bulgaria, and one which transformed it from paganism into a prominent literary culture. The conversion of the Khan Boris to Eastern Christianity in 852 marked the beginning of religious culture among the Bulgarians. Ten years later Constantine and Methodius set out on their Christianizing mission to the Moravians. And after the death of Methodius in 885 the survivors of this mission returned to Bulgaria to form the nucleus of a new religious culture, which included figures like St. Clement of Ohrid, the scholar and author who was responsible for baptizing the future Macedonians. Boris's son Symeon became ruler in 893, and his reign marks the high point of early South Slavic culture. It was during this period that Slavic became the official language of state, and Cyrillic the official script (AD 893).

The Second Bulgarian Empire (1196–1331) was linguistically and culturally more stable, with a literary flowering based on Veliko Tărnovo in the north-east. But the Eastern empire was in decline. Bulgaria eventually fell to the Turks in 1393. The ensuing period of Ottoman rule lasted for five centuries, until 1877. With the fall of Constantinople in 1453, Byzantine culture declined sharply in the old Eastern empire.

In the period before Ottoman rule, Bulgarian Slavic had advanced from being a vassal language to the status of a ruling, official language, and from an unwritten vernacular to an elaborate literary culture. Although the missionary work of Constantine and Methodius took place in Moravia, it was in Bulgaria and Macedonia that the early Slavic written culture and liturgical literature really flourished. The advent of Christianity provided the emerging literary language with access to the wealth and traditions of Greek Byzantine culture. The problem was how much spiritual, cultural and linguistic independence Byzantium would allow its new converts. In the early years there were many difficulties of dogma and practice. The Three Languages "principle", for example, stated that the only languages suitable for religious purposes were Greek, Hebrew and Latin, and the Bulgarian Church had to win acceptance for a Slavic liturgy, following the earlier achievements in Georgia and Armenia. Byzantium capitulated relatively quickly on this issue. After all, it had sent Constantine and Methodius to Moravia to encourage worship in Slavic. And Byzantium was generally more lenient than Rome was in its attitude to vernacular languages: the work of Constantine and Methodius, and their Slavic liturgy, was stamped out in Moravia by papal decree, prompted by the Catholic German clergy and princes (2.4.5).

The religious literature of the First and Second Bulgarian Empires – liturgical, doctrinal and hagiographical – was an important underlying factor in maintaining the Bulgarian language through the years of the Ottoman occupation. Although the church-based literary activity did not die out entirely, it continued only at a reduced level under Islamic rule, reinforced by the authority of the Greek Orthodox Church. Furthermore, as spoken Bulgarian evolved, it became increasingly distinct from the written liturgical language. Early evidence of spoken Bulgarian in the written language is found in the *damaskini*, translations of homiletic and other work from Greek originals, dating from the sixteenth century and named after the Greek author Damaskin the Studite. The *damaskini* reflected local dialects to varying degrees, tended to use more analytic constructions than were typical of the synthetic morphology of Church Slavonic (chapter 5), and permitted the use of Turkish loan-words (chapter 9). But they failed to create a single viable basis for a modern literary Bulgarian, and conflicted with the synthetic morphology of Russian-based Church Slavonic texts, which entered Bulgaria from the seventeenth century as part of an attempt to revive Church Slavonic as a written language.

The language debate of the nineteenth century, and especially during the 1840s, questioned whether the new literary Bulgarian language was to be a consciously historical revival based on Church Slavonic, or should rely rather on the contemporary nineteenth-century vernacular. And if the language were to have a vernacular base, which of the dialects would be selected? The linguistic controversy was intensified by the clear structural differences between Old Church Slavonic and nineteenth-century Bulgarian, which had lost most of its nominal inflexions, replaced the infinitive with subordinate syntactic constructions, developed a postposed definite article and acquired a whole system of renarrative tenses as a result of contact with Turkish. Rilski had published a grammar of Bulgarian in 1835 which moved significantly towards the vernacular, but there were conservative forces which attempted to reinstate Church Slavonic models, partly through an appeal to imported Russian, and Russian Church Slavonic, texts.

The outcome of the controversy was a consensus in favor of the dialect of the more prosperous eastern area, specifically the historically important centre of Veliko Tărnovo. When Ottoman rule came to an end in 1877, this new literary Bulgarian was energetically supported in the wider context of Bulgarian nationalism. In 1879, as part of the post-Ottoman "rejuvenation", Sofia (Blg *Sófija*) became the capital. In spite of the continuing cultural, political and linguistic pre-eminence of Russian, and the strong influence of Russian in the mid-century Bulgarian language revival, strenuous efforts were made then, and continue to be made, to purify Bulgarian from the Turkish, Greek and Russian elements which have accumulated in the language over the years. The Turkish element, indeed, had reached a level of penetration as high as 50 percent (Pinto, 1980: 46). The popularity of Russian texts in the late nineteenth century, which also provided a line of access to Western culture and vocabulary, in its turn was the subject of policies of purification, as nationally conscious Bulgarian writers and linguists moved towards a codification of the language which reflected Bulgarian, rather than imported, models. Authoritative orthographic specifications, first approved in 1899 and updated in 1945, together with the appearance of widely accepted descriptive and prescriptive grammars (Andrejčin, 1942/1978), helped to establish the norms of the language, though today Bulgarian still lacks a complete monolingual defining dictionary (Čolakova, 1977–).

The Church Slavonic literature, therefore, has been important in maintaining the Bulgarians' feeling of ethnic identity and historical continuity. But it has played an interrupted role in the evolution of the modern literary language. The lexis of Contemporary Standard Bulgarian is substantially influenced by Old Church Slavonic, either directly or via Russian Church Slavonic, especially in its abstract and liturgical terminology. But the phonology, morphology and syntax of modern Bulgarian bear clearer evidence of the vernacular. Bulgarian is an example of a dialect-based language revival where analytic vernacular elements competed with, and eventually won over, an established, morphologically synthetic, model of a literary language (Pinto, 1980: 51).

Modern literary Bulgarian, however, is often interwoven with local dialect elements, depending on the geographical origins of each speaker. As Scatton describes it:

> the speech of many educated Bulgarians represents a continuum, with the colloquial, non-literary speech of their native regions at one end and the learned, literary standard at the other. In actual usage, speakers move back and forth between these two poles, incorporating, to various degrees, non-literary features into their formal speech

and vice versa. Since the Second World War, owing to the rapid growth of the population and cultural prestige of Sofia, the westernized conversational speech of educated natives of the city has gained increasing prestige and has come to be regarded by some linguists as a (if not the) standard spoken variant of the literary language. (Scatton, 1993: 189–190)

2.2.3 Macedonian

As de Bray notes:

By an irony of history the people whose ancestors gave to the Slavs their first literary language, were the last to have their modern language recognized as a separate Slavic language, distinct from the neighbouring Serbian and Bulgarian. (de Bray, 1980b: 137)

But this view is opposed by the Bulgarians, who also lay claim to the origins of literacy among the Slavs. And Bosnian (2.2.4.3) has now become the newest Slavic literary language to achieve national status.

The Macedonians identify the origins of their language with the cultural and literary achievements of St. Clement and his followers, and especially the period of the early eleventh century, when the Bulgarian–Macedonian state and church were ruled from Ohrid by Samuilo (also Samuel or Samuil). But between the twelfth and twentieth centuries Macedonian language and culture were almost continuously subjugated to external religious and political pressures. The cultural doldrums of five centuries of Ottoman rule, and of strongly authoritarian religious control from the Greek Orthodox Church, caused a lack of continuity in Macedonian culture and identity. During this period the Macedonians were most sympathetic to the Bulgarians, partly on historical grounds, and partly for reasons of religion: the Bulgarian Independent Church, which was established in 1870, had jurisdiction over the Slav part of Macedonia, and the link between nation and church was strong in 1890, as it had been a millennium before. In addition, Bulgaria had a kind of geopolitical claim to political influence over Macedonia under the short-lived treaty of San Stefano (1878).

However, when Macedonia was annexed by Bulgaria in 1941, as part of the wartime break-up of Yugoslavia, the Macedonians found that the Bulgarians were not sympathetic towards the idea of an independent Macedonia as a political or cultural entity. Tito's promise of an independent federated Macedonia within the new Yugoslav state finally persuaded the Macedonians to ally themselves politically and culturally with the new Yugoslavia, and to abandon their long-standing Bulgarian affiliations. The Macedonian Church declared itself independent in 1967. And the Macedonians have carefully differentiated their language and culture from both Serbian and Bulgarian models, at least at the official level, and assert the origins of their language from their own dialectal resources (a view opposed by Bulgarian linguists):

> Macedonian is structurally related to Bulgarian more than to any other South Slavic languages. But the core of its standard was not formed out of dialects or variants that had ever been covered by the Bulgarian standard. Consequently, its autonomy could not have resulted from a conscious distancing of a variant of a pluricentric language. Like the other South Slavic standards, the Macedonian standard was based on dialects which had never before been covered by a standard.
> (Tomić, 1991: 449)

The contemporary standardization of Macedonian has nonetheless been aware of the need to differentiate Macedonian from Bulgarian.

The period of Ottoman rule marks a low point in the national identity of the Macedonians. When Macedonian finally did begin to re-emerge as an identifiable cultural entity in southern Macedonia in the latter half of the nineteenth century, its revival was based on folk songs and tales, which had escaped the influence of the Greek Orthodox Church. A typical example of the period is Konstantin Miladinov, who, in 1861, published a collection of 600 Macedonian folk lyrics and epics, and who based his own original work on the language of this folk literature. This language revival, centered on the southern dialects of Macedonia, provided evidence of an ethnically identified folk culture. The close connection between folk idioms and modern poetry is much in evidence in contemporary Macedonian literature. On the other hand, the influence of Bulgarian is on the decline. Bulgarian could have played a central role in the emergence of modern literary Macedonian, had the Bulgarians been more sympathetic to proposals for a composite Bulgarian–Macedonian literary language which were put forward by various Macedonians in the latter part of the nineteenth century (a situation which recalls the Slovak overtures to Czech rather earlier in the century: see 2.4.5–6). This was a lost opportunity to create a pluricentric (2.5) South-East Slavic literary language. The partitioning of Macedonia among the victorious Balkan states in 1913, and the subsequent suppression of Macedonian by all the occupying forces, effectively united the Macedonians against all their overlords – including the Bulgarians, with whom the Macedonians historically had the closest cultural and linguistic ties.

The Macedonian language achieved official recognition only relatively recently, at the Second Session of the Anti-Fascist Council for the National Liberation of Yugoslavia, on 29 September 1943. The Macedonians joined the Yugoslav Federation as a separate republic with their own language and literature in 1944. The language which became Contemporary Standard Macedonian was based not on the southern dialects of the Miladinov folk materials, but on the area around Skopje. And it drew its concept and definition of national identity and nationhood to a significant extent from *Za makedonskite raboti* (*On Macedonian affairs*) by Krste Misirkov, a work which, though suppressed shortly after its publication in 1903, argued for the geopolitical–cultural autonomy of Macedonia. Although this work acted as a statement of policy, Macedonian remains very much an *ausbau* language (11.2.1), rebuilt recently on a dialect base and consciously differentiated especially from Bulgarian.

Nonetheless, as Hill describes it, the situation of Macedonia within the federative state of Yugoslavia was in an important sense indeterminate, since it did not 'represent either a political, ethnic or linguistic unit' (Hill, 1982: 47). The problem was not with the political status of the Socialist Republic of Macedonia but rather with the misfit between the geographical territory of this entity and the Macedonian speaking territory, which spreads into Albania, Greece and Bulgaria. This situation has not been resolved by the formation of the autonomous state of Macedonia, or "Former Yugoslav Republic of Macedonia (FYROM)", after the political dismemberment of Yugoslavia in the 1990s.

Since 1945 much attention has been paid to codifying Macedonian orthography, grammar and lexis (though there is still no complete monolingual defining dictionary of the language), and to completing a linguistic description of the Macedonian literary language. In spite of all this, the Bulgarian Writers' Union still does not acknowledge the existence of a Macedonian language, which they regard as a western dialect of Bulgarian. The growth of a national linguistic consciousness, reinforced by educational and legislative authority, should make Macedonian progressively less like Bulgarian in the years to come. The promotion of a unified Macedonian language, however, is not helped by the geographical dispersion of its speakers, and there are substantial minorities of Serbs, Albanians and Bulgarians in FYR Macedonia. In addition, significant émigré communities of Macedonians are to be found in Greece, Bulgaria, North America and Australasia.

Contemporary Macedonia is autonomous, though under pressure from Greece and Bulgaria in establishing its political, economic, cultural and linguistic autonomy. While the standing of the language is reinforced by political independence, Greece opposes the use of "Macedonia(n)" for the country or the language on historical grounds.

2.2.4   Serbo-Croatian, Serbian, Croatian and Bosnian

2.2.4.1   *Orthodoxy and Serbian*

Among the Orthodox believers the dominating partner was Serbia, with
Montenegro and Bosnia-Hercegovina playing a relatively less important role.
Montenegro has a special place in the history of language among the South
Slavs, since it was here that some of the first books in Cyrillic were printed in
1493. The Serbs, who were religiously more homogeneous, were converted to
Byzantine Christianity in 871–875. Their early history was marked mainly by
resistance to Bulgarian influence in the east and south, but the Nemanja dynasty
(1169–1331) established the medieval Kingdom of Serbia, together with a considerable flourishing of literature and the arts. The Christians, however, were defeated at
Kosovo in 1389, and Serbia remained under Turkish control until the late nineteenth century. Many Serbs fled west into Bosnia, Dalmatia and Montenegro, or
north to Vojvodina and even into Hungary. Those who stayed behind found a
linguistic and national rallying-point in the Serbian Orthodox Church. But the
material conditions of life in Vojvodina and in Hungary were such that Serbian
culture prospered there more than in Serbia proper. The first Serbian literary
society was founded in Budapest, and many important figures of Serbian culture,
like the poet Jovanović and the educator and publicist Dositej Obradović, were
Hungarian-born Serbs.

From the fall of Constantinople in 1453, and especially from the eighteenth
century onwards, the Russian element in Serbian culture becomes more clearly
discernible, as Russia emerges as defender of the Orthodox faith and as the focus of
Orthodox Slavic culture. The Russian recension of Church Slavonic was adopted
and adapted for Serbian use. The Serbian language, however, still lacked a political
base, which did not come until the formation of the new Serbian Kingdom following the Kara George uprising (1804–1813). This served to focus the national,
cultural and linguistic aspirations of Serbs all through the Balkans and in
Hungary. And it led to the growth of pan-Slav sentiment, which the Habsburg
empire moved to suppress. Serbia was eventually freed from Turkish control by the
Treaty of Berlin in 1878. The success of Serbia in the Balkan Wars in 1912–1913
had the effect of uniting the Serbs, and of drawing non-Serbian states into a closer
union which eventually emerged as Yugoslavia after the First World War.

The establishment of the Serbian state in 1817 was closely linked to a rise in
Serbian national and linguistic sentiment. Written Serbian was not effectively
standardized. The Cyrillic alphabet was used in its Old Church Slavonic form,
which was not well suited to Serbian. The standard idiom was a "Slavic-Serbian"
hybrid (Unbegaun, 1935; Albin, 1970), produced by mixing Russian Church

Slavonic with Serbian. And the profusion of regional dialects made the spoken language different from what was written. The rallying cry of the new Romantic movement was "Piši kako govoriš, govori kako pišeš!" (Write as you speak, and speak as you write!), in the words of Vuk Karadžić, which recalls the views of the Slovene Kopitar (2.2.5). Vuk's earlier linguistic work, including a Serbian dictionary, was strongly influenced by the need to find a dialect able to act as a focal point for a new, more widely accepted, literary language. Slavic-Serbian was unsuitable, lacking either a recognized standard or a general consensus. Vuk's intention was to identify and promote a single dialect which, written in a fairly phonetic script, could act as a focal point for the linguistic sentiment of both the Serbs and the Croats. The reforms of Vuk (for Serbian) and Gaj (for Croatian) worked in close parallel. They agreed that the dialect of East Hercegovina – the *je-* version of the *što* dialect, or "štokavian" (10.2.2), a central and fairly neutral variant, albeit from the Serbian area – would be the national standard. Vuk reformed Cyrillic by adding new letters and discarding unnecessary ones (appendix B). Gaj's modifications in the Roman alphabet made Serbian Cyrillic and Croatian Roman match almost symbol-for-symbol. The lexis of the new language was purged of many of the Church Slavonic elements which had been so confusingly prevalent in Slavic-Serbian. These reforms achieved national status in the Vienna Literary Agreement ("Bečki dogovor" or "Književni dogovor") of 1850, attended by the major Serbian and Croatian specialists of their day. Serbia had used Serbian as an official language since 1814, and Montenegro even earlier. The unified Serbo-Croatian language did much over the remainder of the nineteenth century to prepare the way for the broader unification of the Yugoslav states.

Nonetheless, the status of Serbian and Croatian vis-à-vis Serbo-Croatian (as it was) or B/C/S (as it is) remains a vexed issue today, both in former Yugoslavia and among the émigré populations of Yugoslavs abroad. There were many Serbs and Croats who denied that Serbo-Croatian existed at all, except as a fiction to unite what they regarded not as variants but as two languages – Serbian and Croatian. Serbo-Croatian has now – since the dissolution of Yugoslavia – divided into three culturally and politically defined languages: Bosnian, Croatian and Serbian. The dual status of Serbian and Croatian in Serbo-Croatian was unusual, though not unique; in some respects it resembles the Hindi–Urdu relationship in modern India and Pakistan. In the Yugoslavian case, although the Hercegovinian basis of Serbo-Croatian remained, there were two parallel norms of the standard language, centred on Zagreb (Croatian) and Belgrade (B/C/S *Beògrad*) (Serbian). At the time of the dissolution of Yugoslavia, there was still no single authoritative grammar or dictionary of the unified language covering both variants. Apart from some differences of phonology, morphology and syntax (10.3.), there was also a tendency for lexical borrowings to differ in policy. Borrowings in the Serbian variant often correspond to calques or Slavic creations in Croatian: Serb *mùzika* 'music' corresponds to Cr *glàzba*, and Serb *bibliotéka* 'library' to Cr *knjîžnica*.

Naylor, writing in 1980, observed that "the linguistic differences between the two variants are no greater than those between British and American English and would not justify separating them into two separate languages" (1980: 68). This linguistic judgment has been overtaken by history, and it is difficult to conceive of a set of circumstances which would reunite Serbian, Croatian and Bosnian.

2.2.4.2   *Catholicism and Croatian*

The dominant group among the Catholics has been the Croats; the Dalmatians, in spite of a cultural flowering in the fifteenth and sixteenth centuries, became increasingly identified with Croatian political and linguistic nationalism from the nineteenth century. The national idea of an independent Croatia dates from about AD 924, when Tomislav led the Croats to freedom from Byzantium. From the late eleventh century until the Battle of Mohács in 1526, however, the Croats were under Hungarian rule, which was followed by 250 years of Turkish domination. In 1790, with the Turks already off Croatian territory, the Croatian Diet formally chose a form of alliance with Hungary, which lasted until the First World War. The language situation in Croatia was characterized by the dominant Hungarian influence. Latin was the official written language. Croatian Church Slavonic was widely used for religious purposes parallel to Latin, and was written in the Glagolitic script (appendix B) until the Renaissance, and increasingly in the Roman script afterwards. These Roman scripts, some of them even based on Hungarian orthography, covered many varieties of Slavic from Church Slavonic to local dialects. But they were ill-coordinated, and there was no consensus about which dialect should be used for official purposes. These difficulties were brought to a head by the growing feelings of Croatian nationalism and pan-Slavism at the time of the Illyrian Province (1809–1814; 2.2.5). During the early part of the nineteenth century, indeed, writers on Croatian often referred to the "Illyrian" language, and there was a widespread feeling that the South Slavs, excluding Bulgaria, were part of one single language culture. This new national spirit was expressed by the poet and publicist Ljudevit Gaj, a Romantic nationalist in the pattern of the Czech and Polish revivals. His work on orthographic reform, based largely on the Czech model, using diacritics, led to standardized orthographies for both Croatian and Slovenian.

The language question, indeed, sparked off one of the bitterest political conflicts of the nineteenth century. Croatian, Hungarian and German were all widely spoken in Croatia at the time, and Latin was still used as the official language in

Hungary and Croatia in the first half of the nineteenth century. In 1846 the Hungarians finally succeeded in having Hungarian, not German, accepted as the official language, and they tried to impose this solution on Croatia. In the short term the Croats lost this particular battle, since both the Hungarians and the Austrians proved unsympathetic to the establishment of the Croatian language as an official medium. In the longer term, however, this episode gave the Croats an awareness of their language-culture which added an important impetus to their political claims for autonomy, and led indirectly to the united Serbia-Croatia after 1918.

The polarization into Serb *vs* Croat culture was of long standing, and had strong religious bases in the opposition of Orthodoxy and Catholicism. It was emphasized by the growing use of Croatian in secondary and tertiary education throughout the nineteenth century – for example, in the Academy of Art and Science (1867–) and the University of Zagreb (1874–). However, the official union of Croatian and Serbian into Serbo-Croatian was enshrined in the Vienna Literary Agreement of 1850 (2.2.4.1). This agreement helped both Croats and Serbs to overcome narrow nationalistic outlooks and to aim for a broader cooperation in politics and culture. The year 1850 did not, however, signal the end of the tension between Serbian and Croatian, which became the two major variants of the new literary language. The theoretically neutral Serbo-Croatian stood between and above them, with two alphabets (Roman for the Croats, and Cyrillic for the Serbs) and agreed differences in phonology, grammar and lexis. This underlying dichotomy was both a dynamic and a difficult factor in the fate of Serbo-Croatian. The fact that the national standard was based on a Serbian dialect had been a source of irritation to the Croats, who had tended to promote Croatian, rather than the Croatian variant of Serbo-Croatian, in the Croatian Republic. In 1967 there appeared a unilateral Croatian declaration proclaiming the autonomous status of the "Croatian literary language". This position was actively supported by many Croatians, especially abroad. The Serbs remained more faithful to the notion of a Serbo-Croatian language: Serbo-Croatian, after all, was based on a Serbian dialect. This linguistic separatism has waxed more strongly whenever political and ethnic tensions between the Serbs and the Croats have been exacerbated, for example during the Yugoslav political crisis of 1991. The two languages are now officially separated.

2.2.4.3 *Islam and Bosnian*

Bosnia's history has been influenced primarily by its religious and ethnic diversity. Bosnia – which consists of two regions, Bosnia in the north and Hercegovina in the south – fell to the Turks in 1463, and many Bosnian noblemen became Muslims. The Arabic script was used to write Bosnian Islamic literature until at least the late nineteenth century (Ivić, 1986: 155). Bosnia nevertheless remained linguistically close to Serbian, and until its autonomy in 1992 Bosnian was seen as a dialectal area of Serbo-Croatian. Its population was predominantly Muslim, a feature it shares with Kosovo, dating from the 500 years of Turkish occupation of the Balkans. During the Tito period the Bosnian Muslims were given the new "ethnic" name *Muslimani* (having previously been simply Serbs or Croats of Islamic faith), but this name has now been dropped in the new state, replaced by *Bòšnjāci* (Eng *Bosniaks*). The Hercegovinian dialect was the one chosen for the standard of Serbo-Croatian.

The current population by ethnic group splits into Bosnian (44 percent), Serb (31 percent), Croat (17 percent) and "other" (7 percent), and by religion into Islam (43 percent), Orthodox (30 percent), Catholic (18 percent) and "other" (9 percent). Contemporary Bosnia has an unusual and difficult political structure, and following the Dayton Accords of 1995 consists of the Federation of Bosnia and Hercegovina, and Republika Srpska ("Republic of Srpska"), covering almost half of Bosnia, to accommodate the Serbian population. The script of Republika Srpska is Cyrillic, its base ekavian/jekavian (Constitution, Article 7), and its orientation is towards Serbia and Belgrade, with 90 percent of the population claiming Serbian allegiance. The remainder of Bosnia is under the new Bosnian government, uses the Roman script, and is developing a new language definition which is still emerging in instruments like dictionaries (Benson, 1998; Uzicanin, 1995).

Modern Bosnian is closest to Croatian, not the least in its use of Roman rather than Cyrillic. In lexis there are clear Turkish admixtures reflecting both historical and cultural realities (2.2.2). The status of the Bosnian language is increasingly recognized by bodies like the United Nations, UNESCO, and translation and interpreting accreditation agencies.

The website of the Bosnian Embassy in Washington offers two language choices: English; and what it calls "B/S/H", or "Bosnian/Serbian/Croatian (Hrvatski)" a single text in Roman script. This recognition of a multilingual, multicultural and potentially pluricentric status quo is unusual, and unlike the single-language focus which has dominated the states emerging from the former Yugoslavia as it fell apart. Whether this will work linguistically and culturally, as well as politically and economically, remains to be seen.

2.2.5   Slovenian

The Slovenes' history, in comparison with that of Serbia, Croatia and Macedonia, has been comparatively peaceful, but also lower key. The Slovenes have been Catholic since the eighth century. Partly because of their relatively small population, they have been almost continuously under the control of Rome or the Habsburgs, and have enjoyed a moderate level of material prosperity. Perhaps for these reasons they have tended to avoid armed insurrection and political revolt, and so have managed to escape political and cultural destruction. In modern times most of the Slovenes live in four major areas in the north-west of former Yugoslavia (Carniola, Styria, Primorska, Prekmurje), and in adjacent areas of Austria and Hungary (Carinthia) and Italy (Venetian Slovenia). About 300,000 Slovenes live abroad, principally in North America.

Slovenian illustrates the difficulty of establishing a written language in a political context with insufficient administrative and educational support and cultural continuity. German-Slovenian diglossia, which has been standard for centuries in Slovenia, has itself helped to retard the emergence of a fully autonomous and articulated Slovenian literary language.

Typically of the "smaller" Slavic languages, the emergence of the Slovenian nation is closely connected with factors of language and culture. The Slovenes were united more by their wish to define their identity apart from the German world than by a wider pan-Slav or Yugoslav sentiment, which became part of Slovene national consciousness only in relatively recent times. Apart from brief periods of allegiance to the Slavic kingdoms of Samo (627–658) and Otakar II (1253–1278), the Slovenes were subject to non-Slavic political rule, and to the religious domination of Rome, from their conversion in 748 until 1945. After 1278 they passed from the control of the Holy Roman Empire into that of the Habsburgs. From the fourteenth century the official policy was one of Germanization and colonization at the expense of Slovenian language and culture. The official languages were Latin, German and Italian, the latter two spoken by the nobility and the middle classes, while the peasantry spoke Slovenian. The Reformation, however, led to a sudden increase in Slovenian linguistic and cultural nationalism. Protestantism was widely accepted in the churches and schools. This religious revolution was accompanied by a spontaneous popular surge of activity in the Slovenian language, symbolized by Primož Trubar, who translated the New Testament into Slovenian and produced a series of hymns and other religious works which were read, admired and imitated by writers like Jurij Dalmatin, the translator of the Old Testament (1584). There was now a model for the Slovenian literary language, supported by the grammar of Bohorič (1584), based on the Lower Carniolan (Dolenjsko) dialect of Trubar and Dalmatin, from the area to the south of Ljubljana. The later admixture of elements from the Gorenjsko dialect of Ljubljana represented an addition rather than a major revision, and in many respects this sixteenth-century idiom remained the principal model for the later development of literary Slovenian.

The Counter-Reformation of the seventeenth century, however, interrupted the nascent national Slovenian language-culture. Slovenian books were burned, and dissidents persecuted. This anti-Slovenian attitude persisted until the Napoleonic Wars, when Slovenia, like many other "smaller" language-cultures, was caught up in the wave of nationalism which swept Europe. Napoleon's plans included the establishment of the Province of Illyria (1809–1814), which was designed to provide a home for the unification of Slovenes, Croats and Serbs. This potential framework for Slovene nationalism was also a spur to pan-Slavic sentiment. In its more local form this idea, which survived even after the fall of Napoleon, included the absorption of Slovenian into Serbian-Croatian (not yet Serbo-Croatian!), also known as the "Illyrian language" (Iovine, 1984). In its wider form, for instance in the writings of the Slovak poet and scholar Kollár, there would be four principal "dialects" of Slavic – Polish, Russian, Czech and Illyrian – unified within a transnational concept of Slavdom. The Illyrian plan could have been a mixed blessing for the Slovenes, since their language could easily have been overshadowed by the numerically and historically stronger Serbian-Croatian axis. But Slovenian escaped this fate, thanks mainly to the union of Serbian and Croatian in 1850, which excluded Slovenian and rendered the Illyrian concept irrelevant, and confirmed Thomson's observation of the tendency of the Slavs to increasing diversification, rather than unification (2.1.1).

The Slovenes were left to work out the shape of their own revived literary language. There were vital contributions from men like Valentin Vodnik, a writer, teacher, publicist, grammarian and lexicographer; Prešeren, a poet of international standing; and Kopitar, an influential Slavic philologist, author of the first full descriptive grammar of Slovenian and promoter of an all-Slovenian language (1809). The key problem was the familiar issue of established literary norms versus the claims of the principal dialects. The Reformation model of literary Slovenian was prestigious and supported by major written texts. But it was increasingly distant from spoken Slovenian, whose dialects had continued to evolve and diverge. This made it difficult for those shaping the new Slovenian language to reconcile it with the popular nineteenth-century trend towards more phonetic orthographies and vernacular-oriented literary languages, a position advocated by Kopitar and opposed by Prešeren's view of a reasonable compromise of historical and contemporary spoken Slovenian, as well as of Slovenian and foreign (especially German) elements (Herrity, 1985). The controversy between the "historical" and the "vernacular" camps was finally resolved in what Stankiewicz (1980: 101) calls a "modern historicism". Modern literary Slovenian is, like Bulgarian, a dialectal artefact, an abstraction not naturally occurring in the dialect base of the language. It is a 'more or less abstract platform to secure the linguistic unification of the language' (Lencek, 1982: 284).

Slovenian was not accepted as an official administrative medium until 1945. The 1920 plebiscite had shown that the majority of the Slovenes living in Styria and Carinthia wished to remain in Austria rather than join the new inter-war Yugoslavia. This result is commonly attributed to the Slovenes' fear of domination by the Serbian and Croatian majorities in Yugoslavia. Either way, it kept a large number of Slovenes outside Yugoslavia until the territorial, national and political changes brought about by the Second World War consolidated the major part of the Slovenes in Tito's Yugoslavia, with full constitutional linguistic rights, as a constituent republic. The language is now fully codified in orthography, grammar and lexicography.

The separation of Slovenia as an independent nation on the break-up of Yugoslavia in 1991 is helping to confirm the status of Slovenian, in the absence of pressure and competition from Serbo-Croatian. Certainly the contexts where Serbo-Croatian was favored in the Republic of Yugoslavia – including television, education and the armed forces, as described by Toporišič (1978) – are now significantly reduced.

2.3   East Slavic

The three modern East Slavic languages are Russian, Ukrainian and Belarusian. As a linguistic group they are more homogeneous than South or West Slavic. Under the Soviet regime they were all part of the USSR. Ukrainian was centered in the Ukrainian Soviet Socialist Republic of the USSR, and Belarusian in the Belorussian (as it then was)[1] Soviet Socialist Republic, situated on the western borders of the USSR. Russian was the language of the Russian Soviet Federal Socialist Republic, which was not only the political and cultural center of the USSR, but also the largest of the republics, covering the expanse from European Russia to the Pacific. Russian was also the *lingua communis* of the entire USSR, as it is of the new Russian Federation, which is territorially still the world's largest nation. All three language cultures and countries are now officially autonomous.

In comparison to the West and South Slavs, the East Slavs have remained politically and culturally more cohesive. Russia and Russian have been the dominant forces. This factor has hindered the emergence of both Ukrainian and Belarusian as autonomous language-cultures. True, the Russian influence has

---

[1] In these sections we use *Belorussia(n)* only for names like the Belorussian SSR or older references to the geographical area. Elsewhere, in spite of anachrony, we favor *Belarus* for the state as it was officially named after independence in 1991, and *Belarusian* as the adjective and name of the language.

been interrupted – first by the Tartar invasion and occupation, and later by the periods of Polish domination in Belorussia and Ukraine; Polish also had an appreciable effect on Russian, especially in the seventeenth and early eighteenth centuries. The main source of this Polish element was the eastward expansion of Poland after the fourteenth century, which brought with it Catholicism, particularly Jesuit Catholicism, and a more Western form of culture. Russia regained control of Ukraine and Belorussia after the Partitions of Poland at the end of the eighteenth century. Both Ukraine and Belorussia, however, had a difficult path to linguistic and cultural autonomy, particularly under Russian rule. Having finally become federated republics of the USSR in the 1920s, they were subjected to Stalin's anti-nationalistic purges in the 1930s, and the subsequent policy of cultural and linguistic Russianization. In *Marxism and the problems of linguistics* (1954) Stalin claimed that linguistic variety within the USSR actually demonstrated that Russian was a national supra-language. The extent of this linguistic imperialism can be judged by the data on publishing (Armstrong, 1962), which favored Russian out of all proportion to the population balance. This was in direct contradiction to Lenin's explicit policy of national cultural self-determination.

All three East Slavic languages lay claim to the same early written records as evidence of their own historicity. East Slavic learning began at a time when the three languages were dialectally similar, and the center of this emerging culture was, at various times, located in Ukraine and Great Russia. From the conversion of the East Slavs to Orthodoxy in 988 until the sacking of Kiev by the Tartars in 1240, the East Slavs were culturally, religiously and linguistically coherent. The written records bear the mark of the Greek Orthodox influence, which was transmitted by the disciples of Cyril and Methodius from Moravia to Bulgaria, and thence to Russia. The earliest documents of East Slavic are in Church Slavonic – a South Slavic language – in both the Glagolitic and the Cyrillic scripts. They are mainly religious, and consist of Gospels, sermons, prayers and hagiography. Only occasional errors on the part of the monk copyists reveal the beginnings of dialect differentiation. Distinct Russian, Ukrainian and Belarusian emerged slowly, following the disorganization of Rus' during and after the Tartar invasion, the absorption of Ukraine and Belorussia into Poland and Lithuania, the later emergence of Novgorod, Moscow and St. Petersburg as centres of Orthodox culture and political influence, and the folklore- and regionally based cultural revivals. Moscow emerged as the dominant East Slavic cultural force with the fall of Constantinople and Bulgaria to the Turks. As a result, Moscow took on the role of the "Third Rome" as the centre of Orthodoxy. Nevertheless, the Russian language did not achieve a viable written literary form, clearly distinguished from Church Slavonic, until the latter part of the eighteenth century. And for

Ukrainian and Belarusian there was the additional burden of establishing and maintaining their autonomy from "Great" Russian. All three languages have had long histories of diglossia, especially involving the vernacular and Church Slavonic.

2.3.1 Russian

The history of Russian (or "Great Russian") shows a language-culture developing from a position of relative strength. The most significant political threat to Russian was the 250 years' occupation by the Tartars between the thirteenth and fifteenth centuries. But in spite of their destructive political and cultural influence, the Tartars were not linguistically hostile to the Russians. The development of the Russian language was characterized by a search for identity. On the one hand, it was necessary to differentiate Russian clearly from Church Slavonic; and, on the other hand, various Western languages (mainly French, Polish and German) had left behind linguistic bric-à-brac in Russian which had to be eclectically discarded from, or integrated with, the emerging written language.

The East Slavs were converted to Orthodox Christianity under Prince Vladimir in AD 988, and literacy among the Russians began with religious and hagiographical writings. The earliest manuscript to contain Russian elements, even if only in copyists' errors, is the Ostromir Gospel of 1056–1057. Here we find the beginnings of a Russianized Church Slavonic, which spread gradually to liturgical, ecclesiastical and chancery documents (see below), where the use of Church Slavonic was obligatory. The non-official records of Russian from this period, like the Novgorod birch-bark inscriptions and some inscriptions on pottery, show even more evidence of a native Russian idiom. The *Igor Tale*, a heroic epic describing a military campaign of 1185, shows stronger Russian elements, though its authenticity is not certain.

With the passage of time Russian dialects became increasingly distinct from the original common East Slavic. After the fall of Kiev, in 1240, the centre of power shifted to Novgorod and then to Moscow (Rus *Moskvá*), which meant that the geographical center of the future Russian literary language was much further to the north. And the Moscow dialect eventually became, from the eighteenth century, the basis for the development of the new literary Russian language. Before this time, however, the model of the literary language was Church Slavonic, maintained in a fairly static state by the authority of the church. The Church Slavonic language, and its cultural tradition, gave to Russian considerable quantities of vocabulary in the form of borrowings and calques, ultimately from Greek. After the loss of Bulgaria to the Turks, and the fall of Constantinople in 1453, Russian Orthodoxy became more self-contained, both dogmatically and linguistically. And if the influence of Church Slavonic is also fundamental to the development of South Slavic literary languages, these latter differ from Russian in that the geographical source of interference was closer to home. As the Russian language evolved, Church Slavonic became progressively more foreign, and the presence of these non-native South Slavic Church Slavonic elements is particularly evident in Russian. The South Slavic component was deliberately emphasized during the "Second South Slavic Influence" of the late fourteenth and fifteenth centuries, when Bulgarian prelates consciously "re-Bulgarized" (Issatschenko, 1980; 1980–1983) the church texts to achieve maximum conformity with the established church norms. In time, however, the Russian recension of Church Slavonic gained increasing acceptance in Russia, and came to influence Serbian and Bulgarian Church Slavonic, and the formation and revival of these literary languages. Nonetheless, a genuinely Russian translation of the gospels did not appear until 1819.

The fifteenth century also marked the opening of regular Russian contacts with the West. The Tartars had left behind only a modest legacy of vocabulary, and little else of cultural value. Russian was still insulated from the Renaissance and the Reformation by distance, poor communications and political isolationism. But the language began steadily to acquire a more Western character, with cultural contact and lexical loans from Polish and Ukrainian, and – often by way of these languages – from German, Italian and French. By the start of the eighteenth century, however, Russia was still culturally backward, with an unsophisticated literature, restricted in scope and sensibility, and written in a heavy and unexpressive idiom. The so-called "Chancery" language (Rus *delovój jazýk*), a bureaucratic register somewhat closer to spoken Russian, was also conservative and inflexible.

The force that Westernized Russia and Russian was Peter the Great (1672–1725), who '[hauled] Muscovy kicking and screaming into the 18th century' (Hingley, 1972: 74). Peter was personally responsible for weakening the authority of the church in areas of Russian culture, education, public life, politics and economic affairs. He imported Western technology and technologists, military advisers, and cultural and linguistic models. Many of his contemporaries, and many subsequent critics, have accused him of being an undiscriminating reformer. This is certainly true in some cases: his technical and cultural importations, for instance, created lexical anarchy in Russian for more than half a century. But Peter, in a linguistic sense, was a kind of latter-day Reformation man. He brought education and writing to the people by reforms of Russian calligraphy, typography and orthography, and he actively encouraged the use of Russian in all areas outside the strict confines of church affairs. The question now was how Russian would create linguistic and artistic forms from properly Russian material, and how these would relate to the Church Slavonic models which had hitherto dominated Russian writing.

The relation between Church Slavonic and Russian is the key to an understanding of the evolution of the modern Russian literary language. Some authors interpret the history of Russian in terms of a steady Russification of Church Slavonic. More recently, however, Issatschenko (1980, 1980–1983) and others have argued that there is, in fact, a break in the evolution of Russian in the eighteenth century, coinciding with the break-down of Russian–Church Slavonic diglossia, and the emergence of new models for literary Russian, especially the written and spoken forms of educated French. This Westernizing movement forms part of the central Russian cultural theme of the eighteenth century. There was a large amount of straight imitation and translation of French, German, Italian and Polish literature, philosophy and publicistic writings. During the course of the century some substantial literary talents were instrumental in bringing Western culture to Russia, and in attempting to form a Russian literary medium which could express all that its foreign models could. The most famous example is probably Karamzin, although his role as a slavish Westernizer is commonly overstated. At the other extreme was a faction known as the Slavophiles, who were in favor of taking over as little as possible from the West, and of exploiting the resources of Slavic to fill the obvious linguistic and literary gaps (Walicki, 1975). The polymath and grammarian Lomonosov first formulated the problem clearly in 1755 in his adaptation of the classical theory of the "three styles" to the balance of Church Slavonic and Russian elements in the literary language: a high style for formal occasions and heroic poems, with substantial Church Slavonic influence; a middle style for informal verse epistles, satires, eclogues and elegies; and a low style for comedy, epigrams, prose and ordinary affairs. This helped to stabilize some of the stylistic confusion in Russian literature of the time. Towards the end of the century, writers like the fabulist Krylov began to make increasing use of Russian and of Russian folklore, and the work of Pushkin in particular was fundamental in the establishment of a workable balance of Russian and non-Russian elements in the new literary language. Pushkin was accused of being an immoderate Westernizer by the Slavophile camp, and it was fortunate for Russian literature that Pushkin's language, and that of later major poets like Lermontov and Tyutchev, and prose writers like Turgenev, Tolstoy and Dostoevsky, showed that the medium was rich and flexible enough to fulfill the role of a major literary language. The Church Slavonic element has nevertheless remained in some aspects of phonology, and in many areas of grammar and particularly lexis. On the other hand, the Russian regional phonological influence on the contemporary standard is evident in the Moscow pronunciation, with its approximate admixture of South Russian vowels and North Russian consonants (10.3.3).

During the nineteenth century the Russian language made two significant advances. In literature, science and other registers it became a much more flexible and sophisticated medium; and in geographical terms Russian greatly expanded its area from Poland to the Pacific. Russian exploration eastwards, and its acquisition of areas to the south and west of Russia proper, led to groups of non-Russian subjects coming under the control of Moscow. The policy of Russification intensified towards the end of the century as rebellious movements became more active. Ukrainian, Polish and Belarusian all underwent periods of partial prohibition in Russian-controlled areas, although these controls were relaxed after the Revolution. Lenin's policy towards minorities was officially one of cultural self-determination. This policy was ideologically sound as well as politically expedient in the early years of the USSR. Under Stalin, however, ethnic language groups suffered badly in the wave of Great Russian nationalism. Although the post-Stalin era reversed many of these injustices, it is still true that Russian monopolized a volume of the cultural and linguistic resources far out of proportion to its numerical status vis-à-vis other languages in the USSR. On the other hand, it did function, in both theory and practice, as a general medium for communication in extra-national affairs within the republics of the USSR, not to mention its role as the major foreign language of the Eastern Bloc, and as an official language of the United Nations and in international politics and commerce.

With the Russian Revolution the Russian language changed in some fundamental ways (Comrie, Stone and Polinsky, 1996). The most obvious was the overdue 1918 reform of the orthography, and the vastly expanded area of literacy. The style and lexis (chapter 9) of the Revolution also had their own particular characteristics, which in turn influenced the Communist movements in others areas of Eastern Europe. There has also been a shift from the so-called "Old Moscow norm", based on the upper class speech of Moscow and accepted as standard Russian since the age of Pushkin, towards a less class-oriented variety with its roots partly in Leningrad/St. Petersburg speech. In spite of the linguistic, social and political upheavals which followed the Revolution, the position of Russian gained in strength, both nationally and internationally, until the fall of European Communism. It has now suffered something of a setback outside Russia, as its role as a *lingua communis* in the former USSR has become anachronistic, and as its status in international affairs has to some extent been eroded by English.

2.3.2   Ukrainian

In its early years Ukrainian (formerly sometimes known also as "Little Russian" or "Ruthenian" (2.3.3)), shared with Russian and Belarusian a common culture and language derived from Bulgarian Orthodox Christianity from the conversion to Christianity in 988 (2.3). After the fall of Kiev (Ukr *Kýjiv*) in 1240, and the departure of the Metropolitan to Russia in 1299, Ukraine enjoyed a short period of uneasy independence in Galicia and Volhynia (–1321), after which Ukraine was absorbed progressively into Lithuania, Poland and Hungary. The major part of Ukraine remained under Lithuanian and Polish domination until the Union of Lublin in 1569, when Poland assumed control. In the Partitions of Poland in the eighteenth century, however, Ukraine and a substantial portion of Poland were annexed by Russia, which banned the use of Ukrainian in much of public life from 1863–1905. Although nominally autonomous from 1917, Ukrainian did not really prosper within the Soviet Union from the 1930s until the formation of the independent modern Ukrainian state in 1991 after the fall of the USSR.

Apart from the early Church Slavonic manuscripts, which show only a small degree of Ukrainian interference, there were only inconclusive stimuli to Ukrainian as a literary language until the late sixteenth century. During this period the written models included the "Euthymian" recension of Church Slavonic, an esoteric, Bulgarian-inspired attempt to re-establish older South Slavic models, which was then replaced by Ruthenian, a written and administrative language based on the Belarusian dialect of Vilno under Lithuanian rule. After the Union of Lublin in 1569, however, the increasing domination of Polish as a written language in the Ukrainian lands progressively took over the functions of Ruthenian, and turned Church Slavonic into a virtually dead liturgical language. Church Slavonic scholarship itself underwent a significant revival, with the production of the Ostrih Bible in 1581, and the appearance of grammars and dictionaries of Church Slavonic by scholars like Zizanij, Smotrytsky (*Smotryc'kyj*) and Berynda. This recension of Church Slavonic replaced Polish as the literary language for those Ukrainians who had not been wholly polonized (Shevelov, 1980: 149), and, in conjunction with allegiance to the Orthodox Church, began to acquire symbolic value associated with national identity. In the western parts of Ukraine there was also a movement towards a more genuinely Ukrainian written language, inspired by the influence of the Reformation and the translation of church books into the vernacular, which resulted in lexical borrowings from Western European cultures. To a limited extent, the Jesuit schools reintroduced written Ukrainian in interludes to plays and in occasional satirical verse.

The anti-Polish and anti-Catholic sentiment eventually came to a head in the Khmelnitsky (*Xmel'nyc'kyj*) riots of 1648, which led to the creation of the Cossack state in eastern Ukraine as a Russian protectorate, and so eventually to the annexation of this area of Ukraine by Russia after the defeat of the Cossacks at the Battle of Poltava (1709). Polish influence in Ukraine declined steadily through the eighteenth century, as Russian political, religious, military and cultural power increased. The partitions of Poland at the end of the eighteenth century transferred control of the major part of the Ukrainian lands to Imperial Russia. With these changes came an increased influence of the Russian recension of Church Slavonic, and of Russian as a cultural and linguistic model.

Ukrainian gained a sense of historical purpose from the Xmel'nyc'kyj uprising, a spirit which was strongly felt in the nationalistic Romantic Ukrainian literature of the nineteenth century, especially in the writings of poets like Shevchenko (*Ševčenko*), Kulish (*Kuliš*) and Franko. During this period the written language was realigned closer to the vernacular, particularly the south-eastern dialects in the Kiev–Poltava–Kharkov area. Elements of Church Slavonic were progressively replaced, since it was now too closely associated with the growing authority of Imperial Russian rule and that of the church in Russia. The Russian attitude towards Ukrainian in the nineteenth century varied from paternalism to suppression. Gogol's Ukrainian-flavored Russian was accepted as part of Russian literature, but distinctly Ukrainian separatist movements met with stern repression. Printing in Ukrainian was restricted, being allowed only in poetry, fiction and drama. Lvov (*L'viv*) became the centre of Ukrainian publishing activity, and Galician (western) Ukrainian was briefly promoted as a literary language. The Kiev variant regained some of its prominence after 1905, however, when printing in Ukrainian was once more permitted, though Ukrainian schools remained closed until 1917.

The story of Ukrainian after the Revolution is similar to that of Belarusian (2.3.3). The establishment of the Ukrainian SSR, and the acceptance of Ukrainian as its official language after the Civil War, were followed by a period of linguistic and cultural construction and reconstruction in the 1920s, and the reconciliation and codification of the various geographically based variants of the language, especially the lexical innovations common in the western (Galician) areas of Ukraine with the phonological elements of the south-eastern dialects. Written Ukrainian, however, was slow to occupy a full range of written roles in public life and official functions. Ukraine was still predominantly an agricultural country, and there was a historical shortage of intellectuals to provide leadership in the re-formation of Ukrainian as a national language-culture. This period of militant Ukrainianization and *laissez-faire* in Ukrainian affairs came to an end in 1930, the beginning of Stalin's purges of regional nationalists and of his campaign against the anti-collectivization attitude of the Ukrainian peasants. Russian was generally used in official business, and was formally installed as the second language of Ukraine. These policies help to explain why many Ukrainians fought with the Germans in the Second World War, in the hope of liberating Ukraine, and why the cultural and linguistic recovery of the Ukrainian SSR after the war was so delayed.

From 1945, however, Ukraine did finally include most speakers of Ukrainian, with the exception of upwards of 3 million who were left in the Russian Republic, and the less numerous but politically active migrant settlements in North America. Modern Ukrainians remain acutely conscious of the cultural and linguistic differences between Russian and Ukrainian.

The post-Communist language situation in Ukraine is currently not a little confused. While de-Russification in the heart of Ukraine is proceeding as predicted, the substantial numbers of Russian residents are posing a problem of policy and equity, in terms of both language rights, ethnic allegiance and the cultural solidarity of Ukraine as a whole. In addition, the pro-Moscow orientation of the Cossacks is contributing to some political destabilization. Nonetheless the reduction of Russian influence is providing a vital stimulus to the Ukrainian language, which is now moving to develop a full range of functional roles (2.5).

2.3.3   Belarusian (formerly Belorussian)

Belarusian emerged from Kievan Rus' in the thirteenth century as a group of dialects not clearly differentiated from Russian and Ukrainian. When the Tartar invasion of 1240 split Kiev from Belorussia, the Belorussians turned westwards to Lithuania for political protection against the Tartars and the Teutonic Knights. From 1386, when the Grand Duchy of Lithuania joined with Poland, Belorussia fell increasingly under Polish domination in secular and religious affairs. The Union of Lublin (1569), and the Union of Churches (1596), brought Polish customs and Catholicism to the upper levels of Lithuanian–Belorussian society, but not to the majority of the people. Belorussia and the Polish Ukraine were seceded to Russia in the Polish Partitions of 1772, 1793 and 1795. The Russians proved to be linguistically even less sympathetic than did their Polish predecessors. The use of the name "Belorussia" was even banned in 1840, and the population was subjected to a policy of Russification and forced re-conversion to Orthodoxy which followed the popular revolt under Kalinoŭski in 1863. After the First World War Poland incorporated a substantial proportion of Belorussian territory, and probably about 3.5 million Belorussian nationals. The remainder of Belorussia had to endure the Civil War (1917–1920) before emerging in the USSR with its own official language after the Peace of Riga in 1921, when the western part of Belorussia was ceded to Poland. These boundaries were readjusted to consolidate Belorussia between 1939 and 1945. While the Belorussian SSR was nominally secure as a constituent republic of the USSR from 1921, Belarusian language and culture underwent more thoroughgoing Russification than did Ukrainian, and were starting to show signs of real weakness by the end of Russian control in 1991.

The Belarusian ("White Russian", "White Ruthenian") language is first recorded as an official language from the fourteenth century, when it was used in literature and administration in a form intermingled with Ukrainian elements. Its first major literary document is Skaryna's translation of the Bible, which appeared in Prague in 1517–1519, and some ecclesiastical writings of the sixteenth century. Until 1596, when the Grand Duchy of Lithuania was absorbed into the Polish commonwealth, Belarusian – sometimes known also as "Ruthenian" (2.3.2) – served 'as the medium for state, diplomatic and private correspondence, as well as for all chancery and legal functions' (McMillin, 1980: 106). This administrative language was initially written but not literary, and its range of functions was restricted. However, as an entity separate from Church Slavonic, it showed some elements of local dialectal variation, and – as is the case with Russian – provided an alternative secular written medium to the language of the church. The contact with the Reformation and Western culture through Polish enriched the vocabulary and range of the language. The next century, however, saw a policy of progressive Polonization, and in 1697 the Polish *sejm* (parliament) officially banned the use of Belarusian in state and court affairs. The public use of Belarusian was intermittently under official interdiction until 1921.

Modern Belarusian literature is generally thought to begin with the early nineteenth-century *Aeneid* by Rovinski, which was prompted by Kotlyarevsky's (*Kotljarevs'kyj*) Ukrainian version of 1798. But it was not until the second half of the nineteenth century that we see the emergence of a substantial vernacular literary culture, which drew more from folk poetry and the spoken language than from prestigious existing literary standards. In the works of poets like Kupala and Kolas, and in the Naša Niva literary circle, the language began to achieve a genuinely literary level of achievement (Karskij, 1955). The journal *Naša Niva* finally decided in 1912 to publish exclusively in Cyrillic, ending a prolonged period of Cyrillic/ Roman parallel use. And Belarusian could not even be referred to as a "language" in Russia until 1917. Belarusian has constantly felt the influence of Ukrainian, Russian and Polish in cultural and religious matters, and much of its evolution has been concerned with establishing the viability of Belarusian as an independent literary language. Subsequent codification of the orthography (1933), grammar (1960s) and lexis (1970s) has made late but important contributions towards regularizing and establishing Belarusian as an autonomous language. With a smaller and more coherent geographical space than Ukrainian, Belarusian has had less of the problem of language revival from multiple dialect bases, and the tendency has been towards a dialectal compromise which reflects the general characteristics of the language around the capital, Minsk.

In theory, Belarusian now had the right to cultural and linguistic self-determination guaranteed by the constitution of the USSR. But Stalin's anti-nationalistic purges of the thirties and the post-war years destroyed much of the Belarusian cultural leadership and intelligentsia as part of the attack on "bourgeois nationalism". This repressive policy had the effect of sending the Belarusian language and literature into a period of retreat for almost twenty years.

Belarusian might have continued to decline had it not been for the fall of Communism and the USSR, since the use of Russian had become so widespread in Belarus. The consolidation and completed codification of the language will certainly reinforce its status (11.2). But President Lukashenko (Bel *Lukašenka*) is moving to strengthen economic, cultural and linguistic ties with Russia, which will tend to restrict the overall vitality of the Belarusian language.

2.4   West Slavic

The West Slavs consist of two principal ethnic and linguistic groups: a Czecho-Slovak group, comprising Czech and Slovak; and a Lekhitic group, including Polish, Kashubian, Upper Sorbian, Lower Sorbian (though this classification of Lower Sorbian is sometimes disputed: see 2.4.2) and the extinct languages: Polabian, a language which became extinct in the eighteenth century in what is now Germany; and Slovincian, which disappeared in Northern Poland in the early twentieth century.

The most potent religious force in the history of the West Slavic languages has been Catholicism, which drove Orthodoxy out of Moravia in the ninth century, triumphed over the Reformation, and made some important inroads into Orthodox strongholds in Ukraine and Belarus. The Catholic Church provided the alphabet, a literary tradition, and administrative and educational structures, which all played a vital role in the establishment of the West Slavic literary languages. The church's role was often linked to political agendas and to German – and Hungarian – national aspirations. The German influence was responsible for expelling Orthodoxy from the Western Slavic lands, and for suppressing the use of Czech in the former Bohemian Kingdom during the Counter-Reformation. German has also been the dominant influence in politics, culture and economics for a thousand years. After 1945 the West Slavs were turned eastwards away from Germany towards the new hegemony of Russia, from which they emerged on the fall of Euro-Communism in 1991.

The West Slavic languages have been characterized by a strong sense of ethnicity. For the East Slavs, linguistic nationhood was concerned with crystallizing intra-Slavic differences into cultural and political units. But for the West Slavs it was a matter of survival, self-determination and self-definition in the face of intermittent repression, especially from the Germans and Hungarians. Czech and Polish were fortunate in emerging early as language-cultures. And if Slovak lacked such an obvious historical tradition, it was at least born in a spirit of nineteenth-century nationalism which gave a solid impetus to differentiating it from the cultural massif of Czech. Sorbian, with a much smaller population and many fewer advantages, has had the hardest struggle to survive. But the German influence has not been consistently antagonistic to the West Slavs. Much of the economic and political, and a good part of the cultural (especially musical), heritage of the West Slavs has derived inspiration from the Germans and Austrians.

2.4.1   Polish

The Polish language has been maintained for more than a millennium by virtue of numbers, historical self-awareness, ethnic loyalty and religious cohesion. The strong and continuous affiliation with Catholicism helped to spare Polish much of the linguistic trauma of the Reformation and Counter-Reformation, which played such an important role in the history of Czech. Of all the West Slavic languages, Polish was the least likely to perish. What Polish required was a permanent political framework, particularly after the restrictions on the use of Polish in public life during the partitions of Poland from 1797 to 1918. As Schenker observes: 'Polish, alone among the Slavic literary languages, has gone through a gradual, unbroken development from the Middle Ages to the present day' (Schenker, 1980: 210).

   The origins of the Polish State, like those of Bohemia and Moravia, are uncertain. We know that the Poles – the name originally meant 'plain-dwellers' – occupied the area between the Oder and the Vistula about the sixth century AD, and were constantly harried by the Germans from the west. In 963 Prince Mieszko finally scored an important victory over the Germans, and brought about the Christianization of Poland in 966 as a result of his subsequent marriage to a Bohemian princess. Kazimierz the Great (r. 1333–1370), the last of the Piast dynasty, established Poland as a viable political entity. He promoted Poland's external security by making peace with Bohemia and the Teutonic Knights, and expanding Poland's boundaries eastwards into the west of the Kievan state. His internal policies included fiscal and legal reform, human rights, religious tolerance, and the promotion of communications, architecture and the arts. His achievements included the founding of the Cracow (Pol *Kraków*) Academy, later the University of Cracow, in 1364. And the Christianization of Lithuania (1386) spread Polish language and influence through all its eastern provinces. This period also saw the start of the fusion of language elements from the original court around Poznań and Gniezno in western Poland (Pol *Wielkopolska*, or 'Great Poland'), with elements from the "Little Poland" (Pol *Małopolska*) area around Cracow in the south, culminating in the establishment of the capital in Warsaw (Pol *Warszawa*), which belongs to the Mazovian dialect area of Poland (10.4.2).

During the early period of Christian rule in Poland the official language was Latin, though there is a possible echo of the Constantine and Methodius tradition in the ancient hymn *Bogurodzica* ('Mother of God'). Polish proper names appear in Latin manuscripts from the twelfth century, some early glosses from the thirteenth century, and psalters and sermons from the fourteenth century, together with some records of local government. The beginnings of a more literary tradition are found in satirical and didactic verse in the fifteenth century. Knowledge of Latin, however, was restricted to the clergy and the upper classes. The language of the court at Gniezno and later at Cracow was evolving in a European context, as can be seen from numerous borrowings from Old Czech, German, Latin, Italian and other languages. The secular use of Polish received an indirect but important stimulus from the insistence of Kazimierz the Great on law and education. From the fifteenth century we find an increasing number of translations, as well as legal and court documents, in Polish. In the Polish Golden Age in the sixteenth century the humanism of the High Renaissance and the Reformation brought Polish culture to a genuinely European level. The spirit of Polish self-awareness was expressed in the famous proclamation by Rey (1505–1569):

> A niechaj narodowie wżdy, postronni znają
> Iż Polacy nie gęsi, że swój język mają.
> And may other nations always know
> That the Poles are not geese, and have their own language.

The sixteenth century also marks the summit of Poland's power in political and military terms. Poland *"semper fidelis"* was the bulwark of Catholic Europe. The strength of the Catholic Church reflected the political stability of Poland: the country benefited enormously from the cultural and linguistic stimulus of the Reformation, without being influenced by Protestantism to a major degree, and was largely spared the Counter-Reformation. The Poles had already achieved a wider use of their language in public affairs, and a certain democratization of the church while maintaining their links with Rome. Sermons were already regularly delivered in Polish, and the secular use of the language had been firmly established through the encouragement of literacy and printing in the Golden Age.

The Jagiellonian dynasty (1370–1572) saw the rise of Poland to the status of a European power, which eventually stretched from the Baltic to the Black Sea. Polish cultural, religious and linguistic influence, partly as a result of the Union of Lublin of 1569, extended eastwards into Lithuania, Belorussia and Ukraine. But the elective monarchy which followed it (1572–1795) ended in Poland's disappearance as a political entity. Poland's political decline was not accompanied by a cultural collapse, as happened in Czechoslovakia. But the eventual partitioning of Poland by Russia, Prussia and Austria in 1772 and 1773, and its total dismemberment in 1795–1797, did pose a genuine threat to the continuation of Polish language-culture. The Poles, unlike the Czechs after the disaster of the Battle of White Mountain in 1620, developed a spirit of Romantic nationalism.

The resilience of the Polish language in partitioned Poland – as championed in the nineteenth century by poets like Mickiewicz – became one of the symbols of Polish nationalism. The three occupying powers were not equally tolerant of the cultivation of the Polish language. The Austrians were at least Catholic, and so had no religious quarrel with the Poles. Their administration was culturally permissive in its attitude towards the use of Polish. Prussia was initially more concerned with the Germanization of the lands west of the Lower Vistula, and with the economic utilization of Polish production. In the nineteenth century, however, the old friction between Catholicism and the Lutheranism of Prussia began to re-emerge, and under Bismarck the policy of *Kulturkampf* was directed towards the systematic de-Polonization of key areas like education. But it was in the Russian-occupied zones that Polish fared worst. Ancient rivalries for control of Belorussia and Ukraine, and between Catholicism and Orthodoxy, found expression in a strongly anti-Polish attitude by the Russian administration. After the 1863–1864 uprising the Russian administration forbade the use of Polish in public places, including churches, and in education.

Education was probably the most sensitive area. The use of Polish language and literature in education was actively supported by the church, but Prussia and Russia restricted its use. All over partitioned Poland education was at a low ebb, with small numbers of ill-equipped schools. The study of German or Russian was made obligatory, and secondary and tertiary education was biased increasingly towards the languages of the occupying powers. The Russians closed the University of Wilno in 1831 – in contrast to the Austrians, who permitted the continuation of the Polish Academy in Cracow. The situation with literature was equally difficult. Polish literature answered the difficulties of the Partitions by going into partial exile. Paris became the home of generations of Polish writers, musicians and artists. The French influence had been strong in Polish political and artistic life since the end of the eighteenth century, particularly since the Napoleonic Wars, and there are important links between French Jacobinism and the Republican and nationalistic-Romantic sentiments which sustained the Polish cause through the Partitions, and eventually emerged in independent Poland in 1918. Writers like Mickiewicz, Słowacki, Norwid, Krasiński, Prus, Żeromski, and the Nobel laureates Reymont and Sienkiewicz, all spent important periods of their creative lives abroad – as did the composer Chopin (Pol *Szopen*) – and published much of their work outside Poland.

After 1918 the fate of the Polish language in the reconstituted Polish state was no longer endangered. But there were significant linguistic problems in the new state which were never solved, particularly the fate of the millions of Ukrainians, Belarusians and Germans, who were systematically disadvantaged in education and ethnic rights. Nowadays most of the East European Poles live within Poland. But there are still millions of Poles and their descendants living overseas. Some of these migrations date from the late nineteenth century and the large-scale exodus of Poles, especially from the impoverished Galician area in the east. There are also substantial groups of Poles who left Poland more recently for ethnic and political reasons, and now live in North America, Britain, Western Europe and Australasia.

The effect of the end of Communism has been less dramatic in Poland than in most other Slavic countries. While there are significant lexical and stylistic changes under way as a result of cultural Westernization, the status of the Polish language in Poland has hardly altered. Rapprochement with the West was already well under way before 1990, and Polish influence – through the work of the trade union Solidarity (Pol *Solidarność*) and the enormous strategic importance of the presence of the Polish Pope, John Paul II, in the Vatican – were among the key factors leading to the post-Communist era.

2.4.2 Sorbian (Upper Sorbian and Lower Sorbian)

The Sorbs represent the smallest officially recognized modern Slavic language(s). During the last hundred years they have declined from 166,000 to probably at most 67,000 speakers (Stone, 1985), and possibly under 30,000. Speakers of Upper Sorbian outnumber speakers of Lower Sorbian by 2:1. Half the Sorbs are Lutheran and a quarter Catholic. Culturally and ethnically distinct from the Poles and Czechs, their nearest Slavic neighbours, they have managed to preserve their language and identity through long periods of Germanization since the tenth century. Since the disappearance of the Polabian language on the lower Elbe in the eighteenth century, the Sorbs have been the last of the Slavs who reached the territory bordered by the Elbe and the Oder some time between the third and sixth centuries AD. They inhabit an area around the River Spree (Sorb *Sprjewja*) to the east of Berlin and Dresden, and west of the Oder–Neisse rivers, barely 90 km × 65 km in extent. This area is known as Lusatia (Ger *Lausitz*, Sorb *Łužica*), hence the alternative, now less common, English name of the language and people: Lusatian(s) (e.g. de Bray, 1980c). The Sorbs are traditionally an agricultural people, and Sorbian has never become a dominant urban language. Even the capital, Bautzen (Sorb *Budyšin*), has only 1,000 Sorbs out of a population of 44,000 (Stone, 1972: 3). Bautzen is the focal point of the Upper Sorbs, who inhabit the southern (upper) reaches of the River Spree. The less numerous Lower Sorbs are centred further to the north, around the town of Cottbus (Sorb *Chośebuz*). Until 1991 the Sorbs constituted an official ethnic minority in what used to be the German Democratic Republic. This status was ratified in the 1990 treaty of the reunification of the Germanies. The replacement in 1992 of the Institut za Serbski Ljudospyt (Institute for Serbian Ethnography) with the Serbski Institut in Bautzen, with a branch in Cottbus for Lower Sorbian, gives Sorbian a permanent institutional home.

The Sorbs have a long history of subjugation. They have passed through periods of Polish, Czech and especially German (Prussian and Saxon) domination, when they often had little or no official civil, legal or ethnic standing. Like most of the other oppressed Slavic peoples, the Sorbs benefited linguistically from the Reformation, which introduced Sorbian into liturgical use and, with its translations of the Bible in both Lower and Upper Sorbian, in that order, dating from the sixteenth century, prompted the beginnings of Sorbian written culture. Lutheranism in both Upper and Lower Sorbian, and Catholicism in Upper Sorbian, both provided stimuli to the development of written Sorbian, a situation which was not helped by periodic suppression of printing in Sorbian. Grammars and dictionaries of both variants of Sorbian appeared during the following century. During the Romantic movements of the early nineteenth century Sorbian began to flourish as a written language, and enjoyed a fine flowering of journalism and literature, especially in the poets Zejler and Bart-Čišinski. The cultural organization Maćica Srbska (Herrity, 1973), founded in 1847, provided a focus-point for the new Sorbian literature. These movements were rebuffed by the pan-German policies of the late nineteenth century. This continued until the Sorbs were finally recognized as an ethnic entity after the Second World War, when, in the terms of the Constitution of the German Democratic Republic, Sorbian achieved the status of an official language, and its people gained education rights extending from primary school to tertiary studies at the Sorbian Institute of the Karl Marx University in Leipzig. Significantly, however, the Constitution of the German Democratic Republic recognized only a single "Sorbian" language – like the "Czechoslovak" language in Czechoslovakia between the two World Wars (2.4.5–6) – so that the Upper and Lower versions were regarded at most as variants, and not as two languages.

The uncertain status of Sorbian as one language or two is reflected in the history of its standardization. Early Bible translations, grammars and dictionaries were in both Upper Sorbian and Lower Sorbian. At this stage the literary language was predominantly ecclesiastical, and its variety mirrored the religious diversity which followed the Reformation. We find in the eighteenth century three standardized Sorbian languages – Catholic Upper Sorbian (strongly supported from Prague), and Protestant Upper and Lower Sorbian. This situation was eventually resolved by the merging of the two Upper Sorbian variants, but only recently:

> The closure of [the newspaper] *Serbske Nowiny* in 1937 marked the end of the era in which Catholic and Protestant Sorbs in Upper Lusatia had each had their own literary language. After the revival of publishing in 1945 all Upper Sorbs used the analogical spelling, but wrote in what was basically the Protestant literary variant.   (Stone, 1972: 121)

The establishment of Sorbian as a literary language in the nineteenth century depended very much – as in Macedonia, Slovenia and Slovakia – on closer links between the literary and spoken language. Maćica Serbska, and newspapers like *Tydźenska Nowina* and *Serbske Nowiny*, provided an outlet for the new literature, and for an increasingly de-Germanized form of Sorbian. And in the twentieth century Domowina (1912–), a publishing house and cultural focal-point, has played the primary role in encouraging publication in Sorbian. In spite of this, the two standard literary variants of Sorbian have remained, as is the case with Czech, at some distance from the spoken language. Although the Gothic alphabet was finally abandoned – by the Catholic Sorbian press in 1910, and the Protestant Sorbian press in 1937 – and the Roman alphabet adopted, attempts at unifying the two languages have been resisted by popular feeling, especially on the part of Lower Sorbs.

It is difficult to gauge the likely effect on Sorbian of the demise of the German Democratic Republic, and the consolidation of East and West Germany. The change will bring Sorbian within the protection of language rights in the European Community, which could certainly help to support the maintenance of the language at an official level. It remains to be seen whether Upper, and particularly Lower, Sorbian are sufficiently vigorous to benefit from this new situation.

There is still the vexed question of whether the two Sorbians constitute one language or two, and even whether they derive from the same source (Polański, 1980). Linguists, and especially philologists, cannot even agree on whether Sorbian constitutes two languages covering two different peoples (Schuster-Šewc, 1959), two standard languages emerging from a single proto-language but covering one people (Lötsch, 1963), or two variants of a single language. Schleicher (1871) located Sorbian within the Czech-Slovak group, while Taszycki (1928) and Stieber (1930) have Sorbian with the Lekhitic grouping of Polish and Kashubian, together with the dead languages Polabian and Slovincian, and explain the similarities between especially Upper Sorbian and Czech on the grounds of later contiguous development and influence. There is no obvious way of resolving this difference of opinion. In sociolinguistic terms, both Upper and Lower Sorbs refer to themselves as *Serbja*. Upper Sorbian is stronger than Lower Sorbian as an official, standardized literary language. As Stone notes (1993a: 599), 'Lower Sorbian has only with great difficulty maintained its separate status as a literary language'. Although it exists in a standard literary form, Lower Sorbian is certainly not as "vital", in the sociolinguistic sense that it is much less used than Upper Sorbian in printed form, has fewer speakers, and is restricted in the social and functional roles that it fulfills, which suggests that it is less than a full language. On the other hand, the degree of differentiation of Lower Sorbian from Upper Sorbian is somewhat greater than the distance between Kashubian and Polish, which favors the analysis of two languages rather than one. Nonetheless, various aspects of language policy and management in the Lower Sorbian written language over the last century have tended to move it towards written Upper Sorbian (Stone, 1985). These include the 1891 grammar of Lower Sorbian by Muka (Mucke, 1965), and that by Šwela of 1906, favoring the Upper Sorbian rule of the genitive-accusative for masculine personal nouns in the plural over the nominative-accusative (6.2.4), although the genitive-accusative is found in no Lower Sorbian dialect. Similarly, the maintenance of the simple imperfect and aorist past tenses in written Lower Sorbian follow the model of Upper Sorbian with no justification in the Lower Sorbian dialects. And in orthography Lower Sorbian has abandoned prothetic written /h/ before /o/ and /u/ in favor of the Upper Sorbian prothetic /w/ (1.3.1.7, 3.2.1.4).

The decision on whether we are dealing with one language or two depends – as it does with Croatian and Serbian – on which set of criteria is considered to be decisive, since the standard criteria for describing language-hood do not resolve this dilemma (11.2). However, a promising new model for the interpretation of the relation between the two variants of Sorbian is offered by the concept of "pluricentric languages" (Kloss, 1967; Clyne, 1991, 1991a–b; Sussex 1994). Pluricentric languages, which include English and German, have multiple standards in different locations. The variant forms (for instance, British, American and Australian English) need not be equally influential, but they do have recognized norms, unify recognized groups of speakers, and may encompass linguistic variation of quite substantial scope. Just as there are proponents of an American language (Mencken, 1919/1936), so also one can speak of two separate Sorbian languages, or of a single pluricentric language, or of a single language with a major sub-variant in Lower Sorbian.

We shall follow de Bray (1980c), Širokova and Gudkov (1977) and others who concentrate on Upper Sorbian as the more prominent variant, referring to Lower

Sorbian particularly in relation to phonology and morphology as a well defined co-variant, and clearly more than a dialect.

2.4.3 Kashubian and Slovincian

Kashubian (or "Cassubian") belongs to the Lekhitic group of West Slavic, stretching from the now extinct Polabian in the west, through Slovincian and Kashubian to Polish in the east. The term "Pomeranian" covers Kashubian and the dialects which were once spoken to its west, notably Slovincian.

According to Ethnologue, Kashubian is spoken by perhaps only 3,000 people in the north-west of Poland around the city of Gdańsk, though up to 500,000 may claim Kashubian ethnicity while speaking Polish. Compared to Slovincian and Polabian, it shows relatively lower levels of Germanization. It has also remained distinct from standard Polish. All in all, Kashubian is a difficult but intriguing case. As Topolińska (1980: 194) shows, its main claim to the status of a literary language is a 'more or less strictly codified spelling standard', though Lorentz's (1919) attempt at establishing this standard was not fully successful. Kashubian still lacks a well-documented standardized form. There is a varied Kashubian literature, including writing of significant scope in the nineteenth century. But it reflects the usage of the Kashubian intelligentsia, and is not the agreed codified standard of the Kashubians. As a group, the Kashubians lack a sense of ethnic identity and separatism, and do not make the strong connection between ethnicity and national language which we find among all the other Slavic languages. The use of Kashubian is restricted on the whole to non-official contexts, and mainly to domestic and local situations. The presence of Polish, a closely related language used for all official purposes, creates a diglossic situation in which the status of Kashubian is subsidiary, and does not seem likely to improve. This situation partly recalls the relation of Belarusian to Russian before 1990. But the difference is that Belarusian has significantly greater numbers, and a well-defined standard language, both of which are missing in Kashubian. The Kashubians themselves refer to Polish as "high speech", on the analogy of Hochdeutsch and Plattdeutsch (Topolińska 1980: 184). For this reason, we shall treat Kashubian as both less than a language and more than a standard Polish dialect, particularly since Kashubian is not as readily understood by other speakers of Polish.

Slovincian, which became extinct early in the twentieth century, is most often considered as a western variant of Kashubian. It was spoken on the Baltic, between Polabian in the west and Kashubian in the east. Slovincian did not attain the status of more than a local variant, though the fact that it has a distinct name serves to identify it, and its Protestant speakers, as something more than just a dialect.

We shall refer occasionally to Slovincian examples, but shall not devote major attention to it.

2.4.4   Polabian

Polabian, once spoken near the mouth of the River Elbe on the Baltic, is the westernmost of the former Baltic Slavic languages, and part of the Lekhitic family together with Polish. The Polabians were descendants of the Drevani, a Slavic tribe whose presence is recorded from the eleventh century. Polabian became extinct in the middle of the eighteenth century, and is only imperfectly known from proper names and records of the language taken down before its disappearance (Polański, 1993).

The 2,800 or so words which constitute our lexical knowledge of Polabian show up to 20 percent German interference. The grammar of the language was also significantly Germanized. Polabian is formally of considerable historical and typological interest, but too little is known of its history and social development.

2.4.5   Czech

The area which is now the Czech and Slovak Republics was occupied by the Slavs only in the sixth century AD. Before this time the country had been successively populated by the Celtic Boii (hence "Bohemia") until 100 BC, and then sporadically by German tribes. The Slavs, led by the mythical hero Čech (hence "Czech" – though spelled in Polish-style orthography), lived in a region dominated by the Avars. Under the leadership of an outsider, Samo, they achieved independence from the Avars in the seventh century. In the ninth century there was established the state of Great Moravia, a kingdom which included Bohemia and parts of modern Slovakia, Poland and Hungary. Its Prince Rostislav was responsible for introducing (Orthodox) Christianity to the region when he invited the Byzantine Patriarch to send missionaries to convert the Western Slavs. Constantine and Methodius (2.2.1) arrived in 863, and converted and baptized the Slavs of Moravia and Bohemia. They brought with them the Orthodox Church's administrative structures, an alphabet and the beginnings of a literary language and culture modelled on Greek (that is, Old Church Slavonic). The Catholic German princes were suspicious of this movement. They conspired to overthrow Rostislav (870), and, with the deaths of Constantine (869) and Methodius (885), Orthodoxy came to a premature end among the West Slavs. The Slavic books and liturgy were burned and proscribed, and German-dominated Catholicism replaced them. Moravia fell to the Hungarians about 900, and the young Slavic culture was driven westwards into Bohemia, where the Benedictine Abbey of Sázava produced some hagiography, the Prague Fragments (eleventh to twelfth century, one of the earliest extant Slavic manuscripts), and the thirteenth-century hymn 'Hospodine, pomiluj ny' (Lord, have mercy upon us) – all of which represented the Old Czech version of Church Slavonic, in the tradition of Constantine and Methodius (Weingart, 1949).

The emergence of the strong Přemysl dynasty in Bohemia, and the Golden Age which it ushered in, made Bohemia partly independent from the politics of the neighboring European powers, and for a time an exception to Bismarck's famous dictum, expressed many years later, that he who controls Bohemia controls Europe. Under the Přemysl (–1306) and Luxemburg (1310–1439) dynasties, Bohemia grew in territory, wealth, and political and religious independence. Charles IV (r. 1342–1378) did much to make Prague (Cz *Praha*) a commercial and intellectual centre. He founded the Charles University in Prague (1348) – soon to become a centre of political and religious nationalism, and encouraged the arts and architecture. The Czech manuscripts of the thirteenth and fourteenth centuries began with Czech glosses included in Latin manuscripts and culminated in a complete translation of the Bible, and in hymns, carols and hagiography.

Hussitism gave Bohemia a pre-eminent intellectual position in Europe. Jan Hus (1369–1415) had a fundamental influence on Czech and Slovak orthography as well as on language and religious dogma and practice. The Hussite movement was prompted by the reforms proposed by Wyclif in England. But in Bohemia it achieved the momentum of a spontaneous national mass movement with a clear religious dimension. Hus opposed the doctrines which excluded the laity from actively taking part in worship, and in their place he proposed the free preaching of the gospels in the vernacular. He encouraged the spread of literacy by the increased reading of the Bible and religious literature, and the use of hymns. And he attempted to make the written Czech language closer to the vernacular.

The installation of the Habsburgs in Bohemia (1526) consolidated the position of Prague as a commercial and intellectual centre. German printing techniques gave an outlet to the cultural activities of the Czech Reformation: the first grammars of Czech, and especially the so-called Kralice Bible (1579–1594), which was produced by a Protestant group. The Kralice Bible appeared within a few years of the Luther and King James Bibles, but was more conservative than its German and English counterparts in its approach to the vernacular. The impetus of this creative activity sparked a wave of linguistic nationalism, which reached a new anti-German peak in 1615 when the Estates decreed that

> All children in Bohemia, of native or foreign-born parentage, should learn Czech, and that only those children who spoke Czech could

> inherit land or immovables of a deceased landholder. Thereafter no
> foreigner who did not know Czech could become a citizen of any town
> in the Kingdom. (Thomson, 1953: 147)

Furthermore, religious dissension between the increasing number of factions, and
the growth of militant Protestantism among the Czech nobles, led to increasing
friction between them and the Catholic Habsburgs. In 1620 the Bohemian forces
were defeated at White Mountain (Bílá Hora). The ensuing Thirty Years' War and
its aftermath saw the enserfment of the Slavic agricultural class, and the destruction
of the Bohemian nobility, Protestantism, writing, free speech, nationalism and
material prosperity. The Catholic Counter-Reformation suppressed and exiled
Protestants and unorthodox Catholics, together with the best Czech writers – like
the writer-educator Komenský (Comenius, 1592–1660). In 1662 the Jesuits completed their domination of the education system by taking over control of the
Charles University, a situation which lasted until the expulsion of the Jesuits in
1773. The prospects for the Czech language were not promising, and Bohemia
entered a period of Germanization which was only relieved by the emergence of
Romantic nationalism, and the rebirth of religious tolerance, towards the end
of the eighteenth century.

The resurgence of Czech was directly related to the German Romantic concept of
language-nation, and directly opposed to the spirit and practice of Metternich's
internal policies. Among the stateless Slavs of Eastern Europe this notion of
language-nation was vital in reasserting the legitimacy and standing of the various
Slav tongues. The first problem was one of codification and standardization, which
required grammars, dictionaries and official recognition. Czech had already been
well served by its grammatical tradition, even during the period of cultural eclipse;
and Dobrovský's *Ausführliches Lehrgebäude der böhmischen Sprache* (1809) was a
landmark in the rehabilitation of literary Czech – not the least in explicitly recog-
nizing the tradition of the Kralice Bible, which helped to create the diglossic
situation of modern written Literary Czech, which is clearly distinct from educated
Czech speech. Dobrovský's grammar was supported by further historical, philological and lexicographical works, by Jungmann's dictionary, by historical studies
showing the authentic historicity of Czech culture and language by scholars like
Palacký, by an original literature (for instance, in the work of the poet Mácha), and
by a rapid increase in translating, and the expansion of the teaching of Czech into
state schools.

Jungmann's influence was crucial in developing the lexical resources of Czech.
Nearly two centuries of German domination had left literary Czech in a lexically
impoverished and confused state. The nineteenth-century Czechs adopted a polity

of re-Slavicizing their lexis, confirming and creating a consistently Slavic vocabulary by reviving Czech and dialectal-Czech words, or adapting Slavic roots, at the expense of "internationalisms" derived from Greek, Germanic and Romance (like Croatian, see 2.2.4). So we have Czech *hudba*, but Russian *múzyka*, Polish *muzyka* 'music'; and Czech *knihovna*, but Russian *bibliotéka*, Polish *biblioteka* 'library'. There were also some important achievements of a more institutional nature. A Chair of Czech Language was established at the Charles University in 1791. But the leading Czech intellectuals, sensing that Vienna would keep close control over the university, wisely diversified their efforts, and set up the Museum of the Bohemian Kingdom (1818) and Matice česká (1830), which was entrusted with the propagation of the Czech language. The vocabulary of Czech expanded rapidly with its increasing use in intellectual spheres, stimulated by the desire of Czech intellectuals and writers to show that their language was a worthy vehicle of intellectual and literary activity. As Bradley (1971) observes, this cultural nationalism was primarily concerned with establishing linguistic equality with German. The political element arrived later, with the growth of pan-Slavism, and the new contact with Slovak nationalists. By the early nineteenth century Prague had already become the intellectual centre of the Western Slavic world. The Charles University was separated as a *Czech* university in 1882 from the newly created German University of Prague. Czech schools, media and the arts grew rapidly. The nineteenth-century Czech revival had a high degree of national self-consciousness. Nevertheless, it took the First World War, and the emergence of leaders like Masaryk and Beneš, to promote the Czechs to nationhood. The Slovaks joined with Bohemia and Moravia in 1918 to form the new Czechoslovak state. Czech and Slovak became official co-variants of the "Czechoslovak language", a situation which has survived the Second World War and the Communist takeover of Czechoslovakia in 1948.

The Czech Republic, comprising Bohemia and Moravia, was separated from Slovakia to form the Czech Republic in 1992. The effect of this change on the Czech language is likely to be minor.

Lachian (or Lakhian), a Czech dialect sometimes claimed as a language, is discussed in 10.4.3.

2.4.6   Slovak

The history of Slovak is very different from that of Czech. Much of it consists of the Slovaks' efforts to lever their language away from Czech, and to establish it on a viable independent basis.

The Slovaks were separated from the Czechs by the Hungarian capture of Great Moravia around AD 900, and until 1918 they had no official ethnic or linguistic standing. They were traditionally an agricultural people, subordinate to the Magyar majority of the Hungarian Kingdom. Until the end of the eighteenth century their spoken language had only the status of a regional vernacular, and until the end of the nineteenth century their written language, when it was not Latin, Hungarian or German, was predominantly Czech.

Slovak is not clearly visible in linguistic terms until the seventeenth century, and its emergence as a national language is a feature more of the Counter-Reformation than of the Reformation. During the Hussite movement the majority of Slovaks became Protestants and followed the Czechs in using the Kralice Bible. This Bible language ("biblčtina") was preserved by the Protestants even through the Counter-Reformation, when they were reduced to an isolated minority, and was an important factor binding the Slovak Protestants to the Czech language and to Czech-Slovak unification during the following centuries.

Slovak is an exception to the generalization that Protestant religions were associated with local vernacular movements and the church in the development of literacy among the Slavs, because a major impetus to Slovak as a written language came from the Catholic Church. The new Jesuit University in Trnava (1613–) trained priests in Slovak, and strove to reverse the Czech-Slovak sentiment which had become attached to works like the Kralice Bible. In the 1750s they produced a Catholic Slovak Bible, which was consciously less like Czech in its language.

This championing of Slovak against Czech faced considerable odds. Czech had been used in philosophical and theological discussion, in the chancery of the Hungarian King Matthias Corvinus, and even in some Magyar local administration. But ethnic and cultural factors slowly started to turn in favor of Slovak. It cannot be said that the Slovaks had yet developed a sufficiently strong or unified concept of national identity, nor that the Slovaks had yet evolved a clearly anti-Czech sentiment. But the Czech language of the eighteenth century was in decline following the Counter-Reformation. The Trnava University Press printed a series of books in which literary Czech was increasingly modified in the direction of Slovak, and eventually formed a *koine* of West Slovak dialects, known as Jesuit Slovak, which was used by both Catholics and Protestants (Auty, 1953). Joseph II (r. 1780–1790) reflected the more tolerant and humanitarian spirit of his age by encouraging vernacular education and the use of Slovak by local government officials. It was during his reign that a Catholic priest, Father Anton Bernolák, published two important pamphlets, *Dissertatio philologico-critica* ... (1787) and *Grammatica slavica* ... (1790). He proposed a new version of "de-Czeched" Slovak which came to be known as "bernoláčtina" or "Bernolák language".

Bernoláčtina was a hybrid of Czech morphology with West and Central Slovak phonology. Bernolák's expressed motives were mixed: Slovak ethnicity and the idea that Slovak was the purest Slav language and maybe even a supra-national Slavic *interlingua* were intermingled with the more practical goal of producing a genuinely Slovak Bible. *Bernoláčtina* was essentially for literate high-class Catholic Slovaks. It became the vehicle for sermons and the work of a major poet in Ján Hollý. But it was not widely accepted by the priests and laity of east and central Slovakia because of its West Slovak bias, and the Protestants, loyal to the language of the Kralice Bible, criticized it for being unrefined and insular. *Bernoláčtina*, however, did give rise to widespread debate, especially in the context of the growth of nationalistic feeling. The poet Ján Kollár expressed not only the idea of Slovak nationality but also the concept of pan-Slavism. Kollár had studied at the University of Jena, and had absorbed German doctrines of linguistic and cultural nationalism. He and the scholar Šafařík now began to put the case for Slovak equality within a Czecho-Slovak community, which they felt reflected the true national affiliation of Slovak. Unlike many separatist movements of the time, they proposed a language community in which both Czech and Slovak, as distinct entities united by a common purpose, would mutually contribute to the formation of a new literary language. The Czechs, however, did not respond to this idea of broader shared unity, which reinforced the developing impetus to move Slovak away from Czech and more in the direction of major Slovak dialects.

The catalyst which eventually brought the Catholic and Protestant linguistic factions together was Ľudovit Štúr. Štúr, though not primarily a philologist, was a first-rate publicist. His goal was Slovak ethnic nationhood, very much in the spirit of Herder's concept of nationalism. During the late thirties and forties he and a group of Protestant friends worked out a new compromise form of Slovak, based this time on Central Slovak dialects but without identifying with any one dialect: it was in effect a codified form of educated Central Slovak, a new *koine*, particularly of phonology and morphology. Lexically and orthographically it was more conservative, and preserved many parallels with Czech. The new proposal was formally announced by Štúr's *Nárečja slovenskuo alebo potreba písaňja v tomto nárečí* (*The Slovak tongue, or The necessity of writing in this tongue*), which appeared in 1846, and was soon followed by his grammar of Slovak (*Nauka reči slovenskej*). Štúr's journalistic and publicistic activity, and his breadth of vision in publishing both Catholic and Protestant writings, led directly to the 1851 compromise between the Catholics' *bernoláčtina* and the new Protestant "Štúr language" or *štúrovčina*. This fusion was based on Štúr's grammar, and was formalized in 1852 by the (Catholic) linguists Hattala and Hodža as "opravená slovenčina" ("revised Slovak"). This compromise received wide acceptance and became the model for modern literary Slovak.

The phonology and orthography of literary Slovak have changed little since 1851, and their codification was consolidated in Czambel's *Rukoväť spisovnej reči slovenskej* (*Guide to written Slovak*) in 1902. There have been some simplifications in morphology, and enormous lexical expansion, often guided by a desire to reinforce the distinction between Slovak and Czech. The obstacles that still lay before the Slovak language reformers in 1851 were more political in nature. The Austro-Hungarian Ausgleich of 1867 placed the Slovaks under Hungarian jurisdiction. The Slovak cultural institution Matica slovenská, founded only in 1862, was closed in 1875, and Slovak schools did not reopen until 1918:

> Until 1918 literary Slovak existed on a very restricted scale. While it served as the medium for a literature whose quality was by no means negligible, especially in the sphere of poetry, it was not used for any official purpose and was almost entirely absent from schools of any but the elementary grade, and it must be remembered that the number of educated Slovaks who used the written language was very small indeed.
>
> (Auty, 1953: 157)

Even after the formation of the new Czechoslovak state in 1918, the constitution's definition of the "single Czechoslovak state" and a "single Czechoslovak language" gave Slovak an equivocal position with respect to Czech. The Czechs and Slovaks numbered barely 65.6 percent of the new state, and the Slovaks did not enjoy the special language privileges accorded to the more numerous Germans, who enjoyed a full education system in German (Fryščák, 1978). And as the minor partner in what was promoted as a single language with two variants, partly as a symbol of national unity, Slovak was in some danger of being overwhelmed by Czech, with its prestige, historicity and key role in intellectual and scientific innovations in language. Some even considered Slovak no more than an eastern dialect of Czech, with a regional literature but few official functions (Fryščák, 1978). During the 1930s there were major tensions between the dominance of Czech and the drive for a separate Slovak language. The journal *Slovenská reč*, founded in 1932, was actively separatist, and sought to differentiate Slovak from Czech and from any concept of Czech as a de facto national standard. During the Nazi occupation, Slovak achieved official status in the Free Slovak State (1939–1945), but this situation was reversed after 1945 when Slovakia was reincorporated into Czechoslovakia. During the 1960s, however, Slovak linguistic sentiment culminated in the publication of a set of principles for the fostering of the Slovak language. These *Tézy o slovenčine* (Ružička, 1970: 169–184) have provided a basis for the establishment of Slovak in its own right, a status solidly guaranteed after the 1968 Prague Spring in the two-language, two-republic state of modern Czechoslovakia.

The separation of Czechoslovakia into the Czech and Slovak Republics occurred in early 1992 in an eminently civilized fashion. The effect of this change has been to confirm the status of Slovak as an autonomous language. Some further conscious distancing from former and current Czech models is already evident in language planning and legislation undertaken as one of the first acts of the new Slovak parliament.

2.5   Overview

The development of the individual Slavic languages has been intensively studied. But the broader factors underlying this development are harder to identify. For instance, the role of the church was crucial for all the Slavic languages which achieved some significant level of codification before the nineteenth century, which includes all but Slovak and Macedonian (and Bosnian, in the sense that it was still part of Serbo-Croatian). The early appearance of canonical texts, translations of at least parts of the Bible, and other liturgical and homiletic writings was fundamental to the establishment of literacy and a written language. Among the Orthodox Slavs this policy was actively supported by the church. For the Catholic Slavs, on the other hand, the vernacularization of religious culture was initially associated with the Reformation and scholars like Hus, though in areas like Lusatia and Czechoslovakia the Catholic Church realized fairly soon that it had to match, rather than merely repress, the power of the vernacular liturgy. It was from these liturgical beginnings that genuinely literary traditions began to emerge. This did not, at least among the East Slavs, necessarily imply the use of the language for administration, since the administrative language of these areas was distinctly more vernacular in origin and character. The Orthodox Slavs used Church Slavonic as a liturgical language, removed to varying degrees from the local vernaculars. The Catholic Slavs used Latin. Codification of the emerging languages required the production, discussion and acceptance of norms for orthography, grammar and lexis. Several important and often vigorous confrontations took place between competing potential standards before the emergence of nationally supported codified norms.

From the late eighteenth century the pivot moves from church to *natio* and *patria*, supported by the ethos of the Romantic movement. The authority of canonical texts is replaced by the authority of the voice of the nation. Sometimes this voice is a collective one, distinguished by adherence to a norm which differentiates it from neighboring, often more powerful and threatening, or authoritarian, norms. Sometimes the voice is rather one of regional dialects, providing not only a direct pipeline to folk culture, but also to bases for the determination and definition of new, potentially national, varieties. The assertion and establishment of these norms as languages has been seen by all the Slavic nations, and language-cultures, as a fundamental component of their identity and viability. We can see recent confirmation of the importance of language to national identity in the campaign of the 1960s and 1970s by the Croats to have Croatian accepted as a language, and not merely a variant (however official) of Serbo-Croatian.

We can now look back over the individual histories of the Slavic languages and consider some more general features of their emergence. We take up the issue of standard languages and their criteria in 11.2.

2.5.1   Patterns of emergence of the standard languages

In relation to models the Slavic languages have followed four broad overlapping patterns of standardization: a revived historical model; a combination of dialects; a single principal dialect base; and different solutions to the purification question.

1. The revived historical model
    All the Slavic languages show at least some evidence of the principle of historical evocation. The clearest examples of explicit historical revival are Slovenian and Czech. In the case of Slovak and Macedonian, on the other hand, we find an assertion of ethnic, linguistic and cultural independence from a dominating neighboring culture with high historicity – Czech in the case of Slovak, and Bulgarian and Serbian in the case of Macedonian.
2. The multiple-dialect model
    Slovak and Macedonian also belong to the group of Slavic languages whose standardized literary form has been deliberately based on a *koine* of dialects rather than on one local variant. The same holds for Polish: here the *koine* which constitutes the contemporary standard was more continuous, and shows the progressive influence and intermingling of the major dialect areas. These languages contrast with Slovenian, a *koine* with more obvious historical-archaizing elements; and with Sorbian, where pluricentric variant-choice was combined with historical components.
3. The single principal dialect model
    Standards based predominantly on the dialect of one area are found in Czech, Russian, Belarusian, Bulgarian and B/C/S, where the establishment of a standard language was a matter of formal negotiation.
4. Purification
    In four cases – Russian, Belarusian, Ukrainian and Bulgarian – the formation of the national standard involved melding a dialect choice

with the issue of Church Slavonic (2.2.1). Of these, Ukrainian is a dialect *koine* language, and the others are single-dialect based. Russian itself has the largest quantum of Church Slavonic in Slavic. The other three languages have moved to limit both Church Slavonic and Russian elements. And Ukrainian and especially Belarusian have also undergone de-Polonization.

Bosnian, officially in existence since 1992, still has to establish its standardization and differentiation (*abstand*) from Croatian and Serbian, and must promote its functional expansion (*ausbau*) (11.2) within a state where there are three official languages (listed there in the order Bosnian, Serbian and Croatian) and a complex multi-ethnic demography. It will be some time before a clearly delineated Bosnian can be identified.

Looking back at the evolution of the individual languages, we can identify five crucial chronological reference points.

1. The first of these time-frames is the establishment of written versions of the languages, and the development of literacy following the conversion of the Slavs to Christianity from the ninth century. Here we find the establishment of Slavic literacy and the written language among the Moravians, where it was quickly suppressed by Catholic and German political pressures, and among the East and particularly the South Slavs. This development was curtailed by the rise of the Ottoman empire in the fifteenth century, leaving Moscow as the "Third Rome" and the East Slavs as the holders of the continuous tradition of Slavic literacy. During this phase many later-established languages find their history effectively within the history of a more powerful neighbor: Slovak, for instance, in relation to Czech.

2. The second point is the Reformation, where the role of the vernacular in the church, in both liturgy and scripture, reinforced movements for literacy among the Catholic West and South Slavs, and in the now Protestant Slavic areas among the West Slavs, giving rise to strong language movements among the Sorbs, Poles, Czechs, Slovenes and Croats. The relation between the vernacular and the liturgy in the Orthodox Slavic lands was closer, and the Reformation did not have the urgency of the counter-Latin movements among the Catholic Slavs.

3. Over time the suppression of many of these developments, for instance among the Czechs after the Battle of White Mountain in 1620, helped to establish the notion that language and nation, in the

ethnic, geographical and political sense, could form a powerful union. This idea, which forms the third chronological anchor-point, was articulated by philosophers like Herder at the start of the Romantic movement in the late eighteenth century, where we find in explicit form the idea that language determines people, and that people have a right to nationhood. These ideas gave rise not only to pan-Slav sentiments – including the proposal that at least some of the Slavs would abandon their vernaculars in favor of a general Slavic *koine* like the Illyrian language (2.2.4–5) – but also to vernacular-based language emergence among all the Slavic languages. In countries where the language was firmly established, as in Russia, the movement was to distance the vernacular from the liturgical language, and to create a new literary language based more on native elements. In the case of Bulgarian this amounted to reinventing a native literacy. In areas like Slovakia and Slovenia there were attempts to establish languages distinct from dominant neighbors. By the late nineteenth century all the modern languages were in a *de facto*, if not *de iure*, position of greater strength than at the start of the century, with the exceptions of Belarusian and Ukrainian (publicly restricted by Russian fiat), Macedonian (still to be clearly separated from Bulgarian), Sorbian (still insufficiently vital for want of numbers and functionality), and Bosnian.

4.   The effect of Communism, which constitutes the fourth stage of this broad-scale periodization, on the Slavic languages was politically radical, but culturally more mixed in its outcomes. While Lenin's policy was based on linguistic self-determination for national groups, by 1939 Russian had been installed as more than just a *lingua communis*, and something more akin to a second mother tongue, in the Soviet Union (Kreindler, 1982, 1985a). And after the 1920s Belarusian and Ukrainian never had the resources or support which they needed for full functionality. After the Communist takeovers of 1944–1948, all the modern Slavic languages had, on paper at least, a basis for existence. The eventual establishment of Slovak within (and now without) Czechoslovakia, and the confirmation of Slovenian and Macedonian in Yugoslavia, may be seen eventually as positive outcomes of language policy under Communism. But Belarusian and Ukrainian may well have been saved by the disintegration of Communism among the Slavs.

5.   The fifth chronological step, the fall of Euro-Communism, was effectively complete by the end of 1991. This brought to an end the

dominance of Moscow as an ideological (as well as cultural and linguistic) model, and also served to reunite the linguistic traditions of Eastern Europe with the mainstream of Western linguistics. Russian was no longer the favored foreign language, and was not the official language of trans-national bodies like Comecon and the Warsaw Pact. Everywhere throughout the former Soviet Union and Eastern Europe Russian is being supplanted by English, and to a lesser extent German and French, in the educational, commercial and cultural domains. This is not to say that Russian has been totally replaced: Russia itself can be expected eventually to return to a position of greater economic and cultural influence, and the linguistic infrastructure of decades of working with Moscow are still evident. In addition the 1994 elections in Ukraine and Belarus, for instance, showed a clear reversion to more Moscow-aligned policies in politics and economics, as did even more strongly the 2002 economic pact between Russia and Belarus. Nevertheless, the new orientation Westwards is having some profound effects on the modern Slavic languages.

Several tendencies can be discerned from the point of view of the current standing of the literary languages. First, with the exception of Sorbian, the smaller languages have benefited by being removed from the authority of neighboring larger languages into new language-states of their own. As we have seen, Belarusian, Slovak, Slovenian and Macedonian are the winners. Ukrainian will benefit from the removal of intrusive Russian models and pressures. The middle-sized languages already with sufficient independence – Polish, Czech, Bulgarian, Croatian and Serbian – will probably not gain a lot from their new status, though in the case of Croatian and Serbian we can expect greater differentiation as the two states diverge politically and culturally, coupled with a decline in the use and status of Serbo-Croatian and the emergence of Bosnian.

There remain Russian and Sorbian. Russian loses from the new political dispositions. Its status as a supra-national language in the USSR has gone, and its role as a trans-national and international language has been reduced. Within Russia, however, there is (as elsewhere throughout the Slavic area) a revival of literature in new, less regimented and more colloquial genres, and the language is anything but languishing. Sorbian, however, is potentially in peril. Some nationalistic pressures in contemporary Germany favor Germanness at the expense of multiculturalism, and it is not at all clear to what extent or in what form Sorbian will continue, the language policies of the European Community notwithstanding, as a fully viable language (or languages) beyond the next generation.

3

Phonology

3.1 Introduction

This chapter begins by examining the equivalences for vowels, consonants, groups of sounds and suprasegmentals with reference to Proto-Slavic (3.2). We then discuss the systems of vowels (3.3), consonants (3.4) and suprasegmentals (3.5) of the modern languages. For conventions of transcription and transliteration, see appendix B.

3.2 Historical evolution and modern equivalences

The first problem in studying the sounds of modern Slavic is one of equivalence: which sound corresponds to which other sound or sounds in the eleven languages? Some sounds show wide variations, like the root vowel in the word for 'white':

(1)   B/C/S *bĕo*, Rus *bélyj*, Pol *biały*, Cz *bílý*, Slk *biely*, Blg *bjal*

But not all Russian words with *e* correspond to Slovak words in *ie*, Polish words in *ia*, Bulgarian words in *ja* or Czech words in *í*, cf. the word for 'day':

(2)   Rus *den'*, Blg, Cz, Slk *den*, Pol *dzień*, B/C/S *dân*

We therefore need a common basis for comparison of equivalent or cognate sounds and their typological description.

We shall use Proto-Slavic as the reference-point. It is neutral with respect to all the other Slavic languages. Using it in this way is linguistically informative, since many of the sound changes which have formed the modern Slavic languages, like palatalization and assimilation, are still living as phonological and morphological processes in the modern languages. And the equivalences for a sound in any language can be recovered by checking in the various equivalence tables in which it occurs. In other words, we are able to discuss both the historical development of Slavic (its genetic evolution) and the internal phonological processes of the modern languages (their synchronic typology) in comparable terms. Combining diachronic and synchronic analyses works well for Slavic. It is very much in the traditions of Slavic linguistics. And it is particularly useful in phonology, where we find wide variations in the data.

In 3.2 we describe the main changes in vowels (3.2.1.), consonants (3.2.2.) and sound-combinations (3.2.3.) which have formed the modern languages from Proto-Slavic; in 3.2.4 we describe the changes in suprasegmental features. For details of the Proto-Slavic system and its features, see 1.3.

3.2.1   Development of the Proto-Slavic vowel system

The late Proto-Slavic vowel system had the following shape (see also table 1.3):

	Front		Central	Back	
High	i		y		u
Mid-high		ь			ъ
Mid-low	e	ę		o	ǫ
Low		ě		a	

Plus fronted allophones of /u/, /ǫ / and /a/ after palatal consonants

Features of special interest are the development of (1) the high-mid vowels ь, ъ (*jers*) (3.2.1.1); (2) the low-mid nasal vowels (ę ǫ)) (3.2.1.2); and (3) low front /ě/ (*jat'*) (3.2.1.3), followed by (4) vowels in word-initial position (3.2.1.4); (5) quality changes (free and contextual) (3.2.1.5); (6) contraction (3.2.1.6); and (7) diphthongs (3.2.1.7).

3.2.1.1   *The jers (ь ъ)*
(On the name 'jer', see 1.3.1.6) These two vowels (derived from IE short *ĭ ŭ*, respectively) are often referred to as "reduced" or "ultra-short" vowels. However, it is unlikely that there were three degrees of length in the system (ultra-short, short and long). More likely, the location of these short vowels in the central area made them weak in the same way as the neutral vowel (*schwa*) is typically weak in many systems, especially those with relatively strong stress. Their disappearance as phonemes was in principle a Proto-Slavic phenomenon, since it occurred in all areas. However, the realization of the disappearance varied widely across the whole Slavic area, indicating that it began right at the end of the Common Slavic period (1.1).

Throughout the Slavic area the *jers* were in principle lost in "weak" position, and virtually throughout fused with other existing vowels when in "strong" position. The two contexts may be summarized as follows:

- a *jer* was weak in word-final position, or where the following syllable contained a vowel other than a *jer*;
- a *jer* was strong where the following syllable contained a weak *jer*.

Complications to this simple rule of alternating strong and weak positions arose from resistance to the consonant clusters which were potentially formed by the loss of a weak *jer*, in which context all the languages retained such a *jer* to some extent or other. The extent of retention is a partial indicator of the relative consonantism *vs* vocalism of each language (for example, the extremes are Sorbian (consonantal) and B/C/S (vocalic), see further below 3.2.3.1).

In addition to creating new and more common consonant clusters, the loss of the *jers* signals the end of the open-syllable structure which had prevailed in Proto-Slavic, since words, and thus syllables, could now end in a consonant. It further signals the start of the assimilation in clusters (especially of voice, but also place and, to a lesser extent, manner of articulation) which occurs in all the languages, and of the devoicing of final voiced obstruents which occurs in all but two languages (B/C/S and Ukrainian) (3.2.3.2).

A development related to the resistance to new clusters was – again to a greater or lesser extent by language – the introduction of fill vowels to obviate the appearance of (even existing) consonant clusters in the new final position. In all cases the fill vowel has the same form as the strong *jer*, meaning that this development pre-dates the completion of the loss of the *jers*, the assumption being that the loss in final position was early and was compensated for by an inserted *jer* while the *jers* were still in the system. In a few cases, initial clusters have been obviated by vowel prothesis (3.2.1.4).

In two modern languages (Bulgarian and Slovenian) the strong position for at least the back *jer* is reflected in a *schwa* ([ə]). However, there is plenty of evidence that *schwa* was the first result in most areas, subsequently to be itself merged with other vowels. Also in many of the Slavic areas the *jers* merged together first (in *schwa*) before the final step, while other areas kept them apart.

Since the loss of internal *jers* was dependent on word shape, the loss gave rise to the vowel ~ zero alternation which is one of the most typical morphophonological features of Slavic (4.2.1).

The realization of the strong *jers* by language is summarized in table 3.1. For Bulgarian and Macedonian we give plural or definite article forms, since they have no declensions.

Table 3.1. *Realization of strong* jers

PSl examples: *sъnъ* 'sleep' NomSg ~ *sъna* GenSg; *dьnь* 'day' NomSg ~ *dьnja* GenSg; *dъždь* 'rain' NomSg ~ *dъždja* GenSg; *mъxъ* 'moss' NomSg ~ *mъxa* GenSg; *pьsъ* 'dog' NomSg ~ *pьsa* NomSg; *lьnъ* 'flax' NomSg ~ *lьna* GenSg

Language	Back *jer* (ъ)	Front *jer* (ь)	Examples (NomSg ~ GenSg)	
Blg	/ə/	/e/	*săn ~ sănját* (Def);	*den ~ dni* (Plur);
			dăžd ~ dăždové;	*măx ~ măxove* (Plur);
			pes ~ pésove (Plur);	*len ~lénăt* (Def)
Mac	/o/	/e/	*son ~ soništa/sništa*;	*den ~ denove/dni*;
			dožd ~ doždovi;	*mov ~ movot*;
			pes ~ psa (dial. *pesovî*);	*len ~ lenot*
B/C/S	/a/	/a/	*săn ~ snẵ*;	*dân ~ dâna*;
			dăžd ~ dàžda;	*mâx ~ mẵxa*;
			pẵs ~ psẵ;	*lẵn ~ lẵna*
Sln	/a ə/	/a ə/	*sèn ~ snà*;	*dán ~ dné*;
			dèž ~ dežjà;	*máh ~ máha*;
			pès ~ psà;	*lán ~ lána*
Rus, Bel	/o/	/'e/	Rus, Bel *son ~ sna*;	*den' ~ dnja*;
			dožd' ~ doždjá;	
			Rus *mox ~ mxa*, Bel *mox ~ móxu* or *imxú*	
	(then *e > o*, 3.2.1.5):		Rus, Bel *pěs ~ psa*;	
			Rus *lën ~ l'na*, Bel *lën ~ lěnu* or *l'nu* or *il'nú*	
Ukr	/o/	/e/	*son ~ sna*;	*den' ~ dnja*;
			došč ~ doščú;	*mox ~ móxu*;
			pes ~ psa;	*l'on ~ l'ónu*
Pol	/e/	/'e/	*sen ~ snu*;	*dzień ~ dnia*;
			deszcz ~ deszczu/dżdżu;	*mech ~ mchu*;
			pies ~ psa;	*len ~ lnu*
USorb	/e/	/e/	*dźeń ~ dnja*;	*deść ~ dešća; len ~ lena*
	(then *e > o* before a hard consonant):		*són ~ sona*;	*moch ~ mocha; pos ~ psa*
LSorb	/e/	/e/	*żeń ~ dnja*;	*dešć ~ dešća; mech ~ mecha*;
	(then *e > o* or *a* before a hard consonant):		*soń ~ sni*;	*pjas ~ psa; lan ~ lana*
Cz	/e/	/e/	*sen ~ snu*;	*den ~ dne*;
			dešt' ~ deště;	*mech ~ mechu*;
			pes ~ psa;	*len ~ lnu*
Slk	/e o a/	/e/	*sen ~ sna*;	*deň ~ dňa*;
			dáž ~ dažd'a;	*mach ~ machu*;
			pes ~ psa;	*l'an ~ l'anu*

(Central dialects and standard; West and East dialects as in Czech)

From table 3.1 we can see that most of West and South Slavic probably first merged the *jers* into [ə]. West Slavic at first retained the hard or soft quality of the preceding consonant, a feature which thereby became phonemic, but was later lost in Czech and Slovak. In most areas the later result was the merging of /ə/ with the low-mid vowel /e/. Only B/C/S and partly Slovenian fused the *schwa* with /a/. Macedonian, with the same results as East Slavic (/o/ *vs* /e/) – though without the hard ~ soft distinction – may reflect what is often said to be the result in Old Church Slavonic, but the latter is more likely to be seen in the Bulgarian retention of *schwa*. It is unclear whether Bulgarian passed through the "merged" *schwa* stage, though this possibility is supported by many examples of [ə] from front *ь* (e.g. *păn* 'tree-stump' from PSl *pьnъ*). Macedonian, on the other hand, has maintained the original quality distinction like East Slavic, and so cannot in the interim have merged the two (though its northern dialects behave like Bulgarian).

One further position of the *jers* needs to be mentioned. In the "tense" position, before a [j], the *jers* tended to be raised rather than lowered. In all areas except Russian these *jers* merged with high /i/ and /y/. In Russian these *jers*, along with /y/ and /i/, were treated as normal *jers*, becoming /o/ and /e/ when strong, and lost when weak. In this case, the position of the stress was a significant factor: in the Proto-Slavic forms *šíja* 'neck' and *mýjǫ* (or *mъ́jǫ*) 'I wash', the vowel was treated as strong, even though clusters of 'consonant + j' would not have been unacceptable in most areas: compare PSl *pijǫ́/pьjǫ́* 'I drink', in which the unstressed *jer* was allowed to disappear (Rus *p'ju*). In PSl *moldъ́jь* 'young' [NomSgMasc] (and all such long adjectival endings, e.g. *dóbrъjь* 'good'), the first *jer* was strong regardless of stress, and never disappeared. In Old Russian such vowels always became /o e/, though subsequently, under the conditions of unstressed vowels (see below 3.3.2.6), only the stressed ones have remained /o/, and the others are now treated as /y/ and /i/ (the RusChSl result). These forms are reflected as follows:

(3)   Rus   *šéja   móju   p'ju   molodój   dóbryj*

All other areas have *šýja, mýj-u/em* (or *šíja, míj-u/em* in languages where /y/ does not exist). Where the long adjectival endings have survived, the forms are -*yj/ij* or contracted -*ý/í*.

The fill vowels (above) also belong here, since they are the same as the results of the strong *jers*. Indeed, we might include here those weak *jers* which did not disappear (see 3.2.3.1), since the motivation for the two is identical. The clusters always involve a final sonorant, since 'obstruent + sonorant' were the typically acceptable Proto-Slavic clusters, based on the principle of rising sonority (see 1.3.1.1). The fill vowel appears only when the cluster is final, that is, where the ending is zero:

(4)   Fill vowels

PSl	*ognь* 'fire'	*větrъ* 'wind'	*myslь* 'thought'		
	ǫglь 'coal'	*osmь* 'eight'	(all NomSg)		
Blg	*ógăn*	*vjátăr*	*mísăl*	(*vắglen*)	*ósem*
Mac	*ogan*	*vetar*	(*misla*)	(*jaglen*)	*osum*
B/C/S	*òganj*	*vètar*	*mîsao*	*ǔgalj*	*ȍsam*
Sln	*ógenj*	*véter*	*mísel*	*ógel*	*ósem*
Rus	*ogón'*	*véter*	*mysl'*	*úgol'*	*vósem'*
Ukr	*vohón'*	*víter*	*mysl'*	*vúhil'*	*vísim*
Bel	*ahón'*	*véter*	*mysl'*	*vúhal'*	*vósem*
Pol	*ogień*	*wiatr*	*myśl*	*węgiel*	*osiem*
Sorb	*woheń*	*wĕtr*	*mysl*	(*wuhlo*)	*wosm*
Cz	*oheň*	*vítr*	*mysl*	*uhel*	*osm*
Slk	*oheň*	*vietor*	*mysel'*	*uhol'*	*osem*

The inconsistency of the fill vowels in such noun contexts in East and West Slavic is readily seen, and only South Slavic, as the most vocalic group, regularly inserts a vowel. A common verbal context for such new clusters was the past participle active NomSgMasc, with the suffix *-l-*: *psenes-lъ* 'carry', *mog-lъ* 'be able'. Such forms are normally regularized morphologically, with or without the inserted vowel: in East Slavic the norm is removal of the suffix /l/ (e.g. Rus *nës* [Fem *nes-lá*], *mog* [Fem *mog-lá*]). In languages with a syllabic /l̥/ no change is necessary (e.g. Cz *nes-l*, *moh-l*, both bisyllabic), though a vowel may still be inserted (e.g. Slk *nies-o-l*, *moh-o-l*). Elsewhere either the cluster is accepted (e.g. Pol *niós-l*, *móg-l*) or not (e.g. B/C/S *trés-a-o* 'shake' (Fem *trés-la*), *mȍg-a-o*, where final /l/ has become /o/; Blg *nés-ă-l*, *mog-ắ-l*).

3.2.1.2   *The nasal vowels (ę, ǫ)*

At the time of syllable opening the nasal vowels of Proto-Slavic had appeared from vowels followed by nasal consonants within the same syllable ("tautosyllabic"), with front and back versions according to the quality of the original vowel (see 1.3.1.7). This meant that they typically alternated with nasal consonants, and were probably not well integrated into the vowel system (cf. Shevelov, 1964: 583). Simultaneously with the reappearance of closed syllables – caused by the loss of the *jers* – the nasal vowels began to lose their nasality. For one thing, new clusters with tautosyllabic nasal consonants began to appear, albeit rarely, but they nevertheless became structurally possible (e.g. PSl *tonьk-ъjь 'thin' > tonk-yj). This, combined with the weak integration and articulatory complexity of the nasal vowels, led to their demise in most of the area fairly early: probably in the tenth century in all East Slavic, in all but Polish and Polabian in West Slavic, and in B/C/S, but somewhat later in the rest of South Slavic. Traces may still be found in some dialects of Bulgarian, Macedonian and Slovenian (10.2).

Of the standard languages, only Polish has retained the nasal vowels, at least at the structural level, and in the orthography. In practice they are usually realized as an oral vowel plus nasal consonant, the articulation of the latter corresponding to that of the following consonant (będę 'I will be' [bɛndɛ]). Only in a few contexts is a nasal vowel the norm: before spirants (mięso 'meat') and in final position for the back nasal (są 'they are'). Otherwise true nasal vowels are heard only in formal, careful speech (3.3.2.3). Such articulations are identical to new (foreign origin) sequences of 'vowel + nasal consonant', which may also produce nasal vowels in the pre-spirant position (kwadrans 'quarter of an hour'). In this same context standard Bulgarian may also have nasalized vowels, though they need not subsume the nasal consonant (ónzi 'that' [ɔzi] or [ɔnzi]).

The quality of the Polish nasal vowels is interesting etymologically, for they have clearly gone through a stage of merging and then one of separation, in which the new quality does not correspond to the old. In stage one the two merged into a central nasal vowel (probably schwa, but perhaps rounded), but the previous quantity distinction was retained, as was the hard or soft quality of the preceding consonant. In stage two, with the loss of phonemic quantity in Polish, the long version (either originally long or newly long through contraction or compensation) moved back (the modern letter ą). The short version moved forward (the modern letter ę), while the consonant palatalization remained phonemic.

In the other languages the quality distinction was usually retained and the denasalized vowels merged with others in the system:

ǫ > u and ę > ä:	Rus, Ukr, Bel, Cz, Slk, Sorb
ǫ > u and ę > e:	B/C/S
ǫ > o and ę > e:	Sln
ǫ > ə and ę > e:	Blg
ǫ > a and ę > e:	Mac

So all East and West Slavic except for Polish had a common result for both nasal vowels (> u/ä), and all South Slavic had a common result for the front nasal vowel (> e). Subsequent changes to the [ä] have separated East and West Slavic some-what, since [ä] became /a/ or /e/ in Czech and Sorbian (and even /o/ in the latter),

Table 3.2. *Nasal vowel reflexes*

a. Proto-Slavic
1. short back (ǫ):
   rǫka 'hand'   zǫba 'tooth' [GenSg]   mǫka 'flour'   idǫ 'I go'
2. long back (ǭ):
   sǭdъ 'court'   zǫbъ 'tooth'   mǫka 'torture'   idǫtь 'they go'
3. short front (ę):
   pętь 'five'   męso 'meat'   językъ 'tongue'   sę 'self' [AccSg]
4. long front (ę̄):
   pętъjь 'fifth'   rędъ 'row'   tęgnǫti 'to pull'   ljubętь 'love'/prosętь
                                                                   'ask' [3 Pl]
(Note: short and long here include later results of suprasegmental processes.)

b. Modern

Blg/Mac	1	răká/raka	zăbi/zabi (Pl)	–	id[ə]/(idam)
	2	săd/(sud)	zăb/zab	măka/maka	idăt/idat
	3	pet	meso	ezík/jazik	se
	4	péti/petti	red	tégn[ə]/tegne	ljúbj[ə]t/ljubat
B/C/S/ Sln	1	rúka/rōka	zùba/zóba	múka/móka	(idēm)
	2	sûd/sód	zûb/zób	mùka/(múka)	ȉdū/(dial. idó)
	3	pêt/pét	mêso/mesó	jèzik/jêzik	se
	4	pêtī/pêti	rêd/réd	Cr tégnuti	ljūbē/ljúbijo
Rus/Ukr/Bel	1	ruká	zúba	muká	idú
	2	sud	zub	múka	idút
	3	pjatʹ	mjáso	jazýk	sja
	4	pjátyj	rjad/Bel rad	tjanútʹ	ljúbjat
Pol	1	ręka	zębu	męka	idę
	2	sąd	ząb	mąka	idą
	3	pięć	mięso	język	się
	4	piąty	rząd	ciągnąć	lubią
Cz/Slk	1	ruka	zubu/zuba	muka	jdu/(idem)
	2	soud	zub	mouka/múka	jdou/idú
	3	pět/pät'	maso/mäso	jazyk	se/sa
	4	pátý/piaty	řád/rad	táhnout/ tiahnut'	prosí/prosia
U/LSorb	1	ruka	zuba	muka	du
	2	sud	zub	–	du
	3	pjeć/pěś	mjaso/měso	jazyk/jězyk	so/se
	4	pjaty	rjad	ćahnyć/śěgnuś	lubja/lubje

and /a/ or /ä/ in Slovak, but always /a/ in East Slavic. Some varieties of Bulgarian and Macedonian may well have initially merged the quality of the two into a nasalized *schwa* and then separated them again in the same way as Polish.

In table 3.2 we give the reflexes of the four Proto-Slavic forms (back ~ front and long ~ short).

3.2.1.3   jat' (ě)

The table of Proto-Slavic vowel phonemes in 3.2.1 makes /ě/ look well integrated as a front partner to /a/. But the reality is that the [ä] position became unstable after the developments which led to phonemicization of palatalization. In the former opposition of hard ~ soft *syllables*, it was the vowel which was dominant, for example in the opposition of, say, /ta/ to /t′ä/. The back ~ front distinction resided mainly in the vowel, supported by the hard or soft nature of the consonant. After the loss of the *jers* and the closing of syllables, the bond between the consonant and vowel was weakened and the single segments became phonemic. In this situation it was the consonants which became dominant within the system, since they were "independently" phonemic, for example in final position where no vowel followed. In the new syllables /t-a/ and /t′-ä/ the quality of the vowel was secondary, and since in the context of simple phonetics the distance between /a/ and /ä/ is small and fragile, /ä/ readily came to be seen as an allophone of /a/. Thus Proto-Slavic /ě/ found itself losing independence. But in several areas it appears to have "defended itself", so to speak, in the short term by shifting to a higher position, in the extreme case (Ukr) ending up as /i/, while original /i/ there moved back to /y/. Former /ě/ is now nowhere a separate phoneme, and is directly traceable only in the *jekavski* (Jekavian) variant of B/C/S, where it is reflected in the phonemic sequences /j-e/ or /i-j-e/. Elsewhere it has coalesced with some other phoneme – most often /e/, sometimes /a/. In the case of Ukrainian it was joined in the /i/ position by new /i/ from other sources (3.2.1.5).

A different view about the systemic weakness of /ě/ is that, unlike the other phonemes, it was phonetically still a complex sound, effectively a rising diphthong of the /ea-ia/ type (Shevelov, 1964: 585). Its complexity within an otherwise "pure vowel" system was therefore its weakness. This does make the actual range of shifts easier to understand. The phonetic nature of /ě/ at the end of Proto-Slavic is open to debate, and the phonemic scenario described in the preceding paragraph can equally well account for its subsequent fate, since the end point of push–pull activity is not necessarily phonetically predictable. So we shall simply note the fact of its weakness and observe its reflexes, which must also be related to the rest of each given vocalic system (examples are given in table 3.3).

/ě/ > /e/:	Rus, Bel, B/C/S(Ekavian), Mac
> /ie/:	Cz, Slk, Sorb, B/C/S(Jekavian), Sln
> /a/(via /ä/):	Pol, Blg
>/i/:	Ukr, B/C/S(Ikavian) (On the variants of B/C/S see 1.5.3 and 10.2.2.)

It is probably no coincidence that the areas which initially "retained" /ä/ (but where it later became /a/) were those which also retained nasality, on the grounds

that the denasalization of the front nasal typically produced /ä/. In a phonemic
view of the motivation for sound change, this could have provided a push for /ě/ to
move upwards. Where nasality remained, this position remained available to /ě/.
Subsequently in all areas /ä/ from whatever source became an allophone of /a/. In
Slovak, which alone now has the phoneme /ä/, its source was, in fact, the front
nasal. In all these areas we find the /a/ result consistently only in a "hard" context,
i.e. followed by a hard consonant or syllable (the position of stress is also relevant in
Bulgarian). In other contexts the result was /e/.

In the other areas the vowel moved upwards. Sometimes it jumped existing /e/ to
become a high-mid [e], for example in Old Russian, where it was supported in some
areas by a back partner [o]. The dialects at the base of standard Russian either did
not acquire that partner or lost it quickly and along with it went /ě/. In some
northern Russian dialects /ě/ is reflected, along with certain reflexes of /e/, in high-
mid [e] or a diphthong of the [i̯e] type, both usually supported by back partners
(10.3.3). And in Ukrainian, as noted above, it continued even higher to dislodge /i/,
which elsewhere in East Slavic remained the dominant variant of the /i/-/y/ pair.
In Ukrainian original /i/ shifted to /y/, eliminating the variation, as /i/ and /y/ are
there unquestionably separate phonemes. (It should be noted that Ukrainian /y/ is
still a front vowel, close to [ɪ], and so not as far back as the /y/ of Russian or
Belarusian.)

For the rest of South and West Slavic positing the stage of /i̯e/ helps to explain
what followed: in those areas which developed vocalic quantity as a phonemic
feature, this diphthong could split into higher and lower versions, e.g. Cz > short
/e/ or long /ī/, while in B/C/S (Jekavian) it gave short /je/ or long /ije/; or it could
remain diphthongal when long, e.g. Slk > short /e/, long /i̯e/, Sorb > short /e/ or /je/,
long > /ie/.

Table 3.3 shows examples of the reflexes. Belarusian orthography reflects
unstressed vowel pronunciation, in this case pretonic /e/ > /a/ (*raká*). Czech uses
the letter *ě* to represent /e/ after palatal stops (including /n/) and /je/ after
other consonants. In Sorbian this letter represents the falling diphthong /ie/ (or a
close /é/). For other orthographic details, including diacritics, see appendix B.

A context of special interest for *jat'* – and for vowels in general (3.2.1.4) – is word-
initial position, where *jat'* essentially behaves the same as internally (table 3.3).
This indicates that its nature was such that it did not require or acquire the prothetic
/j/ which was typical of initial front vowels, since, if it had done so, the resulting sequence of /jě/ would have become /jä/, then /ja/, as happened internally
(1.3.1.6), and as happened to /ě/ where it became /a/ (see below). This supports the
notion that *jat'* was more than just a fronted [ä] and rather a diphthongal [i̯a].
The examples in (5a) show initial /je/ from /ě/ corresponding to internal /e/

Table 3.3. *Reflexes of /ě/*

a. Proto-Slavic (all NomSg nouns or NomSgMasc adjectives)

svě́tъ 'light, world' / tělo 'body'
svě́tja 'candle' / dělo 'affair, thing, work'
věra 'faith' / lě́to 'year, summer'
rěka 'river' / bě̀lъ(jъ) 'white'

b. Modern

	svě́tъ 'light, world'	tělo 'body'	svě́tja 'candle'	dělo 'affair, thing, work'	věra 'faith'	lě́to 'year, summer'	rěka 'river'	bě̀lъ(jъ) 'white'
Blg	svjat (Def svetă)	tjálo (Pl telá)	svešt	(dělo)	vjára	ljáto	reká	bjal (Pl bélı)
Mac	svet	telo	sveḱa	delo	vera	leto	reka	bel
B/C/S (Ek)	svȇt	tȇlo	svéća	dȅlo	vȅra	lȅto	réka	bȇo (Def bȇl)
(Jek)	svìjet	tìjelo	svijéća	djȅlo	vjȅra	ljȅto	rijéka	bȉo/bìjel
Sln	svét	teló	svéča	délo	véra	léto	réka	bél
Rus	svet	télo	svečá	délo	véra	léto	reká	bél-yj
Ukr	svit	tilo	svíčka	dilo	víra	lito	rīka	bilyj
Bel	svet	céla	svéčka	dzéla	véra	léta	raká*	béla
Pol	świat	ciało	świeca	dzíało	wiara*	lato	rzeka	biały
Cz	svět	tělo	svíce	dílo	víra	léto	řeka	bílý
Slk	svet	telo	svieca	dielo	viera	leto	rieka	biely
Sorb	swět	čě́lo / šě́lo	swěca	dzě́ło / žě́ło	wěra	lěto	rěka	bě́ły

Blg: (*ja* only under stress and before [formerly] hard consonant)

Bel: (*pretonic /e/ > /a/ after hard consonant)

Pol: (LocSg *świecie*); (**a* only before [formerly] hard dental)

Sorb: (LSorb *šě́lo, žě́ło*)

(PSl *ĕxati/ĕdǫ 'travel' [Det] Inf/1ps (which appears to have had a Proto-Slavic variant in ja-), *ĕzditi/ĕzda 'travel' [Indet] Inf/noun NomSg, *ĕsti 'eat' Inf/ĕda 'food' NomSg); Russian initial e- means /je/. But those in (5b) show the expected /ja/, as is also found internally, and those in (5c) show /ja/ where it is not expected:

(5)   Initial /ĕ/

(5a)   >je

B/C/S	(jáhati	jášem)	jézditi	Sln jézda	jĕsti	jĕdja (arch.)
Rus	éxat'	édu	ézdit'	ezdá	est'	edá
Cz	jet	jedu	jezdit	jízda	jíst	jídlo

(5b)   >ja/je

Blg	–	(jáxam)	–	jázdene	jam	jádene
Pol	jechać	jadę	jeździć	jeżdżenie	jeść	jadło

(5c)   >ja

Mac	–	(java)	jazdi	–	jade	jadenje
Slk	–	–	jazdit'	jazda	(jest'	jedlo)

This last /ja/ may be explained either as a dialectal alternative, which is better for the inconsistent results of Slovak and Slovenian; or as an indication of the earlier shifting of /ĕ/ to /ä/ in these areas, which is better for the consistent Macedonian results.

3.2.1.4   Word-initial vowels and prothesis

Prothesis   During the open-syllable period of Proto-Slavic (1.3.1.1) there was a hiatus between the compulsory final vowel and any following initial vowel. This led to the regular insertion of a glide, which then became perceived as an initial (prothetic) consonant. The nature of the glide was controlled by that of the initial vowel, namely [i̯] before a front unrounded vowel and [u̯] before back (typically rounded). The only uncertain situation was before initial /a/, which was treated mostly as a back vowel, but also sometimes as a front vowel. The hesitation was probably due to its lack of lip-rounding, which discouraged [u̯]. This was perhaps supported by its contextually fronted variant [ä], though this [ä] would not have occurred initially, since it was induced by the *preceding* consonant. With the syllable restructure (closing) and the new importance of consonants, these glides became consonantal [j] and [w], respectively, and the latter then usually became labio-dental [v].

Examples of each of the possible initial vowels follow (for /ĕ/, see the preceding section). /y/ and the *jers* were impossible initially, having earlier always acquired a prothetic consonant: [u̯] (> /w-v/) to /y/ (from /ū/) and /ъ/ (from /ŭ/), [i̯] (> /j/) to /ь/ (from /ĭ/); further, the sequences /j/ + /ъ/ and /j/ + /ь/ had subsequently become /i/.

/i/   The articulation of /i/ would have made the [i̯] glide very weak. In many areas it did not survive, but in others it actually dominated the vowel:

(6)   Initial /i/
      PSl   *igrati* 'to play' (<*jь-*) *iměti*/*imati* 'to have, take' (<*jь-*)
              iva   'willow' *imę*/*imene* 'name' NomSg/GenSg (<*jь-*)
              idǫ   'I go' (<*jь-*):

Blg	*igrája*	*imam*	*íva*	*íme*/Pl *imená*	*idắ*
B/C/S	*ȉgrati*	*ìmati*	*ȉva*	*ȉme*/*ȉmena*	*ȉdēm*
Rus	*igrát′*	*imét′*	*íva*	*ímja*/*ímeni*	*idú*

(/j/ before (any) stressed /i/ was lost in CS-Russian only in the twentieth century)

Ukr	*hráty*	*máty*	*íva*	*imjá*/*ímeny*	*ídu*
Bel	*ihrác′*	*mec′*	*íva*	*imjá*/*ímeni*	*idú*
Cz	*hrát*	*mít*	*jíva*	*jméno*	*jdu*
Slk	*hrat'*	*mat'*	*jíva*	*meno*	*idem*
Pol	*grać*	*mieć*	*iwa*	*imię*/*imienia*	*idę*
USorb	*hrać*	*měć*	*jiwa*	*mjeno*	*du*
LSorb			*wiwa*	*mě*/*mjenja*	

Retention or loss of /i/, therefore, is unconditional across one of the three groups only in South Slavic. In East and West Slavic the position of stress is relevant. In Sorbian, which is now virtually never without a prothetic consonant, there are only a few examples of prothetic /h/ in this context, e.g. PSl *iti* 'go' Inf > USorb *hić*, LSorb *hyś*; PSl *inakъ* 'other' > USorb *hinak*/*jinak*, LSorb *hynak*.

/e/   The context of initial [i̯] plus /e/ (> /je/) produced one of the earliest major group splits, in that East Slavic converted this sequence to #o- in many words. The other languages retained /je/, Bulgarian and Macedonian later losing the /j/. The development in East Slavic is often explained in terms of phonemics: /o/ and /e/ may have been perceived as back ~ front variants of the same phoneme, with /o/ the more independent one (i.e. less controlled by context) and thus the more natural for initial position. But this argument did not hold good for the whole area, so that there are other issues at play. The new vowel would still have had to meet the "anti-hiatus" principle which was producing the glides in the first place – unless this principle had weakened, which would place the change potentially within the syllable-restructuring period. It is possible that the new vowel did contain a glide of its own, which would have been [u̯]. Alternatively, the strong lip-rounding of the new vowel could have been sufficient to act in the same way as a [u̯] glide. In fact, the change in East Slavic affected only certain roots, and it seems that the nature of the second syllable was relevant, with certain following vowels apparently inhibiting the change. This is an easier case to argue than the converse: that certain following vowels encouraged the change. In a few cases Old Russian shows variation, supported by modern Russian dialects, suggesting that there were more cases of the change than are evident in the early texts, and that the forms with #*je*- are influenced by Old Church Slavonic.

(7) Initial /e/

PSl	*edinъ* 'one'		*ezero* 'lake'		*ežь* 'hedgehog'	
	edlь/edla 'fir'		*estь* 'be' 3 Sg		*ed(ъ)va* 'scarcely':	
OCS	*jedinъ*	*jezero*	–	–	*jestъ*	*jedva*
Blg	*edín*	*ézero*	*ež*	*elá*	*e*	*edvá*
B/C/S	*jèdan*	*jȅzero*	*jȇž*	*jéla*	*je*	*jèdva*
Rus	*odín*	*ózero*	*ëž**	*eľ/jólka*	*est'*	*edvá***
	(*ORus *ježь/ožь*)		(**dial. *odvá*, ORus *jedъva* and *odъva*)			
Ukr	*odýn*	*ózero*	*jižák*	*jalýna*	*je*	(*lédve*)
Bel	*adzín*	*vózera*	*vóžyk*	*élka*	*josc'**	(*lédz've*)
	(*e > o* is a later East Slavic development, see below)					
Cz	*jeden*	*jezero*	*ježek*	*jedle*	*je*	*jedva*

Initial /e/ (with no prothesis) occurs in Russian in only one case – that of the demonstrative *èt-ot* 'this', which derives from a prothetic expletive of the 'hey!' sort, added later to the basic demonstrative root *t-*. This is supported by the Belarusian form *hèt-* ['ɣɛt-].

/ę/   No doubt all areas had initial /ję/ by the time of denasalization, which would produce /jä/. Where this /ä/ moved to /e/ (see above, 3.2.1.3) the reflex is either /je/ (B/C/S, Sln) or /e/ (Blg), the latter matching the loss of /j/ in #*je* (above). Where /ę/ became /a/, the reflex is always /ja/ (East and West Slavic). Polish retained nasalization and has /ję/ or /ją/. The only odd area is standard Macedonian and B/C/S dialects, which do not match the rest of South Slavic – neither standard B/C/S nor Bulgarian – but have /ja/. Other Macedonian dialects have the expected /e/:

(8) Initial /ę/

PSl *ęzykъ* 'tongue'   *ęti* 'to take' (with prefix *pri-*)
       ęčьmy/ęčьmene 'barley' NomSg/GenSg;
       and cf. *jędro* 'kernel',

apparently with original /j/
('d.' = 'dialectal')

Blg	ezík	–		ečemík	jadró
Mac	jazik	–		jačmen (d. ečmen)	jadro
B/C/S	jèzik (Čak. jazȉk)	Sln prijéti	jèčmen		jédro
Rus	jazýk	pri-n-ját'	jáčmén'		jadró
Pol	język	przyjąć	jęczmień		jądro
Cz	jazyk	Slk prijat'	ječmen/Slk jačmeň		jádro

/a/   The most typical result here was prothetic /j/. We rarely find prothetic /w-v/ (see 3.2.2.4). This result is unsurprising, given that /a/ was not rounded. But we do find a few reflexes with no prothesis, again mainly in the Bulgarian/ Macedonian area. The proclitic conjunction a 'and, but' is the only native form never to acquire prothetic /j/ anywhere:

(9)   Initial /a/
PSl   azъ 'I'   ablъko 'apple'   agnę 'lamb'
       aje 'egg'   asenь 'aspen'   ako 'how, as'
       ('d.' = 'dialectal')

Blg	az	jábălka	ágne	jajcé	jásen (d. osen)	OCS ako
Mac	jas	jabolko	jagne	jajce	jasen (d. esen)	(kako)
B/C/S	jâ	jȁbuka	jȁgnje	jáje	jȁsen	(kȁko)
Rus	ja	jábloko	jagn-ёnok	jaj-có	jásen'	Ukr jak
Pol	ja	jabłko	jagnię	jaje	jesień (d. jesion)	jak
Cz	já	jablko	jehně	vejce /Slk vajco	jasan (d. jesen)	jako/Slk ako

/u/   The most rounded vowel is perhaps least likely to acquire a [u̯], since this would be assimilated into the vowel and thus be redundant. Proto-Slavic itself did not have prothesis here, but the prothesis did appear later, though inconsistently, in Ukrainian/Belarusian and Sorbian (see below on the related feature of initial ju-). The preposition u 'next to', being usually proclitic, does not attract the prothesis even where – as happens with Sorbian – the prothesis occurs elsewhere in that region:

(10)   Initial /u/
PSl   uxo 'ear'   umъ 'mind'   uměti 'to know'
       usta/ustьnъ(jь) 'mouth, lips' Pl/'oral'   u 'next to'

Blg/Mac	uxó/uvo	um	uméja/umee	ustá/usta	u
B/C/S/Sln	ŭho/uhô	ûm/úm	uméti/ùmeti	ústa	B/C/S u
Rus	úxo	um	umét'	ustá	u
Ukr	vúxo	um	umíty	(v)ustá	u
Bel	vúxa	–	uméc'	vúsny	u
Pol	ucho	um	umieć	usta	u
Sorb	wucho	um	LS wuměś	LS wusta	wu/LS wu/hu
Cz/Slk	ucho	um	umět/umet'	ústa	u

/ǫ/ Where /ǫ/ was denasalized to /u/ the reflexes are as for /u/. In Slovenian the new /o/ did not acquire a prothesis, but Bulgarian /ə/ (initially nasalized) did usually acquire /w-v/, and Macedonian /a/, like regular /a/, could acquire /j/. In Polish the new back nasal acquired /w-v/ regardless of its shape in Proto-Slavic:

(11) Initial /ǫ/

PSl	ǫg(ъ)lъ 'corner'		ǫžь 'adder'	ǫgorь 'eel'
	ǫzъkъ(jь) 'narrow'		(v)ǫsъ/(v) ǫsy 'beard'/'moustache' Pl	
Blg/Mac	ắgắl/agol	jagúlja/jagula –	–	Blg vắsí
	Mac d. jagol			
B/C/S	ŭgao	ŭgor	(gûž) ŭzak	–
Sln	ôgel	ogór	(góž) ózek	d. vôsi
Rus	úgol	úgor'	už úzkij	usý
Ukr/Bel	vúhol/vúhal	vuhór	vuž vuz'kýj/vúzki	vus
Pol	węgieł	węgorz	wąż wązki	wąs
Sorb	nuheł/nugeł	wuhoŕ	wuž wuski	wusy
Cz/Slk	úhel/uhol	úhoŕ/úhor	užovka úzký/úzky	vous/fúz

The reflexes of (v)ǫs-, in which only Russian has no /v/, suggest that the /v/ was either part of the original root or attached in Proto-Slavic. Indo-European parallels (e.g. OIrish fés 'beard') also suggest the /v/ is old. On why Russian has no /v/, see below (b) on initial u-/ju-. Initial /g/ in B/C/S and Slovenian may be a special case of expressive prothesis or – more likely – the result of "blending" with other words (Shevelov, 1964: 244) (cf. B/C/S gúja 'snake', Sln góž 'rope')

/o/ The same results attach to /o/, which acquires /w-v/ in the same general areas as does /u/: Ukrainian/Belarusian and Sorbian, but this time more rarely in Ukrainian and Belarusian. In East Slavic original /o/, and /o/ from /je/, behave identically. The preposition *o(b)* 'about, concerning, during, against', as with *u* (above), acquires /w-/ only in Sorbian:

(12)   Initial /o/

PSl	*ognь* 'fire'	*oko/oči* 'eye' Sg/Pl	*onъ* 'he'		*ovьca* 'sheep'
	ostrъ(jь) 'sharp'				
Blg/Mac	*ógăn/ogan*	*okó/oko*	on	*ovcá/ovca*	*óstăr/ostar*
B/C/S	*òganj*	*ȍko*	ȏn	*óvca*	*ȍštar*
Sln	*ógenj*	*okó*	òn	*óvca*	*óster*
Rus	*ogón'*	arch. *óko*	on	*ovcá*	*óstryj*
Ukr	*vohón'*	arch. *óko*	vin	*vivcjá*	*hóstryj*
Bel	*ahón'*	*vóka*	jon	*aŭcá*	*vóstry*
Pol	*ogień*	*oko*	on	*owca*	*ostry*
Kash			wön	*wöwca*	*wöstri*
U/LSorb	*woheń*	*woko*	wón	*wowca/wojca*	*wótry/wótšy*
Cz/Slk	*oheň*	*oko*	on	*ovce/ovca*	*ostrý*

In *osmь* 'eight', the appearance of /v/ throughout East Slavic – including Russian *vósem'* – is due to the tonal nature of the vowel; see below, 3.2.1.5.

Ukrainian *hóstryj* 'sharp' is an exceptional example of prothetic /h/.

Czech dialects (Bohemian) show prothetic /v/, e.g. *von* 'he', *vokno* 'window' (10.4.3).

Other word-initial features

i.   Initial /ju/

In this same context a curious feature concerns etymological initial *ju-*, which in East Slavic lost the /j/ and retained an /u/, which did not then acquire a new prothetic /w-v/ in either Ukrainian or Belarusian. But there are very few reliable examples. Several appear in Russian in their Russian Church Slavonic (i.e. South Slavic) form, and there are some in Ukrainian and Belarusian in the Polish form. This develop-ment has been related to the East Slavic loss of /j/ before /e/ (and > /o/, see above), suggesting that initial /j/ became unstable through con-fusion with the prothetic, non-etymological /j/:

(13)   Initial /ju/

PSl	*jugъ* 'south' NomSg	*juxa* 'soup' NomSg	*jutro* 'morning' NomSg (and *za-jutra* 'tomorrow')

Blg/Mac	*jug*	Mac *juva*	*útro*	(*utre*)
B/C/S/Sln	*jǔg*	*júha*	*jǔtro*	*sǔtra*/(Sln *jǔtri*)
Rus	*jug* (RusChSl); ORus *ugъ*	*uxá*	*útro*	*závtra* (< *za utra*)
Ukr/Bel	–	*juxá* (Pol) –		*závtra*/*záŭtra*
Pol/Sorb	–	*jucha*	*jutro*/*jutšo*	(*jutro*/(*jutrě*/*witśe*)
Cz/Slk	*jih*/*juh*	*jícha*/*jucha*	*jitro*/*jutro*	*zítra*/*zajtra* (< *z*(*a*) jutra)

ii. Simplification of initial clusters

In the same way as newly formed final consonant clusters were avoided in most areas by the insertion of a fill vowel (see above, 3.2.1.1), new initial consonant clusters formed through the loss of a *jer* were also not favored. This would be the case especially if the new sequence was 'sonorant + obstruent' – in groups like *rt-*, *ln-*, *mx-*, which is against the principle of rising sonority which had dominated until then. The normal solution was the same as for final clusters – treat the weak *jer* as strong, thus eliminating the alternation with zero which was otherwise the typical result. Examples include PSl *lьna* 'flax' GenSg, *rъži* 'rye' GenSg, *rъžati* 'neigh' Inf, *mъxa* 'moss' GenSg (and see table 3.1). Some areas accept these happily, e.g. Russian (14a). Others do not, e.g. B/C/S (14b). A third solution is a prothetic vowel, and this is adopted by Belarusian, at least in variant (dialectal) forms (14c). And languages with syllabic /r̥/ or /l̥/ may use this solution, e.g. B/C/S and Macedonian (14d):

(14a)	Rus	*l'na*	*rži*	*ržat'*	*mxa*
(14b)	B/C/S	*lana*	*raži*		*maxa*
(14c)	Bel	*il'nú*		(*i*)*ržác'*	*imxú*/*móxu*
(14d)	Mac		*'rž*	*'rži*	
	B/C/S			*r̥žati*	

3.2.1.5 *Quality changes*

a. Non-contextual: /y/

We have noted the non-contextual changes to the major vowels above (*jers*, nasals and *jat'*). The only other vowel to undergo such change was /y/. With the syllable restructure and the separation of consonant and vowel phonemes, all languages had to make decisions, as it were,

about the status of the previously positionally soft consonants
(1.3.1.3). The possibilities were: (1) make them into palatalized phonemes; (2) leave them as allophones controlled by front vowels; or (3)
eliminate the palatalization completely. We shall deal with the details
of this development below (3.2.2.2). The fate of /y/ relates directly to
this problem. In type (1) (e.g. Russian) /y/ became an allophone of /i/,
since the choice of quality depended on that of the preceding consonant, but the separate quality nevertheless remained. In type (2) (e.g.
early Ukrainian) /y/ could survive as a phoneme, since it could control
the quality of the preceding consonant. In type (3) (e.g. B/C/S) /y/ did
not survive at all, since there was no longer any choice of
[±Palatalized] within the system. Intermediate solutions occurred
where languages passed through type (2) into type (3) (e.g.
Ukrainian, Czech, with fusion of /i–y/ and loss of palatalization) or
back into type (2) (e.g. Ukrainian, with the appearance of a new /i/).
Thus we find the following situation with regard to PSl /y/:

1. It is a separate phoneme: in Ukrainian, which shifted from type
   (3) back to type (2), that is, it redeveloped palatalization when /ě/ was
   converted into a new /i/. The original /i/ and /y/ had merged and shifted
   to an intermediate /y/ position. Consonants may now be allophonically
   hard or soft before these vowels. This is also the situation in Sorbian.

2. It is an allophone controlled by the preceding consonant. This is the
   best description of the situation in Russian, Belarusian and Polish,
   where palatalization is clearly phonemic throughout the system, so
   that the choice of [i] or [y] is controlled by the preceding consonant
   rather than being independent.

3. It is an allophone controlled by length: in Czech and Slovak /i/ and /y/
   merged in /i/, but with a long and short version. The short version
   has a retracted or reduced quality which is effectively /y/ (phonetically close to the /y/ of Ukrainian, but lower and more fronted than
   that of Russian and Belarusian (3.4.2)).

4. It no longer exists: all of South Slavic eliminated palatalization and
   /y/ along with it. While Bulgarian has redeveloped some palatalization, this has not affected the /i/ phoneme.

b. Contextual: effects of surrounding consonants

i. Fronting/raising

Contextual changes to vowels are also frequently related to the hard ~
soft nature of surrounding consonants. Given the regressive nature
of Slavic assimilation, the *following* consonant is the main actor in

this scenario, and in particular soft and palatal consonants have a fronting and/or raising effect on vowels. If the *preceding* consonant is *also* soft or palatal, the effect is maximal. Typical effects are:

Phonemic (distributional limitations):

/a/ > /e/   Czech: after soft or palatal consonants *and* not before
                    hard consonants (= *přehláska* 'umlaut')
                    duše 'soul' (PSl/Rus *dušá*)
                    jevit 'to show' (PSl *javiti*, Rus *javíť-sja* 'to seem')
                    běžet 'to run' (PSl *běžati* – from earlier **běgěti*, Rus *bežáť*)

        USorb: between soft consonants
                    jejo 'egg' (PSl *jaje*, Rus *jajcó*)
                    rjeńši 'earlier' (PSl *ranьšьjь*, Rus *rán'šij*)
                    rjad 'row' NomSg ∼ *w rjedźe* LocSg

/o/ > /e/   USorb: between a hard and a soft consonant
                    sel 'salt' (PSl *solь*, Rus *sol'*)
                    zerja 'dawn' (PSl *zorьja*, Rus *zórja*)

/u/ > /i/   Czech: after soft or palatal consonants *and* not before
                    hard consonants (= *přehláska*)
                    lidé 'people' Pl (PSl *ljudьje*, Rus *ljúdi*)
                    cizí 'foreign' (PSl *tjudjьjь*, Rus *čužój*)
                    klíč 'key' (PSl *ključь*, Rus *ključ*)
                    líbit se 'to admire' (PSl *ljubiti*, Rus *ljubíť sja*)

Allophonic   In the languages with extensive phonemic palatalization, raising of front vowels before soft consonants is usually noticeable at least in stressed syllables. In Russian, Belarusian and Polish /e/ is realized here as raised [e] (*vs* [ɛ] otherwise):

(15)   Rus *ètot* 'this' SgMasc ['ɛtət] ∼ *èti* 'this' Pl ['etʲɪ]

When a stressed non-front vowel in Russian is surrounded by soft consonants, it is noticeably fronted:

/a/ > [ä]:   Rus *pjátyj* 'fifth' ['pʲatɨj] ∼ *pjat'* 'five' [pʲætʲ]
/o/ > [ö]:   Rus *tot* 'that' [tɔt] *vs tëtja* 'aunt' ['tʲötʲə]
/u/ > [ü]:   Rus *bljúdo* 'dish' ['blʲudə] *vs ljúdi* 'people' Pl ['lʲüdʲɪ]

ii. Backing caused by a following hard consonant: /e/ > /o/

The reverse phenomenon of backing occurs in Russian, Belarusian and Sorbian, where /e/ has become /o/ when followed by a hard consonant, or rather, when not followed by a soft consonant (thus also in final position). In the case of Sorbian there is no other context, and the affected /e/ may be of any source (PSl /ь/, /ъ/ and /ę/ as well as /e/):

(16a)   Sorb   *žona* 'wife' (PSl/Rus *žená*) ~ *ženić so* 'to get married';
         polo 'field' (PSl/Rus *pól(j)e*);
         pos 'dog' (PSl /ь/)   *ćelo* 'calf' (PSl /ę/)
         (*zeleny* 'green' is inconsistent, see Rus/Pol below)

In the case of Russian and Belarusian this effect occurs only under stress:

(16b)   Rus   *sëla* 'villages' Pl ~ *sél'skij* 'rural' ~ *seló* 'village'
         (PSl *sel-*)
         zelënyj 'green' ~ *zélen'* 'greenery' (PSl *zelen-*)
         licó 'face' (PSl *lice*)

(16c)   Bel   *sëly* 'villages' Pl ~ *sél'ski* 'rural' ~ *sjaló* 'village'
         zjalëny 'green' ~ *zélen'* 'greenery'

In these examples the source of /e/ may also be /ь/: Rus/Bel *ovës/avës* 'oats' (PSl *ovьsъ*), but not /ě/, which always remains /e/: Rus/Bel *les* 'forest'.

For Polish the additional restriction is that only following hard dentals have produced the change, so that backing does not occur in word-final position either:

(16d)   Pol   *žona* 'wife' (PSl/Rus *žena*) ~ *żeński* 'feminine'
         zielony 'green' ~ *zieleni* 'green' PlMasc
         But: *pole* 'field'

In Polish the only source of the backed /o/ is /e/, not /ъ/ or /ь/, which remain /e/: *sen* 'sleep' (PSl *sъnъ*), *pies* 'dog' (PSl *pьsъ*).

iii. Effects caused by closed syllables and word boundaries
     Phonemic In Ukrainian, apart from /ě/, the other sources of the new high front /i/ were /o/ and /e/ in (new) closed syllables. This change is usually interpreted as the result of compensatory lengthening on this vowel for the loss of the *jer* in the next syllable. The interim stages were diphthongs of the [ụo] type, seen in some texts and still in some dialects (10.3.2). In addition to providing new sources of /i/, this development produced new alternations of /i/ ~ /o/ or /e/:

(17)   Ukr   *nis ~ nósa* 'nose'   NomSg ~ GenSg   (PSl *nos-*);
               sim ~ semí 'seven'   NomSg ~ GenSg   (PSl *sedm-*)

Proto-Slavic /ь/ did not participate in this change, remaining /e/: *pes* 'dog', *den'* 'day'; nor did bookish or foreign words participate.

In Polish, with the loss of phonemic vowel length (3.2.4.2), long /ō/ became /u/ in closed syllables, mainly where the following consonant was a voiced phoneme, even though, if this consonant was an obstruent, it would be phonetically devoiced in final position. The etymology and alternation are preserved orthographically by the letter *ó*:

(18a)   Pol   *gród* (/grud/, [grut]) ~ *grodu* 'castle' NomSg ~ GenSg
               pole ~ pól 'field'   NomSg ~ GenPl
               móc ~ mogę 'be able' Inf ~ 1 Sg

Later the new /u/ would be extended to open syllables by analogy:

(18b)   Pol   *król ~ króla* 'king' NomSg ~ GenSg
               pióro ~ piór 'pen' NomSg ~ GenPl

And the same change has occurred in Upper Sorbian, where long /ō/ has become the falling diphthong ['uo] (orth. *ó*):

(19a)   USorb   *hród ~ hroda* 'castle' NomSg ~ GenSg

And similarly long /ē/ has become ['ie] (orth. *ě*):

(19b)   USorb   *pěc ~ pjecy* 'stove' NomSg ~ GenSg.

Allophonic   In Ukrainian and Belarusian the high vowels are reduced to semivowels when they occur initially after a word-final vowel within the same syntagma, especially where there is a clitic involved, including a prefix. /i/ and /y/ become [i̯], and /u/ becomes [u̯]. Both languages indicate [u̯] in the orthography, Ukrainian with the letter *в* (*v*, normally for /v-w/), Belarusian with the special letter *ў* (*ŭ*). Ukrainian also indicates [i̯] with the letter *й* (*j*, normally for /j/), while Belarusian leaves *i* (i.e. with no orthographic marker of reduction):

(20a)   Ukr   *Ivána ~ do Jvána*   '(to) Ivan' [GenSg];
               idé ~ voná jdé   '(she is) going'
               učýtelja ~ do včýtelja '(to) the teacher' [GenSg];
               umíju ~ ne vmíju   'I can(not)'

(20b)   Bel   *Ivána* ~ *do Ivána*   '(to) Ivan' [GenSg];
              idzé ~ *janá idzé*   '(she is) going'
              v hóradze ~ *žyli ŭ hóradze* '(they lived) in the town';
              uvážyć ~ *zaŭvážyć*   'respect' [Imprfv ~ Prfv]

iv. Backing caused by the preceding consonant

The effect noted above (b(ii)) of /e/ > /o/ appears in Ukrainian in a different context, namely *following* mainly a palatal consonant. This effect is extended also to some positionally palatalized consonants, regardless of stress or the following consonant. It is believed that this was the initial Common East Slavic ("Old Russian") step, related to the unpaired status of the palatals and of /e/-/o/. Belarusian and Russian then moved beyond to different rules as their vowel systems changed in relation to stress:

(21)   Ukr   *čolovík*   'man'   (Rus *čelovék*);
             žonátyj   'married'   (Rus *ženátyj*);
             johó   'he' [GenSg] (Rus *jegó*);
             s'ohódni 'today'   (Rus *segódnja*)

c. The effects on vowels of suprasegmental developments, especially stress

i. Stress

Russian and Belarusian are the most unusual within the group in respect of stress, for they developed such an intense degree of stress that most unstressed vowels have become markedly reduced in quality. This is the phenomenon known as *ákan'e* in Russian, meaning specifically the non-distinction of the unstressed low back vowels /a/ and /o/. The unstressed front vowels /e/ and /i/ are also not distinguished, a phenomenon known in Russian as *íkan'e*. The high /u/ and [y] are not affected. There is a very large range of varieties of this phenomenon across the Russian and Belarusian dialects (10.3), so we shall restrict ourselves to the two standard languages. In both languages, unstressed /o/ and /a/ merge after hard consonants into [ə] or [ʌ] (by position) in Russian, and into [a] in Belarusian ("strong *akan'e*"). Belarusian reflects this effect in its orthography. Russian does not, and its orthography shows the (morpho)phoneme:

(22)   Rus   *golová* 'head' [gəlʌ'va]
             travá 'grass' [trʌ'va]
             kórotko 'short' Adv ['kɔrətkə]
       Bel   *galavá* [ɣala'va]   *travá* [tra'va]   *kóratka* ['kɔratka]

After soft consonants /o/ and /a/, and also /e/, become [ɪ] in both languages in post-tonic position. This also happens in Russian in all pretonic syllables, but Belarusian has [a] only in the first pretonic syllable:

(23) Rus /e/: *zelënyj* 'green' [zʲɪˈlʲɔnɨj]
          /o/: *seló* 'village' [sʲɪˈlɔ]
          /a/: *pjatí* 'five' [GenSg] [pʲɪˈtʲi];
     Bel *zjalëny* [zʲaˈlʲɔnɨ] *sjaló* [sʲaˈlɔ] *pjací* [pʲaˈt͡sʲi]

In Bulgarian there is a degree of change to unstressed vowels, mainly in informal style, involving a loss of quality distinction towards the narrower of a pair. Unstressed /o/ tends to be raised to /u/ and /a/ to /ə/, and to a lesser extent also /e/ to /i/. This last is considered non-standard.

(24) Blg *vodá* 'water' [vʊˈda]; *blagodarjá* 'thank you'
          [blagʊdarˈjə]
          kraká 'foot' [Pl] [krəˈka], *ímam* 'I have' [ˈiməm];
          berá 'I take' (Colloq) [bɪˈrə] (Standard [bɛˈrə])

In Slovenian dialects there is a similar raising of unstressed /o/ to /u/, /e/ to /i/ and /a/ to /ə/, but the standard language retains the quality of the underlying stressed vowel.

Shifts of stress position have sometimes produced quality changes in the newly stressed vowel, initially prosodic changes such as a new rising pitch, which is then resolved into a new quality. In Proto-Slavic retraction of stress from a weak stressed *jer* produced just such a new rising pitch, known as the 'neo-acute' (see also below, 3.2.4). This is reflected in various ways, among them quality changes, e.g. NRus /o/ and /e/ became high-mid [o], [e], and then the rising diphthongs [u̯ɔ], [i̯ɛ], all still in evidence in the dialects (e.g. *stol* 'table' from PSl **stolь* is [stu̯ɔl]). The unexpected prothetic /v/ in Rus *vósem'* 'eight' (with [u̯ɔ] > [vɔ]) (see above) is a rare reflection of the neo-acute in the standard language. And the Ukrainian development of /o/ and /e/ > /i/ noted above is probably a continuation of the same process, extended to any context before a weak *jer* regardless of stress, so that we are dealing simply with compensatory lengthening. However, when the source was indeed the neo-acute, there is an additional effect: the inserted /o/, /e/ in the *polnoglasie* forms are lengthened to /i/ *only* where the lost *jer* had been stressed, e.g. Ukr *horód* 'town', from PSl **gôrdъ*, but *holív* 'head' [GenPl] from PSl **golvъ*.

Later changes of this sort are discussed below (3.2.4) as essentially suprasegmental in result as well as motivation.

ii. Vowel quantity/length

The common quality changes related to vowel length are in evidence in several areas, of which the most interesting are in West Slavic, where all but Sorbian have gone through processes of diphthongization and change of monophthongal quality. West Slavic redeveloped quantity as a phonemic feature after its near loss in Proto-Slavic (see below, 3.2.4). Quantity remains a prominent feature in Czech and Slovak, but has been lost in Polish and Sorbian. In Czech and Slovak we observe the conversion of some long vowels into diphthongs which function within the system as long vowels, e.g. in Czech long /ū/ (from either /u/ or /ǫ/) > /ou/ [ɔu̯]:

(25)   PSl   *dubъkъ*   'oak' [Dim] > Cz *dūbek* > *doubek*
         PSl   *nesǫtь*   'they carry' > Cz *nesū* > *nesou*

In the Bohemian dialects, including Common Czech (2.4.5, 10.4.3), the front vowel has done the same, i.e. long /ī/ > /ei/ [ei̯]:

(26)   PSl *byti* 'to be' > Common Cz *bei̯t* (but Standard Cz *být*)

There have also been shifts in quality, partly of a push–pull nature, e.g. in Czech long /ō/ has taken the place of the older long /ū/ (cf. (25)):

(27)   PSl   *stolъ*   'table' > Cz *stōl* > *stůl*
         PSl   *možeši*   'you [Sg] can' > Cz *mōžeš* > *můžeš*

Long /ē/ has similarly become long /ī/:

(28)   PSl *květъkъ* 'flower' [Dim] > Cz *kvētek* > *kvítek*

The literary standard shows many exceptions to the last development, with retained /ē/:

(29)   PSl *nesti* 'to carry'   >   Cz *nést*
         PSl *lětati* 'to fly'   >   Cz *létat*
         PSl *lěto* 'year'   >   Cz *léto*

Phonological contexts appear to be mainly responsible, notably after /l/. In the colloquial language and Bohemian dialects, such forms have more regularly given /ī/: *nýst, lítat, líto*.

Slovak has made even more use of diphthongs. The normal (but not the only) long partner of /a/, /e/ and /o/ is a diphthong, and a diphthong is also a possible partner of /u/. Only /i/ has no diphthongal partner:

(30)   Slk   *pät'* 'five' ~ *piaty* 'fifth' (Cz *pátý*)

   nesú 'they carry' ~ *niest'* 'to carry' (Cz *nést*)

   moja 'my' [FemSgNom] ~ *môj* (Cz *můj*) [MascSgNom]

See further below (3.2.1.7) on diphthongs.

iii. Tone/pitch

The effect of tonal changes on vowels – other than that of the neo-acute mentioned above – is always still connected to the new prosodic shape, and so we leave it until discussion of the suprasegmental features (3.2.4).

3.2.1.6   *Contraction*

While the status of /j/ changed with the syllable restructure (see 3.2.1.7 below), it remained – in articulatory terms – in many areas a glide or semivowel rather than a full consonant, at least in the intervocalic context. In this context it could in some systems be so weak that it could disappear, and the area of such developments is an interesting one for the Slavic group as a whole. It appears that the centre for the loss of this /j/ was the Czech area, with Russian and Bulgarian at the outer extremes, so that it may be regarded as starting in the former Czech area and weakening as one moves away from this centre (Marvan, 1979). When /j/ disappeared, the typical result was a long vowel rather than hiatus, though the latter would have been the direct interim result. The simplest statement of the process is that the new vowel quality was that of the vowel after the /j/, which could then be affected by the (morpho)phonemics of a given word. Examples from Czech, Russian and Bulgarian illustrate the effects (31a) (Russian written 'vowel + *e*' = /Vjᴄ/):

(31a)	PSl			Cz	Ru	Blg
	moja	'my'	[NomSgFem]	*má*	*mojá*	*mója*
	moje		[NomSgNeut]	*mé*	*moë*	*móe*
	mojego		[GenSgMasc]	*mého*	*moegó*	–
	dobraja	'new'	[NomSgFem]	*dobrá*	*dóbraja*	(*dobrá* = short)
	ženojǫ	'woman'	[InstrSg]	*ženou* (< -ū)	*ženój* (< -óju)	–
	znajetь	'he knows'		*zná*	*znáet*	*znáe*
	znajǫtь	'they know'		*znají*	*znájut*	*znájat*
	pojasъ	'belt, waist'		*pás*	*pójas*	*pójas*
	stojati	'stand' Inf		*stát*	*stoját'*	*stojá* [1Sg]

Between these two stand mixtures ((31b–e), with contracted forms on the left of the colon, uncontracted on the right):

(31b) Pol   *dobra, żoną, pas, stać : moja, moje, mojego/mego, znaje*
        (also Sorb)
     Ukr   *mohó, dóbra*: the rest as Rus (incl. *mojemú* [DatSgMasc])
     B/C/S *môga, dôbrā, žènōm, znâ(m), pâs: mòja, mòje, znȁjū, stȁjati*
     Sln   as B/C/S, except: *státi*

Interesting are Macedonian and Belarusian. In Macedonian the /j/ has gone, but the vowels have often not fused, a result found in Bulgarian only in 3Sg verbs, e.g. *znáe*:

(31c) Mac   *moe, znae, znaat, ovaa* 'that' [NomSgFem]: *moja, pojas, stojat*

Belarusian is normally like Russian, but has sometimes retained the /j/ and lost the second vowel:

(31d) Bel   *majá, majë, majhó, majmú*

Similarly, Slovak, normally like Czech, has for the same grammatical forms:

(31e) Slk   *moja, moje, môjho, môjmu*

The Macedonian type of hiatus occurs also in North Russian dialects, where it represents a relatively later loss of intervocalic /j/. All the above stages may be seen in these dialects: hiatus (['znaet]), hiatus with assimilation (['znaat]), fusion into long ([zna:t]), and ultimate short ([znat]) (10.3.3).

3.2.1.7   Diphthongs

Proto-Slavic /j/ became freer in distribution after the syllable restructure. In the open-syllable period it could occur only before vowels, having derived from earlier '/i/ + vowel'. After the reappearance of closed syllables, /j/ could appear in (syllable-)final position:

1.   as a weak *jer* disappeared:
     (32)   PSl *mojь* 'my' > *moj*

2.   as unstressed /i/ (especially post-tonic) after a vowel was reduced:
     (33)   PSl *znái(te)* 'know' [2Sg/Pl Imper] > *znáj(te)*

Thus /j/ became a phoneme as free as any other consonant and was able to form large numbers of diphthongs, since structurally a final post-vocalic /j/ was not distinguished from [i̯].

This structural possibility was easily extended to the back position in those areas where /w-v/ was phonetically bilabial (see below, 3.2.2.4), giving new diphthongs of 'vowel + [u̯]'. Where /w-v/ was phonetically labio-dental, such diphthongs were unlikely to develop, though they could arise later from other sources (e.g. Cz /ū/ > /ou/). These falling diphthongs are therefore common throughout the Slavic area, and with any nuclear vowel.

The sequences /ie/ and /uo/ may occur as either falling or rising diphthongs. The falling type – /i̯e/ and /úo/ – occur only in Sorbian, where they reflect long /e/ (or /ě/) and /o/, respectively. The rising type – /i̯e/ and /u̯o/ – are also the result of the reallocation of vowel length, as noted in 3.2.1.6.

3.2.2   Development of the Proto-Slavic consonant system

The late Proto-Slavic consonant system is shown in table 3.4 (see also table 1.3). Forms in brackets may or may not have been still present at the late Proto-Slavic stage. In other words, they may already have been dialectal: the labial forms with /l'/ (/bl'/ etc.), where they existed, were morphophonemes in alternation with the simple labial, the palatal /l'/ being in effect the reflex of a following /j/ (1.3.1.4). The palatal stops were most likely unchanged, their further development being a major feature in the typology of the sound systems. The quality of the voiced velar and the labial fricative are almost certainly old dialectal features, so that they are marked here (bracketed) as variants. And the voiced affricate and soft (palatalized) dental fricatives probably also existed as such only in some areas. All of these points will be taken up below.

Table 3.4. *The late Proto-Slavic consonant system*

	Labial	Dental	Palatal	Velar	Glottal
Plosive	p (pl')	t	(t')	k	
	b (bl')	d	(d')	(g)	
Nasal	m (ml')	n	n'		
Fricative		s (s')	š'	x	
	(v) (vl')	z (z')	ž'	(ɣ)	
	(w)		j		
Affricate		c'	č'		
		(dz')	(dž')		
Liquid		r	r'		
		l	l'		

In this section we focus on the development of:

1. palatal consonants (the result of fusion with /j/ or of velar palatalization);
2. positionally palatalized consonants and the status of the feature [±Palatalized];
3. the voiced velar stop/fricative;
4. the labial fricative;
5. the quality of /l/; and
6. the syllabicity of the liquids /r/ and /l/.

3.2.2.1   *Palatals*

Velars   The process of the appearance of the palatal consonants was relatively early Proto-Slavic (for details see 1.3.1.4–5). Throughout the Slavic area /š/ and /ž/ had resulted from (1) /sj/-/zj/ and (2) /x/-/g/, followed by either /j/ or a front vowel, and /č/ from /k/ in the same contexts (the '1st Palatalization of the Velars', PV1). Also throughout, the dental affricate /c'/ belongs to the same process, deriving primarily from /k/ followed by the new front vowels formed during the mono-phthongization of the diphthong /oi/ as syllables were opened (the '2nd Palatalization of the Velars', PV2). This also occurred in some other contexts in which the *preceding* vowel was operative (the '3rd Palatalization of the Velars', PV3).

More uncertain as to its areal distribution is /dz'/, which derived from /g/ in the last two contexts (PV2 and PV3). The end reflexes are often /z'/, even though the voiceless partner never ends up as /s'/. This suggests that the quality of /g/ varied (see below).

West Slavic differed from East and South Slavic in the realization of PV2 and PV3 for /x/ only, the reflex in West Slavic being palatal /š/ as opposed to the dental /s'/ elsewhere. A common example of PV3 is the Proto-Slavic root *vьx- 'all' (the *jer* was strong in the NomSgMasc, weak elsewhere) (see 1.3.1.5 for other examples):

(34)   PSl   *vьx-* 'all'
       SSl: Blg *vsí-čk-* Mac *si-* (loss of /v/) B/C/S *s(a)v-* (inversion) Sln *v([ə])s-*
       ESl: Rus, Ukr   *v(e)s(')-* Bel *uv(e)s(')-*
       WSl: Cz *vše-ch(e)n-* Slk *vše-t(o)k-* Pol *wszy-st(o)k-* Sorb *wš-(ón-)*

This is the source of what structurally should be a palatalized /s'/ in East and South Slavic, which would match /c'/ and either /dz'/ or /z'/ as the earliest palatalized phonemes. Like the velar area, this is a set of three phonemes which might pair up in either way (hard ~ soft was not yet a possibility): /s'/-/z'/, with /c'/ alone, or /c'/-/dz'/, with /s'/ alone. In either case there was a systemic imbalance which might lead to the removal of one, and this may explain the absence or loss of /s′/ in West Slavic or that of /dz′/ almost everywhere, though the picture outside West Slavic is untidy. Consider the reflexes of Proto-Slavic *nogě 'foot, leg' LocSg:

(35) PSl *nogě* 'leg' LocSg
    ESl: OR *no(d)zě* (Rus *nogé*) Ukr *nozí*   Bel   *nazé*
    SSl: OCS *nodzě* Blg *nozé* [Pl]   Mac *noze* [Pl] B/C/S *nózi* (Sln *nôgi*)
    WSl: Cz *noze*   (Slk *nohe*) Pol *nodze*   Sorb *noze*

Polish is now the only language with /dz/ from this source, and it is clear that many languages converted /dz/ to /z/ only later.

/t/ and /d/ + /j/ Matching the de-affrication of /dz/ to /z/ is that of /dž/ to /ž/, which has occurred also in many areas. The many reflexes of /t+j/ and /d+j/ indicate that they were reached after the Proto-Slavic period, which is why it is simpler to say that late Proto-Slavic still had (unchanged) palatal stops /t′/ and /d′/, which only after the break-up of Slavic unity gave their modern results, which are not always a related articulatory pair. (The affrication of these to /c′/-/dz′/ is also possibly Proto-Slavic.) A second source of the same reflexes as /t+j/ are the clusters /kt/ and /gt/ before front vowels, occurring mainly on the boundary between (velar) verb stem and infinitive ending or deverbal suffix. These had both become /t′/ in Proto-Slavic. Reflexes are unified for East (36a) and West (36b) Slavic, but not for South Slavic (36c–f). There is some dispute about whether the last examples of (36a) in Ukrainian and Belarusian represent an old /dž/ or a new one, since this form appears only in deverbal forms. On balance, the "old" argument is rather more convincing (see Carlton, 1990: 140).

(36)   PSl *tj/dj* (> *t′/d′*)
            PSl *svě-tja* 'candle' *xot-jǫ* 'I want' *pek-ti* 'to bake' (or *pek-tь* 'oven')
                mog-ti 'to be able' (or *mog-tь* 'power') *med-ja* 'boundary'
                sad-ja 'soot' *xod-jǫ* 'I go'

(36a) ESl: /t′/ > /č/ and /d′/ (> /dž/) > /ž/

Rus	*svečá*	*xočú*	*peč′* (N, V)	*moč′*	*mežá*	*sáža*	*xožú*
Ukr	*svičá*	*xóču*	*péči*	(*mohtý*)	*mežá*	*sáža*	*xodžú*
Bel	*svéčka*	*xačú*	*pjačý*	(*mahčý*)	*mjažá*	*sáža*	*xadžú*

(36b) WSl: /t′/ > /c/ and /d′/ > /dz/ (> /z/)

Cz	*svíce*	*chci*	*péci*	*moci*	*mez(e)*	*saze*	(*chodím*)
Slk	*svieca*	*chcem*	*piect′*	*môct′*	*medza*	*sadza*	(*chodím*)
Pol	*świeca*	*chcę*	*piec*	*móc*	*miedza*	*sadza*	*chodzę*

	USorb	*swěca*	*chcu*	*pjec*	*móc*	*mjeza*	*sazy*	*chodźu*
	LSorb	*swěca*	*cu*		*pjac*	*moc*	*mjaza*	*caze*	*chojžim*

(36c)　B/C/S:　/t'/ > new /ć/ and /d'/ > new /dź/

　　　　B/C/S　*svéća   xòću   pèći   mòći   mèdja*　(d. *sadja*)　(*hòdīm*)

(36d)　Sln, B/C/S (Kajk):　/t'/ > /č/ and /d'/ > /j/

　　　　Sln　*svéča   hóčem   pêči   môči   mêja   sáje*　(*hódim*)

(36e)　OCS, Blg:　/t'/ > /št/ and /d'/ > /žd/

　　　　OCS　*svěšta   xoštǫ   pešti   mošti   mežda*　(*sažda*) *xoždǫ*

　　　　Blg　*svešt   šta   pešt* (N)　*mošt* (N)　*meždá   sážda*　(*xódja*)

(36f)　Mac:　/t'/ > /ḱ/ and /d'/ > /ǵ/

　　　　Mac　*sveḱa   ḱe   –   moḱ* (N)　*meǵa   saǵa*　(*odam*)

It would be attractive to see the Macedonian reflexes – which are those of its northern dialects – as old, as this would mean that they had moved least of all the languages, since /ḱ/ and /ǵ/ are in effect palatal stops, and this approach is taken by some (e.g. Friedman, 1993: 256). The traditional view, however, is that they are, in fact, new, that is, they have developed later, from either: (1) affricate forms (/c'/-/dz'/ or /ć/-/dź/, seen as the initial common South Slavic reflex), which then again lost the affrication (e.g. Bernštejn, 1961: 228; Shevelov, 1964: 215); or (2) the /št/-/žd/ of the southern dialects through influence of Serbian /ć/-/dź/, ending up in the central dialects in a lowest common denominator form (Koneski, 1967: 81; Carlton, 1990: 139). Variant (2) is based on the evidence of Old Macedonian (OCS) texts as well as the dialectal results (both centering on the Ohrid area). However, it seems more plausible that at least some dialects never went through the Bulgarian pattern, but either retained the original stops or went through the affricate stage (variant [1]). The result in B/C/S (Čakavian) – /t'/ > /t'/ and /d'/ > /j/ – indicates a similar effect for /t'/ at least.

Labials + /j/　The most common, and possibly universal, result of this group was the appearance of an epenthetic /l'/: the palatal element of the labial articulation apparently produced a liquid element strong enough to be generalised. The extra /l/ is now a regular part of the morphophonology of all East Slavic and the western South Slavic languages (B/C/S and Slovenian), as can be seen in (37a):

(37)　Labial + /j/

　　　PSl　*zem-ja* ~ *zem-ьsk-*/*zem-ьn-* 'earth' [NomSg] ~ Rel Adj stem

　　　　　ljub-iti ~ *ljub-jǫ* 'love' [Inf ~ 1Sg]

　　　　　(*po*)*stav-iti* ~ (*po-*)*stav-jen-* 'put' [Inf] ~ PPP stem

(37a)   (i) with /l'/

       Rus (+ Ukr/Bel) *zemljá zémsk-*   *ljubít' ljubljú postávit'*   *postávlen-*

       B/C/S (+ Sln)   *zèmlja zĕmn-*   *stàviti*   *stàvljen-*

(37b)   (ii) without /l'/:

       Blg (+ Mac)   *zemjá zemn-*   *postávja* (Blg [1Sg]) *postáven-*

       Cz (+ Slk)   *zemĕ zemsk-*   *postavit*   *postaven-*

       Pol (+ Sorb)   *ziemia ziemsk- lubić lubię postawić*   *postawion-*

The case for the /l'/ having been general, and then removed in some areas, rests on a few root forms, including place-names, in group (ii). The most consistent lexeme is that for the verb 'spit', with the Proto-Slavic root **peu̯- > pju-*, with the reflex *plju-* in every area:

(38)   PSl root *peu̯- > pju-* 'spit'

(38a)   Rus, Ukr, Bel, B/C/S, Sln   *pljun-*

(38b)   Blg   *pljuv-*   Mac *pluk-*   Cz *plivn-*

            Slk   *pl'u(v)-*   Pol *plun-*

            Sorb   *plun-/pluw-*

The age of this inserted /l'/ is perhaps evidenced in its appearance in non-/j/ forms, already in the Proto-Slavic form **plьv-* (Rus *plevát'*, Pol *plwać*), which might suggest that the epenthetic /l'/ is here something other than the effect of /j/, possibly a sort of onomatopoeia. But this could also simply be a later derived form, since it occurs only in Russian, Belarusian and Polish, the rest having *pljuv-*.

The only other common lexeme with a general /l'/ is *b(l)judo* 'dish', a borrowing from Germanic, which must have acquired the /l'/ in early Proto-Slavic, and was possibly borrowed into East Slavic first (Rus *bljúdo*, Sorb *blido*, Blg, Mac *bljúdo*).

Perhaps the relevant factor in both of these is the word-initial position, since it has no alternation with a simple consonant, and so the trend towards /l'/ was unhindered (Shevelov, 1964: 221).

One other argument for the generality of epenthetic /l'/ lies in OCS texts from the Bulgarian/Macedonian area, where /l'/ does appear, and more often in older than in younger texts. However, the earliest texts are still from the eleventh century, by which time Russian and Serbian versions would have had the /l'/, so that this evidence is also unreliable.

A probable explanation (Shevelov, 1964) is that there was hesitation or inter-changeability in the presence of the /l'/. This was reflected directly in the mixed OCS evidence, which was then eliminated according to either phonetic motivation (giving /l'/) or morphological (giving variation by individual word, favoring the initial position and allowing place-names to remain unaffected).

An alternative result for /m/ + /j/ in non-/l'/ areas is /mn'/, seen in some Bulgarian dialects in *zemnjá* (for standard *zemjá*). This result is also seen in more modern form in the Czech realization of the same sequence, e.g. *město* 'town' is phonemically /mjesto/, but phonetically ['mɲɛstɔ].

/r/ + /j/ Of the three dental sonorants – /r/, /l/ and /n/ – the last two do not present major problems in respect of a following /j/. They are continuants, and so easily became palatal without losing their basic quality, and their reflexes throughout either remain palatal or, much more commonly, join with the positionally soft equivalents (see below, 3.2.2.2).

/r/ was more complex. The addition of /j/ would have made for a truly complex sound, one which has not survived as a palatal /r'/in any area. The range of reflexes is: (1) /r/+/j/, that is, a sequence of two phonemes (Ukrainian, Sorbian); (2) /r'/, that is, palatalized alveolo-dental (Russian); (3) hard /r/ (South Slavic, Belarusian, Slovak); (4) (post-)alveolar fricative /ř/ (Czech), which has been reduced to (5) a simple fricative /ž/ in Polish (with the etymology reflected in the spelling *rz*), both devoiced to [ř̥] and [ʃ] respectively in certain contexts (3.4.3.2). Slovenian has a mixture of (1) and (3), and Sorbian of (1), (3) and (4), including in the last the unique reflex /s'/ (after /t/ in Upper Sorbian, after /p t k/ in Lower Sorbian) (*ibid.*). No distinction was maintained anywhere between palatal /r'/ and palatalized /r'/ (39).

(39)   /r/ + FV, /r/ + /j/

/r'/: PSl   *rędъ* 'row' *rěka* 'river' *tvarь*   'creature, thing' *tri* 'three'
/r'/: PSl   *morje* 'sea' *burja* 'storm' *lěk-arjь* 'doctor' (agentive suffix)

B/C/S/Sln	*rêd*	*réka*	*tvâr*	*trî*	*môre/morjé*	*búra/búrja ljèkar/lekár*
Blg/Mac	*red*	*reká/réka*	*tvar*	*tri*	*móre*	*búrja/bura lékar*
Rus	*rjad*	*reká*	*tvar'*	*tri*	*móre*	*búrja* *lékar'* (arch.)
Ukr	*rjad*	*riká*	*tvar*	*try*	*móre*	*búrja* *líkar*
Bel	*rad*	*raká*	*tvar*	*try*	*móra*	*búra* *lékar*
Cz	*řád*	*řeka*	*tvář*	*tři* [ř̥]	*moře*	*bouře* *lékař*
Slk	*rad*	*rieka*	*tvár*	*tri*	*more*	*búra* *lekár*
Pol	*rząd*	*rzeka*	*twarz*	*trzy* [ʃ]	*morze*	*burza* *lekarz*
Sorb	*rjad*	*rěka*	*twar*	*tři* [sⁱ]	*morjo*	– *lěkar*

3.2.2.2 Palatalized (soft) consonants

Within the Proto-Slavic syllable, the harmony between consonant and vowel (1.3.1.3) meant that consonants before front vowels were automatically palatalized to some extent wherever this was possible (e.g. not palatals, which were inherently soft; or velars, which had earlier become palatals in such a context). When the syllable restructure occurred, consonants could occur without a following vowel and became independent phonemes. At this point the languages could either retain or not retain the underlying palatalization of consonants previously followed by a weak front *jer*. At first there was probably some retention everywhere; then the status of such consonants was sorted into phonemic or allophonic, or they were removed entirely. In East and West Slavic phonemic palatalization first developed strongly, then was reduced in extent in several areas (Czech/Slovak and Ukrainian), but kept in the rest (Russian/Belarusian, Polish/Sorbian). In South Slavic it developed weakly in Bulgarian/Macedonian, and not at all in B/C/S and Slovenian.

Another context in which palatalization could become phonemic prior to the loss of the *jers* was where the front nasal was denasalized to [ä]. This was then seen as an allophone of /a/, meaning that there was an opposition between 'hard consonant + old /a/' and 'soft consonant + new /a/'. However, while the syllable was still open – which it was until the loss of the *jers* – the true opposition can be interpreted as between hard and soft *syllables*, in this case between 'hard consonant + [a]' and 'soft consonant + [ä]'. So while the denasalization provided a potential case for phonemically soft consonants, they really became established only with the loss of the *jers*. In a similar way, where /ě/ became /ä/-/a/ – i.e. in the areas which did not denasalize – /ě/ would have provided the same impetus, but would have remained unrealized before the loss of the *jers*, and after the loss, would simply have reinforced the new situation. The extent of the hard/soft opposition in different areas will be taken up in the "modern" section (3.4.1).

3.2.2.3   *Velars (g/ɣ)*

The articulation of the voiced velar consonant in Proto-Slavic is traditionally said to have been initially occlusive [g], which then became fricative [ɣ] or laryngeal [ɦ] in many areas ("lenition"). We cannot say whether this is so, or whether some areas always had the fricative version, but the areal division is certainly very old, and looks as follows:

[g]:	ESl: N-Rus	WSl: Pol, LSorb	SSl: all standard languages
[ɣ]:	ESl: S-Rus, Bel		SSl: NW-Sln, NW-Čak
[ɦ]:	ESl: Ukr	WSl: Cz, Slk, USorb	

One interpretation of this picture is that the lenition was a feature of the centre of the Slavic area, perhaps earliest in the third ([ɦ]) group, which may have reached the laryngeal [ɦ] via the velar [ɣ].

Within the system, there was no pressure either way, since the velar set was tripartite, with /k ∼ g ∼ x/. From one view-point, /g/ was odd by being voiced, leaving /k/ and /x/ as a voiceless pair opposed as stop ∼ fricative; from another, /x/ was odd, with /k/ and /g/ opposed as voiced ∼ voiceless. The articulation of /g/ therefore simply promoted one or other of these equally valid scenarios, going better with /k/ if a stop, better with /x/ if a fricative.

Given that the fricative variant was early, in relation to the palatalizations of the velars, it is more likely that its presence was the reason for the different results for /g/ – either /dž/ or /ž/ for PV1, /dz′/ or /z′/ for PV2 and PV3. The fricative version would have produced directly a fricative palatal /ž/ matching the result of /x/ (/š/), and the stop version an affricate /dž/ matching that of /k/ (/č/). The uncertainty in the (Old Russian) textual evidence may reflect the presence of the two variants in important areas like N-Rus *vs* S-Rus + Ukr + Bel. In other words, we do not have to posit the traditional 'de-affrication' of /dž/ and /dz′/ to account for the modern /ž/ and /z′/ (see also 1.3.1.5).

3.2.2.4   *Labials (v/w)*

A similar division occurs across the area in respect of the bilabial *vs* labio-dental articulation of /v/ (which range we shall refer to as /w-v/). Again an early division is certain, and we cannot be sure that there was initially a unified version which split. While earlier Proto-Slavic, and probably PIE, would have had [w], traditionally, [v] is said to be the starting-point, at least in Late Proto-Slavic, reducing – again by a sort of lenition – (back) to [w] (probably actually [β], a bilabial fricative, but we will follow the convention and use [w]). It is true that in some modern languages an underlying [v] alternates directly with [u̯] (e.g. Belarusian), but one might equally suggest that it is the [v] which is new (e.g. in this case through the influence of Russian). The distribution is as follows (for details of distribution and allophones in each language, see 3.4.1):

[v]	devoiced to [f] before a word boundary or voiceless obstruent (see 3.4.3.2): Blg, Mac, Rus, Cz, Pol
[v]	not devoiced: B/C/S
[v]	becoming [u̯] before a word boundary or consonant: Sln, Bel, Slk
[v]/[w]	becoming [u] initially before a consonant (Bel) or between consonants (Ukr)
[w]	becoming [u̯] before a word boundary or consonant: Ukr, Sorb
[w]	becoming [vʲ] before [i]: Ukr

Examples showing the open (pre-vocalic) form *vs* the closed (pre-consonantal or pre-pausal) form are given in (40) with the /w-v/ in phonetic transcription. The orthography frequently disguises the pronunciation, some using *v* to represent [w], others *w* to represent [v], etc.:

(40) /w-v/

PSl	*volja*	'will'	*vьdova*	'widow'	*gněvъ*	'anger'
	pravьda	'truth'	*lavъka*	'bench, counter'		
Blg/Mac	[v]*ólja*	[v]*dó*[v]*íca*	*gnja*[f]/*gne*[f]	*prá*[v]*da*	*lá*[f]*ka*
B/C/S	[v]*ȍlja*	[ȕ]*dova*	*gn*(*j*)*ȇ*[v]	*prȃ*[v]*da*	–
Sln	[v]*ólja*	[w]*dó*[v]*a*	*gnè*[u̦]	*prá*[u̦]*da*	*lá*[u̦]*ka*
Rus	[v]*ólja*	[v]*do*[v]*á*	*gne* [f]	*prá*[v]*da*	*lá*[f]*ka*
Ukr	[w]*ólja*	[u]*do*[w]*á*	*hni̦*[u̦]	*prá*[u̦]*da*	*lá*[u̦]*ka*
Bel	[v]*ólja*	[u]*da*[v]*á*	*hne*[u̦]	*prá*[u̦]*da*	*lá*[u̦]*ka*
Cz	[v]*ůˌe*	[v]*do*[v]*a*	*hně*[f]	*pra*[v]*da*	*lá*[f]*ka*
Slk	[v]*ȏl'a*	[v]*do*[v]*a*	*hne*[u̦]	*pra*[u̦]*da*	*la*[u̦]*ka*
Pol	[v]*ola*	[v]*do*[v]*a*	*gnie*[f]	*pra*[v]*da*	*ła*[f]*ka*
Sorb	[w]*ola*	[wu]*do*[w]*a*	*hně*[u̦]	*pra*[u̦]*da*	*ła*[u̦]*ka*

(See also the examples of prothetic /w-v/ noted in 3.2.1.4.)

3.2.2.5 *Quality of /l/*

Again as a result of the phonemicization of consonants and vowels out of the earlier syllabic units (1.3.1), the new hard and soft versions of /l/ caused problems. The nature of the "hard syllables" of Proto-Slavic was probably not simply neutral (*vs* palatalized for the "soft" ones), but a positive (labio-)velarization. In the subsequent development of the hard ~ soft opposition, the hard members became the unmarked ones, with palatalization being the marked feature. But in /l/ the velarization remained in many areas, probably because a neutral [l] – the basic "European" one – was not distinct enough from the soft. So where there is still an opposition, it is normally between a strongly palatalized and a strongly velarized version (East Slavic) or between a medium [l] and a velarized one (Blg, Mac), the latter having sometimes gone on to lose its lingual contact and become [w] (Pol, Sorb). The opposition may also be between medium and palatalized (or palatal), whether as separate phonemes (Slk, B/C/S, Sln) or allophones (Pol). In some areas there is a single medium /l/ from both sources (Cz). Where the /l/ is velarized, it may be reduced by context only to [u̦] (Ukr, Bel, Slk, Sln), or even to vocalic [ɔ] (B/C/S).

In the examples in (41), we again use phonetics for the articulation of the former /l/: [ł] for velarized, [lʲ] for palatalized, [ʎ] for palatal:

(41) /l/

PSl *lъbъ* 'forehead' *lěsъ* 'forest' *listъ* 'letter, page'
     ljudьje 'people' Pl *stolъ* 'table'

Rus	[ɫ]*ob*	[lʲ]*es*	[lʲ]*ist*	*sto*[ɫ]	[lʲ]*udi*
Ukr	[ɫ]*ob*	[lʲ]*is*	[ɫ]*yst*	*sto*[u̯]	[lʲ]*udy*
Bel	[ɫ]*ob*	[lʲ]*es*	[lʲ]*ist*	*sto*[u̯]	[lʲ]*udzi*
Cz	[l]*eb*(*ka*)	[l]*es*	[l]*ist*	*stú*[l]	[l]*ide*
Slk	[l]*ebka*	[ʎ]*es*	[ʎ]*ist*	*sto*[l] (coll. [u̯])	[ʎ]*udia*
Pol	[w]*eb*	[l]*as*	[lʲ]*ist*	*stó*[u̯]	[l]*udzie*
Sorb	–	[l]*ěs*	[l]*ist*	*sto*[u̯]	[l]*udzio*
Blg/Mac	[ɫ]*ob*	[l]*es*	[l]*ist*	*sto*[ɫ]	[lʲ]*ude*/[l]*uǵe*
B/C/S	–	[l]*es*	[l]*ist*	*stô* (< oo)	[lʲ]*udi*
Sln	(arch) [l]*eb*	[l]*és*	[l]*íst*	*stò*[u̯]	[l] *judjé*

3.2.2.6 *Syllabicity of /r/, /l/*

In 1.3.1.7 we opted for the view that Proto-Slavic developed syllabic liquids, and so now we must consider the extent to which these were retained or restructured after the break-up.

As syllables again became closed through the loss of the *jers*, all areas had to cope with the new clusters previously separated by a weak *jer*, including those with /r/ or /l/ (types *CRъC*, *CRьC*, where 'R' means /r/ or /l/). Many areas extended existing syllabic /r̥/ and /l̥/ to these contexts, while others did not allow the weak *jer* to disappear. The first group thus strengthened the range of the syllabic liquids, while the second tended to abandon even the existing range. But there is, in fact, quite a range of treatments between these two extremes.

The extreme "syllabic" type is seen in South Slavic generally and in (Central) Slovak, with only two results from the twelve possibilities (four each of syllabic, strong *jer* and weak *jer* – see (42)). At the other extreme are Ukrainian and Belarusian, with eleven results from the twelve. In between, it appears that the rest of West and East Slavic maintained some syllabic forms for a time, and then abandoned them. The Lekhitic group (Polish, Sorbian) accepted consonantal clusters (involving consonantal /r/ and /l/), and both they and Czech converted the syllabic segments into a range of vowels dependent on the surrounding context. Later on, the range of syllabic forms was reduced in different ways even in the 'southern' group, especially /l̥/, which survived only in Czech and Slovak; /r̥/ continues not only in Czech and Slovak, but also in B/C/S and Macedonian, and structurally also in Bulgarian and Slovenian, though here it is phonetically (and probably phonemically) [ə] + [r] (3.4.1–2). In (42a) we find:

a. the example of Pol *wierzch*, in which the *rz* reflects a former soft or palatal /r/, is believed to indicate that initially Polish – and thus perhaps others – solved this problem by inserting a vowel after the /r/, in the manner of syllables with a full (i.e. non-*jer*) vowel (cf. *polnoglasie*, 1.3.1.7.). However, the retention of the softness of syllabic /r̥'/ could also account for this effect;

b. the various inserted vowels in Polish and Czech are related to the articulation of the surrounding consonants;

c. /č/ > /c/ before /r̥'/ is a special feature of B/C/S and Macedonian;

d. Bulgarian normally inverts the /r/ and /ə/ in (new) closed syllables (to avoid final clusters).

(42) Syllabic /r̥/, /l̥/

(42a) CR̥C (or C + *jer* + R + C):

PSl:	*gr̥dlo* 'throat, neck'	*vr̥'xъ*'summit'	*čr̥'nъ(jь)* 'black'		
	tl̥stъ (*jь*) 'fat'	*vl̥'kъ* 'wolf'	*žl̥'tъ(jь)* 'yellow'		
Blg	*gắrlo*	*vrắx*	*čérăn*	*tlắst*	*vắlk*	*žắlt*
		([Def] *vărxắt*)				
Mac	*grlo*	*vrv*	*crn*	–	*volk*	*žolt*
B/C/S/Sln	*gr̃lo/gŕlo*	*vȓh/vŕh*	*cȓn/čŕn*	*tȗst/tólst*	*vȗk/vólk*	*žȗt/žólt*
Rus	*górlo*	*verx*	*čërnyj*	*tólstyj*	*volk*	*žëltyj*
Ukr	*hórlo*	*verx*	*čórnyj*	*tovstýj*	*vovk*	*žóvtyj*
Bel	*hórla*	*verx*	*čórny*	*tóŭsty*	*voŭk*	*žóŭty*
Cz	*hrdlo*	*vrch*	*černý*	*tlustý*	*vlk*	*žlutý*
Slk	*hrdlo*	*vrch*	*čierny*	*tlstý*	*vlk*	*žltý*
Pol	*gardło*	*wierzch*	*czarny*	*tłusty*	*wilk*	*żółty*
USorb	*hordło*	*wjerch*	*čorny*	*tołsty*	*wjelk*	*žołty*
LSorb	*gjardło*	*wjerch*	*carny*	*tłusty*	*wjelk*	*žołty*

In (42b) we see:

a. the Belarusian examples with /ry/-/ly/ in unstressed syllables (and Ukrainian has similar ones, as well as /lu/ in *jabluko*) are taken to indicate a preceding stage of syllabic /r̥ l̥/;

b. there are examples in East Slavic of a third possible strategy for avoiding undesirable clusters: to elide the sonorant as well as the weak *jer*, e.g. the town name ORus *Plьskovъ* has become *Pskov*.

(42b)   C + R + jer + C (strong/weak sets)

PSl: krъvь/krъvi 'blood' [NomSg/GenSg]   krьstъ 'cross'
krьstiti 'to baptize'
plъtь/plъti 'flesh' [NomSg/GenSg] (j)ablъko 'apple'
slьza 'tear'

(Note: /r̩/ (phonemic) = syllabic; [r̥] [r̥̩] (IPA) voiceless; [r̩] (IPA) = syllabic)

	krъvь 'blood' NomSg	krъvi GenSg	krьstъ 'cross'	krьstiti 'to baptize'	plъtь 'flesh' NomSg	plъti GenSg	(j)ablъko 'apple'	slьza 'tear'
Blg	krăv	–	krăst	krăstja	plăt	–	jábălka	sălzá
Mac	krv	–	krst	krsti	–	–	jabolko	solza
B/C/S	krȓv	kȓvi	kȓst	kȑsta	pȕt	pȕti	jȁbuka	sȕza
Sln	krí	krví	kŕst	kŕsta	pólt	pólti	jábolko	sólza
Rus	krov'	króvi	krest	krestít'	plot'	plóti	jábloko	slezá
Ukr	krov	króvi	xrest	xrestýti	plot'	plóti	jábluko	sľozá
Bel	kroŭ	kryví	–	chryscíc'	ploc'	plóci	jáblyk	sljazá
Cz	krev	krve [r̩]	křest [ř̩]	kŕtit [ř̩]	plet'	pleti	jablko	slza
Slk	krv	krvi [r̩]	krst	krstit'	plet'	pleti (lit.)	jablko	slza
Pol	krew	krwi [r̩f]	chrzest [ʃ]	chrzcić [ʃ]	płeć	płci	jabłko [pk]	łza
USorb	krej	krwě [rw]	–	křćić [ʃ]	–	–	jabłuko	sylza
LSorb	kšej	kšwě	–	kšćiś (arch.)	–	–	jabłuko	łdza

In summary, of the twelve contexts we find the following distribution of results (for further details see below, 3.4.1, modern systems):

South Slavic and Slovak:

1.   /r̩/ for all forms with /r/ and /l̩/ for all forms with /l/;
2.   Slovenian and Macedonian convert /l̩/ to /ol/; B/C/S converts it to /u/;
3.   Bulgarian converts both to sequences of 'consonant + /ə/', the order being controlled by word shape: avoidance of syllable-final clusters causes /ərCC-/ to become /rəCC-/, and /əlCC-/ to become /ləCC-/.

Czech: retains /r̩/; converts /l̩/ to /lu/ except in the limited context after labials (e.g. vlk); retains the distinction between strong and weak jer, with the latter giving syllabic forms, except that soft /r'/ > consonantal /ř/ after velars and labials (e.g. křtu).

Polish and Sorbian: retain the distinction between the two sets: the first > 'vowel + liquid' (except Pol /l/ after dental, e.g. tłusty); the second > 'liquid + /e/' when the jer is strong (3.2.1.1) (e.g. krew), and simple liquid when it is weak (e.g. krwi, płci).

East Slavic: retains the distinction between the two sets: the first > 'vowel + liquid'; the second > 'liquid + vowel'; Ukrainian and Belarusian distinguish between strong and weak jer, the latter > /y/, /i/ (e.g. Bel kryví, jáblyk); stressed jers are here strong (Ukr króvi, plóti).

3.2.3 Development of Proto-Slavic sound combinations

3.2.3.1 *Simplification and new clusters*

As noted in 1.3.1.1 and 1.7.1, while clusters of 'stop + sonorant' were normally accepted in Proto-Slavic, as conforming to the Law of Rising Sonority, the treatment of the clusters /tl/ and /dl/ represents one of the features distinguishing West Slavic from the rest. The dental stop remained in West Slavic, but was eliminated elsewhere:

(43) *tl, dl*

PSl	*plet-la* 'plait' [PPA FemSg]	*ved-la* 'lead' [PPA FemSg]
Rus	*plelá*	*velá*
Blg	*pléla*	*do-véla*
Cz	*pletla*	*vedla*
Pol	*plotła*	*wiodła*

Some former transitional dialects are out of step with the modern group, e.g. N-Sln (Carinthian) with /tl/, /dl/ (10.2.1), Central Slovak with /l/, at least inside roots (10.4.4). And an odd early variant in NW-Russian (Pskov region) has /tl/ > /kl/ and /dl/ > gl/ – which is clearly not just simplification (10.3.3).

When the syllable was restructured, the principle of rising sonority ceased to operate: there could now be closed final syllables and also internal closed syllables (where the second might be less sonorous than the first [e.g. 'sonorant + non-sonorant' – **mъx-* 'moss' > *mx-*, 'stop + fricative' – **pьs-* 'write' >*ps-*]). "Desirable" clusters were welcomed (e.g. 'fricative + sonorant' – **sъn-* 'sleep' > *sn-*; 'fricative + stop' – **sъt-* 'hundred' > *st-*). But resistance to "undesirable" clusters continued to some extent in all areas, with a broad spectrum of preference. Polish at one extreme accepted almost all, and B/C/S at the other rejected almost all. In particular many areas resisted word-final clusters, sometimes of any sort (e.g. B/C/S even now often converts such clusters in borrowed words: *àkcent* > *àkcenat* 'accent'). All areas resisted final clusters of 'consonant + sonorant' some of the time (e.g.**ognь* 'fire' acquired a fill vowel everywhere, even Pol *ogień*), but few did this all of the time (e.g.**myslь*, 'thought', see above 3.2.1.1 (4)).

Examples of new initial clusters structurally matching the old are:

(44a) fricative or stop + sonorant: *s(ь)rebr-* 'silver' *(k)ъnęg-*'prince'

$\qquad\qquad\qquad\qquad\qquad\qquad\quad$ *s(ъ)n-* 'sleep'

$\qquad$ fricative + stop: *ž(ь)d-*'wait' *s(ь)de* 'here' (> *zd-* see below)

The same could occur internally, where 'sonorant + stop' or any geminate cluster would mean a closed syllable, the others not:

(44b) sonorant + stop or fricative: *zem(ь)sk-* 'earth' [Adj]
　　　 kon(ь)sk- 'horse' [Adj]   *prav(ь)d-* 'truth'
　　　 fricative + sonorant: *(po)s(ъ)l-* 'send'
　　　 stop + sonorant: *sed(ь)l-* 'saddle' (new *dl* even
　　　　　　　　　　　　　　　　　　　　　　　　　　　　　　　　　　　　in East and South Slavic)
　　　 fricative + fricative (inc. new geminate):   *rus(ь)sk-* 'Russian' [Adj]

Examples of new initial clusters which do *not* structurally match the old:

(45) sonorant + sonorant: *m(ь)r-* 'die'   *l(ь)n-* 'flax' (see above 3.2.1.1)
　　　 fricative + fricative
　　　 (inc. new geminate):   *s(ъ)sa-* 'suck'   *v(ъ)ved-* 'lead in'
　　　 stop + stop: *k(ъ)de* 'where'

Examples of final clusters:

(46) *most(ъ)* 'bridge'   *mozg(ъ)* 'brain'

3.2.3.2   *Assimilation, devoicing*

No doubt as a direct result of the new syllabic structure, the consonantal elements within and across syllable boundaries became closely connected, as reflected in the various types of (regressive) assimilation. From then on they occur in all areas: of voice, place of articulation and – to a lesser extent – manner of articulation.

In respect of voice, in almost every area – with two exceptions – obstruents in a new cluster acquired the voice status of the final member of the group. New final voiced obstruents became devoiced, except that the word boundary was usually also perceived as simply a syllable boundary, so that a voiced obstruent in the following word (within the same syntagma) would preserve the voice and indeed cause the voicing of a preceding voiceless one. The sonorants, being inherently voiced, do not normally participate in this assimilation, either actively (i.e. causing voicing) or passively (i.e. being devoiced).

The phoneme /w-v/ behaves in a special fashion, since in Proto-Slavic it was a sonorant without a voiceless partner. After the final devoicing began, /w-v/ tended to become an obstruent partnered by [f] – which usually became a new phoneme /f/ – in those areas where it was [v]. Elsewhere it remained a sonorant with no voiceless partner. Its ambiguous status is reflected well in Russian, where it is devoiced to [f] before voiceless obstruents (here behaving like an obstruent), but does *not* cause the assimilative voicing of preceding voiceless obstruents (here behaving like a sonorant).

For modern examples of these features see below, 3.4.3.2.

3.2.4 Development of the Proto-Slavic suprasegmental features

The late Proto-Slavic situation in regard to suprasegmental features was as follows (and see 1.3.1.8):

- stress was free and mobile;
- quantity (length) was now phonemic on most vowels (from diphthongs); in word-final position there occurred a short version of the long vowels, but still with no choice available;
- tone (rising ~ non-rising pitch) was phonemic on stressed initial vowels (carried over after the monophthongization of diphthongs, which alone had had such an opposition. This means that only the vowels /i, u, ě, ǫ, ę/ showed phonemic tone, since /a/ and /y/ did not derive from diphthongs). The rising pitch was the marked feature.

We now consider the main lines of development of each of these features.

3.2.4.1 *Stress*

Stress remained free and mobile in East Slavic and most of South Slavic, though in most areas it underwent positional changes. Some of these were purely phonological: e.g. in B/C/S (Štokavian) the stress was retracted globally by one syllable. But most related to morphology: e.g. regularization within the paradigm. This meant a loss of mobility of stress, that is, opposition within parts of a paradigm, for example between the singular and plural of nouns.

The B/C/S retraction meant a limitation on the freedom of stress, for example it could not fall on the final syllable of any polysyllabic word. This change also gave rise to a new rising pitch on the newly stressed syllable, which revitalized the feature of pitch in this area.

In Slovenian stress shifts – this time in both directions, related to existing pitch and quantity – produced either different quality or a new pitch, according to the different dialects. This led to the present situation in which the standard has both a tonal and non-tonal variant.

The exception in South Slavic is Macedonian, in which the stress is fixed in relation to the word boundary, possibly through a stage similar to the B/C/S retraction, which then became generalized on a non-final syllable. In the modern standard the position of stress is on the antepenultimate, while in dialects the position may be penultimate (south and south-west) or free (east) (10.2.3).

In West Slavic stress also became fixed, in this case on the initial syllable of all words, no doubt through the same stage as B/C/S and Macedonian. Later, Polish alone shifted the fixed stress to the penultimate syllable.

Note that where the stress is fixed in relation to the beginning of the word, the stress is also not mobile. But it remains mobile in those languages with the stress fixed in relation to the end of the word, since endings within a paradigm may have varying numbers of syllables. For Polish in particular this is an important feature, and possibly one which was a motive force in the shift from initial to penult. It is less important for Macedonian, since the nominal system is now substantially without inflexion, so that mobile stress is really meaningful only for verbs. Ultimately this sort of mobility is of limited importance, since the opposition between forms must be signalled by segmental differences, not suprasegmental ones (cf. Russian, where mobility of stress can be meaningful, e.g. *ruki* 'hand' may be [GenSg] or [NomPl] depending on stress position (4.2.4)).

3.2.4.2   *Quantity*

Vowel length became phonemic (again) in West and part of South Slavic, but ceased to be related to quality almost everywhere, including East Slavic. In the areas with free stress, it tended to be a concomitant of the stressed syllable, and this is the case in the "strong-stress" languages – Russian, Belarusian and Bulgarian, and to a lesser extent in Ukrainian.

Quantity developed most strongly as a phonemic feature in West Slavic, at the expense of free stress, and supported by extensive contraction, of which Czech was the centre (see 3.2.1.6). It survived, however, only in Czech and Slovak, and was lost (*c.* sixteenth century) in Polish and Sorbian. Slovak subsequently weakened the range of quantity with the so-called "Rhythmic Law", whereby two consecutive long syllables are avoided (diphthongs behave like long vowels: 3.5.2).

In South Slavic quantity became phonemic in B/C/S and Slovenian, though never independently of either stress or pitch. The retraction of stress in B/C/S (above) made pitch a much more important feature, and it also restricted the domain of length as it did that of stress, since no pretonic vowel may be long (though there are relatively few pretonic vowels, given the rarity of non-initial stress). However, the length of originally long stressed syllables was retained, so that there could still be an opposition in post-tonic position. Slovenian is the one language in which length has remained associated with quality to a small extent, since its phoneme /ə/ may not be long. For other vowels length is limited to stressed position.

The remaining languages (East Slavic and Bulgarian/Macedonian) have abandoned length as a potential phonemic feature. There are some indications that Ukrainian did develop it briefly in the Common East Slavic (Old Russian) period through compensatory lengthening of vowels in a syllable before a lost *jer*. This is the normal explanation for the development of /o/ and /e/ to /i/ in such positions

(3.2.1.5). And some North Russian dialects may have done the same at least in the context of a lost stressed *jer*, which had produced, already in Proto-Slavic, the so-called "neo-acute" or new rising pitch, which resulted in diphthongs of the /ųo/, /ie̯/ type (see 3.2.1.5 and 1.6.2).

3.2.4.3   *Tone*

The simple Proto-Slavic opposition of rising ∼ non-rising became complicated with the appearance of the neo-acute, since this seems to have differed from the old acute (rising pitch), thus presenting a potential three-way system. It appears that this situation was unacceptable everywhere and it was resolved in two basic ways:

> a.   merge the old and new acutes in opposition to the non-rising (circumflex), as adopted in: (i) Czech, Upper Sorbian and Slovenian, where the opposition was converted to one of quantity: acute > long, circumflex > short; (ii) East Slavic, Bulgarian and Macedonian, where after stage (i) the new quantity opposition was then lost and in some cases reinterpreted as one of stress position (e.g. in Russian *polnoglasie* forms);
>
> b.   merge the old acute and circumflex in opposition to the new acute, adopted in: (i) Slovak, Polish, Lower Sorbian, likewise then converting the opposition to one of quantity: neo-acute > long, the rest > short; (ii) B/C/S and Slovenian, where it became a new pitch opposition: neo-acute > rising, the rest > falling. Subsequently, as noted above, part of B/C/S underwent a retraction of stress which produced a new tonal opposition: newly stressed syllables (i.e. former pretonic) > rising, formerly stressed (i.e. initial syllables) > falling.

For the modern picture of phonemic suprasegmental features across the area see 3.5. For information on dialectal differences, see Chapter 10.

3.3   **Modern vowel systems**

3.3.1   Phonemes

The Slavonic vowel systems contain from five to perhaps twenty-four phonemes, depending on how they are analysed. All the languages have /i e a o u/, and may include additional vowels like high-mid /é ó/ or /ə/, nasal vowels /ę ą/, syllabic liquids /r̥ l̥/, a parallel system of unstressed vowels, and the suprasegmental features of stress, pitch and length. A language may also have marginal phonemes, which occur in foreign borrowings, and which have been only partially assimilated. And there are some sounds whose phonemic status is a matter of disputation. The

Table 3.5. *Modern vowel systems*

Language	Segmental vowel phonemes (ISO/Slav transliteration)	Suprasegmental features
PSl	i ь y e ę ě a o ǫ ъ u	Free, mobile pitch accent
	ī ȳ ę̄ ě̄ ā ǭ ū	Length
Blg	i e a ǎ o u	Free, mobile stress
Mac	i e a o u r̥	Fixed (antepenultimate) stress
B/C/S	i e a o u r̥	Free, mobile pitch accent
	ī ē ā ō ū	Length
Sln	i e a ə o u	Free, mobile pitch or stress
	ī ē ệ̄ ā ō ộ̄ ū (r̥)	Length
Bel	i (y) e a o u	Free, mobile stress
Ukr	i y e a o u	Free, mobile stress
Rus	i (y) e a o u	Free, mobile stress
Cz	i e a o u r̥ l̥	Fixed (initial) stress
	ī ē ā ō ū	Length
	ou (eu au)	Diphthongs
Slk	i e ä a o u r̥ l̥	Fixed (initial) stress
	ī ē ā ō ū r̥̄ l̥̄	Length
	ia ie iu ô (eu au)	Diphthongs
Sorb	i y a o u	Fixed (initial) stress
	ě ó	Diphthongs
Pol	i (y) e ę a ą o u	Fixed (penultimate) stress

systems of vowel phonemes, seen from a standard "phonetic-phonological" viewpoint and based on contrasts in minimal pairs, are shown in table 3.5 (with marginal or disputed phonemes in brackets).

This inventory is close to the maximum number of phonemes, based on minimal pairs, which can be postulated for each language. Many analyses aim for lower figures by using distribution (e.g. treating *i* and *y* as one phoneme) or by abstracting suprasegmental features (e.g. B/C/S has not 24, but 6 vowel phonemes, plus phonemic length and phonemic pitch). The phonemic status of vowels is also affected by the relation between vowel quality and suprasegmentals. Vowel quality is not radically affected by pitch, but vowel quality and length show some important correlations. Slovak /ō/-[ɔː], for instance, occurs only in words of foreign origin like *nóta*, *tón* and *morfológia*. The native Slovak /ô/-[u̯ɔ] is the proper long counterpart of short /o/-[ɔ] on historical, typological and morphophonological grounds:

(47a) Cz *kůň*   Slk *kôň* 'horse'
        cf.

(47b) Cz *dům* Slk *dom* 'house' Cz *bol* Slk *bôl'* 'pain'

(47c) Slk *hlava* 'head' [GenPl] *hláv*
            voda 'water' [GenPl] *vôd*
            stôl 'table' [GenSg] *stola*
            osem 'eight' *ôsmy* 'eighth'

The vowel /o/ is consequently unpaired in respect of length, and is more marginal in the system of Slovak vowels. Sorbian /ě/ ['ie] and /ó/ ['uo] present a similar problem. Like Slovak /ô/, they are pronounced as diphthongs (though falling). Although Sorbian lacks phonemic length, the distribution of /ě/ and /ó/, and their behavior in morphophonological alternations, show that they are diphthong phonemes:

(48a) USorb *čech* 'a Czech' *čěski* [Adj]

(48b) USorb *kóń* 'horse' *konja* [GenSg]

Diphthongs, indeed, are phonemically problematic. All Slavic languages have *phonetic* diphthongs, composed of two separate phonemes, like the common sequence 'vowel + /j/':

(49) Rus *čitáj*! 'read!' /čitaj/ [t͡ʃɪ'taj]

Such diphthongs must be clearly distinguished from diphthong phonemes, where a combination of vocalic or semi-vocalic sounds forms a single phoneme, like Slovak /ô/, Sorbian /ě/ /ó/ or Czech /ou/:

(50) Cz *sud* 'barrel' *soud* 'court'

The diphthong functions like a single phoneme in distribution, minimal pairs and morphophonology. In Slovak, for instance, the diphthongs /ia ie iu/ participate in the Slovak Rhythmic Law (3.5.2), and alternate with short vowels in paradigms:

(51a) Slk *chlieb* 'bread' [GenSg] *chleba*

(51b) Slk *žaba* 'frog' [GenPl] *žiab*

So these are diphthong phonemes. But Slovak /eu/ and /au/ only occur in words of foreign origin, like *pneumatika* and *autor*, and do not alternate with short vowels, and so are vowel phoneme sequences – as are also *ie, ia, iu* in foreign words (Pauliny *et al.*, 1968: 76).

Vowel phonemes are also affected by phonotactics. In particular, some vowels cannot occur next to, or between, palatal sounds (3.4.3). There is also a close relationship between vowel quality and stress. Some of the languages show two vowel systems: one larger system for stressed syllables; and another smaller system for unstressed syllables, showing neutralization of some of the oppositions of the full stressed system (3.5.1).

There are three vowel heights in all but Slovenian and Ukrainian, which have four (also Sorbian, if its diphthongs are treated as simply high vowels); and oppositions of [±Round] and [±Front], usually interdependent (table 3.6).

The status of vocalic /r̥/ is not beyond doubt in Slovenian and Macedonian, where it is regularly pronounced [ər]. The phonemic analysis could take either

Table 3.6. *Stressed vowel inventories*

1. Russian, Belarusian, Polish and Sorbian (all in one analysis) B/C/S, Macedonian, Czech

	− Round		+ Round
High	i		u
Mid	e		o
Low		a	
	+ Front		− Front

2. Russian and Belarusian in a second analysis

	− Round		+ Round
High	i	y	u
Mid	e		o
Low		a	
	+ Front		− Front

3. Ukrainian (and Polish in a second analysis)

	− Round		+ Round
High	i		u
High Mid		y	
Low Mid	e		o
Low		a	
	+ Front		− Front

4. Slovak

	− Round		+ Round
High	i		u
Mid	e		o
Low	ä	a	
	+ Front		− Front

Table 3.6. (*cont.*)

5. Bulgarian

	– Round			+ Round
High	i			u
Mid	e	ə		o
Low		a		
	+ Front			– Front

6. Slovenian

	– Round			+ Round
High	i			u
High Mid	é ([e])			ó ([o])
Low Mid	e	ə		o
Low		a		
	+ Front			– Front

7. Sorbian in a second analysis

	– Round			+ Round
High	i			u
High Mid	ě ([ie])			ó ([uo])
Low Mid	e			o
Low		a		
	+ Front			– Front

alternative: admit /r̥/ as a phoneme and omit /ə/ (supported by the orthography), or admit /ə/ as a phoneme and omit /r̥/ as a vowel phoneme. In Slovenian the presence of /ə/ in other contexts makes the latter option preferable, as in Bulgarian, which also has /ə/, and where the orthography additionally makes this the only reasonable solution. /r/ remains as a consonant phoneme in both. The absence of /ə/ elsewhere in Macedonian makes the vocalic /r̥/ solution preferable for it. Czech, Slovak and B/C/S have an indisputable vocalic /r̥/ phoneme. Phonetic evidence supporting these solutions may be found in the relative length and energy of the [ə]–[r] elements across these languages (Cubberley, 1987).

3.3.2   Phonetics

Generally speaking, the Slavic vowels are closer to cardinal vowels than their English counterparts: the Slavic high back rounded vowel /u/ is higher, backer and rounder than the English /u/, and so on. Differences in pronunciation between the Slavic languages are related to the number and distribution of phonemes, and to the range of allophones, particularly in conjunction with factors like stress.

3.3.2.1 Stressed vowels

We begin with stressed vowels in positions where they are not affected by surrounding phonemes. The vowels /i a u/ are similarly pronounced in all the languages, as is /ə/ in Slovenian and Bulgarian. Other vowel phonemes, however, do show some important differences:

> /y/ Russian and Belarusian have a high central unrounded vowel [ɨ], which contrasts with a vowel more like English [ɪ] in Ukrainian, Polish and Sorbian.
>
> /e/ Most commonly [ɛ], but raised to [e] before palatalized sounds in East Slavic, Polish and Sorbian, the languages which keep large series of hard/soft consonants: Pol *cień* [t͡ɕenʲ] 'shadow' *vs len* [lɛn] 'linen, flax'. When long and stressed /e/ also tends to [eː] in Czech and B/C/S: Cz *léto* 'summer' [eː] *vs len* 'flax' [ɛ], also unstressed: *dobrého* [eː]; B/C/S *déte* 'child', *lêp, lépa* 'beautiful' [NomSgMasc/Fem] both [eː] *vs ȉdēm* 'I go' [eː].
>
> /o/ is strongly lip-rounded in Russian, and may even be pronounced [u̯ɔ] (3.2.1.7).

3.3.2.2 Diphthongs

As noted above, Slavic contains numerous phonetic diphthongs of the form 'vowel + /j/' and 'vowel + /w/', which are not diphthong phonemes. Czech and Slovak have some genuine 'vowel + glide/semivowel' diphthong phonemes (see above). Other diphthong phonemes are:

(52a) ['ie]: Sorbian /ě/: Sorb *pěkny* ['pieknɪ] 'obedient'

(52b) [u̯ɔ]: Slovak /ô/: Slk *kôň* [ku̯ɔɲ] 'horse'

(52c) ['uo]: Sorbian /ó/: Sorb *kóń* ['kuonʲ] 'horse'

The Sorbian diphthongs tend to be reduced to simple high mid [e] and [o] at conversational speed, but the diphthongal pronunciation is the literary norm.

3.3.2.3 Nasal vowel phonemes

Polish /ę ą/ preserve their nasal vowel quality only before fricatives, where they are usually pronounced as rounding diphthongs [ɛ̃u̯ ɔ̃u̯]. They retain this nasal pronunciation also at the end of words in formal speech, and at slow tempi. Elsewhere the nasal quality is reduced (see 3.3.2.7).

3.3.2.4 *Other vowel phonemes*
Other vowel phonemes found in individual languages are:

(53a)	Slk /ä/ [æ] or [ɛ]:	*pät'* '5'
(53b)	Sln /é/ [eː]:	*pét* [peːt] '5'
	cf. Sln /ê/ [ɛː]:	*žêna* ['ʒɛːna] 'woman'
(53c)	Sln /ó/ [oː]:	*pót* [poːt] 'road, way'
	cf. Sln /ô/ [ɔː]:	*nôž* [nɔː ʃ] 'knife'
(53d)	Blg and Sln /ə/:	Blg *pǎt* 'road'
		Sln *pès* 'dog'

3.3.2.5 *Prepalatalization*
From a phonological point of view, in some Slavic languages the vowels /i/ and /e/ are preceded only by palatal or palatalized consonants. Orthographically this is sometimes interpreted as the vowels "prepalatalizing" the consonants:

/i/ [i] (orth. *i*) prepalatalizes: all consonants in hard/soft pairs:
Ukrainian, Sorbian
labials, velars and /l/: Polish
velars and /l/: Bulgarian, Macedonian

[i] (orth. *i*) (of /i/) indicates a preceding soft phoneme: Russian, Belarusian

/e/ prepalatalizes: all consonants in hard/soft pairs (native words):
Russian, Belarusian
dentals (which become palatal): Slovak (with some exceptions)
velars and /l/: Bulgarian, Macedonian

orth. *ě* (/e/) indicates a preceding palatal phoneme: Czech

/ě/ prepalatalizes: all consonants in hard/soft pairs: Sorb

3.3.2.6 *Stressed (or pitched) vs unstressed vowels*
Stressed vowels are usually louder, longer and higher in pitch than comparable unstressed vowels, very much as in English. Unstressed vowels may show modifications of vowel quality. As a general rule, the greater the contrast of energy between stressed and unstressed syllables, the more the unstressed vowels will be "reduced". The fixed-stress languages have relatively weaker stress. Their vowels tend to preserve their quality in unstressed syllables. The free-stress languages tend

Table 3.7. *Stressed* vs *unstressed vowel systems*

		i	(y)	é	e	ə	a	ó	o	u	(r̥)
Slovenian:	Stressed system:	i		é	e	ə	a	ó	o	u	(r̥)
	Unstressed system:	i			e	ə	a		o	u	(r̥)
Bulgarian:	Stressed system:	i			e	ə	a		o	u	
	Unstressed system:	i			(e)	ə				u	
Belarusian:	Stressed system:	i	(y)		e		a		o	u	
	Unstressed system:	i	(y)		(e)	ə				u	
Russian:	Stressed system:	i	(y)		e		a		o	u	
	Unstressed system:	i	(y)				a			u	

to have a stronger contrast between stressed and unstressed syllables, and the unstressed vowels tend to be reduced (Bulgarian, Slovenian, Russian, Belarusian). Ukrainian is an exception to this generalization: unstressed vowels suffer only a minor reduction in quality. The same applies to B/C/S, in this case no doubt related to the pitched nature of its stress.

Reduction of unstressed vowels may occur anywhere in the word, or may be conditioned by the position of the unstressed syllable with respect to the stressed ("tonic") syllable of the word. Such unstressed vowels result in the neutralization of oppositions in the vowel system, and in a reduction in the number of distinctive vowel sounds. Reduced vowels are marked in the Belarusian orthography, but in the other languages one must predict the vowel quality on the basis of the known phonetic properties of the vowel system.

The reduction of unstressed vowels in the four languages creates a second vowel system (a sub-system) with fewer contrastive phonemes (table 3.7).

In Slovenian the close versions /é ó/ merge with the open /e o/ in unstressed position:

(54)   Sln   *kóst* 'bone' [koːst]
            kostí [GenSg] [kɔˈstiː]
            kôsti [DatSg] [ˈkɔːsti]

Unstressed /e/ is raised in Bulgarian (sub-standardly) and Russian (after soft consonants) to [ɪ], in Russian to [ɨ] after hard consonants, by a process known by its Russian name *ikan'e* (3.2.1.5):

(55)   Rus   *sem'* '7' [sʲemʲ]   *semí* [GenSg] [sʲɪˈmʲi]
            cen 'price' [GenPl] [t͡sɛn]   *cená* [NomSg] [t͡sɨˈna]

But in Belarusian unstressed /e/ after hard consonants is *lowered* to /a/ (*akan'e*):

(56)   Bel   *čérap* 'skull', [Pl] *čarapý*

Unstressed /e/ after soft consonants is also lowered to /a/, but only in pretonic syllables (*jákan'e*):

(57)   Bel   *zjamljá* 'earth'   [Pl] *zémli*
       bjazzúby 'toothless'   *bezadkázny* 'irresponsible'   *póle* 'field'

Unstressed Bulgarian /a/ merges with unstressed /ə/ as [ə]:

(58)   Blg   *brat* 'brother'   *brátăt* 'the brother' ['bratət]
             grad 'city'   *gradăt* 'the city' [grə'dət]

Unstressed Bulgarian /o/ fuses with unstressed /u/ as [ʊ]:

(59)   Blg   *okó* 'eye' [ʊ'kɔ]   *uxó* 'ear' [ʊ'xɔ]

But in Belarusian unstressed /o/ merges with unstressed /a/ as /a/ ("strong *akan'e*"):

(60)   Bel   *zólata* 'gold'   *zalatý* 'golden' [NomPl]

In Russian, unstressed /o/ and /a/ after hard consonants are pronounced [ʌ] in absolute initial or first pretonic position, but [ə] elsewhere (also *akan'e*):

(61)   Rus   *molokó*   'milk' [məlʌ'kɔ]
             karandáš   'pencil' [kərʌn'da ʃ]
             oknó   'window' [ʌk'nɔ]
             abrikós   'apricot' [ʌbrɪ'kɔs]
             slóvo   'word' ['slɔvə]
             máma   'Mum' ['mamə]

These four languages give the clearest evidence of the interaction of stress and reduction in vowel quality. However, the other languages may also show some variation in vowel quality in conjunction with stress or length. In first pretonic position, Ukrainian /o/ takes on something of the [ʊ] quality of unstressed Bulgarian /o/ (especially before stressed /u/):

(62)   Ukr   *holúbka* 'little dove' [fiʊ-]

Sorbian /ó/ ['uo] or [o] is normally pronounced [ɔ] in unstressed syllables:

(63)   USorb   *rozpóznać*   'recognize' ['rɔspɔznat͡ɕ]
         cf.   *póznać*   'recognize' ['puoznat͡ɕ]

And long Czech and Slovak vowels tend to be more extreme (higher, fronter, etc.) than their corresponding short vowels, and especially in stressed (initial) position (3.3.2.1). The most perceptible is /i/, whose short version tends to [ɨ] or [ɪ], but these and similar phonetic variations are generally not as perceptible as the major variations listed above. B/C/S long and stressed /e/ likewise tends to be higher than short or unstresed /e/ (3.3.2.1).

3.3.2.7   *Position in the word*

Vowels may also be affected by their position in a word (other than in relation to stress). Except in careful speech, the Polish nasal vowel /ę/ normally loses its nasal quality in word-final position:

>   (64)   Pol   *proszę* 'please' ['prɔʃɛ]

And the nasal vowel /ą/ may either preserve its nasal quality or lose it (both standard), or give rise to a final *-m* (non-standard):

>   (65)   Pol   *śpiewają* 'they sing' [-jɔ̃], [-jɔu̯], [-jɔ̃u̯], [-jɔm]

Before consonants other than fricatives, the nasal vowels are regularly followed by an epenthetic homorganic nasal consonant (3.4.2), and the vowel may lose its nasality:

>   (66)   Pol   *będę* 'I will be' ['bɛ̃ndɛ], ['bɛndɛ]

Other properties of word position which affect vowel phonetics involve adjacent and surrounding consonants, and features of secondary articulation. Palatal or palatalized consonants in particular may alter vowel quality, and not only in Czech *přehláska*, or Polish and Sorbian vowel mutation in *C'VC'* sequences, which are matters of phonotactics (3.4.3). Even in Russian, surrounding palatalized consonants can cause fronting of a vowel (3.2.1.5):

>   (67)   Rus   *pjátyj* 'fifth' ['pʲatɨj]   *pjat'* '5' [pʲætʲ]
>   And in Slovenian: short /e/ > [e] before final /-j/:   *jèj* [jej] 'eat'
>   short /o/ > [o] before final [u̯]:   *stòl* [stou̯] 'table'

The spoken language often diverges considerably from the official standard in vowel pronunciation, and not only in dialects. Educated colloquial Prague Czech, for example (11.3.2), regularly makes the following changes:

>   /ī/ (orth. *ý*) > [ei]:   *velký mlýn* 'big mill' ['vɛlkei mlein]
>   /ē/ > [iː]:   *dobrého mléka* 'good milk' [GenSg] ['dobriːɦɔ
>   'mliːka]
>
>   /ū/ > [ou̯]:   *úřad* 'office' ['ou̯ɾat]

(in the written standard /ou/ is the regular morphophonemic partner of short /u/ in all but initial position, where long *ú* (/ū/) is the only possibility, even for etymological long /ō/).

3.4   Modern consonant systems

3.4.1   Phonemes

The Slavic consonant phonemes show less diversity than the vowels. Table 3.8 presents a classification by manner and place of articulation, based on oppositions in minimal pairs, of all the phonemes which appear across the standard languages; sounds which are never phonemes, but only allophones, are enclosed in square brackets (including semivowels). Many pairs of sounds in this set are mutually exclusive, e.g. a language does not have both dental and uvular /r/, or both velar /g/ and glottal /h/. Foreign sounds are not indicated here, as there are no common sounds which are foreign to the whole Slavic area; they are shown in table 3.10.

/r/ and /l/ may also be vocalic phonemes in many systems. /m/ and /n/ may also be vocalic allophones in a few systems (3.3.1), and all four of these may be devoiced (3.4.3.4).

Nineteen of the phonemes are common to all the languages (table 3.9).

Table 3.8. *Slavic consonant phonemes*

	Labial	Dental	Post-Alveolar	Alveolo-Palatal	Palatal	Velar/Uvular	Glottal
Stop	p p′ b b′	t t′ d d′			t' k' d' g'	k k′ g g′	[ʔ]
Nasal	m m′	n n′			n'	[ŋ]	
Fricative	f f′ v v′	s s′ z z′	š š′ ž ž′	ś ź		x x′ ɣ ɣ′	h h′
(or Semivowels)	w w′ [u̯]				j [i̯]		
Affricate		c c′ dz dz′	č č′ dž dž′	ć dź			
Liquid		r r′	ř [r̝]		r'	[ʁʲ] ʁ	
		l l′			l'		

Table 3.9. *Consonant phonemes common to all Slavic languages*

	Labial	Dental/Alveolar	Post-Alveolar	Palatal	Velar	Glottal
Stops	p b	t d			k (g)	
Nasals	m	n				
Fricatives	(v) (w)	s z	š ž	j	x (ɣ)	(h)
Affricates		c	č			
Liquids		r l		•		

Table 3.10. *Non-common phonemes; allophones; distribution of /w-v/ and /g-ɣ-h/*

	Labial	Dental/Alveolar	Post-Alveolar	Alveolo-Pal	Palatal	Velar	Glottal
Blg	v; H/S all; f	H/S all; (dz)	[dž]		k' g' n'	g (ɣ) (ŋ) / H/S k/g	
	(Some descriptions interpret soft as 'palatalized +j', see 3.4.1.1)						
Mac	v f	ľ (dz)	[dž]			g (ɣ) (ŋ)	
B/C/S	v [f]	(dz)	[dž]			g (ɣ) (ŋ)	
Sln	v [f] (u̯)	(dz)	[dž]			g (ɣ) (ŋ)	
Pol	v f; H/S all / w (H only) (<PSl l)	(dz) (l')	[dž]	ś ź ć dź	n'	g (ɣ) (ŋ) / (k') (g')	
USorb	w; H/S all / (w < v/l) [v] [f]	H/S n/c; (r > uvular) / (dz)	dž			(ŋ) H/S ʁ / (ɣ) [g]	h / (?)
LSorb	As USorb	H/S n/l/r (dz)	(dž)	ś ź ć dź		g (ɣ) (ŋ) / (k') (g')	
Cz	v f	(dz)	ř [r̝] (dž)		t' d' n'	(ɣ) (ŋ) [g]	h (?)
Slk	v [f] (u̯)	dz	dž		t' d' n' ľ	(ɣ) (ŋ) [g]	h
Rus	v f; H/S all	H/S all exc. c (dz)	(dž)			g (ɣ) H/S all	
Bel	v [f] (u̯) / H/S all exc. u̯	H/S n/s/z/c; H/S dz	dž			ɣ [g] H/S all	
Ukr	w (v) [f] / H/S all	H/S all; [dz] dz'	dž			[g] H/S all	h

Notes:

'H/S' = 'Hard/Soft', i.e. ±Palatalized; 'all' = the common sounds listed in table 3.9 in that place of articulation; round brackets indicate allophones, square brackets foreign

The brackets in table 3.9 mean that all languages have *either* /v/ *or* /w/; and *either* /g/, /ɣ/ *or* /h/. The distribution of these and the main remaining parts of each language's system are shown in table 3.10.

All Slavic languages contain sizeable quantities of foreign words, which have been integrated into the native Slavic phonological systems to differing degrees. Sometimes, as with the Slovak diphthongs /au eu/ (3.3.1), they occur only in obviously foreign words, and so remain present but marginal in the language's phonemic system. But there comes a point where the quantity of such words makes this treatment insufficient. Determining this point often depends on distribution. We discuss these phonological processes in 3.4.3 below, and illustrate some of the problems by the feature of palatalization.

3.4.1.1   *Palatalization*

The most highly palatalized languages in Slavic are East Slavic, Sorbian and Polish, and in some descriptions Bulgarian. There are increasingly severe limitations on the distribution of palatalized consonants as we move from Russian to Belarusian and Ukrainian, and further to Bulgarian, especially the ability of palatalized consonants to occur in final position (3.4.3.4).

Of the paired hard/soft consonants in final position, Polish has only the palatal nasal /n'/. But Polish shows a more advanced state of phonetic palatalization than any of the other languages. This fact is mirrored in the analyses of Šaumjan (1958) and Koschmieder (1977), who give Polish a full double series of hard and soft consonants:

Paired:	Hard:	p	b	t	d	k	g	f	v	s	z	n	m	r	l	c
	Soft:	p'	b'	t'	d'	k'	g'	f'	v'	s'	z'	n'	m'	r'	l'	c'
Unpaired:	Hard:	š	ž	x	č	dz	dž									
	Soft:	ś	ź		ć	dź										

for which Koschmieder supplies minimal pairs like:

(68)   Pol   *wara* 'beware!'   *wiara* 'belief'
          mara 'apparition'   *miara* 'measure'
          wiza 'visa'   *wizja* 'vision'
          pana 'man' (GenSg)   *piana* 'foam'

The opposite analysis is proposed by Jassem (1964: 335) and Bidwell (1969), who re-analyse most of the paired series as 'consonant + /j/', with the sole exception of /k' g'/. Bidwell cites phonetic data which show a pronunciation of 'consonant + [j]' for historically palatalized consonants:

(69)   Pol   *piasek* ['pjasek]   cf. Rus *pesók* [pʲɪˈsɔk] 'sand'

The phonetic data do not square with Koschmieder's palatograms, which show clearly the palatalizing influence of the /j/ on preceding consonants, and so favor the /C'/ analysis. From the typological point of view, the analysis in two paired series makes Polish look more like East Slavic. But the analysis with 'consonant + /j/' makes it easier to relate Polish progressively to Sorbian, and thence to Czech and Slovak, on a scale of declining palatalization. The unpaired soft phonemes noted by Koschmieder (ś ź ć dź), while phonetically palatal, are the soft alternants of the hard /s z c dz/ (e.g. *gród* ~ *grodu* ~ *grodzie* 'castle' [NomSg ~ GenSg ~ LocSg]: /t/ ~ /d/ ~ /dź/); the same applies to /n'/, phonetically palatal, but the soft partner of /n/ (e.g. *żona* ~ *żonie* 'wife' [NomSg ~ LocSg]: /n/ ~ /n'/). In this view, written forms with *j* (e.g. *wizja*) – all foreign in origin – represent a sequence of 'consonant + /j/', in which the consonant is allophonically palatalized.

3.4.2   Phonetics

At the phonetic level – that is, including allophones – we can measure each language as a sub-set of the maximum number of phones occurring across the whole group, expressed in rounded percentage terms, with the following results (since different descriptions will produce different numbers of phonemes, this comparison is possible only for the phonetic level):

- the range is 34–59 percent;
- lowest is Slovenian, highest Ukrainian (and Russian in one standard variant (with both soft and hard post-alveolar fricatives, see 11.3.1 – noted below as Russian[2]; Russian[1] has only hard post-alveolar fricatives);
- under 40 percent: Slovenian (34 percent), B/C/S (35 percent), Slovak (39 percent);
- 40–50 percent: Macedonian (40 percent), Upper Sorbian (41 percent), Czech (44 percent), Lower Sorbian (49 percent);
- over 50 percent: Polish (51 percent), Bulgarian (54 percent), Belarusian/Russian[1] (56 percent), Ukrainian/Russian[2] (59 percent).

South Slavic – except for Bulgarian – and Slovak are lowest, and East Slavic highest. The main reason for the differences lies in the extent of the feature of palatalization.

Beyond the basic phonetics of Slavic sounds, which are indicated sufficiently by the phonemic descriptions in tables 3.8–3.10, the process of palatalization and the palatal region itself are the area of greatest differentiation.

As noted above, the palatalization of non-palatal consonants may vary, on the one hand, between "genuine" co-articulation palatalization – as in Russian and

Belarusian, and, on the other hand, articulations closer to a sequence of 'consonant + /j/' – as in Ukrainian, Bulgarian and Sorbian. In the latter areas, palatalization is largely allophonic, occurring only (and automatically) before front vowels and /j/ (as for Polish in foreign borrowings, above), and before back vowels it may be interpreted as phonemic or as a sequence. Elsewhere, it is often very limited in its range of activity, e.g. only in dentals, or not in final position.

In the palatal region, stops are rare, confined to Czech and Slovak in West Slavic (with /t'/, /d'/, /n'/, as well as /l'/) and Macedonian in South Slavic (with /ḱ/ and /ǵ/), the latter alone reflecting the Proto-Slavic palatal stops resulting from /t, d + j/ (3.2.2.1). As for the fricatives, the Proto-Slavic "palatals" /š/ and /ž/ are reflected everywhere as post-alveolars (also called "palato-alveolars"), mostly with low tongue position (i.e. "hard", e.g. East Slavic, Polish), sometimes high (i.e. "soft", e.g. Upper Sorbian). Only Polish and Lower Sorbian have developed new alveolo-palatal fricatives (/ś/, /ź/), from previous palatalized /s'/, /z'/. The affricates are slightly different, partly because the voiced one (/dž/) is frequently missing. They are also normally post-alveolar, but more often have high tongue position ("soft", e.g. Russian), though low tongue position ("hard") is also found (Belarusian, Ukrainian). Polish and Lower Sorbian have developed the alveolo-palatal affricates /ć/, /dź/ from palatalized /t'/, /d'/. B/C/S also has alveolo-palatal /ć/, /dź/, but from /t, d + j/ (/t' d'/).

3.4.3 Phonotactics and limitations on distribution

Limitations on the appearance of particular phonemes are most often related to clusters and word- or syllable-final position. Only a few are related to CV contexts, and we treat them first.

3.4.3.1 *Palatalization*

Among the languages with a hard/soft opposition, this opposition is often neutralized before certain vowels, usually the front vowels /i/ and /e/. In the case of /i/, it is normal for such languages to have two audible variants: [i] (/i/) after soft (palatalized) consonants, and [ɨ] (/i/ or /y/) after hard consonants. This allows the hard/soft consonant opposition to operate (as in East Slavic, Polish, Sorbian). The absence of the second variant tends to prevent it (as in Bulgarian), though some languages oppose hard/palatal: Czech /t d n/, Slovak /t d n l/ and Polish /n/ before /i/, and Slovak also before /e/. In most cases, and normally in the case of /e/, the soft member of the pair occurs here automatically (as in Russian, Belarusian, Polish, Sorbian). Bulgarian and Ukrainian have only hard consonants before /e/, and Bulgarian also before /i/ (in each case the velars are exceptions, the soft variant occurring before both vowels). But the soft velars are rarely freely opposed to hard velars, being normally positional variants, even in languages like Russian with a strongly developed hard/soft opposition.

3.4.3.2   *Assimilation*

The general rule is that consonants within a cluster will adopt the voice and place of articulation of the final member of the cluster. This situation arose at the end of the Proto-Slavic period with the reappearance of closed syllables and the formation of new clusters (3.2.3.1), both of which were brought about by the loss of the *jers* (3.2.1.1). Thus, while assimilation represented a broad trend, not every area or language was certain to follow it.

1.   Assimilation of voice

Regressive assimilation of voice among obstruents is the norm throughout: voiced obstruents are devoiced before voiceless obstruents, and voiceless obstruents are voiced before voiced obstruents (for word-final position, see 3.4.3.4). The single exception in the standard languages is Ukrainian, in which the second rule applies, but not normally the first:

(70a)   Rus, Bel   *nóžka* 'foot' [ˈnɔʃka]; Ukr *nížka* [ˈnʲiʒka]

(70b)   Rus, Bel, Ukr   *prós′ba* 'request' [ˈprɔzʲba]

Ukrainian optionally devoices only the final /z/ of prefixes before a voiceless root-initial obstruent, e.g. *róz-kvit* 'daybreak' [-skv-] or [-zkv-]. The prefix *z-* is normally devoiced: *z-čýstyty* 'to clean' [ʃt͡ʃ-] (assimilation of voice and place).

It is in this general situation that allophones otherwise not phonetically present may appear, e.g. [dz], [dž], [ɣ] as voiced versions of the voiceless phonemes /c/, /č/, /x/ (table 3.10).

Sonorants do not participate in these rules of assimilation: normally they do not themselves devoice and they do not cause voicing of preceding obstruents. The common sonorants /r l m n/ stand apart in every language except Slovak, at least within a word. In Proto-Slavic, clusters with sonorants second were common, and they continue to be so and to show no assimilation in the modern languages:

(71)   Rus   *tri* 'three' [trʲi]   *sloj* 'layer' [slɔj]   *sneg* 'snow' [snʲɛk]

In Slovak, /m/ and /n/ at least may cause voicing where internal morpheme boundaries are clear:

(72)   Slk   *tak-mer* 'almost' [ˈtagmɛr]   *naš-mu* 'our' [DatSgMasc] [ˈnaʒmu]

but this is inconsistent, and never occurs when boundaries are not clear. It is, therefore, a boundary-related feature, and we return to it below (3.4.3.4).

One Proto-Slavic sonorant which behaves idiosyncratically is /w-v/. In many areas where /w-v/ was labio-dental /v/ (Russian, Czech, Polish, Bulgarian, Macedonian) it found itself partnered phonetically by [f], which often was well represented in the foreign lexicon (especially from Greek via Old Church Slavonic) and which often became a separate phoneme itself. In these areas the status of /v/ as a sonorant became compromised, and it began to behave at least partly like an obstruent. For example, in Russian it behaves like an obstruent and is devoiced to [f] when followed by a voiceless obstruent, but it behaves like a sonorant when in last position in a cluster and does not cause voicing:

(73)   Rus   *lávka* 'counter, shop' ['lafka]   *tvoj* 'your' [tvɔj]

Where this phoneme is bilabial /w/, but also in some cases where it is /v/, it continues to function as a sonorant. In both cases it usually becomes [u̯] when in first position in a cluster (Belarusian, Ukrainian, Slovak, Sorbian, Slovenian), in one case remaining [v] (B/C/S):

(74a) 'sheep':   Bel *aŭcá* [au̯ˈt͡sa]   Ukr *vivcjá* [vʲiu̯ˈt͡sʲa]
                 Slk *ovca* [ˈou̯t͡sa]   Sln *ôvca* [ˈɔːu̯t͡s a]
                 USorb *wowca* [ˈwou̯t͡s a]   B/C/S *óvca* [ˈɔːvt͡sa]

cf. /v/ > [f]:
(74b)   Rus *ovcá* [ʌfˈt͡sa]   Blg *ovcá* [ufˈt͡sa]   Mac *ovca* [ˈɔft͡sa]
        Pol *owca* [ˈɔft͡sa]   Cz *ovce* [ˈɔft͡sɛ]

In the first group (74a) [f] remains a foreign sound – that is, a phoneme at best only in the foreign sub-system. It appears as a native allophone only in one limited context – in Slovak in word-initial position:

(75)   Slk   *vták* 'bird' [ftaːk]

Similarly, in many areas, /l/ becomes [u̯] in closed syllables, but this is not an effect of voice or change of status.

As to the spelling of this feature, most languages follow the morphological principle and so do not mark assimilation of voice. The exception is B/C/S, which normally (with a few exceptions) does mark it:

(76)   B/C/S *ȕzak* ~ *ȕska* 'narrow' [NomSgMasc/Fem]
        ȕčiti 'teach' ~ *ȕdžbenīk* 'textbook'

Some non-alternating common roots may show the voicing, e.g. Proto-Slavic *kъde 'where' is spelt gd- in Russian, Belarusian, Polish and B/C/S; or Proto-Slavic *sьde(sь) 'here' is spelt zde- in Russian, Czech and Slovenian. And some prefixes may regularly spell their assimilated form, e.g. Rus raz- > ras-: ras-skáz 'story'.

The related feature of final devoicing is treated in 3.4.3.4.

2.   Progressive assimilation

While the normal Slavic assimilation is regressive, there are occasional cases of progressive assimilation, especially of voice. Examples are the loss of voice in /v/ in Polish and Macedonian following voiceless obstruents (in Macedonian only after /s/):

(77)   'candle':   Pol świeca ['ɕfʲɛt͡sa]   Mac sveḱa ['sfeca/'sfekʲa]

or the loss of voice in /ř/ in Czech:

(78)   Cz   tři 'three' [tr̝̊i]

or of /ž/ in Polish (when it comes from Proto-Slavic /r'/ (spelt rz), as does Czech /ř/):

(79)   Pol   trzy 'three' /tžɨ/ [tʃɨ] (a sequence, not [t͡ʃ],
        cf. czy [Q particle] [t͡ʃɨ])

Upper Sorbian also has the letter ř, pronounced /š/ after /p k/, and /s'/ after /t/ (thus, tři = [tsʲi]); Lower Sorbian has /ś/ in all these contexts, spelt ś: tśi.

        See 3.4.3.4 on special cases of these phenomena in the context of word boundaries.

3.   Assimilation of place

The common context for this sort of assimilation is in clusters of 'dental + palatal', e.g. /s/ + /š/, /t/ + /č/ etc., when the dental also becomes palatal (> šš, t'č). Typically, such clusters will involve 'prefix + stem' contexts:

(80)   Rus   sšiť 'sew' [ʃʃitʲ]   ótčestvo 'patronymic' ['ɔt͡ʃɪstvə]

In rare cases the shift is induced by non-sibilants:

(81)   Sln   z njim 'with him' [ʒɲim] (commonly also spelt ž njim)

Uncommon also is the reverse, where palatals become dentals:

(82)   Bel   dačcé 'daughter' [dat͡st͡sɛ]

In languages with the hard/soft opposition, assimilation of palatalization is possible, but not common. Russian perhaps typifies the process in its current gradual loss of such assimilation:

(83)   Rus   *ésli* 'if': older ['jesʲlʲɪ] > newer ['jɛslʲɪ]

The appearance of the velar nasal [ŋ] as an allophone of /n/ before velar stops is general in West and South Slavic, but not in East Slavic, where it remains dental. Nowhere is it a phoneme:

(84)   Cz, Slk, Pol, Sorb, B/C/S, Sln, Blg, Mac *banka* 'bank' ['baŋka]
    cf. Rus, Bel, Ukr   *bank* [bank]

4.   Assimilation of manner
Other than assimilation of voice, assimilation of manner of articulation is rarer. The few cases involve nasality, e.g. oral stop > nasal stop (= assimilation of nasality):

(85)   Bel   *ammán* 'deceit' < *ab-man* (cf. Rus *obmán*)

or stop > semivowel (= loss of lingual contact):

(86)   Pol   *koński* 'horse' [Adj] [kɔj̃skɪ]

Occasionally one finds *dissimilation* of manner, in 'stop + stop' clusters, but usually only at the colloquial level:

(87)   Rus   *mjágkij*   'soft'   ['mʲæxʲkʲɪj]   (standard)
           kto   'who'   [xtɔ]   (non-standard)

3.4.3.3   *Simplification of clusters*
We find some languages continuing the Proto-Slavic tradition of simplification of clusters, whether by dissimilation or elision. Where such changes are old the orthography usually reflects it, making the only descriptive requirement a mor-phophonological explanation of the alternation (chapter 4). Colloquial developments are not reflected in the orthography, are usually lexically limited and do not represent general rules. Geminate consonants are normally acceptable, but are sometimes an exception, e.g. in Czech, where they are regularly contracted to a single one, even across morpheme boundaries:

(88)   Cz   *Anna* ['ana], *oddech* 'rest' ['ɔdɛx]

and sporadically in Macedonian:

(89)   Mac   *raseče* 'chop up' < *raz-seče*
    cf. Rus   *Ánna* ['anna], *ótdyx* ['ɔddɨx], *rasséč'* [rʌs'sʲetʃ͡]

3.4.3.4   *Word-final features*

These include limitations on palatalization and voice not only in the absolute final context, but also in the effects occurring across a word boundary.

1. Palatalization

   In languages with the hard/soft opposition, many soft consonants cannot occur in word-final (or syllable-final) position. In some languages no soft consonant may occur in these positions, e.g. Bulgarian:

   (90a)   Blg   *den* 'day'
       cf.   Rus, Ukr   *den′*   Pol, USorb *dzień*

   Soft velars do not occur finally in any language, and final soft labials occur only in Russian, and even then only in word-final, and not internal syllable-final, position:

   (90b)   Rus *sem′* 'seven' *krov′* 'blood' *step′* 'steppe' *gólub′* 'pigeon'

   but compare the derived words with hard consonants internally (90c) and the absence of all soft labials in other languages (90d):

   (90c)   Rus   *króvnyj* 'bloody'   *stepnój* 'steppe'   *golúbka* 'dear'

   (90d)   Bel   *sem*   *kroŭ*   *stèp*   *gólub*
       Ukr   *sim*   *krov*   *step*   *hólub*
       Pol   *siedem*   *krew*   *step*   *gołąb*

2. Voice

   In only two standard languages is the opposition of voice maintained in absolute word-final position – that is, where there is a pause after the word, namely B/C/S and Ukrainian. In all other languages, voiced paired consonants are devoiced in final position (with /v/ behaving as noted above (3.4.3.2), even when a language also has /f/). This rule can produce homonyms with at least one particular form of a word, typically forms with a zero ending – most often NomSg of masculine nouns or GenPl of feminine/neuter nouns – alternating with the voiced consonant in other forms:

   (91)   Rus   *rog* 'horn' and *rok* 'fate' [NomSg] [rɔk]
       ~ *róga* [GenSg] ['rɔga], *róka* [GenSg] ['rɔka]
       Rus   *serb* 'Serb' and *serp* 'sickle' [NomSg] [sʲɛrp]
       ~ *sérba* [GenSg] ['sʲɛrba], *sérpa* [GenSg] ['sʲɛrpa]
       Cz   *Srb* 'Serb' and *srp* 'sickle' [NomSg] [sr̩p]
       ~ *Srba* [GenSg] ['sr̩ba], *srpu* [GenSg] ['sr̩pu]

cf.   B/C/S   *Sȓb* 'Serb' [sr̩b] *vs sr̓p* 'sickle' [sr̩ːp]
      Ukr   *serb* [sɛrb] *vs serp* [sɛrp]

Note the effect of devoicing on /h/: in three of the four languages with this
phoneme, the devoiced version is [x], that is, it merges with the phoneme /x/:

(92a)   Ukr   *rih* 'horn' [rix]   Cz, Slk *roh* [rɔx]
        Ukr   *mih* 'he was able' ∼ *mix* 'fur', both [mʲix]

In the fourth – Upper Sorbian – /h/ is silent in final position:

(92b)   USorb   *róh* 'horn' [rʲuo]

Belarusian's result is as expected – [ɣ] > [x]:

(92c)   Bel   *roh* 'horn' [rɔx]

The sonorants are unpaired for voice, and normally do not participate in this
rule. But where they follow a voiceless obstruent in this position they may be
(progressively) devoiced, though this is most often resisted. For example, in
Russian /r/ and /l/ may either be devoiced or become syllabic:

(93)   Rus   *mysl'* 'thought'   [-sʲl̥ʲ] or [-sʲl̩ʲ]
              teátr 'theatre'   [-tr̥] or [-tr̩]

with the syllabic pronunciation now more common. /m/ and /n/ are now
virtually always syllabic:

(94)   Rus   *ritm* 'rhythm' [-tm̩], *žizn'* 'life' [-znʲ]
              (older: standard [-tm̥], non-standard [-sʲn̥ʲ])

In the native lexicon such clusters have usually been avoided by fill vowels (see
above 3.2.1.1), even in the most consonantal languages, e.g. 'seven' (PSl
*sedmь) and 'eight' (PSl *osmь).

(95)   Pol   *siedem   osiem*

While Czech appears not to do this in these lexemes – based on the
orthography:

(96)   Cz   *sedm   osm*

the standard pronunciation of these is, in fact ['sɛdʊm], ['ɔsʊm].
   As expected, however, Polish normally has consonantal sounds here,
including devoicing after voiceless obstruents:

(97)   Pol   *myśl* 'thought' [miɕl̥]   *wiatr* 'wind' [vʲatr̥]

Languages with [u̯] have this sound word-finally for /v/ or /l/ as in syllable-final position (see above for /v/). This may be reflected in orthography (98) or not (99):

(98)   Bel *daŭ*   Ukr *dav* '(he) gave'   (cf. both *dalá* '[she] gave')

(99)   Sln *stòl* 'chair'   *dál* 'give' [PastActivePart]

B/C/S, which does not have [u̯], has converted /l/ in final position to the vowel /o/:

(100)   B/C/S *stô* 'table' (< *stoo) *dão* '(he) gave'
                (cf. [GenSg] *stòla*, [Fem] *dála*)

3.   Clusters
     Final clusters may be simplified or avoided, mainly in B/C/S and Bulgarian/Macedonian, the most "vocalic" languages. B/C/S may break the cluster with a vowel:

(101)   B/C/S *àkċenat* 'accent'   (but *stùdent* 'student')

while Bulgarian and Macedonian may elide, at least colloquially:

(102)   Blg   *most*   'bridge'   [mɔs]
        Mac   *radost*   'joy'   ['radɔs]

or, in the case of clusters involving /r/ and /l/, Bulgarian may invert (metathesize) the cluster:

(103)   Blg   *prăv* 'first' [Masc] ~ *pắrva* [Fem]

which it does also internally before a third consonant:

(104)   Blg   *krăvtá* 'blood' [Def] ~ *kắrvi* [Plur]

4.   Word boundary; juncture (sandhi)
     a.   Voice
          In word-juncture contexts, the realization of the final consonant matches that of internal clusters: if voiceless the consonant is voiced by a following (initial) voiced obstruent. If it is voiced, its voice is retained in this context:

(105)   Pol   *las brzozowy* 'birch forest'   ['laz bʒɔ'zɔvɨ]
        Rus   *brát býl*   '(my) brother was'   ['brad bɨl]
              déd stoít   'grandfather is standing' ['dʲɛt stʌ'it]

If the final consonant is followed by a sonorant or vowel, the norm is also as for internal clusters, that is, no voicing occurs, nor is voice retained:

(106a)   Rus   *brát Níny*   'Nina's brother'   ['brat 'nʲinɨ]

                brát ušël   '(my) brother left'   ['brat u'ʃɔl]

                déd Níny   'Nina's grandfather'   ['dʲɛt 'nʲinɨ]

                déd ušël   'grandfather left'   ['dʲɛt u'ʃɔl]

(106b)   Pol (North)   *brat Ryśka*   'Rysiek's brother'   ['brat 'rɨɕka]

                      brat ojca   'father's brother'   ['brat 'ɔjt͡sa]

                      sad ojca   'father's garden'   ['sat 'ɔjt͡sa]

(106c)   Blg   *zdráv móst*   'a sturdy bridge'   ['zdraf mɔst]

                grád Várna   'the city of Varna'   ['grat 'varnə]

                grád Óxrid   'the city of Ohrid'   ['grat 'ɔxrit]

However, there are some exceptions here, first in Slovak – which we noted above (72) could also undergo voicing by following sonorants internally, at a morpheme boundary:

(107)   Slk   *vlak meškà*   'the train's late'   ['vlag 'mɛʃkaː]

             vlak ide   'the train's coming'   ['vlag 'ije]

But also in Polish (in its southern variant; see also 10.4.2.1):

(108)   Pol (South)   *brat Ryśka* 'Rysiek's brother'   ['brad 'rɨɕka]

                     brat ojca   '(my) father's brother'   ['brad 'ɔjt͡sa]

b. Clusters

Clusters occurring across a word boundary may occasionally be simplified in similar ways to internal ones. Languages which do this more than others are Belarusian and Ukrainian, where the reduction of /w-v/ to [u̯] in absolute final position may be mirrored by initial /w-v/ between a final vowel and a following consonant:

(109a)   Bel   *žýli ŭ hóradze* '(they) lived in town' < *v horadze*

(109b)   Ukr   *žýly v místi* [-lɪ u̯ mʲi-]

Further, /w-v/ becomes the vowel /u/ between two consonants across a boundary (marked orthographically also). These are also now the "initial", citation forms:

(110a)   Bel   *ën usë* 'he everything [AccSg] (+ verb)'

                     (< *vsë*, [NomSg] *usë*)

(110b)   Ukr   *tám **udová*** 'there (is the) widow'
          (< *vdova*, [NomSg] *udová*)

Another approach used by Belarusian is adding prothetic /i/ before initial
groups beginning with sonorants following final consonants:

(111)   Bel   *janá lhála* 'she lied' ~ *ën ilháŭ* 'he lied'

c. Hiatus and prothesis

The avoidance of two vowels across a boundary is an old Proto-
Slavic principle, which led in Proto-Slavic to the introduction of prothetic
consonants (1.3.1, 3.2.1.4). This principle has continued to be operative in
many areas, with prothetic consonants only one solution. Perhaps the most
interesting example is the use in Czech and Upper Sorbian of a non-
phonemic glottal stop before all initial vowels (almost certainly modelled
on neighboring German). It is most consistent precisely where it avoids
hiatus:

(112)   Cz   *já a on* 'he and I' ['ja: ʔa 'ʔɔn]

But, as in German, it has been generalized as a boundary marker, even after
final consonants, and even where these consonants belong to a proclitic form,
indeed even a prefix. Furthermore, the glottal acts at least like a sonorant in
failing to prevent devoicing of the preceding consonant:

(113)   Cz   *lov a hon* 'fishing and hunting' ['lɔf ʔa 'fiɔn]

But the fact that this in turn is generalized to cause the devoicing of
proclitic-final consonants means that the glottal is functioning as a voiceless
obstruent:

(114)   Cz   *v Americe* 'in America' [f 'ʔamerit͡se]
          bezoký 'eyeless' ['bɛsʔɔki:]

This last example also shows that the glottal has become an initial marker of
(root) morphemes, not only words.

The use of the glottal is, however, not an obligatory standard form, and is
regarded by some as a conservative feature (Kučera, 1961: 104). Its "demise"
may indicate a greater preparedness to accept hiatus, though in the Czech
case, that was already no longer its primary purpose.

In the case of Upper Sorbian, /h/ is an alternative to the glottal, and this /h/ used to be the norm in Lower Sorbian. But here it has gradually been removed and been either replaced by /w/ or dropped.

An alternative to prothesis used in Belarusian and Ukrainian is the reduction of an (unstressed) initial vowel to a semivowel. This affects only the high vowels /i/ and /u/, the latter even though /u/ typically acquired prothetic /w-v/. In those cases where it did not (notably when unstressed), /u/ is susceptible to the reduction solution:

(115a) Bel *janá idzé* 'she is coming' [ja'na i̯'d͡z ʲɛ]
              ne ŭméju 'I cannot' [nʲɛ u̯'mʲeju] < *umeju*

(115b) Ukr *voná jde* [wo'na i̯'dɛ]
              ne vmíju [nɛ u̯'miju]

3.5 Suprasegmentals

The three suprasegmental features of Slavic phonemics are stress, quantity and tone. Position of stress is able to distinguish different words, as in English:

(116a) Eng *ínsight ~ incíte, éxport ~ expórt*

(116b) Rus *zámok* 'castle' ~ *zamók* 'lock'

Length is able to distinguish words in four Slavic languages (Slovenian, B/C/S, Czech, Slovak), though virtually only in the vowel system (for consonants, see 3.5.2):

(117a) Sln   *spì* 'sleep!' 2 Sg   *spí* 'he sleeps'

(117b) B/C/S *grâd* 'town' (long + falling) *grȁd* 'hail' (short + falling)

(117c) Cz   *dráha* 'road'   *drahá* 'dear' [NomSgFem]

(117d) Slk   *naraz* 'suddenly'   *náraz* 'blow'

The term "pitch accent" is used in roughly the same sense of phonemic tone, and "pitch" refers to its phonetic realization. B/C/S and one variant of Slovenian have this feature:

(118a) B/C/S 'village': *sèlo* [NomSg] (short + rising)
                           sèla [GenSg] (short + rising)
                           sȅla [NomPl] (short + falling)

(118b) Sln   'town'   *mẹ́sta* [GenSg] (long + rising)
                           mẹ̑sta [NomPl] (long + falling)

The development of suprasegmental features in Proto-Slavic is treated in 3.2.4. All three features have been eliminated, at some time, by at least one of the Slavic languages. In the modern languages, furthermore, we find important interrelations between the three features. Stress and pitch are directly related in Slovenian and B/C/S, and the two always occur on the same vowel. In languages with phonemic stress, stressed vowels are generally longer than the unstressed ones, as in English. Pitch and length can function separately, as in B/C/S, where posttonic vowels may be long or short. They can be partially interdependent, as in Slovenian, where only long vowels may carry a tonal opposition. B/C/S quantity is therefore freer (= less conditioned) than that of Slovenian. Similarly, the existence of the Slovak Rhythmic Law (3.5.2) means that quantity in Slovak is less free than in Czech.

By combining these factors, we arrive at the following classification of the modern Slavic languages according to their suprasegmental features (see also 3.2.4):

No distinctive suprasegmental features: Polish, Sorbian, Macedonian
Stress only: East Slavic, Bulgarian
Quantity only: Czech (free), Slovak (limited)
Stress and (limited) quantity: Slovenian (non-tonal variant)
Stress, tone and quantity: B/C/S, Slovenian (limited quantity and pitch)

Sentence intonation is also a prosodic feature of Slavic. But there are few comparative studies of Slavic intonation (Nikolaeva 1977; Bahmut, 1977 for East Slavic), and no generally agreed framework for analysis or description. We consequently omit intonation from our discussion of phonology, though some aspects will be noted in chapter 7.

3.5.1   Stress

While early Proto-Slavic probably developed fixed penultimate or final stress, later stress was determined by the location of pitch while this could still appear on any syllable. Eventually it became associated with particular morphemes and inflexional patterns, and became free, at which point pitch became limited to the stressed syllable, and so was secondary. The pitch accent has given way to stress in nine of the eleven languages, and five of them now have fixed stress.

The accent pattern of the modern Slavic languages can be classified as follows.
Stress (free and mobile):

1.   Intensity: East Slavic, Bulgarian, Slovenian non-tonal
2.   Pitch: B/C/S, Slovenian tonal

Stress (fixed):
Initial: Czech, Slovak, Sorbian
Penult: Polish
Antepenult: Macedonian

Dialects may exhibit transitional phenomena: Eastern Slovak has penultimate stress, like Polish; Lower Sorbian has such a strong secondary stress on the penult that the exact status of the stress position is a matter of some dispute (indeed, all the West Slavic languages have a marked secondary stress on the "other" syllable – initial or penultimate – in longer words). Some Kashubian dialects have initial, some penultimate and some free stress (10.4.2.1).

The intensity-stress languages differ considerably in the nature of their stress. The fixed-stress languages exhibit a less energetic type of stress, and there is relatively less difference in energy between stressed and unstressed syllables. Little contrastive information is available on the relative strength of stress, though Stieber (1969: 65), for instance, claims that Polish stress is stronger than Czech. The higher degree of stress mobility involved in antepenultimate as opposed to initial stress (e.g. Pol 'student, stu'denta, studen'tami) may suggest a potentially freer, and therefore stronger, stress. The unstressed vowels consequently retain much of the phonetic quality which they would have under stress. The primary acoustic component of this stress is pitch. On the other hand, the free-stress languages show a more energetic stress, with a more perceptible difference in phonetic quality between stressed and unstressed vowels. Ukrainian probably has the weakest stress of the free-stress languages, while Russian, Belarusian and, to a lesser extent, Bulgarian and Slovenian exhibit stronger contrast between stressed and unstressed vowels. This stress is acoustically signalled by energy and length rather than by mere pitch. Stressed vowels tend to be longer than unstressed vowels.

Two important questions arise over the placing and identity of stress or pitch:

1.   Do fixed-stress languages have stress exceptions?
2.   Do free-stress languages have predictable stress – and if so, to what extent?

3.5.1.1   *Exceptions in fixed-stress languages*

The fixed-stress languages do have stress exceptions, which fall into two major classes: lexical irregularities and clitics. (In this section stress on the fixed-stress languages is indicated by a preceding prime – as in IPA, since the acute has other functions in most of these languages.)

a.   Lexical
      Words with atypical stress are mostly of foreign origin, and may resist assimilation to native stress patterns over long periods of time.

It is sometimes possible to isolate such exceptions by their language of origin, or by their form in the receiving language. Šewc (1968: 27) reports several classes from Sorbian:

1. Antepenultimate rather than initial stress:
   a. Words in *-ita* (Ger *-ität*) and some in *-ija* (Ger *-ei*, *-ion*):

      (119a)   Sorb   *aw'torita, uni'wersita, demon'stracija*

   b. Verbs in *-ować* or *-erować* with foreign stems:

      (119b)   Sorb   *tele'fonować, 'studować, mar'kerować*

2. Words which preserve the stress of the language of origin:

   (119c)   Sorb   *te'orija, litera'tura, stu'dent*

Polish has a number of nouns stressed on the antepenult. Most of these words are foreign, including most nouns in *-ik-/-yk-*:

   (120a)   Pol   *uni'wersytet, 'opera, 'muzyka, po'lityka, 'klinika*
             [GenSg]

They also include a few native Polish phrases:

   (120b)   *w'ogóle* 'in general'

and some forms of verbs with appended enclitic forms of the auxiliary:

   (120c)   *'byliście* 'you [Pl] were'

Many of these exceptions are now commonly regularized in educated speech, either by dropping the post-tonic syllable (*uni'werstet, w'ogle*) or by simply shifting the stress (*uniwer'sytet*).

   Macedonian also shows some "irregular" stress, mainly in foreign words. The regular Macedonian stress is antepenult:

   (121a)   Mac   *'sinovi* 'sons'   *si'novite* 'the sons'

But some recent foreign borrowings may show different stress:

   (121b)   Mac   *litera'tura* 'literature'   *litera'turen* 'literary'

In one morphological class the stress is penultimate, namely the verbal noun in *-jki* (the result of fairly recent ellipsis from *-eki*):

   (121c)   Mac   *no'sejki* 'carrying'

In contrast, irregular lexical stress in Czech and Slovak is less frequent. These languages exert a strong unifying pressure on foreign words to conform to initial-stress patterns, and non-initial stress is felt to have an obviously foreign nature. The possibility of secondary stress on the penult and the availability of long vowels are alternatives to irregular stress:

(122)   Cz   ꞌ*litera,tura*   *ensemble* ([ꞌansaːmbl̩])

b.   *Clitics*

The fixed-stress languages, however, do have other, native, exceptions to "normal" stress, particularly in respect of clitics and affixes related to clitics. Clitics are by default unstressed. As individual words they bear no stress, but when combined with adjacent words they may cause the stress to shift, including onto themselves, since in principle they form one "phonetic word" with their host.

1. *Proclitics*

Proclitics, e.g. prepositions, attach to the following word. In initial-stress languages, proclitics naturally attract the stress in 'preposition + noun' phrases:

(123)   'to town'   Cz, USorb ꞌ*do města*   Slk ꞌ*do mesta*

The negative particle *ne* in these languages is stressed and is even joined orthographically:

(124)   'I don't think'   Cz, Slk ꞌ*nemyslím*   Sorb ꞌ*njemyslim*

This also affects a preposed auxiliary:

(125)   'I won't write'   Cz   ꞌ*nebudu psát*   Slk ꞌ*nebudem písat'*
                            USorb ꞌ*njebudu pisać*

In penult and antepenult stress languages the same effect may occur on short host forms:

(126)   Pol   ꞌ*nie wiem* 'I don't know' ꞌ*raz* ꞌ*na rok* 'once a year'

(127)   Mac   ꞌ*ne znam* 'I don't know' ꞌ*što sakaš* 'what do you want?'

In some free-stress languages, prepositions in adverbial 'preposition + noun' phrases may also attract the stress:

(128a)   Rus ꞌ*na gory* 'to (up into) the mountains', cf. Bel *na* ꞌ*hory*

(128b)   Rus ꞌ*za ruku* '(take) by the hand'

While shifts of this sort (being originally effects of the Proto-Slavic pitch system) used to occur generally in Russian, they are slowly being removed, as they already have been in Belarusian, and are now firmly retained only in clearly adverbial phrases like (128b) above, but not (128a).

2. *Enclitics*

Enclitics attach to the preceding word. They are usually particles or conjunctions, but may also be pronouns, and they tend to occupy the second or "Wackernagel" position, the first unaccented position in the sentence. The orthography may treat enclitics as separate words or as affixes. The main classes of Slavic enclitics are:

a. Personal and reflexive pronouns

Enclitic personal and reflexive pronouns (5.5.3) are found in all but East Slavic, where the reflexive pronoun -*sja* is now attached as an affix (or 'postfix') after endings; one also finds enclitics in dialects and colloquial usage. Enclitics are usually in the oblique cases:

(129)   Slk 'zdalo   by   sa ti   'to   'tak
              seem – CondEncl – ReflEnclAccSg –
              you-EnclDatSg – *it*-NomSg – *so*
              'it would seem so to you'

These clitic pronouns can sometimes be stressed, for example when the word order makes them proclitic and they occupy the naturally stressed position:

(130)   Pol   'jak 'się masz? 'how are you?' (*się* [Refl AccSg] is
                  normally enclitic, cf. [Inf] 'mieć się 'to feel')

But they do not normally attract the stress rightwards towards or on to themselves:

(131)   Mac   no'sejǩi mu go 'bringing it to him'
                  (enclitics *mu* 'to him' [DatSg], *go* 'it' [AccSg])

Macedonian clitic pronouns can also be proclitic when anticipating a full noun object (7.4.3.3), but they do not attract the stress, even when appropriately placed (i.e. antepenult):

(132a)   Mac   'vidav go   'I saw him' (enclitic *go*)

(132b)   Mac   *go 'vidav 'Grozana*
          him Procl-Obj – *I saw* – *Grozan* Obj
          'I saw Grozan' (proclitic *go*)

A related usage is found in Bulgarian with Object–Verb – Subject order (7.4.3.3).

b. Clitic forms of the auxiliary 'be'
    Clitic forms of 'be', used as auxiliaries to make compound tenses, are found in all of West and South Slavic, but not East Slavic. As clitics they are written together with the main verb in Polish, where they look more like inflexions, but still fail to attract or affect the stress:

(133)   Pol   *'byliśmy* 'we were'   *czy'talibyśmy* 'we would have read'

They may even be attached to forms other than the verb, that is, they do remain separable, tending to the second position in the clause:

(134)   Pol   *'Gdzieście 'byli?*
                where + Aux-2Pl-Encl – were
                'Where were you?'

In other languages they are written separately:

(135a)   Cz   *'Ukázal jste mu ho?*
                shown – Aux-2Pl-Encl – to him-DatSg-Encl – it-AccSg-Encl
                'Have you shown it to him?'

(135b)   Cz   *'Koupil byste si ho?*
                bought – Cond-2Pl-Encl – self-DatSg-Encl – it-AccSg-Encl
                'Would you have bought it for yourself?'

In Macedonian the auxiliary is sometimes enclitic and sometimes proclitic, but never stressed:

(136a)   Mac   *'ti si 'begal* (*si* enclitic)
                  '(they say that) you have been running'

(136b)   Mac   *si 'begal* (*si* proclitic)

c. Other enclitics
    The Slavic languages contain a variety of other enclitics, including:

    i. question particles (Rus, Cz, Sorb, B/C/S, Blg, Mac)
        (137a)   B/C/S   *li*:   *Jȅ li ôn tȁmo?*   'Is he there?'

(137b)　Rus *li*:　*Býl li ón tám?*　'Was he there?'

　　　　　cf. Pol　*czy*:　'*Czy* 'on '*jest* '*tam*? 'is he there?' (non-clitic)

　ii. conditional particles:

　　　(138)　Rus　*by*:　*Iván by znál*　'Ivan would know.'

　iii. additional markers of imperatives, or other intensifiers:

　　　(139)　Rus *-ka*: *Slúšaj-ka*　'**Listen** (to me, do)!' (Intensive)

　　　　　　Rus　*že*: *Ón že zdés'!* '**He**'s here!

　iv. vocative reinforcers:

　　　(140)　Blg　*be*:　*Iváne be!* 'Ivan!'

None of these enclitic words regularly attracts stress. But virtually any syllable in a word or sentence can be emphasized, and virtually any stressed syllable can lose at least part of its stress in rapid speech.

3.5.1.2　*Predictability in free-stress languages*

In East Slavic and Bulgarian, stress is free – it can occur on any syllable of the word:

(141)　Rus　*skovorodá*　　　　　　'frying-pan'

　　　　　ukládyvajut　　　　　　'they pack'

　　　　　výlitografirovavšiesja　'having been lithographed' [Pl]

Free stress is also mobile – it can move to another syllable in different forms of the same word, whether within an inflexional paradigm:

(142)　Bel　*pisác'* 'to write'　*pišú* 'I write'　*píšaš* 'you [2 Sg] write'

　　　　　Bel　*raká* 'river'　　*réki* [NomPl]

or in word-formation processes:

(143)　Bel　*zólata* 'gold' [Noun]　　*zalatý* 'golden'

　　　　　Bel　*sóxnuc'* 'to dry' [Imprfv]　*výsaxnuc'* [Prfv]

Even native speakers make mistakes with stress. There are some guidelines to stress location: for example, foreign words often have non-mobile stress, and the stress is often located in the same place as in the donor language, particularly with recent borrowings. Most of the clues to stress are morphophonological (rather than lexical or phonological): it is sometimes possible to locate the stress, given certain information about the inflexional pattern of a given root or its affixes.

Within a paradigm the stress may stay on the stem ("fixed-stem stress"):

(144)　Bel 'cloud': *vóblaka*　*vóblaku* [DatSg]　*vóblaki* [NomPl] on the inflexion ("fixcd-end stress"):

> (145)   Bel   'sparrow':   *verabéj* [NomSg] *verab'já* [GenSg] *verab'í* [NomPl]

on the prefix:

> (146)   Bel 'to write out' [Prfv]:   *výpisac'* [Inf]   *výpišu* 'I shall write out'

or on the suffix:

> (147)   Bel 'pupil (fem.)':   *vučaníca* [NomSg] *vučanícy* [NomPl]
> *vučaníc* [GenPl]

These are relatively easy instances, defined lexically: in a given stem, the stress has a given position. Often, however, stress is mobile, and subject to morphophonological alternation. The Russian and Belarusian prefix *vy-* 'out of' is always stressed in perfective verbs (143, 146), and usually in nouns derived from the perfective stem:

> (148)   Rus   *vý-zvat'* 'to call' [Prfv]   *vý-zov* 'call'

but not normally in imperfectives:

> (149)   Rus   *vy-zyvát'* 'to call' [Imprfv]

But *vy-* is the only Russian or Belarusian prefix to behave in this way. More frequent are shifts between the grammatical forms of stem and inflexion. Of the five free-stress languages, Bulgarian is the least complex, thanks largely to the loss of its case system:

> (150a)   Blg   *dušá* 'soul'   *dušé* [VocSg] *duší* [NomPl]
> *dušáta* 'the soul'
>
> (150b)   Blg   *kost* 'bone'   *kósti* [Pl]   *kosttá* 'the bone'
>
> (150c)   Blg   *vésel* 'happy'   *veselják* 'happy man'

Stress shifts occur within the verb system:

> (151a)   Blg   *móga* 'I can'   *možáx* 'I could' [Aor]
>
> (151b)   Rus   *mogú* 'I can'   *móžeš'* 'you [Sg] can'

It is possible to identify areas of individual paradigms where stress shifts are more likely to occur. The plural of nouns, for instance, may differ from the singular:

> (152a)   Bel   'brother':   *brat* [NomSg]   *bráta* [GenSg]   *bratý* [NomPl]
> 'window':   *aknó* [NomSg]   *vókny* [NomPl]
>
> (152b)   Rus   'wall':   *stená* [NomSg]   *stený* [GenSg]   *stény* [NomPl]

The accusative singular of feminine nouns may differ from the rest of the singular paradigm:

(153)   Rus   *ruká* 'arm'   *rúku* [AccSg]   *rukí* [GenSg]   *rúki* [NomPl]

Russian masculine nominative plurals in *-a* are always end-stressed, and the inflexions of the rest of their plural paradigm are also stressed:

(154)   Rus 'professor':   *proféssor* [NomSg]   *proféssora* [GenSg]
                             professorá [NomPl]   *professoróv* [GenPl] (etc.)

Feminine inflexions for short-form adjectives and *l*-participles are more likely to attract stress than other inflexions:

(155)   Rus   *žit'* 'to live'; Past tense *žil, žilá, žílo, žíli*

Furthermore, some roots are inherently marked as fixed-end-stressed. In these, if the suffix or ending is zero, the stress falls on the last syllable of the root:

(156a)   Rus 'table': *stol* ({stol + ǿ})   *stolá* [GenSg]   *stolý* [NomPl]

(156b)   Ukr 'was':   *buv* [buṷ] [Masc] ({bul + ǿ})
                        bulá [Fem] *buló* [Neut] *bulý* [Plur]

The citation forms (infinitive for verbs, nominative singular for nouns, etc.) are not reliable guides to the location or behavior of stress, and there is no simple rule for determining it. There have, however, been many valuable attempts at formalizing stress behavior in these languages.

3.5.2   Quantity

Length is not a distinctive property of Slavic consonants. In some Slavic languages (morpho-)phonological rules can give rise to double consonants, like the instrumental singular of some feminine *i*-stem nouns in Ukrainian (5.5.1.4):

(157)   'night': Ukr   *nič* [NomSg]   *níččju* [InstrSg]
                 cf. Rus   *noč'*   *nóč'ju*

Double consonants may also occur intervocally across morpheme boundaries, specifically 'prefix + root' and 'root + suffix':

(158a)   Slk *pod-daný* 'subjected' (cf. *po-daný* 'handed to')

(158b)   'judge':   Bel *suddzjá*   Ukr *suddjá*   (cf. Rus *sud'já*)

(158c)   Rus *napísan-nyj* 'written'

and root-internally in borrowings:

    (159)   Rus   *Ánna* 'Anna'   *grúppa* 'group'

But such native geminates are often pronounced as a single consonant, and always in Czech (see above 3.4.3.3). In Russian single pronunciation is relatively rare, but interestingly it occurs in the root *ross-*: *Rossíja* 'Russia', *rossíjskij* 'Russian' (and in the parallel "ethnic" root *russk-*, but here regularly because of the adjacent consonant /k/); otherwise (intervocal) native geminates always have a morpheme boundary and are pronounced long.

Vowel length was phonemic in Indo-European and in late Proto-Slavic. In the modern Slavic languages it is phonemic only in Czech, Slovak, Slovenian and B/C/S. It survived in Polish until the sixteenth century. Slovenian shows the weakest utilization of length, which is contrastive only in stressed final syllables and monosyllables. Other stressed syllables have been uniformly lengthened and unstressed have been shortened. In the tonal variant of Slovenian, only falling tones contrast for length (since there is no short rising tone):

    (160)   Sln

Short	Long: Tonal	Long: Non-tonal
bràt 'brother'	*brȃt* 'read' (Supine)	*brát*
spì 'sleep!' (2 Sg)	*spȋ* 'he sleeps'	*spí*
kùp 'stack, heap'	*kȗp* 'purchase'	*kúp*

The vowel /ə/ is always short, and vocalic /r̥/ (or /ər/) always long, while the other vowels may be either short or long.

In B/C/S length is a more important part of the phonological system. The two tones are contrasted for length, making four types of pitch accent in all, as seen in (161a–b). The quantity is phonemically contrastive, as in these minimal pairs:

    (161a)   B/C/S   *grȁd* (short falling) 'hail'   *grȃd* (long falling) 'town, city'

    (161b)   B/C/S   *vàljati* (short rising) 'to be good'   *váljati* (long rising) 'to roll'

In addition, any post-tonic syllable may also be long or short, and here length is distinctive also:

    (162a)   B/C/S   *stvȃr* 'thing'   [LocSg] *stvári*   [GenPl] *stvárī*

This length contrast is often accompanied by tonal changes elsewhere in the word:

    (162b)   B/C/S   *žèna* 'woman'   [GenPl] *zénā*

Vocalic /r̥/ also may be long or short:

    (163a)   B/C/S   *Tȓst* (short falling) 'Trieste'   *tȓst* (long falling) 'cane'

    (163b)   B/C/S   *tȑpati* (short rising) 'to throw'   *tŕpeti* (long rising) 'to endure'

In Czech and Slovak we find minimal pairs which contrast for length:

(164a)   Cz   *vada* 'fault'   *váda* 'quarrel'

(164b)   Cz   *piji* 'I drink'   *pijí* 'they drink'

(164c)   Slk   *pas* 'passport'   *pás* 'belt'

Like B/C/S, Czech and Slovak also have contrastive length on unstressed (= post-tonic) vowels. Any syllable in Czech or Slovak may be long, including in Slovak the vocalic /r̥ l̥/, which are only short in Czech. The long and short vowels are not fully paired, since the long partner is often a diphthong:

(165a)   Cz   Short   i   e   a   o   u   r̥   l̥
                Long   ī   ē   ā   ū/(ō)   ū/ou̯   –   –

(165b)   Slk   Short   i   e   a   ä   o   u   r̥   l̥
                Long   ī   ē/i̯e   ā/i̯a   i̯a   ō/u̯o   ū/i̯u   r̥̄   l̥̄

In Slovak the long/short contrast is neutralized by a special Slovak Rhythmic Law: long vowels, which include the diphthongs, cannot occur in consecutive syllables. The second syllable is usually shortened:

(166)   Slk   *pekný* 'nice' ~ *krásny*   'beautiful' cf. Cz *krásný*
                 myslím 'I think' ~ *chválim* 'I praise'   cf. Cz *chválím*

The exceptions often involve diphthongs, and most occur in 'prefix + root' or 'root + suffix' combinations:

(167a)   Slk   compound: *tisíc-násobný* 'a thousandfold'

(167b)   Slk   'prefix + root':   *zá-sielka* 'parcel' (i.e. not *záselka)

(167c)   Slk   'root + inflexion': *chvál-ia* 'they praise'

(167d)   Slk   'root + suffix':   *mliek-ár* 'milkman' *páv-í* 'peacock's'

The length of comparable vowels between these four languages does not always agree. Such variations arise from several causes: the lengthening of non-final stressed syllables in Slovenian, and its lack of atonic length; the leftwards movement of stress and new rising tones in B/C/S (3.5.3); and the non-parallel evolution of individual sounds. The Slovenian ~ /B/C/S correspondences are given in 3.5.3 below. In Czech and Slovak vowels agree for length in the majority of cases. The exceptions are partly covered by the Slovak Rhythmic Law, and by regular phonological rules, like the equivalence of Cz *ů* and Slk *ô*. Others include:

	Czech	Slovak
'to give'	*dát*	*dat'*
'summer'	*léto*	*leto*

'end'	*konec*	*koniec*
'lower'	*níže*	*niže*
'house'	*dům*	*dom*

Long unstressed vowels in Czech and Slovak are approximately as long as short stressed vowels; long stressed vowels are about twice as long. Only Czech and Slovak regularly mark length in their orthography, B/C/S and Slovenian mark it (as with tone) only in lexicographical and pedagogical works.

3.5.3 Tone

Both Indo-European and Proto-Slavic had phonemic tone, but it survives in modern Slavic only in B/C/S and Slovenian. The historical development of tone (see 3.2.4.3) is closely linked to stress. In Late Proto-Slavic tone was found on only one syllable per word. The tonic syllable had the same phonetic properties as stressed syllables in the modern languages.

Standard Slovenian is presented in two variants: the stress (non-tonal) type and the tonal type. The tonal type was formalized and sanctioned by the Academy in Ljubljana, although it is not a compulsory part of the school curriculum. The two variants are parallel for the location of the prominent syllable, and for length. There is some controversy about whether Slovenian has pitch at all, especially since the pitches are perceptually less evident than in B/C/S. The pitch variant contains a long rising (´), short falling (`) and long falling (^) pitch. Short falling pitch is found mainly on final syllables and monosyllables:

(168)　Sln　*pès* [pəs] 'dog' (PSl *pьsъ*)　*precèj* 'rather' [-ej]

In the non-tonal variant this pitch is simply short, and is marked in dictionaries by the grave (a double grave in Pleteršnik's version).

Pitch is therefore contrastive only between the two long pitches, which can occur in any position in the word. In the non-tonal variant, /a i u r/ are simply long and are marked by the acute; long open /e/ and /o/ and close /é/ and /ó/, the latter marked in the Pleteršnik version by a subscript dot, are marked by the (round) circumflex and acute respectively. In the discussion of pitch we disregard the quality of /e/ and /o/.

In standard B/C/S, following the model of Vuk Karadžić, there are two pitches, and vowels may also be either long or short. The combined features are marked: long rising (´), short rising (`), long falling (^) and short falling (ˇ). The falling tones can occur only on initial syllables or in monosyllables (representing the original stress position):

(169)　B/C/S　*zȁmak* (short falling)　cf. Rus *zámok* 'castle'

No final syllable (of a polysyllabic word) can be stressed:

(170)   B/C/S   *stòla* [GenSg] (short rising)   cf. Rus *stolá* 'table'

Rising tones reflect a leftwards movement of the stress by one syllable, when compared to Proto-Slavic or the other free-stress languages (see 3.2.4.3). The underlying length of the new stressed vowel was retained:

(171a)   B/C/S   *povréditi* 'to harm' [Prfv]   cf. Rus *povredít'*

(171b)   B/C/S   *ùčitelj* 'teacher'   cf. Blg *učítel*   Sln *učítelj*   Rus *učítel'*

The major dialects (Štokavian) are all consistent with this pattern, provided that we remember that the Jekavian variant will show the falling pitch on the first of its two syllables, and the rising on the second:

(172a)   'hay':   PSl *sêno* (falling)   Rus *séno*   Sln *senô*   B/C/S *sêno, sîjeno*

(172b)   'river':   PSl *reká* (rising)   Rus *reká*   Sln *réka*   B/C/S *réka, rijèka*

Non-standard dialects, however, vary widely in their tonal properties. The *kaj*-variant (Kajkavian) is a compromise with Slovenian, and the *ča-* variant (Čakavian) is much closer to Proto-Slavic (10.2.2).

Some studies have cast doubt on the maintenance of the full four-tone system in modern standard B/C/S. Magner and Matejka (1971) claimed that while tones were passively understood, and were part of the literary standard, the speech of educated (and some less educated) people of the central Serbian-Croatian region showed that it was stress, not tone, which was the crucial functional category of Serbo-Croatian phonology. Nonetheless, the Karadžić model continues to be taught, and is widely received as the official standard, at least of Serbian.

When we compare the tones of Slovenian and B/C/S, we find some important differences. The location of the stressed syllable in Slovenian agrees moderately well with that in the free- and mobile-stress Slavic languages, especially in the fact that any syllable in the word may be stressed. In B/C/S, however, final syllables cannot be stressed, except in monosyllables within a phrase. Where possible the stress has moved leftwards by one syllable. The same leftwards shift occurred also in Slovenian, but only from short final syllables. It is counterbalanced in Slovenian by a rightwards shift from a falling pitch, which could land on the final syllable. The retracted stress always gave a rising pitch in B/C/S, as it did also in Slovenian except when landing on /ə/. In contrast, the rightwards shift in Slovenian gave a long falling pitch. Stressed syllables also differ in length: they are usually long in Slovenian, but in B/C/S may be either long or short. Examples of differences thus produced are:

(173)   PSl   B/C/S   Sln (tonal)   (non-tonal)
'ninth'   *devêtъjь*   *dèvētī*   *devêti*   *devêti*
'hay'   *sêno*   *sêno*   *senộ*   *senó*
'village' *se'lo*   *sèlo*   *sêlo*   *sêlo*
'measure' *méra*   *mȅra*   *mẹ́ra*   *méra*
'brother' *brátrъ*   *brȁt*   *bràt*   *bràt*

Pitch, like length, is phonetically relative. Just as stressed short syllables may be longer than unstressed long syllables (3.5.2), so a high pitch may be phonetically lower than a low pitch within the intonation contour of the sentence or phrase.

4

Morphophonology

4.1 Overview

Morphophonology (North American "morphonology") is richly exemplified in Slavic, for example:

(1a) PREFIX ALTERNATION IN PREFIX + ROOT
B/C/S *bez-* 'without' + *právo* 'right' (+ -*n-* [Adj])
= *bèsprávan* 'without rights'
(i.e. regressive assimilation of voicing of /z/ to /s/, caused by the following voiceless /p/; this is standard in Slavic, though often not reflected in orthography)

(1b) ROOT ALTERNATION IN PREFIX + ROOT
Rus *pred-* 'pre-' + *istórija* 'history' = *predystórija* 'prehistory'
(i.e. *i* becomes *y* after the hard *d* of *pred-*)

(1c) ROOT ALTERNATION IN ROOT + SUFFIX
Rus *knig-* 'book' [Noun] + -*n-yj* [Adj] > *knížnyj* 'bookish'
(i.e. regressive mutation of /g/ to /ž/ = First Palatalization of Velars)

(1d) ROOT ALTERNATION IN ROOT + INFLEXION
Pol *matka* 'mother' + Dat Sg -*e* > *matce*
(i.e. *k* > *c* by the Second Palatalization of Velars)

The standard approach in Slavic linguistics is to view alternations as processes. One form is changed to another form by means of a rule: mutation is such a rule, which – for instance – changes /g/ to /ž/ in (1c). Alternations occur in prefixes, roots and suffixes, in specific combinations of these three elements.

Such alternations show many processes identical with automatic phonological change, like palatalization and assimilation. But some morphophonological alternations, like many vowel alternations, do not have an obvious phonological rationale. English has a common Indo-European vowel alternation in examples like *swim, swam, swum*. In Slavic we find similar examples:

(2a) Slk   *niest'* 'to carry' [Determinate] *nesiem* 'I carry'
               nosit' 'to carry' [Indeterminate]

(2b) Slk   *chlieb* 'bread' [NomSg]   *chleba*   [GenSg]

(2c) Rus   *brat'* 'to take'   *berú*   'I take'
             -birát' verbs, with prefixes   *podbirát'* 'to select'
             -bor nouns, with prefixes   *podbór* 'selection'

Alternations within inflexions or across morpheme boundaries can present patterns of a different order:

(3) Bel   [NomSg]   [LocSg]   [NomPl]

     'young man' *junák* [-k]   *junakú* [-ku]   *junakí* [-k^{j}i]
     '(river) bank' *bérah* [-x]   *béraze* [-z^{j}ɛ]   *berahí* [-ɣ^{j}i]

The nominative plural forms are phonologically transparent, and follow the phonological rules for *i/y* after velars. But in the locative singular forms the /h ~ z/ alternation in *berah* is historically the /g ~ z/ alternation of the Second Palatalization of Velars (PV2; 1.3.1.5), with the regular modern spirantized Belarusian reflex of Proto-Slavic */g/. This, as well as the selection of the endings *-e* in *béraze* and *-u* in *junakú*, are governed by morphological factors.

Morphophonological alternations can be classified in two main ways: by the surface phonological properties of the alternations themselves; and by the morphological factors in which the alternations occur. We present a descriptive summary of the vowel (4.2) and consonant (4.3) alternations and their conditioning morphological environments (4.4–4.5) before relating these alternations to underlying forms and derivational rules (4.6). Some of these alternations date from before the period of Proto-Slavic, and are found in all the Slavic languages. Others are more recent, and their application (or not) forms part of the morphophonological typology of the individual languages.

4.2   Vowel alternations

Vowel alternations ("ablaut") follow the Indo-European pattern: change of vowel quality, vowel loss, cluster simplification (via vowel insertion) and alternation of length and pitch. Czech also has a later umlaut (Cz *přehláska*, or alternation of quality, 4.2.6).

4.2.1   Vowel ~ zero alternations

Vowel ~ zero alternations arise in most cases from the preservation or deletion of the *jers*, the original Proto-Slavic short vowels ъ and ь, especially in original final and penultimate syllables (3.2.1.1). These deletions destroyed the Proto-Slavic pattern of open syllables, and created new consonant clusters as well as classes of words ending in consonants. They also created the conditions for alternation in words with *jers* in the final two syllables. (For further examples, see 3.2.1.1.)

In nouns the main context of realized vowels in vowel ~ zero alternations is before zero inflexions (a, b, d, f):

a.   masculine singular nominative, e.g.:

(4)   'dog' (PSl *pьsъ* [NomSg] ~ *pьsa* [GenSg]):
     Rus *pës* ~ *psa* Cz *pes* ~ *psa* Pol *pies* ~ *psa* B/C/S *pȁs* ~ *psȁ*

b.   the genitive plural of some feminine and neuter nouns:

(5a)   'light' (PSl *svĕtьlo* [NomSg] ~ *svĕtьlъ* [GenPl]):
      Slk *svetlo* ~ *svetiel* Cz *svĕtlo* ~ *svĕtel* Pol *światło* ~ *świateł*

(5b)   'sentry-box' (PSl *budъka* [NomSg] ~ *budъkъ* [GenPl]):
      Rus, Ukr *búdka* ~ *búdok*   Bel *búdka* ~ *búdak*

c.   the instrumental singular of III-declension nouns, which have vowel inflexions in the nominative-accusative singular *vs* most of the other forms, as in (a), but in the instrumental singular the inflexion also contained a (weak) *jer*, and so also gives a vowel alternant (optionally regularized in Belarusian):

(6)   'love' (PSl *ljuby* [NomSg] ~ *ljubъvь* [AccSg] ~ *ljubъvi* [GenSg] ~ *ljubъvьjǫ* [InstrSg]):
     Rus   *ljubóv′* [Nom-AccSg] ~ *ljubví* ~ *ljubóv′ju*
     Bel   *ljubóŭ* [Nom-AccSg] ~ *ljubví/ljubóvi* ~ *ljubóŭju*

d.   In adjectives the zero ending occurs in the short form (nominative) masculine singular:

(7)   'narrow' (PSl *ǫzъkъ* [NomSgMasc] ~ *ǫzъka* [NomSgFem]):
     Rus *úzok* ~ *uzká* B/C/S *ȕzak* ~ *ȕska* Sln *ózek* ~ *ózka*

e.   Consonant-final prepositions and prefixes may also insert a fleeting vowel (usually originally a weak *jer*) before a following consonant

cluster where the new enlarged cluster would otherwise violate phonotactic rules (see 3.4.3). There is some variation between languages:

(8)   Cz   *skočit* [Imprfv] (*seskočit* [Prfv]) *s mostu* 'to jump off the bridge'
      sklidit [Prfv] (*klidit* [Imprfv]) *se stolu* 'to clear the table'
      Rus *v srédu* 'on Wednesday' ~ *vo vtórnik* 'on Tuesday'

f.   In verb systems vowel ~ zero alternations occur in asyllabic verb roots
     (i.e. roots not containing a surface vowel) when a consonantal inflex-
     ion (e.g. infinitive) follows: Rus *terét'* 'to rub', *tr-u* 'I rub' (these are not
     originally "asyllabic", but *jers* – e.g. *tьr-* – and they usually belong in
     the "pre-Slavic" vowel alternation group like *br-/ber-/bor-* in (2c))

Some inserted vowels do not derive from *jers*, but are "fill vowels" (see 3.2.1.1),
whose role is to simplify (especially final) consonant clusters:

a.   early insertions, at the time of the loss of the *jers*:

(9)   'fire' (PSl *ognъ* [NomSg] ~ *ognja* [GenSg]):
      Rus *ogón'* ~ *ognjá*   Pol *ogień* ~ *ognia*

b.   in clusters not contrary to the Proto-Slavic rule of rising sonority, later
     insertions by the more vocalic languages (3.2.3.1: those less tolerant of
     consonant clusters, especially finally), notably B/C/S:

(10a) 'good' (PSl *dobrъ* [MascNomSg] ~ *dobra* [FemNomSg]):
       B/C/S   *dȍbar* ~ *dòbra*
       Blg   *dobǎr* ~ *dobrá*
       cf. Rus *dobr* ~ *dobrá*

(10b) 'theatre':
       B/C/S   *teȁtar* [NomSg] ~ *teȁtru* [LocSg]
       cf. Rus *teátr* ~ *teátra*

Neither of these types of inserted vowels is determined by purely phonological
factors. Some of the consonant clusters which they interrupt are indeed possible,
but are not permitted in precisely the morphological environments where these
alternations occur in parallel to those from *jers*. Russian, for instance, allows final
/-ml'/ in *Kreml'* 'Kremlin' [NomSg] but not in *zemél'* 'earth' [GenPl] (not *zeml'*)
(PSl *zem(l)jь*); and Polish allows /-sł/ in *niósł* 'he carried', but not in *wiosło* 'oar'
[NomSg], *wioseł* [GenPl] (not *wiósł*).

A common context illustrating this uncertainty is the former *l*-participle (like Pol
niósł), which is now either the full past tense (East Slavic) or the form of the main

verb used in compound forms (West and South Slavic). Historically, this is an adjectival (short) form (5.5.2.1) in which the *l*-suffix is added directly to the infinitive stem, without any *jer*. The range of development includes deletion, that is, a consonant (/l/) ~ zero alternation:

(11) 'be able' (PSl *mog-* :   *moglъ* [Masc] ~ *mogla* [Fem]):
    a. vowel ~ zero   Slk *mohol* ~ *mohla*
    b. consonant ~ zero   Rus *mog* (**mogl*) ~ *moglá*
    c. vowel ~ zero AND vowel ~ consonant B/C/S *mȍgao* ~ *mȍgla*
    d. vowel (syllabic consonant) ~ consonant Cz *mohl* (syllabic /l̥/) ~ *mohla*
    e. no alternation   Pol *mógł* ~ *mogła*
    (consonantal /w/: phonetically in colloquial speech > type (b): *mógł* > [muk])

The alternation *e* ~ *ø* (12a), and the less extensive *i* ~ *ø* (12f), may be accompanied by palatalization of the preceding consonant(s), depending on the capacity of /e/ and /i/ to cause prepalatalization in individual languages (3.4.1). There may also be simplification of consonant clusters in those forms where the fill vowel does not appear:

(12a)   e ~ ø

Rus	'earth'	*zemél'*	[GenPl]	*zemljá*	[NomSg]
	'cold'	*xóloden*	[Short]	*xolódnyj*	[Long, MascNomSg]
	'lad'	*páren'*	[NomSg]	*párnja*	[GenSg]
Pol	'dog'	*pies*	[NomSg]	*psa*	[GenSg]
	'tear'	*łez*	[GenPl]	*łza*	[NomSg]
	'without me'	*beze mnie*	'without us'		*bez nas*
	'mother'	*matek*	[GenPl]	*matka*	[NomSg]
Slk	'soap'	*mydiel*	[GenPl]	*mydlo*	[NomSg]

(12b)   o ~ ø

Rus	'bonfire'	*kostër*	NomAccSg	*kostrá*	[GenSg]
	'window'	*ókon*	[GenPl]	*oknó*	[NomSg]
Pol	'donkey'	*osioł*	[NomAccSg]	*osła*	[GenSg]
Sorb	'dog'	*pos*	[NomSg]	*psa*	[GenSg]
	'to take'	*wozmu*	'I take'	*wzać*	[Inf]
Slk	'cap'	*čiapok*	[GenPl]	*čiapka*	[NomSg]

(12c)   a ~ ø

B/C/S	'flexible'	*gȉbak*	[MascNomSg]	*gȉpka*	[FemNomSg]
	'notebook'	*svȅzākā*	[GenPl]	*svȅska*	[NomSg]

	Mac	'good'	*dobar*	[MascNomSg]	*dobra*	[FemNomSg]
		'theatre'	*teatar*	[Sg]	*teatri*	[Pl]
(12d)	ă ∼ ø					
	Blg	'theatre'	*teátăr*	[Sg]	*teátri*	[Pl]
		'dead'	*mắrtăv*	[MascSg]	*mắrtvi*	[Pl]
(12e)	ô ∼ ø					
	Slk	'bowl'	*misôk*	[GenPl]	*miska*	[NomSg]
(12f)	i ∼ ø					
	Rus	'third'	*trétij*	[MascNomSg]	*trét′ja*	[FemNomSg]
				(= /tret′-j-ø/)		
		'ravine'	*uščélij*	[GenPl]	*uščél′e*	[NomSg]
						(= /l′j-e/)

Vowel ∼ zero alternations can form part of a series of alternations involving a number of vowels, especially in derivations from asyllabic (mainly former weak *jer*) verb roots, as in the *ø* ∼ *e* ∼ *i* series in Czech: *brat* 'to take [Imprfv]', *beru* 'I take', *vybirat* 'to choose [Imprfv]'.

4.2.2   Vowel lengthening

The languages with contrastive length in modern Slavic are Czech, Slovak, B/C/S and Slovenian (3.5.2). In Czech and Slovak alternations involving length are often associated with changes in vowel quality, including the effects of *přehláska* (umlaut) in Czech (4.2.6) and diphthongization in Slovak.

Vowel lengthening occurs in somewhat different morphological environments from vowel ∼ zero alternations. Apart from the typical zero ∼ non-zero ending condition, we also find some vowel lengthening in word formation, and a more extensive use in verb inflexion and aspect derivation. In Slovak some alternations are caused by the Slovak Rhythmic Law (3.5.2), a phonological rather than morphophonological process (Slovak diphthongs count as long vowels):

(13a)	ā ∼ a (all four languages)				
	Cz	'frost'	*mráz*	[NomAccSg]	*mrazu*	[GenSg]
		'contented'	*spokojená*	[FemNomSg]	*spokojena*	'satisfied' [Pred]
	Slk	'rain'	*dážd′*	[NomAccSg]	*dažd′a*	[GenSg]
		'voice'	*hlások*	[Dim]	*hlas*	[NomAccSg]
		'to seat'	*sádzat′*	[Imprfv]	*sadzač*	'typesetter'
	B/C/S	'town'	*grâd*	[Sg]	*grȁdovi*	[Pl]

(13b) ē ~ e (Cz, B/C/S, Sln); ie ~ e (Slk)

Cz	'bread'	*chléb*	[NomAccSg]	*chleba*	[GenSg]
B/C/S	'honey'	*mêd*	[NomAccSg]	*mȅda*	[GenSg]
Sln	'bread'	*hléba*	[GenSg]	*hlèb*	[NomAccSg]
Slk	'bread'	*chlieb*	[NomAccSg]	*chleba*	[GenSg]

(13c) ī ~ e (Cz)

Cz	'belief'	*víra*	[NomSg]	*věřit*	'to believe' [vjɛ-]

(13d) ū ~ o (Cz)

Cz	'house'	*dům*	[NomAccSg]	*domu*	[GenSg]
	'my'	*můj*	[MascNomSg]	*moja*	[FemNomSg]

(13e) ȳ ~ y (Cz, Slk)

Slk	'to breathe'	*dýchat'*	[Imprfv]	*dych*	'breath'
Cz	'to be'	*být*		*byl*	'he was'

(13f) ā ~ a ~ o (all four languages)

Slk	'to go out'	*vycházat'*	[Imprfv]	*vychodit'*	[Prfv]
B/C/S	'to answer'	*odgovárati*	[Imprfv]	*odgovòriti*	[Prfv]
Sln	'to give to drink'	*napájati*	[Imprfv]	*napojíti*	[Prfv]

(The other main imperfectivizing suffixes with -*va*- are discussed below.)

4.2.3   Vowel tone alternations

Alternations of tone occur in B/C/S and Slovenian (and also often operate together with alternations of quality, especially high ~ low /e ~ o/ in Slovenian):

(14)	B/C/S	'father'	*òtac*	*ȏče*	[VocSg]
		'to throw'	*báciti*	*bâcen*	[Past Part Pass]
	Sln	'town'	*mésto*	*mẹ̑sta*	[Pl]
		'to twist'	*víti*	*vît*	[Sup]

4.2.4   Stress alternations

At the phonetic level, stress alternations result in quality alternations in those languages in which quality is related to stress. These are treated in the next section (4.2.5). The primary function of stress alternation lies in the shifting of stress position within paradigms, which is possible only in languages with mobile stress. In the two languages with fixed but mobile stress, that is, Polish and Macedonian, the patterns are usually predictable on the basis of word shape.

In the free-stress languages – all of East and South Slavic except for Macedonian –
the patterns are often not predictable. In both types the most common opposition
is between stem- and inflexion-stress, with three basic patterns of "fixed-stem",
"fixed-inflexional (fixed-end)" and "mobile", the last having potentially a large
number of "patterns", but in practice restricted to 'singular ~ plural' in nouns and
'1Sg ~ rest' in the non-past tense of verbs. These patterns are discussed and
exemplified in 5.5.

4.2.5 Vowel quality alternations

Vowel quality alternations take several forms, some of which may occur
simultaneously:

a. alternations of quality *per se* (ablaut)
b. alternations of stress: unstressed vowels may have different quality,
    particularly in Russian, Belarusian and Bulgarian (3.3.2.6, 3.5.1)
c. combined alternations of quality and length

There are relatively few combinations of sounds in alternations of this last type.
Their morphological environments are approximately the same as those in vowel ~
zero alternations, though alternations of vowel quality combine with other types of
alternation in various forms of the verb, especially in aspect formation.
Palatalizations often occur with such alternations of vowel quality:

(15) Vowel quality alternations

o ~ e	Blg	*duxóven*	'spiritual'	*dušéven*	'emotional'
	Ukr	*vozýty*	'to convey' [Indet]	*vézty*	'to convey' [Det]
	Sorb	*žona*	'wife'	*ženić*	'to marry' (of a man)
	Pol	*aniol*	'angel'	*aniele*	'angels'
	Cz	*nosit*	'to carry' [Indet]	*nést*	[Det]
a ~ e	Blg	*bjal*	'white'	*béli*	[Pl]
	Rus	*sadít'sja*	'to sit down' [Imprfv]	*sest'*	[Prfv]
	Pol	*bialy*	'white'	*bieli*	[MascAnim NomPl]
		kwiat	'flower'	*kwiecie*	[LocSg]
	Sorb	*pijach*	'I drank' [Imperf]	*piješe*	[2–3 Sg]
		rjad	'row'	*rjedźe*	[LocSg]
e ~ i	Rus	*bréju*	'I shave'	*brit'*	'to shave'
	Ukr	*letíty*	'to fly' [Det]	*litáty*	'to fly' [Indet]

o ~ u	Rus	*sóxnuť*	'to dry'	*suxój*	'dry'[Adj]
	Pol	*pokoju*	'room' [LocSg]	*pokój*	([-uj])
					[NomSg]
		grožba	'threat'	*gróžb*	[GenPl]
o ~ i/y	Rus	*móju*	'I wash'	*myť*	'to wash'
	Ukr	*konjá*	[GenSg]	*kiń*	'horse'
o ~ a	Ukr	*stojáty*	'to stand'	*statý*	'to become'
	Rus	*sprosíť*	'to inquire' [Prfv]	*sprášivať*	'to inquire'
					[Imprfv]
a ~ i/y	Rus	*sadíťsja*	'to sit down'	*sidéť*	'to sit'
					[Intrans]
	Ukr	*sadýty*	'to seat' [Trans]	*sydíty*	'to sit'
					[Intrans]
u ~ e	Pol	*przyjaciół*	'friend'	*przyjaciele*	[Pl]
ą ~ ę	Pol	*ząb*	'tooth'	*zęba*	[GenSg]
		rąk	'hand' [GenPl]	*ręka*	[NomSg]
o ~ ó/ô	Slk	*stola*	'table' [GenSg]	*stôl*	[NomAccSg]
		noha	'leg, foot' [NomSg]	*nôžka*	[Dim]
	Sorb	*loda/lodu*	'ice' [GenSg]	*lód*	[NomAccSg]
vowel ~ nasal consonant					
	Rus	*načáť*	'to begin'	*načnú*	'I shall begin'
	B/C/S	*nàčēti*	'to begin'	*nằčnēm*	'I shall begin'

There are also many instances of complex alternations involving several vowels,
sometimes including both zero and quality alternations:

(16)	Rus	**dux**	'spirit'	**dýšit**	'he breathes'
		vzdyxáť	'to breathe'	**vzdox**	'sigh'
		brať	'to take'	**berú**	'I take'
		vybirát	'to choose'	**výbor**	'choice'

4.2.6   Czech *přehláska* (umlaut)

Czech *přehláska* (umlaut) (1.7.3.3, 3.2.1.5, 3.4.3.1) is an automatic phonological rule operating irrespective of the morphological environment. However,
it also affects morphophonology across the boundary between stems and endings, and so has had an important effect on the formation of "soft" inflexional
types (5.5).

Vowels mutate after the Czech palatal consonants /ď t' n' ř j/ and the formerly
palatal consonants /č š ž/ (now post-alveolar) and /c/ (now dental). Using

the standard examples *žena* 'woman', *duše* 'soul', *město* 'town' and *moře* 'sea', they include:

(17) Czech *přehláska*

y > e	*ženy*	*duše*	[GenSg]
a > e	*žena*	*duše*	[NomSg]
á > í	*ženám*	*duším*	[DatPl]
o > e	*ženo*	*duše*	[VocSg]
u > i	*ženu*	*duši*	[AccSg]
ou > í	*ženou*	*duší*	[InstSg]
ů > í	*městům*	*mořím*	[DatPl]

Most of the changes involve raising (as we would expect from the Slavic tendency to (syn-) harmony (1.3.1.3) after palatals) or fronting, and have the effect of markedly reducing the variety of distinct inflexions, as can be seen from the listing of "soft" noun and adjective inflexion types in chapter 5.

4.3 Consonant alternations

The majority of consonant alternations involve palatalization, mainly a direct result of the velar and /j/ palatalizations of Proto-Slavic (on which see 1.3.1.5 and 3.2.2.3), but also of the phonemicization of additive palatalization where this occurred. These alternations are found in inflexion, usually before *j/i/e*, and in some word-forming elements which cause mutation. The main question in palatalizing contexts is how far the palatalization will go: as far as additive palatalization (C ~ C'), which is found mainly in nouns and adjectives?; or as far as mutation (or "replacive palatalization")? The degree of palatalization is restricted by the phonological rules of individual languages. Russian, for instance, shows the effects of the First Palatalization of Velars (PV1), but not of PV2. At other times the deciding factor is morphological, or a combination of morphological and phonological. For example, in Slovak PV2 effects occur only in the nominative plural of masculine nouns ending in -*k* or -*ch* (see (20)).

4.3.1 Palatalization

4.3.1.1 *Additive palatalization*

(18) Additive palatalization (*syllables* are bolded where appropriate)

p ~ p'	Pol	'peasant'	*chłop* [NomSg]	*chłopi* [Pl]
b ~ b'	Pol	'weak'	*słaby* [NomSgMasc]	*słabi* [MascPersNomPl]

m ∼ m′	Pol	'dumb'	*niemy* [NomSgMasc]	*niemi* [MascPersNomPl]
w ∼ w′	Sorb	'grave'	*row* [NomSg)	*rowje* [LocSg]
f ∼ f′	Rus	'telegraph'	*telegráf* [NomSg]	*telegrafírovat'* [Verb]
v ∼ v′	Rus	'cart'	*voz* [NomSg]	*vĕz* 'he conveyed'
t ∼ t′/t'	Cz	'hut, cabin'	*chata* [NomSg]	*chatĕ* [Dat-LocSg]
d ∼ d′/d'	Cz	'bear'	*medvĕd* [NomSg]	*medvĕdi* [NomPl]
n ∼ n′/n'	Slk	'splinter'	*trnka* [Dim]	*tŕň* [NomSg]
s ∼ s′	Rus	'I carry'	*nesú*	*nesëš'* 'you [Sg] carry'
z ∼ z′	Bel	'I gnaw'	*hryzú*	*hryzéš* 'you [Sg] gnaw'
l ∼ ł	Sorb	'happy'	*wjesoły* [MascNomSg]	*wjeseli* [PersNomPl]
l ∼ l′/l'	Bel	'table'	*stalá* [GenSg]	*stalé* [LocSg]
r ∼ r′	Rus	'beaver'	*bobr* [NomSg]	*bobré* [LocSg]
k ∼ k′	Blg	'torment'	*mắka* [Sg]	*mắki* [Pl]
g ∼ g′	Pol	'horn'	*rogu* [GenSg]	*rogi* [Pl]
x ∼ x′	Bel	'fly'	*múxa* [NomSg]	*múxi* [GenSg]
h ∼ h′	Ukr	'dear'	*dorohýj* [MascNomSg]	*dorohí* [NomPl]

4.3.1.2   *Mutation of labials (/l/ epenthesis)*

Labials in East Slavic, Slovenian and B/C/S generally insert /l/ before /j/ in the 1 Person singular non-past (East Slavic only), past participle passive and verbal noun:

(19)	p ∼ pl′	Rus	'to buy'	*kupít'*	[Prfv]	*kupljú*	'I will buy' [Prfv]
	cf.	Pol	'to buy'	*kupić*	[Prfv]	*kupię*	'I will buy' [Prfv]
	b ∼ bl′	Rus	'to love'	*ljubít'*	[Imprfv]	*ljubljú*	'I love'
	f ∼ fl′	Bel	'to rule'	*hrafíc'*	[Imprfv]	*hrafljú*	'I rule' (paper)
	v ∼ vl′	Rus	'I live'	*živú*	[Imprfv]	*oživlénie* 'animation'	
	m ∼ ml′	Bel	'to feed'	*karmíc'*	[Imprfv]	*karmljú*	'I feed'

4.3.1.3   *Mutation of dentals and velars*

(20)	t ∼ č	Rus	'notice'	*zamétit'*	[Prfv]	*zamečát'*	[Imprfv]
	t ∼ ć	Sorb	'pond'	*hat*	[Nom AccSg]	*haće*	[LocSg]
	t ∼ c	Cz	'to shine'	*svítit*		*svíce*	'candle'
	t ∼ ḱ	Mac	'flower'	*cvet*	[Sg]	*cveḱe*	[Pl]
	d ∼ ž	Rus	'to go'	*xodít'*		*xožú*	'I go'
	d ∼ z	Cz	'to be born'	*narodit se*		*narození*	'birth'

d ~ dž	Ukr	'to go'	*xodýty*		*xodžú*	'I go'
d ~ dź	Pol	'neighbor'	*sąsiad*	[NomSg]	*sąsiedzi*	[Pl]
d ~ žd	Blg	'sight'	*vid*		*víždam*	'I see'
d ~ dz	Slk	'to go'	*chodit'*		*chodza*	'journey'
d ~ ǵ	Mac	'the city'	*gradot*		*graǵanec*	'citizen'
d ~ j	Sln	'to bear'	*rodíti*		*rôjen*	'born' (children) [MascNomSg]
k ~ c	Cz/ Sorb/Bel	'hand, arm'	*ruka*	[NomSg]	*ruce*	[LocSg]
k ~ č	Blg	'weep'	*plákax*	[1SgAor]	*pláča*	[1SgPres]
k ~ c ~ č	Slk	'bird'	*vták*	[Sg]	*vtáci*	[Pl]
					vtáčí	[Adj]
g ~ z ~ ž	Rus	'friend'	*drug*	[NomSg]	*druz'já*	[Pl]
					drúžeskij	[Adj]
	B/C/S	'friend'	*drûg*	[NomSg]	*drûže*	[Pl]
g ~ dz	Pol	'enemy'	*wróg*	[NomSg]	*wrodzy*	[NomPl]
g ~ dž	Slk	'bulldog'	*buldog*	[NomSg]	*buldodží*	[Adj]
s ~ ś	Pol	'orderly'	*ordynans*	[NomSg]	*ordynansi*	[Pl]
s ~ š	Mac	'high'	*visok*	[MascSg]	*viši*	[Compar]
	Sorb	'to ask'	*prosyć*		*prošu*	'I ask'
z ~ ź	Pol	'marquis'	*markiz*	[NomSg]	*markizi*	[Pl]
z ~ ž	Blg	'say'	*kázax*	[Aor]	*káža*	[Prfv non-past]
	Rus	'to convey'	*vozít'*		*vožú*	'I convey'
x ~ ś	Pol	'a Czech'	*Czech*	[NomSg]	*Czesi*	[NomPl]
x ~ s ~ š	Slk	'a Czech'	*Čech*	[NomSg]	*Česi*	[NomPl]
					Češka	[FemNomSg]
	B/C/S	'sin'	*grêh*	[NomSg]	*grési*	[NomPl]
					grěšnīk	'sinner'
h ~ z ~ ž	Bel	'leg, foot'	*nahá*	[NomSg]	*nazé*	[LocSg]
	Slk	'leg, foot'	*noha*		*nôžka*	[Dim]
r ~ ř/ž	Pol	'Hungarian'	*Węgier*	[NomSg]	*Węgrzy*	[NomPl]
	Cz	'good'	*dobrý*	[MascSg Nom]	*dobří*	[PersNomPl]
c ~ č	Slk	'night'	*noc*		*nočný*	[Adj]
	Mac	'sheep'	*ovca*		*ovčar*	'shepherd'
c' ~ č	Bel	'to roll'	*kacíc'*		*kačú*	'I roll'
dz ~ dž	Slk	'to throw'	*hádzat'*		*hádžem*	'I throw'
dz' ~ dž	Bel	'to go'	*xadzíc'*		*xadžú*	'I go'

4.3.1.4   Compound alternations (of clusters)

This class contains either compound palatalization or regressive assimilation of palatalization:

(21)	sk ~ šć	Sorb	'Sorbian'	*serbski* [MascNomSg]	*serbšćina*	'Sorbian (lang.)'
	sk ~ šč	Rus	'to seek'	*iskát'*	*iščú*	'I seek'
	sk ~ št'	Slk	'Polish'	*pol'ský* [NomSgMasc]	*pol'ština*	'Polish language'
	st ~ šć	Pol	'Communist'	*komunista* [NomSg]	*komuniści*	[NomPl]
	st ~ šč	Sln	'to leave'	*zapustíti* [Prfv]	*zapuščáti*	[Imprfv]
	st ~ šć	B/C/S	'to entertain'	*gòstiti*	*gòšćen*	[PPP]
	st ~ št'	Cz	'to clean'	*čistit*	*čištěn*	[MascNom SgPPP]
	sl ~ šl'/šlj	Sln	'to ponder'	*premísliti* [Prfv]	*premišljeváti*	[Imprfv]
		Rus	'to send'	*poslát'*	*pošljú*	'I will send'
	sn ~ šnj	Sln	'to delay'	*zakasníti* [Prfv]	*zakašnjeváti*	[Imprfv]
	zg ~ žd'	Blg	'I bit'	*glózgax* [Aor]	*glóždja*	'I bite'
	zd ~ žd'	Cz	'to be late'	*opozdit se* [Prfv]	*opožděný*	[PPP]
	zł ~ źl	Pol	'bad, evil'	*zły* [MascNomSg]	*źli*	[MascAnim NomPl]
	ck ~ ct'	Cz	'English'	*anglický* [MascNomSg]	*anglicti*	[MascAnim NomPl]

4.3.2   Other simplex alternations

(22a) v ~ š Mac *strav* 'fear' *strašen* 'terrible'
v ~ s Mac *Vlav* 'a Vlach' *Vlasi* 'Vlachs'
(these are historically the x ~ š/x ~ s alternations (PV1/PV2), with Mac x > v)
s ~ c Mac *pes* 'dog' *pci* [Pl]

In Macedonian the following alternations occur before c/č in derivation:

(22b)	s(t) ~ f	'bridge'	*most* [Sg]	*mofče*	[Dim]
	š ~ f	'mouse'	*glušec* [Sg]	*glufci*	[Pl]
				glufče	[Dim]
	z ~ v	'train'	*voz* [Sg]	*vovče*	[Dim]
	j ~ v/ø	'scarf'	*šamija* [Sg]	*šami(v)še*	[Dim]

4.3.3 Epenthetic /n/

With the exception of Belarusian, all Slavic languages insert *-n-* between a preposition and a following 3 Person personal pronoun:

(23) Ukr *vin* 'he'   *johó* [GenSg]   *bez n'óho* 'without him'
cf. Bel *ën* 'he'   *jahó* [GenSg]   *bez jahó* 'without him'

The epenthetic *-n-* is now standard for all non-enclitic 3 Person pronouns, with or without a preposition, in South Slavic (B/C/S *njègov*, Blg, Mac *négov* 'his'), and in the instrumental in Ukrainian, Polish, Slovak and Sorbian (5.5.2.3):

(24)		InstrSgMasc-Neut	InstrSgFem	InstrDu	InstrPl
	Ukr	*nym*	*néju*		*nými*
	Pol	*nim*	*nią*		*nimi*
	Slk	*ním*	*ňou*		*nimi*
	Sorb	*nim*	*njej*	*nimaj*	*nimi*

4.3.4 Voice alternations

As we have seen, voiced obstruents at the end of a word are phonologically devoiced, except in Ukrainian and B/C/S, according to the rule discussed in 3.4.3.4:

(25) Sorb *muž* [-ʃ] 'man'   *muža*   [GenSg]
Rus *borodá* 'beard'   *boród* [-t]   [GenPl].

Morphophonologically driven alternations of voice may also be caused by regressive assimilation of voice before suffixes (3.4.3.2), sometimes marked in the orthography:

(26) B/C/S *Srbin* 'a Serb'   *srpski* 'Serbian'
Rus *svátat'* 'to propose as a husband'   *svád'ba* 'wedding'.

4.3.5 Consonant ~ zero alternations

The most important types of consonant ~ zero alternations involve the dropping of consonants before the perfective suffix *-nu-* in East Slavic:

(27) Ukr 'to move'   *dvýh-aty* [Imprfv]   *dvý-nuty* [Prfv]
Rus 'to touch'   *tróg-at'* [Imprfv]   *tró-nut'* [Prfv]
cf. Pol *dźwig-nać* ('to lift'), Blg *tróg-na*

although there are some cases of restoration by analogy:

(28)   Rus   'to perish'   *pogib-át'* [Imprfv]   *pogíb-nut'* [Prfv] (not **poginut'*)

We also find some simplification of consonant clusters. Many of these occur in any case in allegro speech, but some of the languages additionally authorize such changes in their orthography:

(29)   Mac   'leaf'   *list*   [Sg]   *lisje*   [Pl]
                'local'   *mesten*   [MascSg]   *mesna*   [FemSg]
                'grape'   *grozd*   [Sg]   *grozje*   [Pl]
        B/C/S   'ill'   *bȍlestan*   [MascNomSg]   *bȍlesna*   [FemNomSg]

This is particularly clear in East Slavic (and some West Slavic) *l*-participle forms, where final 'consonant + /l/' results in the loss of the *l*:

(30)   Rus   *nës*   'he carried'   *neslá*   'she carried'
        cf. Pol *nióst* [nʲus(w)]   'he carried'   *niosła*   'she carried'

In the case of the suffix *-nu-* (see above), it may itself be deleted in this form, leading in turn to the deletion of /l/ (cf. 28):

(31)   Rus   *pogíb-nut'* 'to perish'   *pogíb* [PastMasc]   *pogíbla* [Fem]

The deletion is regular where the verb is derived from an adjective, when *-nu-* has the meaning 'become *x*':

(32)   Rus   *slep-* 'blind':
              o-slép-nut' 'go blind'   *oslép* [PastMasc]   *oslépla* [Fem]

For further discussion on phonological cluster simplification, see 3.2.3.1 and 3.4.3.3.

4.4   Combined vowel and consonant alternations

4.4.1   Liquids

B/C/S show *l* ~ ø and *l* ~ *o* alternations at the end of words and syllables:

(33)   B/C/S   'salt'   *sȏ*   [NomAccSg]   *sȍli*   [GenSg]
                'fell'   *pȁo*   [Masc]   *pȁla*   [Fem]
                'rural'   *sȅoskī*   [MascNomSg]   *sȅlo*   'village'

There is also an important liquid/vowel set of alternations in roots. These fall into two main types.

4.4.1.1 *Pleophony*

Particularly in Russian, Church Slavonic roots contrast in some words with East Slavic roots which have undergone pleophony (see 1.3.1.7, 1.6.1). It is possible to view such forms as part of morphophonology, or to see them as semi-suppletive roots in word formation. Such pairs may occur in different derivations from the same root, or they may provide stylistic alternatives or may even have different meanings:

(34)   Rus *-oro-*, RusChSl *-ra-*: Rus *górod*   'city, town' *grad* (poetic)

                         Rus *storoná* 'side'   *straná* 'country'

    Rus *-olo-*, RusChSl *-la-*: Rus *vólost'* 'rural district' *vlast'* 'power'

    Rus *-ere-*, RusChSl *-re-*: Rus *pere-dát'* 'transfer'   *pre-dát'* 'betray'

    Rus *-olo-*, RusChSl *-le-*: Rus *molóčnyj* 'milk' [Adj] *mléčnyj* (poetic);

                                    cf. *Mléčnyj Put'* 'The Milky Way'

A related alternation within Russian proper (that is, not Russian Church Slavonic), and also Belarusian and Ukrainian, is *oro ~ or* etc., sometimes additionally with no vowel (simple *r*):

(35) *oro ~ or*   Rus *borót'sja* 'to fight' *borjús'* 'I fight'

                       bor'bá 'struggle'

    olo ~ ol   Rus *kolót'*   'to stab' *koljú*   'I stab'

    ere ~ er ~ r Rus *terét'*   'to rub'   *tër*   [PastMasc]

                       tru   'I rub'

    olo ~ el   Rus *molót'*   'to grind' *meljú* 'I grind'

4.4.1.2 *Metathesis*

Similar alternations occur in West and South Slavic, deriving from the metathesis which is the equivalent to East Slavic's pleophony:

(36) *or ~ ra*   Blg   *orá*   'I plough' *rálo* 'a plough'

                Sln   *pôrjem* 'I undo' *práti* 'to undo'

    ol ~ la   Blg   *kólja*   'I stab'   *klax* 'I stabbed'

                Slk   *kole*   'he stabs' *klat'* 'to stab'

    ol ~ ło   USorb *kolje*   'he stabs' *kłóć* 'to stab'

    er/ar ~ re ~ r Pol   *mrzeć* 'to die'   *marł* 'he died'

                               mrę   'I die'

    el ~ la   Blg   *mélja*   'I grind' *mljax* 'I ground' [Aor]

    el ~ le   Pol   *mielę*   'I grind' *mleć* 'to grind'

And Bulgarian shows an alternation, deriving from Proto-Slavic syllabic /r̥ l̥/, related to syllable- and word-final position (avoiding final clusters):

(37) ă ~ ră   Blg *grăk*   'a Greek'   *gărci*   [Pl]
      ă ~ lă   Blg *gắltam*   'I swallow'   *glắtna* [Prfv]

4.4.2   Approximants (j, v–w) and diphthongs

There is also the important *ov* ~ *uj* alternation in verbs: finite forms of imperfective verbs replace *-ov-/-ev-* with *-uj-/-juj-* immediately before the present-tense inflexion. Historically, the /j/ is a present-tense suffix or theme whose presence caused the diphthongs /ou eu/ to form a closed syllable and thus undergo monophthongization (1.3.1.7 and 5.5.5.4). The /ov/ form appears almost exclusively in the infinitive suffix *-ova-*:

(38) Rus   *plevát'*   'to spit'   *pljujú*   'I spit'
             kovát'   'to forge'   *kujú*   'I forge'
      Sorb   *lubow-ać*   'to love'   *lubu-ju* 'I love'
             lubowany   [PPP]   *lubuješ* 'you [Sg] love'
             lubowanje   [Verbal noun]   *lubuj!*   'love!' [2 Sg]

4.5   **Morphological typology of alternations**

In this section we describe the typical morphophonological alternations of Slavic, relating the above alternations to morphological contexts (inflexion and word formation in the noun (table 4.1), adjective (table 4.2), verb and adverb (tables 4.3–4.4)).

4.5.1   Nouns: inflexion

See table 4.1. In addition to mutation, there is also automatic additive palatalization of consonants before /i/ and sometimes /e/ in East and West Slavic (3.4.3.1).

Special forms outside the area of palatalization, and some more within morphology than morphophonology, include:

a.   Suppletive forms, mainly distinguishing singular and plural:

(39) Cz   *člověk*   'man, person'   *lidé*   [Pl]
      Slk   *človek*   'man, person'   *l'udia*   [Pl]
      Rus   *rebënok* (*ditjá*) 'child'   *déti*   [Pl]

Table 4.1. *Alternations in the inflexion of nouns*

Case	Conditions	Alternation		Examples
NomSg Masc	Zero ending	Fleeting vowel	B/C/S Rus	*větar* 'wind' ∼ *větra* [GenSg] *son* 'sleep' ∼ *sna* [GenSg]
		Vowel quality	Slk Pol	*stôl* 'table' ∼ *stola* [GenSg] *róg* 'horn' ∼ *rogu* [GenSg]
		Vowel length	Slk	*dážd'* 'rain' ∼ *dažd'a* [GenSg]
DatSgFem	-e	Mutation	Sorb Bel	*sotra* 'sister' ∼ *sotře* *raká* 'river' ∼ *racé*
LocSgFem	-i/-e	Mutation	Bel Ukr	*straxá* 'roof' ∼ *strasé* *fábryka* 'factory' ∼ *fábryci*
VocSgMasc	-e	Mutation	Slk Pol	*chlapec* 'lad' ∼ *chlapče* *profesor* 'professor' ∼ *profesorze*
NomPl	Sec. gender -i	Mutation	Blg Pol	*vojník* 'soldier' ∼ *vojníci* *Czech* 'Czech' ∼ *Czesi*
GenPl	Zero ending	Fleeting vowel	Cz	*pračka* 'washerwoman' ∼ *praček*
Nom/AccDu	Sorb only	Mutation/ palatalization	Sorb	*wóčko* 'eye' ∼ *wóčce* *ryba* 'fish' ∼ *rybje* *woda* 'water' ∼ *wodźe*

Table 4.2. *Alternations in the inflexion of adjectives*

Case	Conditions	Alternation	Examples
NomSg Masc	Zero ending	Fleeting vowel	B/C/S *dõbar* 'good' (Rus *dobr*) cf. B/C/S Rus *dobra* [FemSg]
		C ∼ ø	Mac *mesten* 'local' ∼ *mesna* [FemSg]
NomPl	Sec. gender	Mutation	Cz *český* 'Czech' ∼ *čeští* Cz *dobrý* 'good' ∼ *dobří*
		Vowel quality	Pol *wesoły* 'happy' ∼ *weseli* [MascPersNomPl] ∼ *wesołe* [Other NomPl]

Table 4.3. *Alternations in the inflexion of verbs*

Form	Conditions	Alternation		Examples
Inf/Past *vs* Non-past	Asyllabic Root	Fleeting vowel or pleophony V/nasal C	Rus Slk	*terét'* 'to rub' ~ *tru* 1Sg ~ *tĕr* Past Masc *žat'* 'to reap' ~ *žnem* 1Sg
Finite *vs* Inf	Asyllabic root	Fleeting vowel	Slk	*brat'* 'to take' ~ *berem* 1Sg
1Sg Non-past *vs* rest		Stress	Bel	*hnac'* 'to chase' ~ *hanjú* 1Sg ~ *hóniš* 2Sg
1Sg Non-past *vs* rest and Inf (not WSl, Blg, Mac)	Root in Lab	*l*-epenthesis	Rus	*ljubít'* 'I love' ~ *ljubljú* 1Sg ~ *ljúbiš'* 2Sg
Infinitive *vs* Non-past *vs* Past		Vowel length	Slk Cz	*klást'* 'to put' ~ *kladiem* 1Sg *pít* 'to drink' ~ *piji* 1Sg ~ *pil* Past Masc
Inf *vs* Non-past		Vowel tone	B/C/S	*mòliti* 'to ask' ~ *mȍlīm* 1Sg
Infinitive *vs* Non-past *vs* Past Masc/Fem *vs* Part		Vowel tone	B/C/S	*kléti* 'to curse' ~ *kùnēm* 1Sg ~ *klȅo* ~ *kléla* Past *klȇt* [PPP]
Infinitive *vs* Non-past *vs* Past		Vowel quality	Rus	*ryt'* 'to dig' ~ *róju* 1Sg *brit'* 'to shave' ~ *bréju* 1Sg *peč'* 'to cook' ~ *pĕk* Past M
Infinitive *vs* Non-past		*ov ~ uj*	Slk	*pracovat'* 'to work' ~ *pracujem* 1Sg
Infinitive and 1Sg Non-past *vs* rest		Additive pal.	Rus	*nestí* 'to carry' ~ *nesú* 1Sg ~ *nesëš'* 2Sg
1Sg Non-past *vs* rest	Root in Dent or Vel	Mutation	Cz Rus	*mohu* 'I can' ~ *možeš* 2Sg *plačú* 'I pay' ~ *plátiš'* 2Sg
Infinitive *vs* 1Sg Non-past *vs* rest	*〃*	Mutation	Pol	*piec* 'to bake' ~ *piekę* 1Sg ~ *pieczesz* 2Sg
Aorist *vs* Imperfect	*〃*	Mutation	Blg	*písax* 'I wrote' ~ *píšex* 'I was writing'
Infinitive *vs* Imperative and Non-past	*〃*	Mutation	Rus	*pisát'* 'to write' ~ *piší* 2Sg *pišú* 1Sg, *píšeš'* 2Sg

Table 4.4. *Alternations in the word formation of verbs*

Form	Conditions	Alternation		Examples
Aspect		Stress	Rus	*uznajú* 'I recognize' ∼ *uznáju* [Prfv] 1Sg
		Vowel quality (+ length)	Slk	*spojit'* 'to combine' [Prfv] ∼ *spájat'* [Imprfv]
		Mutation	Slk	*odrazit'* 'repel' [Prfv] ∼ *odrážat'* [Imprfv]
Determinate action		Vowel quality	Ukr	*nestý* 'to carry' [Det] ∼ *nosýty* [Indet]
Prefixed Prfv		Vowel quality	Rus	*podobrát'* 'to select' [Prfv] ∼
vs Imprfv and derived noun		incl. zero		*podbirát'* [Imprfv] *podbór* 'selection'

b. Nouns in *-anin* drop the *-in* in the plural (this element having been originally a singulative suffix, related to 'one'):

(40) Bel *minčánin*   'inhabitant of Minsk'   *minčáne* [Pl]
         hramadzjánin   'citizen'   *hramadzjáne* [Pl]

c. Some stems show atypical palatalization when followed by certain inflexional forms. These may derive from collective forms:

(41) Rus *brat* 'brother'   NomPl *brát'ja* cf. Sorb *brat, bratra*

4.5.2 Nouns: word formation

Some word-forming suffixes may cause:

a. regressive assimilation of voice: B/C/S *bêg* ∼ *bèk-stvo* 'flight'
b. palatalization/mutation:

(42) Cz *knih-a* 'book' *kníž-nost* 'bookishness' *kníž-ka* 'book' [Dim] cf. *knih-ovna* 'library'
         Rus *bél-(yj)* 'white' *bel-'ë* 'linen'

c. pleophony, in East Slavic, where non-pleophonic South Slavic roots alternate in some words with pleophonic East Slavic forms (see also (34) above):

(43) Rus *górod* 'town, city' (RusChSl) *graždanín* 'citizen'
cf. Rus *gorožánin* Ukr *horodjányn* 'town-/city-dweller'

4.5.3 Adjectives: inflexion

See table 4.2.

4.5.4 Adjectives: word formation

1. Short-form adjectives (indefinite (B/C/S, Sln); predicative adjectives (ESl, WSl); and standard adjectives (Blg, Mac) show the changes listed in table 4.2 under [NomSg].
2. Gradation: some forms palatalize the final consonant of the root in forming the comparative and superlative, together with vowel changes preceding the palatalized consonant. This category contains the largest group of suppletive roots (cf. Eng *good* ~ *better/best*) in Slavic (8.4.4) (and see below on adverbs.)
3. Other word-formation processes with adjectives show:
    a. regressive assimilation of voice:

(44) B/C/S *téžak* 'heavy' [MascSg] *téšk-a* [FemSg]

b. palatalization/mutation:

(45) Pol *wron-a* 'crow' *wron-i* [-ɲi] (Adj)
                           Wroń-ski [ɲ]/[j̃] (Name)
      Cz *knih-a* 'book' *kníž-ní* [Adj]

c. vowel quality, often along with patalalization:

(46) Pol *kościół* 'church' *kościel-ny* [Adj]
      Sorb *pol-o* 'field'   *pól-ny*   [Adj]

4.5.5 Adverbs

Adverbs are relatively less complex in the alternations found in their roots. In the positive degree the suffixal formations with *-o* and *-e* are widespread and productive. Those with *-e*, when this is derived from PSl *-ě* (in WSl), show palatalization:

(47) Cz   *dobr-ý* 'good'   *dobř-e* 'well'
      USorb *słab-y* 'weak'   *słab-je* 'weakly'

Normally, however, the -*e* is simply the fronted version of -*o* after a (formerly) palatal root:

(48) Rus   *krájn-ij* 'extreme'   *krájn-e* 'extremely'

Beyond this, they produce root changes which fall mainly within regressive assimilation of palatalization, for instance Pol *zły* 'bad', *źle* 'badly', where the "softened" (i.e. de-velarized) /l/ regressively transfers its palatal quality to the initial /z/. There are a few suppletive forms like 'much' ∼ 'more': Cz *mnoho* ∼ *více*, Ukr *baháto* ∼ *bíľš(e)*, but these normally unite with the root of the cognate adjective in gradation forms.

In the graded forms of adverbs we find mutation where the suffix involved a /j/, as in the basic comparative -*je*:

(49) Rus   *tíxo* 'silently'   *tíše* 'more silently'
      Sln   *blízu* 'near'   *blíže* 'nearer'

For other suffixes, see 8.5.

4.5.6   Verbs: inflexion

The morphophonology of Slavic verbs is very complex. The list in table 4.3 gives typical alternations. Some general patterns emerge, for instance: the vowel ∼ zero alternation in roots like Slk *brat'* 'to take' ∼ *beriem* 'I take', where the vowel is absent in the infinitive and the past active and passive participles. A similar pattern is found with the -*ov*- formant, alternating with -*uj*-:

(50) Slk *pracovat'*   'to work'   *pracujem* 'I work'
           pracoval   'worked' [PPA]   *pracuj*   'work!'
           pracovaný   'worked' [PPP]   *pracujúc* 'working' [Pres Ger]
                                           pracujúci 'working' [PPA]

and in palatalization, where the non-palatalized forms occur in the first group of forms (infinitive and past participles). But in Russian Class IV verbs like *brodít'* 'wander' the only form to palatalize is the 1SgPres: *brožú* 'I wander'. These patterns are discussed in 5.5.5. At this point, we are interested in establishing some typical contrasts within the paradigms, in order to show the extent and nature of the morphophonology of verb inflexion.

4.5.7   Verbs: word formation

See table 4.4.

4.6   Underlying forms and derivational rules

Slavic is one of the key disciplines for the development of theories of underlying structures and derivational rules in modern linguistics. The intellectual forebears include Baudouin de Courtenay (Stankiewicz, 1972), Trubetzkoj and Jakobson. Jakobson's paper on the one-stem Russian verb (Jakobson, 1948) laid the foundations for Slavic morphophonology, and contributed later to the development of generative phonology (Halle, 1959).

Jakobson's insight concerned the fact that many Russian verbs appear to have two stems:

(51) *ži-t'*   'to live'   *živ-ú*   'I live'
      ži-l   Past Masc   *živ-út*   'they live'
                                  živ-í!   'live!'
                                  živ-úščij   'living' [PresPartAct]
      ves-tí   'to lead'   *ved-ú*   'I lead'
      vë-l   Past Masc   *ved-út*   'they lead'
                                  ved-í!   'lead!'
                                  ved-úščij   'leading' [PresPartAct]

while other verbs cover the same set of conjugational forms with just one stem:

(52) *govor-í-t'*   'to speak'   *govor-jú*   'I speak'
      govor-í-l   [Past Masc]   *govor-ját*   'they speak'
                                    govor-í!   'speak!'
                                    govor-jáščij   'speaking' [PresPartAct]

Jakobson proposed a mechanism for uniting both patterns in a single conjugational model, by showing how both stems of the two-stem verbs can be derived from a single underlying form: underlying forms had to be also surface alternants themselves, which limited the level of abstraction which was permitted. His analysis was applied by his students to other areas of Russian (Stankiewicz, 1968a, 1979), and to other Slavic languages (Schenker, 1954, 1964).

In practical terms, Jakobson's proposals amount to this (Townsend, 1975: 82): if a word has two stems, the longer is basic. If the stems are of the same length, as with the *vesti* example above, the 3 Person plural non-past provides the basic stem. For the three verbs exemplified above, then, the basic forms are respectively *živ-, ved-* and *govor-*. The stem is the root, together with its prefixes and suffixes, to which inflexions are added.

In the following chapters we shall favor surface-based representations of roots and affixes. However, the underlying forms are often identical to actual proto-forms (below), so where it seems helpful we shall adduce the Proto-Slavic forms (as is done extensively in chapter 3). Jakobson's proposals are, by contemporary standards, both conservative and surface-oriented. Lipson's (1968) adaptation of the one-stem verb into a pedagogical grammar of Russian brought these ideas into the classroom (especially in the USA), and Townsend's (1968/1975) textbook on word formation helped to make the linguistics of word formation part of the basic training of students of Russian.

Jakobson's ideas have provided a fundamental stimulus to generative phonology. Scholars like Halle, Lightner, Lunt and Rubach have proposed models of phonology which extend beyond the notion of abstractness represented in Jakobson's work, more in the spirit of Chomsky and Halle's *The sound pattern of English* (1968) and its successors. One of the most interesting features of some of this work has been the postulation of some underlying forms which are closer to the phonology of Proto-Slavic in a number of key respects. Synchronic derivation therefore mirrors diachronic evolution, in a way which is typical of the traditional orientation of Slavic linguistics not to follow Saussure in making a rigid distinction between synchrony and diachrony.

4.7 Morphophonology and Slavic orthographies

Seen in the light of our discussion of underlying forms, Slavic orthographies fall into two groups. One, the older, group is more historically motivated and morphophonemic in orientation. It includes all but the more recently codified orthographies: Belarusian, B/C/S and Macedonian. The morphophonemic systems preserve the unity of the underlying morpheme at the expense of phonetic transparency. This makes them easier to read and comprehend, but harder to pronounce, since the reader has to bear in mind such late-level phonetic output rules as final devoicing of obstruents; (mainly regressive) assimilation of voice and in some cases place and manner of articulation; the simplification of consonant clusters; special pronunciations for /v/ and /l/ in positions other than before a vowel; synharmony requirements of palatal consonants and following vowels; and the differences of vowel quality caused by movement of stress. (On all of these, see 3.4.3.)

Of the more phonetically oriented orthographies, B/C/S and Macedonian provide more phonetically faithful spellings for devoicing (B/C/S) and simplified
consonant clusters (both) (4.3.4–4.3.5):

(53)   B/C/S   *ŭzak*   'narrow'   *ŭska*   [Fem]
                rădostan 'joyful'   *rădosna* [Fem]
        Mac   *list*   'leaf'   *lisje*   'foliage'

B/C/S's lack of devoicing in final voiced obstruents makes the marking of devoicing
simpler for it – as for Ukrainian (54). Belarusian goes furthest in representing
vowels accurately, particularly *akan'e*:

(54)   Rus   *górod*   ['gɔrət]   'town'
        Ukr   *horód*   [ɦɔ'rɔd]   'kitchen garden'
        Bel   *hórad*   ['ɣɔrat]   'town'

Belarusian also deals explicitly with /v/, which is [v] only before a vowel, by the use
of the letter *ŭ* (Cyrillic ỹ) for other positions. While the Belarusian system is
pedagogically helpful for beginners, it can cause problems later with the identification of forms which share a common base, since the identity of the base is obscured
by the variety of written forms.

We describe the Slavic orthographies in more detail in appendix B.

5

Morphology: inflexion

5.1 Overview

Slavic is a morphology-rich language family, in the mainstream Indo-European tradition, with highly articulated systems of prefixes, roots and suffixes. While Slavic as a whole has a very Indo-European system of synthetic inflexional paradigms, there is some movement towards a more analytic approach in verb and especially nominal morphology, in both national standard languages and regional and social variants. This differentiation of Slavic within the Indo-European language family makes Slavic morphology an area of particular theoretical and empirical interest.

This chapter will concentrate on four aspects of morphology: the morphological categories of Slavic (5.2), morphological word-classes (5.3), the inflexional categories (5.4) and the paradigms for the major inflexional types (5.5).

5.2 Morphological categories and structures

The Slavic word consists of one or more roots – the central component of the word – and affixes (prefixes and suffixes), which may accompany the root. For the major categories, the word contains an inflexional suffix, or ending. As this chapter is concerned only with inflexion, we shall simply summarize the other aspects of word structure, with references to chapters 8 and 9 for examples and discussion. Roots can be combined in apposition or by joining with a so-called "link-vowel" -o- (8.1.3, 9.5.2), or by truncation to create so-called "stump compounds" and acronyms, and in mixed formations (8.2.3, 9.5.3).

Slavic also has a wealth of affixes which occur before the root (prefixes) or after the root (suffixes). Prefixes generally modify or add to the root's meaning. They have a role in three domains: in inflexional morphology and the creation of paradigms (this chapter); in word-formation (8.2.1, 8.3.1, 8.4.1); and in lexicology (9.4).

Suffixes follow the root, and come in three main types: derivational, inflexional (= endings), and post-inflexional, which occur in that order. Derivational suffixes are of several sub-types. First after the root are suffixes which change the part or sub-part of speech in familiar processes like abstract and agent nominalization, verbalization, adjectivalization and adverbialization (8.2.2, 8.3.2, 8.4.3). The root's final consonant or internal phonological composition may be modified as a result of the addition of the suffix (chapter 4; 8.1.5, 8.4.3.2). In addition to prefixes, roots and suffixes, there are the link vowels, which are used to join the members of a compound (8.1.3), and the so-called "thematic vowel", which indicates the conjugation to which a verb belongs (8.3.2.1). In some analyses this vowel is included in the stem, while in others it appears as a further ordered suffix, as with the -*a*- and -*i*- formants in these two Sorbian verbs:

(1) *Thematic vowel*
    Sorb   *dźěl-a-* 'work'   *dźěl-a-ć* [Inf]   *dźěl-a-š* [2SgPres]
            pal-i- 'burn'   *pal-i-ć* [Inf]   *pal-i-š* [2SgPres]

After these come inflexions, or endings, which mark categories like infinitive, person, number, tense, case and gender, as appropriate to the word-class of the stem (for aspect, see 5.4.7, 6.2.5). Several inflexional suffixes may occur in a fixed order:

(2) *Inflexions*

Sorb	Infinitive	*dźěl-a-ć*	'to work'	[Inf]
	Person	*njes-u*	'I carry'	[1SgPres]
		njes-eš	'you carry'	[2SgPres]
	Number	*wóčk-o*	'eye'	[Sg]
		wóčc-e		[Du]
		wóčk-a		[Pl]
	Tense	*pij-u*	'I drink'	[Pres]
		pij-ach	'I was drinking'	[Imperf]
	Case	*wóčk-o*	'eye'	[Nom]
		wóčk-a		[Gen]
		wóčk-u		[Dat]
	Gender	*now-y*	'new'	[MascSgNom]
		now-a		[FemSgNom]
		now-e		[NeutSgNom]

Last of all comes the post-inflexional reflexive (sometimes called a "postfix"), a clitic pronoun which has developed into a suffix in East Slavic (while remaining a separable pronoun, and so not part of inflexion, elsewhere):

(3)   *Reflexive clitic suffix (postfix)*
      'wash (oneself)'
      East Slavic: Rus   *mýt'-sja*   Ukr   *mýty-sja*
      West Slavic: Slk   *umyvat' sa*   Sorb *myć so*
      South Slavic: B/C/S *m̃ti se*   Blg   *míja se*

The stem, by definition, includes the root together with all its word-forming affixes, but excluding inflexions and the reflexive. The form of both roots and affixes may be modified, when certain elements are combined, for phonological (chapter 3) or morphophonological (chapter 4) reasons.

The examples in (3) show that Slavic has important parallels with other European languages of the "synthetic" morphological type (e.g. Latin, German and the verb system of French), where individual affixes simultaneously realize several morphological categories, in contrast with the more "analytic" patterns of English. Nonetheless, some complex verb forms in Slavic have developed a more analytic structure (5.5.5.): compare (4a) to (4b) within one language, and (5a) to (5b–c) across languages:

(4)   *Synthetic and analytic structures*
      'I shall read' [Imprfv]:

(4a) Ukr   *čyt-*   *á-*   *ty-*   *mu*
            read   thematic vowel   Inf   Fut 1Sg

(4b) Ukr   *búd-*   *u*   *čyt-á-*   *ty*
            be + Fut   1Sg   read   Inf

(5)   'I would have read' [Masc]

(5a) Pol   *prze-*   *czyt-*   *a-*   *ł-*   *by-m*
            Prfv   read   thematic-vowel MascSg   Cond-1Sg

(5b) Rus   *já*   *by*   *pro-*   *čit-*   *á-*   *l*
            I   Cond   Prfv   read   thematic-vowel   MascSg

(5c) Blg   *štjáx*   *da*   *săm*   *pro-*   *čé-*   *l*
            AuxCond-1Sg   that   Aux-1Sg   Prfv   read   MascSg

Similar examples are found in the virtual loss of cases in Bulgarian and Macedonian, which has made these languages more of the analytic type, and has forced prepositions to carry a heavier semantic and functional load, as in English. While Czech has a genitive plural of *věda* 'science' in *Akademie Věd* 'Academy of Sciences', Bulgarian has *Akadémija na Naúkite*, literally 'Academy of Sciences [PlDef]'.

While case and verbal agreement are seen as part of inflexional morphology, prepositions and particles are usually allocated to syntax. In the Slavic linguistic tradition, however, there is a focus on the word (Rus *slóvo*) as a grammatical unit in both morphology and phrase and sentence structure which emphasizes the central position of the word in the Slavs' conception of their language-structure.

5.3   Morphological word-classes

It is convenient to begin a discussion of morphological word-classes with the traditional division of words into those which inflect and those which do not. Non-inflecting words include conjunctions, prepositions, various invariant particles, interjections and exclamations:

(6)   *Invariant parts of speech*

(6a)   Conjunctions

'and'   Rus, Bel, Blg, Mac, B/C/S *i*; Cz, Slk, Sorb *a*; Ukr *ta*; Sln *in*

'that'   Rus *čto*, Bel *što*, Ukr *ščo*, Cz, Slk *že*; Pol *że*; Blg *če*, Mac *deka*, B/C/S, Sln *da*

(6b)   Prepositions

'in'   Rus, Blg, Mac, Sln, Cz, Slk *v*; Ukr, Bel *v/u*; B/C/S *u*; Pol, Sorb *w*

'before'   Rus, Ukr *péred*; Bel *pérad*; Cz, Sorb *před*; Blg, Mac, B/C/S, Sln, Slk *pred*; Pol *przed*

(6c)   Particles

Conditional   EastSl, Slk, Sln *by*

Question   Rus, Bel, Cz, Slk, Blg, Mac, B/C/S *li*; Sorb *-li*; Sln *ali*; Pol *czy*; Ukr *cy*; Bel *ci*

(6d)   Interjections

'perhaps'   Pol *chyba*; Blg *xíba*

(6e)   Exclamations

'well'   Bel *ox, oj*; Sorb *ach*; Rus, Bel *nu*; Sorb *no*

'hop, jump'   Sorb *hop*

'splash'   Sorb *plumps*

Most simplex words in these categories are non-inflecting, and have the same form in any position in the sentence. Exceptions, like the Belarusian variation between *v, u* and *ŭ* in the form of the preposition 'in', are due to phonological factors (4.4.2). However, the inflecting word-classes have historically contributed many words to the invariant categories in the modern Slavic languages (7a–d). Prepositional phrases, consisting principally of Preposition + Noun, generally governing a following noun phrase in the genitive (in those languages where it is still available), continue to provide a productive source of compound preposition-like expressions (7e). Impersonal constructions also show forms which may be identical to inflected endings, but they do not form full paradigms (7f). Adverbs can be formed from gerunds (7g) and from Preposition + Noun combinations which have become calcified (7h):

(7)   *Invariant parts of speech derived from inflected forms*

(7a)   Conjunctions
'because'   Rus *potomú čto*, Pol *dlatego że*
(lit. "for it, [that]")

(7b)   Prepositions
'thanks to'   Sorb *dźakowano*, Rus *blagodarjá* (+ Dat)
'in spite of'   Rus *nesmotrjá na* (+ Acc) (*smotréť* 'look')

(7c)   Interjections
'of course'   Bel *práŭda* (lit. "truth" [NomSg])
'absolutely'   Bel *bezumóŭna* (lit. "without condition")

(7d)   Exclamations
'goodness'!   Bel *bácjuxny!*; Rus *bátjuški!* (lit. "fathers!")
'hell'!   Bel *čort*, Rus *čërt* (lit. "the devil!")

(7e)   Compound prepositions
'during'   Rus *v tečénie* [Acc] (lit. "in the course (of)")
Ukr *na prótjazi* [Loc] ('')

(7f)   Impersonal forms
'I am sorry that …'
Rus *mne*   *žalʹ*, *čto* …
to-me pity, that …
'my feet are cold'
Ukr *mení* *xólodno* *v* *noháx*
to-me cold in feet

(7g)   Adverbs from gerunds
'lying down'   Sorb *ležo*
'standing up'   Sorb *stejo*

(7h)   Adverbs from prepositional phrases
'meanwhile'   Sorb *mjez-tym* (lit. "between that")
'in the afternoon'   Sorb *po-połdnju* (lit. "after mid-day")

5.4   Inflexional categories

The inflecting word-classes, on the other hand, take different forms in different grammatical contexts, depending on grammatical roles like subjects and objects, and on agreement:

(8a)   Rus   *ja   ljubí-l   krasív-uju   dévušk-u*
              I   love-PastMascSg   beautiful-FemSgAcc   girl-AccSg
              'I loved a/the beautiful girl'

(8b)   Rus   *krasív-aja   dévušk-a   ljubí-la   menjá*
              beautiful-FemSgNom   girl-NomSg   love-PastFemSg   me
              'the beautiful girl loved me'

From the point of view of the morphological categories expressed in their inflexions (5.4), and the forms which these inflexions take in paradigms (5.5), we find a broad division into two main types of inflecting words: the verbs; and the "nominals", which include nouns, adjectives, pronouns, determiners, numerals, participles and, to a limited extent, Czech gerunds, and which display these features – although not all of these categories are represented in all forms of the relevant word-classes:

(9)	**Verbs only**	**Verbs and nominals**	**Nominals only**
	Tense	Person	Case
	Aspect	Gender	Definiteness
	Mood (incl. Renarration)	Number	Deixis
	Voice		

5.4.1   Number

The inflexional category of number is marked in Slavic on all inflecting parts of speech, including the Bulgarian and Macedonian articles, and gerunds in Czech (but not in the other languages). In personal and some other pronouns, number is a lexical rather than an inflexional category (5.5.2–5.5.3). Number is an inherent category in nouns, pronouns and nominalized forms of adjectives and participles. It occurs through concord (6.2.1) in non-head members of the noun phrase, and in predicates through agreement (6.2.2).

Indo-European and Proto-Slavic had three numbers: singular, dual (for two objects, especially parts of the body), and plural. Only Sorbian and Slovenian now preserve the dual number as a living category, and the other Slavic languages now have only the opposition of singular and plural.

In modern Slavic the ability of the various numbers to refer to real-world entities is largely similar to the situation in English. Singular noun phrases in Slavic, apart from their expected ability to refer to singular countable and non-countable mass referents, can also refer to what in English may be designated by plural nouns, for instance 'potatoes' (as a dish to be eaten: Rus *kartófel'* [Sg]). Such singular-only ("*singularia tantum*") words function as mass nouns. There are other words for individual potatoes, which are pluralizable in the regular way, for instance by using a related diminutive form (Rus *kartóška* '(a) potato', Pl *kartóški*). There are also collective nouns which are grammatically singular (Bel *zver* 'beast', *zvjar'ë* 'wild beasts'), and a generic singular:

(10)   *Generic singular*

(10a)   Blg   *rabótiš,*   *níšto*   *ne*   *izlíza*
              work-2SgPres   nothing   Neg   emerge-3SgPres
              'you work, and nothing comes of it'

(10b)   Blg   *dărvóto*   *e*   *rasténie*
              tree-Def   be-3SgPres   plant
              'the tree is (a) plant'

Unlike English and like most European languages, referents which are distributed on a "one each" basis are in the singular in Slavic where English has a plural:

(11)   *"Distributed plural"*
        Rus   *bežáli*   *sobáki,*   *podnimája*   *xvóst*
              run-PastImprfv-Pl   dog-Pl   raising-Ger   tail-AccSg
              'the dogs were running (along), with their tails raised'

Plural number refers to multiple entities, with the principal exceptions of the "authorial" 'we', and the polite use of 2 Person plural pronouns, found everywhere except in Polish, which uses the words *pan* 'man', *pani* 'woman' and *państwo* 'people', with 3 Person agreement (11.4.2):

(12)   *Politeness and plural number*

(12a)   Rus   *tý ne znáeš'*   'you [Sg = Familiar] don't know'
              vý ne znáete   'you [Pl = Polite] don't know'

(12b)   Pol   *ty nie wiesz*   'you [Sg = Familiar] don't know'
              pan nie wie   'man (= you [Sg = Polite]) don't know'

There are also "generalized plurals", but without an expressed subject and with 3 Person plural inflexions, corresponding functionally to French *on*, German *man*:

(13)   *Generalized plurals*
  Blg   túk   prodávat   zelenčúk
         here   sell-3PlPres   vegetables [SgColl]
         'here they sell vegetables/vegetables are sold here'

Plural-only nouns ("*pluralia tantum*") are more numerous in Slavic than they are in English. They refer not only to nouns with plural component parts, like eyeglasses and underpants (Blg *očilá* 'eyeglasses', *gášti* 'underpants'), but also to what to the anglophone mind are semantically singular entities like watches and cabbage soup. A given object may have different numbers in different languages:

(14)

	Pluralia tantum	Singular forms
Proper names		
'Bohemia (+ Moravia)'	Cz *čechy*	
'Czechoslovakia'		Cz *Československo*
Materials:		
'firewood'	Rus *drová*	Slk *drevo*
Realia:		
'watch'	Slk *hodinky*	Pol *zegarek*
		B/C/S *ūra*
	Cz *hodiny*	Blg *časóvnik*
	Rus *časý*	
'cabbage soup'	Rus, Ukr *šči*	Ukr *kapusnják*
Collectives:		
'peas'		Rus *goróx*, Pol *groch*
Most abstracts:		
'music'		Cz *hubda*, Rus *múzyka*

In many parts of the declension systems the expressions of number in the various Slavic paradigms have continued to be significantly distinct. In Bulgarian there is even a special set of nominal inflexions for impersonal masculine nouns used only with numerals (5.5.1). However, distinct inflexions associated with number are not found in personal pronouns; in some relative ('who', 'which'), interrogative ('who?', 'which?', 'what?'), indefinite ('someone', 'something') or negative ('no-one', 'nothing') pronouns, all of which have inflexions typical of either singular or plural paradigms (5.5.2.2); or in a small number of non-inflecting nouns and adjectives, where number is shown only through concord and agreement (6.2.1–6.2.2).

There is also the decline of the dual and its tendency to merge with the plural, even in Sorbian and Slovenian, as it has done in all the other Slavic languages. One of the main relics of the dual inflexion across many Slavic languages is found in the palatalized plural forms of parts of the body: compare the singular and plural forms of 'eye', 'ear' and 'hand', where the palatalization of the stem-final velars /k/ and /x/ (orthographically Cyrillic *x*, Roman *h, ch*) results in /c č š/, a typical feature of the former dual:

		'eye'	'ear'	'hand'
(15)	Rus	*óko, óči* (poetic)	*úxo, úši*	(*ruká, rúki*)
	Bel	*vóka, vóčy*	*vúxa, vúšy*	(*ruká, rúki*)
	Ukr	*óko, óči*	(*vúxo, vúxa*)	(*ruká, rúky*)
	Pol	*oko, oczy*	*ucho, uszy*	*ręka, ręce*
	Cz	*oko, oči*	*ucho, uši*	*ruka, ruce*
	Slk	*oko, oči*	*ucho, uši*	(*ruka, ruky*)
	B/C/S	*ȍko, ȍkči*	*ȗho, ȗši*	*rúka, rúce*
	Blg	*okó, očí*	*uxó, uší*	*răká, răcé*
	Mac	*oko, oči*	*uvo, uši*	*raka, race*

Some of these forms are obviously cognate with the regular duals of modern Sorbian and Slovenian:

			'eye'	'ear'	'hand'
(16)	Sorb	Sg	*woko*	*wucho*	*ruka*
		Du	*woči*	*wuši*	*ruce*
		Pl	*woči*	*wuši*	*ruki*
	Sln	Sg	*okó*	*uhó*	*rôka*
		Du	*očési*	*ušési*	*rokí*
		Pl	*očí*	*ušésa*	*roké*

Other forms, however, show regularized plurals (bracketed in (15)). And even where the old dual remains, there is sometimes a regularized plural for special uses, usually metaphorical: Slovak has regular *oká* 'metaphorical eyes', *uchá* 'metaphorical ears', as in *morské oká* 'sea eyes' (e.g. in the name of a lake) and *uchá na hrncoch* 'ears [= handles] on cooking pots'. More regular survivals of the dual are found in specific case forms of nouns, like the dative/instrumental/locative plural in B/C/S *žènama* 'women' or *prózorima* 'window', or the *-ma* form in the instrumental plural of colloquial Czech *knihama* 'books' [InstrPl] for Standard Czech *knihami* (10.4.3). Another survival of the dual is found in the standard use in Slavic of what looks like a genitive singular – actually the old masculine nominative dual – of masculine and neuter nouns with the numbers 2–4: Bel *pésnjar* 'singer', *dva pesnjará* '2 singers' (sometimes referred to as a "paucal" form). The dual number in Sorbian and Slovenian is also becoming unstable in dialectal and colloquial use, giving way to the plural (Stone, 1993a: 614; Priestly, 1993: 448). It is likely to remain operational in the standard languages by virtue of being enshrined in the authoritative prescriptive grammars of these languages: as Lencek observes (1982: 186), the dual has been saved in Slovenian through the 'intervention of grammarians'. On the other hand, the remains of the dual are also being slowly eroded in languages like Slovak by pressure from the other, now regular, inflexional paradigms (Mistrík, 1985).

We discuss concord and agreement with numerals in the context of morphosyntax in chapter 6, and number as a lexical category, including the typically Slavic collective numerals, in chapter 9.

5.4.2   Case

Case is an inflexional category of all the inflecting parts of speech in Slavic: even the verb shows case in the declension of participles, though not in the gerunds. The number of cases and the number of distinct case forms differ between languages, parts of speech and their paradigms. Proto-Slavic had seven cases: nominative, vocative, accusative, genitive, dative, instrumental and locative.

Of these, the vocative was found only in singular nouns. Though it is not a "case" in the syntactic sense, for our purposes it will be treated as such on the basis of having a distinct inflexion. This is also the traditional approach.

Case forms, where they did exist, showed considerable syncretism. The plural, and even more so the dual, showed fewer distinct case forms than the singular; and feminine *i*-stem nouns and neuter *consonant*-stem nouns showed fewer distinct forms than nouns of the *a/ja* or *o/jo* declensions (5.5.1).

This general pattern of distinctive forms has been handed down to modern Slavic with several changes. The most drastic change is found in Bulgarian and Macedonian, which have lost all but some remains of the vocative, and an "oblique" case which occurs only in some paradigms:

(17)   *Non-nominative cases: Bulgarian and Macedonian*
        Bulgarian:
            Oblique case: masculine singular nouns with the definite article
            Vocative case: masculine and feminine singular nouns
        Macedonian:
            Oblique case: masculine names and nouns denoting persons and
                            relationships (optional accusative, singular only)
            Vocative case: masculine and feminine singular nouns denoting
                            persons

The form of the vocative varies with gender and number:

(18a) *Bulgarian: Nominative ∼ Vocative*

		Nom		Voc
Blg	Masculine:	*učítel*	'teacher'	*učítelju*
		otéc	'father'	*ótče*
		junák	'youth'	*junáko/junáče*
	Feminine:	*sestrá*	'sister'	*séstro*
		Bălgárija	'Bulgaria'	*Bălgárijo*

(18b) *Macedonian: Nominative ∼ Vocative*

	Nom		Voc
Mac Masculine Personal:	*vnuk*	'grandson'	*vnuku*
Feminine:	*žena*	'wife'	*ženo*

The non-oblique ("full") definite form is found in subjects and nominal predicates, while the oblique ("short") form occurs in other contexts. Paradigms lacking the oblique form use the full form regardless (note that Bulgarian orthography uses *a* for word-final /ă/ (5.4.3, 5.5.1):

(19a) Blg *gradắt* [full form] *e málăk*   'the town is small'

(19b) Blg *Dimítăr e mexánikăt* [full form]   'Dimitar is the mechanic'

(19c) Blg *víždam mexánika* [short form]   'I see the mechanic'

(20a) Mac *sin mi gleda konjot* [full form]   'my son sees the horse'

(20b) Mac *konjot gleda sina* [short form]   'the horse sees my son'

In the other languages, the general reduction of the number of different paradigms has resulted in considerable interference by individual paradigms and case forms on others, especially as parts of speech changed their inflexional paradigm. The feminine *a/ja* inflexion -*ax*, for the locative plural, for instance, has become widely used in East and West Slavic for all classes of nouns: compare Rus *kostjáx* 'bones' [LocPl], *konjáx* 'horses' [LocPl], to the Proto-Slavic forms (5.5.1). Other changes have involved the number and distribution of cases. The vocative has been largely lost in Russian, Belarusian, Slovak and Slovenian, reducing the number of cases to six. And the locative has tended to disappear as a separate form, becoming identical with the dative or instrumental:

B/C/S   locative = dative singular and plural in all nouns
Slovenian   locative = dative singular in all nouns

| Ukrainian | locative = dative singular in most nouns, dative *or* instrumental singular in all pronouns |
| Polish | locative = instrumental singular in all masculine and neuter adjectives. |

On the other hand, in some nouns Russian shows a second (partitive) genitive in *-u* and a second locative in stressed *-ú* (Masc) or *-í* (Fem), so bringing up the maximum number of cases to eight (*syr* 'cheese', *sýra* GenSg, *sýru* GenSg^2; *sad* 'garden', *sáde* PrepnlSg, *sadú* LocSg^2; *króvi* 'blood' PrepnlSg, *kroví* LocSg^2). There is a terminological issue here, since some grammars of Russian use the term "prepositional" for the locative. We shall follow the convention in Slavic by using "locative", as in Proto-Slavic. We shall keep the term "prepositional" for those instances where there is a distinction between the locational and non-locational meanings.

Of the six or seven (counting the vocative) common cases across modern Slavic, the nominative is the citation form. It is marked either by a zero inflexion, for instance in the masculine *o*/*jo*-declension or the feminine *i*-declension; or by an inflexion which is often used as a label for the paradigm, for instance in the feminine *a*/*ja*-declension. The only other case which can have a zero inflexion is the genitive plural. With feminines, for instance, if the nominative singular has a zero inflexion the genitive plural will normally not, and vice versa:

(21)		NomSg	GenPl	
	Rus	*dám-a* 'lady'	*dam-ø*	
		njánj-a 'nanny'	*njan-ø*	(phonologically /n'an'a ~ n'an'/)
		kost'-ø 'bone'	*kost-éj*	

All other cases are marked by (non-zero) inflexions. The distinctiveness of these systems of inflexions varies considerably within and across paradigms.

Within paradigms the question of the distinctiveness of case forms is a central one. Leaving aside the dual, some paradigms, like the masculine/neuter *o*/*jo* and feminine *a*/*ja*, have retained much of the distinctiveness of their forms: compare the Proto-Slavic forms in tables 5.1 and 5.4 with those of the modern languages (tables 5.2, 5.5). Other paradigms, however, show lower, and in some instances declining, distinctiveness, as in the feminine *i*-declension (tables 5.6, 5.7). Distinctive case forms allow the carriage of distinctive grammatical functions and meaning. Syncretic case forms (the identity of case distinctions following loss) throws the onus back on the syntax, and/or the lexicon and the context, for the expression of meaning. The limiting case of syncretism is the word which lacks inflexions altogether, as happens with borrowed words and some home-grown neologisms, particularly acronyms (8.2.3, 9.5.3, 9.6.1), before they establish their

Table 5.1. *Proto-Slavic* o/jo-*stems:* rabъ *'slave'*, konь *'horse' [Masc]'*; město *'place'*, pole *'field' [Neut]*

		o Masc	*jo* Masc	*o* Neut	*jo* Neut
Singular	Nom	*rab-ъ*	*kon-ь*	*měst-o*	*pol-e*
	Voc	*rab-e*	*kon-ju*	=NOM	=NOM
	Acc	=NOM	=NOM	=NOM	=NOM
	Gen	*rab-a*	*kon-ja*	=MASC	=MASC
	Dat	*rab-u*	*kon-ju*	=MASC	=MASC
	Instr	*rab-omь/rab-ъmь*	*kon-emь*	=MASC	=MASC
	Loc	*rab-ě*	*kon-i*	=MASC	=MASC
Dual	Nom	*rab-a*	*kon-ja*	*měst-ě*	*pol-i*
	Voc	=NOM	=NOM	=NOM	=NOM
	Acc	=NOM	=NOM	=NOM	=NOM
	Gen	*rab-u*	*kon-ju*	*měst-u*	*pol-ju*
	Dat	*rab-oma*	*kon-ema*	*měst-oma*	*pol-ema*
	Instr	=DAT	=DAT	=DAT	=DAT
	Loc	=GEN	=GEN	=GEN	=GEN
Plural	Nom	*rab-i*	*kon-i*	*měst-a*	*pol-ja*
	Voc	=NOM	=NOM	=NOM	=NOM
	Acc	*rab-y*	*kon-i*	=NOM	=NOM
	Gen	*rab-ъ*	*kon-ь*	=MASC	=MASC
	Dat	*rab-omъ*	*kon-emъ*	=MASC	=MASC
	Instr	*rab-y*	*kon-i*	=MASC	=MASC
	Loc	*rab-ěxъ*	*kon-ixъ*	=MASC	=MASC

place in the language. One of the signs of the acceptance of a word in a Slavic language (apart from Bulgarian and Macedonian) is its development of a full set of case forms, as well as derivational morphology.

Significant syncretism of case forms is evident within a number of Slavic paradigms. In tables 5.1 5.9, examples of paradigms with significant levels of non-distinctiveness of forms include the singular of the *i*-declension, especially feminine, and the dual of all nouns (in which there is always syncretism of nominative and accusative, genitive and dative, and locative and instrumental).

The extreme cases, as we saw above, are Bulgarian and Macedonian, which have eradicated all but a skeleton of their original case systems. This has brought about a fundamental change in the means of expression of grammatical relationships, and has made the nominal systems of these languages, and the grammatical constructions in which they are engaged, more analytic. We take up the role of prepositions and other phenomena, including clitic object-marking in Bulgarian and Macedonian, in chapter 6 (6.1.2.4). Bulgarian and Macedonian make up for their lack of cases principally by using either simple apposition:

Table 5.2. *The* o/jo *declension in the modern languages, using PSl* gordъ *'town'*, мужь *'man, husband'*, město *'place'*, sr̩′dьce *'heart'. Modern meanings are not given, but they have often changed. Neuter forms are given only where different from masculine. Other forms, including variants and other languages, are added as extra lines as necessary: Rus* sad *'garden'*, sáxar *'sugar'*, póle *'field'; Cz* chlap *'fellow'*

		B/C/S		Russian		Czech	
SgNom	Masc	*grȃd-ø*	*mȗž-ø*	*górod-ø*	*múž-ø*	*hrad-ø*	*muž-ø*
	Neut	*mȅst-o*	*sȑc-e*	*mést-o*	*sérdc-e*	*měst-o*	*srdc-e*
Voc	Masc	*grȃd-e*	*mȗž-u*	=NOM	=NOM	*hrad-e*	*mu-ži*
	Neut	=NOM	=NOM	=NOM	=NOM	=NOM	=NOM
Acc		=NOM	=GEN	=NOM	=GEN	=NOM	=GEN
Gen		*grȃd-a*	*mȗž-a*	*górod-a* GS²	*múž-a* *sáxar-u*	*hrad-a*	*muž-a*
Dat		*grȃd-u*	*mȗž-u*	*górod-u*	*múž-u*	*hrad-u* *chlap-ovi*	*muž-i* *muž-ovi*
Instr		*grȃd-om*	*mȗž-em*	*górod-om*	*múž-em*	*hrad-em*	*muž-em*
Loc		*grȃd-u*	=DAT	*górod-e* LS²	*múž-e* *sad-ú*	*hrad-ě*	*muž-i,* *muž-ovi*
PlNom	Masc	*grȁd-ovi*	*mȕž-evi*	*gorod-á* *sad-ý*	*muž′-já*	*hrad-y* *chlap-i*	*muž-i*
	Neut	*mȅst-a*	*sȑc-a*	*mest-á*	*sérdca*	*měst-a*	*srdc-e*
Voc		=NOM	=NOM	=NOM	=NOM	=NOM	=NOM
Acc	Masc	*grȁd-ove*	*mȕž-eve*	=NOM	=GEN	=NOM *chlap-y*	*muž-e*
	Neut	=NOM	=NOM	=NOM	=NOM	=NOM	=NOM
Gen	Masc	*grȁd-ōvā*	*mȕž-ēvā*	*gorod-óv*	*muž-éj*	*hrad-ů*	*muž-ů*
	Neut	*mȅst-ā*	*sȑc-ā*	*mést-ø*	*serdéc-ø* *pol-éj*	*měst-ø*	*srdc-í*
Dat	Masc	*grȁd-ovima*	*mȕž-evima*	*gorod-ám*	*muž′-jám*	*hrad-ům* Sorb	*muž-ům* *-am*
	Neut	*mȅst-ima*	*sȑc-ima*		*sérdc-am*		*srdc-ím*
Instr		=DAT	=DAT	*gorod-ámi*	*muž′-jámi*	*hrad-y* Pol Sorb	*muž-i* *-ami*
Loc		=DAT	=DAT	*gorod-áx*	*muž′-jáx*	*hrad-ech* Pol Sorb	*muž-ích* *-ach*

(22)   'a litre of milk':   Blg *lítăr mljáko*; cf. Rus *lítr moloká* [GenSg]

or by transferring the meaning of the case to appropriate prepositions, which therefore function in these languages more like the prepositions of English and modern Romance languages:

Table 5.3. *Proto-Slavic* ŭ-*stems:* synъ *'son'*

	Sing	Du	Pl
Nom	*synъ*	*syny*	*synove*
Gen	*synu*	*synovu*	*synovъ*
Dat	*synovi*	*synъma*	*synъmъ*
Acc	=NOM	=NOM	*syny*
Instr	*synъmь*	=DAT	*synъmi*
Loc	*synu*	=GEN	*synъxъ*
Voc	*synu*	=NOM	=NOM

Table 5.4. *PSl* a/ja-*stems:* žena *'woman, wife'*, duša *'soul'*, sǫdьja *'judge' [Masc]*

		a		*ja*
Singular	Nom	*žena*	*duša*	*sǫdьja*
	Voc	*ženo*	*duše*	*sǫdьje*
	Acc	*ženǫ*	*dušǫ*	*sǫdьjǫ*
	Gen	*ženy*	*dušě/dušę*	*sǫdьjě/sǫdьję*
	Dat	*ženě*	*duši*	*sǫdьji*
	Instr	*ženojǫ*	*dušejǫ*	*sǫdьjejǫ*
	Loc	*ženě*	*duši*	*sǫdьji*
Dual	Nom	*ženě*	*duši*	*sǫdьji*
	Voc	=NOM	=NOM	=NOM
	Acc	=NOM	=NOM	=NOM
	Gen	*ženu*	*dušu*	*sǫdьju*
	Dat	*ženama*	*dušama*	*sǫdьjama*
	Instr	=DAT	=DAT	=DAT
	Loc	=GEN	=GEN	=GEN
Plural	Nom	*ženy*	*dušě/dušę*	*sǫdьjě/sǫdьję*
	Voc	=NOM	=NOM	=NOM
	Acc	=NOM	=NOM	=NOM
	Gen	*ženъ*	*dušь*	*sǫdьjь*
	Dat	*ženamъ*	*dušamъ*	*sǫdьjamъ*
	Instr	*ženami*	*dušami*	*sǫdьjami*
	Loc	*ženaxъ*	*dušaxъ*	*sǫdьjaxъ*

Note on variants: endings in ě/ę are early North *vs* South developments (1.4.1).

(23) 'mother is proud of her work'
　　Rus *mát' gordítsja svoím trudóm* [InstrSg]
　　Blg *májka se gordée **săs** svója trúd* (lit. 'with …')

The case decline of Bulgarian and Macedonian is dramatic. But it is nonetheless across paradigms that the most striking changes in Slavic have taken place,

Table 5.5. a/ja *declension in modern languages: PSl* žena *'woman'*, duša *'soul'*

		B/C/S		Russian		Czech	
Sing	Nom	*žèn-a*	*dúš-a*	*žen-á*	*duš-á*	*žen-a*	*duš-e*
	Voc	*žèn-o*	*dûš-o*	=NOM	=NOM	*žen-o*	=NOM
	Acc	*žèn-u*	*dûš-u*	*žen-ú*	*dúš-u*	*žen-u*	=DAT
	Gen	*žèn-ē*	*dúš-ē*	*žen-ý*	*duš-í*	*žen-y*	=NOM
	Dat	*žèn-i*	*dúš-i*	*žen-é*	*duš-é*	*žen-ě*	*duš-i*
	Instr	*žèn-ōm*	*dúš-ōm*	*žen-ój*	*duš-ój*	*žen-ou*	*duš-í*
	Loc	=DAT	=DAT	=DAT	=DAT	=DAT	=DAT
Plur	Nom	*žèn-e*	*dûš-e*	*žèn-y*	*dúš-i*	*žen-y*	*duš-e*
	Voc	=NOM	*dûš-e*	=NOM	=NOM	=NOM	=NOM
		žèn-e					
	Acc	=NOM	=NOM	=GEN	=NOM	=NOM	=NOM
	Gen	*žén-ā*	*dúš-ā*	*žèn-ø*	*dúš-ø*	*žen-ø*	*duš-í*
	Dat	*žèn-ama*	*dúš-ama*	*žèn-am*	*dúš-am*	*žen-ám*	*duš-ím*
	Instr	=DAT	=DAT	*žèn-ami*	*dúš-ami*	*žen-ami*	*duš-emi*
	Loc	=DAT	=DAT	*žèn-ax*	*dúš-ax*	*žen-ách*	*duš-ích*

Table 5.6. *Proto-Slavic* ĭ*-stems:* kostь *'bone'*, gostь *'guest'*

		Fem	Masc
Singular	Nom	*kost-ь*	*gost-ь*
	Voc	*kost-i*	*gost-i*
	Acc	=NOM	=NOM
	Gen	*kost-i*	*gost-i*
	Dat	=GEN	=GEN
	Instr	*kost-ьjǫ*	*gost-ьmь*
	Loc	=GEN	=GEN
Dual	Nom	*kost-i*	*gost-i*
	Voc	=NOM	=NOM
	Acc	=NOM	=NOM
	Gen	*kost-ьju*	*gost-ьju*
	Dat	=GEN	=GEN
	Instr	*kost-ьma*	*gost-ьma*
	Loc	=INSTR	=INSTR
Plural	Nom	*kost-i*	*gost-ьje*
	Voc	=NOM	=ACC
	Acc	=NOM	*gost-i*
	Gen	*kost-ьjь*	*gost-ьjь*
	Dat	*kost-ьmъ*	*gost-ьmъ*
	Instr	*kost-ьmi*	*gost-ьmi*
	Loc	*kost-ьxъ*	*gost-ьxъ*

Table 5.7. i-*declension in modern languages: PSl* костъ *'bone'*, gostь *'guest'*

		B/C/S		Russian		Czech	
Sing	Nom	*kôst-ø*	*gôst-ø*	*kóst'-ø*	*góst'-ø*	*kost-ø*	*host-ø*
	Voc	= GEN	*gôst-e*	= NOM	= NOM	*kost-i*	*host-e*
	Acc	= NOM	= GEN	= NOM	= GEN	= NOM	= GEN
	Gen	*kôst-i*	*gôst-a*	*kóst-i*	*góst-ja*	*kost-i*	*host-a*
	Dat	= GEN	*gôst-u*	= GEN	*góst-ju*	= GEN	*host-u*
	Instr	= GEN	*gôst-om*	*kóst-'ju*	*góst-em*	*kost-i*	*host-em*
		kôšć-u					
	Loc	*kòst-i*	*gòst-u*	= GEN	*'gost-e*	= GEN	= DAT
Plur	Nom	*kôst-i*	*gôst-i*	*kóst-i*	*góst-i*	*kost-i*	*host-i*
							host-é
	Voc	= NOM	= NOM	= NOM	= NOM	= NOM	= NOM
	Acc	= NOM	*gôst-e*	= NOM	= GEN	= NOM	*host-y*
	Gen	*kòst-ī*	*gòst-ijū*	*kost-éj*	*gost-éj*	*kost-i*	*host-ů*
		kòst-ijū	*gòst-ī*				*host-í*
	Dat	*kòst-ima*	*gòst-ima*	*kost-jám*	*gost-jám*	*kost-em*	*host-ům*
	Instr	= DAT	= DAT	*kost-jámi*	*gost-jámi*	*kost-mi*	*host-y*
	Loc	= DAT	= DAT	*kost-jáx*	*gost-jáx*	*kost-ech*	*host-ech*

Table 5.8. *Proto-Slavic* ū-*stems:* cṛ'ky *'church'*

	Sing		Du		Plur	
	PSl	Cz	PSl	PSl	Cz	
Nom	*cṛ'k-y*	*církev-ø*	*cṛ'kъv-i*	*cṛ'kъv-i*	*církv-e*
Gen	*cṛ'kъv-e*	*církv-e*	*cṛ'kъv-u*	*cṛ'kъv-ъ*	*církv-í*
Dat	*cṛ'kъv-i*	*církv-i*	*cṛ'kъv-ьma*	*cṛ'kъv-amъ*	*církv-im*
Acc	*cṛ'kъv-ь*	= NOM	= NOM	= NOM	= NOM
Instr	*cṛ'kъv-ьjǫ*	*církv-í*	= DAT	*cṛ'kъv-ami*	*církv-emi*
Loc	*cṛ'kъv-e*	= DAT	= GEN	*cṛ'kъv-axъ*	*církv-ich*
Voc	= NOM	= GEN	= NOM	= NOM	= NOM

since they affect so many of the languages, in some cases across the board. The richness of Proto-Slavic has given way to a significantly simplified set of paradigms, where Czech remains on the conservative side. Of the six original declensional paradigms of Proto-Slavic (5.5.1.1–6), only three – the *i*, *a/ja* and *o/jo*-declensions – survive as vital components of the modern systems. The *consonant*-declension, including *ū/v* (see below), is restricted, and the

Table 5.9. *Proto-Slavic* consonant-*stems:* kamy *'stone'* (n) *[Masc]*, imę *'name'* (n) *[Neut]*, matь *'mother'* (r) *[Fem]*, slovo *'word'* (s) *[Neut]*, telę *'calf'* (nt) *[Neut]*

		n		r	s	nt
Sg	Nom	*kam-y*	*im-ę*	*mat-i*	*slov-o*	*tel-ę*
	Voc	= NOM	= NOM	= NOM	= NOM	= NOM
	Acc	*kamen-ь*	= NOM	*mater-ь*	= NOM	= NOM
	Gen	*kamen-e*	*imen-e*	*mater-e*	*sloves-e*	*telęt-e*
	Dat	*kamen-i*	*imen-i*	*mater-i*	*sloves-i*	*telęt-i*
	Instr	*kamen-ьmь*	*imen-ьmь*	*mater-ьjǫ*	*sloves-ьmь*	*telęt-ьmь*
	Loc	*kamen-e*	*imen-e*	*mater-e*	*sloves-e*	*telęt-e*
Du	Nom	*kamen-i*	*imen-ě*	*mater-i*	*sloves-ě*	*telęt-ě*
	Voc	= NOM	= NOM	= NOM	= NOM	= NOM
	Acc	= NOM	= NOM	= NOM	= NOM	= NOM
	Gen	*kamen-u*	*imen-u*	*mater-u*	*sloves-u*	*telęt-u*
	Dat	*kamen-ьma*	*imen-ьma*	*mater-ьma*	*sloves-ьma*	*telęt-ьma*
	Instr	= DAT	= DAT	= DAT	= DAT	= DAT
	Loc	= GEN	= GEN	= GEN	= GEN	= GEN
Pl	Nom	*kamen-e*	*imen-a*	*mater-i*	*sloves-a*	*telęt-a*
	Voc	= NOM	= NOM	= NOM	= NOM	= NOM
	Acc	*kamen-i*	= NOM	= NOM	= NOM	= NOM
	Gen	*kamen-ъ*	*imen-ъ*	*mater-ъ*	*sloves-ъ*	*telęt-ъ*
	Dat	*kamen-ьmъ*	*imen-ьmъ*	*mater-ьmъ*	*sloves-ьmъ*	*telęt-ьmъ*
	Instr	*kamen-ьmi*	*imen-y*	*mater-ьmi*	*sloves-y*	*telęt-y*
	Loc	*kamen-ьxъ*	*imen-ьxъ*	*mater-ьxъ*	*sloves-ьxъ*	*telęt-ьxъ*

ŭ-declension has largely been absorbed into *o/jo*, though with several of its distinctive inflexions retained to a greater or lesser extent. In contrast, the pronoun system's expression of case has been kept fairly well. Indeed, by adding clitic pronominal endings to adjectives, some of the Slavic and Baltic languages have created new ("long" and/or "definite") paradigms (5.5.2). Taken as a whole, Slavic has been conservative in its retention of case systems, and stands with the Baltic languages against, say, Romance and Germanic. But it has been reformist in its approach to the management of paradigms in which case-based distinctiveness can be expressed.

A great deal of attention has been paid in Slavic linguistics not only to the evolution and distinctiveness of the various case forms but also to the meanings of the cases. Since these issues have to do with the ways in which morphological constituents and material combine with other elements above the level of the word, we shall leave this discussion to chapters 6–7, together with the question of the syntactic uses and semantic properties of cases.

5.4.3   Definiteness and deixis

The category of definiteness is expressed in Bulgarian and Macedonian by a post-posed definite article (originally a Proto-Slavic demonstrative/deictic pronoun) (Blg *zemjá* 'earth', *zemjáta* 'the earth'), a typically Balkan phenomenon found also in Romanian and Albanian. The Bulgarian and Macedonian article is a suffix which follows whatever inflexion is present in the noun or adjective. However, since the articles also inflect, we shall discuss them under the heading of inflexion. The definite marker is affixed to the leftmost inflecting member of a noun phrase. An unmodified noun takes the definite suffix itself (24b), but when there is a modifying adjective, the definite suffix attaches itself to the leftmost adjective (24c):

(24)   *Bulgarian post-posed article*

(24a)   Blg   *vízdam kón/kónja*   'I see a horse/the horse'

(24b)   Blg   *kónjat vízda cárja*   'the horse sees the Tsar'

(24c)   Blg   *xúbavata i plodoródna zemjá*   'the beautiful and fertile land'

In Macedonian there is not only a definite article suffix, but also two deictic suffixes for "this" [Proximate] and "that" [Non-proximate]:

(25)   *Macedonian post-posed definite and deictic suffixes*

Mac	*žena*	'woman'
	ženata	'the woman'
	ženava	'this woman'
	ženana	'that woman'

For details of the articles, see 5.5.1. Other Slavic languages have no articles, though some use the numeral '1' for indefinites (e.g. Bulgarian: Scatton, 1984: 41), and determiners like 'this' for definiteness (11.3); such usages are often not recognized by the official grammars. Dialectal North Russian has a post-posed article like that of Bulgarian and Macedonian, but this phenomenon is not found in the standard language (10.3.3).

Slavic languages lacking articles handle definiteness through lexical deictics and the manipulation of word order (7.4), aspect (5.4.7) and Functional Sentence Perspective (7.5).

5.4.4   Gender

Gender is an inherent property of nouns, nominalized forms and some personal pronouns. It is also marked, by concord and agreement, on adjectives, participles, ordinal numerals, determiners, concording quantifiers, some cardinal numbers, the *l*-participle forms of verbs and Czech gerunds.

Proto-Slavic possessed the three genders of Indo-European: masculine, feminine and neuter, which have passed into all the modern Slavic languages as the "primary" genders:

(26)   Ukr   Masculine: *vin* 'he, it'; *kit* 'cat'; *kúxar* 'cook'
             Feminine: *voná* 'she, it'; *bezžálistnisť* 'ruthlessness'; *bloxá* 'flea'
             Neuter: *vonó* 'it'; *dno* 'bottom'; *móre* 'sea'; *obnimánnja* 'embrace'

In general, the genders of nouns are correlated with the final sound of the citation form (nominative singular):

Masculine: hard consonant; some soft consonants (if present in the language)
Feminine: *-a, -ja*; some soft consonants (if present in the language)
Neuter: *-o, -e*

The modern Slavic languages also have words of common gender ("epicenes"), nouns which are masculine or feminine according to the entity they refer to (cf. Fr *enfant*):

(27a)   Pol   *ten biedny* [Masc]/*ta biedna* [Fem] **kaleka** *nie może chodzić*
             'this poor cripple cannot walk'

(27b)   Rus   *šéľma poslál* [Masc]/*poslála* [Fem] *sčët*
             'the **rogue** sent a bill'

Across the languages a number of such nouns in *-a* are epicenes.

The presence of a cognate root in two languages is no guarantee that the words will have the same primary gender. Differences of gender in certain cognate words, in fact, are one of the cues which distinguish nouns in closely related languages (whether in native (28a) or borrowed (28b) lexical items):

(28a)   Serb   *svěska* [Fem], Cr *svězak* 'a volume' [Masc]

(28b)   'system':   Rus, Blg *sistéma*, Ukr *systéma*, Bel *sistèma* [Fem];
                  Sorb, Pol *system*, Cz, Slk *systém*, B/C/S *sistēm*, Sln *sistém*, Mac *sistem* [Masc]

Primary grammatical gender is closely related to sex in those instances where the reference is to biological gender. Masculine nouns may designate referents of either sex, though they usually refer to male or asexual (animate or inanimate) entities:

(29a)   Rus   *sekretár'* 'secretary', *dóktor/vrač* 'doctor' [Masc/Fem]

(29b)   Ukr   *kúxar* 'cook', *xlópec'* 'lad', *myslývec'* 'hunter' [Masc]

(29c)   Ukr   *dub* 'oak', *mist* 'bridge', *mózok* 'brain', *velosypéd* 'bicycle'
         [Masc]

Feminine nouns (*a/ja* or *i*) as a rule do not refer to male humans, with a few exceptions, especially for honorifics and insults, usually through reference to an animal (30c); most are common gender:

(30a)   Ukr   *hoduvál'nycja* 'wet-nurse'   Sln   *tájnica* 'secretary'
         Rus   *vladýka* 'bishop', *sud'já* 'judge', *kolléga* 'colleague'

(30b)   Slk   *osoba, osobnost'* 'person', *Veličina* 'eminence', *Vysost'* 'excellency'

(30c)   Rus   *Iván? Èta svin'já ...* 'Ivan? That pig ...'

Feminine or masculine names of animals may refer to either males or females (that is, the non-specific, generic name):

(31)   Generic animal names

(31a)   Rus   *obez'jána* 'monkey', *výdra* 'otter' [Fem]

(31b)   Rus   *volk* 'wolf', *medvéd'* 'bear' [Masc]

In the latter case, the female is normally marked by an added suffix:

(31c)   Rus   *volč-íc-a/volč-íx-a* 'she-wolf', *medvéd-ic-a* 'she-bear'

Neuters may exceptionally refer to humans, notably in diminutives and augmentatives, and in honorifics:

(32)   Rus   *Váše Prevosxodítel'stvo* 'Your Excellency'

But neuters usually refer to inanimates or abstracts:

(33)   Bel   *aknó* 'window', *bezrabócce* 'idleness, being out of work'

or to young animals or children:

(34)   Cz   *dítě* 'child   Ukr   *teljá* 'calf', *porosjá* 'piglet'

Abstracts may occur in any primary gender.

Proportions of the genders differ somewhat across the languages, but the ratio of masculine:feminine:neuter is about 3:2:1 (Schupbach, 1984; Corbett, 1991). There is an interesting relationship between gender and word-formational suffixes (8.2.2). New words in Slavic are predominantly masculine or feminine, with productivity in the neuters being restricted, apart from deverbal abstract action nominals. As a result, the neuter is falling further behind the feminine, which is, in turn, falling somewhat behind the masculine in the overall development of nouns.

Modern Slavic also has a system of "secondary gender", involving the features [Animate], [Personal] (i.e. referring to humans) and [Masculine Personal]. The secondary genders affect only the nominative plural and the accusative (and marginally the genitive singular – see below), and then not in all the numbers and not in all the languages. In the singular, [Animate] affects the accusative of masculine nouns: animates take the form of the genitive in all but Bulgarian and Macedonian (no cases), and the Kajkavian variant of B/C/S, to express the accusative:

(35a) Sln *poznám tá glás*   'I know that voice'   [MascInan]

(35b) Sln *poznám téga fánta*   'I know that boy'   [MascAnim]

Grammatical animacy is not the same as physical animacy. There are some "honorary animates" in a small number of semantic classes, which act as if they were animate in the masculine singular, and in the nominative-accusative plural:

(36) 'corpse':   Rus *trup*, Pol *nieboszczyk* 'cadaver', Rus *mertvéc*
                           'dead man'
      mushrooms: Sorb *prawak, brězak, kozak* (all designating types
                           of mushrooms; but *hrib* 'mushroom' is a regular
                           inanimate)
      playing cards
      and game pieces: Pol *pionek* 'pawn', *koń* 'knight', Rus *tuz* 'ace'
      dances: Pol *mazurek* 'mazurka'   Rus *gopák* 'gopak'
      games: Pol *tenis* 'tennis' (*grać w tenisa* 'to play tennis')
      cars: Pol *Fiat* 'Fiat car'

B/C/S, which includes here only the names of chess pieces, has the smallest number of honorary animates. Ukrainian and Belarusian exclude the names of animals, but Ukrainian includes many semantic inanimates, apparently centred on the notion of 'well-shaped object' (Shevelov, 1993: 958). In West Slavic and Ukrainian, animate masculines tend to take the genitive singular in -*a*, and inanimate masculines tend to take the genitive singular in -*u*.

In the plural, gender is marked only in the nominative and the accusative. Primary gender is found in the nominative and accusative plural of concording modifiers in B/C/S and Slovenian, and partly in Czech. Secondary gender occurs in the plural in East and West Slavic. The features which control its selection are:

(37) *Plural: secondary gender*

	Nominative plural	Accusative plural
East Sl	–	[±Animate]
Sorb, Pol, Slk	[±Masculine Personal]	[±Masculine Personal]
Cz	[Masculine Animate]	–
	vs [Neuter, Other]	

The inflexional form of concording modifiers like determiners and adjectives is controlled by the gender of the head noun (35b: *téga* is [MascAcc = GenSg]).

When gender distinctions are made, they usually follow a two-way distinction, like [+Animate] *vs* [−Animate]. But Slovenian and B/C/S have a three-way division into the primary genders, and Czech has a unique three-way split into masculine animates, neuters, and a third group ('Other' in (37)) consisting of masculine inanimates and feminines.

The forms of the various gender markings follow these general rules:

5.4.4.1 *Nominative plural*
There is no fully reliable rule, though the marked secondary gender (masculine personal or masculine animate) will often show palatalization, as in *mili* in (38a):

(38a) Pol *miły student* [Sg] 'nice student'   *mili studenci* [Pl]

(38b) Pol *miły portret* [Sg] 'nice portrait'   *miłe portrety* [Pl]

(38c) Pol *miła studentka* [FemSg] 'nice student' *miłe studentki* [Pl]

The *l*-participle shows similar gender distinctions:

(39) Pol 'they did': *oni robili* [MascPersPl]
                        one robiły [Other]

5.4.4.2 *Accusative plural*
In East Slavic, Sorbian, Polish and Slovak, the marked gender ([Animate], etc.) usually takes the same form as the genitive plural. The unmarked gender takes the same form as the corresponding nominative plural:

(40a) Rus *krasívye dévuški* [NomPl] *ljúbjat menjá*
            '(the) beautiful girls love me'

(40b) Rus *eë krasívye portréty* [NomPl] *naxódjatsja v Èrmitáže*
            'her beautiful portraits are in the Hermitage'

(40c)   Rus   *já ljubljú   krasívyx dévušek* [AccPl = GenPl]/
                 krasívye portréty [AccPl = NomPl]
                 'I love beautiful girls/beautiful portraits'

In Czech the accusative plural shows secondary gender differently. Masculine animate nouns have an accusative plural different from both the nominative plural and the genitive plural, while for other nouns the two case forms of the nominative and accusative plural are the same. Adjectives and modifiers have a neuter accusative plural in -*a*, and all other genders in -*e*:

(41a)   Cz   [NomPl]:   *ti vysocí lvi*   'these tall lions'
                           ty vysoké domy   'these tall houses'
                           ta velká města   'these big towns'

(41b)   Cz   [AccPl]:   *viděl jsem ty vysoké lvy/ty vysoké domy/ta velká města*
                           'I saw these tall lions/houses/big towns'

B/C/S and Slovenian operate with a primary gender distinction which does not involve the genitive plural at all. Bulgarian and Macedonian show gender only with "direct quantification", where masculines take the "secondary" plural endings from the old dual (referred to as the "number/counting form"):

(42a)   Blg   *učeník* 'teacher' [Masc], [Pl] *učenici*; BUT *četiri učeníka* '4 teachers'

(42b)   Blg   *učeníčka* 'teacher' [Fem], [Pl] *učeníčki*; *četiri učeníčki* '4 teachers'

The dual in Slovenian shows an identical nominative and accusative, with masculines in -*a* distinct from the other two genders. Sorbian is more complex. In Upper Sorbian, masculine animates show an accusative = genitive in the noun and adjective, and a [±Masculine Personal] distinction in the nominative of the adjective:

(43)   Sorb   'good men'   [NomDu]   *dobraja mužej*
                               [AccDu]   *dobreju mužow*
                'good worms'   [NomDu]   *dobre čerwjej*
                               [AccDu]   *dobrej čerwjow*
                'good oaks'   [NomDu]   *dobre dubaj*
                               [AccDu]   *dobrej dubaj*

Lower Sorbian operates with the feature [Masculine Animate] for the nominative and accusative of dual nouns, but the adjectives do not vary for secondary gender.

Gender may have a curious effect on numerals. Polish numbers under 1,000, and Slovak numbers under 100, have masculine animate forms. In Upper Sorbian it is obligatory to mark the feature [MascPers] with '3–4', and optional with '5–99'.

Compare the numeral '3' in (44a), modifying a masculine animate subject, with the non-masculine animate subject of (44b):

(44a)   Slk   ***traja*** *chlapi*   '3 boys'

(44b)   Slk   ***tri*** *dievčatá*   '3 girls'

With these exceptions, Slavic numerals do not show distinctions of primary gender above '2'. The numeral '1' has all three genders, and is treated like a determiner; and '2' operates with a [±Fem] contrast in East Slavic, Polish and B/C/S, with [±Masc] in the rest (as in Proto-Slavic) (see 5.5.4.1).

Of the three Slavic genders, the neuter is clearly the most at risk. It has been lost in some Russian (Stankiewicz, 1968b) and Slovenian dialects (Stankiewicz, 1965; Priestly, 1983: 353–355), and is distinguished mostly by its ability to express abstracts, especially deverbals, via suffixes (Schupbach, 1984). In Russian neuters have only about 13% of the stock of nouns, and are declining (Corbett, 1991: 317). Relatively few new words created from within Slavic languages or borrowed from without (9.5–6) enter as neuters. In addition, the neuter is the most weakly distinguished of the genders in terms of distinctive inflexions or agreement (Corbett, 1991). While it will certainly be retained as a grammatical category, if only by the prescriptive and educational policies of language maintenance in the Slavic countries (11.2), the neuter is likely to become progressively less vital. It has already been lost in Romance and in Lithuanian.

5.4.5   Person

Person in Slavic is a lexical category of personal pronouns, and an inflexional category of verbs:

(45)   B/C/S   *mȍlīm*   'I ask'

                       mȍlīš   'you [Sg] ask'

                       mȍlī   'he/she/it asks'

though it is not marked in all the categories of the verb, including the past tense forms of East Slavic:

(46)   Ukr   *já/tý/vín znáv*   'I [Masc]/you [MascSg]/he knew'

In personal pronouns the category of person is a lexical category, and is marked by different root forms:

(47)   Sln   *jàz*   'I'   *tí*   'you [Sg]'   *òn/óna/óno*   'he/she/it'

                  mí   'we'   *ví*   'you [Pl]'   *óni/óne/óna*   'they'

There are three persons:

> First Person ([1Pers]), 'I' and 'we', including the speaker
> Second Person ([2Pers]), 'you', including the hearer(s)
> Third Person ([3Pers]), 'he/she/it/they', referring to neither the
> speaker nor the hearer.

Person is marked for all three numbers in verbs and many pronouns. Gender is marked only on the 3 Person pronouns, and in the Slovenian dual. For Slavic impersonal constructions, which are widely used in Slavic see 7.3.3.

5.4.6   Tense

Tense is found in all the finite parts of the verb, including the participles and gerunds. Tenses may be simplex or complex (5.5.5.2). By convention [Tense] is the category around which the verbal paradigms are organized.

All eleven languages have a single present tense, which expresses both the "does" and "is doing" forms of the English present. But there are important differences in the past and future tenses. The languages are usually divided into two groups, based on the inventory of their tenses. This classification aligns Sorbian with South Slavic, and Slovenian with East and West Slavic:

a.   Languages which preserve the Proto-Slavic imperfect (repeated, habitual or ongoing past actions) and aorist (single or completed past actions): B/C/S, Bulgarian, Macedonian and Sorbian show the following tenses:

   present
   past: imperfect, aorist, perfect, pluperfect
   future: imperfective, perfective, perfect
   conditional: regular, past

   (Bulgarian also has a more remote future perfect tense known as the "future-in-the-past", translated by 'I was on the point of having done'; in B/C/S the imperfect and aorist are now literary forms only.)

   The term "perfect", which must not be confused with the perfective aspect (8.3), refers to tenses formed with an auxiliary (usually 'be') and the *l*-participle.

b.   Languages which have lost the imperfect and aorist: the languages in this group are East Slavic (Russian, Ukrainian, Belarusian), West Slavic excluding Sorbian (Polish, Czech, Slovak), and Slovenian:

present
past: imperfective, perfective, pluperfect
future: imperfective, perfective
conditional: regular, past

(Russian has no pluperfect, and Russian and Belarusian have no past conditional. The auxiliary has been lost in the past in East Slavic.)

When we consider the tenses themselves, we find that they divide into a past ~ non-past grouping rather than into past ~ present ~ future. Particularly in East Slavic, the past tenses are formed from *l*-participles and do not mark [Person], having lost the auxiliary. The present and future do mark [Person], and indeed share the same inflexions for the present and future perfective:

(48a)   Rus   *já guljál*   'I was going for a walk'   [PastImprfv, MascSg]

(48b)   Rus   *já poguljál*   'I went for a walk'   [PastPrfv, MascSg]

(49a)   Rus   *já guljáju*   'I am out for a walk'   [Pres, 1Sg]

(49b)   Rus   *já poguljáju*   'I shall go for a walk'   [FutPrfv, 1Sg]

In West Slavic, however, the formal dichotomy of past ~ non-past is less obvious. The past tenses also mark [Person], the inflexion appearing in the auxiliary:

(50)   Cz   *procházel*   *jsem*   *se*
            was going for a walk-MascSg   AuxCl-1Sg   ReflCl
            'I was out for a walk'

And in B/C/S, Bulgarian, Macedonian and Sorbian the presence of the imperfect and aorist, with inflexional patterns more like those of the present, makes the system less a matter of past *vs* non-past than in West, and especially East, Slavic. Note, however, that B/C/S has a present perfective *dôdjēm* 'I (often) come': using present-tense inflexions with perfective stems does not result in a future, as in West and East Slavic (cf. the Russian future perfective *dojdú* 'I shall reach'). This factor places B/C/S partly with the B group as well, and the rise of aspect at the expense of tense in B/C/S is pushing it increasingly in this direction, as is the colloquial loss of the imperfect and aorist.

The contrast between the (a) and (b) systems, however, goes deeper than this. In the first system, there are two ways of expressing repeated, habitual or ongoing past actions: the imperfect, and the perfect formed with the imperfective *l*-participle:

(51a)   Blg   *pătúvax*   [Imperf]   'I was going/used to go'

(51b)   Blg   *pătúval săm*   [Perf Imprfv]   'I was going/used to go'

And there are two ways of expressing single complete(d) past actions: the aorist, and the perfect formed with the perfective *l*-participle:

(52a) Blg *popătúvax*   [Aor]   'I went'
(52b) Blg *popătúval săm* [Perf Prfv] 'I went'

This overlap is commonly supposed to have brought about the development of the B system, which eliminated the imperfect and aorist in favor of the *l*-participle forms. We can even see this process at work in modern B/C/S, where the imperfect and the aorist have been almost totally replaced in the spoken language by the forms with the *l*-participle, and are optional even in the literary language (Browne, 1993: 330).

The result of this reorganization of the tense system can be expressed in another way. In the A system the verbs are organized very much around the tenses; aspect is operative, but only as one component of verb forms. But in the B system aspect has become much more prominent, particularly in the past tenses. Both aspect and tense are present in both the A and B systems, just as they are in English. But in the new B system there has been a certain shift which has given aspect a more obvious, often dominant, role.

5.4.7   Aspect

Since aspect is discussed in some detail in 6.3 and 8.3, we restrict ourselves here to a basic overview of the issue. There are two aspects: perfective and imperfective, which are not to be confused with the perfect and imperfect tenses (5.4.6). As a first approximation, perfective verb forms express an action or state which is seen as complete, completed, total, or unified, or with reference to a specific location in space and time, or to the completion of a specific goal ("telic"). The imperfective expresses actions or states which are incomplete, still in progress, repeated or habitual (6.3, examples 114–115).

The present tense is therefore normally imperfective (except in a few instances, especially in B/C/S and Czech, see 6.3, examples 117, 200). Past and future tenses, as well as the participles, gerunds and imperatives, can be either perfective or imperfective. Past perfectives share inflexions with past imperfectives, and future perfectives share inflexions with the present (6.3, examples 118–119).

Differences in aspect are signalled by the verb stem, where word-forming processes are used to construct perfective stems from imperfective stems (mainly by pre-fixation), and imperfective stems from perfective stems (mainly by suffixation) (see 8.3). Aspect therefore belongs partly with inflexional morphology, and partly with word formation (8.3). We discuss aspect as a morphosyntactic category in 6.3.

5.4.8 Voice

Slavic can express both the active and passive voices. Although it does not possess passive inflexions as such, certain of the expressions of the passive are closely related to inflexional patterns.

1. AUXILIARY + PAST PASSIVE PARTICIPLE

The auxiliary is usually 'be' for both actions and states, as in English:

(53) Rus *kníga bylá pródana* 'the book was sold' (action and state)

In Polish *zostać* 'become, remain' is used for actions, and *być* 'be' for states (cf. German *werden* and *sein*):

(54a) Pol *książka została sprzedana*   'the book was sold' (action)

(54b) Pol *książka była sprzedana*   'the book was sold' (state)

In this construction the participle is usually perfective.

The passive construction can express a single (not habitual or repeated) action, or a steady ongoing state:

(55a) Ukr *sád búv posádženyj účnjami*   'the garden was planted by the pupils'

(55b) Sorb *kniha worduje čitana*   'the book is read'
(from German *werden*: dialectal and sub-standard in Sorbian)

Macedonian uses this construction as an active perfect tense with the *n/t* past "passive" participles of intransitive verbs (5.5.5.6)

2. VERB + REFLEXIVE

The formal reflexive is a verbal affix in East Slavic, and a clitic pronoun in West and South Slavic. In (56) the reflexive is marked by the suffix *-sja*:

(56) Rus *úlicy nášix gorodóv i sël **osvetljájutsja** èlektríčestvom*
'the streets of our cities and villages are lit by electricity'

This construction expresses habitual or repeated passive actions or states. Animate agents tend to make the whole structure reflexive rather than passive (57a), while inanimate agents tend to occur with the proper passive interpretation (57b):

(57a) Rus *já **mójus'** xolódnoj vodój*   'I wash (myself) in cold water'

(57b) Rus *ókna **mójutsja** xolódnoj vodój*   'the windows are washed with cold water'

The morphology of the reflexive affix in East Slavic makes it a marginal inflexional category of verbs, while [Reflexive] is marked by a clitic pronoun in West and South Slavic:

(58)   'I wash myself': Ukr *mýjusja* cf. Cz *myji se* Blg *míja se*

The reflexive marker even occurs with derived verbal nouns in Polish:

(59)   'changing one's clothes':   Pol *przebieranie się*
                                       cf. Ukr *pereodjahánnja*

The reflexive form also expresses reciprocal or mutual actions:

(60)   Rus *oní perepísyvajutsja* 'they correspond' (by mail)

Slavic also has a number of verbs which are reflexive in form, but semantically active:

(61)   Bel *ón rádavaŭsja* 'he rejoiced/was glad'

Such deponent-reflexive verbs, however, may correspond to non-reflexive forms in another Slavic language:

(62)   'hurry':
        Pol *śpieszyć się*   Blg *spéša se*
    cf. Rus *spešít'*   Ukr *pospišáty*

The other expressions of the passive are syntactic, and are not directly inflexional. They involve the use of the indefinite-personal and impersonal constructions, as well as word order (7.3.3, 7.4).

5.4.9   Mood

Slavic possesses an imperative, which usually expresses commands:

(63a)   Sorb   **njezabudźće na nana a maćer**
                 'do not forget [Pl] your father and mother'
(63b)   Sorb   **pójmoj domoj!**

Imperatives may be softened by the inclusion of a subject pronoun:

(64a)   Pol   **pomóż matce**
                'help mother!'
(64b)   Pol   **a ty pomóż matce**
                'and you'd better help mother'

or may be emphasized by imperative enclitic particles (65b). Imperatives may express other notions, including irony, exclamations and a historic present:

(65a)   Rus   *edvá mý vídeli rodítelej kak pribeží* [Imper2Sg]*Vánja*
        'no sooner did we see the parents than Vanja came running up'

(65b)   Rus   *pojdëm-te*! [Imper1Pl + particle]
        'let's go!'

Commands may also be expressed by forms other than the imperative, including *l*-participles, infinitives, periphrastic 3 Person constructions, and the conditional:

(66a)   Rus   *poéxali*! [PastPl]
        'let's go!'

(66b)   Rus   *ne kurít'* [Inf]
        'no smoking'

(66c)   Rus   *púst' ón pridët* [particle – he – 3SgFutPrfv]
        'let him come'

The conditional mood fulfills many of the functions of a subjunctive. It is expressed by the *l*-participle, with the conditional of the auxiliary 'be', or with a conditional particle (*bi* in (67) derived from the conditional of 'be'):

(67)   'I would begin/I would have begun'
       Sln   *jàz bi začél; bi bíl začél*
       B/C/S *jâ bih pòčeo; pòčeo bih*

The conditional can express conditions, hypothetical statements and mild commands. And it is used to introduce subordinate clauses of non-factual events, notably after verbs of wishing, desiring and fearing:

(68)   Cz   *bojím se, **uby lékař nepřišel** pozdě*
       'I am afraid that the doctor may come (too) late'

It is sometimes claimed that the optative, which expresses a wish ('would that ...'), is a category of Slovenian. In form it is the same as the periphrastic 3 Person imperative in the other languages:

(69)   Sln   *náj bi bíl pádel*   'would that he had fallen' [Past Optative]

The renarrative, which is used for the reporting of facts vouched for by someone other than the speaker, is a morphological category in the verb paradigms of Bulgarian and Macedonian, and is probably due to the influence of Turkish. While not called a "mood" in Bulgarian or Macedonian grammars – but simply a conjugation – it is common, and useful, to treat it so in English-based descriptions (some linguists call it the "Indirect Mood"). It affects only some tense forms:

Bulgarian: perfect past, pluperfect, conditional, future, future perfect
Macedonian: perfect past, past conditional, future

The renarrated forms are used not only to report "distanced" (Lunt, 1952) facts, but also to express doubt, incredulity or unexpectedness. They are the standard verb form for fairy tales and legends, and in this way suggest neatly that the events described are not historically attested; the renarrated forms in (70) are in bold type:

(70a)   Blg *Ednó vréme v njákoe si cárstvo **ímalo** edná cárska dǎšterjá ...*
        *Tjá **bíla** xúbava, očíte i **bíli** čérni kató tája čérna nóšt ...*
        'Once in a kingdom there was a king's daughter. She was beautiful, her eyes were as black as this black night ...'

(70b)   Blg *Vojnícite **bíli** v pǎlno bójno snarjažénie*
        'They say that the soldiers were in full battle dress'

5.5   Paradigms

We present below the paradigms of the inflecting parts of speech in Slavic, first the nominals (nouns (5.5.1), adjectives and determiners (5.5.2), pronouns (5.5.3) and numerals (5.5.4)), and then the verbs (5.5.5–5.5.6). We shall start from Proto-Slavic, particularly in the case of the nominals, since the Proto-Slavic forms provide an indispensable basis for an understanding of the ways in which the modern paradigms have simplified and mixed the original patterns and categories.

Slavic morphology is rich in sub-classes and exceptions. We shall present only the major patterns and typical exceptions, in order to illustrate the underlying nature of the paradigms. More detailed information about the paradigms of individual languages can be found in the standard grammars of each language, and in the works listed in the bibliography.

5.5.1   Nouns

Proto-Slavic nouns formed six inflexional paradigms (or five, for those who include the ū-stems in the *consonant*-declension), whose traditional names reflect the Indo-European and early Proto-Slavic themes or suffixes. (Note that, while it is common to refer to these declensions as 'stems' (*a/ja*-stems, etc.), we shall use the term 'declension'.) Later Proto-Slavic converted long and short vowels into different qualities (see 1.3.1), and the relevant equivalences – which we shall use for these and all subsequent examples (other than the declension names themselves) are:

Early PSl	Late PSl
jo	e
ŭ	ъ
ū	y
ĭ	ь
o	o (no change)
a	a (no change)
ja	ja (no change)
ī	i

The six paradigms, with the standard model examples, are:

1. *o/jo*-declension: [Masc] *rabъ* 'slave'   *konь* 'horse'
                                   [Neut] *město* 'place'   *pole* 'field'
2. *u-* (= ŭ) declension: [Masc] *synъ* 'son'
3. *a/ja*-declension: [Fem] *žena* 'woman'   *duša* 'soul'
4. *i-* (=ī) declension: [Fem]   *kostь* 'bone'
                                   [Masc] *gostь* 'guest'
5. *u/v-* (=ū) declension: [Fem]   *kry* 'blood'   *ljuby* 'love'
6. *consonant*-declension: (n) *kamy* [Masc] 'stone' *imę* [Neut] 'name'
                                   (r)   *mati*   [Fem] 'mother'
                                   (s)   *slovo* [Neut] 'word'
                                   (nt) *telę*   [Neut] 'calf'

Some classify the *u/v* group as a member of the *consonant*-declension on the grounds that the *ū* (> *y*) of the NomSing appears as consonantal *v* elsewhere, on the same pattern as the other consonant types. For our purposes, we shall retain the notional distinction, as this group has occasionally a distinct reflex.

     The modern Slavic languages have reduced this rich morphological variety in several different ways.

Modern paradigms   The six declensions of Proto-Slavic have been mainly reduced to the *i*, *a/ja* and *o/jo*-declensions as living, productive categories. The *consonant*-declension has left a few survivals, but has mostly been absorbed into the *i*-declension, as has the *u/v*-declension – usually via the *consonant* type, and the *u*-declension has been largely absorbed into the *o/jo*-declension. Various inflexions have migrated between declensions with the re-classification of nouns, and have sometimes established themselves for some or all nouns of the new declension. Czech, which is morphologically rather conservative, retains more extensive traces of the *consonant* and *u/v*-declensions as well.

Inflexional categories   The three categories of number, case and gender are described above, 5.4.1–5.4.4. In respect of nouns, gender is usually the property of the stem. But the different paradigms are clearly arranged according to patterns which correlate moderately well with primary gender: feminine with the *i*-declension and with most nouns in *-a*; masculine with some nouns in *-a*, and with *o/jo*-declension nouns which end in a consonant in the nominative singular; and neuter with those ending in *-o* and *-e*. Secondary gender operates on the accusative singular masculine, the accusative dual masculine, and the nominative and accusative plural. The correlation between gender and paradigm has led many descriptive, especially pedagogical, grammars to call the declensions by gender names (e.g. the "feminine declension" for the *a/ja* type).

These three categories normally occur throughout the noun paradigms. There are, however, some areas where their application is restricted.

1. Indeclinable nouns
    A noun may be indeclinable, especially if
    a. it ends in a vowel unknown to a Slavic nominative singular, like *-u*:
       Rus *Bakú* (place name), Cz *emu* 'emu'
    b. its form disagrees with its "supposed" gender or number: Rus *kófe* 'coffee' [Masc], though *-e* is the usual marker of a neuter; or a final hard consonant referring to a female person: Rus *gospožá Bráun* 'Mrs [NomFem] Brown', *gospožú Bráun* [AccFem]; Pol *profesor* '(female) professor'.
    c. it is formed from, and pronounced as, initials: Rus *KGB* [kagɛ'bɛ] 'the KGB'.

    Most indeclinable nouns (other than abbreviations) are borrowed words or foreign proper names. Only occasionally are local place-names or surnames indeclinable, e.g. Rus *Púškino* 'the town of Pushkino' (so avoiding confusion with the town *Púškin* in all its case forms), *Evtušénko* (surname (Yevtushenko), whose suffix is of southern, or Ukrainian, origin), *Dolgíx* (surname, whose form is an oblique case, here GenPl).

2. Defective paradigms
    Bulgarian and Macedonian have kept number as an inflexional class, but their case systems have been severely reduced. They show no case

in the plural, but in the singular there may be a vocative in *a/ja* and *o/jo* nouns (5.5.1.3, 5.5.1.1). There is also an oblique case, which is found in

a. Bulgarian, but only with the article (5.4.3);

b. Macedonian, as an optional suffix with masculine personal nouns, including proper names and names of relatives ending in a consonant (5.5.1);

c. Mixed paradigms.

Some nouns have some inflexional forms borrowed from the adjective-determiner declension (5.5.2). Proper names with adjective endings have only adjectival inflexions (Rus *Tolstój, Dostoévskij*, Pol *Penderecki*). And in some of the languages proper names, particularly those in *-in/-ov* (Fem *-ina/-ova*), have adjectival endings for some inflexional forms:

(71)   Rus   Masc: *Petróv* [Nom], *Petróvym* [InstrSg] (= adjectival)
                     (not nominal **Petróvom*)
              Fem: *Petróva* [Nom], *Petróvu* [AccSg] (= nominal),
                     Petróvoj [Gen-Dat-Instr-LocSg] (= adjectival)

We discuss the noun-like elements in adjective paradigms in 5.5.2.

Noteworthy are the Bulgarian definite article suffix, and the Macedonian definite article and deictic suffixes, since they are found with all noun paradigms (as well as with the adjective-determiner paradigm, see 5.5.2). The article and deictic suffixes are not ordinary word-forming suffixes, since they follow the inflexions. In Bulgarian the article suffix can show an oblique case (one form for all but the nominative and vocative) in the masculine singular (this form – or at least the distinction – is not present in all regions or registers):

(72a)   *Bulgarian article suffix*

		Masc	Fem	Neut
SingNom:	Hard	*-ăt*	*-ta*	*-to*
	Soft	*-jat* (= /jăt/)	*-ta*	*-to*
SingOblique:	Hard	*-a* (= /ă/)	*-ta*	*-to*
	Soft	*-ja* (= /jă/)	*-ta*	*-to*
Plural:		*-te*	*-te*	*-ta*

The above forms show also (in brackets) the phoneme /ă/ where it is "hidden" under orthographic *a* – in final position or after soft consonants, so that the letter *ă* appears only in the NomSing.

(72b)   Blg   *zăb* 'tooth'   *zăbăt* [Def]   *zăbá* [DefObl]   *zăbite* [DefPl]
              kon 'horse'   *kónjat* [Def] *kónja* [DefObl] *kónete* [DefPl]

> rádost 'joy'   rádostta [Def]   rádostite [DefPl]
> sélo 'village'   séloto [Def]   sélata [DefPl]

Macedonian has not only an article suffix but also proximate ('this') and non-proximate ('that') deictic suffixes. They inflect for gender and number, but not for case:

(73a)   *Macedonian article and deictic suffixes*

		Masc	Fem	Neut
'the':	Sing	-ot	-ta	-to
	Plur	-te	-te	-ta

Similarly: -ov 'this';   -on 'that'

(73b)   Mac   *noǩ*   'night' [Fem]
         noǩta   'the night'   *noǩite*   'the nights'
         noǩva   'this night'   *noǩive*   'these nights'
         noǩna   'that night'   *noǩine*   'those nights'

In both Bulgarian and Macedonian masculine nouns in -a and -o take the appropriate "gender" suffix, that is, the *form* of the noun determines that of the article.

(74a)   Blg   *bášta*   'father' [Masc]   *báštata*   'the father'
         čičo   'uncle' [Masc]   *čičoto*   'the uncle'

(74b)   Mac   *buržoá* 'bourgeois' [Masc]   *buržoáta* 'the bourgeois'

The syntax of the article/deictic suffix depends on the structure of the noun phrase in which it occurs. If the head noun is modified by adjectives and/or determiners, the article/deictic suffix is attached to the leftmost concording modifier (4.2.1).

5.5.1.1   *The o/jo-declension*

The Proto-Slavic forms are shown in table 5.1, and sample modern forms in table 5.2 – one language from each group (B/C/S, Rus, Cz) plus special forms for other languages. This pattern is followed for all paradigms in this section.

The *o/jo* paradigm is now often known as the "consonant" paradigm, since the nominative singular of most masculine nouns ends in a consonant, or as the "masculine" declension, since it represents the bulk of masculine nouns. It forms a hard (*o*) and soft (*jo*) series in East and West Slavic. South Slavic shows mainly hard inflexions.

In the modern languages, some inflexional endings have been borrowed from the *a/ja*-declension (e.g. the vowel -a- in the Dat-Instr-LocPl), and from the *u* (*ŭ*)-declension (genitive and locative singular in -u, genitive plural in -ov). The dative in -ovi (Pol -owi) in some East and South Slavic languages also comes from the former *u*-declension.

Gender: Masculine in *-ø*, and *-o* (the latter mainly with proper names); neuter in *-o* and *-e*. Some masculines have been absorbed from the *u*-declension (5.5.1.2: PSl *synъ* 'son'), and *consonant*-declension (5.5.1.6: PSl *kamy* 'stone'). Masculines may express any secondary gender. The neuters are inanimate. Neuters include a large number of verbal nouns in *-n/t-i(j)e* (Cz *-í*). Secondary gender (5.4.4) operates in the masculine in the accusative singular, nominative-accusative dual and nominative-accusative plural; and in the neuter in the accusative plural. Belarusian neuters are like the masculines: the neuter gender in Belarusian is considerably weaker than the other two genders (at least partly due to phonetic fusion of unstressed endings), something which is also happening in non-standard Russian (Schupbach, 1984).

Case: This is the most varied paradigm of Slavic, including a vocative, and a second genitive and locative in the singular in Russian. Czech neuters in *-í* show fewest distinct case forms in this paradigm.

Masculines and neuters have the same case forms, except in the nominative singular, nominative plural, and genitive plural. The vocative singular and second genitive and locative are not found in the neuters.

Morphophonology   Typical alternations are listed below (for a full list, see chapter 4):
Stems:

1.   Alternations related to the zero ending in the nominative singular of masculine nouns, and the genitive plural of some neuters:
a. Vowel ~ zero:

    (75a)   Mac   *lakot-ø* 'elbow'   *lakt-i* [Pl]

    (75b)   Rus   *kámen'-ø* 'stone'   *kámn-ja* [GenSg]

    b. Vowel quality and quantity alternations:

    (76)   Pol   *mióɗ-ø* 'honey' [NomSg]   *miod-u* [GenSg]

2.   Vowel quality alternations before palatalized consonants:

    (77)   Pol   *miast-o* 'city, town' [NomSg]   *mieści-e* [LocSg]

3.   Palatalization of velars and dentals:
a. PV1 before *-e* of VocSg:

    (78a)   Rus   *Bóg-ø* 'God' [NomSg]   *Bóž-e* [VocSg]

    (78b)   B/C/S   *òtac-ø* 'father' [NomSg] (*c* < *k*)   *òč-e* [VocSg]

b.   PV2 before -*ě* of LocSg and -*i* of NomPl:

(79a)   Cz   *mlék-o* 'milk' [NomSg]   *mlé-ce* [LocSg]

(79b)   B/C/S   *ǔčenīk-ø* 'pupil' [NomSg]   *ǔčenīc-i* [NomPl]

c.   Dentals before -*ě* of LocSg:

(80)   Pol   *miast-o* 'city, town' [NomSg]   *mieści-e* [LocSg]

4.   Stems may shorten, particularly with the suffix -(*an*)*in* 'member of group':

(81)   Bel   *balhár-yn-ø* 'Bulgarian' [NomSg]   *balhár-y* [NomPl]

       Rus   *gospod-ín-ø* 'gentleman, master' [NomSg]   *gospod-á* [NomPl]

       B/C/S   *grȁdan-in-ø* 'citizen' [NomSg]   *grȁdān-i* [NomPl]

5.   Stress alternation is common between the singular and the plural. The Russian LocSg in -*ú* and NomPl in -*á* are always stressed; the latter sets the stress pattern for all the plural forms:

(82)   Rus 'teacher *učítel'-ø* [NomSg]   *učitel-já* [NomPl]
                     učítel-ja [GenSg]   *učiteléj-ø* [GenPl]
                                             učitel-jám [DatPl]
       Note also: Bel *bérah* 'bank (river)', Pl *berahí, berahóǔ* . . .

6.   Suppletion in some common stems:

(83)   'person':
       Cz   *člověk* [NomSg]   *lidé* [NomPl]
       Blg   *čovék* [NomSg]   *čovéci/xóra/ljúde* [Pl]

Inflexions   This exceptionally varied paradigm includes some inflexions which merit special comment (especially those adopted from the *u*-declension):

NomSg: masculines in -*a*, mainly practitioners of a trade or profession, belong formally to the *a/ja* declension (5.5.1.3): Pol *poeta* 'poet'; Rus *djádja* 'uncle'.

AccSg: masculines have the form of either the nominative or the genitive, on the basis of animacy (5.4.4).

GenSg: masculines have -*u* (from the *u*-declension, 5.5.1.5) or retain -*a*. Where both forms are available, -*a* is more common with animates. B/C/S and Slovenian have only -*a*. Of the other languages, Russian has the lowest use of -*u*, which occurs only in genitive[2] (partitive) with mass nouns: *čáška čáj-u* 'a cup of tea' (*vs zápax čáj-a* 'the smell of tea').

DatSg: -*u* is more common when the GenSg ends in -*a*, and -*ovi* (from the *u*-declension) when the GenSg ends in -*u*, thus avoiding syncretism.

LocSg: -*u* (from the *u*-declension) is general in B/C/S and Slovenian, and is sometimes available in the other languages, including the locative[2] of Russian in -*ú*: Rus *sad* 'garden', *v sad-ú* 'in the garden'.

VocSg: -*u* (from the *u*-declension, though supported by the *jo* form) is usual for hard stems, especially velars; and -*e* for all, but especially soft, stems, with pre-palatalization (either replacive or additive: 4.3.1): Cz *Bůh* 'God', [VocSg] *Bože*. Velars and (formerly) soft stems may take -*u* in Ukrainian and Polish: Pol *człowiek, człowiek-u* 'person'. Sorb -*o* occurs with soft and velar stems, and stems in -*s* -*z* -*c*: *Bóh* 'God', *Bož-o*. On Bulgarian and Macedonian see 5.4.2 and below.

NomPl: masculines have -*i* or -*y*, though Russian has a growing number of nouns in stressed -*á* like *gorod-á* (table 5.2). -*ovi* (from the *u*-declension) is found mainly with practitioners: Cz *filolog* 'philologist', [NomPl] *filolog-ovi*. Neuters generally retain -*a*, including in Bulgarian and Macedonian: Blg *mjást-o* 'place', Pl *mest-á*.

GenPl: the masculines which have the -*ov* ending, or variations of it, have taken it from the *u*-declension. The zero ending has survived in the neuters, where there is no risk of syncretism with the NomSg.

Dat/Loc/InstrPl: many languages have generalized the *a/ja* endings here: East Slavic, Slovak and Sorbian have -*am*/-*ax*/-*ami*, Polish has -*ach*/-*ami*, but has retained the old dative -*om*. B/C/S has generalized further, with -*ima* for all three. Only Slovenian and Czech have retained the old forms (Sln -*om*/-*ih*/-*i*, Cz -*ům*/-*ech*/-*y*).

Of the remaining cases, the InstrSg has retained -*om* in all languages, and the AccPl varies by animacy as in the singular (see above, 5.4.4).

Bulgarian and Macedonian are rather different from the other languages. In definite masculine nouns they may distinguish a "Direct" from an "Oblique" case (see also 5.4.2, 5.5.1):

Masculine oblique singular
    Macedonian nouns in -*e* take -*ta:*

            Mac *Blaže* (man's name) [MascDirSg], *Blažeta* [MascOblSg]

    And other nouns take -*a*:

            Mac *tatk-o* 'father' [MascDirSg], *tatk-a* [MascOblSing]

    In Bulgarian only nouns in a consonant can have the oblique form, -*a* ([ə])

            Blg *sínăt* 'the son' [MascDirSg], *sín-a* [MascOblSing]

In both languages the oblique case is frequently replaced by the nominative. They also retain a vocative, which has partially survived the loss of the case system in these languages:

Vocative singular

Bulgarian:	-*ju* with formerly soft stems:	*kon* 'horse', *kón-ju*
	-*o* after velars and hushings:	*măž* 'man, husband',
		mắž-o
	-*e* elsewhere:	*otéc* 'father', *ótč-e* (PV1)
Macedonian:	-*u*, also -*e* and -*ø*, sometimes in the same noun: *brat*	
	'brother', [Voc] *brat, brat-u, brat-e*	

Czech verbal nouns in -(*n*/*t*)-*í* are cognate with other verbal nouns in -*i*(*j*)*e*, but have undergone contraction. Their paradigm shows exceptional neutralization in case forms, particularly in the singular:

(84)	Cz	'building':	*staveni*
	Sing:	Nom Gen Dat Acc Loc:	*staveni*
		Instr:	*stavením*
	Pl:	Nom Gen Acc	*staveni*
		Dat	*stavením*
		Instr	*staveními*
		Loc	*stavenich*

5.5.1.2   *u (ŭ)-declension*

The Proto-Slavic *ŭ*-stem nouns (table 5.3) were all masculine. They have now merged into the *o*-declension, based on gender (all were masculine), but they have sometimes left traces of their original inflexions (see above).

5.5.1.3 *a/ja-declension*

Although many Cyrillic grammars treat these as two distinct types – an approach which is motivated by the orthography – they are, in fact, hard and soft versions of the one declensional type in East and West Slavic, where the hard ~ soft distinction remains. In South Slavic we find only the *a* type. The *a/ja*-declension has influenced several standard forms of the *i*, *o* and *jo*-declensions, has absorbed many *u/v*-declension words, and has also taken over many *i*-declension words, especially in Sorbian. For forms, see tables 5.4, 5.5.

Gender Mainly feminine, with an important subgroup of masculines, both native: Rus *djádja* 'uncle', B/C/S *slúga* 'servant', *vȍjvoda* 'commander; and borrowed, many (now) common gender: Pol *poeta* 'poet', Rus *kolléga* 'colleague'. Secondary gender is marked in the accusative plural for East Slavic feminines, and for non-singular masculines as if they were *o/jo*-declension words.

Case Case distinctions are well preserved, including the vocative. Important differences for nominative plural and accusative plural are found in individual languages: Cz *hrdina* 'hero', *hrdinové* [NomPl], *hrdiny* [AccPl].

Morphophonology
1. Alternations related to the zero-ending (genitive plural)
   a. Vowel ~ zero alternations:
      'sister': [NomSg] Cz Slk *sestr-a*, Pol *siostr-a*, Rus *sestr-á*
      [GenPl] Cz *sester-ø*, Slk *sestier-ø*, Rus *sestër-ø*,
      cf. Pol *sióstr-ø*
   b. Vowel quality and quantity alternations:
      Pol *drog-a* 'road', [GenPl] *dróg-ø;* Slk *slza* 'tear', [GenPl] *sĺz-ø*
2. Other vowel quality alternations:
   a. In the dative-locative singular, before palatalization, in Polish and Sorbian:
      Pol *wiara* 'belief' [NomSg], *wierze* [Dat-LocSg]
   b. Czech shows *přehláska* (3.2.1.5) in the *ja* inflexions (after soft and formerly soft palatals):
      Cz *ulice* 'street' [NomSg], *ulici* [Acc-Dat-LocSg], *ulicí* [InstrSg]
3. 2nd Palatalization of Velars (3.2.2.3), and mutation of dentals and labials (*a*-declension only) in:
   [Dat-LocSg] in Ukr, Bel; Pol, Cz, Sorb; B/C/S:

   Cz *míra* 'measure', [Dat-LocSg] *míře*
   Bel *straxá* 'roof', [Dat-LocSg] *strasé*

   [Nom-AccDu] in Sorb: Sorb *ruka* 'hand', [Nom-AccDu] *rucy*

4.   Stress and pitch. Alternation of stress between stem and desinence is common, especially with native Slavic monosyllabic roots, in East Slavic, Slovenian, B/C/S and Bulgarian. The alternations may oppose singular to plural, or individual case forms in any number:

Rus *vodá* 'water', [AccSg] *vódu*, [NomPl] *vódy*, [LocPl] *vodáx*

Changes in stress may also change the quality of a vowel:

Bel *raká* 'river', [NomPl] *rèki*

5.5.1.4   *i(ĭ)-declension*

This productive class is often signalled in East Slavic by the "soft sign", which is historically the Proto-Slavic front *jer* (ь) and phonologically a "zero" ending. The other languages do not give an overt signal for the *i*-declension. The *i*-declension has gained some former *u/v*-declension nouns (PSl *kry* 'blood', 5.5.1.5). It contains the highly productive *-nost* abstract nouns, and, in some languages, the numerals from '5' to '19', and the 'tens': '20', '30', etc. The *ja*-declension (5.5.1.3) shows some influence on the *i*-declension (especially Cz/Slk, see table 5.7), and in Sorbian it has largely absorbed it (Stone 1993: 619). For forms, see tables 5.6, 5.7.

Gender   Masculine nouns, with some exceptions for PSl **pǫtь* 'road', have joined the *jo*-declension. Feminine nouns have usually remained a distinct declension. Secondary gender (5.4.4) operates with the accusative plural, according to the individual languages.

Case   The vocative is retained in B/C/S, Polish, Czech and Ukrainian. Much of the Proto-Slavic syncretism has been retained.

Morphophonology
   a.   Stems
      1.   Alternations related to the zero-ending (nominative singular):
         a.   Vowel ~ zero alternation (subject to the phonotactic rules of the language): Cz *krev* 'blood', [GenSg] *krve*, Rus *lož'* 'a lie', [GenSg] *lži* (cf. Rus *krov'*, *króvi*).
         b.   *ø ~ l* alternation in B/C/S: B/C/S *sô* 'salt' [MascSg], *sòli* [GenSg].
         c.   Vowel quanitity and quality alternations: Cz *sůl* 'salt' [NomSg], *soli* [GenSg]; Pol *gałąź* 'branch' [NomSg], *gałęzi* [GenSg].
         d.   Stress and pitch may alternate, especially with monosyllabic Slavic roots: B/C/S *stvâr* 'thing' [NomSg], *stvári* [LocSg], *stvâri* [Nom-AccPl], *stvárī* [GenPl], *stvárima* [Dat-Instr-LocPl].

2. Ukrainian doubles certain stem-final consonants (from older 'consonant +*j*') in the instrumental singular: Ukr *nič* 'night' [NomSg], *níččju* [InstrSg].
b. Inflexions
1. Czech and Slovak have a genuine (feminine) *i*-declension as well as a mixed *i-ja* type, with zero nominative singular but the remainder as in the *ja* type: Cz *laň* 'roe deer' [NomSg], *laně* [GenSg]; Slk *dlaň* 'palm of hand' [NomSg], *dlane* [GenSg].
2. The instrumental plural shows -(')*mi* in only a few nouns: Rus *lóšad'* 'horse' [NomSg], [InstrPl] *lošad'mí*, Cz *kostmi* (table 5.7).

5.5.1.5   *u/v-declension (ū-stems)*

The *u/v*-declension originally contained a small number of feminine nouns, which have now migrated to the other primarily feminine declensions – *a/ja* or *i*. Like the *consonant*-declension (5.5.1.6), all forms other than nominative singular had a consonant theme, in this case /v/, while the nominative singular had /y/ from Proto-Slavic /ū/ (from older /ŭu̯/, giving /ŭv/ in pre-vocalic position, cf. the alternation *ov* ~ *u*, 4.4.2). The typical migration has been to the *i*-declension, and the accusative singular, containing /v/, has become the new nominative singular. The sole example of retained -*y* in the nominative singular is Sln *krí* 'blood':

(85) 'blood':

	PSl	B/C/S	Sln	Rus	Pol
[NomSg]	*kr-y*	*kr̄v-ø*	*kr-í*	*króv'-ø*	*krew-ø*
[AccSg]	*krъv-ь*	= NOM	= NOM	= NOM	= NOM
[GenSg]	*krъv-i*	*kr̄v-i*	*krv-í*	*króv-i*	*krw-i*

The best traces of the original paradigm remain in modern Czech, though the endings are close to the Czech "mixed" *ja*-declension. Table 5.8 shows the Proto-Slavic and modern Czech forms.
    Examples of the shift of this group into the *a/ja* or *i*-declensions are:

(86) 'church':
    a/ja: LSorb *cerkwja*, Bel *carkvá*, Ukr *cérkva*, B/C/S *cr̄kva*, Blg *čérkva*, Mac *crkva*;
    i: USorb *cyrkej*, Slk *cirkev*, Pol *cerkiew*, Rus *cérkov'*, Sln *cérkev*.

5.5.1.6   *The consonant-declension*

Proto-Slavic nouns of this declension had an additional (epenthetic) -VC- in all cases but the nominative singular, hence the name "consonant" declension. (This syllable was originally a suffix, in some cases functioning as a lexical classifier (e.g. -(*t*)*er* 'close kin', -*nt* 'young animal'), which had been lost in the nominative singular of Proto-Slavic.) This type is not productive in modern Slavic, and is best preserved in Czech.

The consonants appearing in Proto-Slavic are: -*n*- (masculine and neuter); -*r*- (feminine); -*s*- (neuter); and -*nt*- (neuter). The Proto-Slavic forms are shown in table 5.9; the modern forms are discussed in non-tabular form.

The tendency has been to remove the *consonant*-declension, mainly by re-adjustments of inflexional class. Sometimes a suffix, in another declensional class, has become the regular form, as in the (*n*)*t*-stems (below). Alternatively, nouns have taken the expanded stem as the norm, have back-formed a new nominative and given the new formation a new set of endings, usually preserving the original gender, and following the hard/soft pattern of the original paradigm:

> Rus *kámen'* [NomSg]   *kámnja* [GenSg]   (*jo* Masculine)
> Ukr *kámin'* [NomSg]   *kámenja* [GenSg]   (*jo* Masculine)

A similar evolution is found in the transfer of *u/v*-stem feminines like PSl *cr̩'ky* 'church' (OCS *crъky*) to *i*-stems, where the oblique case forms provide a new stem for the nominative (5.5.1.5).

The *consonant*-declension types or their remnants in modern Slavic include:

a.   *n*-stems: a separate neuter declension only (87a), except for a few masculines in Czech (87b), the rest having shifted mainly into the masculine *i* type, then further into *jo* (cf. Rus *kamen'* above):

> (87a)   'name':   Bel   *imjá* [Nom-AccSg]   *ímeni* [Gen-Dat-LocSg]
>   (or: *imjá* [GenSg] *ímju* [Dat SG], *ími* [LocSg])
>   *ímenem* or *ímem* [InstrSg]
>   *imëny* or *imí* [NomPl]
>   Rus   *ímja* [Nom-AccSg]   *ímeni* [Gen-Dat-LocSg]
>   *imená* [NomPl]
>   'seed'   Cz   *símě/sémě* [NomSg] (also now *semeno*)
>   *semene* [GenSg]   *semena* [NomPl]
> (87b)   'day':   Cz   *den* [NomSg Masc] *dne* [GenSg]
>   *dni/dnu* [Dat/LocSg]
>   *dni/dny* [NomPl] *dní/dnů* [GenPl]

Bulgarian and Macedonian, with only singular ~ plural endings, have retained the "consonant" look of the neuter ones, Bulgarian with the old nominative plural endings, Macedonian with a new suffix:

(87c)   'seed'   Blg   *séme* [Sg]   *semená* [Pl]
                Mac   *seme* [Sg]   *seminja* [Pl]

b.   *r*-stems: feminine, two words only: 'mother' and 'daughter'. Most languages retain the irregularity of the nominative singular (88a), but some have preferred the regular *a*-declension diminutive (88b):

(88a)   'mother': Sln *máti* [NomSg]   *máter* [AccSg]   *mátere* [GenSg]
                Ukr *máty* [Nom-AccSg]   *máteri* [GenSg]

(88b)   'mother': Pol   *matka* [NomSg]   *matki* [GenSg]

c.   *s*-stems: neuter, now regular *o*-declension inflexions, but with stem alternations retained in a few common words, and in their derived adjectives, e.g. the concrete and abstract variants of the root *neb-* in Russian:

(89)   'sky':   Rus   *nébo*   [NomSg]   *néba* [GenSg]
                          nebesá [Nom-AccPl]
      'celestial':   Rus   *nebésnyj*
      'palate':   Rus   *nëbo* [NomSg]   *nëba* [GenSg]
                          nëba [Nom-AccPl]
      'palatal':   Rus   *nëbnyj*

d.   (*n*)*t*-stems (the vowel of the extra syllable is the nasal /ę/, derived from pre-consonantal /n/, hence this type is usually called *nt*-stem): neuter, lexically (originally and mostly still) the names of young domestic animals. Inflexions are normally *o*-declension; in some languages the stem alternation is retained, and in Czech this includes even the "suffixal" vowel changes, undergoing *přehláska* only in the singular:

(90)   'calf':   B/C/S   *tèle* [NomSg]   *tèleta* [GenSg]
               Cz   *tele* [NomSg]   *telete* [GenSg]   *telata* [NomPl]

Russian has the *nt*-stem suffix (with neuter endings) only in the plural. The singular is replaced by the masculine *o*-declension diminutive suffix *-ën(o)k-*, originally applied to young wild animals:

(91)   'piglet':   Rus   *porosënok* [NomSg]   *porosënka* [GenSg]
                     porosjáta   [NomPl]

Polish has the same, but with the singular lacking a specific diminutive form:

(92)   'piglet':   Pol   *prosię*   [Nom-AccSg]   *prosia* [GenSg]
                    prosiata   [Nom-AccPl]

Though for this word it has a parallel masculine with diminutive suffix for both the singular and plural:

(93) 'piglet':   Pol   *prosiak* [NomSg]   *prosiaka* [Gen = AccSg]
                         prosiaki [Nom-AccPl]

Bulgarian and Macedonian again retain the stem alternation between singular and plural; as with *n*-, one has the old suffix, one a new suffix:

(94) 'lamb':   Blg   *ágne* [Sg]   *ágneta* [Pl]
                 Mac   *jagnje* [Sg]   *jagninja* [Pl]

5.5.2   The adjective and determiner declension

The adjective and "determiner" paradigm, with some variations, covers a variety of word classes:

1. Long-form adjectives (East and West Slavic)
2. Definite adjectives (B/C/S and Slovenian)
3. The numeral '1'
4. Determiners like 'this', 'that', 'such'
5. Quantifiers like 'some', 'all'
6. Nouns with adjectival endings (substantivized adjectives), including many proper names:
    Rus *parikmáxer-sk-aja* 'hairdresser's', *Tolst-ój*, Pol *Sław-sk-i*
7. Nominalization of any of the above categories:
    Pol   *ci dobrzy ludzi* 'these good people'
          ci dobrzy 'these good ones'
          ci 'these (ones)'
8. Non-personal pronouns
9. Personal pronouns (3 Person)

Their inflexional properties differ somewhat from those of nouns (see below on the noun-like forms of the short-form adjectives):

Case: No distinct vocative. Bulgarian and Macedonian show case only in the personal pronouns (here 3 Person, type 9).

Number: is not an inherent category in types 1–5.

Gender: is not an inherent category in types 1–5 and 7. Secondary gender (5.4.4) is crucial, and combines with primary gender in the nominative and accusative (see below).

If secondary gender occurs in the nominative, the marked category has a special distinct form:

(95a)   Cz   [NomPl]:   *noví* 'good' [MascAnim] *vs* unmarked *nové*

(95b)   Pol   [NomPl]:   *nowi* 'good' [MascPers] *vs* unmarked *nowe*

But in the accusative, the forms showing secondary gender are like the corresponding genitive:

(96a)   Cz   [AccSg]:   *nového* [Anim] *vs nový* (= Nom)

(96b)   Rus   [AccPl]:   *nóvyx* [Anim] *vs nóvye* (= Nom)

Apart from the question of gender, the forms of the adjective-determiner declension fall within two extremes: noun-like and adjective proper:

1. *Noun-like inflexions (o/jo and a/ja): the short-form and indefinite adjective* Adjectives in early Proto-Slavic had the form of nouns, each with three patterns by gender. Most stems ended in a hard consonant and followed the noun patterns *o*-Masc, *a*-Fem and *o*-Neut; relatively few had soft stems and followed the corresponding *jo* or *ja* patterns. Models (NomSg only) are shown in table 5.10.

The short-form adjective of modern East and West Slavic follows this pattern, though it survives only in the nominative – and in the oblique cases in a few fixed idiomatic expressions (e.g. Rus *sredí béla dnjá* [GenSg] 'in broad daylight', lit. 'in the midst of white day'), and is only hard. It is principally used as part of an expanded predicate after 'be':

(97)   Cz   *je povinen-ø to zaplatit* 'he must pay for it' ('is obliged to ...')

In Russian, short-form adjectives include the short predicative forms of the passive past participles (98b) (the citation form is the long form):

(98a)   Rus   *gotóv-yj* 'ready'
                   ón gotóv-ø prijtí 'he is ready to come'

(98b)   Rus   *očaróvan-n-yj* 'enchanted'
                   já očaróvan-ø 'I am enchanted (by ...)'

Table 5.10. *Proto-Slavic short adjectives*

	Masc	Fem	Neut
'new'	*nov-ъ*	*nov-a*	*no-vo*
declined as:	*rabъ* (5.5.1.1)	*žena* (5.5.1.3)	*město* (5.5.1.1)
'blue'	*sin-jь*	*sin-ja*	*sin-je*
declined as:	*konь* (5.5.1.1)	*duša* (5.5.1.3)	*sr̥ce* (5.5.1.1)

Ukrainian has effectively lost a functional short form in that it has only short, contracted forms in the nominative singular feminine and neuter and nominative plural. Only a few adjectives can have a short form in the nominative singular masculine, where the regular form is uncontracted (e.g. *kóžnyj*/*kóžen* 'each'):

(99)   Ukr   'new'   *nov-ýj* [Masc], *nov-á* [Fem], *nov-é* [Neut], *nov-í* [Pl]

The other languages have many fewer short predicative forms. Czech, like Russian, has short forms of the passive past participle, as well as a few other short forms where the adjective is expanded by a following element:

(100)   Cz   *dům je postaven-ø znova* 'the house has been rebuilt'
             je hotov-ý 'he is ready'
             je hotov-ø k službam 'he is ready to serve (lit. 'for service')'

In Russian, too, in simple predicates the short form is giving way to the long form, at least in neutral style, the short form marking an expressive function:

(101)   Rus   *on (óčen') sláb-yj* 'he is (a very) weak (person)' (factual)
                on (óčen') slab-ø 'he really is (very) weak' (figurative, emotive)

but this is not the case where the adjective has only a short form (being always semantically expanded by a following element):

(102)   Rus   *já óčen' rád-ø vás vídet'* 'I am very pleased to see you'

2. *Adjective inflexions: formation of the long adjective.* The long-form adjective was formed in Proto-Slavic by adding 3 Person pronouns to the declined short adjective (i.e. with its inflexions). The original pronoun forms (including some early local variants) are shown in table 5.11.

One assumes that there would have been contraction from the start, especially of forms with a reduplicated consonant (e.g. InstrSg, LocPl), including the reduplicated /j/ of the pronoun itself (in Fem):

InstrSgMasc   **novomъ + jimь > novoimъ*
LocPl   **nověxъ + jixъ > nověixъ*
GenSgFem   **novy + jejě/jeję > novyjě/novyję*

Nominal forms with a single vowel (e.g. GenSg, DatSg) were a lesser problem, treated in different ways in accordance with the general approach (by area) to contraction of intervocalic /j/:

GenSgMasc   **nova + jego > novajego, novajago, novaago, novaego* and further to:
novago (OCS), *novego* (West), *novogo* (East, by morphological analogy with *tъ* 'that', 5.5.2.2), *novega* (South, the *-a* perhaps by analogy with the GenSing of (*o*) nouns).

Table 5.11. *Proto-Slavic 3 Person pronouns*

		Masc	Fem	Neut
Sg	Nom	*-jь*	*ja*	*je*
	Acc	= NOM	*jǫ*	= NOM
	Gen	*jego*	*jejě/jeję*	= MASC
	Dat	*jemu*	*jeji*	= MASC
	Instr	*jimь*	*jejǫ*	= MASC
	Loc	*jemь*	*jeji*	= MASC
Du	Nom	*ja*	*ji*	*ji*
	Acc	= NOM	= NOM	= NOM
	Gen	*jeju*	= MASC	= MASC
	Dat	*jima*	= MASC	= MASC
	Instr	= DAT	= DAT	= DAT
	Loc	= GEN	= GEN	= GEN
Pl	Nom	*ji*	*jě/ję*	*ja*
	Acc	*jě/ję*	= MASC	= MASC
	Gen	*jixъ*	= MASC	= MASC
	Dat	*jimъ*	= MASC	= MASC
	Instr	*jimi*	= MASC	= MASC
	Loc	*jixъ*	= MASC	= MASC

Note: as for *a/ja* stem nouns, the endings in *ě/ę* are early north *vs* south (1.4).

The modern Slavic languages have thus simplified to a greater or lesser extent the complex new inflexions. The nominative and accusative singular and the nominative plural created few phonological problems, and so tend to show more noun-like forms:

NomSgMasc **novъ + jь > novъjь*:
Rus *nóvyj*, Ukr *novýj*, Bel *nóvy*, Pol, Sorb *nowy*,
Cz, Slk *nový*; Blg, Mac *nov*, B/C/S *nȍv*, Sln *nòv*

NomSgFem **nova + ja > novaja*:
Rus, Bel *nóvaja*, Ukr *nová*, Blg, Mac *nóva*,
B/C/S *nȍva*, Sln *nôva*, Pol, Sorb *nowa*, Cz, Slk *nová*

NomSgNeut **novo + je > novoje*:
Rus *nóvoje*, Bel *nóvaje*, Ukr *nové*, Blg, Mac *nóve*,
B/C/S *nȍve*, Sln *nôve*, Pol, Sorb *nowe*, Cz, Slk *nové*.

East Slavic and most of West Slavic have removed primary gender distinctions in the plural, using typically the feminine nominative plural form:

NomPlFem **novy + jě/ję > novyjě/novyję*:
Rus *nóvye*, Bel *nóvyja*, Ukr *noví*, Pol, Sorb *nowe*, Slk *nové*

cf. NomPlMasc *novi+ji > noviji

NomPlNeut *nova+ja > novaja.

Czech has retained the three genders in the nominative plural by using the old masculine form for secondary gender [MascPers]: *noví*, and keeping Fem *nové* and Neut *nová*. Slovak, Polish and Upper Sorbian (not Lower Sorbian) have also used the old masculine for secondary gender [MascPers]: *noví/nowi*, but used the feminine for all others: *nové/nowe*.

B/C/S has retained all three genders in the nominative-accusative plural – in both long and short forms, the two sets distinguished by pitch and quantity:

(103) B/C/S   Masc   Fem   Neut

NomPl short: *nòvi*   *nòve*   *nòva*

NomPl long: *nȍvī*   *nȍvē*   *nȍvā*

Slovenian, too, has retained all three genders in the nominative-accusative plural, but only in a single (short) form:

(104) Sln   Masc   Fem   Neut

NomPl: *nóvi*   *nóve*   *nóva*

B/C/S and Slovenian preserve some of the Proto-Slavic indefinite paradigm in their indefinite adjectives. In Slovenian only the masculine singular nominative shows a distinct indefinite form (*nòv* 'new' [Indef], *nȏvi* [Def]), all other forms being identical to the long (definite) forms. B/C/S has special indefinite forms in the masculine and neuter singular, excluding the instrumental (adjectival inflexion only), and the neuter nominative (consistent with either long or short forms). The feminine forms differ from the corresponding definite forms only in pitch, and sometimes in length in the inflexional vowel (also (103) and table 5.12).

(105) B/C/S   Masc/Neut   Fem

GenSg short: *nòva/nòvōg(a)*   *nòvē*

GenSg long: *nȍvōg(a)*   *nȍvē*

Finally, Bulgarian and Macedonian have only short forms, and, of course, no cases.

A regular pattern of shortened nominative and accusative is found with determiners (5.5.2.2.) and 3 Person pronouns (5.5.2.3).

With two exceptions, the adjective/definite inflexion is the last morpheme in the word. The exceptions are:

a.   The East Slavic reflexive *-sja* (always post-inflexional) with participles:

(106)   Rus *vozvraščájušč-ij-sja* 'returning' [NomSgMasc]

vozvraščájušč-aja-sja [NomSgFem]

(Inf *vozvraščát'sja* 'to return')

Table 5.12. *Modern adjective paradigms*: nov- *'new'* (*long forms*)

	B,C/S		Russian		Czech	
Sg	**Masc/Neut**	**Fem**	**Masc/Neut**	**Fem**	**Masc/Neut**	**Fem**
Nom	*nòv-ī/nòv-ō*	*nòv-ā*	*nóv-yj/nóv-oe*	*nóv-aja*	*nov-ý/nové*	*nov-á*
Acc	=NOM/GEN	*nòv-ū*	=NOM/GEN	*nóv-uju*	=NOM/GEN	*nov-ou*
Gen	*nòv-ōg(a)*	*nòv-ē*	*nóv-ogo*	*nóv-oj*	*nov-ého*	*nové*
Dat	*nòv-ōm(e/u)*	*nòv-ōj*	*nóv-omu*	=GEN	*nov-ému*	=GEN
Instr	*nòv-īm*	*nòv-ōm*	*nóv-ym*	=GEN	*nov-ým*	=GEN
Loc	=DAT	=DAT	*nóv-om*	=GEN	*nov-ém*	=GEN
Pl	**MascAnim/Neut:**	**Fem**	**Masc/Neut**	**Fem**	**Masc/Neut**	**Fem**
Nom	*nòv-ī/nòv-ā*	*nòv-ē*	*nóv-ye*		*nov-í/nová*	*nov-é*
Acc	*nòv-ē/*=NOM	=NOM	NOM/GEN		*nov-é/*=NOM	=NOM
Gen	*nòv-īh*		*nóv-yx*		*nov-ých*	
Dat	*nòv-īma*		*nóv-ym*		*nov-ým*	
Instr	DAT		*nóv-ymi*		*nov-ými*	
Loc	DAT		GEN		*nov-ých*	

b. The article/deictic suffixes of Bulgarian and Macedonian, which attach to the leftmost concording member of the noun phrase:

(107)   Mac *žén-a-ta* 'the woman', *ubáv-a-ta žéna* 'the beautiful woman'

5.5.2.1   *Adjectives*

The adjectives of East and West Slavic retain a hard and a soft paradigm. B/C/S has only a hard paradigm, and Slovenian only a soft paradigm (inflexions begin with front vowels). The remains of the inflexions in Bulgarian and Macedonian reflect the hard paradigm in most of their forms. The choice of paradigm for a given adjective depends on the final consonant of the stem and on phonotactic rules, especially after palatals and velars (3.4.3, 4.2.5). As examples we show in table 5.12 the hard long forms in our sample languages, and in table 5.13 the hard and soft paradigms in Slovak:

Morphophonology
1. Vowel ~ zero alternation
    A short-form adjective, indefinite adjective (B/C/S, Sln) or regular adjective of Bulgarian and Macedonian, may show a fleeting vowel in the masculine singular:

(108)   Blg   *dobắr* 'good', *dobrá* [Fem], *dobró* [Neut], *dobrí* [Plur]
        B/C/S   *dòbar* 'good', *dòbra* [Fem], *dòbro* [Neut], *dòbri* [Plur]

Table 5.13. *Slovak* nový *'new' (hard) and* cudzí *'foreign' (soft)*

		Masc		Neut		Fem	
Sg	Nom	*nov-ý*	*cudz-í*	*nov-é*	*cudz-ie*	*nov-á*	*cudz-ia*
	Acc	= NOM/GEN		*nov-é*	*cudz-ie*	*nov-ú*	*cudz-iu*
	Gen		*nov-ého*	*cudz-ieho*		*nov-ej*	*cudz-ej*
	Dat		*nov-ému*	*cudz-iemu*		= GEN	= GEN
	Instr		*nov-ým*	*cudz-ím*		*nov-ou*	*cudz-ou*
	Loc		*nov-om*	*cudz-om*		= GEN	= GEN
		MascPers/Other		Neut		Fem	
Pl	Nom	*nov-i/nov-é*	*cudz-í/cudz-ie*	*nov-é*	*cudz-ie*	= NEUT	
	Acc	= GEN/NOM		= NOM		= NOM	
	Gen		*nov-ých*	*cudz-ích*			
	Dat		*nov-ým*	*cudz-ím*			
	Instr		*nov-ými*	*cudz-ími*			
	Loc		= GEN				

2. Vowel quality alternation may occur, as with the Polish/Sorbian mutation of vowels before palatals:

(109)   Pol   *wesoły* 'happy', *weseli* [MascPers NomPl]

3. Vowel length and stress are very stable in the adjective paradigm, and the main alternations occur between the long and short forms or within the short forms (table 5.12).

4. Palatalization: 2nd Palatalization of Velars, and mutation of dentals, in marked secondary gender in the nominative plural (4.3.1):

(110)   Cz   *anglický* 'English', NomPl *angličtí*
             Cz   *dobrý*   'good',   NomPl *dobří*

Czech soft stems with the *i*-inflexion (from *přehláska*) show particularly few distinct forms in the singular, e.g. *cizí* 'foreign' has this form for all genders in NomSg and all cases of FemSg; in the plural they show regular soft endings:

cizí [Nom/AccPl], *cizích* [Gen/LocPl], *cizím* [DatPl] and *cizími* [InstrPl]

5.5.2.2 *Determiners*

Determiners – their declension is sometimes known as the "special adjective declension" – include deictics ('this', 'that'), some non-personal pronouns ('who', 'what'), and concording quantifiers ('one', 'all'). The nominative and accusative singular, and the nominative plural, are the only forms which do not have adjective-like endings. Among the other cases there are some irregularities, especially with inflexional vowels, and with mixed hard and soft paradigms. The interrogative/relative 'who' is hard (*o*-declension), but 'what' is mainly soft (*jo*-declension). In each the nominative has been extended by *-to*, probably since the loss of the final *jer* would have left unpronounceable forms (tables 5.14, 5.15):

'This' and 'that' show a different mixture of the soft and hard paradigms (tables 5.16 for both paradigms in Proto-Slavic, 5.17 for hard paradigms in the modern languages). The morphophonological alternations of the stem generally follow the pattern of the

Table 5.14. *Proto-Slavic interrogative pronouns*

Nom	*k-ъ-to* 'who'	*č-ь-to* 'what'
Acc	= GEN	= NOM
Gen	*k-ogo*	*č-eso/č-ьso*
Dat	*k-omu*	*č-emu*
Instr	*c-ěmь* (PV2)	*č-imь*
Loc	*k-omь*	*č-emь*

Table 5.15. *Modern Slavic interrogative pronouns: 'who', 'what'*

		B/C/S		Russian		Czech	
Sg	Nom	(t)k-ŏ̀	št-ŏ̀/št-à̊	k-to	č-to	k-do	c-o
	Acc	= GEN	= NOM	= GEN	= NOM	= GEN	= NOM
	Gen	k-òga	č-èga	k-ogó	č-egó	k-oho	č-eho
	Dat	k-òmu/k-òme	č-èmu	k-omú	č-emú	k-omu	č-emu
	Instr	k-ȋm/k-ȋme	č-ȋm/č-ȋme	k-em	č-em	k-ým	č-ím
	Loc	= DAT	= DAT	k-om	č-ëm	k-om	č-em

Table 5.16. *Proto-Slavic demonstrative pronouns* tъ *'that'* sь *'this'*

		Masc		Fem		Neut	
Sg	Nom	tъ	sь(jь)	ta	si/sьja	to	se/sьje
	Acc	= NOM/GEN		tǫ	sьjǫ		= NOM
	Gen	togo	sego	tojě/toję	sejě/seję		= MASC
	Dat	tomu	semu	toji	seji		= MASC
	Instr	těmь	simь	tojǫ	sejǫ		= MASC
	Loc	tomь	semь	toji	seji		= MASC
Du	Nom	ta	sьja	tě	si/sьji	tě	si
	Acc	= NOM/GEN		= NOM/GEN		= NOM
	Gen	toju	seju	= MASC		= MASC
	Dat	těma	sima	= MASC		= MASC
	Instr	= DAT		= DAT		= DAT
	Loc	= GEN		= GEN		= GEN
Pl	Nom	ti	si/sьji	ty	sьjě/sьję	ta	si
	Acc	= NOM/GEN		= NOM/GEN		= NOM
	Gen	těxъ	sixъ	= MASC		= MASC
	Dat	těmъ	simъ	= MASC		= MASC
	Instr	těmi	simi	= MASC		= MASC
	Loc	těxъ	sixъ	= MASC		= MASC

adjectives, with the nominative plural showing special forms for secondary gender. Notice also the "nominal" forms in the nominative and accusative singular.

Inflexional forms of note include the nominative singular masculine, where the loss of the weak *jer* would again have made the form unpronounceable, and we find either reduplication (Rus *tot*, OCS *sьsь*), the addition of the "long" ending -*j* (B/C/S *tâj*, Mac, Ukr *toj*, OCS *sii*, RusChSl *sej*), or the addition of another (demonstrative) element (Cz, Slk, Pol, LSorb *ten*, Blg *tózi*).

Semantically, the *t-* form is now usually non-contrastive, or non-distinctive in respect of proximity. Most languages have made lexical substitutions for proximate 'this',

Table 5.17. *Modern demonstrative* t- *'this/that'*

		B/C/S			Russian			Czech		
		Masc	Neut	Fem	Masc	Neut	Fem	Masc	Neut	Fem
Sg	Nom	*t-âj*	*t-ô*	*t-â*	*t-ot*	*t-o*	*t-a*	*t-en*	*t-o*	*t-a*
	Acc	=NOM/GEN		*tû*	=NOM/GEN		*t-u*	=NOM/GEN		*t-u*
	Gen	*t-ŏg(a)*		*tê*	*t-ogó*		*t-oj*	*t-oho*		*t-é*
	Dat	*t-ŏm(e/u)*		*tôj*	*t-omú*		=GEN	*t-omu*		=GEN
	Instr	*tîm, tíme*		*tôm*	*t-em*		=GEN	*t-ím*		*t-ou*
	Loc	=DAT		=DAT	*t-om*		=GEN	*t-om*		=GEN
Pl	Nom	*t-î*	*t-â*	*t-ê*	*t-e*			*ti/ty*	*ta*	*ty*
	Acc	*t-ê*	=NOM	=NOM	=NOM/GEN			*ty*	=NOM	=NOM
	Gen	*t-îh*			*t-ex*			*t-ĕch*		
	Dat	*t-îm, t-íma*			*t-em*			*t-ĕm*		
	Instr	=DAT			*t-émi*			*t-ĕmi*		
	Loc	=DAT			=GEN			=GEN		

replacing *sъ* with an adapted form of *tъ*, e.g. with added -*to* in Czech and Slovak (*tento, tato, toto*), added emphatic initial [ɛ] or [ɣɛ] in Russian and Belarusian (Rus *ètot, èta, èto*, with the inflexions of *t-*, but in the plural the vowel of the soft stem: *èti-* vs *te-*; Bel: *hèty, hèta (ja), hèta (e)*). Ukrainian added emphatic initial *ot-* to the forms of *sej-*, then elided the initial vowel: *cej, cja, ce*. In all of East Slavic the new form is now the non-contrastive one, with *t-* marked as contrastive or non-proximate. In the others, the non-proximate 'that' form is either affixed: Cz, Slk, Pol *tamten* (*tamta, tamto*), Sln *tísti* (*tísta, tísto*); or lexically different: Blg *ónzi*, Mac *onoj*, B/C/S *ònāj*, Sln *óni*.

5.5.2.3   3 Person pronouns

The 3 Person pronouns show obvious parallels, apart from the nominative singular and plural, with the long-form adjective and determiner paradigms, which were originally formed by suffixing these pronouns to the adjective/determiner stem.

The full Proto-Slavic forms are given in table 5.11. All languages have since substituted a former demonstrative/deictic pronoun for the nominative (singular and plural), either *on-* 'that (non-proximate)' or *t-* 'that (proximate)' (Blg, Mac):

Rus, Cz, Slk, Pol, B/C/S, Sln *on-*; Ukr *vin, von-*; Bel *jën, jan-*;
Sorb *wón, won-*; Blg *toj, tja, to*; Mac *toj, toa, toe/tie*

The remaining forms are close to those of Proto-Slavic (table 5.11):

(111)   3 Person Pronoun, GenSgMasc and Fem
B/C/S *njèga, njê*; Rus *egó, eë* (/jejo/); Cz *jeho, jí*

Table 5.18. *Full and clitic accusative and dative forms of 3 Person pronoun*

		Accusative (Dir Obj)		Dative (Indir Obj)	
		Full	Clitic	Full	Clitic
Blg	M	*négo*	*go*	(*na négo*)	*mu*
	F	*néja*	*ja*	(*na néja*)	*i*
	Pl	*tjax*	*gi*	(*na tjáx*)	*im*
Mac	M	*nego*	*go*	*nemu*	*mu*
	F	*neja*	*ja*	*nejze*	*i*
	Pl	*niv*	*gi*	*nim*	*im*
B/C/S	M	*njèga*	*ga*	*njèmu*	*mu*
	F	*njẽ*	*je*	*njôj*	*joj*
	Pl	*njȋh*	*ih*	*njȋm*	*im*
Sln	M	*njéga*	*ga*	*njému*	*mu*
	F	*njó*	*jo*	*njèj/njéj/njì*	*ji*
	Pl	*njìh*	*jih*	*njìm*	*jim*
	Du	*njíju/njú*	*ju*	*njíma*	*jima*
Cz/Slk	M	*jeho*	*ho*	*jemu*	*mu*
Pol	M	*jego*	*go*	*jemu*	*mu*

Case: no vocative

Gender: singular: primary gender

dual and plural: primary and secondary gender

masculine = neuter, except for the nominative singular, and under the control of gender factors for the nominative dual and plural.

West (except Sorbian) and South Slavic show clitic pronouns for the major oblique cases of all three numbers. Even Bulgarian and Macedonian retain old case forms (table 5.18).

After prepositions there is a special "prothetic *n*-" form of the pronoun in all but Belarusian, where the *n*- never occurs, and in South Slavic, where the *n*- is standard for all full forms of the pronouns (but missing in the clitic forms):

(112a)   'him' (Acc):   Rus *egó*, Bel *jahó*, B/C/S *njèga*

(112b)   'without him': Rus *bez negó*, Bel *bez jahó*, B/C/S *bez njèga*

5.5.3   1–2 Person pronouns and the reflexive pronoun

The 1 and 2 Person pronouns, and the reflexive pronoun, are somewhat different from the other pronoun paradigms, though their inflexional categories are similar (table 5.19). On 'short' forms, see below and table 5.20.

Table 5.19. *Proto-Slavic 1–2 Person pronouns:* (j)azъ *'I'*, ty *'you'*
[Sing], my *'we'*, vy *'you' [Pl]*, sebe *'self' (substitute s- for t- of*
2 Person Sing)

		1 Person		2 Person	
		Full	Clitic	Full	Clitic
Sg	Nom	*(j) azъ*		*ty*	
	Acc	= GEN	*mę*	= GEN	*tę*
	Gen	*mene*		*tebe*	
	Dat	*mьně*	*mi*	*tebě*	*ti*
	Instr	*mъnojǫ*		*tobojǫ*	
	Loc	= DAT		= DAT	
Du	Nom	*vě*		*va/vy*	
	Acc	*na*	*ny*	*va*	*vy*
	Gen	*naju*		*vaju*	
	Dat	*nama*		*vama*	
	Instr	= DAT		= DAT	
	Loc	= GEN		= GEN	
Pl	Nom	*my*		*vy*	
	Acc	*nasъ*	*ny*	*vasъ*	*vy*
	Gen	*nasъ*		*vasъ*	
	Dat	*namъ*	*ny*	*vamъ*	*vy*
	Instr	*nami*		*vami*	
	Loc	*nasъ*		*vasъ*	

Case: no vocative;
the reflexive pronoun has no nominative.

Gender: no gender, except for the nominative dual and plural in Slovenian:
e.g.   *mídva* 'we two' [Masc], *mídve/médve* [Other]
mí 'we' [Masc], *mé* [Other]

Number: inherent and lexical, not an inflexional category;
the reflexive pronoun has no dual or plural.

The accusative and dative have clitic (short form) pronouns in West and South
Slavic. In the plural these differ from the full forms only in South Slavic (not
Slovenian) (table 5.20).

5.5.4   Numerals

The declension of numerals mainly follows patterns of nouns or pronouns presented
above. The word formation of the numerals themselves is presented in 8.6.1.

Table 5.20. *Full and clitic accusative and dative forms of 1–2 Person pronoun and reflexive*

		Accusative (Dir Obj)		Dative (Indir Obj)	
		Full	Clitic	Full	Clitic
Blg	1Sg	*méne*	*me*	*(na méne)*	*mi*
	2Sg	*tébe*	*te*	*(na tébe)*	*ti*
	Refl	*sébe*	*se*	*(na sébe)*	*si*
	1Pl	*nas*	*ni*	*(na nás)*	*ni*
	2Pl	*vas*	*vi*	*(na vás)*	*vi*
Mac	1Sg	*mene*	*me*	*mene*	*mi*
	2Sg	*tebe*	*te*	*tebe*	*ti*
	Refl	*sebe*	*se*	*sebe*	*si*
	1Pl	*nas*	*ne*	*nam*	*ni*
	2Pl	*vas*	*ve*	*vam*	*vi*
B/C/S	1Sg	*mène*	*me*	*mèni*	*mi*
	2Sg	*tèbe*	*te*	*tèbi*	*ti*
	Refl	*sèbe*	*se*	*sèbi*	*si*
	1Pl	*nâs*	*nas*	*năma*	*nam*
	2Pl	*vâs*	*vas*	*văma*	*vam*

Sln = B/C/S, but no length difference in the plural

Cz	1Sg	*mne*	*mě*	*mně*	*mi*
	2Sg	*tebe*	*tě*	*tobě*	*ti*
	Refl	*sebe*	*se*	*sebě*	*si*
Slk	1Sg	*mňa*	*ma*	*mne*	*mi*
	2Sg	*teba*	*t'a*	*tebe*	*ti*
	Refl	*seba*	*sa*	*sebe*	*si*
Pol	1Sg	*mnie*	*mię*	*mnie*	*mi*
	2Sg	*ciebie*	*cię*	*tobie*	*ci*
	Refl	*siebie*	*się*	*sobie*	*se*
USorb	1Sg	*mnje*	*mje*	*mni*	*mi*
	2Sg	*tebje*	*će*	*tebi*	*ći*
	Refl	*sebje*	*so*	*sebi*	*sej*

5.5.4.1   *Cardinal numerals*

The Proto-Slavic numerals had the following shape:

‘1’ had a determiner (Special adjective) declension (table 5.16) on the root *jedin-*:

(113)   Proto-Slavic ‘one’
Nom: *jedin-ъ* [Masc] *jedin-a* [Fem]   *jedin-o* [Neut]
Gen: *jedin-ogo* [Masc, Neut]   *jedin-oě/jedin-oę* [Fem]

Table 5.21. *Proto-Slavic numerals '2–4'*
dъva 'two' (like *tъ* dual, table 5.16); *trьje* 'three' (*i*-stem plural); *četyre* 'four' (*consonant (-r)*-stem)

	Masc	Fem/Neut	Masc	Fem/Neut	Masc	Fem/Neut
Nom	*dъva*	*dъvě*	*trьje*	*tri*	*četyre*	*četyri*
Acc	= NOM		*tri*	= NOM	*četyri*	= NOM
Gen	*dъvoju*		*trьjь*		*četyrъ*	
Dat	*dъvěma*		*trьmъ*		*četyrьmъ*	
Instr	= DAT		*trьmi*		*četyrьmi*	
Loc	= GEN		*trьxъ*		*četyrьxъ*	

Table 5.22. *Proto-Slavic numerals '5–1,000'*
pętь '5' (*i*-stem FemSg)'; *desętь* '10' (mixed *i*-stem feminine and *consonant (-t)*-stem)'; *sъto* '100' (*o*-stem Neut)

	Sg	Sg	Du	Pl	Sg	Du	Pl
Nom	*pętь*	*desętь*	*desęti*	*desęte*	*sъto*	*sъtě*	*sъta*
Acc	= NOM	= NOM	= NOM	*desęti*	= NOM	= NOM	= NOM
Gen	*pęti*	*desęti*	*desętu*	*desętь*	*sъta*	*sъtu*	*sъtъ*
Dat	= GEN	= GEN	*desętьma*	*desętьmъ*	*sъtu*	*sъtoma*	*sъtomъ*
Instr	*pętьjǫ*	*desętьjǫ*	= DAT	*desętьmi*	*sъtomъ*	= DAT	*sъty*
Loc	= GEN	*desęte*	= GEN	*desętьxъ*	*sъtě*	= GEN	*sъtěxъ*

'2–4': '2' had the dual of the determiner declension, '3' was *i*-stem plural, and '4' *consonant (-r)*-stem (table 5.21).

'5–1,000': The units '5, 6, 9, 10' had the suffix -*t*-, and '7, 8' had the suffix -*m*-. They belonged mostly to the *i*-stem feminine; '100' was *o*-stem neuter, and '1,000' *ja*-stem feminine. Sample forms are shown in table 5.22.

'11–19' had the shape '*x*-on-ten' (*x* declined, the second element had the locative of 'ten': *na-desęte*), '20–90' had the form '*x* tens' (*x* declined, the second had the same case as *x* for '2–4', but was GenPl for '5–9'), as did also '200–900' and the thousands ('*x* hundreds/thousands'):

(114)   Proto-Slavic teens, tens, hundreds and thousands

'12': *dъva na desęte*   '15': *pętь na desęte*
'20': *dъva desęti*   '30': *trьje desęte*   '50': *pętь desętь*
'200': *dъvě sъtě*   '300': *tri sъta*   '500': *pętь sъtъ*
'2,000': *dъvě tysęt'ě*   '3,000': *tri tysęt'i*   '5,000': *pętь tysęt'ь*

Table 5.23. *'2–4' in the modern languages*

	B/C/S				Russian				Czech			
	2		**3**	**4**	**2**		**3**	**4**	**2**		**3**	**4**
	M/N	F			M/N	F			M	F/N		
Nom	*dvâ*	*dvê*	*trî*	*čètiri*	*dva*	*dve*	*tri*	*četýre*	*dva*	*dve*	*tři*	*čtyři*
Acc	=NOM				=NOM/GEN				=NOM			
Gen	*dvàjū*	*dvéju*	*trijū*	*četirìjū*	*dvux*		*trëx*	*četyrëx*	*dvou*		*tří*	*čtyř*
Dat	*dváma*	*dvèma*	*trìma*	*čètirma*	*dvum*		*trëm*	*četyrëm*	*dvěma*		*třem*	*čtyřem*
Instr	=DAT				*dvumjá*		*tremjá*	*četyr'mjá*	=DAT		*třemi*	*čtyřmi*
Loc	=DAT				=GEN				=GEN		*třech*	*čtyřech*

The modern situtation generally differs only in having fused and often contracted the elements of compounds together, but often still declining both parts of the tens and hundreds. Other points of interest include the following.

Bulgarian and Macedonian distinguish primary gender with '1' and '2', and have no cases. The other languages have:

'1': like determiners, distinct gender:

(115)   'one': NomSgMasc and GenSgMasc

Ukr *odýn, odnohó*; Sln *êden/èn, ênega*; Pol *jeden, jednogo*

'2–4': the inflexions resemble plural adjectives, though with an unusual inflexional vowel in the oblique cases (derived from the dual forms inherent in '2'). Likewise, the instrumental in *-ma* echoes the dual form. The languages form two groups:

a.   East Slavic, Czech, Slovenian and B/C/S: '2' distinguishes primary gender in all forms (Bel, B/C/S) or only in the non-oblique cases.

b.   Slovak, Polish, Sorbian: distinguish primary and secondary gender.

The modern inflexions are listed in table 5.23.

'5–19', '20–90': some numerals, like Rus, Ukr *sórok*, Bel *sórak* '40' (masculine *o*-declension) lie outside the general pattern, which is that of an *i*-declension feminine noun. Sample forms are given in table 5.24. For the rest:

a.   B/C/S, Bulgarian, Macedonian: do not decline

b.   Russian, Ukrainian, Czech: decline generally like *i*-declension singulars, with some irregularities in the instrumental: '5' Rus *pjat'*, Ukr *p'jat'*, Cz *pět*; Instr: Rus *pjat'jú*, Ukr *p'jat'má*, Cz *pěti*. Ukrainian has an optional variant, used with animates, with forms like those of '2': *p'jat'*, Gen *p'jat'óx*, etc.

Table 5.24. '5', '11', '20'

	B/C/S			Russian			Czech		
	5	11	20	5	11	20	5	11	20
Nom	*pĕt*	*jedànaest*	*dvádesēt*	*pjat'*	*odínnadcat'*	*dvádcat'*	*pĕt*	*jedenáct*	*dvacet*
Acc		=NOM			=NOM			=NOM	
Gen		=NOM		*pjatí*	*odínnadcati*	*dvadcatí*	*pĕti*	*jedenácti*	*dvaceti*
Dat		=NOM			=GEN			=GEN	
Instr		=NOM		*pjat'jú*	*odínnadcat'ju*	*dvadcat'jú*		=GEN	
Loc		=NOM			=GEN			=GEN	

    c. Belarusian, Slovak, Sorbian, Slovenian: decline generally like *i*-declension plurals: '5' Sln *pét*, Gen-Loc *pêtih*, Dat *pêtim*, Instr *pêtimi*

    d. Polish: all oblique cases in -*u*: '5' *pięć*, oblique *pięciu*

'100': is indeclinable in Slovenian (*stó*), otherwise like masculine *o*- (table 5.2) or feminine *a*-declension (table 5.5) nouns, depending on the language.

'200–900': written as two words in Czech (*dvě stě*), Sorbian, Slovenian and B/C/S, and as one word elsewhere (Ukr *dvísti*). The 'hundreds' component is invariant in Slovenian, and the whole numeral optionally declines in Belarusian. Other languages show full declensions, with both components in the same case: Belarusian *dzevjac'sót* '900', [Dat] *dzevjacistám*, etc.

'1,000': not declined in Slovenian; elsewhere it follows the *i*- or *a*- noun pattern. The Proto-Slavic lexeme is replaced by the Greek root *xiljad*- in Bulgarian and Macedonian, and also as a Serbian variant (9.2.2–9.2.3).

'1,000,000': *million*: is not declined in Slovenian; elsewhere it is an *o*-stem noun.

Secondary gender A special group of cardinal numerals shows secondary gender as follows:

    '2–99': Slovak, in non-oblique case forms:

        '5': MascPers Nom *traja*, Acc=Gen)

        Other   Nom *tri*,   Acc=Nom, Gen *troch* ...

    Other case forms, like *troch*, do not distinguish gender.

Lower Sorbian, in all case forms, with -*o*- for masculine animates and -*i*- elsewhere:

        '5': MascPers *pĕśo*, Gen *pĕśoch*, Dat *pĕśom* ...

        Other   *pĕś*, Gen *pĕśich*, Dat *pĕśim* ...

(The parallel forms in Upper Sorbian are now archaic [Stone, 1993a: 633].)

'2–999': Polish, in non-oblique case forms.

'2':   MascPers *dwaj/dwóch/dwu*, Fem *dwie*, Neut *dwa*; (Gen *dwóch*, etc.)
'3':   MascPers *trzej/trzech*, Other *trzy*; (Gen *trzech*, etc.)
'5':   MascPers *pięciu*, Other *pięć*; (Gen *pięciu*)

5.5.4.2   *Ordinal numerals*

Ordinal numerals are declined like hard or soft adjectives, with concording gender. Most are hard and have the suffix *-t* (PSl **pętъ(jь)* 'fifth'). Others (the long form being more common given the definite meaning) are:

PSl **pьr̥'vъ(jь)* 'first', **vtorъ(jь)* 'second', **tretь(jь)* 'third' (soft stem), **sedmъ(jь)* 'seventh', **osmъ(jь)* 'eighth'. The root *drug-* 'other' is now used for 'second' by all but Bulgarian, Macedonian and Russian.

5.5.4.3   *Collective numerals*

Collective numerals are used with *pluralia tantum* nouns, and with collections of entities which form groups, like children, pairs of animals and so on, within the range of '2–10' (for '1 [Coll]' the "plural" form is used). The common suffix for '2–3 [Coll]' is *-j-* (e.g. Rus *dvó-j-e* '2 [Coll]', *tró-j-e* '3 [Coll]'), for '4–10 [Coll]' *-er-*, attached to either the cardinal (usually) or ordinal stem (Rus *čétv-er-o* 'four [Coll]' with ordinal stem, *sém-er-o* 'seven [Coll]' with cardinal stem). Their inflexions may show:

a.   no case: Bulgarian, Macedonian
b.   plural adjectival inflexions: Czech, Sorbian
c.   oblique cases like those of cardinal numerals or determiners: East Slavic and Slovak
d.   special forms: Pol '2 [Coll]' *dwo-j-e*, Gen *dwoj-ga*, Dat-Loc *-gu*, Instr *-giem*;
     B/C/S '2 [Coll]' *dvȍ-j-e*, Gen *dvó-ga*, other cases *-ma*

5.5.5   Verbs

5.5.5.1   *Verbs: Morphological categories*

The verb paradigms contain the morphological categories:

Person: 1, 2, 3
Number: singular, dual (Sorbian and Slovenian), plural
Gender: primary and secondary, according to the pattern of genders in the nominative in the individual languages (5.4.4).

Tense:	present, past, future, imperfect, aorist, pluperfect, as well as various combinations, like the Bulgarian future-in-the-past.
Voice:	active, passive, reflexive
Mood:	indicative, conditional, imperative
Renarration:	"authentic", renarrated (Bulgarian and Macedonian)
Case:	as for adjectives; case is marked in verbs only on participles.

These are the inflexional morphological categories of Slavic. Although aspect is conventionally treated with paradigmatics, it is formally more closely related to word formation, and we discuss it in 6.3 and especially in 8.3.

These inflexional categories divide into two types: those which the verb "acquires" by agreement from the subject (number, person, gender, case); and those which are inherent in the verb. The acquired characteristics are marked on the various verb forms as follows:

1. No acquired characteristics: non-finite forms of the verb:
   infinitive (not in Macedonian or Bulgarian)
   supine (only Czech and Slovenian)
   gerund (though Czech gerunds inflect for gender and number)
2. Gender and number:
   Tense forms with the *l*-participle, and lacking an auxiliary on which [Person] would be marked: East Slavic past and conditional tenses, as well as the 3 Person past which lacks the auxiliary in Czech, Slovak, Polish and Macedonian.

   (116) Rus *já/tý/ón vernú-l-sja* 'I [Masc]/you [Masc]/he returned

   Czech gerunds also mark gender and number:

   (117) Cz 'doing': *dĕlaj-e* [Masc], *dĕlaj-íc* [Fem-Neut], *dĕlaj-íce* [Pl]
   'having done': *dĕlav-ø* [Masc], *dĕlav-ši* [Fem-Neut], *dĕlav-še* [Pl]

3. Gender, number and case:

   (118) Participles:
Rus	*zanimájušč-ij*	'occupying'	[Pres Act]
	zanimávš-ij/zanjávš-ij	'having occupied'	[Past Act]
	zanimáem-yj	'being occupied'	[Pres Pass]
	zánjat-yj	'occupied'	[Past Pass]

4. Person and number:
    All finite verbs forms except the past in East Slavic:

    (119)   Sln present: *drž-ím* 'I hold', *drž-íta* 'you [dual = two] hold',
            drž-ijo 'they hold'

    (120)   Rus future perfective: *ja otpráv-lju* 'I shall send',
                                     ty otpráv-iš' 'you [Sg] will send'

    (121)   Rus imperative: *piš-í*: 'write' [2Sg]; *napíš-em* 'let us write'

5. Person, number and gender:
    All *l*-participle forms with the auxiliary as a separate and inflecting
    word; and in Polish, the *l*-participle forms with the affix-auxiliary:

    (122)   Sorb past perfective:

sym dźělal-ø	'I have worked'
smój dźělal-oj	'we [Du MascPers] have worked'
smy dźělal-i	'we [Pl MascPers] have worked'

In contrast, the *inherent* morphological categories of the verb combine to form
the various "parts of the verb", including the tenses, moods, voices and so on, as
well as the non-finite parts of the verb like the gerunds, infinitive and supine.
Table 5.25 shows which parts of the verb are present in which language, and also
specifies basic information about their form and currency. This table should also be
used for orientation purposes. There are so many variations in verb forms that it is
not practicable to put them all into a single table of conjugational forms. So once it
is known from this table that a given category is present in a language, the actual
forms of the paradigm can be retrieved from the individual sections on the infinitive, present tense and so on.

5.5.5.2   *Verbs: Morphological forms (conjugation)*

The simplex verb form consists of a stem plus an optional derivational suffix
(absence = non-derived root) and theme (usually a thematic vowel; absence =
"athematic"), plus an inflexion and optional reflexive postfix. The forms of these
parts of the verb differ significantly from one language to another and from one
verb paradigm to another. The traditional ("Leskien") description of Proto-Slavic
and Old Church Slavonic has five verb paradigms, based on the thematic vowel or
'consonant + vowel' syllable of the present tense (table 5.26).

The five classes of Proto-Slavic still provide a useful point of reference for
modern typologies, even though there have been four major types of change to
the Proto-Slavic system:

Table 5.25. *Verbs: inherent morphological categories*

	Pres	Fut	FutPerf	Aor	Impf	Perf	Plupf	Imper	Cond	PastCond	Inf	Sup
B/C/S	S	C	C	(S)	(S)	C	C	S	C	C	S	–
Sln	S	C	–	–	–	C	(C)	S	C	C	S	S
Blg	S	C	C	S	S	C	C	S	C	–	–	–
Mac	S	C	C	S	S	C	C	S	C	–	–	–
Bel	S	S/C	–	–	–	S	–	S	C	–	S	–
Russ	S	S/C	–	–	–	S	–	S	C	–	S	–
Ukr	S	S/C	–	–	–	S	C	S	C	–	S	–
Pol	S	S/C	–	–	–	S	–	S	S	(C)	S	–
Sorb	S	S/C	–	S	S	C	C	S	C	–	S	–
Cz	S	S/C	–	–	–	C	–	S	C	–	S	(S)
Slk	S	S/C	–	–	–	C	C	S	C	C	S	–

Notes:

S = simplex form

C = complex form, i.e. formed with at least one auxiliary

S/C = simplex or complex according to perfective/imperfective aspect

– = absent form or paradigm (note in addition that gerunds, the past conditional, pluperfect, and all the remote past tenses are not usually found in the spoken language)

( ) = rare or not commonly used form

'S' under 'Imper' refers to 2 Person imperative; 1 Person imperative forms are S or C; 3 Person forms are always C.

Bulgarian and Macedonian have in addition a "future in the past" and a "future perfect in the past", as well as "renarrative" forms (5.5.5.8).

Table 5.26. *Proto-Slavic conjugational classes*

Class	Theme	PSl examples (stems)
I	-e-	*nes-* 'carry', *mog-* 'be able'
II	-ne-	*dvig-* 'move', *gib-* 'bend'
III	-je-	a. stem in vowel: *zna-* 'know', *my-* 'wash'
		b. stem in consonant: *pis-* 'write', *plak-* 'cry'
IV	-i-	*pros-* 'ask', *vid-* 'see', *lež-* 'lie' (< earlier **leg-*)
V	-ø- ("athematic")	(*j*)*es-* 'be', *da*(*d*)- 'give'

1. The collapse of Classes I–III into one class: (a) in Russian and Belarusian by the prepalatalization of consonants before *e*; and (b) in Bulgarian and Macedonian through the merging of *e* and *je* into *e*.

2. The development of a new class of -*a*- verbs in West and South Slavic (which we shall call Class VI), through the contraction of *aje* to *a* (Rus *délaeš'*, Cz *děláš* 'you [Sg] do').

3. Lower Sorbian has a unique new paradigm with the theme *j*, derived mainly from roots in *j*: *stojaś* 'to stand', *stojm* 'I stand', *stojš* 'you [Sg] stand'. We shall call this Class VII.

4. Diversification of inflexions through stress alternations, especially in Russian and Belarusian, resulting in differences of vowel quality: 'I take': Rus *berú* [bʲɪ'ru], Bel *bjarú'*; 'you [Sg] take': Rus *berëš'*, Bel *bjarèš*.

We shall continue to use these class names (I–V, plus VI–VII) for the modern languages.

The modern languages therefore show (excluding athematic verbs):

a. two paradigms (I + II + III (*e*), and IV (*i*)): Rus, Bel, Ukr

b. three paradigms (I + II + III (*e*), IV (*i*), VI (*a*)): Blg, Mac, B/C/S, Sln, Cz, Slk, USorb, Pol

c. four paradigms (I + II + III (*e*), IV (*i*), VI (*a*), VII (*j*)): LSorb

(*e* thus now includes *ne* (II) and *je* (III) in all languages; the traditional description in some languages may distinguish one or both of these, but the range of possibilities is essentially the same across the whole group).

Stem   The stem can undergo morphophonological alternations in different parts of the verb, and, in order to predict the correct forms of even regular verbs, one must know four forms: the infinitive, 1 Person singular present, 2 Person singular present, and past passive participle (e.g. Rus *peč'* 'to bake', *pekú*, *pečëš'*, *pečënnyj*). In this example the palatalization apparently shows two major stems for the same verb, and this is the traditional approach. The "one-stem" approach developed by Jakobson (4.6), while a most attractive and powerful idea, is complicated enough for Russian, and very complicated for all eleven languages. It also raises theoretical issues which are beyond the scope of this book. So when we speak of the "stem" of a verb, we shall mean only the appropriate form to which the given inflexions are added in the paradigm under discussion.

5.5.5.3 *Infinitive*

The infinitive is absent in Macedonian, and effectively also in Bulgarian, where it is present only in a now rare vestigial form (see below). These languages use either the 1 Person singular present (Blg) or the 3 Person singular present (Mac) as the citation form, where the other nine languages use the infinitive.

The infinitive may be imperfective or perfective, and is formed from the stem by the addition of a thematic vowel and a suffix/ending (PSl *-ti*). Although the infinitive (where present) is the regular citation form, it is not a reliable guide to all the other forms of the verb, and itself shows certain irregularities.

Ending Slovak and Ukrainian have generalized the infinitive ending for all classes of verb (*-t'*, *-ty* respectively). The other languages have special endings for Class I velar stems (resulting from the early Proto-Slavic change of the clusters *kt* and *gt* to *tj/t'*), and Belarusian and Russian also have special endings (*-ci*, *-ti* respectively) in Class I non-velar stems against the regular reduction of the final vowel to *-c'*, *-t'*, respectively. The Russian *-ti*, unlike the Belarusian *-ci*, is always stressed. All of West Slavic has also lost the final vowel, Czech only now completing this process (*-ti* > *-t*, e.g. *psáti* 'to write' > *psát*); the unreduced form is now literary, and resists best in the velar stems (*péci* 'to bake', alongside new *péct*).

Thematic vowel The thematic vowel of the infinitive shows up again in the past, and to some extent controls the form of the past participle passive. It is more varied in Classes III and IV.

Typical examples of infinitives include:

Class I non-velars: 'to take' (PSl *bьra-ti*): Rus *brat'*, Ukr *bráty*, Bel *brac'*, Pol Sorb *brać*, Cz *brat*, Slk *brat'*, B/C/S, Sln *bráti*.

Class I velars: 'to bake' (PSl *pek-ti*): Rus *peč'*, Ukr *pektý*, Bel *pjačý*; Pol *piec*, Cz *péci/péct*, Slk *piect'*, Sorb *pjec*, B/C/S *pèći*, Sln *péči*.

Class II: 'to move' (PSl *dvig-nu-ti*): Rus *dvínut'*, Ukr *dvýnuty*, Bel *pasunúc'*, Pol *dwignąć*, Cz *hnout*, Slk *posunút'*, Sorb *hibnyć* 'touch', B/C/S *d'ïgnuti* 'lift', Sln *dvígniti* 'lift'.

Class III

1. Verb roots in *-a.* 'to be acquainted with' (PSl *zna-ti*): Rus *znat'*, Ukr *znáty*, Bel *znac'*, also Sorb *znać*; West and South Slavic have contracted the present *-aje-* in these verbs to *-a-*, making them Class VI.

2. Verbs in *-o-/-e-* (PSl roots in *-or/-ol/-er/-el*): 'to grind' (PSl *mel-ti*): Rus *molót'*, Ukr *molóty*, Bel *malóc'*, B/C/S *mlèti*, Sln *mléti*, Cz *mlít*, Pol *mleć*, Slk *mliet'*, Sorb *mlěć*.

3. Verbs in 'vowel + suffix *-va-*': 'to sign': Rus *podpísyvat'*, Ukr *pidpýsuvaty*, Bel *padpísvac'*, B/C/S *potpisívati*, Sln *podpisováti*, Pol *podpisywać*, Cz *podpisovat*, Slk *podpisovat'*, Sorb *podpisować*.

Class IV

1. Verbs in *-i-*: 'to praise' (PSl *xval-i-ti*): Rus *xvalít'*, Ukr *xvalýty*, Bel *xvalíc'*, B/C/S Sln *hvaliti*, Pol *chwalić*, Cz *chvalit*, Slk *chvalit'*, Sorb *chwalić*.

2. Verbs in *-e-* (< PSl *ě*): 'to see' (PSl *vid-ě-ti*): Rus *vídet'* (Ukr *vertíty* 'to turn': *ě* > *i*, Bel *vjarcéc'* 'to turn'), B/C/S *vìdeti*, Sln *vídeti*, Pol *widzieć*, Cz *vidět*, Slk *vidiet'*, Sorb *widzeć*.

3. Verbs in *-a-* (< PSl *ě*, stems in palatals, including *j*): 'to lie' (PSl *lež-a-ti* < **leg-ě-ti*): Rus *ležát'*, Ukr *ležáty*, Bel *ljažác'*, B/C/S *lèžati*, Sln *ležáti*, Pol *leżeć*, Cz *ležet*, Slk *ležat'*, Sorb *ležeć*.

Class V: (athematic) verbs are idiosyncratic: 'to eat' (PSl *ěs-ti/jas-ti*): Rus *est'*, Ukr *jísty*, Bel *ésci*, B/C/S *j̈èsti*, Sln *jésti*, Pol *jeść*, Cz *jíst*, Slk *jest'*, Sorb *jěsć*.

Class VI: Verbs in *-a-*, former Class III: 'to know' (of people) (PSl *zna-ti*): B/C/S *znàti*, Sln *znáti*, Cz *znat*, Pol *znać*, Slk *znat'*; Sorb *džěłać* 'to work' (Sorb *znać* has remained in Class III).

Class VII: Verbs in *-j(a)-*, former Class IV: 'to stand' (PSl *stoj-a-ti*): LSorb *stojaś;* 'to undo' (PSl **por-ti*), LSorb *projś.*

The Bulgarian "infinitive" is used only after two modal verbs, and only optionally, always replaceable by the normal *da* + present. It is formed as a bare verb root, identical to the 2–3 Sg Aorist (*xváli* 'praise'). Verbs ending in a dental lose that as well (*ja* 'eat' < root *jad-*).

5.5.5.4   *Present tense*

Slavic has only one present tense, which expresses both 'I do' and 'I am doing'. In Slovenian it is the only simplex tense. It is formed from the imperfective stem,

Table 5.27. *Proto-Slavic present-tense inflexions*

	Endings I–IV	Examples I–IV	Endings V	Examples V	
				(roots *jes-, dad-*)	
1Sg	-ǫ	*nes-ǫ, piš-ǫ, proš-ǫ*	-mь	*jes-mь*	*da-mь*
2Sg	-ši	*nes-e-, piš-e-, pros-i-*	-si	*je-si*	*da-si*
3Sg	-tь	*nes-e-, piš-e-, pros-i-*	-tь	*jes-tь*	*das-tь*
1Du	-vě	*nes-e-, piš-e-, pros-i-*	-vě	*jes-vě*	*da-vě*
2Du	-ta	*nes-e-, piš-e-, pros-i-*	-ta	*jes-ta*	*das-ta*
3Du	-te	*nes-e-, piš-e-, pros-i-*	-te	*jes-te*	*das-te*
1Pl	-mъ	*nes-e-, piš-e-, pros-i-*	-mъ	*jes-mъ*	*da-mъ*
2Pl	-te	*nes-e-, piš-e-, pros-i-*	-te	*jes-te*	*das-te*
3Pl	Class I, II, III: -ǫtь; Class IV: -ętь;		Class V mixed:		
		nes-ǫtь, piš-ǫtь, pros-ętь		*s-ǫtь*	*dad-ętь*

which may undergo a number of characteristic morphophonological alternations. The inflexions themselves also show certain differences between languages – and between paradigms in individual languages, though not as much as with nouns. The same inflexions occur with the simplex future perfective, formed like the present but with the perfective stem, in East and West Slavic (hence the use of "non-past" for this set of inflexions). We omit here the present tense of irregular and athematic verbs (5.5.6).

The stem is often different from that of the infinitive, which is not a reliable guide to the present tense (typical stems are listed above). Then follow the thematic forms determining the class of the verb, as noted above, and then the endings. Table 5.27 shows the Proto-Slavic endings.

Morphophonology

1. Alternations occurring between the present-tense and infinitive stems are:

   a. vowel quality or even syllable structure, especially in Classes I–III:

   (123)   *ova ~ uj:* Cz *kup-ova-t* 'to buy', 1Sg *kup-uj-i*, 2Sg *kup-uj-e-š* . . .

   b. alternations associated with 'vowel + liquid' combinations:

   (124)   Cz *mlí-t*   'to grind',   1Sg *mel-u;*
            Rus *umeré-t'* 'to die' (Prfv), 1Sg *umr-ú*

   c. alternations reflecting old ablaut:

   (125)   Pol *br-a-ć* 'to take', 1Sg *bior-ę*

d. "concealed" nasal consonants:

(126)   Rus   *nač-á-t'*   'to begin' [Prfv],   1Sg *nač-n-ú*;
        Pol   *ciá-ć*   'to cut',   1Sg *tn-ę*

e. quality/quantity alternations: Pol *mó-c* 'to be able', 1Sg *mog-ę*

2. The alternations occurring *within* the present-tense stem involve pala-
    talization. Stem-final consonants may undergo PV1 before thematic *-e-*
    (Class I):

(127)   Rus *moč'* 'to be able', 1Sg *mog-ú*, 2 Sg *móž-eš'*

and mutation of dentals and labials, in three patterns:

a. only 1Sg is palatalized (Class IV): Rus *xod-ít'* 'to go', 1Sg *xož-ú*, 2Sg
    xód-iš' 'you go'; Rus *ljub-ít'* 'to love', 1Sg *ljubl-jú*, 2Sg *ljúb-iš'*.
b. 1Sg and 3Pl are palatalized (Class IV): Pol *prosić* 'to request', 1Sg
    proszę, 2Sg *prosisz*, 3Pl *proszą*; Ukr (labial stems only): 1Sg *ljubl-jú*,
    2Sg *ljúb-yš*, 3Pl *ljúbl-jat'*.
c. all the present is mutated (Class III): B/C/S *pís-ati* 'to write',
    1Sg *píš-ēm*, 2Sg *píš-ēš* 'you write'.

3. Alternations involving the thematic vowel:
    Classes I–III
    When stressed in Russian (and Belarusian, 1 Person plural only) *-e-*
    becomes *-ë-* (= /o/):

(128)   Rus *sme-ë-m-sja*, Bel *smja-ë-m-sja* 'we laugh'
        Rus *nes-ú*, 'I carry', *nes-ë-š'* 'you carry'; Bel *njas-ú*, *njas-é-š*
        (cf. Cz *nes-u*, *nes-e-š*)

Thematic vowel   The thematic vowel operates in the 1 Person singular only with
the new *-m* ending (Class VI):

(129)   Rus *piš-ú* 'I write', *píš-e-š'*; B/C/S *píš-ē-m*, *píš-ē-š*

In Macedonian the 1 Singular vowel is always *-a-*: *mož-am* 'I can', *mož-eš* 'you can'.
   In the 3 Person plural the thematic vowel is retained only in Macedonian:
vik-a-at 'they shout'; and (optionally) in Slovenian: *sed-í-jo/sed-é* 'they sit'.

Inflexions
1 Person singular
The 1 Person Singular has widely adopted the *-m* once found only in athematic
verbs, but not in East Slavic and restricted in West Slavic, except Slovak, which has

generalized it. Lower Sorbian has it in all but Class I, Czech has it in Classes IV and VI, Polish and Upper Sorbian in Class VI only:

'I do, I work' (Class VI): all have -*m*: Cz *dĕl-ám*, Pol *dział-am*, Sorb (*d*)*źĕl-am*;
'I hear' (Class IV): Cz *šlyš-ím*, Pol *słysz-ę*, USorb *słyš-u*, LSorb *šlyš-ym;*
'I give' (Class III): Cz *daruji*, Pol *daruję*, USorb *daruju*, LSorb *studuju/studujom* 'I study'.

3 Person singular

The 3 Person singular shows no final consonant (that is, the ending is zero after the theme) except in East Slavic.

Ukrainian has -*t'* for Classes IV and V: *pitá-je-ø* 'he asks' (III), *xvál-y-t'* 'he praises' (IV).

Belarusian has -*c* with reflexive verbs, but -*ø* elsewhere: *smjaé-c-ca* 'he laughs', *édz-e-ø* 'he goes/travels'.

Russian always has -*t*: *zná-e-t* 'he knows', *éd-e-t* 'he travels', *xód-i-t* 'he goes'.

2–3 Person dual

The 2 and 3 Person dual show secondary gender in Sorbian: -*taj* for [MascPers], -*tej* elsewhere: *njes-e-taj* 'you two [MascPers] carry'.

3 Person plural (PSl Class I–III: -*ǫt*-; Class IV -*ęt*-; Class V mixed)

Sln: -*jo* for all classes; some classes allow alternatives in -*e* and -*jo*: *drž-í-jo/drž-é* 'they hold', in -*o* and -*jo*: *bér-e-jo/ber-ó* 'they take'.

Cz: -*í* for Class IV and after *j; -jí* after *a* (Class VI); -*ou* elsewhere: *ved-ou* 'they lead', *pros-í* 'they ask'.

Slk: -*ia* for Class IV; -*ú* after consonant stems; -*ju* elsewhere: *ved-ú* 'they lead', *pros-ia* 'they ask'.

Sorb: -(*j*)*a* for Class IV, -(*j*)*a*/-(*j*)*u* elsewhere: *njes-u* 'they carry', *słyš-a* 'they hear'. Lower Sorbian has -*e* in Classes IV and VII: *słyš-e* 'they hear', *stoj-e* 'they stand'.

Pol: -*ją* if the stem ends in a vowel; -*ą* elsewhere: *prosz-ą* 'they ask'.

East: retain the Proto-Slavic vowel and the consonant (-*ut*('), -*jat*(')): Rus *nes-út* 'they carry', *prós-jat* 'they ask'.

Both stem and inflexion may be affected by variations of stress or pitch:

a.   stem stress: Rus *dél-a-t'* 'to do', *dél-a-ju*, *dél-a-eš'*, ... *déla-jut*;
b.   desinence (end) stress: Rus *br-a-t'* 'to take', *ber-ú*, *ber-ëš'*, ... *ber-út*;
c.   1Sg desinence stress, elsewhere stem stress: Rus *pis-á-t'* 'to write', *piš-ú*, *píš-e-š'*, ... *píš-ut*.

5.5.5.5   *Future tenses*
a. *Simplex future tenses*
    1.   *Perfective future*

In East and West Slavic the perfective future is formed by adding present-tense endings to the perfective stem:

(130)   Cz   *za-zpívat*   'to sing' [Prfv]
           za-zpívám 'I shall sing, I shall have sung'

    2.   *Imperfective future*

Ukrainian and Belarusian have a special simplex imperfective future as well as a complex formation. It is formed from the infinitive plus forms of the verb 'to take/have', the two /i/s being contracted:

(131)   'to praise': Ukr   *xval-ý-ty* (+ *im-u 'I (shall) have),
                       xvalýty-mu 'I shall praise'

In Ukrainian the simplex form is more common than the complex form, while in Belarusian the simplex form is now archaic. In Czech, Slovak and Sorbian, with a few verbs of determinate motion and conveying, the prefix *po-* does not perfectivize the stem:

(132)   Cz   *hn-á-t* 'to drive'   *po-žen-u*   'I shall be driving'
           pl-ou-t 'to swim'   *po-pluj-i*   'I shall be swimming'
           růst 'to grow'   *po-rost-u*   'I shall be growing'

    3.   *Bi-aspectual*

South Slavic has only one simplex future tense (also as alternative to the complex forms): B/C/S affixes enclitic forms of the verb *htèti* 'to want' (full present *hòć-u*, etc.) to the imperfective verb stem (a pattern also found in Romanian):

(133a)   B/C/S future suffixes
         1Sg *-ću*   1Pl *-ćemo*
         2Sg *-ćeš* 2Pl *-ćete*
         3Sg *-će*   3Pl *-će*

(133b)   B/C/S   *písa-ti* 'to write' *písa-ću* 'I shall write, I shall be writing'
                 ùme-ti 'to know how' *ùme-ću* 'I shall know how'

Only the positive future here is simplex, since the negative form attaches *ne-* to the clitic form:

(134)   B/C/S   *néću písati* 'I shall not write'

b. *Complex future tenses*

1. *Imperfective future*

    a. The formation of this tense shows three complex alternatives:

      (i) Future of 'be' + imperfective infinitive (East and West Slavic)

          (135a)   Ukr *búdu* (*búdeš* ...) *hovorýty* 'I (etc.) shall be speaking'

          (135b)   Pol *będę* (*będziesz* ...) *mówić* 'I (etc.) shall be speaking'

          Bulgarian, which usually follows model (c) below, has a rarer alternative form with the inflected future auxiliary (a short form of 'to want', like B/C/S above) with the vestigial infinitive:

          (135c)   Blg *šta* [ʃtə] (*šteš* ...) *vídja* 'I (etc.) shall be seeing'

      (ii) Future of 'be' + imperfective *l*-participle (Slovenian; Polish, alternative to (a))

          (136a)   Sln *vídel bóm, vídel bóš* ... 'I (etc.) shall be seeing'

          (136b)   Pol *będę* (*będziesz* ...) *mówił* 'I (etc.) shall be saying' (non-clitic auxiliary)

      (iii) Invariant future particle + present tense (Bulgarian, Macedonian)

          (137a)   Blg *šte kázvam, šte kázvaš* ... 'I (etc.) shall be saying' (cf. (a), where the auxiliary inflects)

          (137b)   Mac *ḱe kážuvam, ḱe kážuvaš* ... 'I (etc.) shall be saying'

          Negative forms are expressed in Bulgarian by *njáma da* or *ne šte* (colloq.) + present, and in Macedonian by *néma da* or *ne ḱe* + present.

2. *Future perfective*

    a. Bulgarian and Macedonian possess complex forms of the future perfective, with the invariant future particle and the perfective "present":

          (138a)   Blg *šte napíša*   'I shall write, I shall have written'

          (138b)   Mac *ḱe nápišam* 'I shall write, I shall have written'

    b. Future of 'be' + perfective *l*-participle (Slovenian, as for imperfective):

          (139)   Sln *bóm kúpil* 'I shall buy'

3. *Future perfect*

The future perfect is a step further into completed actions in the future than the future perfective: the future perfect translates only 'I shall have -ed'. It is found in Belarusian and South Slavic.

a. The Proto-Slavic form was the future of 'be' + *l*-participle, which is continued in B/C/S, virtually imperfective only:

> (140)   B/C/S   *bȕdēm govòrio*   'I shall have spoken'

b. Bulgarian has the future of auxiliary 'be' (= invariant particle + present or future) + the aorist *l*-participle, in either aspect:

> (141a)   Blg   *šte săm písal*   'I shall have been writing' [Imprfv]
>
> (141b)   Blg   *šte băda písal*   'I shall have been writing' [Imprfv]
>
> (142a)   Blg   *šte săm napísal*   'I shall have written' [Prfv]
>
> (142b)   Blg   *šte băda napísal*   'I shall have written' [Prfv]

c. Macedonian uses the invariant future particle + perfect in *imam* ('have') *-no* (below) (either aspect):

> (143a)   Mac   *ḱe ímam píšano* 'I shall have been writing' [Imprfv]
>
> (143b)   Mac   *ḱe ímam napíšano* 'I shall have written' [Prfv]

4. *Future in the past*

Bulgarian is also able to form a "future in the past" – that is, a future action viewed from a point of time in the past, and which translates into English as 'I would have done ...', 'I was on the point of doing ...'. They are therefore close in meaning, and sometimes in form, to the past conditional (5.5.5.7). The Bulgarian future in the past is formed from the aorist of the auxiliary 'be' + *da* + present (normal) or perfect (rare) of the verb:

> (144a)   Blg   *štjáx da píša*   'I would have written'
>
> (144b)   Blg   *štjáx da săm napísal*   'I would have written'

Other languages, including Macedonian, use the past conditional (5.5.5.7) to express this tense form.

5.5.5.6   *Past tenses*

a.   *Simplex past tenses*

The simplex past tenses are: (a) the imperfect and the aorist; and (b) the imperfective and perfective past in East Slavic. Polish represents a special case of the past: the *l*-participle is present along with the auxiliary, but they are fused together as one word. Since the form is parallel to the auxiliary of the other languages, we shall discuss this tense under complex past tenses below.

1. *Imperfective and perfective past* (*East Slavic*)

The past tenses in East Slavic have lost the auxiliary from the former perfect and are formed with the "bare" *l*-participle (5.5.5.10):

(145a) Imperfective: Rus *pe-l* [Masc], *pé-la* [Fem],
                            pé-lo [Neut], *pé-li* [Pl]
                      Ukr *spivá-v, spivá-la, spivá-lo, spivá-ly*
                            'I/you/he/she/it was, we/you/they were singing'

(145b) Perfective: Rus *propé-l, propé-la, propé-lo, propé-li*
                      Ukr *prospivá-v, prospivá-la,*
                            prospivá-lo, prospivá-ly

Aspects of the morphophonology of these tenses are discussed under past participle active (5.5.5.10).

2. *Imperfect*

The Proto-Slavic imperfect is retained in Sorbian, B/C/S, Bulgarian and Macedonian. Like the past imperfective, it refers to a past action in progress ('I was doing') or repetition ('I used to do'). A thematic vowel and inflexions are added to the root, which is imperfective except occasionally for a Bulgarian perfective. The base stem is that of the infinitive, or its equivalent (*l*-participle) in Bulgarian and Macedonian. Inflexions are then added after a thematic vowel (which was complex in Proto-Slavic (table 5.28), but is now simplified in all [table 5.29]). The inflexions are very similar to those of the aorist (table 5.30), excepting the 2–3 Singular.

B/C/S has two qualifications:

a. all verbs with infinitives in *-ati* have *-ā-*: *pèvati* 'to sing', *pèvāh*';
b. verbs where the infinitive and present stems are identical have either *-ijā-* or *-ā-*: *pèći* 'to cook', *pècijāh/pèčāh* 'was cooking';

Note the Sorbian secondary gender in the 2–3 Du: *-štaj* = [MascPers].

Morphophonology

a. The modern thematic vowel is determined by language, verb class and ending (see table 5.28). Bulgarian has /a/ before /x/ in Class I and II,

Table 5.28. *Proto-Slavic imperfect tense*

Class	I	I	III	IV	IV	V
Theme	*-ĕa-/-aa-*	*nes-ĕa-*	*mož-aa-*	*pis-aa-*	*vid-ĕa-*	*noš-aa-*	*b-ĕa-*
Endings 1Sg	*-xъ*					
(all classes) 2Sg	*-še*					
3Sg	*-še*					
1Du	*-xově*					
2Du	*-šeta*					
3Du	*-šete*					
1Pl	*-xomъ*					
2Pl	*-šete*					
3Pl	*-xǫ*					

Table 5.29. *The modern imperfect tense*

	Blg	Mac	B/C/S	Sorb
Themes				
Class I/II	*ja/e*	*e*	*ijā*	*e*
	tres-já-x	*tres-e-v*	*trésijāh*	*třasech*
	tres-é-še	*tres-e-še*	*trésijāše*	*třaseše*
Class III	*e*	*e*	*jā*	*e*
	píš-e-x	*piš-e-v*	*bȉjāh*	*bijach*
Class IV	*e*	*e*	*jā*	*a*
	mól-e-x	*mol-e-v*	*mȍljāh*	*słyšach*
Class VI	*a*	*a*	*ā*	*a*
	djál-a-x	*čit-a-v*	*dȅlāh*	*dźěłach*
Endings				
1Sg	*-x*	*-v*	*-h*	*-ch*
2Sg	*-še*	*-še*	*-še*	*-še*
3Sg	*-še*	*-še*	*-še*	*-še*
1Du				*-chmoj*
2Du				*-štaj/-štej*
3Du				*-štaj/-štej*
1Pl	*-xme*	*-vme*	*-smo*	*-chmy*
2Pl	*-xte*	*-vte*	*-ste*	*-šće*
3Pl	*-xa (/ă/-[ə])*	*-a*	*-hu*	*-chu*
		(tres-e-a, čit-a-a)		

otherwise /e/: *čet-já-x, čet-é-še* 'was reading'. Sorbian shows regular vowel mutation between palatals: *bij-a-ch, bij-e-še* 'was hitting';

b. Palatalization of the stem follows the present-tense pattern. B/C/S has a choice in verbs with either *-ijā-* (*pècijāh* 'was cooking' PV2) or *-ā-* (*pèčāh* PV1).

3. *Aorist*

The aorist, like the imperfect, is found only in Sorbian, B/C/S, Bulgarian and Macedonian. It designates a past action seen at a single point in time, like the English 'I did', 'I said'. It is formed from the perfective infinitive stem in all four languages; Bulgarian and B/C/S also allow its formation from the imperfective stem. Since Bulgarian and Macedonian have no real infinitive, the aorist forms a good guide to the form of this stem.

In Proto-Slavic, the oldest form of the aorist (often called the "root aorist") had been replaced by a form involving a thematic *-s-*, known therefore as the "sigmatic aorist", in all forms except the 2–3 Singular, which never shows this theme. In the following, we show only the sigmatic form (the root form can be retraced by deleting the *-s-* and recovering underlying root consonants lost because of it). Where the stem ended in a consonant (Class I, Class II without the suffix *-n-*), the clusters with *-s-* were often simplified by the deletion of the stem consonant. Further, the *-s-* itself underwent change in some forms: to *-x-* (initially after /i/, then after all vowels by analogy), and to *-š-* before the front vowel ending *-ę* in the 3 Plural. In a further development, the consonant stems of Classes I and II also acquired the *-s-*, at the same time inserting the fill vowel *-o-* (these forms being referred to as the "second sigmatic aorist"). The Proto-Slavic forms of this last pattern are shown in table 5.30; the modern forms are shown in table 5.31.

Morphophonology

1. Stems ending in a vowel keep that vowel for all aorist forms; stems ending in a consonant add:

    1Sg, 1–3Pl: Blg, Mac, B/C/S: *-o*; Sorb *-e*:

    Blg *pék-ó-x*, Sorb *pjek-e-ch* 'I baked'

    2–3Sg: all languages *-e*: Blg *péč-e*, Sorb *pječ-e* 'he/she/it baked'

2. 1st Palatalization of Velars in 2–3Sg (preceding example);

3. Sorbian   a. secondary gender in 2–3Du (as imperfect)

    b. regular vowel mutation between palatals:

    poběž-a-ch 'I ran', *poběž-e-šće* 'you [Pl] ran';

Table 5.30. *Proto-Slavic aorist tense*

Theme		Inf stem ending in consonant: -o-/-e#;				Inf stem ending in vowel: ø	
Class	I	I	III	III	IV	V
Endings						
1Sg	-xъ	nes-o-xъ	rek-o-xъ	napisa-xъ	pozna-xъ	promysli-xъ	by-xъ
2Sg	-(e)ø	nes-e	reč-e	napisa-ø	pozna-ø	promysli-ø	by-ø
3Sg	-(e)ø	all = 2Sg					
1Du	-xově	nes-o-	rek-o-	napisa-	pozna-	promysli-	by-
2Du	-sta	etc.					
3Du	-ste						
1Pl	-xomъ						
2Pl	-ste						
3Pl	-šę						

Table 5.31. *The modern aorist tense*

	Blg	Mac	B/C/S	Sorb
1Sg	-(o)x	-(o)v	-(o)h	-(e)ch
	trés-o-x	tres-o-v	trés-o-h	-třas-e-ch
	písá-x	piša-v	písa-h	-pisa-ch
	móli-x	-moli-v	mŏli-h	modlich so
2Sg	-e/ø	-ø	-ø	-ø
	trés-e	tres-e	três-e	-třas-e
	písá	piša	písa	-pisa
	mólí	moli	mŏlī	modli so
3Sg	-ø	-ø	-ø	-ø
1Du				-(e)chmoj
2Du				-(e)štaj/-(e)štej
3Du				-(e)štaj/-(e)štej
1Pl	-(o)xme	-(o)vme	-(o)smo	-(e)chmy
2Pl	-(o)xte	-(o)vte	-(o)ste	-(e)šće
3Pl	-(o)xa [ə]	-(o)a	-(o)še	-(e)chu

4. Macedonian: *x* has become *v*, except in the 3Pl, where it becomes *j* between *i* and *a*: *stori-v* 'I did', *stori-ja* 'they did' (< *storix, *storixa), otherwise it is lost: *treso-v* 'I shook', *treso-a* 'they shook'.

5. Stress and length: note differences between the two tenses in:

   Bulgarian stress: Blg *váljáx* [Aor] 'I rolled' (variants)';
                         valjáx [Imperf]

   B/C/S length: B/C/S *ìmah* [Aor] 'I had'; *ìmāh* [Imperf]

b.   Complex past tenses

 1. *Compound past (perfect)*

The compound past adds an auxiliary to the *l*-participle, either imperfective or perfective. The auxiliary is 'be' (5.5.6). The only exception is Macedonian, which has special forms of its own. The auxiliary may be either clitic (Cz, Slk, B/C/S, Sln, Blg):

(146)   Cz   *vědě-l jsem, vědě-l jsi, vědě-l ø* 'I/you [Sg]/he knew'

or non-clitic (Mac, Sorb):

(147)   Sorb   *sým/sí/jé wědźe-ł* 'I/you/he knew'

The 3 Person auxiliary is omitted in Czech, Slovak, Macedonian (and Polish – see below). While subject pronouns are normally omitted with 1–2 Person forms in languages with the compound past, in the 3 Person the pronoun usually stands, since otherwise there would be no clear marker of [Person] in the sentence. The participle undergoes regular alternations, as in the simplex past tense. In Polish we find a special case. Here the auxiliary has been reduced to an affix, which is attached directly to the *l*-participle:

(147)   Pol   *śpiewa-ł-e-m* 'I [Masc] sang'
              śpiewa-ł-a-sz 'you [Fem Sg] sang'
              i.e.: *śpiewa-ł* + vowel marking gender + person
              and/or number

cf. (148)   Cz   *zpíva-l-ø jsem, zpíva-l-a jsi* ...

Unlike East Slavic, [Person] is clearly marked on all forms except the 3 Person, which consists of the bare *l*-participle with its marking for gender and number:

(149)   Pol   *śpiewa-ł-ø* 'he sang', *śpiewa-ła* 'she sang'

Macedonian has special forms of the compound past. Here the *l*-participle form can express the renarrative (5.5.5.8), and the auxiliary is clitic:

(150a)   Mac   *(ti) si písa-l*   'they say that you were writing'

(150b)   Mac   *(ti) si nápisa-l* 'they say that you have written'

though these forms can also be interpreted as non-renarrative. This tense, known in Macedonian as the "past indefinite", contrasts with the past definite, which is an active tense formed from the past participle *passive* of *intransitive* verbs. This construction has a clitic auxiliary and an agreeing participle:

(151a)   Mac   *ne sme rúča-ni*   'we haven't had dinner'

(151b)   Mac   *doktorot e ótid-en*   'the doctor has left'

Yet another Macedonian form of the compound past has the auxiliary 'have' and the neuter singular of the past participle passive of *transitive* verbs:

(152)   Mac   *imame napisa-no dva pisma* 'we have written two letters'

Polish has a somewhat similar construction, but the participle agrees with the object, like an attributive adjective:

(153a)   Pol   *mam książk-ę przeczyta-ną*   lit. 'I have the book (all) read'

(153b)   Pol   *mam przeczyta-ną ksiáżk-ę* lit. 'I have a read book'

2. *Pluperfect*

The pluperfect is found in all the languages except Russian. It is formed from an auxiliary with the *l*-participle of either aspect: the imperfective translates as 'had been doing', and the perfective as 'had done'. Bulgarian has only the aorist participle of either aspect. The auxiliary has two principal forms, both of which were used in Proto-Slavic:

a. Past tense of 'be': Ukr, Cz, Pol, B/C/S, Sln (154a)
b. Imperfect of 'be': Blg, Mac, B/C/S (rare), Sorb (154b)

(154a)   Ukr   *voná pišlá bulá*   'she had gone' [Prfv]

(154b)   Blg   *te bjáxa došlí*   'they had arrived' [Prfv]

The omission of the auxiliary in the complex form of 'be' follows regular rules, as outlined under the perfect tense above. Special alternative forms are found in Macedonian, with the imperfect of 'be' + the perfective past of the verb:

(155)   Mac   *beše sum storil* 'I had done'

And in Belarusian the only form is the past tense of 'be' + the past gerund:

(156)   Bel   *janá bylá pračytáŭšy*   'she had read'

The word-order of the elements in the pluperfect may vary. Languages with a clitic auxiliary in the past perfect of 'be' must locate this clitic in second position:

(157a)   B/C/S   *jâ sam b̃io sȋigao* OR *b̃io sam sȋigao* OR *sȋigao sam b̃io* 'I had arrived'

Non-clitic elements may simply invert (cf. 154a):

(157b)   Ukr   *voná bulá xodýla* 'she had gone'

5.5.5.7   *Conditional and past conditional*

a.   *Simple conditional*

The conditional expresses "would VERB". It is formed with the *l*-participle of either aspect (in Bulgarian, the aorist participle) plus one of:

a. an invariant clitic particle:

Rus, Ukr, Bel, Slk, LSorb: *by*; Sln, Mac: *bi*

(158)   Rus   *ja by poležál*   'I would lie down for a while'

b. the inflected conditional of the auxiliary 'be', either clitic (B/C/S, Cz, Pol) (159a) or non-clitic (Blg, USorb) (159b):

(159a)   Pol   *poczekałbym*   'I [Masc] would wait'
          Cz   *žil bych*   'I [Masc] would live'

(159b)   Blg   *bíx napísal*   'I [Masc] would write'

b.   *Past conditional*

This rather literary tense, which is absent in East Slavic, is formed with the *l* participle and the past conditional of the auxiliary 'be':

a. invariant *by/bi*:

(160)   Slk   *byl bi som 'robil*   'I [Masc] would have done'

b. clitic auxiliary:

(161)   Pol   *byłbym 'zrobił* OR *'zrobiłbym był*   'I [Masc] would have done'

c. non-clitic auxiliary:

(162)   Sorb   *'bych 'byl 'zdźělał*   'I [Masc] would have done'

Table 5.32. *Renarration in Bulgarian and Macedonian (all forms are 1Sg [Masc])*

	Bulgarian		Macedonian	
	Indicative	Renarrative	Indicative	Renarrative
Present	*píša*	*píšel săm*	*pišam*	*pišal sum*
Aorist	*písax*	*písal săm*	*napišav*	*napišal sum*
Perfect	*písal săm*	*bíl săm písal*	*sum pišal, imam pišano*	*sum imal napišano*
Future	*šte píša*	*štjál săm da píša*	*ḱe pišam*	*ḱe sum pišel*

Bulgarian and Macedonian have special forms for this tense. Bulgarian has either the imperfect of the auxiliary *šta + da +* present/perfective present:

(163a)   Blg   *štjáx da pătúvam*   'I would have gone'

or a new form which adds imperfect endings to the aorist (perfective) stem:

(163b)   Blg   *pročitá-še*   'you [Sg] would have read'

(Both these forms also normally express the future in the past [5.5.5.5].) In Macedonian the usual form is *ḱe +* imperfect:

(164a)   Mac   *da me sákaše, ne **ḱe ímaše** stráv*
            'if you loved me you wouldn't be afraid'

Macedonian also has a special form using imperfect endings on the aorist stem, like that of Bulgarian except that the future particle *ḱe* is retained:

(164b)   Mac   *ḱe izbégaše*   'he would have run out'

5.5.5.8   *Renarrative*

The renarrative forms of literary Bulgarian and Macedonian denote events which the speaker did not witness or cannot vouch for. The renarrative shows elaborate adaptation of existing morphological material into complex paradigms. It is marked by the absence of the 3 Person auxiliary in compound tenses (cf. past perfect), and in some forms by special renarrative participles: the "imperfect" participle, which adds participial endings to the imperfect stem (*piše-x/-v* [Imperf 1Sg]: participle *píšel* [MascSg]); and the Macedonian "hybrid" participle, which adds an imperfective theme to the aorist (perfective) stem (*napiš-a-v* [Aor 1Sg]: participle *napiš-e-l* [MascSg]). The correlations between indicative and renarrative forms are complex, and in table 5.32 we show only the common forms – those of present, aorist, perfect and future (Scatton, 1984: 337).

5.5.5.9   *Imperative*
The simplex imperative is found in the 2 Person, and in the 1 Person dual and
plural. A periphrastic imperative like the English 'let him go' is found with the
3 Person (7.1.4). The simplex imperative is formed from the present-tense stem.
Proto-Slavic forms are shown in table 5.33.

The modern form of the imperative inflexion depends on the last sound of the
stem, and the 2 Person singular is formed as follows:

a.   Add -*j* if the stem ends in a vowel (all languages)

  (165a)   Pol *kocha-ć* 'to love', *kocha-sz* 'you love': [Imper] *kocha-j* 'love'
       Rus *déla-t'* 'to do', 2 Sg *déla-ješ'*:   [Imper] *déla-j* 'do'

  (165b)   'to buy': Ukr *kupuvá-ty*, Pol *kupowa-ć*, Sln *kupová-ti*, Mac
       kupuv-a: [Imper]: Ukr, Pol, Sln, Mac *kupuj*

b.   Soften the final consonant (not South Slavic)
   If a consonant can be softened (3.4), it may undergo this process in
   imperative formation:
   East Slavic: if the stem ends in a single consonant, and the stem is
   stressed in the 1 Person singular:

  (166a)   Rus *vsta-t'* 'to stand up' [Prfv], 1Sg *vstán-u*:
       [Imper] *vstan'* 'stand up'

   West Slavic: if the stem ends in a single consonant:

  (166b)   Pol *bronić* 'to defend', [1Sg] *bron-ię*: [Imper] *broń*

c.   Add -*i*
   South Slavic: if the stem ends in one or more consonants:

  (167a)   Sln *trésti* 'to shake', [1Sg] *trés-em*: [Imper] *trés-i*

Table 5.33. *Proto-Slavic imperative*

Class	I	II	III	IV	V
Endings					
2Sg	-*i*	-*i*	-*i*	-*i*	-*i*
1Du	-*ěvě*	-*ěvě*	-*ivě*	-*ivě*	(*bud*)-*ěvě*, (*dad*)-*ivě*
2Du	-*ěta*	-*ěta*	-*ita*	-*ita*	-*ěta*/-*ita*
1Pl	-*ěmъ*	-*ěmъ*	-*imъ*	-*imъ*	-*ěmъ*/-*imъ*
2Pl	-*ěte*	-*ěte*	-*ite*	-*ite*	-*ěte*/-*ite*

Czech, Slovak, Sorbian: if the stem ends in more than one consonant:

(167b)   Slk   *myslet'* 'to think', [1Sg] *mysl-ím*: [Imper] *mysl-i*

East Slavic (Rus, Bel *-i*, Ukr *-y*):

1. if the stem ends in a single consonant and the inflexion is stressed in any form:

> (167c)   Rus *ljubít'* 'to love', [lSg] *ljublj-ú*, 2Sg *ljúb-iš'*: [Imper] *ljub-í*

2. on perfective verbs with the prefix *vý-*, always stressed, which are treated as the non-prefixed form:

> (167d)   Rus *vý-zvat'* 'to summon' [Prfv], [1Sg] *výzov-u*: [Imper] *výzov-i*
> cf. Imprfv. *zvat'* 'to call', *zovú, zoví*

3. if the stem ends in more than one consonant:

> (167e)   Rus   *pómnit'* 'to remember' [Prfv], [1Sg] *pómn-j* u: [Imper] *pómn-i*

d.   Add *-ij* (Polish: if the stem ends in more than one consonant):

(168)   Pol   *ciągnąć* 'to pull' [Prfv], [1Sg] *ciągn-ę*: [Imper] *ciągn-ij*

Once the 2 Sg imperative is known, the other imperative forms can normally be derived by adding appropriate endings (e.g. 1 Pl *-m*, 2 Pl *-te*). Note: (1) in Bulgarian, Macedonian and Czech the *i* of the 2 Person singular is replaced by *e/ě* in the plural (reflecting PSl *-i/-ě*):

(169)   Mac   *nos-i* 'he carries', [Imper 2Sg] *nos-i*: [2Pl] *nos-e-te*

(2) Bulgarian, Macedonian and Russian have no special 1 Person plural forms, and may use instead the 1 Person future perfective indicative (Russian), or a periphrastic form with a particle (all three languages):

(170)   'let us write':   Rus   *napíš-em* [Prfv], *daváj-te pisá-t'* [Imprfv]
                           Blg   *néka (da) napíš-em* [Prfv]/*píš-em* [Imprfv]

Morphophonology

1.   Sorbian secondary gender: *-taj* for masculine personal, *-tej* elsewhere.
2.   Vowel quality alternation: regularly in Polish in final syllables (zero-endings): *rob-ić* 'to do', [Imper 2Sg] *rób-ø*.
3.   Vowel length: Czech shortens long stem vowels: Cz *píš-i* 'I write', [Imper 2Sg] *piš-ø*.

4. Palatalization follows the pattern of the 2 Person singular present (5.5.5.4).
5. Stress follows the pattern of the 1 Person singular present in mobile stress languages (167c).

5.5.5.10 Participles

Present active (Not found in B/C/S or Macedonian.) Formed from the present-tense stem: delete any final consonant in the 3 Person plural present and add:

Rus	-*ščij*	Pol	-*cy*	Sln	-*č*
Ukr	-*čyj*	Sorb	-*cy/ty*	Blg	Class VI: -*št*
Bel	-*čy(j)*	Slk	-*ci*	Blg	other: final vowel *e/ja* + *št*
		Cz	-*cí*		

(171a) 'they read': Rus *čitáju-t* Pol *czytają* Blg *čet-át*

(171b) 'reading': Rus *čitáju-ščij* Pol *czytają-cy* Blg *čet-éšt*

cf. (171c) Blg *gléda-t* 'they look' *gléda-št* 'looking'

Past active (I) Russian alone has retained the genuinely adjectival past participle active of Proto-Slavic, which is formed from the infinitive stem of either aspect by adding -(*v*)*š*-(*ij*): (*pro*) *čitá-t'* 'to read', (*pro*) *čitá-l* 'he read', (*pro*) *čitá-vš-ij* 'having read'.

Past active (II) (*the "l-participle"*) This past participle active is of either aspect, and is formed from the infinitive stem. It is used with auxiliaries to form the simplex imperfective/perfective past, and most compound verb paradigms (above). In East Slavic it is usually just the "past tense", since there is no auxiliary. Bulgarian has two imperfective forms: one from the aorist stem, which is the normal one; and one from the imperfect stem, which is used only in renarration (5.5.5.8). The formation rules are:

1. Class II–VI verbs: add the *l*-participle inflexions to the infinitive stem (i.e. minus the infinitive inflexion) (the stem in these verbs always ends in a vowel):

Masc Sg:	Rus, Cz, Slk, Sln, Blg, Mac:	-*l*
	Pol, Sorb:	-*ł*
	Ukr:	-*v* (= [u̯])
	Bel:	-*ŭ*
	B/C/S:	-*o*
Fem Sg:	Pol, Sorb -*ła*, others -*la*	

Neut Sg:	Pol, Sorb *-ło*, others *-lo*
Du:	Sorb	Masc Pers *-łoj*, other *-lej*
	Sln	Masc *-la*, other *-li*

The plural shows no gender in Russian, Belarusian, Bulgarian (*-li*), Ukrainian (*-ly*) and Macedonian (*-le*). Other languages show secondary gender as for their adjectives. This affects the final vowel, and in Polish and Sorbian mutates the *ł* to *l* before *-i*:

(172)   Pol 'we wrote': *napisa-li-śmy* [MascPers] *napisa-ły-śmy* [Other]

2.   Class I verbs: consonant stems reinstate the final velar (all languages) or dental (West Slavic) which is "hidden" in the infinitive, but which shows up in the 1 Person singular present:

(173)   'bake':   Rus   *peč'* [Inf]: *pëk-ø* [Masc], *pek-lá* [Fem]
               Pol   *piec*: *piek-ł*, *piek-ła*
               B/C/S   *pèći*: *pèk-ao*, *pèk-la*

East and South: remove *t* and *d* before *l* in all forms:

(174)   'lead':   (PSl   *ves-ti* < *ved-ti*):
               Rus   *vestí* [Infin]: *vë-l* [Masc], *ve-lá* [Fem]
               Blg   *dovedá* [1Sg]: *dové-l*, *dové-la*
               Cz   *vést*: *ved-l*, *ved-la*

The endings are as for Class II–VI verbs in the feminine, neuter, dual and plural. In the masculine singular there is variation and alternation:

East Slavic: omit *-l* after velars and dentals (except /t d/, see (174)):

(175)   'he baked':   Rus, Bel *pëk-ø*   Ukr *pik-ø*   cf. Cz *pek-l*
       'he carried':   Rus, Bel *nës-ø*   Ukr *nis-ø*   cf. Cz *nes-l*

All languages potentially insert a fill vowel before final *-l*:

B/C/S	*-a-*:	*pèk-a-o*
Slk	*-o-*:	*piek-o-l*
Sln	*-e-* ([ə]):	*skúb-sti* 'to pluck', *skúb-e-l*
Blg	*-ă-*:	*rék-ă-l* 'said'

Syllabic liquids may appear in the stem: Sln, B/C/S *mréti* 'to die', Sln *mŕl* ['məru̯], B/C/S *nȑo* ['mr̩ɔ], or in the desinence: Cz *nést* 'to carry', *nesl* ['nɛsl̩]).

Other morphophonological alternations include stress variation:

(176) Rus 'was' *by-l* [Masc], *by-lá* [Fem], *bý-lo* [Neut], *bý-li* [Pl]

and vowel-quality alternation between palatals in Polish and Sorbian:

(177) Pol *nieść* 'to carry': *niós-ł* [Masc], *nios-ła* [Fem],
               nios-ło [Neut], *nies-li* [MascPers], *nios-ły* [Other]

The *l*-participle is not used regularly as an adjective/predicate, except in some fossilized forms like Rus *ustál-yj* 'tired'.

Present passive Also now found only in Russian, this participle adds the adjectival suffix *-m-(yj)* to the present-tense stem of some transitive verbs (or, as pedagogical texts tend to say, the adjectival ending to the 1 Person plural present):

(178) Rus *vvódi-m* 'we introduce', *vvodí-m-yj* 'being introduced'

Many such participles in Russian and other languages are now adjectives:

(179a) Rus *ljubímyj* 'favorite' (*ljubít'* 'to like, love')

(179b) Pol *rodzimy* 'native' (*rodzić* 'to give birth')

When formed from a perfective stem (and less commonly from imperfective), they are adjectives meaning '(un ...)-able':

(180) Rus (*ne*)*ispravímyj* '(in)corrigible' (*isprávit'* [Prfv] 'to correct')

Past passive The past participle passive is usually perfective, though it may be imperfective. It is formed only from transitive verbs, and is used in the passive construction (7.1.5, 7.3.5), and as an attribute, and also to make compound past tenses in Macedonian (151–2). Its stem is normally the infinitive stem. The most common ending is '(vowel) + *n* + adjective desinence', but some verbs take *-t-* in place of the *-n-*. The three forms are distributed among the classes of verb stems as follows:
   -t-:
   a.   monosyllabic stems ending in a vowel (where the vowel is part of the root, not a suffix):

(181) Cz *mý-t* 'to wash', [PPP] *my-t*
          Rus *vzja-t'* 'to take', [PPP] *vzjá-t-yj*

   b.   Class II verbs (not Sorbian or Slovenian):

(182a) Rus *protjanú-t'* 'to stretch' [Prfv], [PPP] *protjánu-t-yj*
           Slk *ukradnú-t'* 'to steal' [Prfv], [PPP] *ukradnu-t-ý*

c.   stems ending in *r* or *l*:

(182b)   (PSl *-per/pьr-*):   Bel   *zapér-ci* 'to lock' [Prfv], [PPP] *zapé-r-ty*
         (PSl *mel-*):   Bel   *maló-c'* 'to grind',   [PPP] *maló-t-y*

-(*n*)*n*- (double -*nn*- in Russian and Ukrainian):
verbs with infinitives in -*a*-, notably in classes III, IV and VI:

(183)   Rus   *sdéla-t'* 'to do' [Prfv], [PPP] *sdéla-nn-yj*
        Rus   *na-pisát'* 'to write' [Prfv], [PPP] *napísa-nn-yj*
        Sln   *napísa-ti, napísa-n*

-*en*-:
all other verbs, mainly Class IV, but including Sorbian and Slovenian
Class II verbs:

(184)   Sorb   *wukn-y-ć* 'to learn', [PPP] *wuknj-en-y*

Morphophonology

1.   Palatalization in the root: all languages show PVl in Class I verbs:

(185)   Cz   *péci* (PSl *pek-*) 'to bake', [PPP] *peč-ený*

2.   Mutation of dentals and labials in Class IV:

(186)   Rus   *zaprosí-t'* 'to request', [PPP] *zapróš-enn-yj*

3.   B/C/S has an epenthetic *j/v* to avoid 'vowel + vowel' sequences in
     Class III verbs with -*en* in place of -*t*:

(187)   'to hit'   B/C/S   *bȉti*, [PPP] *bȉ-j-en* and *bȉ-v-en*
              cf. Rus   *bi-t'*, PPP *bí-t-yj*

4.   Alternations of vowel quality: stressed -*en*- becomes -*ën*- in Russian
     and Belarusian:

(188)   Rus   *udiv-ít'* 'amaze', [PPP] *udivl-ënnyj* (with mutation)

And Polish and Sorbian show this alternation between palatals and
hard consonants:

(189)   Pol   *prosić* 'to ask', [PPP] *proszeni* [MascPers], *proszony* [Other]

5.   Predicative forms: only Russian and Czech have special predicative
     forms of this participle. Russian "removes" one -*n*- (in fact a single -*n*- is

the older form) and the adjective ending (or just the ending after -*t*-),
and Czech removes the ending:

(190)   Rus *sdéla-nn-yj* 'done' [Masc],   predicative *sdéla-n-ø*
        Cz   *vypi-t-ý*   'drunk (up)' [Masc], predicative *vypi-t-ø*

6.   Macedonian uses this formation with transitive verbs to form the past
tense (5.5.5.6).

5.5.5.11 *Gerunds and supine*

The Slavic gerunds (also "verbal adverbs" or "adverbial participles") are invariant,
except in Czech where they inflect for gender and number. Slavic gerunds can only
refer to the subject of the main sentence (see 7.3.5):

(191)   Rus *sídja na stúle, on uvídel eë* '**sitting** on a chair, he caught sight of
         her' (has to be that *he* was sitting on the chair)

Gerunds are virtually restricted to the written languages, except when they form
other parts of speech and then fossilize, like Rus *blagodarjá* (+ dative) 'thanks to'.
While the primary distinction is actually one of aspect, we shall refer to the two
types as 'present' and 'past', as a reflection of their formal derivation.

Present gerund (all languages)   The present (imperfective) gerund is very close in
form to the present participle active. It is formed in a number of different ways for
different languages and classes of verbs, with many irregularities. Principal formation types include:

1.   Add to the present-tense stem the same vowel as in the 3 Person plural
present and a suffix with mutated /t/ (< PSl *t'*/*tj*)):

     Bel   -*čy* Slk, Pol -*c*   B/C/S -*ći*
     Ukr -*čy*   Sln Class I -*č*

   (192) Bel *sjadzéc'* 'to be seated', [3Pl] *sjadzjá-c'*, [PresGer] *sjadzjá-čy*

2.   Add this suffix to the present-tense stem:
    Blg, Mac: add -*jki*/-*jḱi*, respectively, to vowel stems, -*ejki*/-*ejḱi*
    (Mac also -*ajḱi*) to consonant stems:

   (193) Blg *píš-a* 'I write', [PresGer] *píš-ejki*

    Sorb (alternative to (3) below): add -*jcy* to vowel stems, -*icy* to con-
    sonant stems (or -*o*, as Russian -*a*/*ja* in (3))

(194)   Sorb   *stupać* 'to step',   [3Pl] *stupa-ju*, [PresGer] *stupa-jcy*
        słyšeć 'to hear', [3Pl] *słyš-a*,   [PresGer] *słyš-icy*

3. Add a vowel to the present-tense stem (reflex of PSl *-ę*, then
    [NomSgMasc]):

Russian: *-a/ja*:   *čitát'* 'to read', [3Pl] *čitá-jut*, [PresGer] *čitá-ja*
                    sidét' 'to be seated', [3Pl] *sid-ját*, [PresGer] *síd-ja*
Sln (Class III–IV): *e/je*:   *délati* 'to do', [3Pl] *déla-jo*, [PresGer] *délaje*
                              molíti 'to ask', [3Pl] *móli-jo*, [PresGer] *molé*
Sorb (alternative to 2): *-o*:   *stupać* 'to step', [3Pl] *stupa-ju*, [PresGer]
                                 stupajo
                                 njesć 'to carry', [3Pl] *njes-u*, [PresGer] *njeso*

4. Czech gerunds inflect for number and gender, and add the endings:

Hard: [Masc] *-a*, [Fem/Neut] *-ouc*, [Pl] *-ouce*:
        vést 'to lead', *veda, vedouc, vedouce*
Soft: [Masc](*-e*), [Fem/Neut] *-íc*, [Pl] *-íce*:
        mazat 'to smear', *maze, mazíc, mazíce*

Past gerund (not in Bulgarian or Macedonian)   The past (perfective) gerund is
usually formed from the perfective infinitive stem. With the exception of Russian

Table 5.34. *Proto-Slavic athematic verbs*

	byti 'be'	*ěsti/jasti* 'eat'	*dati* 'give'	*věděti* 'know'	*iměti* 'have'
Infinitive	*byti* 'be'	*ěsti/jasti* 'eat'	*dati* 'give'	*věděti* 'know'	*iměti* 'have'
Inf stem	*by-*	*ěd-*	*da-*	*vědě-*	*imě-*
Future stem	*bud-(e)-(I)*	–	–	–	–
Present stem	(*j)es-*	*ěd-/jad-*	*dad-*	*věd-*	*ima-(/im-)*
	(1. *d > s* before *t*; *d > ø* before other consonant; 2. *s > ø* before *s*)				
Pres 1Sg	*es-mь*	*ě-mь*	*da-mь*	*vě-mь*	*ima-mь*
2Sg	*es-i*	*ě-si*	*da-si*	*vě-si*	*ima-si*
3Sg	*es-tь*	*ěs-tь*	*das-tь*	*věs-tь*	*ima-tь*
1Du	*e-vě*	*ě-vě*	*da-vě*	*vě-vě*	*ima-vě*
2Du	*es-ta*	*ěs-ta*	*das-ta*	*věs-ta*	*ima-ta*
3Du	*es-te*	*ěs-te*	*das-te*	*věs-te*	*ima-te*
1Pl	*es-mъ*	*ě-mъ*	*da-mъ*	*vě-mъ*	*ima-mъ*
2Pl	*es-te*	*ěs-te*	*das-te*	*věs-te*	*ima-te*
3Pl	*s-ǫtь*	*ěd-ętь*	*dad-ętь*	*věd-ętь*	*im-ǫtь*
Imper	*bud-i/ě-te*	*ěd'-i/ěd-i-te*	*dad'-i/dad-i-te*	*věd-i/ě-te*	(*imě-i-te*)
Pres Part Act	*s-y/s-ǫt'-*	*ěd-y/ěd-ǫt'-*	–	–	*imy/im-ǫt'-*
Past Part Act I	*by-v-/-vš-*	*ěd-/-š-*	*da-v-/-vš-*	*vědě-v-/-vš-*	*iмě-v-/-vš-*
Past Part Act II	*by-l-*	*ěd-l-*	*da-l-*	*vědě-l-*	*imě-l-*

Table 5.35. *Modern irregular verbs*

A. **'be'** (East Slavic has only 3Sg, in the sense of "emphatic presence": Bel *ësc'*, Rus *est'*, Ukr *je (st')*;
Russian has also an archaic 3Pl copula: *sut'*)

	Blg	Mac	B/C/S	Sln	Sorb	Pol	Cz	Slk
			(non-)clitic		U\L			
Pres 1Sg	*săm*	*sum*	*(jè)sam*	*sèm* [ə]	*sym\som*	*jestem*	*jsem*	*som*
2Sg	*si*	*si*	*(jè)si*	*sì*	*sy*	*jesteś*	*jsi*	*si*
3Sg	*e*	*e*	*jēst(e)/je*	*jè*	*je\jo*	*jest*	*je*	*je*
1Du				*svà*	*smój\smej*			
2Du				*stà*	*staj/stej\stej*			
3Du				*stà*	*staj/stej\stej*			
1Pl	*sme*	*sme*	*(jè)smo*	*smò*	*smy*	*jesteśmy*	*jsme*	*sme*
2Pl	*ste*	*ste*	*(jè)ste*	*stè*	*sće\sćo*	*jesteście*	*jste*	*ste*
3Pl	*sa* [ə]	*se*	*(jè)su*	*sò*	*su*	*są*	*jsou*	*sú*

B. Other former athematic and 'want' (the Proto-Slavic root *xъt-*)

	Blg	B/C/S	Russian	Polish	Czech
'eat'					
Infin	–	*jēs-ti*	*es-t'*	*jeś-ć*	*jís-t*
1Sg Pres	*ja-m*	*jēd-ēm*	*je-m*	*je-m*	*jí-m*
3Pl Pres	*jad-át*	*jēd-ū*	*jed-ját*	*jedz-ą*	*jí-ø*
Imper 2Sg	*ja-ž*	*jēd-i*	*jež'-ø*	*jedz-ø*	*jez-ø*
'give'					
Infin	–	*dȁ-ti*	*da-t'*	*d-ać*	*dát*
1Sg Pres	*da-m*	*dȁ-m/dád-ēm*	*da-m*	*da-m*	*dá-m*
3Pl Pres	*dad-át*	*dȁ-jū/dád-ū*	*dad-út*	*dadz-ą*	*da-jí*
Imper 2Sg	*da-j*	*dȃ-j*	*da-j*	*da-j*	*de-j*
'know'	*(zna-)*	*(zna-)*	*(zna-)*		
Inf				*wiedz-ie-ć*	*věd-ě-t*
1Sg Pres				*wie-m*	*ví-m*
3Pl Pres				*wiedz-ą*	*věd-í*
Imper 2Sg				*wiedz-ø*	*věz-ø*
'have'					
Inf	–	*ìma-ti*	*im-é-t'*	*m-ie-ć*	*mí-t*
1Sg Pres	*ím-am*	*ìm-ām*	*im-é-ju*	*m-a-m*	*m-á-m*
3Pl Pres	*ím-at*	*ìma-jū*	*im-é-jut*	*m-a-ją*	*m-a-jí*
Imper 2Sg	*ím-aj*	*ìm-aj*	*im-éj*	*m-ie-j*	*m-ě-j*
'want'	(PSl *xъt-ě-ti*, 1Sg *xъt'-ǫ* 3Pl *xъt'-ǫtь/xъtę-tь*)				
Inf	–	*htě-ti*	*xot-é-t'*	*chc-ie-ć*	*cht-í-t*
1Sg Pres	*št-a*	*hòć-u\ću*	*xoč-ú*	*chc-ę*	*chc-i*
3Pl Pres	*št-at*	*hòć-ē\ćē*	*xot-ját*	*chc-ą*	*cht-ě-jí/cht-í*

Note: in A: \ separates USorb and LSorb forms;
in B: \ separates full and clitic forms;
in A and B: / marks variant forms

and B/C/S, which have alternative forms in -*v*, the gerund ends in -*ši* or -*vši*. Only Czech gerunds inflect. The rules for formation are:

for vowel stems add -*v*- (Pol, Sorb -*w*-, Bel -*ŭ*-), for consonant stems add nothing; then add -*ši* (Pol -*szy*, Bel -*šy*):

(195)   Bel   *zrabí-c'*   'to do',   [PastGer] *zrabí-ŭšy*
               pračytá-c' 'to read', [PastGer] *pračytá-ŭšy*

Czech gerunds inflect. For vowel stems add -*v*- as described above. Then for both consonant and vowel stems add:

(196)   [Masc] -*ø*, [Fem/Neut] -*ši*, [Pl] -*še*:
        říc-i   'to say', [PastGer] *rek-ø, rek-ši, rek-še*
        koupi-t 'to buy', [PastGer] *koupi-v-ši/-še*

Note that some past (perfective) gerunds may have the formation of the present gerund:

(197)   Rus   *vojtí* [Prfv] 'to enter', [3Pl] *vojd-út*, [PastGer] *vojd-já*

Supine   The supine survives only in Czech and Slovenian, and has effectively now disappeared in Czech. It is used after verbs of motion in place of the infinitive, though the infinitive itself is preferred (7.2.2.1).

The supine is formed by deleting the -*i* from the infinitive:

Cz: infinitive   *spát* 'to sleep', supine *spat* (with its different quantity, the only
        form still quoted as being distinct from the infinitive)
Sln: infinitive   *pêči* 'to bake'   supine *pêč*
                 píti 'to drink'   supine *pít*

5.5.6   Athematic and auxiliary verbs

The athematic verbs 'be', 'eat', 'give', 'know' and 'have' of Proto-Slavic showed -*m* in the 1 Singular present. This and the other endings were attached directly to the present-tense stem, without a thematic vowel, hence the name 'athematic'. The generalization of the -*m* to many other verb classes has helped to make these verbs more irregular than athematic in the modern context. We list below the main parts of the verb 'be', which is also important as an auxiliary, as well as 'eat', 'give', 'know' and 'have' in Proto-Slavic (table 5.34), and those plus 'want' (regular in Proto-Slavic) in sample languages (all still have some irregularity in the paradigms, if only in the relationship between the infinitive and present-tense stems) (table 5.35).

6

Syntactic categories and morphosyntax

6.1 Syntactic units

A central notion of Slavic syntactic studies has been the word, as we can see from the terminology of Russian morphology and syntax: *slovoizmenénie* ('word-changing', i.e. inflexion), *slovoobrazovánie* ('word formation') and *slovosočetánie* ('word combination'). The word is consequently seen as a bridge between morphology and syntax. Slavic shows less variation in its syntactic structures than in its morphology, and especially its phonology. And, as we shall see, an important part of the syntactic differences which do occur can be linked to the morphological categories and structures of the languages.

This chapter, like the preceding chapters, tries to be as theory-neutral as possible. We begin with the syntactic word and word-classes (6.l), and the formal markers that bind them together in syntactic constructions: concord, agreement and government, together with the complex question of aspect. Sentence structure and word order are described in chapter 7.

6.1.1 The syntactic word

Traditional Slavic linguistics defined the word mainly on morphological-paradigmatic and semantic grounds. The syntactic word can also be defined by formal criteria. Bloomfield's (1933: 178) "minimum free form" criterion works with major word-classes (noun, verb, adjective, adverb). But the notion of "standing alone" is problematic with inflected words, and with function words like conjunctions, and also allows more than just words in some special contexts:

(1)   Pol   *Powiedział, żebyśmy **przepisali** wszystko jeszcze raz.*
             Prze-? *Ja nawet nie napisałem raz.*
             'He told us to **re-write** everything once more.'
             '**Re-?** I haven't even written it once.'

The uninterruptability criterion states that if a sequence of sounds (or morphemes) can be interrupted, then it contains at least two words. However, clitics cannot stand alone, but they can be separated from their "hosts" by other clitics and so have an equivocal word-status:

(2a)   Slk   *urobil som **mu** to*   'I have done that **for him**'

(2b)   Slk   *urobil bi som **mu** to*   'I would have done that **for him**'

The non-permutability criterion states that if a sequence of sounds or morphemes cannot occur in a different order, it is a word. If it can be inverted, then it contains more than one word. But prepositions and following nominals cannot be inverted. However, Preposition + Noun sequences can be interrupted, for instance by modifiers, which demonstrates their status as words. Working together, then, the formal definitions of the word are viable (Krámský, 1969). Orthographies reflect this agreement with varying degrees of fidelity, depending often on historical chance (appendix B).

6.1.2   Syntactic word-classes

Slavic has a very European array of grammatical word-classes: the open classes – nouns, verbs, adjectives and adverbs; and the closed word-classes – auxiliaries, determiners, pronouns, prepositions, conjunctions and interjections. These correspond broadly to familiar word-classes in Romance and Germanic languages. And there is a substantial similarity of word-classes across the Slavic languages. We shall therefore concentrate here on four aspects of Slavic word-classes which are morphosyntactically interesting: adjectives, expressions of possession, numeral expressions and clitics.

6.1.2.1   *Adjectives*

In Old Church Slavonic there were two forms of the adjective. The short form had a regular nominal declension, and probably expressed an attribute which was indefinite, or which had not previously been associated with a given noun (Lunt, 1959: 125):

(3)   OCS   *vъ peštь **ognjьnǫ*** [AdjShort] 'into **a fiery** furnace'

The long form added the forms of the third person pronoun to the adjective stem, with the meaning of an attribute known to be associated with the noun:

(4)   OCS   *vъ geono **ognjьnǫjǫ*** [AdjLong] 'into **the fiery** hell'

In modern Slavic the definite-indefinite opposition has been preserved only in Slovenian and B/C/S, and even here the short-form adjective is giving way to the long form. In Slovenian this development may be connected with the low level of differentiation between the two systems (5.5.2.1), though it does not explain why the long form should predominate. In B/C/S the short form is obligatory with predicative adjectives (5a), and is also well preserved with predicate nominals (5b):

(5a) B/C/S *Vlâdo je stàr* 'Vlado is **old**'
           [AdjShort]

(5b) B/C/S *Vlâdo je stàr* 'Vlado is **an old** man'
           [AdjShort] *čòvek*

(5c) B/C/S *Vlâdo je stârī* 'Vlado is **an old** man'
           [AdjLong] *čòvek*
           [stylistically marked]

(5d) B/C/S *stârī* [AdjLong] '**the old** man is singing'
           čòvek pèvā

In East and West Slavic some languages have preserved the contrast of long and short adjectives. The short-form adjective is used primarily in predicates, and remains as an attributive only in possessive adjectives, and in some idioms and fixed expressions:

(6) Cz *adamovo* [AdjShort] *jablko* '**Adam's** apple'

(7) Rus *na bósu* [AdjShort] *nógu* '**bare**foot, without socks'
           [Adv] (lit., 'on **bare** foot')

The long-form adjective is gaining ground in the predicate at the expense of the short-form adjective, and is now commonly used there as well as in its usual attributive role:

(8) Rus *rebënok byl poslúšen* [Short]/*poslúšnyj* [Long]
           'the boy was **obedient**'

The decline of the short-form adjective is evident across the Slavic languages, apart from Bulgarian and Macedonian, which already have only short forms. In Russian and Czech the short forms are best preserved, but even here usage is tending towards the long form. The short form is strongest in its more verb-like uses in predicates, particularly when it follows the copula and governs a noun phrase, prepositional phrase, or infinitive:

(9a) Cz *jsme hotovi* [AdjLong/Short] *vam pomoci*
           'we are **ready** to help you'

(9b) Cz *je hotov* [AdjShort]/*hotový* [AdjLong] *prinést jakoukoli obět'*
           'he is **ready** for any sacrifice'

(10)   Rus   *já vsegdá **gotóv** [AdjShort]/*gotóvyj [AdjLong] vám pomóč'*
'I am always **ready** to help you'

In such qualified contexts the short form is obligatory in Russian.

6.1.2.2   *Expressions of possession: pronouns and adjectives*
Slavic possessives can be formed with possessive adjectives and pronouns (1–2
Persons, 3 Person reflexive) (see 5.5.2–5.5.3); or with personal pronouns (3 Person)
in the genitive, normally preceding the head noun. Emphasis can allow post-
position, as in (11b):

(11a)   Slk   *nastavá* [Verb] ***naša*** [PossAdj] *chvíl'a* [Noun] '**our** time is coming'

cf. (11b)   Slk *zo šiestich koní* [Noun] ***jeho*** [PossPron] *dva boli najbystrejšie, najkrajšie*
(lit. 'of six horses his two were fastest, most beautiful')
'of **his** six horses two were the fastest and the most beautiful'

The personal pronoun, however, may be in the form of the possessive dative in
Bulgarian and Macedonian, and also Slovak, and in all three persons. In
Macedonian the possessive usually occurs only with single, unmodified nouns
denoting family relations, and follows this noun (*mi* = 'to me'):

(12a)   Mac   *go* [Cl-O] *najde* [V] *brat* [S] ***mi*** [Dat]
'**my** brother found him'

and in Slovak also with single nouns, expressing similarly close ownership:

(12b)   Slk   *vlasy*   ***mu*** [DatSg]   '**his** hair'
záhrada   ***im*** [DatPl]   '**their** garden'

But in Bulgarian the dative possessive pronoun may occur with longer noun
phrases, where it follows the first inflected constituent:

(13a)   Blg   *stólăt **im*** [DatPl]   '**their** canteen'

(13b)   Blg   *nóvijat **im*** [DatPl] *studéntski stól*   '**their** new student canteen'

(There is also the "dative of the interested person": 7.1.7). The situation is different
with a noun expressing possession. Here the noun is usually in the genitive, and
usually follows the head nominal:

(14a)   Bel   *mjákkae svjatló **mésjaca** [Gen] zaliló ljasnúju paljánu*
'the soft light **of the moon** lit up the forest clearing'

(14b)   Sorb   *namjet **dobreho přećela** [Gen], **wjesneho wučerja** [Gen]*
'the plan **of (our) good friend, the village teacher**'

But Slovak may still use the dative with a single noun:

(14c) Slk *záhrada susedom* [DatPl] 'the neighbors' garden'

The "heavier" or more complex the possessive noun phrase, the more likely it is to be post-nominal. Conversely, short-noun or Adjective + Noun expressions of possession may precede the head noun, though this usage is emphatic:

(15) Pol *to jest naszej ciotki* [Gen] *pies* 'that is our aunt's dog'

But most Slavic languages prefer one of two alternatives to such premodifying possessives: either the genitive occurs post-nominally, as in (14a–b), or a pre-posed possessive adjective is formed from the noun. Not all nouns are morphologically able to form this less common possessive adjective, and there are some syntactic restrictions on its use. In East Slavic, and West Slavic except Sorbian, the possessive adjectives are less productive in the standard languages, except in idioms and set expressions:

(16a) Rus *máma* 'mother'; *mámin sýn* 'mother's son, cry-baby, etc.'

(16b) Rus *súka* 'bitch'; *súkin sýn* 'son of a bitch'

– though the possessives are more common in dialectal speech. In the other languages the nouns which form such possessives are usually proper names (especially given names), and words referring to kinship, close domestic animals and the like. Such possessives may appear as predicates, though they are more common as attributes. But they are usually formed only from single nouns, with the exception of Sorbian (below):

(17a) Blg *Vázov* (surname); *Vázovite săčinénija* 'Vazov's works'

(17b) Blg *sestrá* 'sister'; *séstrina dăšterjá* 'niece, sister's daughter'

Sorbian also has a regular post-posed genitive:

(18a) Sorb *dźěći mojeho bratra* [Gen] 'the children of my brother'

(18b) Sorb *drasta stareje žony* [Gen] 'the clothes of the old woman'

but when the noun is turned into a possessive adjective, the modifier of the noun keeps its original agreement (a construction also extant but now archaic in Slovak):

(19a) Sorb *mojeho* [Gen] *bratrowe* [Nom] *dźěći* [Nom]
       'my brother's children'

(19b) Sorb *stareje* [Gen] *žonina* [Nom] *drasta* [Nom]
       'the old woman's clothes'

6.1.2.3   *Numeral expressions*

Slavic has the usual array of cardinal and ordinal numerals, and a variety of nouns and adverbs derived from them. It does, however, have a more unusual class of collective numerals (5.5.4.3), which is used to designate a group or certain number of individuals. Collective numerals occur with *pluralia tantum*:

(20a)   Cz   *dvoje rukavice*   'two pairs of gloves'

and with groups of individuals which have some cohesion, notably in groups like the family or groups of animals:

(20b)   Pol   *pięcioro kurcząt*   'five chickens'

There are strict limitations on the productivity of collective numerals. The numbers up to about (4) are used moderately frequently, but the numbers from (5) to (10) are less common, and collective forms of higher numbers are rare. For *pluralia tantum* over this figure, and in other contexts, Slavic uses numeral classifiers. This class is not often recognized, especially since it is not widely known in Indo-European. But it is common in languages of South-East Asia. It is marginal in English, in constructions like

(21a)   John had five head of cattle

(21b)   How many cattle did John have? – Five head

Slavic uses numeral classifiers, both in the structure Numeral + Numeral classifier + Noun, like (21a), and in the PRO-form omitting the noun, like (21b):

(22a)   Rus   *u negó býlo pját' štúk karandšéj*
             'he had five CLASSIFIER pencils'

(22b)   Rus   *u negó býlo pját' štúk*
             'he had five CLASSIFIER'

The classifier varies with semantic-grammatical classes:

(23a)   Rus   *u negó býlo pját' golóv skotá*
             'he had five **head** = CLASSIFIER of cattle'
             (*skot*: 'cattle' [Coll])

(23b)   Rus   *v klásse sidélo pját' čelovék studéntov*
             'in the classroom sat five **person** = CLASSIFIER students'

The origin of this construction in Slavic is obscure: Polish has a restricted construction with *sztuka*, borrowed from German *Stück* 'piece':

(24a)   Pol   *Jan kupił dziesięć sztuk probówek*
             'Jan bought five CLASSIFIER test-tubes'

(24b)   Ger   *er hat 5 **Stück** Brötchen gekauft*
'he bought five CLASSIFIER bread rolls'

6.1.2.4   *Clitics*

Slavic grammars and dictionaries make much use of the term "particle", which commonly includes not only interjections and exclamations but also some conjunctions, and a variety of proclitics and enclitics. We examine the types of clitics in the morphological systems of Slavic pronouns and verb auxiliaries in 5.4, and their word-order properties are examined in 7.4.3.3. Here we concentrate on the use of proclitic pronouns, and on the enclitics, which form a significant component in the Slavic inventory of word-classes. It should be noted that, while it is a normal phonological property of clitics that they be unstressed, this needs to be qualified: they form a "phonetic word" (that is, a phrase with only one primary accented syllable) with their host word, but the position of stress in this unit is often mobile and can, in fact, fall on the clitic, especially on to prepositions (see also 3.5.1). On the other hand, words which are unstressed may or may not be called clitics, for example most basic conjunctions: when they occur in first position in the clause (like Eng *that*) they may be called simply unstressed words or sentence (pro)clitics; when they occur in second position (the "Wackernagel" position), conjunctions or particles are commonly called sentence (en)clitics (see below).

Proclitic pronouns in Slavic are found only in Macedonian and Bulgarian. Their use in these languages is linked to the decline of the case system, which restricted the means available to mark subjects and objects. The languages could have evolved in the same direction as English, using word order as the only means of marking such syntactic relations. Instead, they evolved proclitic pronouns – and the pronouns are the one nominal class where case has maintained a substantial semblance of an inflexional category in these two languages. There is, however, a vital difference between the two languages in their use of the proclitic pronouns. In Macedonian the proclitic pronoun is usual in all sentences with direct or indirect objects. In Bulgarian, however, this proclitic is in regular use only with inverted word order, where object and subject have been inverted around the verb for reasons of emphasis and/or Functional Sentence Perspective (7.5). In such instances, Bulgarian introduces the proclitic pronoun to mark the object:

"Regular" SVO order:

(25a)   Blg   *namérix* [V-1Sg] *knígata* [O] *na Iván*
'I found Ivan's book' ...

(25b)　Mac　*devójkata* [S] *gi* [Cl-O] *nápi* [V] *góstite* [O] *i gi* [Cl-O]
　　　　　　　pósluži [V] *slátko* [O]
　　　　　　　'the girl gave the guests something to drink and served them
　　　　　　　some preserves'

cf. "Inverted" OVS/OV order:

(26a)　Blg　*négo* [O] *go* [Cl-O] *víkat* [V-3Pl]　'they are calling him'
　　　　　　　('it is him that they are calling')

(26b)　Mac　*drúgarot Mítre* [O] *ne go* [Cl-O] *glédam* (V-1Sg)
　　　　　　　'I can't see comrade Mitre' [OV(S)]

These proclitic forms, however, are used only with definite nouns in Macedonian – in other words, proper nouns, nouns with the definite article, or anaphoric nouns referring to an antecedent in the preceding linguistic or immediate extra-linguistic context.

Subject personal pronouns are not proclitic, and the majority of Slavic proclitics are prepositions, which, like English prepositions, attach themselves to the following noun phrase both syntactically and phonologically. Some proclitics, particularly prepositions, can even attract stress under special conditions (3.5.1.1). There are only relatively few proclitics attached to a single host word outside pronouns and prepositions, but these may occasionally include emphatic particles: compare the clitic *i* in Ukrainian (reduced post-vocalically to *j*) with the non-clitic, stressed Russian one:

(27a)　Ukr　*ne móžu j podúmaty pro cé*　'I can't **even** think about that'

(27b)　Rus　*í dúmat' ob ètom ne mogú*

In B/C/S, which has a particularly rich enclitic system, most of these emphatic particles are less clitic-like:

(28a)　B/C/S　*ôn me je prätio čäk do kũćē*
　　　　　　　'he accompanied me **right** up to the house'

cf. (28b)　Pol　*on prowadził mię aż do domu*

(28c)　B/C/S　*ta vî znáte*　'but you know (very well)'

But B/C/S also shows emphatic enclitics, like all other Slavic languages:

(29a)　B/C/S　*ǎko pak žèlāte*　　　'if you wish'

(29b)　B/C/S　*ôn pak nìje nìšta govòrio*　'**but** he said nothing'

(29c)　Rus　*ón že znál èto*　　　'**but** he knew that'

Enclitics attach themselves to the preceding constituent. They usually occur in the "Wackernagel position", the first unaccented position in the sentence.

The sentence-enclitics (i.e. the Wackernagel enclitics) are semantically very varied, and express, among other things:

1. *Yes/no questions*

    B/C/S, Bulgarian, Macedonian, Russian and Czech have *li*, where the other languages have a sentence-initial particle (see 7.1.2):

(30a)	Rus	*znáet **li** Pëtr o vášem priézde?*
		'Does Peter know of your arrival?'
(30b)	Rus	*Pëtr **li** znáet o vášem priézde?*
		'Does PETER know of your arrival?'
(31a)	Rus	*zdoróv **li** tý?*
		'are you well?'
cf. (31b)	Ukr	*čý tý zdoróv?*
(31c)	Pol	***czy** jestesz zdrowy?*

2. *Vocatives*

    Although they might seem to be functionally redundant, since Bulgarian has preserved the vocative better than most other cases, Bulgarian does show enclitic particles which act as vocative reinforcers:

(32)	Blg	*Ivánе **be**!*	'Ivan!'

3. *Emphatic-contrastive enclitics*

    These are widely used, particularly in East and West Slavic, to emphasize a preceding constituent, or to express contrast or emphasis:

(33a)	Rus	*já-**to** ne zabýl ničegó*	'**but** I forgot nothing'
(33b)	Cz	*kolik let **že** studoval?*	'**and** how many years did he study?'

    Some enclitics in this semantic class are not only sentence-enclitic:

(34a)	Sorb	*Naš Petr (**dźě, traš, wšak**) to činil njeje*
		'Our Peter (**certainly**) didn't do that'
(34b)	Sorb	*Naš Petr to **tola** (**dźě, traš, wšak**) činil njeje*
		'Our Peter **certainly** didn't do *that*' (Šewc, 1968: 237)

    B/C/S and Slovenian have *pak*, which functions as a sentence-enclitic (see (29b)). Bulgarian and Macedonian are, perhaps surprisingly (in view of their rich clitic systems) much less endowed in this area.

4. *Imperative markers*

In Russian there is no special form of the 1 Person plural imperative, and in Belarusian this form is not fully part of the literary language. It is in East Slavic that we find imperative markers most frequently, and not only with 1 Person imperatives:

(35a)   Rus   *pojděm-te* (*pojděm-ka*)   'let's go!'

Most such reinforcers are colloquial. They are also found in other, especially West, Slavic languages:

(35b)   Pol   *chodż no*!   'do come here!'

6.2   Syntactic roles and relations

In English, syntactic relations are formally marked mainly by word order: as a matter of convention, the subject precedes the verb (36a) and adjectives and modifiers usually precede the noun which they modify (36b):

(36a)   Barbara hugged John/John hugged Barbara

(36b)   these fine old German iron bridges

In Slavic, word order is less important for specifying syntactic relations than three types of inflexions: concord (6.2.1), agreement (6.2.2) and government (6.2.3). They all work on the principle that one word controls the form of other words which occur in its construction. In concord the head noun controls (Corbett, 1983) the inflexion of its modifiers in the noun phrase for number, gender and case:

(37a)   Slk   *Jana odišla* [V] *bez* [Prep] *d'alšieho* [Adj-NeutSgGen]
              vysvetlenia [N-NeutSgGen-Controller]
              'Jana left without further **explanation**'

The subject "agrees with" (i.e. controls the inflexion of) the verb or predicate in number, person and gender:

(37b)   Slk   *Vŕby* [3Pl] *a rakyty* [3Pl] *začinajú* [3Pl] *pučat' pri potokoch*
              '**the willows and brooms** are beginning to blossom by the streams'

And the verb "governs" (i.e. controls) the case of the object(s), with or without a preposition:

(37c)   Slk   *učit'* deti [child-Acc] *slušnosti* [obedience-Dat]
              '**to teach** children obedience'

(37d)   Slk   *starat' sa o* [Prep] *nieco* [Acc]   'to try for something'

Word order (7.4–7.5) usually functions as a second-line signal of syntactic relations. It is important when inflexions do not mark syntactic relations clearly, as happens in the case-reduced noun systems of Bulgarian and Macedonian. The same difficulty arises in the other nine languages, whenever an accusative has the same form as a nominative, a situation which makes it impossible to identify the subject by inflexion alone. Here the language has the default Subject–Verb–Object (SVO) interpretation, though contrastive intonation or context may make it OVS (38b, where *ő* indicates emphatic stress):

(38a)   Rus   [SVO]   *mát' ljúbit dóč'* 'the mother loves her daughter'

(38b)   Rus   [OVS]   *mát' ljúbit dőč'* 'the mother is loved by her daughter'/
                         'it is the daughter that loves the mother'
                         also 'it is the daughter that the mother loves'

6.2.1   Concord

The elements of the noun phrase concord – that is, have a uniform morphological marking – for case, gender and number. Concord is often seen as part of agreement. But subjects agree with their predicates not only in number and gender but also in person, a category not found in the concord of the Slavic noun phrase. The principal difference between concord and agreement, however, is that concord is internal to the noun phrase, while agreement is external to it.

In Slavic concord, the head nominal passes its marking for case, gender and number on to determiners, adjectives, participles, some quantifiers and some numerals, in attributive and appositive constructions:

(39a)   Rus   *vsé èti krásnye i bélye cvetý*   [all Nom-AccPl]
                'all these red and white flowers'

(39b)   Rus   *vsé èti cvetý, krásnye i bélye*   [all Nom-AccPl]
                'all these flowers, red and white'

Concord does not operate in certain constructions:

1.   *Morphological availability*
     Some adjectives, possessive pronouns and nouns do not inflect, and so cannot concord.

2.   *Modifiers of modifiers and phrasal modifiers*
     These do not concord. If an adjective is modified by an element like an adverb or prepositional phrase, these elements will not concord, nor

will the dependent parts of an expanded participial construction, or a phrase in another case:

(40a)   Slk   *starec* [NomSg] *s bielymi* [InstrPl] *vlasami* [InstrPl]
'an old man with white hair'

(40b)   Slk   *starec* [NomSg] *bielych* [GenPl] *vlasov* [GenPl]

cf. (40c)   Slk   *bielovlasý* [MascNomSg] *starec* [MascNomSg]
'a white-haired old man'

(40d)   Rus   *dalekó ne vsémi* [InstrPl] *studéntami* [InstrPl]
pročítannaja [FemNomSg]
staťjá [FemNomSg]
lit. 'a far from by all the students read article'

Sorbian shows a special non-concording determiner with possessives. The modifier of the possessive adjective takes its form from the parallel genitive phrase, and does not necessarily concord with the head noun of its own noun phrase (see also above on possession):

(41a)   Sorb   *žona* [FemNomSg] *stareho* [MascGenSg]
wučerja [MascGenSg]
'the wife of the old teacher'

(41b)   Sorb   *stareho* [MascGenSg] *wučerja* [MascGenSg]
žona [FemNomSg]
'of the old teacher the wife'

(41c)   Sorb   *stareho* [MascGenSg] *wučerjowa* [NomFemSg]
žona [NomFemSg]
'of the old teacher's wife'

3.   *Pronouns and following modifiers*
With the exception of examples like Rus *my vse* 'we all', the modifiers of pronouns occur predominantly in the singular. Animate pronouns take masculine modifiers, and non-animate pronouns take neuter modifiers. With negative pronouns the modifier need not concord for case:

(42)   Cz   *nic* [Nom] *dobrého* [Gen] 'nothing good' (cf. Fr *rien de bon*)

4.   *Quantifiers and numerals in the noun phrase*
These cause the greatest complications with concord. Some quantifiers concord, particularly in the *some/each/any* series. Other quantifiers do not concord, are impersonal, usually take neuter

agreement of the predicate, and require a genitive singular for non-count nouns, and a genitive plural for count nouns, in the remainder of their noun phrase. In other words, they act more like personal constructions with a governing noun of measure or quantity:

(43a) B/C/S *lȋtra/mnȍgo dȍbrōga pȋva* [NeutGenSg]
           'a litre/lot of good beer'

(43b) B/C/S *grȕpa/mȁlo dȍbrīh žénā* [FemGenPl]
           'a group of/few good women'

Bulgarian and Macedonian follow this rule for number, but use apposition without prepositions:

(44) Blg *pakét sól, pakét cigári*
        'a packet of salt, a packet of cigarettes'

Numerals are more complicated. With ordinal numerals there is no difficulty, since they function like adjectives. But cardinal and collective numerals present much greater complexity. Cardinal numbers concord in part with the head of the noun phrase. But they can also control the case (and number) of the rest of the noun phrase.

The eleven languages differ in their treatment of numerals. The controlling effect of the numeral only applies to the nominative and accusative = nominative; elsewhere the case of the noun phrase is controlled by its function in the sentence. A final complication is that modifiers and nouns can react differently to the presence of a numeral in the noun phrase.

The form of the numeral (non-oblique cases only) (The following comments apply to the numbers '1'–'9' and all larger numerals ending in them, excepting '11'–'19'. Only the last digit may concord for gender.)

'1' syntactically an adjective, and concords fully with the head nominal and other modifiers. Reverse-order numerals (like 'one-and-twenty' etc. in Czech, Slovak and Slovenian (45b)) have only a single masculine form of the '1' (in Slovenian a reduced form: *en- vs êden* '1'); this reverse order form is most common in non-oblique cases:

(45a) Cz '21': *dvacet jeden* [Masc]/*jedna* [Fem]/*jedno* [Neut]

(45b) Cz '21': *jedenadvacet* [all genders]

though there is also a newer Czech pattern *dvacet jedna* followed by the genitive plural with all genders (Short, 1993a: 521).

'2' distinguishes gender:

[+Fem]: East Slavic, B/C/S

(46a) Rus   *dvá studénta*   '2 students' [Masc]
       dvé studéntki   '2 students' [Fem]
       dvá okná   '2 windows' [Neut]

[+Masc]: Slovenian, Czech, Sorbian, Bulgarian, Macedonian

(46b) Sorb   *dwaj konjej*   '2 horses' [Masc]
       dwe chěži   '2 houses' [Fem]
       dwě jeji   '2 eggs' [Neut]

Once again, there is a newer Czech pattern *dvacet dva* followed by the genitive plural with all genders (Short, 1993a).

Masculine Personal *vs* Masculine *vs* Other: Slovak, Polish

(46c) Pol   *dwaj Polacy*   '2 Poles' [MascPers]
       dwie kobięty   '2 girls' [Fem]
       dwa koty   '2 cats' [Masc]
       dwa okna   '2 windows' [Neut]

Polish also has the masculine personal form *dwóch* (see (52) and 6.2.2).

Similar forms are found in the relevant words for 'both'.

'3' and above:

Concord operates for gender only in Slovak and Polish, where the masculine personal concord may reach '999'; in Bulgarian, where the masculine personal numerals are in use up to about '6'; and in Upper Sorbian, where the special masculine personal numbers are available, but are much less used than the normal numerals (Lower Sorbian does not have masculine personal forms). The special masculine personal forms again apply only to the non-oblique cases:

(47) Slk   *traja bratia* '3 brothers' [MascPers]
       tri ženy   '3 women'

The form of the concording modifier   The form of the concording modifier differs according to the numeral:

'1': modifiers concord fully with the head noun and the numeral

'2': Slovenian and Sorbian: the modifier takes the dual, and so concords fully with the head noun:

(48) Sorb   *dwaj dobraj konjej*   'two good horses'

'2' (not Slovenian or Sorbian) and '3'–'4' (all languages):

Bulgarian, Macedonian: plural modifier
West Slavic, East Slavic (except Russian non-feminines)
Slovenian, B/C/S: nominative plural
Russian: genitive plural [all genders], nominative plural [Fem]

(49a) Mac *tri ubavi* [Pl] *ženi* [Pl] '3 beautiful women'

(49b) Rus *tri krasívye* [NomPl]/*krasívyx* [GenPl] *dévuški* [GenSg]
            '3 beautiful girls'

In Russian there is a preference for the genitive when the genitive singular and nominative plural of the noun are differentiated by stress, as in *gorá:* [GenSg] *gorý*, [NomPl] *góry* (Wade, [1992]/2000: 201).

'5 +': with all the numbers from '5' to '20' inclusive, and any number containing the final digits '0', '5'–'9', the modifiers concord in case, gender and number with the head noun (see following section). Bulgarian and Macedonian modifiers do not mark case or gender in the plural, and so simply show the plural form of the modifier. Numbers above '20' containing the final digits '1'–'4' inclusive follow the rules for '1'–'4', except in Bulgarian and Macedonian, where they take the plural form of the modifier.

The form of the head noun For all oblique cases, the head nominal controls the case of the entire noun phrase, including the numeral. But with a noun phrase in the nominative, or the accusative=nominative, the numeral can control the number and case of the rest of the noun phrase. Head nouns react with numerals: '1': the head noun controls the noun phrase, and all concordable elements concord with it:

(50) Pol *jeden wysoki żołnierz* [all MascNomSg]
           'one tall soldier'

'2' Slovenian and Sorbian: the head noun is in the dual (see (46));
'2' (not Slovenian or Sorbian) and '3'–'4' (all languages). A variety of forms is possible:

Russian, B/C/S: genitive singular
Ukrainian, West Slavic, Slovenian: nominative plural

Most of the special non-plural forms found in this position are associated with the old dual. In Russian and B/C/S the genitive singular forms (sometimes called "paucal") reflect the dual. Note that in Belarusian, masculines occur in the nominative plural (as in Ukrainian) but non-masculines occur in the old dual (as in

Russian). And Bulgarian and Macedonian have masculines in the "secondary plural" (known variously as the "counting form", "count plural", "quantitative plural"), which is also identical to the old dual, and often also to the modern oblique case singular of the noun with the definite article:

(51a)   Blg   *tri stóla* '3 chairs' (cf. *stolóve* 'chairs')

cf. (51b)   Blg   *čas*   'hour'
                    časắt   'the hour'
                    časá   'the hour' [Obl]
                    tri čása '3 hours'

'5 +': Bulgarian and Macedonian use the plural or, for masculines, the counting form – and this is also the number they show with numerals from '1'–'4' above '20': '21', etc. Other languages use the genitive plural. Large numbers like '1,000' or '1,000,000' also function like head nouns, and control the genitive plural (Bulgarian and Macedonian: plural). Bulgarian prefers the normal plural in general, while Macedonian prefers it when it is accompanied by a plural modifier:

(51c)   Blg   *pét učenici* [Plur]   *pét učeníka*   [Count] '5 pupils'

(51d)   Mac *pet toma*   [Count] *pet debeli tomovi* [Plur]   '5 large volumes'

Polish has a special form of the head noun with masculine personal nouns in noun phrases containing a numeral. While Sorbian and Slovak, which also have this gender category in numerals, show the numeral concording with the head noun, the Polish alternative form *dwóch* ... (etc.) takes the noun in the genitive plural, and the verb in the neuter singular (52a), although the alternative form is also available (52b):

(52a)   Pol   *dwóch Polaków* [GenPl] *przyjechałoby* [NeutSg]
                '2 Poles would have come'

(52b)   Pol   *dwaj Polacy* [MascPersNomPl] *przyjechaliby* [MascPersNomPl]

Other types of numerals fall into two classes. Most of them, like the collectives, function as head nouns and take a genitive plural of all the following elements of the noun phrase. Others – like the ordinals – concord like adjectives.

So far we have dealt only with noun phrases containing a single noun. But it often happens that a noun will contain a conjoined subject, and in such instances there may be a conflict of gender and/or number within the noun phrase.

(53a)   Rus   *v rússkom* [LocSg] *i anglijskom* [LocSg] *jazykáx* [LocPl]
                'in the Russian and English languages' [conflict of number]

(53b)   Pol   *dobrzy* [MascPers] *muzykanci* [MascPers] *i kobiȩty* [Fem]
                  'good musicians and girls'

(where 'good' refers to both the musicians and the girls: there is conflict of gender, and agreement of the adjective is with the nearest noun phrase).

The Slavic languages have several strategies in such cases. One is to make the adjective concord with the nearest noun (53b). Another solution is to resolve the conflict of gender or number – perhaps by having the noun in the plural as in (53a).

6.2.2   Agreement

Agreement occurs between subjects and predicates. The principal syntactic function of agreement is to identify the grammatical subject of a sentence. The subject transfers to the predicate its number, as well as its person and gender where appropriate. The transfer is limited by several factors.

1. Which morphological categories can the predicate mark?
2. Is there an expressed copula or predicate? (e.g. in East Slavic the present tense of 'be' is often omitted, leaving only the nominal or adjectival [part of the] predicate)
3. Is there an expressed subject? Here we must distinguish impersonal sentences from "subjectless" sentences. An impersonal sentence (7.3.3) can have no subject, and the verb is in the neuter singular. A "subjectless" sentence is one where the subject is potentially present, but is actually missing. But in some languages the marker of person, number and perhaps gender as well may be clear in the inflexion of the verb, in which case the pronominal subject is more often omitted.

We shall begin with a predicate consisting of a verb, since this is the most common type of agreement.

GENDER AGREEMENT occurs only with the *l*-participle verb forms (i.e. compound tenses which do not contain an infinitive, and simplex imperfective and perfective past tenses). Gender agreement may mark primary gender [Masc, Fem, Neut] or secondary gender [MascPers, etc.]:

(54a)   Slk   *Jana písala* [FemSg]
                  'Jana wrote'

(54b)   Slk   *žiaci boli chvaleni* [all MascPers]
                  'the pupils were praised'

PERSON AGREEMENT occurs in all tenses except those simplex past tenses (especially the East Slavic imperfective and perfective) where the auxiliary has been lost. Person agreement occurs only between subjects and verbs:

(55a)   Slk   (*ja*) *píšem* [1Sg], (*ty*) *píšeš* [2Sg]
'I write, you write'

(55b)   Pol   *pisałem* [1Sg], *pisałesz* [2Sg]
'I wrote, you wrote'

(Examples like Polish *powinienem* 'I must' (*powinien* 'obliged' + -*em* '1Sg') are special cases where the auxiliary has become morphologically attached to the predicative adjective as a clitic.)

NUMBER AGREEMENT is found in all subject-verb agreement:

(56a)   Ukr   *vín tjanúv* [MascSg]
'he pulled'

(56b)   Ukr   *vоný tjanúly* [Pl]
'they pulled'

These basic patterns may be changed by a variety of factors. We shall mention briefly only two: the question of subject noun phrases containing numerals; and the resolution of conflicts of number, gender and person (for a fuller treatment, see Corbett, 1983, chapter 10).

Number agreement poses some intriguing problems. Unlike English, Slavic strongly favors grammatical agreement. In English it is common (and acceptable) to find semantic agreement, where plural verbs occur with singular nouns referring especially to groups of people (e.g. 'the government is/are intent on raising duties'). In Slavic the grammatically singular noun preserves grammatically singular agreement in the majority of examples, at least in formal usage. The major exception to this rule occurs when the subject contains a numeral. Corbett (1983: 221) presents the following table of predicate agreement with noun phrase subjects containing a numeral:

(57)   Predicate Agreement with Numeral Phrases

	2	3	4	5–10	100
Bulgarian	P	P	P	P	P
Macedonian	P	P	P	P	P
Slovak	P	P	P	S/P	S
Sorbian	D	P	P	S/P	S
OCS	D	P	P	S(P)	
Polish	99% P	91% P	100% P	7% P	

B/C/S	97% P	89% P	83% P	7% P	
Czech	P	P	P	S	S
Slovenian	D	P	P	S	S
Belarusian	92% P	78% P	63% P	39% P	50% P
Russian	86% P	77% P	76% P	50% P	
Ukrainian	83% P	79% P	74% P	38% P	21% P

P plural, S singular, D dual

The table shows a progressive differentiation of the languages. Bulgarian and Macedonian show plural agreement for '2' and all higher numbers, (including, incidentally, compounds with '1' like '21', '31', etc.). Sorbian, Old Church Slavonic and Slovenian have dual agreement for '2'. With this exception, Slovenian and Sorbian show identical patterns for numbers above '5', with plural agreement for masculine personal forms, and singular agreement elsewhere. (The figures for OCS are difficult to establish, since the extant MSS give insufficient evidence.) The other languages all show progressively declining percentages of plural agreement for '2–4', with the singular favored for '4' more than '3', and for '3' more than '2'; and roughly progressively declining proportions of singular agreement for numbers of '5' and above. The factors affecting the choice of number agreement in these examples are rather complex. Plural agreement is favored by noun phrases containing animate nouns, and with those where the subject precedes the predicate. But the opposite is found in Polish:

(58a)   Rus   *dvá poljáka* [GenSg] *prišlí* [Pl]
        '(the) two Poles came'

(58b)   Pol   *dwóch Polaków* [GenPl] *przyszło* [NeutSg]

Noun phrases containing numerals therefore show a "conflict" of number – the plurality of the concept versus the status of the numeral itself: as numbers (digits) grow larger, they tend increasingly to function like head nouns, and take a governed genitive plural.

A different problem occurs with agreement with the honorific second person pronoun *vy*, which is grammatically plural but semantically singular. Comrie (1975) and Corbett (1979) have both observed another gradient in agreement with *vy*. In Russian, for example, nominal predicates (and long-form adjectives) take singular or semantic agreement (59a), while verbal predicates (and short-form adjectives) take plural or grammatical agreement (59b):

(59a)   Rus   *kakój vý génij* [NomSg]   *kakój vý úmnyj* [MascNomSgLong]
              'what a genius you are'   'how intelligent you are'

(59b)   Rus   *kák vý umný* [PlShort]   *kák vý poëte* [2Pl]
'how clever you are'   'how (well) you sing'

There are other conflicts of agreement. Conflicts of person agreement in noun phrases containing conjoined subjects are perhaps the easiest to resolve. If a noun phrase contains any 1 Person pronoun, it takes 1 plural (or dual) agreement:

(60a)   Sorb   *my a Jan pijemy* [1Pl]
'we and Jan are drinking'

If the noun phrase contains no 1 Person pronoun, but does contain a 2 Person pronoun, it takes 2 plural (or dual) agreement:

(60b)   Sorb   *wy a Jan pijeće* [2Pl]
'you [Pl] and Jan are drinking'

Otherwise it takes 3 plural or 3 dual agreement:

(60c)   Sorb   *woni a Jan pija* [3Pl]
'they and Jan are drinking'

The resolution of gender conflicts is somewhat more complex. The general pattern seems to involve a hierarchy of genders something like:

(61)   Masculine Personal
Masculine Animate
Animate
Masculine
Feminine
Neuter

Depending on the categories employed in a given language, the presence of even one "higher" gender will switch gender agreement to that higher gender for the whole conjoined subject:

(62)   Slk   *otec* [Masc], *matka* [Fem] *a diet'a* [NeutSg] *sú zdraví* [MascPers]
'father, mother and child are healthy'

In this example, the presence of one masculine personal noun (*otec* 'father') is sufficient to cause the adjective to occur in the male personal form as well. There are, however, many complications to this generalization (Corbett, 1980).

In non-verbal predicates, consisting of Copula + Adjective or Copula + Noun, the case of the adjective or noun is governed by the copula (6.2.3.), but the gender and number are rather matters of agreement. In gender agreement, for instance, masculine subjects may never take feminine complements – though the reverse can happen, especially with epicenes, if only colloquially:

(63) Rus   *Máša* [Fem] – *xoróšij* [Masc]/*xoróšaja* [Fem]
             kolléga [Common]
             'Masha is a good colleague'

Adjective predicates have agreement at the same level as the highest-ranked gender in the subject:

(64a) Pol   *studentki* [Fem] *i górnicy* [MascPers] *są mądrzy* [MascPers]
              'the female students and the miners are intelligent'

(64b) Cz   *hrady* [MascInan] *a církve* [Fem] *jsou krásné* [MascInan]
              'the castles and churches are beautiful'

All these generalizations, however, are subject to an overall restriction: the greater the syntactic distance from the subject, the more semantic agreement is likely to override grammatical agreement. Attributive adjectives show near-total grammatical agreement, while relative pronouns and especially personal pronouns show a greater probability of semantic agreement:

(65) Rus   *Núžno znát', čto odnó značítel'noe licó* [Neut] *nedávno*
             sdélalsja [Masc] *značítel'nym licóm, i do togó vrémeni ón*
             [Masc] *býl neznačítel'nym licóm.* (Gogol, *Šinel'*)
             'It is necessary to know that a certain distinguished person
             (only) recently became a distinguished person, and before that
             he was an undistinguished person.'

Putting all these facts together, Corbett has proposed an "agreement hierarchy". The lesser the syntactic distance between nominals and concording or agreeing constituents, as with attributive adjectives, the more likely is grammatical agreement. Conversely, the greater the syntactic distance, the more probable is semantic agreement:

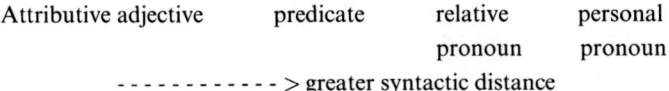

Attributive adjective   predicate   relative   personal
                                           pronoun   pronoun
- - - - - - - - - - - - > greater syntactic distance

This hierarchy covers not only number agreement but also gender agreement, and in structures like relative clauses and anaphora (reference) in personal pronouns, often in subsequent sentences.

Only finite verb forms can express agreement (examples from Horálek (1992: 258). Agreement is not expressed when – somewhat colloquially – infinitives are used in place of finite verbs:

(66)   Cz   *to*   *by*   *tak*   *bylo,*   *my*
            that   Cond   so   be-3SgPast   we-Nom
            dělat   *a*   *on*   *si*   *chodit   na   procházku*
            work-Inf and   he-Nom   Refl-Dat   go-Inf   on   walk-AccSg
            'that's the way it would be, we'd have to work and he'd go for a walk'

Imperatives used in place of finite verbs, including those expressing conditions, agree in number:

(67a)   Rus   *a*   *já*   *i*   *pridí*   *k*   *nemú*   *ne*   *vóvremja*
              and   I   Emph   come-2SgImper   to   him   Neg   in time
              'I did not come to him in time'

(67b)   Rus   *udár'*   *tepér'*   *moróz*   –   *ózimi*
              strike-2SgImper   now   frost-NomSg   crop-NomPl
              vsé   *propadút*
              all- NomPl   fail-3PlFut
              'if frost comes now all the winter crops will be lost'

6.2.3   Government

In government – unlike concord or agreement – the controlled construction takes on a feature which is dictated by, but not contained in, the controller itself. Traditional Slavic grammarians view government predominantly in terms of cases: a given verb is said to 'govern' an accusative, genitive, dative or instrumental:

(68a)   Sorb   *wječorne słóncko pozłočuje **tu płódnu lětnju krajinu*** [Acc]
               'the evening sun gilds **this fruitful summer land**'

(68b)   Cz   *nemáte se **čeho*** [Gen] *bát* 'you have **nothing** to fear'

(68c)   Ukr   *dyván právyv **jomú*** [Dat] *za lížko* 'the couch served **him** as a bed'

(68d)   Ukr   *právyty **avtomobílem*** [Instr] 'to drive **a car**'

A verb may also govern a preposition with a specified case:

(69a)   Blg   *pomágam **na njákogo*** [Acc]   'I help **someone**'

(69b)   Rus   *podpísyvajus' na literatúrnyj žurnál* [Acc]
         'I subscribe **to a literary journal**'

or a verb may govern more than one object, with or without prepositions, and with specified cases:

(70)   Rus   *já pródal emú* [Dat] *mašínu* [Acc] *za trídcat'* [Acc] *rubléj*
        'I sold **him** [Dat] **the car** [Acc] **for 30 roubles** [Acc]'

Some verbs may be able to govern several cases, sometimes interchangeably, or may vacillate between pure case government and 'preposition + case' government:

(71a)   Pol   *poblogoslaw mię* [Acc]/*mi* [Dat], *Panie*
         'bless **me**, O Lord'

As we would expect from the decline of case forms in Bulgarian and Macedonian, these languages contain many more examples of prepositional objects than the other Slavic languages do:

(71b)   Blg   *aboníram se za véstnik*   'I subscribe **to a newspaper**'

Not only verbs govern cases. Nouns, and especially action, agent or abstract nouns derived from verbs, can govern objects. If the verb takes an accusative, the derived noun often governs the 'objective genitive':

(72a)   Slk   *otvorenie výstavy* [Gen]   'the opening **of the exhibition**'

(72b)   Slk   *pisatel' listu* [Gen]   'the writer **of the letter**'

though some derived nouns take other cases, with or without a preposition:

(73a)   Rus   *ljubóv' máteri* [Gen]   'love **of a mother**' (ambiguous)

(73b)   Rus   *ljubóv' k máteri* [Dat]   'love **for a mother**'

Verbs which do not govern the accusative usually form derived nouns which govern the same case as the verb:

(74a)   Rus   *ón zavéduet káfedroj* [Instr]   'he heads **the department**'

(74b)   Rus   *ón – zavédujuščij káfedroj* [Instr]
         'he is the head **of the department**'

(Note that the governed case is retained even in the abbreviation: *zàvkáfedroj* 'head of a department'; see 8.2.3)

Non-derived nouns may also show government, especially if they are semantically like verbs – e.g. action nouns:

(75a) Cz *naděje na výhru* [Acc] 'the hope **of a win**'

(75b) Cz *naděje vyhrát* [Inf] 'the hope **to win**'

Adjectives govern cases, most obviously in predicative position:

(76a) Rus *ón blagodáren nám* [Dat] 'he is grateful **to us**'

(76b) Rus *ón nedovólen námi* [Instr] 'he is dissatisfied **with us**'

(76c) Rus *ón sklónen k bojú* [Dat] 'he is inclined **to fighting**'

(76d) Rus *ón sklónen borót'sja* [Inf] 'he is inclined **to fight**'

Prepositions and prepositional phrases can also govern cases, and can occur outside controlled environments. Both are illustrated in:

(77) Pol *on nie jest w stanie* [Loc] *wystȩpować*
      'he is not able (not **in a condition**) to perform'

Some adverbs, adjectives, nouns and prepositional phrases can govern one or more of the types of subordinate sentence, an indirect question or command, just as they govern noun phrases and cases.

(78a) Cz *nehledě na to* [Acc], *že měl moc práce, musel tam jít*
       'in spite **of the fact** that he had a lot of work, he had to go there'

(78b) Rus *já soobščíl vám* [Dat] *o tom* [Loc], *kak* + SENTENCE
       'I told you **about (it)**, how + SENTENCE

Government and agreement operate simultaneously on complements after copulae and semi-copulative verbs. The verb may govern a nominative or an instrumental case, which may be accompanied by a preposition. In languages with a choice between the nominative and the instrumental, as in East Slavic, the instrumental tends to designate a more temporary state:

(79a) Rus *ón býl filósof* [Nom]
       'he was **a philosopher**'
       (permanent characteristic, i.e. he was a philosopher by disposition)

(79b) Rus *ón býl filósofom* [Instr]
       'he was **a philosopher**'
       (non-permanent state, as in a profession)

(79c) Sorb *stać so z wučerjom* [Instr] 'to become **a teacher**'

Slavic has many such quasi-"be" predicates like 'pass for', 'be known as', and others.

The second extension of combined government and agreement involves "predicate attributes" or "adjuncts". The same pattern applies, with the verb governing the case, and the gender and number agreeing with the subject. In one type of adjunct the agreeing-governed word refers to the subject, and the verb is a verb of motion:

(80) Sorb *dźěći chodźa w lěću bosy* [NomPl]
         'the children go about **barefoot** in summer'

In the other type the adjunct refers to the direct object (the "Second Object"):

(81a) Sorb *Widźach plakat* [Acc] *na wrota přibity* [Acc]
         'I saw a notice **stuck** on the gate'
(81b) Rus *já znál egó* [Acc] ***studéntom*** [Instr]
         'I knew him **as a student**'

There is also the so-called "Second Dative":

(82) Rus *ostavát'sja odnomú* [Dat] *menjá ne privlekáet*
         'to remain **alone** does not attract me'

6.2.4 Case

The case system of Slavic has presented a major arena of linguistic research. Notions of markedness have been extended to morphological markedness and the relation between zero and expressed desinence, for instance in the genitive plural (6.2.4.4; and Greenberg, 1969; Bethin 1984), and the relation of morphosyntactic marking to functional communicative needs (Comrie, 1978). There has also been intensive investigation of the meanings of the cases, stemming in particular from Jakobson's 1936 "Beitrag" paper, an attempt to show that the apparently disorganized surface meanings of cases express more coherent underlying meanings. Wierzbicka (1980), on the other hand, argues for the coherence of surface case. This study of case has been one of the powerful integrative forces in Slavic language studies, bringing together formal and functional approaches in a way paralleled only by studies of word order (7.4).

6.2.4.1 *Nominative*

The nominative is used as the grammatical subject, and agrees with the predicate as outlined in 6.2.2. It doubles for the vocative where that case is formally missing (6.2.4.2). The nominative singular is also the citation form for nouns and pronouns; and the nominative masculine singular is the citation form for adjectives. It is morphosyntactically relevant that the nominative is not always distinct from the accusative.

Some non-inflecting nouns, almost always borrowed words, have their syntactic role marked by agreement and concord (such nouns are rare outside East Slavic and, to some extent, Polish):

(83)   Rus   *kófe **vkúsnyj*** [Masc] 'the coffee is **good**'
     Rus   *máèstro **vošël*** [Masc] 'the conductor **came in**' (naturally [Masc])
     Pol   *tam **stał*** [Masc] *kiwi* 'a kiwi **was standing** there'
                             (masculine from: *ptak* 'bird' [Masc])

Infinitives can also be used as grammatical subjects (also (82) above):

(84)   Rus   ***slúšat'*** *takíe véšči menjá vozmuščáet*
            '**to hear** such things upsets me'

An important non-subject use of the nominative is in "be" predicates in B/C/S, Slovenian and Sorbian (in all of which the instrumental is now archaic or literary). In the other Slavic languages (East and West except Sorbian) there is a choice between nominative and instrumental cases in the predicate. Here the instrumental tends to express a meaning which is located in time and space, while the nominative expresses atemporal, or metaphorical, meanings. In East Slavic only the nominative is possible when the copula is present tense:

(85)   Rus   *mój otéc býl **póvarom*** [Instr]   'my father was **a cook**'
     Rus   *mój otéc býl **angličánin*** [Nom]   'my father was English
                                     (**an Englishman**)'
     Rus   *mój otéc **póvar/angličánin*** [Nom]
             'my father is **a cook/an Englishman**'

while in West Slavic, the selection is not controlled by tense:

(86)   Pol   *mój brat jest **studentem*** [Instr]   'my brother is **a student**'
     Cz   *náš soused je **bankéř*** [Nom]/***bankéřem*** [Instr]
             'our neighbour is **a banker**'

And in some Russian dialects it can function as the direct object of infinitives (10.3.3):

(87)   Dial-Rus   *nádo **lódka*** [Nom] *kupít'*
                  'we must buy **a boat**' (lit.: 'necessary **boat** to buy')

6.2.4.2   *Vocative*

The vocative has been lost in Russian in East Slavic; in Slovak in West Slavic; and in Slovenian in South Slavic (see 5.4.2). In these languages the vocative is replaced by the nominative, though it may be maintained in the dialects and in the colloquial language, and even extended as a zero-ending form:

(88)   Colloq-Rus *Natáš, idí sjudá* 'Natasha, come here!'

instead of the standard *Natáša*. The vocative is syntactically less integrated with the structure of the sentence than the other cases, and is excluded by Jakobson (6.2.4.8) from his formal model of the case system. In Slavic descriptions, too, it is often referred to as a 'form' and not a 'case' (Ukr *klýčna fórma* [*vs vidmýnok* 'case'], Cz *vokativní tvar* [*vs pád*]).

6.2.4.3   Accusative
The accusative occurs both without prepositions and with prepositions. Without prepositions, its main function is the direct object, and it is also used in time expressions to answer 'how long?':

(89)   Sln *vès dán*   'all day'
         Rus *mý razgovárivali vsjú nóč'*   'we talked all night (long)'
         Bel *havarýc' hadzínu*   'to talk for an hour'
         Slk *čakal chvíl'ku na odpoved'*   'he waited a moment for an answer'

And sometimes 'when?':

(90)   'every day':
         B/C/S *svàki dân*   Sln   *vsák dán*
         Rus   *kážd yj dén'*   Ukr   *kóžnyj dén'*
         Cz   *každý den*   Sorb *kóždy dźeń*

With prepositions the accusative most often expresses direction (especially with *v* and *na*) or in time, answers to 'when?':

(91)   B/C/S   *pùt u sèlo*   'the road to the village'
         B/C/S   *ići na pòsao*   'to go to work'
         Rus   *poédem v górod*   'let's go to the city'
         Rus   *idëm na koncért*   'we're going to a concert'
         Pol   *wychodzić na ulicę* 'to go out' (lit. 'into the street')
         Cz   *jdu na univerzitu*   'I'm going to the University'
         'on Wednesday': B/C/S *u srêdu*   Rus *v srédu*
                                Pol   *w środę*   Cz   *ve středu*

These same prepositions can express location with the locative (below). Others expressing the accusative of direction have locational parallels with the instrumental, notably *za* and *pod*:

(92)   B/C/S   *záći za ŭgao*   'to go round (lit. 'behind') the corner'
       B/C/S   *stăviti pod zâštitu dřžavē*   'to place under the protection of the state'
       Rus   *zajtí za úgol*   'to go round (lit. 'behind') the corner'
       Rus   *položíť pod krováť*   'to put under the bed'
       Pol   *wyjechać za miasto*   'to go out of (lit. 'beyond') town'
       Pol   *rzucić się pod samochód*   'to throw oneself under a car'

6.2.4.4   *Genitive*

The primary function of the genitive – without prepositions – is to express possession (see above). It also expresses negation (for example, a negative direct object may be genitive – a feature now archaic in B/C/S and Czech and losing ground everywhere) and absence (see 7.1.3):

(93)   Sln   *ní razbíl ôkna*   'he didn't break the window'
       Rus   *já ne našël tám déneg*   'I didn't find any money there'
       Rus   *apeľ sínov nétu*   'there are no oranges'
       Sorb   *nimamy žanoho chlěba wjac*   'we have no more bread'
       (Ger   *kein Brot mehr*)
       Sorb   *ani kamenja tam njebě*   'there wasn't even a stone there'
       Slk   *nemám peňazí*   'I have no money'
   cf. Cz   *ani slovo neřekl*   'he didn't say a word'

In time expressions, it may answer 'when?', especially in respect of dates:

(94)   'on the 2nd of April':
       B/C/S   *drŭgōga apríla*   Sln   *drúgega apríla*
       Rus   *vtorógo aprélja* Bel   *druhóha krasavíka*
       Cz   *druhého února*   Pol   *drugego kwiećnia*

With prepositions it denotes separation ('from', 'off', 'out of', using *ot, s, (i)z*), or achievement of a goal, including a destination ('reach', using *do*). In each case the verbal prefix is also highly relevant; 'absence' is further exemplified by *bez* 'without':

(95a) B/C/S   *vrátiti se iz ràta*   'to return from war'
       Rus   *oná uéxala iz góroda*   'she has left town'
       Pol   *idę z kina*   'I'm coming from the cinema'
(95b) B/C/S   *pût do grâda*   'the road to town'
       Rus   *oná došlá do uglá*   'she reached the corner'
       Pol   *pojechał do miasta*   'he's gone to town'

(95c) B/C/S *déte **bez roditéljā*** 'orphan' (lit. 'child **without parents**')

Rus *ón ostálsja **bez déneg*** 'he was left **without money**'

Pol ***bez żony*** 'without a wife'

Slk *byt' **bez peňazí*** 'to be **without money**'

An extension is separation, propinquity, or small distance, without movement, for example with *u* 'next to, *chez*':

(96) B/C/S *stàjati **kod stòla*** 'to stand **by the table**'

Rus *stojátʼ **u okná*** 'to stand **by the window**'

Pol *mieszkać **u brata*** 'to stay **at one's brother's place**'

Cz *sedĕt **u okna*** 'to sit **by the window**'

Partitive genitive   In all languages except Russian the partitive genitive is formally the same as the normal genitive, and can express the notion 'some' by itself:

(97) B/C/S *dâj mi **tòga vína*** 'give me some of **that wine**'

Slk *napadlo **snehu*** 'some **snow** fell'

Pol *daj mi **wody*** 'give me some **water**'

Russian in addition has a small number of distinct partitive forms of masculine nouns used mostly as optional variants in this meaning. While some high-frequency words are commonly found in this form, most may now also use the normal genitive, that is the separate forms are slowly disappearing, surviving best with quantity words. Formally, the special form (GenSg^2, see 5.5.1.1) has the former *u*-stem ending *-u*:

(98) Rus *čáška **čáju*** 'a cup **of tea**'

*kiló **sáxaru/sáxara*** 'a kilo **of sugar**'

Rus *kupite **čája(čáju)*** 'buy some **tea**';

cf. *kupíte **xléba*** 'buy some **bread**'

*kusók **xléba*** 'a piece **of bread**' (neither can have *xlebu)

Genitive-accusative   The so-called "genitive-accusative" is one of the classic problems of Slavic morphosyntax. It belongs to the "secondary gender" system of Slavic, according to which a noun phrase which syntactically expects an accusative takes the morphological form of the genitive (5.4.4). This affects nouns (in all languages except Bulgarian and Macedonian) and all concording parts of the noun phrase, as well as pronouns (including Bulgarian and Macedonian):

(99)   B/C/S   *znâm tõga stârõga čõveka*   'I know **that old man**'
       Rus   *mý uvídeli vysókogo strógogo milicionéra*
               'we saw a **tall stern-looking policeman**'
       Pol   *widzę ładnego kota*   'I (can) see a **handsome cat**'

In the personal pronouns all languages have common forms for accusative and genitive for 1 Person and 2 Person. For 3 Person, some retain some distinction, either in relation to animacy (Czech, Slovak), the clitic/non-clitic forms (Polish, Sorbian), or in the feminine only (B/C/S, Slovenian); the rest make no distinction (see 5.5.2.3).

There are several proposed explanations for this phenomenon. One approach is phonological: with the rearrangement of the phonological system in relation to hard and soft consonants, the consequent effect on /i/ and /y/, and the reorganization of the declensions as hard/soft variants, a form like PSl NomPl *rabi* was perceived as out of place in a hard declension and pressured to become *raby*, that is, to merge with the accusative plural and partner the soft NomPl *koni*. In turn, the soft equivalent of the accusative plural should be *koni*, and not *koně* (5.5.1.1). Slavic had therefore to face the decision of resisting these pressures so as to maintain the nominative ~ accusative distinction, giving in to them and losing the distinction, or finding a morphological solution. This account overlaps with arguments from morphology, since marked categories are expected to hold or acquire desinences, while unmarked categories like the nominative do not (Greenberg, 1969; Bethin 1984). Or there are more functional-syntactic arguments which refer to syntactic ambiguity and the prominence of animate actors and patients (Comrie, 1978).

On the other hand, the (personal) pronouns had no such problems, yet had clearly gone in this direction already in Proto-Slavic, as evidenced by OCS forms, where only the enclitic forms retained separate accusatives (see 5.5.3), which means that the motive and solution were in the first place syntactic, with the nouns making use of the existing pattern as a solution to their newly developed homophony.

As this was a Proto-Slavic problem, all languages became involved in the genitive–accusative change, even those which did not subsequently develop the hard ~ soft phonological or morphological opposition (5.5).

Why should this development not affect the neuters, at least in the nouns? Comrie (1978) argues plausibly that a major factor was the foregrounding of animate agents and patients in the structure of the noun phrase: particularly since so many verbs can take both animate subjects and animate objects, and since word order was relatively free and driven by pragmatic rather than grammatical needs, it was important to separate out the grammatical roles of (animate) agents and patients. There was no homophony in the singular forms of the other major class of animates, the feminines of the *a/ja*-declension (5.5.1.3).

The development of the different forms of secondary gender, especially in the plural, is another, more complex, issue. The special animate nominative forms of Czech and Slovak, and the differences between virile and animate which distinguish Polish and Upper Sorbian, look like an extension of the same principle, that animate agents require special attention, and human agents most of all. Perhaps because the homophony of nominative–accusative in feminine nouns was old (Proto-Slavic), it did not attract attention, whereas the old distinction in the masculines provided an opportunity for retaining a special nominative form, used by the West Slavic languages for either animate masculine or virile masculine, extended further to the accompanying adjectival system.

6.2.4.5 *Dative*

The dative's primary function is that of indirect object, which it does without prepositions (except in Bulgarian and Macedonian nouns, which require prepositions; for inflexion, see 5.4.2). Its use without prepositions for directional motion is rare:

(100a) B/C/S *priblížiti se grâdu* 'to approach **the town**'

The "attributive dative" may be used for possession:

(100b) B/C/S *òna je Mìlošu sèstra* 'she is **Miloš's** sister'
         Slk *rodičia ti ešte žijú?* 'are **your** parents still alive?'

With prepositions it is used for the expression of direction 'toward' (using especially *k-*), ending up close(r), but not necessarily 'in' or 'on', as opposed to the assumed arrival and entry of the accusative. This distinction is, however, not a clear one except in the case of personal destinations (arriving at someone's place):

(101) B/C/S *krénuli smo k vároši* 'we set off **for town**'
     Rus *mý šli k séveru* 'we were walking **northwards**'
            pojdëm k Váne 'let's go **to Vanya's place**'
     Pol *droga ku miastu* 'the road **to town**'
     Slk *blízit' sa ku chlapcom* 'to approach **the boys**'

Otherwise, there is no consistency of prepositional use across the area.

6.2.4.6 *Instrumental*

The instrumental (Wierzbicka, 1980) without prepositions expresses instrument ('with') (102a), means ('by') (102b), and the agent in passive constructions (102c):

(102a) B/C/S *sèći sàbljōm* 'to cut **with a sword**'

(102b)   Slk   *íst' autobusom*   'to go **by bus**'

(102c)   Bel   *ščásce stvaráecca ljudz'mí*   'happiness is created **by people**'

Some of these meanings are realized only by prepositions, not always with the instrumental case:

(103a)   Sln   *peljáti se z vlákom* [Instr]   'to **go by train**'

(103b)   Sorb   *pisać z kulijom* [Instr]   'to write **with a ball-point pen**'

cf. (103c)   Pol   *uniwersytet został założony przez kobietę* [Acc]
                     'the university was founded **by a woman**'

The instrumental can also be used in the predicate after the copula or semi-copulative verbs, often as a free variant, but in principle expressing notions of non-permanence (see 6.2.4.2).

With prepositions most common is the expression of accompaniment ('with', using *s/z*):

(104)   Rus   *oná ušlá s brátom*   'she's gone out **with (her) brother**'

         Slk   *chlieb s maslom*   'bread **with butter**'

In location, it expresses relative location, for example 'above' (*nad*), 'below' (*pod*), 'behind' (*za*), 'in front of' (*p(e)red*) (the last also usable in the time sense of 'before' or 'ago', (105b)) (some of these may take the accusative where motion is involved – see 6.2.4.3):

(105a)   B/C/S   *za vrátima*   'behind the door'

                   nad vòdōm   'over the water'

          Slk   *pod stolom*   'under the table'

                   za domom   'behind the house'

(105b)   B/C/S   *pred ùlazom*   'in front of the entrance'

                   pred òdlaskom   'before one's departure'

          Sln   *pred híšo*   'in front of the house'

                   pred 14 dnévi   'a fortnight ago'

                   pred odhódom   'prior to departure'

6.2.4.7   *Locative*

The locative is in many ways the least problematic of the cases. It is now used only with prepositions, hence its common name "prepositional case", and takes its meaning predominantly from the preposition. The key area of interest is when the same preposition can also govern a case other than the locative. There are two principal types: when the preposition can also govern an accusative; and when there are two forms of the locative itself.

A preposition can govern either an accusative or a locative in expressions of direction and location, respectively. Compare the examples above under accusative with the following examples of the locative:

(106) B/C/S   *u pózorištu* 'in the theatre'   *na pózornici* 'on the stage'

Rus   *mý býli **v górode** vés' dén'*   'we were **in town** all day'

       *mý včerá býli **na koncérte***   'we were **at a concert** yesterday'

Pol   *studiować **na uniwersytecie***   'to study **at university**'

Slk   *v kute* 'in the corner'   *na stole* 'on the table'

However, while all the Slavic languages with a locative (i.e. excluding Bulgarian and Macedonian) use this case for expressing location, some of the languages use different prepositions (and cases) for direction ('to'), notably *do* (+Gen) in West Slavic and Ukrainian:

(107) Cz   *do města* 'to town'   cf. *v městě* 'in town'

     Pol   *do szkoły* 'to school'   cf. *w szkole* 'in school'

The high-frequency preposition *po*, used among other things for motion within a confined space (108a) or over a surface (108b), takes the locative everywhere except Russian, where it takes the dative. In many paradigms the endings of the dative and locative are identical:

(108a) B/C/S   *hódati **po sòbi*** [Loc]   'to walk **about the room**'

Bel   *xadzíc' **pa pakói*** [Loc]   'to walk **about the room**'

Rus   *guljác' **po párku*** [Dat]   'to stroll **in the park**'

Slk   *prechádzat' se **po lese*** [Loc]   'to stroll **in the forest**'

Pol   *chodzić **po ulicach*** [Loc]   'to walk **about the streets**'

(108b)   'books are strewn **over the whole table**':

B/C/S   *knjìge su razbácane **po čìtavom stòlu*** [Loc]

Bel   *kníhi razlóžany **pa ŭsím stalé*** [Loc]

'to thump **on the shoulder**':

Rus   *xlópnuc' **po plečú*** [Dat]

Cz   *poplácat **po rameni*** [Loc]

The most common non-locational meaning of the locative case is 'about', 'concerning' (*o(b)*) (only Slovak has (additionally) the accusative):

(109) B/C/S   *govòriti **o ùmetnosti***   'to speak **about art**'

Rus   *mý razgovárivali **o górode***   'we talked **about the city**'

	ob ètom nel'zjá *govorít'*	'one can't talk **about that**'
Pol	*opowiadanie* **o psach i kotach**	'a story **about cats and dogs**'
Cz	*snít* **o cestě**	'to dream **about a/the trip**'
Slk	*hovorit'* **o bratovi** [Loc]	'to talk **about one's brother**'
	o čo [Acc] *ide?*	'**what**'s it (the topic) **about**?'

The situation of the "second locative" (LocSg^2, 5.5.1.1–2) is typically Russian, and involves the old *-u* ending from the *u*-stem in the locational meaning, contrasting with the *o*-stem ending *-e* in other uses of the "locative" case:

(110) Rus *o sáde*   'about (concerning) the garden'
       v sadú   'in the garden'
       o móste 'about the bridge'   *na mostú* 'on the bridge'

In other Slavic languages this choice of forms has been resolved by the languages selecting either the *-e* or the *-u* form for the appropriate paradigms, similarly to the choices made between the *o*-stem and *u*-stem endings *-a* and *-u* in the genitive and *-u* and *-ovi* in the dative (respectively). The Russian locative in *-ú* (always stressed) is used only with a small number of monosyllabic masculine inanimates of the *o/jo*-declension. It is still standard in Russian in these words, and is surviving better than the partitive genitive (GenSg^2, see 6.2.4.4 above and 5.5.1.1–2). An even rarer parallel exists within the feminine *i*-declension, in which a few nouns have a stressed ending in the locative meaning against the stressed stem of the non-locative (semantically rare) and the rest of the singular:

(111) Rus *o dvéri* 'concerning the door'   *na dverí* 'on the door'
       o stépi 'about the steppe'   *v stepí* 'in the steppe'

6.3   Aspect

Aspect, together with case, presents as the most controversial grammatical category in Slavic. In the first place, it occupies a complex position between inflexion, paradigmatics and word formation. We have chosen to cover morphological aspect under word formation (8.3), since the aspect-forming components are principally associated with prefixation and suffixation. The inflexional properties attached to those stems are treated under inflexional morphology (5.5.5). In this section we take up the syntax and morphosyntax of aspect, and the related issues of semantics and pragmatics.

Analyses of aspect have been dominated by a search for an orderly mapping between grammatical forms and semantic interpretations. The first assumption has been that since most imperfectives are formally distinct from perfectives, therefore there should be semantically distinct interpretations. Conventionally the perfective is held to describe actions which are (or will be) complete, completed, or have reached an end-point. In contrast, imperfectives refer to actions in process, ongoing, repeated or habitual – or, in the present tense, also atemporal and/or generic: *beavers build dams*. Perfectives should therefore be only past or future, while imperfectives should appear in any of the three tenses. In English glosses this amounts to:

(112)   Imperfective   Perfective
    past: did, used to do, was doing   did, have done, had done
    present: do (both ongoing and atemporal)   –
              am doing
    future: will do, will be doing   will do, will have done

Sorbian, B/C/S, Bulgarian and Macedonian retain the imperfect and the aorist tenses (5.4.6), which further complicates the relation of tense to aspect.

A commonly accepted view is that the perfective is semantically the marked member of the aspect opposition. If an action is not specifically viewed as complete(d), the (unmarked) imperfective is used. The variety of meanings available can be summarized in Comrie's (1976: 25) diagram (6.1).

The process/completion (achievement, etc.) opposition captures neatly a compact use of the perfective which requires periphrastic structures in English:

(113)   Rus   *ón dólgo rešál* [Imprfv] *zadáču i nakonéc rešíl* [Prfv] *eë*
               he long resolved problem and finally resolved it
               'he worked on the problem for a long time and finally solved it'

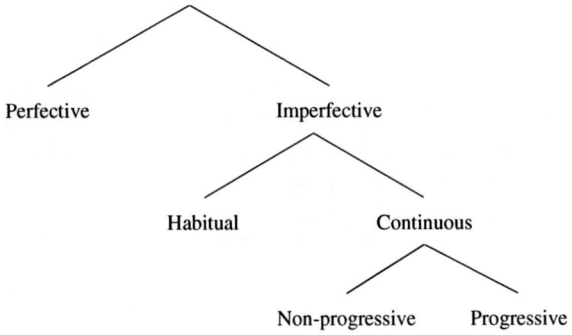

Diagram 6.1

Some data confirm this broad characterization in terms of activities and completed actions. Adverbs like *gradually* tend to occur with imperfectives, while *at once* favors the perfective. Verbs of states or activities like 'sit' will favor the imperfective, while verbs of actions and accomplishments like 'build' allow either aspect, and punctual verbs like 'kill' will favor the perfective. The "procedurals" or Aktionsarten (8.3.1.3) fit here: in Rus *oná zapéla* [Prfv] 'she began singing, she burst into song' the beginning is completed, even if the singing is not. This also seems to line up with the notion of goal-directed activity or telicity. Perfectives tend to prefer a direct object: Rus *čitát'* 'to be engaged in reading [Imprfv]', *čitát' román* 'to be engaged in reading [Imprfv] a novel', *pročitát'* [Prfv] *román* 'to read through a novel to the end', but *pročitát'* [Prfv] does not comfortably stand on its own without an object or appropriate terminating adverbial to situate it in time and/or space. An action can also be interpreted as complete by being explicitly placed at a single location in space and time. Such adverbs often require a perfective:

(114)   Rus   *oná prinjalá* [Prfv] *vánnu v 5 časóv véčera*
'she took a bath at 5 p.m.'

Perfective actions occur within the time-scope of imperfective actions:

(115)   Rus   *poká oná prinimála* [Imprfv] *vánnu, oná propéla* [Prfv] *pésnju*
'while she was taking a bath she sang through the song'

Negative imperatives tend to be imperfective, since they order us to avoid actions or prevent them from occurring:

(116a)   Cz   *neplač!* [Imprfv] 'don't cry!'

Negative perfectives express the undesirability of results, thus are often warnings:

(116b)   Rus   *ne upadíte!* [Prfv] 'don't fall/be careful not to fall!'

There are some significant exceptions to these general tendencies. Slavic languages typically can use the present as a historic present, very much as in Romance. And especially in South Slavic there are some important idiosyncrasies of the relation between tense and aspect. In Bulgarian, for instance, the use of certain aspects with certain tense inflexions switches the verb into the renarrative mood (5.4.9). In B/C/S there is a present perfective, which can be used with the meaning of a present tense, especially for repeated or hypothetical events in the present:

(117a)   B/C/S   *i dēsī se* [Imprfv] *pònekad: zàstanē* [PrfvPres] *čòvek* ...
'and it sometimes happens that a man stops...'

or in subordinate clauses, where it has the expected future sense:

(117b)   B/C/S   *òstani* [Prfv] *óvde, dok se vrátīm* [PrfvPres]
                   'stay here till I return'

And Russian, too, can use the present perfective in the former sense (repetition, cf. the English future in this sense, 'Often you'll see ...'):

(117c)   Rus   *byváet, prideš'* [PrfvPres] *domój i uznáeš'* [PrfvPres], *čto* ...
                 '(it happens that) you'll (sometimes) arrive home to find
                 (lit. 'and will find') that ...'

The claim that aspect is formally marked has led to attempts to identify the semantic markedness of the perfective. It is not difficult to attack this position. Some verbs lack perfectives for no apparent formal or semantic reason (8.3). Some verbs are bi-aspectual: the same form can express either aspect (8.3), so breaking the mapping between form and meaning. And "ongoing *vs* completed" – even granting that this is an over-simplification – turns out to be unable to capture some uses of the imperfective to express events which are completed:

(118a)   Rus   *ón otkryvál* [Imprfv] *oknó*
                 he opened the window (but now it's shut again)
(118b)   Rus   *ón otkrýl* [Prfv] *oknó*
                 he opened the window (and it is still open)

There has consequently been a major effort to refine and reorient the semantic dichotomy of the two aspects. Some proposals have tried to replace "ongoing *vs* completed" with another single, more accurately tuned, binary opposition. One useful perspective involves serial events, which have time boundaries between the completion of one and the start of the next: the "What's next?" criterion:

(119a)   Cz   *ten román jsem četl* [Imprfv] *dávno*
                'I read this novel a long time ago' (I am in the post-reading
                state, I reflect on it ...)
(119b)   Cz   *ten román jsem přečetl* [Prfv]
                'I have read this novel' (what am I to do next?)

The languages can also show aspectual differences in expressing identical events: in Czech it is possible for the formal perfective to express present tense (Townsend, 1984: 291):

(120a)   'I can't stand him'
          Cz   *já ho nesnesu* [formally Prfv], more common than
                já ho nesnáším [regular Imprfv Pres]

This may even occur with habitual or repetitive contexts, even when marked by an adverb. Only particular emphasis on the duration or frequency make the imperfective more likely (Townsend, 1981: 202):

(120b)   'he always arrived late'
        Cz *přišel* [Prfv] *vždycky pozdě*, or
              vždycky přicházel [Imprfv] *pozdě*

So either aspect can have different "meanings" in different languages, or there are multiple factors at work. Recent research, e.g. by Benacchio (2002) on imperatives (7.1.4), shows that we need to supplement a time/space oriented vector with contextual, pragmatic and interpersonal vectors if we are to capture the variability of aspect usage in a methodical way.

The formation of the aspects is closely linked to verbal paradigms. For this reason most grammars of Slavic languages treat aspect together with inflexion (5.5.5) as part of the verbal paradigms. But the actual formation of the aspects is accomplished mainly by prefixation and suffixation, and we therefore treat aspect formation separately under word formation (8.3).

7

Sentence structure

7.1 Sentence structure: overview

In this chapter we deal with the structure of the Slavic sentence: the simple sentence (7.1), complex sentence (7.2), specific construction-types (7.3), word order (7.4) and Functional Sentence Perspective (7.5).

The basic simple sentence contains no coordination and no subordination. In the initial description of the simple sentence we omit clitics and other particles which affect the word order of the sentence, and concentrate on neutral word order. Many of these sentence patterns look like English. For differences in word categories (e.g. articles, clitics) see 6.1.

The sentence contains a predicate, and usually a subject, which normally precedes the predicate (7.4). The subject may not be present, as happens with apersonal and impersonal sentences and ellipsis (7.3.7). If the subject is present, it consists of a noun phrase containing a nominal head, which may be a noun or a pronoun, or another part of speech acting as a nominal (e.g. an infinitive); and zero, one or several modifiers. Not all modifiers can occur with all head nominals: mass and abstract nouns can take numerals only in special circumstances. And the order of modifiers varies somewhat between languages, and for stylistic and special purposes within individual languages as well.

The first element in the noun phrase is the quantifier:

(1) QUANTIFIER + NOUN
     Rus   *vsé ópery*   'all the operas'

Then comes the determiner [Det], consisting of deictics ('this', 'that' (2a)) and possessive adjectives ('my ...'; B/C/S *mâjčin* 'mother's' < *mâjka* 'mother' etc.: (2b)). In addition to word-deictics Macedonian also has suffix-deictics (33a–c). These, like the suffixed articles found in both Bulgarian and Macedonian, are generally attached to the leftmost concording member of the noun phrase (2c–d).

The determiner slot may even be filled by a possessive noun phrase, which would otherwise normally follow the noun (2c):

(2)   DETERMINER + NOUN

(2a)   Rus   *èti druz'já*   'these friends'

(2b)   B/C/S   *njègov kõnj* (*mâjčin kõnj*)   'his horse' ('mother's horse')

(2c)   Pol   *moj-ej*   *ciotk-i*   *star-y*   *koń*
        my-GenSgFem   aunt-GenSg   old-NomSg Masc   horse
        'my aunt's old horse' (stylistically marked, emphatic)

Next comes the numeral or numeral phrase, consisting of a numeral and an optional (and not very frequent) numeral classifier:

(3)   NUMERAL + (CLASSIFIER +) NOUN

(3a)   Blg   *dvé knígi*   'two books'

(3b)   Blg   *dvéte knígi*   'the two books'

(3c)   Rus   *pját'* (*čelovék*) *p'jányx rabótnikov*
        '5 (CLASSIFIER) drunken workmen'

Then follows an adjective phrase, containing as many adjectives as are required, with or without conjunctions like 'and' and 'or'. They may also be accompanied by degree and other modifiers. Unlike English, there may also be objects, infinitives and other complements:

(4)   ADJECTIVE PHRASE + NOUN

(4a)   Cz   *pravdivý   starý   český   rukopis*
        'a real   old   Czech   manuscript'

(4b)   Pol   *bardzo   silny   w ramionach   chłopak*
        very   strong   in shoulders   lad
        'a lad very strong in the shoulders'

(4c)   Rus   *dostójnyj   nášego   uvažénija   učíteľ*
        worthy   our-Gen   respect-Gen   teacher
        'a teacher worthy of our respect'

The nominal head follows; and then, in order, a group of noun phrases with dependent case marking; and then prepositional phrases, and even a few adverbs, fulfilling various syntactic roles; infinitives; and relative clauses and complements:

(5)   NOMINAL HEAD + NOUN PHRASE/PREPOSITIONAL PHRASE

(5a)   Blg   *načálnik na otdelénie* 'director of (the) department'
       Rus   *diréktor škóly* 'principal of the school'

(5b)   Blg   *razširjávane na demokratízăm*
              'spreading of democracy'

(5c)   Blg   *v ímeto   na kralícata*
              in name-Def of queen-Def
              'in the name of the queen'

(5d)   Cz   *Praha dnes*   'Prague today'

(6)   NOMINAL HEAD + INFINITIVE
       Slk   *úmysel bojovat'* 'intention to fight'

(7)   NOMINAL HEAD + RELATIVE CLAUSE/COMPLEMENT

(7a)   Rus   *vsé té stárye rússkie rúkopisi 18-go véka v nášej bibliotéke,*
              kotórye [Pl] *učiteljá xotját prodát'*
              'all those old Russian manuscripts of the 18th century in our
              library, which [Pl = the manuscripts] the teachers want to sell'

(7b)   Ukr   *vín ták rozhubívsja, ščo nemíh ničóho vidpovísty*
              he so be_upset-Past that Neg-able nothing answer
              'he was so upset that he couldn't answer anything'

Some attributive adjective modifiers may also follow directly after the noun. Such
adjectives are standard in Polish. In the other languages post-nominal adjectives
are more commonly found with some technical and fixed expressions, and for
stylistic emphasis (7.4).

The head of the noun phrase may also be a pronoun. Personal pronouns may
be intensified by a following "self" word, but not by adjectives (8a). Negative and
indefinite pronouns, as in English, may be modified by a following adjective or
adjective phrase (8b–c), and may have a following relative clause (8d):

(8)   PRONOUN + MODIFIER

(8a)   Rus   *já sám ne   znáju*
              I self Neg know-1Sg
              'I don't know myself'

(8b)   Cz   *není   v   něm nic   dobrého*
              Neg-be in him nothing good-Gen
              'there is nothing good in him'

(8c)   Rus   *któ-nibuď s širókim krugozórom*
'someone with a broad perspective'

(8d)   Mac   *taa,   bez   koga   ne   možam   da   rabotam*
she   without whom   Neg   able-1Sg   that   work-1Sg
'she, without whom I cannot work'

A noun phrase may consist of a "free relative" (7.2.2):

(9a)   Pol   *kto   wypił   dwie butelki,   lezał   pod   stołem*
who   drank   two bottles   lay   under   table
'(he) who had drunk two bottles was lying under the table'

More commonly, a relative may reduce to a participial clause with a nominalized head:

(9b)   Rus   *ležáščij   pod   stolóm výpil   užé   dvé butýlki*
lying MascSgNom   under   table   drunk already 2   bottles
'the man lying under the table had already drunk 2 bottles'

Infinitives can be the subject (10) or object (11) of a sentence:

(10)   Slk   *začat'   budovat'   je   t'ažšie   ako   kritizovat'*
begin-Inf   build-Inf   be-3Sg   hard-Compar   than   criticize-Inf
'beginning to build is harder than criticizing'

(11)   Ukr   *ljubýty   muzýku,   rozhovórjuvaty*
love-Inf   music-Acc   chat-Inf
'to love music, (to love) to chat'

Subordinate clauses in Slavic literary languages are almost always introduced by a complementizer (7.2.2; cf. 11.3.1), and many such sentences require *to* in the main sentence. Such subordinate clauses may also form the subject (12a) or object (12b):

(12a)   Rus   *tó, čto   ón akadémik, nám kážetsja neverojátnym*
it, that   he ...
'the fact that he is an academician seems incredible to us'

(12b)   Sorb   *z wulkej njesćerpliwosću čakaše na to, zo* + SENTENCE
'with great impatience he waited for [it, that] ... + SENTENCE'

The verb phrase is more complex than the noun phrase in several respects. It contains more varied elements, and the elements are subject to wider variation in word order. We give only simple types of predicate, and leave problems like the negative and question sentence-types, impersonal sentences, and other special problems, for separate discussion below. We also postpone, for the time being, consideration of clitics and particles (7.1.2, 7.1.4, 7.4.3.3).

The Slavic predicate shows many fundamental similarities to the English predicate in both the selection and arrangement of its constituents. First comes the auxiliary. Two kinds of auxiliary must be distinguished: verbal auxiliaries in compound tenses (13a) and auxiliary verbs proper (13b–c). This second type governs an infinitive except in Macedonian and Bulgarian, and standardly in Serbian, where it is followed instead by *da* and a subordinate clause (for the Bulgarian infinitive in (13c) see 5.5.5.3):

(13)   AUXILIARY + VERB

(13a)   Cz   *byl*   *jsem*   *viděl*
             be-MascSgPastPart   Aux-3Sg   see-MascSgPastPart
             'I had seen' [Pluperf]

(13b)   Ukr   *vý povýnni   bulý   z'javýtysja   včásno*
              you obliged   be-Past-Pl   appear-Inf   on time
              'you should have come on time'

(13c)   B/C/S   Croatian   *hòću   ìći   u   kàzalīšte*
                            I want   to go   to (the) theatre
                 Serbian   *hòću   da ìdēm u   pózorīšte*
                            I want   that I go to (the) theatre

After the auxiliary comes either a full verb or a copula. The verb, which includes 'be' in its non-copulative senses of 'be located' and 'take place', may be accompanied by several types of governed noun phrase or prepositional phrase, which are divided according to their role as objects:

(14a)   INTRANSITIVE VERB
        Bel   *snéh kružýcca* 'the snow whirls around'

(14b)   TRANSITIVE VERB + OPTIONAL DIRECT OBJECT
        Bel   *špák spjaváe (pésnju)* 'the starling sings (a song)'

(14c)   TRANSITIVE VERB + OBLIGATORY DIRECT OBJECT
        Bel   *salavéjka   létnjaj   nóčkaj   razliváe*
              nightingale   summer-Instr   night-Instr   pour_out-3Sg
              svajú   trèl'
              Poss-Acc   trill-Acc
              'the nightingale pours out its trill on a summer's night'

(14d)   TRANSITIVE VERB + NON-ACCUSATIVE OBJECT(-S)
        Bel   *ën   néčaha   spadzjáecca*
              he   something-GenSg   await-3SgPres
              'he is waiting for something'

(14e)   TRANSITIVE VERB + MIXED OBJECTS

Bel   *špák   spjaváe   sóncu   svajú   pésnju*
      starling sing-3Sg sun-Dat Poss-Acc song-Acc
      'the starling sings its song to the sun'

(14f)   VERB + PREPOSITIONAL OBJECTS

Bel   *hljadzjáć   bjarózy na   mjané   z   usméškaj*
      look-3Pl   birch-Pl at   me-Acc with   smile-Instr
      'the birches look at me with a smile'

The distinction between prepositional and non-prepositional objects may be useful in some constructions in some of the eleven languages. But Bulgarian and Macedonian have more prepositional objects than the other nine languages because of their poorer case systems for marking objects, and in general for indicating grammatical roles.

The verb may also be followed by an infinitive (or supine, in Czech and Slovenian, after a verb of motion (5.5.5.11)):

(15)   VERB + INFINITIVE/SUPINE

(15a)   Slk   *nakázali   mu   prestat'   fajčit'*
              order-PlPast   he-Cl-Dat stop-Inf   smoke-Inf
              'they ordered him to stop smoking'

(15b)   Slk   *panov   sluchat'   sa   nevyplaca*
              man-AccPl   listen-Inf   ReflEncl   Neg-pay-3Sg
              'it is not worth listening to men'

(15c)   Cz   *jdu   spat/spát*
             go-1Sg   sleep-Sup/sleep-Inf
             'I am going to sleep'

(15d)   Sln   *móram   spát/spáti*
              must-1Sg   sleep-Sup/sleep-Inf
              'I must go to bed'   'I must sleep'

Alternatively, the verb may be followed by a subordinate clause, introduced by a complementizer (7.2.2):

(16)   VERB + COMPLEMENTIZER + SUBORDINATE CLAUSE

(16a)   Slk   *hovoril som vám, že bude treba opravit' niekol'ko mostov*
              'I told you **that** it would be necessary to repair several bridges'

(16b)   Slk   *boji sa,   aby   pri   prechode*
              fear-3SgRefl   in-order-that(-3Sg)   at   crossing-over

nedostal *gul'ku* *odzadu*
Neg-get-MascPast bullet from_behind
'he is afraid that in crossing over he might be hit by a bullet from behind'

(see below on 'in-order-that'). The predicate can also consist of the copula 'be'; quasi-copulative verbs which have the same semantic, and in part syntactic, function as the copula (e.g. Rus *javlát'sja* 'be'); and semi-copulative verbs like 'appear, become, seem, look', all of which express specially modified forms of being. Such predicates do not occur alone, but must be accompanied by a noun phrase, adjective or prepositional phrase. As with verbs proper, an auxiliary may occur as well:

(17) 'BE' + NOUN PHRASE

(17a) Slk *Slovensko je etnologickým uzlom v Slovanstve*
'Slovakia is an ethnological grouping in Slavdom'

(17b) Blg *áz săm studént* 'I am (a) student'

(17c) Rus *já studént* 'I (am a) student'

(17d) Rus *ón býl vysokógo rósta*
he-Nom be-MascSgPast tall-GenSg stature-GenSg
'he was of tall stature/tall in stature/tall'

(18) QUASI-COPULA + NOUN PHRASE
Rus *neobyknovénnaja odarënnost'*
unusual-NomSgFem giftedness[Fem]-NomSg
javljáetsja pričínoj egó udáči
be-3Sg cause-InstrSg his success-GenSg
'unusual giftedness is the cause of his success'

(19) SEMI-COPULA + NOUN PHRASE

(19a) Ukr *vín uvažájet'sja znavcém*
he pass_for-3Sg connoisseur-InstrSgMasc
'he passes for a connoisseur'

(19b) Bel *Jánko stáŭ kupcóm*
Janko become-MascSgPast merchant-InstrSg
'Janko became a merchant'

In East Slavic the copula 'be' is usually not expressed in the present tense except for emphasis or formula-like definitions (20b). Polish also shows a decline of 'be' in the present tense, sometimes replacing it in the written language with a dash (as in East Slavic) or with the invariant *to*, followed by the nominative case, and not by the instrumental case, which is regular for nouns after *być* 'be' (20c–e):

(20)   ZERO COPULA

(20a)   Ukr   *témno v póli*   '(it is) dark in the field'

(20b)   Rus   *Bóg ést' ljubóv'*   'God is love'

(20c)   Pol   *Wisła – wielka rzeka w Polsce*
         'the Vistula is a big river in Poland'

(20d)   Pol   *Wisła to wielka rzeka w Polsce*
         'the Vistula is a big river in Poland'

(20e)   Pol   *ujrzeć* [Inf] *to uwierzyć* [Inf] 'seeing is believing'

The structures of copulae and semi-copulae are similar with following adjectives and prepositional phrases:

(21)   COPULA + ADJECTIVE/PREPOSITIONAL PHRASE

(21a)   Bel   *dzén' vydáŭsja sonéčny*   'the day appeared sunny'

(21b)   Blg   *nošttá e čérna i zlovéšta, nošttá e lédna kató smărt*
         'the night is dark and menacing, the night is cold as death'

(21c)   Blg   *nošttá e kató smărt*   'the night is like death'

(21d)   Rus   *mý v otčájanii*   'we (are) in despair'

And these expressions in turn may be accompanied by objects, usually prepositional phrases, and infinitives. They may also introduce subordinate clauses:

(22)   COPULA + ADJECTIVE/PREPOSITIONAL PHRASE

(22a)   Cz   *Jiří   byl*   *rád*   *té*
         Jiří   be-MascSgPast   glad-MascSg   this-DatSgFem
         pochvale
         praise[Fem]-DatSg
         'Jiří was pleased with this praise'

(22b)   Slk   *nie   som   v   stave   odpovedat'*
         Neg   be-1Sg   in state   reply-Inf
         'I am not in a fit state to reply'

(22c)   Slk   *som presvedčený, že* + SENTENCE
         'I am convinced that + SENTENCE'

Adverbs (in **bold**) are usually optional:

    (23a)   Slk   *nehl'adel ani **napravo** ani **nal'avo***
                    'he looked neither to the right nor left'

    (23b)   Mac *doruček bev doma, **odruček** izlegov **nadvor***
                    'in the morning I was at home, in the afternoon I went out'

Adverbs form many classes, and occur more with verbal predicates than with copulae. Degree adverbs occur with adjectives, adverbs, verbs and some predicate-noun expressions, are closely tied to the heads of their construction, and usually permit less variation in word order for this reason:

    (24)   Sorb *Michał ma **jara** bohatu zbĕrku*
                   'Michael has a very rich collection'

Other types of adverbs/adverbials are more mobile. Slavic grammars differ in their classification of adverbs, though the basis is usually semantic (8.5). The array of semantic types of adverbs is significantly larger than that usually proposed for English. The 1980 Academy grammar of Russian (Švedova, 1980: 703–705), for instance, identifies:

    (25)   ADVERBS (Russian examples)

PLACE:		
place-where	*gde*	'where'
place-whither	*kudá*	'where, to where, whither'
place-whence	*otkúda*	'from where, whence'
TIME:		
time-when	*kogdá*	'when'
time how-long	*dólgo*	'for a long time'
time how-often	*částo*	'often'
MANNER	*býstro*	'quickly'
DEGREE	*óčen'*	'very'
GOAL	*naróčno*	'on purpose'
CAUSE	*sozlá*	'from spite'
ACCOMPANIMENT	*vméste*	'together'

Adverbials may be expressed by an adverb, including an adverb derived from a gerund:

    (26a) B/C/S ôn   je   vȅć   dòšao
                    he   Aux already come-PastPart-MascSg
                    'he has come already'

(26b)   Rus   *ón čitál sídja* [Ger]   'he was reading sitting down'

a case-marked noun phrase:

(27)   Pol   *zabili go karabinem* [Instr]   'they killed him with a rifle'

a prepositional phrase:

(28a)   Mac   *so   puška   go   udrija*
              with rifle   he-Cl-Acc   kill-3PlPast
              'they killed him with a rifle'

(28b)   Sorb   *po   słónčku   do   hribow   hić   je*
               after   sunrise   to   mushrooms   go-Inf   be-3Sg
               zapozdźena   wěc
               be-late-FemSgNomPastPart   thing[Fem]-NomSg
               'to go looking for mushrooms after sunrise is too late'

an expanded or modified version of any of the above:

(29)   Rus   *Máša prosnúlas' ráno útrom*
             'Masha awoke early in the morning'

or by a subordinate sentence introduced by a conjunction:

(30)   Rus   *Máša prosnúlas' útrom,* **kogdá** *sólnce tól'ko čto vstálo*
             'Masha woke in the morning, when the sun had just risen'

There are two other slots in the simple sentence which are not adverbial, but which
look semantically rather like adverbs. These are the "predicative attributives" or
"adjuncts", which agree with the subject in gender and number, and are simultaneously governed in case by the verb. They may refer to either objects or subjects,
and express a notion of "accompanying condition":

(31a)   Sorb   *hólc   přińdźe   wjesoły   ze   šule*
               boy   arrive-3Sg   happy-NomSgMasc   from   school
               'the boy arrives happy from school'

(31b)   Bel   *Mítka   pajšóŭ   péršy*
              Mitka   go-MascSgPast   first-MascSgNom
              'Mitka went first'

(31c)   Sorb   *my   jemy   hriby   syre*
               we   eat-1Pl   mushroom-AccPl   raw-AccPl
               'we eat mushrooms raw'

7.1.1 Definiteness

Bulgarian and Macedonian share with Romanian and Albanian the typically Balkan feature of the post-posed definite article (32a–b), a pattern also found in dialectal North Russian (32c):

(32a) Blg   *žená* 'woman, wife'   *ženáta* 'the woman, wife'

(32b) Mac   *vol* 'ox'   *volot* 'the ox'

(32c) CS-Rus *kníga* '(a/the) book'
       N-Rus *kníga-ta* 'the book'

The Bulgarian and Macedonian article attaches to the leftmost concording member of the noun phrase (5.5.1). If there is only one noun, the suffix attaches to that noun; otherwise it attaches to the first adjective, and so on:

(32d) Blg *Xrísto Bótev e náj-velíkijat   bǎlgarski poét*
            Christo Botev is most-great-Def   Bulgarian poet
            'Xristo Botev is the greatest Bulgarian poet'

The post-posed 'this, that' deictics of Macedonian work in the same way (33a–b). All the Slavic languages, including Macedonian, have lexical (as opposed to affixal) deictics for expressing 'this' and 'that'; and in Macedonian they may even co-occur with the suffix-deictic (33c):

(33a) Mac *volot* 'the ox'   *volov* 'this ox'   *volon* 'that ox'

(33b) Mac *knigata* 'the book' *knigava* 'this book' *knigana* 'that book'

(33c) Mac *ov-ie   naš-i-v-e*
            this-Pl   our-Pl-this-Pl
            'these fellows of ours'

The Macedonian suffix deictics are semantically weaker than the word-deictics, and can often be translated merely by the definite article in English. This connection between the deictics and definiteness recalls Proto-Germanic and Proto-Romance, where deictics were the source of modern articles, as in Latin *illa* 'that' [Fem], French and Italian *la*, Romanian *-la*. In modern Polish *ten* 'this' is increasingly being used to mean [Definite] as well as 'this'; there are parallel developments in Upper Sorbian and Czech (11.3):

(34) Pol *widziałaś tego nowego nauczyciela?*
           'have you seen the/this new teacher?'

To mark a noun phrase as clearly indefinite, most Slavic languages can use the numeral 'one', like Czech *jeden*, or forms like Rus *nékij* 'a certain' (the latter mainly in high style):

(35) Cz *byl tu jeden muž*   'there was a man here'

The pattern of suffixing articles and deictics in Bulgarian and Macedonian is also found, in a slightly different form, in the definite–indefinite adjectives in Common Slavic, Old Church Slavonic, and modern Slovenian and B/C/S (5.4.3, 5.5.2). The other means of marking definiteness in Slavic are not lexical but syntactic and pragmatic, and are concerned with word order and the organization of information in the sentence (7.5).

7.1.2 Questions

The Slavic languages possess three means for constructing questions: by intonation, particles and question-words, with relevant adjustments of word order. Yes/no questions can be formed by applying a marked question intonation to an ordinary declarative sentence. The words affected by the contrastive intonation are in small capitals:

(36a) Blg *Bălgarski-jat   ezík   prinadlež-i   kăm seméjstvo-to   na*
             Bulgarian-Def language belong-3Sg   to   family-Def   of
             SLAVJÁNSKI-TE   EZÍC-I?
             Slavic-DefPl   language-Pl
             'does the Bulgarian language belong to the family of **the Slavic languages?**'

This structure questions the whole sentence ('is it the case that' + Sentence). It is also possible to question individual constituents or words in the sentence by applying the marked part of the question intonation to them:

(36b) Blg [. . .] *SEMÉJSTVOTO na slavjánskite ezíci?*
             '[. . .] to **the family** [i.e. not sub-family, etc.] of the Slavic languages?'

If a sentence is already in a non-neutral word order, the question intonation questions the constituents or words emphasized in the declarative sentence:

(36c) Blg *kăm seméjstvoto na slavjánskite ezíci prinadleží BÁLGARSKIJAT EZÍK?*
             'Is it to the family of Slavic languages that the **Bulgarian language** belongs?' or 'Does **Bulgarian** belong to . . .'

A second method for forming Yes/no questions involves the use of particles. All Slavic languages can ask Yes/no questions by this means. The particles are either sentence-initial or enclitic. Polish *czy*, Ukrainian *čy*, Belarusian *ci* and Slovenian *ali* are sentence-initial:

(37)   Ukr   *čy   zdoróvyj   tý?*
                 Q   healthy   you
                 'are you well?'

All the other languages have the enclitic *li*, and Slovenian also preserves it as a marked stylistic alternative to *ali*:

(38)   B/C/S   *gláva   li   ga   bòlī̄?*
                  head   Q   his   hurt
                  'does his head hurt?'

The enclitic *li* questions the preceding word or constituent. In order to question the sentence as a whole, *li* usually follows the verb, which requires the word order V-*li*-S (39a) or V-*li*-S-O (39b):

(39a)   Rus   *zdoróv   ø   li   tý?*
                 healthy   (be)   Q   you
                 'are you well?'

(39b)   Rus   *otvétil   li   studént   na   vsé   voprósy?*
                 answer-MascSgPast   Q   student   to   all   questions
                 'did the student answer all the questions?'

Other word orders are emphatic, and question the word or phrase to the left – that is, the one to which *li* is attached:

(39c)   Rus   *studént   li   otvétil   na   vsé   voprósy?*
                 student   Q   answer-MascSgPast   to   all   questions
                 'was it the **student** who answered all the questions?'

South Slavic languages possess both sentence initial and *li* questions. Slovenian has *ali*; in the other three South Slavic languages we find *da li/dali* in sentence-initial position, using the *da* 'that, in-order-that' complementizer:

(40a)   B/C/S   *da   li   si   ga   vìdeo?*
                  Q   Q   Aux-2Sg   him   see-MascSgPastPart
                  'have you seen him?'

Dali is particularly used in indirect questions (7.3.4):

(40b)   Blg   *ne   znám,   dalí   šte   bắda   útre   svobóden*
             Neg know-1SgPres   Q   Fut   be-1SgFut   tomorrow   free
             'I don't know whether I shall be free tomorrow'

Tag questions in Slavic are of the German *nicht wahr*? (lit. 'not true?') type:

> (41a) Rus *ón   priéxal,   ne   právda   li*?
>   he   come-MascSgPast Neg truth   Q
>   'he has arrived, hasn't he?

or merely use the word for 'truth' (e.g. Pol *prawda*) with question intonation:

> (41b) Pol *przyjechał, prawda*? 'he has arrived, hasn't he?'

or the negative particle, again with rising/question intonation:

> (41c) Cz *už   bychom   se   měli   vrátit domů, ne*?
>   already be-1SgCond   Refl have-PlPast   return home   Neg
>   'I should have gone home already, shouldn't I?'

Information questions, as opposed to Yes/no questions, are formed with special question words, the "k-/j-words" (8.6.2), which function like the "wh-" words of English. They express notions like *who? what? whose? how? why? where? when? how much*?, and are preceded in the sentence only by prepositions and conjunctions. The other members of the sentence then follow in normal declarative order:

> (42a) Cz *v   kolik   hodin   přijdeš*?
>   at which   hour   come-2SgFut
>   'at what time will you come?'

> (42b) Blg *kák   ne   se   setíx   za   tová   pó-ráno*?
>   how   Neg Refl guess-1SgAor   about that   earlier
>   'how didn't I guess about that earlier?'

Note the special word order with *èto* 'this' [Neuter Singular] and the copula in Russian (43a):

> (43a) Rus *č'já*   *èto*   *kníga*?
>   whose-FemNomSg   this-NeutSg   book[Fem]-NomSg
>   'whose book is this?'

> cf. (43b) Rus *č'já*   *èta*   *kníga*?
>   whose-FemNomSg   this-FemSg   book[Fem]-NomSg
>   'whose is this book?'

7.1.3   Negation

It is usual to find the negative particle *ne* (etc.), which functions as a proclitic, immediately before the verb or auxiliary when the whole sentence is negated. When not functioning as a prefix in word formation (8.2.1, 8.3.1, 8.4.1), *ne* is usually written as a separate word, and as a proclitic is not normally stressed. But in Czech, Slovak and Sorbian the negative particle is attached to the verb (or the auxiliary, if present) and attracts to itself the word-initial stress:

(44a) Sorb 'nje-chodź-u   dźensa   na   dźěło
            Neg-go-1SgPres   today   to   work
            'I am not going to work today'

(44b) Sorb to   'njej-sym   nihdy   prajił
            that   Neg-Aux-1Sg   never   say-MascSgPast
            'I have never said that'

Individual constituents can be negated by placing the negative particle directly before them:

(45a) Cz   přijeli   autem,   ne   vlakem
            come-PlPast   car-Instr   Neg   train-Instr
            'they came by car, not train'

(45b) Cz   muž   ne   v   lepších   letech
            man   Neg   in   best   years
            'a man not in his best years'

(45c) Ukr   ne   já   ne   míh   pomítyty   vášoji   pomýlky
            Neg I   Neg   able-MascSgPast   observe   your   error
            'It wasn't I who couldn't observe your error'

(45d) Ukr   tý   ne   míh   ne   znáty
            you   Neg   able-MascSgPast   Neg   know
            'you couldn't not know'

Apparently the only language not to have this type of constituent negation is Sorbian (Šewc-Schuster, 1976: 14–15). Here the negative particle is placed with the main verb or its auxiliary, and the constituent being negated receives contrastive stress:

(46a) Sorb   wón   nas   ʜɴʏᴅᴏᴍ   spóznał   njeje
            he   us   at once   recognize-MascSgPast   Neg-Aux
            'he didn't recognize us **at once**'

cf. (46b) Rus   ón   ne   srázu   nás   uznál
            he   Neg   at once   us   recognize-MascSgPast
            'he didn't at once recognize us'

Negative pronouns, and adverbs and determiners like 'no-one', 'nowhere' and 'none', have double syntactic negation. The Slavic negative pronouns, adverbs and determiners are prefixed by the negative ni- (8.6.2), and have ne (etc.) after (though not necessarily directly after) the negated word, and directly preceding the auxiliary or main verb. It does not matter how many such negated forms there are in a sentence – there can be only one *ne* (*nje*, etc.), unless the sentence contains a semantically double negative, as in (45d):

(47a) Sorb *nichtó njeje   ničo   wědźał*
        no-one Neg-Aux-3Sg nothing know-MascSgPast
        'no-one knew anything'

(47b) Pol *nikt   mi   nic   o   żadnym   zjeździe*
        no-one I-Cl-Dat nothing about no   conference
        nie mówił
        Neg say-MascSgPast
        'no-one has told me anything about any conference'

Negated pronouns and determiners with *ni-* can allow a preposition to occur between the negative prefix and the pronoun/determiner; this is also required with indefinite pronouns/determiners with *ne*. So that while the Russian pronoun for 'no-one' is *niktó*, instrumental *nikém*, when governed by a preposition the pronoun is interrupted:

(48) Rus *ón   ni   s   kém   ne   razgovárivaet*
       he   NegPref with who-Instr Neg   talk-3SgPres
       'he talks to no-one'

'Neither ... nor' requires *ni ... ni* (*ani ... ani*), with each *ni/ani* occupying the proclitic position of a normal negative; the proclitic *ne* is still required before the verb:

(49) Ukr *ni Čípka, ni Hálja ne zhódžuvalyś*
       'neither Čipka nor Galja agreed'

Slavic, as in English, has a "negative raising" construction where the negative can be attached to the verb of the subordinate (50b) or the superordinate (50a) sentence:

(50a) Rus *já ne dúmaju, čto ón angličánin*
       'I do not think that he is an Englishman'
(50b) Rus *já dúmaju, čto ón ne angličánin*
       'I think that he is not an Englishman'

7.1.4 Imperatives

Commands in Slavic are usually expressed by the imperative. The subject pronoun is normally omitted with 1 and 2 Person imperatives, and the verb, depending on the language, may have a special imperative form (5.5.5.9):

(51a)	Blg	*četéte!*	'read'	[2PlImprfv]
		pomógnete!	'help!'	[2PlImprfv]
(51b)	Rus	*sjad'!*	'sit down!'	[2SgPrfv]
		sadís'!	'be seated!'	[2SgImprfv]
(51c)	Sorb	*dajmy!*	'let us give!'	[1PlPrfv]
		dajmoj!	'let us give!'	[1DuPrfv]

Imperatives occur in both aspects (5.4.7, 6.3), but with complex meanings, which remain controversial. Conventional aspectual meanings coexist, and in some cases are overlaid by, factors of pragmatics, interpersonal communication and politeness. Positive imperfective imperatives are variously described as more polite, more urgent and vulgar. Positive perfective imperatives may indicate completion, e.g. with telic constructions, or may also be brusque (or neutrally polite). Negative imperatives show the same preference for the imperfective as negative declarative sentences, for instance with telic constructions: an action not to be undertaken will not be completed. South Slavic, apart from Slovenian, hardly uses perfectives in this construction. Elsewhere analyses differ. Kučera (1984) finds imperfectives preferred in Czech with verbs expressing voluntary agency, and perfectives with verbs where the subject has less voluntary control over the outcome (e.g. catching a cold). Benacchio's (2002) analysis shows the Russian perfective imperative as distancing, and so more neutral as to politeness in more formal contexts, while in more informal contexts the imperfective is less distanced, and can be either positively polite or downright rude. Her association of communicative distance, pragmatics and politeness looks promising for future investigations of other Slavic languages.

Morphological imperatives can also be used pragmatically to express exhortations, injunctions and desired actions. Negative imperatives can express prohibitions, warnings, cautions and permission.

There are also several periphrastic imperative constructions, like the English *let's go!* They involve invariant particles, and occur in 3 Person imperatives, and also with other imperative forms, especially 1 Person plural/dual:

(52a)	Mac	*neka*	*vika/vikaat!*		
		ImperParticle	shout-3Sg/shout-3Pl		
		'let him/them shout!'			
(52b)	Ukr	*xáj*	*žyvút'*	*náši*	*heróji!*
		ImperParticle	live-3PlPres	our-NomPl	hero-NomPl
		'long live our heroes!'			

(52c) Pol *njech*   *zaśpiewają*!
            ImperParticle   sing-3PlFutPrfv
            'let them sing!'

In Polish, with the polite *pan/pani/państwo/panowie/panie* (11.4.2) in 2 Person
address, 3 Person imperatives serve for commands as well:

(52d) Pol *niech   pani   mi   powie*
            Particle   lady/you[FemSg]   I-Cl-Dat   tell-3SgFutPrfv
            wszystko
            everything
            'tell [Fem] me everything!'

Such periphrastic constructions express a strong desire or wish rather than a
command. The same effect is found in many exclamations, using a 2 Person
imperative of the verb with a 3 Person noun-address, often referring to the
deity:

(53a) Sorb *Pomhaj Bóh*!   'God help (us)!'

(53b) Sorb *Bóh knjez přewódz Was ...*   'May Almighty God guide you'

The three languages without special morphological forms for 1 Person plural
imperative have analytic constructions instead (Bulgarian, Macedonian, Russian):

(54a) Blg *néka   da   glédame*!
            ImperParticle   that   look-1PlPres
            'let us look!'

(54b) Mac *da/neka   vikam/vikame*!
            that/ImperParticle   shout-1Sg/shout-1Pl
            'let me/us shout!'

(54c) Rus *davájte   popróbuem*!
            give-2PlImper   try-1PlPrfv
            'let us try!'

In spite of the presence of genuine morphological imperatives, periphrastic forms
may also be available in the other languages. B/C/S, for instance, has *hàjde* [2Sg],
hàjdemo [1Pl], *hàjdete* [2Pl], parallel to the negative imperatives in *nèmōj, nèmōjmo,
nèmōjte* (64).

There are several ways in which the force of a command can be modified and
mollified, apart from merely adding "please". One method involves enclitic particles like Russian *-te, -ka*, Ukrainian *-no, -bo*, which make the command more
intimate, friendly and shared when added to the regular imperative:

(55a)	Rus	*pojdëm-te/pojdëm-ka*	'let's go!'
(55b)	Ukr	*idý-no*	'go on!'
		skažý-bo	'do tell!'

Commands can also be modified by appropriate use of intonation, or by including the pronoun subject with the imperative form of the verb. This weakens the command to the level of a strong recommendation, sometimes with overtones of a warning:

| (56) | Pol | *a ty słuchaj!* | 'you'd better listen!' |

Slavic commands can also be expressed by the infinitive (57a–b). If uttered directly to a person, however, such an order is authoritarian, brusque or rude (57c):

(57a)	Rus	*ne kurít'!*	'no smoking'
(57b)	Sorb	*začinić!*	'begin!'
		(e.g. in an examination, addressing a class of students)	
(57c)	Pol	*siadać i milczeć!*	'sit down and shut up!'

Impersonal sentences, which express commands by means of statements, often use the reflexive form of the verb (58a). The same command can be expressed by a personal sentence (58b–c) or by an apersonal one, more of a gentle request (58d):

(58a)	Pol	*tu*	*się*	*nie*	*pali!*
		here	ReflCl	Neg	smoke-3SgPres
		'no smoking here!'			

(58b)	Pol	*palenie wzbronione*	'smoking prohibited'
(58c)	Slk	*fajčit'* [Inf] *zakázane*	'smoking prohibited'
(58d)	Rus	*zdés' ne kúrjat* [3PlPres]	'no smoking please'

Conditional constructions may, as questions, convey a polite request or exhortation:

(59)	Pol	*Czy*	*byłaby*	*pani*	*taka*
		Q	be-CondFemSg	you[Fem]	so-FemSgNom
		łaskawa	*i . . .*		
		kind-FemSgNom	and		
		'Could you [Fem] be so kind as to . . .'			

In some languages the past active participle/past tense in *-l* can also be used to express command or volition (60a–d); atypically in Russian it may express a 1 Person imperative (60e):

(60a)   Blg   *ubíl*   *te*   *Góspod!*
              kill-MascSgPart   you-AccSg   God
              'may God strike you dead!'

(60b)   B/C/S   *pròklet*   *bȉo!*
                damn-MascSgPart   be-MascSgPart
                'be damned!'

(60c)   B/C/S   *žívela*   *nȁša*   *dòmovina!*
                live-FemSgPart   our-FemSgNom   country[Fem]-SgNom
                'long live our country!'

(60d)   Pol   *poszedł*   *mi*   *stąd!*
              go-MascSgPast   I-Cl-DatSg   from-here
              'go away!'

(60e)   Rus   *poéxali!*
              go-PlPastPrfv
              'let's go!'

Various particles may add command elements to declarative sentences, turning them into a kind of optative (5.4.9):

(61a)   Cz   *at'*   *se*   *tam*   *pěkně chováš*
             ImperParticle   ReflCl   there   well   behave-2SgPres
             'behave yourself well there'

(61b)   Cz   *až*   *se*   *děje,*   *co*   *děje*
             ImperParticle   ReflCl   do   what   do
             'whatever will be, will be'

Negative imperatives deserve special mention. The simplest means of forming them is to add the negative particle to the sentence in the normal way (7.1.3). In Czech, Slovak and Sorbian the particle is attached to the verb:

(62a)   Sorb   *njekur!*   'don't smoke!'

(62b)   Ukr   *xáj/nexáj prýjde!*   'let him come!'

(62c)   Ukr   *xáj/nexáj ne prýdje*   'let him not come!'

The negative imperative with the negative particle is available in all Slavic languages. In Bulgarian, Macedonian and B/C/S, however, there is a parallel form derived etymologically from the verb 'be able' or 'do' with the infinitive. In Bulgarian this formation is one of the few cases where the (vestigial) infinitive

(63a–b) is found (Scatton, 1993: 226): the alternative with *da* + Sentence (63c) is also available and is preferred. The 'be able/do' negative imperatives are found in the 2 Person in Bulgarian and Macedonian (63), and in the 1 Person plural as well in B/C/S (64):

(63a)	Blg	*nedéj se smé*	'don't laugh'	[Sg]
(63b)	Blg	*nedéjte kázva*	'don't say'	[Pl]
(63c)	Blg	*nedéj da glédaš*	'don't look'	[Sg]
(64a)	B/C/S	*nèmōjmo písati*	'let's not write!'	
(64b)	B/C/S	*nèmōjte písati/nèmōjte da pîšēte*	'don't write!'	[Pl]

The imperative forms of the verb do not always have the communicative force of a command. Imperative forms may be used like the historic present to indicate sudden or dramatic action:

(65a) Mac *tamo   imaše   mnogu   svet   pred*
there   have-3SgAor much   people before
vratata: edni   vlezi,   drugi   izlezi
doors-Def some-Pl   enter-2SgImper others exit-2SgImper
'there, there were many people at the door: some were going in, others were coming out' (de Bray, 1980b: 205)

Russian has a special construction with two imperatives, meaning something like 'went and . . .':

(65b) Rus *a   sobáka voz′mí   da   i   prýgni . . .*
and dog   take-2SgImper Particle and jump-2SgImper
'and the dog went and jumped . . .'

Imperative forms can also express conditions, even with 1 Person subjects (66a); they can also express irony (66b):

(66a) Ukr *prýjdy   já   sjudý   včásno,   ničóho*
come-1SgFutPrfv I-Nom here   in-time   nothing-Gen
b   tóho   ne   buló
Cond this-Gen Neg   by-NeutSgPast
'If I had come here in time, nothing of this would have happened'

(66b) Rus *ždí   ot   takógo   pómoščí!*
expect-2SgImper from such-GenSg help-Gen
'It's useless to expect help from a man like him'

7.1.5   Passives

The passive in Slavic is expressed in two principal ways: a morphological passive, and a reflexive.

The formation of the morphological passive is described in 5.4.8 and 5.5.5.10. Since the imperfective passive past participle is so little used, the morphological passive is uncommon in the present tense, when the reflexive construction is normal (below). However, the morphological passive is regularly found in both the past and the future, especially with the perfective passive participle. The agent is less often expressed in this construction than in English:

(67)   Blg   *vratáta   e   otvórena   ot   lékarjat*
              gate-Pl-Def Aux-3Sg open-NeutPlPastPart by doctor-Def
              'the gate has been opened by the doctor'

The morphological passive is more written than spoken. It is more to be found in formal, scientific and technical prose.

The reflexive, on the other hand, is more like the middle voice in Greek. It is most used in the present tense to express habitual or imperfective passives:

(68a) Rus   *ètot*   *žurnál*
               this-NomSgMasc   journal[Masc]-NomSg
               čitáetsja   *vsémi*
               read-3SgPresRefl   all-InstrPl
               'this journal is read by everyone'

(68b) Slk   *reči   sa   hovoria   a   chlieb*
               speech-Pl ReflCl   speak-3PlPres and   bread-Sg
               sa   je
               ReflCl   eat-3SgPres
               'speeches are spoken and bread is eaten' (saying)

Two other constructions are used in Slavic as intermediate steps between activity and passivity, and as a means of reducing the explicit agentiveness of actions. One is the apersonal construction (7.3.3), where the generalized subject is not lexically expressed:

(69)   Blg   *túk   prodávat   zelenčúk*
              here   sell-3PlPres   vegetable
              'here they sell vegetables/here vegetables are sold'

The second pseudo-passive, which is not evenly distributed across Slavic, involves the past passive participle of both transitive and intransitive verbs and the impersonal construction:

(70) Blg *túk e xódeno*
        here Aux-3Sg walk-NeutSgPastPart
        'someone has walked here' (lit. 'here it has been walked')

The Slavic passive, whether the morphological passive or the reflexive, is less common than the passive construction in a language like English. One of the key roles of the passive in English is to provide a way of inverting the new/old information distribution in the sentence (7.5). In Slavic a natural way to do this is to use OVS word order, particularly when the agent is expressed.

7.1.6 Conditionals

The conditional (5.5.5.7) is formed with the *l*-participle of either aspect (in Bulgarian, the aorist participle) plus either an invariant particle, usually enclitic (71a), or the inflected conditional of the auxiliary 'be', which may be either clitic (71b–c) or non-clitic (71d):

(71a) Rus *já by ležál*
         I CondCl lie-MascSgPast
         'I [Masc] would lie'

(71b) Pol *poczeka-ł-by-m*
         wait-MascSg-CondCl-1Sg
         'I [Masc] would wait'

(71c) Cz *žil bych*
        live-MascSgPast be-CondCl-1Sg
        'I [Masc] would live'

(71d) Blg *bíx napisál*
         be-Cond-1Sg write-MascSgPart
         'I [Masc] would write'

The past conditional, a rather literary tense not found in Russian and Belarusian, belongs properly with the more complex constructions treated below under 7.2. It is formed with the *l*-participle and the past conditional of the auxiliary 'be'. Once again, the condition can be expressed by an invariant particle (72a), or a variant clitic (72b) or non-clitic (72c) construction:

(72a) Slk *byl bi som robil*
         be-MascPastPart Cond Aux-1Sg do-MascPastPart
         'I [Masc] would have done'

(72b)	Pol	*był-bym* be-MascSgPast-CondCl-1Sg	*zrobił* do-MascSgPast
	or:	*zrobił-bym* do-MascSgPast-CondCl-1Sg	*był* be-MascSgPast
		'I [Masc] would have done'	

(72c)	Sorb	*bych* be-1SgCond	*był* be-MascSgPast	*zdźěłał* do-MascSgPast
		'I [Masc] would have done'		

Bulgarian and Macedonian have special forms for this tense. Bulgarian has either the imperfect of the auxiliary *šta* + *da* + Present/Perfective Present (72d), or a new form which adds imperfect endings to the aorist (perfective) stem (72e; both these forms also express the "future in the past": 5.5.5.5):

(72d)	Blg	*štjáx* Aux1SgImperf	*da* that	*pătúvam* go-1SgPres
		'I would have gone'		

(72e)	Blg	*pročitáše* read-2SgImperf-PrfvStem
		'you would have read'

In Macedonian the usual form is *ḱe* + Imperfect (72f), though Macedonian also has a special form, constructed like that of Bulgarian (72e), except that the future particle *ḱe* is retained (72g):

(72f)	Mac	*da* Q	*me* I-Acc	*sakaš,* love-2SgImperf	*ne* Neg	*ḱe* Fut	*imaš* have-2SgImperf	*strav* fear
		'If you loved me you wouldn't be afraid'						

(72g)	Mac	*ḱe* Fut	*izbegaše* run-out-2SgImperf-PrfvStem
		'he would have run out'		

7.1.7   Possession

Slavic is not as prone to expressing possession explicitly as English is. For this reason body parts, relatives and other inalienable possessions, as well as obvious personal possessions, are often specified without an explicit possessive unless possession is contrastively emphasised or specifically assigned to someone else (7.3.1). When it is explicitly expressed, the possessive expression can also be a dative personal pronoun, which may also indicate involuntary involvement, or the "dative of the interested person":

(73) Rus *ón   mné   ukrál   čemodán*
           he   I-Dat stole-MascSg   trunk
           'he stole my trunk'

7.2 More complex constructions

The simple sentence can be expanded by coordination (the "compound" sentence, 7.2.1) or subordination (the "complex" sentence, 7.2.2). Coordination is marked by conjunctions like 'and', 'or' and 'but', and the coordinated sentences are of equal grammatical status – neither dominates the other:

(74) Bel [*Na šýbax snéh ljažýc' iskrýstym púxam*], *a* [*ŭ xáce páxne*
                                                        čýsty mëd]
           '[On the roofs snow is lying like a sparkling powder], and
           [in the hut is the smell of fresh honey]'

The complex sentence consists of a superordinate sentence and a subordinate sentence, which may be introduced by a conjunction/complementizer:

(75a) Bel [*mné dúmalasja*], *čto* [*Vasíl' vernécca dadómu*]
            '[I thought] that [Vasil' would return home]'

(75b) Rus [*ón ne znál*], [*slúšaet* (*li*) *egó Ígor' íli nét*]
            (no complementizer = more colloquial; *li* = more literary)
            '[he didn't know] (whether) [Igor was listening to him or not]'

Or the subordinate sentence may contain infinitives and gerunds which do not have an expressed subject:

(75c) Bel *Symón sabráŭsja iscí sékčy dróvy*
            'Simon was getting ready to go and cut some wood'

(75d) Bel *Daŭnó ne býŭšy u ródnaj vëscy, Vasíl' ubáčyŭ tám šmát peramén*
            'not having been in his native village for a long time, Vasil'
            noticed there a lot of changes'

7.2.1 Coordinate constructions

Coordinating constructions are conventionally divided into conjunction and disjunction.

7.2.1.1   Conjunction

Conjoined constructions in Slavic, as in English, may be signalled by the conjunction 'and', or by the juxtaposition of the conjoined constituents. Only the "logical" *and* allows the inversion of the two components (76a):

(76a)   Cz   *vy   odjedete,   a   my zůstaneme*
'you will leave, and we shall stay'

(76b)   Cz   *řekl, že se brzo vrátí, (a) odešel*
'he said that he would come back quickly, (and) left' (i.e. 'and then')

(76c)   Cz   *zlomil se nohu, a nemůže chodit*
'he broke his leg, and cannot walk' (i.e. 'and therefore')

Slavic tends to omit the coordinating conjunction more often than English, including the last 'and' in a series of conjuncts:

(76d)   Rus   *šël rédkij snég, fonarí ne goréli, tëmnaja úlica bylá perečérčena polosámi svéta iz ókon*
'a light snow was falling, the street lights were not on, (and) the dark street was criss-crossed by strips of light from the windows'

Doublet conjunctions of the 'both ... and' and 'neither ... nor' types place the first conjunction before the first of the conjoined constituents:

(77a)   Blg   *bilí*   *sme*   *záedno*   *i*   *v*   *štástie,*
be-PlPastPart   Aux-1Pl   together   both   in   happiness
i   *v*   *bedá*
and   in   misfortune
'we were together both in happiness, and in misfortune'

(77b)   Bel   *ni*   *mésjac-a,*   *ni*   *zórak*   *ne*   *byló*
neither   moon-GenSg   nor   star-GenPl   Neg   be-NeutSgPast
vidác'   *za*   *hustými*   *xmárami*
see-Inf   behind   thick-InstrPl   cloud-InstrPl
'neither the moon nor the stars was visible behind the thick clouds'

7.2.1.2   Adversative conjunction and disjunction

These types are signalled by a conjunction:

(78)   Rus   *Pëtr, Máša ili Irína = Pëtr ili Máša ili Irína*
'Peter, Masha or Irina = Peter or Masha or Irina'

The typical adversative conjunction is 'but', whether as a word or as a clitic:

(79a) Blg   *ne   sámo   tój,   no   i   áz*
               Neg only he but also I
               'not only he, but I also'

(79b) Rus   *já   uezžáju,   ón   že   ostaëtsja*
               I-Nom leave-1SgPres he however-Encl remain-3SgPres
               'I am leaving but he is staying'

East Slavic *a* is used when the second element is not totally opposed to the first, but simply contrasted:

(80a) Bel   *[nékal'ki dzën býŭ dóždž]*, *a* *[sënnja svécic' sónca]*
               '[for several days there was rain], and/but [today the sun is shining]'

while Russian *no* 'but' implies a stronger opposition of the conjuncts (e.g. contrary to expectations):

(80b) Rus   *[oní býli tám]*, *no* *[ón íx ne vídel]*
               '[they were there], but [he didn't see them]'

In Czech, Slovak and Sorbian, however, *a* has the meaning of both East Slavic *i* (Ukr *i, ta*) 'and' and *a* 'and/but':

(81)   Cz   *[je listopad]*, *a* *[je teplo jak na jaře]*
               '[it is November], and/but [it is warm as in the spring]'

Other types include the temporal disjunctive 'now ... now':

(82)   Blg   *tu* *[pláče]*, *tu* *[se smée]*
               'now [he weeps], now [he laughs]'

the limiting 'only':

(83)   Slk   *[všetci sa zasmiali]*, *iba* *[slečna sa odvrátila]*
               '[all laughed], only [the girl turned away]'

the concessive 'though, although':

(84)   Pol   *[było ciemno]*, *choć* *[świec paliło się dużo]*
               '[it was dark] although [many candles were burning]'

and the explanatory 'that is':

>   (85)   Rus   [*krýši zdés' plóskie*], *tó est'* [*domá postróeny po-aziátski*]
>   '[the roofs here are flat], that is, [the houses are built in the Asian
>   fashion]'

as well as logical disjunctions 'or' and 'either ... or':

>   (86)   B/C/S   *ìli* [*u sèlu*] *ìli* [*u grâdu*] 'either [in the village] or [in the city]'

7.2.2   Subordinate constructions

Slavic has two main types of subordinate constructions: complements and relatives. In complements the subordinate sentence is introduced by a word or phrase, usually followed by a complementizer:

>   (87a)   Slk   [*no vidím*], *že* [*už davno myslí na to*]
>   '[but I see] that [he has already been thinking about that for a
>   long time]'

>   (87b)   Cz   [*citíl*], *jak* [*ho někdo zatahal ze-zadu za rukáv*]
>   ('[he felt] how [someone ...]')
>   'he felt someone pulling him from behind by the sleeve'

Infinitive complements lack both the complementizer and the subject of the subordinate sentence:

>   (88a)   Rus   *mý ubedíli egó pojtí k vračú*
>   'we persuaded him to go to the doctor'

>   cf. (88b)   Rus   *mý*   *ubedíli*   *egó*   *v*   *tóm,*   *čtóby*
>   we   persuade-PlPrfv   he-Acc   Prep   it-Loc   in-order-that
>   *ón*   *pošël*   *k*   *vračú*
>   he   go-MascSgPrfv   to   doctor
>   'we persuaded him (of it that he [should]) go to the doctor'

Relative clauses are attached to a nominal in the main clause (except for a small class of "free" relatives – see below). Traditional grammars recognize only a small number of relative types, based on the k-/j- (wh-) words like 'who', 'which', 'whose' (5.5.5.2, 8.6.2). A relative pronoun introduces the subordinate clause:

>   (89)   Slk   *tento Bartoš, ktorý/čo*   *pracuje*   *na dvore, . . .*
>   that   Bartoš who-MascNomSg/that work-3Sg in yard-LocSg
>   'that Bartoš who is working in the yard . . .'

Traditional Slavic grammars add a third class of subordinate sentences, covering adverbial subordination for place, time, manner and so on:

(90a) Slk *spíš,*   *kedy*   *chceš*
            sleep-2SgPres   when   want-2SgPres
            'you sleep when you want'

(90b) Mac *toj* *me*   *praša,* *kolku*   *godini* *imam*
             he   me-Acc asked   how many years   have-1SgPres
            'he asked me how old I was'

as well as cause, goal, comparison, condition, concession:

(91) Slk *ujst'*   *som*   *musela*   *od*   *neho,*
            go-away-Inf   Aux-1Sg   must-FemSgPast   from   he-Gen
            aby   *nevidel*   *moje*   *slzy*
            in-order-that   Neg-see-MascSgPast   my-AccPl   tear-AccPl
            'I [Fem] had to leave him so that he would not see my tears'

The structure of Slavic conjunctions shows how these "inter-sentence" subordinations are connected to relatives. In (92) the conjunction *potomú čto* 'because' is morphologically decomposable into "for it that", a paraphrase more clearly shown in *iz-za togó, čto* ... "because of it, that ...":

(92) Rus *ón* *perestál*   *kurít',*
             he   stop-MascSgPast   smoke-Inf
            potomú čto (iz-za togó, čto)   *boítsja*   *ráka*
            because   fear-3SgPres   cancer-GenSg
            'he has stopped smoking because he is afraid of cancer'

For this reason we shall discuss such types of subordination under the general heading of relatives. Adverbs in particular have often been treated in this way by Slavic grammars in the past: words like 'when' are often classed with "pronouns" rather than as adverbs or conjunctions.

7.2.2.1 *Infinitival constructions*
Slavic grammars do not usually treat infinitival constructions as complex sentences, but describe them as "adjunction" (Rus *primykánie*) to the governing word or expression. The similarity of infinitives to both sentence-objects and subordinate sentences is seen in paraphrases like:

(93a) Sorb *kazaše*   *młodymaj*   *čiše*   *dychać*
              order-3SgAor   young-DatDu   quieter-Adv   breathe-Inf
              'he ordered the young people [Du] to breathe more quietly'

(93b) Sorb *kazaše młodymaj* *ćiche*   *dychanje*
              (...)   quiet-NeutSgAcc breathing[Neut]SgAcc
              'he ordered the young people to breathe quietly'

(93c) Sorb *kazaše młodymaj* *zo*   *byštaj*   *ćiše*
              (...)   that Aux-Cond-3Du   quieter-Adv
              dychałoj
              breathe-DuPastPart
              'he ordered the young people to breathe more quietly'

Infinitival constructions are limited by morphological availability: Macedonian has no infinitives, and Bulgarian has only a vestigial infinitive which may be used after a negative command (94a). This vestigial infinitive can also be used with the uncommon inflected form of the usually invariant future auxiliary, in *šta, šteš* ... (5.5.5.5) – this form is now literary and obsolescent (94b); and with the verbs 'dare' and 'be able' (94c):

(94a) Blg *nedéjte píta*!   'don't ask!'

(94b) Blg *vídja šteš*   'you [2 Sg] will see'

(94c) Blg *ne*   *sméja/móga*   *naprávi* *tová*
            Neg   dare-1SgPres/be-able-1SgPres do-Inf   that
            'I don't dare to/can't do that'

But we also find the alternative construction of a subordinate clause introduced by *da*:

(95a) Blg *nedéjte*   *da*   *se*   *sărdite*!
            NegImper   that   ReflCl   be-angry-2Pl
            'don't be angry!'

(95b) Blg *ne sméja da naprávja tová*   'I don't dare do that'

Bulgarian, Macedonian and Serbian, especially in its eastern dialects, regularly show *da* + Sentence constructions where the other Slavic languages have infinitives.

Infinitives can occur like a noun phrase as the subject of a simple sentence (10). And infinitives can occur in impersonal sentences (7.3.3) expressing commands, requests, exclamations and so on. Their use as complements requires them to depend on a predicate expression like a verb, adjective, noun, prepositional phrase, predicative impersonal and even 'be'. The imputed subject of the infinitive construction is the same as that of the dominating word or expression, except when the dominating verb governs an object as well as the infinitive:

(96a) Cz *začal*   *padat*   *sníh*
           began-MascSgPast fall-Inf snow[Masc]-NomSg
           'snow began to fall'

(96b) Sorb *mi*   *chce*   *so*   *spać*
             I-Cl-DatSg   want-3SgImpers   self-Cl-Acc   sleep-Inf
             'I feel like sleeping'

(96c) Sorb *dowolich*   *jemu*   *wotpočnyć*
             allow-1SgAor   he-DatSg   rest-Inf
             'I let him rest'

If a given language has a special predicative (short-form) adjective, then this is the form which is preferred with a following infinitive:

(97a) Rus *já*   **soglásen**   *zaplatíť*
            I-Nom   agreeable-MascSg   pay-Inf
            'I agree to pay'

(97b) Ukr *já*   *bíľ še* *ničóho*   *ne*   **hóden**
            I-Nom more   nothing-GenSg   neg   worthy/able-MascSg
            slúxaty
            listen-Inf
            'I am not capable of listening to anything more'

Nouns may occur as predicates with 'be', or in Verb + Noun + Infinitive constructions:

(98) Ukr *vý*   *májete*   *námir*   *prodáty avtomobíľ*?
           you-Pl   have-2Pl   intention-AccSg   sell-Inf car[Masc]-AccSg
           '(do) you have any intention of selling the car?'

Prepositional phrases often have parallels with verbs when followed by an infinitive:

(99) Pol *on*   *nie*   *jest*   *w*   *stanie*
           he-NomSg   Neg   be-3SgPres   in   condition
           (*nie może*)   *przyjechać*   *dzisiaj*
           (Neg be-able-3SgPres)   come-Inf   today
           'he isn't in a fit state to (he can't) come today'

Predicative impersonals are particularly common with infinitives:

(100a) Slk *nebolo*   *mi*   **možno**   *odíst'*
             Neg-be-NeutSgPast   I-Cl-Dat   possible-NeutSg   leave-Inf
             'it wasn't possible for me to leave'

(100b)   Cz   *není*   **třeba**   *se*   *obávat*
         Neg-be-3Sg   necessary   ReflCl   fear-Inf
         'there is no need to be afraid'

And 'be' is found, though more marginally, in some infinitival constructions:

(101)   Slk   *bolo*   *badat',*   *že*   *sa*   *premenila*
         be-NeutSgPast   see-Inf   that   ReflCl   change-FemSgPast
         'it could be seen that she had changed'

The nouns which can govern infinitives are in most instances either derived from verbs (Ukr *námir* 'intention' (98)), or adjectives, or are semantically related to them:

(102a)   Rus   *sklónnosť zabluždáťsja*   'tendency to get lost/go astray'

(102b)   Pol   *szansa wygrać*   'a chance to win'

There are also some restricted Agent + Infinitive constructions, with a small and closed list of nouns (103a), though a noun phrase or prepositional phrase after a nominal is more usual (103b):

(103a)   Rus   *máster   igráť*   *na*   *skrípke*
          master   play-Inf   on   violin-LocSg
          'a master at playing on the violin'

(103b)   Rus   *specialíst po obščéstvennym naúkam*
          'a specialist in the social sciences'

A few languages also show a dialectal or non-standard Common noun + Infinitive, where the infinitive carries the meaning of 'goal'. The construction in (104b) is more correct and more common:

(104a)   Rus   *gvózdik   véšať*   *paľtó*
          nail   hang-Inf   coat
          'a nail to hang a coat on'

(104b)   Rus   *gvózdik   dlja   véšanija*   *paľtó*
          (...)   for   hanging-GenSg   (...)
          'a nail for hanging a coat (on)'

Goal-infinitive expressions show several typically Slavic properties. Verbs of motion with tautosubject infinitives (infinitives with the same subject as the dominating word or expression) may optionally include the 'in-order-that' complementizer (105a). In East and West Slavic this complementizer is otherwise used with heterosubject structures, where the subordinate clause has a different subject from that of the dominating word. It often occurs as an alternative to the infinitive with subordinate-goal clauses (105b–c), whereas other dominating verbs expressing facts rather than wishes or orders show the 'that' complementizer (105d):

(105a)   Rus   *já prišël (, čtóby) kopáť v sadú*
                   'I came (in order) to dig in the garden'

(105b)   Rus   *já poprosíl egó prijtí*
                   'I asked him to come'

(105c)   Rus   *já poprosíl egó, čtóby prišël*
                   'I asked him to (that he might) come'

(105d)   Rus   *já poobeščál, čto mý pozvoním pósle p'ésy*
                   'I promised that we would ring after the play'

(105e)   Rus   *já poobeščál pozvoníť pósle p'ésy*
                   'I promised to ring after the play'

Subordinate goal clauses in Czech and Slovenian also show an archaic supine (5.5.5.11) after verbs of motion (see (15c–d) above).

Heterosubject infinitives can have a passive reading (106a). This passive reading, however, depends on the individual construction, as can be seen from the elliptical structure of (106b), where the infinitive structure is semantically active rather than passive:

(106a)   Rus   *já*   *ótdal*   *časý*   *(íx)*   *počiníť*
                   I-Nom   give_up-MascSgPast   watch-Acc   (it-Acc)   fix-Inf
                   'I handed (it) over my watch to be fixed'

(106b)   Rus   *já*   *dál*   *emú*   *zakuríť*
                   I-Nom   give-MascSgPast   he-Dat   begin_to_smoke-Inf
                   'I gave him a light'

Sorbian and Slovak possess a Latin-type Accusative + Infinitive construction with verbs of perception, where other Slavic languages use the 'as' Complementizer + Sentence, an alternative also available in Sorbian and Slovak:

(107a)   Sorb   *widźach*   *ju*   *na*   *klawěrje*   *hrać*
                   see-1SgAor   she-Acc   on   piano-LocSg   play-Inf
                   'I saw her playing (on) the piano'

(107b)   Sorb   *widźach*   *ju,*   *kak*   *na*   *klawěrje*   *hrje*
                   see-1SgAor   she-Acc   as   on   piano-LocSg   play-3SgPres
                   'I saw her playing (on) the piano'

In one important area, however, Slavic is less permissive than English with infinitives, since verbs of volition may not take heterosubject infinitives, and must use the 'in-order-that' complementizer:

(108)   Pol   *ja*   *chcę,*   *żeby*   *poszedł*
             I-Nom   want-1SgPres   in-order-that   go-MascSgPast
             'I want him to go' (**ja chcę jego pójść*)

The 'in-order-that' complementizer is also important in distinguishing Serbian and Croatian. There is virtually free variation between infinitives and *da* + Sentence with many verbs in B/C/S, including cases of infinitives with the same imputed subject as the subject of the main clause (unlike West and East Slavic):

(109a) B/C/S *pòčex*   *čìtati*   */da*   *čìtām*
                begin-1SgAor   read-Inf   /in-order-that   read-1SgPres
                'I began to read'

(109b) B/C/S *ne mògu náći/da nâdjēm*   'I can't find (it)'

(109c) B/C/S *ȁko smȉjēm pítati/da pítām*   'if I dare to ask'

But there is an increasing tendency to use *da* as one nears the Bulgarian frontier in the south and east (the Torlak dialects: 10.4.2), while the infinitive prevails much more in Croatia. There is consequently a long and gradual dialect chain of usage from west (biased toward the Infinitive) to east (biased toward *da* + Sentence).

7.2.2.2   *Complements*

True Slavic complements involve four types of complementizer: 'that', 'as', 'in-order-that' and 'question' (for indirect questions, see 7.3.4). The complementizer introduces the subordinate sentence, and is itself introduced by a word or phrase. It is this word or phrase which governs the choice of complementizer, and the type of subordinate sentence:

(110a) Rus   *koróľ*   *slýšal,*   *čto   priéxali*
              king[Masc]-NomSg   hear-MascSgPast   that   arrive-PlPastPrfv
              'the king heard that they had arrived'

(110b) Rus   *koróľ*   *slýšal,*   *kak*
              king[Masc]-NomSg   hear-MascSgPast   as
              priezžáli
              arrive-PlPastImprfv
              'the king heard them arriving'

(110c) Rus *koról'*   *prikazál,*   *čtóby*
             king[Masc]-NomSg   order-MascSgPast   in-order-that
             priéxali
             arrive-PlPastPrfv
             'the king ordered that they arrive/come (... them to come)'

(110d) Rus *koról'*   *sprosíl,*   *priéxali*
             king[Masc]-NomSg   ask-MascSgPast   come-PlPastPrfv
             li   oní
             Q   they-Nom
             'the king asked whether they had arrived'

The 'that' complementizer (110a) follows expressions of saying, believing, knowing, and implies a non-physical sensation/perception, as of experiencing or perceiving a fact or result. The 'as' complementizer (110b) follows expressions of sensation and perception (of a process), making the whole construction similar to the English construction with *-ing*. The 'in-order-that' complementizer (110c) follows expressions of ordering, wishing, doubting, fearing, and some expressions of obligation and necessity. It uses the past of the verb plus the hypothetical/conditional *-by*-element (5.5.5.7), which may also express person:

(111a) Cz *chtěl*   *by-ch,*   *aby*   *se*
             want-MascSgPast   Aux-1SgCond   in-order-that-3Sg   ReflCl
             ti   *u   nás*   *líbilo*
             you-Cl-DatSg   at   we-Gen   please-NeutSgPast
             'I would like you to enjoy it here with us'

(111b) Cz *bál*   *se,*   *aby-ch*   *se*
             fear-MascSgPast   ReflCl   in-order-that-1Sg   ReflCl
             o   tom   *někdo*   *nedověděl*
             about   that-LocSg   someone-Nom   Neg-know-MascSgPast
             'he was afraid that someone would find out about it'

(111c) Cz *je*   *třeba,*   *aby-s*   *to*
             be-3SgPres   necessary   in-order-that-2Sg   it-NeutSg
             viděl
             see-MascSgPast
             'it is necessary that you see it'

The use and structure of subordinate sentence-types with Slavic complements is not unlike English, though Slavic has fewer types. The 'that' type is often preceded by the pronoun *to*, with or without a preposition, especially when the expression introducing the subordinate clause is not transitive (112a). This *to* also occurs when sentences function as the subject of another sentence (112b):

(112a) Cz *nehledě na*   *to,*   *že*   *měl*   *moc*
        in-spite-of   it-AccSg   that   have-MascSgPast   much
        práce,   *musel*   *tam*   *jít*
        work-GenSg   must-MascSgPast   there   go-Inf
        'in spite of the fact that he had a lot of work, he had to go there'

(112b) Rus *tó,*   *čto*   *ón*   *uméet*   *govorít'*
        it-NeutNomSg   that   he-Nom   know-3SgPres   speak-Inf
        po-kitájski,   *óčen'*   *vážno*
        in-Chinese   very   important-NeutSg
        'the fact that he can speak Chinese is very important'

The 'in-order-that' type is very common in Bulgarian and Macedonian, and in the south-east dialects of Serbian, where the infinitive is missing, and the whole range of infinitive expressions is transferred to this construction, whatever the subject; the 'in-order-that' complementizer is *da*:

(113) Mac *sednav*   *da*   *si*   *počinam*
        sit-1SgAor   in-order-that   self-Dat   rest-1SgPres
        'I sat down to rest'

As we saw in 7.2.2, in languages with an infinitive the subordinate sentence cannot have a subject identical to the subject of the main sentence, as in English:

(114a) Rus *já prikazál egó ujtí*   'I ordered him to leave'

(114b) Rus *já prikazál, čtóby ón ušël*   'I ordered that he leave'

(114c) Rus **já xočú, čtóby já prišël*   '*I want that I come'

(114d) Rus *já xočú prijtí*   'I want to come'

The 'in-order-that' complementizer may be followed by an infinitive if the subject of the infinitive is the same as the subject of the main sentence. Some verbs of motion can even dispense with the complementizer:

(115) Pol *Janek przyszedł (, żeby) próbować nasze wina*
        'Janek came (in order) to try [Inf] our wines'

But some verbs do not occur with the infinitive. In Sorbian there is quite a different relation of infinitival constructions to complementizer constructions, since Sorbian has a special Accusative + Infinitive (above). But the verbs *stać* 'stand', *ležeć* 'lie', *sedźeć* 'sit', *spać* 'sleep', and *tčeć* 'be, be located' occur with a present gerund, rather like the English *-ing* (116a). In such instances the other Slavic languages would have either an 'as' or a temporal complementizer (116b) or a participial construction (116c). This use of a gerund modifying something other than the subject of the sentence is unusual in Slavic (7.3.6):

(116a) Sorb woni   su   nas   widźeli   w   busu
             they-Nom Aux-3Pl we-Acc   see-PlPast in   bus
             sedźo
             sit-PresGer
             'they saw us sitting in the bus'

(116b) Rus   oní   vídeli   nás,   kak/kogdá mý
             they-Nom see-PlPast we-Acc as/when   we-Nom
             sidéli   v   avtóbuse
             sit-PlPast in   bus
             'they saw us as we sat in the bus'

(116c) Rus   oní vídeli nás, sidjáščix   v avtóbuse
             (...)   sit-AccPl-PresPartAct (...)
             'they saw us sitting in the bus'

7.2.2.3 Relative clauses

Relative clauses in Slavic work on the same general principle as in English. A relative pronoun, which concords in number and gender with the nominal to which it refers, introduces a subordinate clause. Its case is controlled by its syntactic role in the relative clause:

(117a) Ukr   šáfa,   v   jakíj   ležát'
             cupboard[Fem]-NomSg   in   which-FemLocSg   lie-3PlPres
             knýžky
             books-NomPl
             'the cupboard in which the books are lying'

(117b) Sorb kupich   knihu,   kotruž   na
             buy-1SgAorist   book[Fem]-AccSg   which-FemAccSg   at
             wustajency   widźach
             exhibition-LocSg   see-1SgAor
             'I bought the book that I saw at the exhibition'

Word order in subordinate clauses is dictated by the syntactic role of the relative pronoun. This pronoun is usually in first position in the relative clause, particularly when it is either subject or object:

(118a)   Ukr   *ljudýna,*   *jaká/ščo*
         person[Fem]-NomSg   who-FemNomSg/that-Inv
         pryxódyla   *včóra*
         come-FemStPast   yesterday
         'the person who came yesterday'

(118b)   Blg   *velikolépnata*   *panoráma,*   *što*   *predstávja*
         magnificent-FemDef   panorama   which   present-3SgPres
         dolínata
         valley-[Fem]-Def
         'the magnificent view which the valley presents'

As a genitive the relative pronoun may come first, as is regularly the case in Polish (119a) (and in Czech (121)):

(119a)   Pol   *pani,*   *której*   *mąż*
         lady[Fem]-NomSg   who-FemGenSg   husband[Masc]-NomSg
         wyjechał   *niedawno*
         leave-MascSgPast   recently
         'the lady whose husband left recently'

Or it may follow the governing noun phrase, as is usual in the other languages:

(119b)   Rus   *mužčína,*   *žená*   *kotórogo*
         man[Masc]-NomSg   wife[Fem]-NomSg   who-MascSgGen
         uéxala   *nedávno*
         leave-FemSgPast   recently
         'the man whose wife left recently'

The only two word-classes which regularly and obligatorily precede the relative pronouns are prepositions and conjunctions:

(120a)   Blg   *sreštnáx*   *poznáti,*   *s*   *koíto*   *otdávna*   *ne*
         meet-1SgAor   friend-Pl   with   who-PlDef   long   Neg
         săm   *se*   *víždal*
         Aux-1Sg   ReflCl   see-MascSgPastPart
         'I met some friends that I hadn't seen for a long time'

(120b)   Sorb   *njeznaju*   *nikoho,*   *pola   kohož*
         Neg-know-1SgPres   no-one-GenSg   chez   who-GenSg
         bych   *so*   *móhła*   *schować*
         Aux-1SgCond   ReflCl   able-FemSgPastPart   hide-Inf
         'I know no one at whose home I could hide'

The relative pronoun itself is usually of the k-/j- type, a form which is only used for the relative and certain question structures. Some languages, however, have special forms for the possessive relative pronoun. Czech has a literary form *jenž*, originally from the pronoun 'he' plus the particle *že*. This word also provides possessive relative forms, which follow prepositions in spite of their being morphologically genitive in form (a type of modifier which is normally post-posed in Slavic):

(121a) Cz *spisovatel,*   *jehož*   *dílo*
            author[Masc]-NomSg   whose[MascSg]   work[Neut]-AccSg
            čteme
            read-1PlPres
            'the author whose work we are reading'

(121b) Cz *univerzita,*   *jejíž*   *fakulta ...*
            university[Fem]-NomSg   whose[FemSg]   faculty ...
            'the university whose faculty ...'

It is also the possessive which shows variation in B/C/S, Bulgarian and Macedonian, and also in literary Russian, where the interrogative 'whose?' form is available for use as a relative. Note that in Bulgarian the definite article–suffix *-to* converts the interrogative into a relative; Macedonian adds *-što*:

(122a) B/C/S *tô*   *je*   *Pètar,*   *čijā*
               this-NeutSgNom   be-3SgPres   Peter   whose-FemSgNom
               je   *sèstra*   *râdnīca*
               Aux-3SgPres   sister[Fem]-NomSg   worker[Fem]NomSg
               'that is Peter, whose sister is a worker'

(122b) Blg *éto*   *e*   *lékar,*   *čijto*
             this-NeutSg   be-3SgPres   doctor   whose[Masc]-Sg
             sín   *e*   *pisátel*
             son[Masc]-Sg   be-3SgPres   writer[Masc]-Sg
             'this is the doctor whose son is a writer'

(122c) Mac *pisatelot*   *čiišto*   *pesni*   *peat*   *ovie*
             writer[Masc]-Def   whose-Pl   song-Pl   sing-3PlPres   this-Pl
             devojki
             girl-Pl
             'the writer whose songs those girls are singing'

The invariant *čto/co* can also be used as a relative form for animate referents in all eleven languages:

(123) Blg *xórata, čto vidjáx* 'the people whom/that I saw'

Czech and B/C/S possess a construction which is superficially similar, but which introduces another basis altogether for the construction of relative clauses:

(124)   Cz   *přinesl*   *jsem*   *ti*   *knihu,*
        bring-1SgPrfv   Aux-1Sg   you-DatSg   book[Fem]-AccSg
        co   *jsme*   *o*   *ní*   *včera*   *mluvili*
        which   Aux-1Pl   about   it-FemLocSg   yesterday   talk-PlPast
        'I have brought you the book about which we were talking
        yesterday' (lit. '... that we about it yesterday talked')

There are also structures where the head (= referent) in the main clause is not a noun, but a pronoun or an abstract – for example, a whole sentence. Reference to a whole sentence is made by the neuter singular of the appropriate relative pronoun, or by the *čto/co* form:

(125a)   Rus   *pósle obéda šël dóžď, čto udivljálo nás vséx*
         'after dinner rain fell, which (i.e. which fact) astonished us all'

The more common form of such constructions, however, is by means of the typically Slavic Double Pronoun + Relative, where the first element is one of the *t*-series of pronouns, and the second is one of the *k-/j*-series (5.5.5.2, 8.6.2):

(125b)   Rus   *tó,*   *čto*   *pósle*   *obéda*   *šël*
         it   that   after   dinner-GenSg   went-MascSgPast
         dóžď,   *udivljálo*   *nás*   *vséx*
         rain[Masc]-NomSg   amaze-NeutSgPast   we-Acc   all-AccPl
         'that (lit. it that) after dinner rain fell astonished us all'

This "that ... which" construction is also found with unspecified objects in the main clause:

(125c)   Rus   *já*   *vdrúg*   *vspómnil*   *tó,*   *o*
         I-Nom   suddenly   remember-MascSgPast   it   about
         čëm   *mý*   *užé*   *zabýli*
         which-LocSg   we   already   forgot-PlPast
         'I suddenly remembered what (that about which) we had already
         forgotten'

If there is a nominal object, it may be preceded by a determiner of the *t*-series, and the relative clause is again introduced by the appropriate form of the relative pronoun:

(125d)   Rus   *mý   vstrétilis'   s   **tém**   studéntom,   u*
         we   meet-Past   with   that-InstrSg   student-InstrSg   at (chez)
         kotórogo   *mý   býli*   *rán'še*
         who-GenSg   we   be-PlPast   earlier
         'we met the (that) student at whose house we had been earlier'

This "*t-* ... *k-/j-*" pattern also applies to determiners in both the main and the subordinate clause:

(125e)   Rus   *mý   vídeli*   *tám*   **takíe**   *mašíny,*   **kakíx**
         we   see-PlPast   there   such-AccPl   car-AccPl   which-GenPl
         tý   *nikogdá   ne   vídel!*
         you-NomSg   never   Neg   see-MascSgPast
         'we saw there such cars as you have never seen!'

and to a whole range of other determiners and adverbials. As with the basic *to* ... *čto* construction discussed above, the first element can sometimes be omitted. But there is a strong tendency in Slavic to include both, particularly in syntactically complex sentences.

(126a)   Cz   *jdi*   **tam**, **odkud**   *jsi*   *přišel*
         go-2SgImper   there   whence   Aux-2Sg   come-MascSgPastPart
         'go (there) where you came from'

(126b)   Cz   *dělejte*   **tak**, **jak**   *vám*   *říkám*
         do-2PlImper   thus   how   you-DatPl   say-1SgPres
         'do as I tell you'

(126c)   Sorb   *namakach*   *ju*   **tam**, **hdźež**   *ju*
         find-1SgAor   it-FemAcc   there   where   it-FemAcc
         pytat   *njeběch*
         seek-MascSgPastPart   Neg-Aux-1SgCond
         'I found it (there) where I wouldn't have looked for it'

The same type of construction occurs with quantifiers:

(127)   Cz   *dostanete*   **tolik**,   **kolik**   *potřebujete*
         receive-2PlFutPrfv   so_much   how_much   need-2PlPres
         'you will get as much as you need'

And there is the common use of the 'that ... which' pronominal structure (7.2.2.2), with a preceding preposition, for instance where English uses a preposition or a conjunction:

(128a)   Rus   *péred tém, kak ...*   'before (it, that) + Sentence'

(128b)   Rus   *pósle togó, kak ...*   'after (it, that) + Sentence'

In these examples the total structure, with the syntactic role of a conjunction, uses a "dummy" pronoun (*tem, togo*, etc.). But "relative adverbs" can also refer not to "dummy" pronouns, but to nouns themselves:

(129a)   Sorb   *w dobje, hdyž ...*   'at a time when ...'

(129b)   Sorb   *do cuzeho kraja, hdźež ...*   (*w kotrymž*)
                                                 'to a foreign land, where ...   (in which)'

In the majority of examples cited thus far, the *t-* word in the main clause precedes the *k-/j-* word in the subordinate clause. This order is not always followed, especially in proverbs:

(130a)   Sorb   **kelkož**   hłowow,   **telko**   myslow
                how_many   head-GenPl   so_many   thought-GenPl
                ('there are as many opinions as there are heads') [saying]

(130b)   Sorb   **hdźež**   so   kuri,   **tam**   je   woheń
                where   ReflCl   smoke-3SgPres   there   be-3Sg   fire-Nom
                'where there is smoke (there) there is fire'

Furthermore, the *t*-word may be omitted entirely – not only, as we have seen, in adverbial constructions but also with the relative pronoun. This is particularly common in 'he ... who' sentences, and in the "free" relative:

(131a)   Mac   **što**   sum   kažal   e   vistina
                what   Aux-1Sg   say-MascSgPast   be-3Sg   truth
                'what I have said is the truth'

(131b)   Mac   **koj**   prv   ḱe   dojde,   prv   ḱe   svrši
                who   first   Fut   arrive-3Sg   first   Fut   finish-3Sg
                'he who comes first will finish first'

(131c)   Rus   *blažén,*   **kto**   prázdnik   žízni   ráno   ostávil ...* (Pushkin)
                happy   who   festival   life-Gen   early   leave-MascSgPast
                'happy is he who has left the festival of life early ...'

(131d)   Pol   **co**   napisałem,   zostało   przyjęte
                what   write-1SgPast   Aux-NeutSg   accepted-NeutSgPass
                'what I wrote was accepted'

although the *t*-word is often included in such inverted structures:

(131e) Rus *któ   pérvyj   skážet,   tót   polúčit*
             who   first   say-3SgFut that_one   receive-3SgFut
             nagrádu
             reward-Acc
             'who says (it) first, he will receive the reward'

7.3 Specific construction types

In this section we discuss seven topics of specific typological interest: pronouns (7.3.1), reflexives (7.3.2), apersonal and impersonal constructions (7.3.3), indirection (7.3.4), participial (7.3.5) and gerundial (7.3.6) constructions, and ellipsis and deletion (7.3.7).

7.3.1 Pronouns and anaphora

Slavic pronouns occur in circumstances similar to English. In general, if a noun is identical in reference to a preceding noun, a pronoun can occur in its place (anaphora):

(132a) Ukr *Andríj pryjšóv raníše. Vín* ... 'Andrij arrived earlier. He ...'

Less commonly, it can be the first of two such nominals which may be replaced by a pronoun if the nominal occurs in a pre-posed subordinate clause (cataphora):

(132b) Ukr *kolý vín cé káže, znáčyť u profésora je pidstávka*
             'if he says that, it means that the professor has a reason'

Slavic differs from English in that the pronoun often may not occur in the sentence if the verb carries explicit person-number marking, or in colloquial style; examples of both types of subject-omission are given in the discussion of ellipsis (7.3.7).

Slavic has a characteristic "anticipatory plural" use of pronouns in conjoined subjects containing at least one pronoun, sometimes called the "comitative"(133b). In such cases the first pronoun is often plural, and 'and' becomes 'with':

(133a) Rus *já i Iván pošlí na koncért*
             'I and Ivan went to the concert' (unusual)

(133b) Rus *mý   s   Ivánom   pošlí   na   koncért*
             we   with Ivan-InstrSg go-PlPast to   concert (preferred)
             'Ivan and I went to the concert'

Forms like (133b) are ambiguous, since they may refer to two persons or more than two persons: to me, Ivan and perhaps also other persons unspecified ('we and Ivan').

Pronouns are not the only words which can refer back to words in previous sentences in this way. Adjectives or determiners may also do so. The noun with which it occurred in the preceding sentence, or to which it refers, is omitted, and the construction is translated by the English 'ones':

> (134) Pol *U nas w ogrodzie rosną białe i czerwone kwiaty.*
> **Białe (Takie)** *potrzebują dużo wody.*
> 'In our garden grow white and red flowers.
> **The white ones (Such ones)** need a lot of water.'

Certain uses of pronouns are not referential. In Macedonian the proclitic "double object" pronoun is a marker of case and grammatical function, and not of anaphora (6.2.3):

> (135) Mac *go*   *gledam*   *Grozdana*
> he-ProclAcc   see-1SgPres   Grozdan-Acc
> 'I see Grozdan'

Some pronouns are used in non-personal constructions, where the reference is general and unspecified. In certain such cases even the pronoun itself is deleted, leaving only the verb as a marker of person and number:

> (136) Rus *kogdá vídiš'* [2Sg] *takíe véšči, ne znáeš'* [2Sg], *čtó dúmat'*
> 'when you see things like that, you don't know what to think'

Possessive adjectives ('my', 'your', 'his') and possessive pronouns ('mine', 'yours', 'his') follow similar rules for forming pronouns as normal personal pronouns – though unlike English, the two series of forms are identical (5.5.2–3). The one special case is the "reflexive" possessive (corresponding to Latin *suus*), which may refer to a psychological subject (if there is no nominative subject), even if the subject is not expressed at all:

> (137) Rus *nádo ljubít'* **svojú** *ródinu*
> 'it is necessary to love one's country'

But possessive adjectives are usually omitted with nouns referring to family relatives, parts of the body and close personal possessions (7.1.7). In such sentences all possessive relations are understood to refer to the subject of the sentence, unless otherwise stated, or unless some ambiguities are present, in which case the possessor can be explicitly identified:

> (138a) Rus *ón napisál máteri*
> 'he wrote to (his own) mother'

(138b) Rus *ón napisál **svoéj** máteri*
             'he wrote to his own mother' (emphatic)

(138c) Rus *ón napisál **egó** máteri*
             'he wrote to his (someone else's) mother'

7.3.2 Reflexives

The reflexive may take several forms. East Slavic has lost the reflexive as a clitic pronoun, and it is now a verbal suffix which is not separated from the verb (5.5.3). In the other languages the clitic may attach itself to many different hosts in the first unaccented position of the clause (7.4.3.3):

(139) Slk *pozrite,   co   som   si   našla*
             look-2PlImper what AuxCl-1Sg self-Cl-Dat find-FemSgPast
             'look what I've found myself'

It does not matter that the reflexive belongs to an infinitive: it will still occur in second position in the sentence. Consider the alternative ordering of the clitic *się* 'self' with Polish *umyć się* 'to wash (oneself)' and *patrzyć się* 'to look':

(140)   'I want to wash myself'
        Pol *chcę   się   umyć*
              want-1Sg ReflCl wash
              or:
              chcę   umyć   się

(141)   'Janek wants to have a look at the garden'
        Pol *Janek   się   chce   popatrzyć   na   ogród*
              Janek ReflCl want-3SgPres look-InfPrfv at garden
              or:
              Janek   chce   się   popatrzyć   na   ogród

As this example of *popatrzyć się* 'to look[Prfv]' shows, verbs bearing the reflexive marker can have a variety of meanings. Some of these meanings will be genuinely reflexive, and the verbs to which the reflexive marker is added are usually ordinary transitive verbs:

(142) Blg ***míe se** ot vodíte na čérno moré*
             '(he) washes (himself) in the waters of the Black Sea'

In addition, however, verbs with the reflexive formant may also be syntactically active, like Polish *patrzyć się* 'to look'. Verbs with a reflexive form may also express impersonal constructions or passives (7.1.5, 7.3.3).

Apart from the affix/clitic reflexive there is also a "strong", non-clitic, reflexive pronoun in all eleven languages. This pronoun occurs especially after prepositions and in some examples shows a different meaning from the clitic pronoun, with the full reflexive pronoun expressing a stronger notion of responsible agency:

(143a)   Rus   *čúvstvovat'sja*   'to be a feeling, an impression'
                 čúvstvovat' sebjá   'to feel (physically)'

(143b)   Rus   *sprášivat'sja*   'to wonder'
                 sprášivat' sebjá   'to ask oneself'

(143c)   Rus   *lišít'sja žízni*   'to lose one's life'
                 lišít' sebjá žízni   'to take one's life'

The "dative of the interested person" may also occur with the reflexive:

(144a)   Rus   *Mstisláv predložíl sýnu stróit'* **sebé** *dóm*
                 'Mstislav suggested to (his) son to build himself (*sebe*: i.e. for the son) a house'

(144b)   Rus   *Mstisláv predložíl sýnu stróit'* **emú** *dóm*
                 'Mstislav suggested to (his) son to build him (*emu*: i.e. for Mstislav) a house'

Reflexive verbs may also express mutual actions, where subject and object exchange similar actions, perhaps with an implied mutual dative:

(145)   Rus   *oní perepísyvajutsja*   'they exchange letters/correspond'

The reflexive possessive refers to the subject of the clause in which it occurs, whether it is in the form of the determiner or the dative-possessive clitic pronoun:

(146a)   Blg   *znáeš*   *svóite*   (*tvóite*)   *zadălžénija*
                 know-2SgPres   own-PlDef   your(Sg)-PlDef   obligations
                 'you know your obligations'

(146b)   Blg   *obíčam*   *rodínata*   *si*
                 love-1SgPres   country[Fem]-Def   ReflCl-Dat   •
                 'I love my country'

In subject noun phrases like 'John and his brother ...' the *his* does not refer to the whole subject, and is therefore not the reflexive possessive (i.e. the reflexive cannot itself be the subject, since it refers back to it):

(147)   Blg   *Stójko i négov* (*négovijat*) *brát*   (**Stojko i svoj brat*)
                 'Stojko and his brother'

7.3.3   Apersonal and impersonal constructions

Very typical of Slavic are the apersonal construction and the many types of impersonal constructions. Both these types have no expressed subject. In apersonal constructions, also called "indefinite-personal" sentences in several Slavic grammatical terminologies, the verb is in the 3 Person plural and the structure is approximately equivalent to the English 'people/they' + Verb, or constructions with French *on*, German *man:*

(148)   Rus   *govorját,   čto   èto   nevozmóžno*
         say-3PlPres   that   this-NeutSg   impossible-NeutSg
         'they say that this is impossible'

Such apersonal constructions express a reduced notion of agency, and so are midway between actives and passives (7.1.5).

The apersonal construction is distinguished (a) from sentences where the subject is absent because it is understood from the context of discourse or by anaphora from a preceding sentence:

(149)   Pol   *ale jak pracuje!*   '(but) how he works!'

and (b) from sentences containing a neuter singular subject which are not impersonal. In such cases the neuter pronoun may refer back to a sentence or part of a preceding sentence:

(150)   Rus   (SENTENCE).   *Èto udivljálo nás.*
         '(SENTENCE).   This astonished us.'

or may be part of a sentence which is itself the subject of another sentence:

(151)   Slk   *prestat' hrešit' je t'ažšie*   'to stop swearing is more difficult'

The true impersonal construction cannot have a subject – unlike English, where in comparable constructions a "dummy" *it* occurs, as in *it is raining* or *it is stuffy*. In Slavic impersonal constructions the verb or predicate is in the 3 Person neuter singular. From the formal point of view, the main types of Slavic impersonal constructions include:

1.   Impersonal verbs

      (152a)   Cz   *těší   mě*
                please-3Sg   I-Cl-Acc
                'delighted (to meet you)' (in response to an introduction)

(152b)   Ukr *doščýt'*   Cz *prší* Pol *pada*   B/C/S *kíší*
          'it is raining'

(152c)   Rus *xvatáet*   'it/there is enough'
          ne   xvatáet   xléba
          Neg suffice-3SgPres   bread-GenSg
          'there is not enough bread'

2.   Personal verbs used impersonally, especially with the reflexive.
      If a person is indicated, they are in the dative case (153b):

(153a)   Cz *dnes   se   nedělá*
          today   ReflCl   Neg-work-3SgPres
          '(there is) no work today'

(153b)   Rus *mné   ne   spítsja*
          I-Dat   Neg   sleep-3Sg-Refl
          'I don't feel like sleeping'

(153c)   Blg *razbíra   se*   (cf. Mac: *se razbira*)
          understand-3Sg   ReflCl   (ReflCl understand-3Sg)
          'of course'

3.   Numerals

(154)   Pol *pięciu   panów   wchodziłoby*
          5-MascPers   man-GenPl   enter-NeutSgPast-Cond
          '5 men would come in'

There are, however, important variations in the use of personal forms
of the verb with subject noun phrases containing a numeral (6.2).

4.   Quantifiers

(155)   Mac *kolku   luǵe   bea   tamu*
          how-many   people-Pl   be-3PlImperf   there
          'how many people were there'

All Slavic languages, however, have some concording quantifiers
which allow the subject noun phrase to function in personal constructions (see (1) above).

5.   Negated 'be' sentences of existence or presence

(156a)   Ukr *ni   krápli   nemá   vodý*
          Neg drop-GenSg Neg-be/have-3Sg water-GenSg
          'there is not a drop of water'

(156b) Pol *nie*   *ma*   *go*   *w*   *kuchni*
              Neg   be/have-3Sg   he-Cl-GenSg   in   kitchen
              'he isn't in the kitchen'

The comparable personal forms mean not pure absence or non-existence, but rather something like 'he hadn't *gone* there':

(156c) Rus *ón* *né* *byl* *v* *teátre*
              'he wasn't at the theatre' = 'he didn't go/hadn't been to the theatre'

cf. (156d) Rus *egó né bylo v teátre*   'he wasn't in the theatre'
                   (i.e. was missing, e.g. when something happened)

6. Predicative neuter adjectives

(157) Sorb *je* *ćěmno*   'it is dark'   *je ćicho*   'it is quiet'
                je *dźiwno* 'it is strange' *je móžno* 'it is possible'

This class, particularly those words referring to natural phenomena and atmospheric conditions, was and is often called the "category of state" by Soviet and Russian linguists, since it expresses a state or condition rather than an action.

7. Predicative neuter (short-form) past passive participles

(158) Pol *ukradziono*   *mi*   *samochód*
              steal-NeutSgPastPassPart   I-Cl-Dat   car-AccSG
              'my car has been stolen'

8. Predicative nouns

(159) Rus *mné*   *ø*   *žáľ*   *egó*
              I-DatSg   (be)   pity[Noun]   he-Acc
              'I am sorry for him'

9. Agent–patient impersonals

(160a) Rus *reká*   *uneslá*   *lódku*
               river[Fem]-NomSg   carry_away-FemSgPast   boat-AccSg
               'the river carried the boat away'

(160b) Rus *rekój*   *unesló*   *lódku*
               river[Fem]-InstrSg   carry-away-NeutSgPast   boat-AccSg
               'the boat was carried away by the river'

In (160b) the agentive force of *reká* is reduced. Such constructions usually only occur with nouns referring to the irresistible forces of nature.

10.   Infinitival impersonals

(161a)   Sorb *ze   wotewrjeneho   wokna   je*
from open-GenSgPastPassPart window-GenSg be-3Sg
wšo   słyšeć
everything   hear-Inf
'everything can be heard from the open window'

Such impersonal sentences may centre on an infinitive, or may depend as well on the presence of other elements in the sentence, like an agent in the dative case:

(161b)   Rus *ne   mné   skazát'   emú,   čto* ...
Neg   I-Dat   say-Inf   he-Dat   that
'it isn't for me to tell him that ...'

or the meaning 'there was someone/no-one to do X':

(161c)   Pol *jest   komu   to   zrobić*
be-3SgPres   who-DatSg   it-Acc   do-Inf
'there is someone to do that'

(161d)   Ukr *pospišáty   nikudý*
hurry-Inf   Neg-whither
'there is nowhere to hurry to'

This classification by the forms of the impersonal categories and constructions is supplemented and expanded by the more customary semantic classification. Numerals, quantifiers and negated 'be' sentences are semantically self-explanatory. But other semantic categories cut across the formal classification:

1.   Physical states of sentient beings

(162a)   Ukr *mení   nezdoróvyt'sja*
I-Dat   be-ill-3SgPres
'I feel ill'

(162b)   Pol *jest   mi   niedobrze/zimno*
be-3Sg   I-Cl-Dat   bad-NeutSg/cold-NeutSg
'I feel ill/cold'

(162c) Blg *mărzí*   *me*
           freeze-3Sg I-Cl-Dat
           'I feel frozen'

2. Mental states of sentient beings

    (163) Rus *mné*   *nelóvko*
               I-Dat maladroit
               'I feel uncomfortable/embarrassed'

3. Natural phenomena

    (164a) Sorb *je*   *zymno*
                 be-3Sg cold-NeutSg
                 'it is cold'
           Blg   *gromí*
                 thunder-3Sg
                 'it thunders'

    (164b) Slk *stmieva*   *sa*
              grow-dark-3Sg ReflCl
              'it is growing dark'

4. Obligation/duty, with or without an expressed agent

    (165a) Sorb *je*   *trjeba*   *wo*   *tym*   *přemyslować*
                  be-3Sg necessary about it-LocSg think-Inf
                  'it is necessary to think about it'

    (165b) Rus *sléduet*   *napisát'*   *emú*   *pis'mó*
              necessary-3Sg write-Inf he-Dat letter-Acc
              'one (we, you) must write him a letter'

5. Possibility/chance/permission

    (166a) Ukr *ne*   *móžna*   *skazáty,*   *ščob ...*
                Neg possible say-Inf in-order-that
                'one cannot say that ...'

    (166b) Slk *smie*   *sa*   *tu*   *fajčiť*
               dare-3Sg ReflCl here smoke-Inf
              'may one smoke here?'

6.   Fitness/suitability

(167)   Ukr   *várt*   *pryjizdýty*
                worthwhile   come-Inf
                'it is worthwhile coming'

7.   Inclination or disinclination

(168a)   Rus   *mné*   *ne*   *torópitsja*
                  I-Dat   Neg   hasten-3Sg
                  'I don't feel like hurrying'

(168b)   Ukr   *xóčeťsja*   *ráduvatysja, ják sónce sjáje*
                  want-3SgPres-Refl   rejoice-Inf   how sun shine-3SgPres
                  'one feels like rejoicing at how the sun shines'

8.   Regret

(169)   Cz   *bylo*   *škoda,*   *že*   *nepřišel*
                be-NeutSgPast   pity   that   Neg-come-MascSgPast
                'it was a pity that he didn't come'

9.   Action with backgrounded or unexpressed agent

(170)   Ukr   *tám*   *dóbre*   *žyvéťsja*
                there   well   live-3SgPres-Refl
                'it's good living/life is good there'

7.3.4   Indirection

We use the term "indirection" to cover indirect commands, indirect questions and indirect speech. They all report a speech event at a later time, and from a different speech-act perspective, from the original utterance. As a result, 1 and 2 Person address is reformulated as 3 Person in indirect speech acts. Proximate deictics ('this') are converted to non-proximate deictics ('that').

In indirect commands we find infinitival constructions (7.2.2.1) and complements (7.2.2.2). The original imperative is replaced in indirect commands by either an infinitive (except in Macedonian, where there is no infinitive, and in Bulgarian, where there is only a marginal vestigial infinitive), or an 'in-order-that' clause, depending on the verb of command and the syntactic construction:

(171a)   Rus   *čitájte!*   'read!'

(171b)   Rus   *já*   *emú*   *skazál,*   *čtóby*   *ón*
                  I-Nom   he-Dat   tell-MascSgPast   in-order-that   he

čitál
read-MascSgPast
'I told him to read'

Indirect questions are prefixed by a verb or expression of questioning, and the question then follows in its original form and order, with only the person-conversion from 1/2 to 3. Purely intonation questions do not occur as indirect questions in indirect speech acts, and Yes/no questions require an explicit question particle (172b). Information questions keep their original form (173b):

(172a) Rus *– Tý prigotóvil obéd? – sprosíl koról' Ivána*
                 ' "Have you prepared dinner?" the king asked Ivan'

(172b) Rus *koról' sprosíl, prigotóvil **li** Iván obéd*
                 'the king asked if/whether Ivan had prepared dinner'

(173a) Rus *– Któ prigotóvil obéd? – sprosíl koról'*
                 ' "Who (has) prepared dinner?" asked the king'

(173b) Rus *koról' sprosíl, któ prigotóvil obéd*
                 'the king asked who had prepared dinner'

Indirect speech replaces quoted statements with reported statements.

(174a) Blg *kák e stánálo*   'how did it happen?'

(174b) Blg *tój săobští, kák e stánálo* 'he said how it (had) happened'

Indirect questions and indirect speech in Slavic share a feature of tense selection which differs from English. In English an indirect expression requires the replacement of the tenses, especially present by past, according to the familiar rules of the "sequence of tenses":

(175a) I **am** reading *War and Peace*

(175b) he said that he **was** reading *War and Peace*

In Slavic only the first of these conversions takes place – the conversion of person. The tense remains that of the original utterance or question:

(176a) Rus *já*   ***čitáju***   *«Vojnú*   *i*   *mír»*
                 I-Nom   read-1SgPres   War[Fem]-AccSg   and   peace-AccSg

(176b) Rus *ón*   *skazál,*   *čto*   *(ón)*   ***čitáet***
                 he-Nom   say-MascSgPast   that   (he)   read-3SgPres
                 «Vojnú   *i*   *mír»*
                 War[Fem]-AccSg   and   peace-AccSg

7.3.5   Participial constructions

Participles occur in several types of constructions: in predicates, appositions, and participial attributes:

(177a)   Pol   *wiersze   zostały   wydrukowane*
              poem-Pl   Aux-PlPast   publish-PlPastPassPart
              'the poems were published' [Pass]

(177b)   Pol   *wiersze,   wydrukowane   w   Ameryce*
              'the poems   published   in   America'

(177c)   Pol   *wydrukowane   wiersze   imponowały   wszystkim*
              'the published   poems   impressed   everyone'

Participles may also function as adjectives without their temporal meaning:

(178)   'cultured/educated': PAST PASSIVE PARTICIPLE:
        B/C/S *òbrazovan*   Blg *obrazóvan*   Rus *obrazóvannyj*
        Slk *vzdelaný*

And they may function as nouns:

(179)   'defendant' (at law):
        [PresPass]   Rus *obvinjáemyj*
        [PastPass]   Cz, Slk *obžalovaný*   Pol *oskarzony*
                     Ukr *obvynuváčenyj*   Sorb *wobskorženy*

The syntax of Slavic participial constructions depends in the first place on the availability of participial forms (5.5.5.10). Present active participles are not available in Macedonian, and though present in Ukrainian and Belarusian, they are not in common usage. In Bulgarian (Scatton, 1993: 215) they are strictly literary. They occur in apposition and as attributes, and may adjectivalize and nominalize:

(180)   Rus   *trudjáščiesja*   *vséx*   *strán,*
              work-NomPl-PresActPart   all-GenPl   country-GenPl
              soedinjájtes'!
              unite-2PlImper
              'workers of all countries, unite!'

(181)   'chairman, head': Pol *przewodniczący*   Rus *zavédujuščij*

Past active participles occur in all eleven languages, though their use is not common in Ukrainian and Belarusian, and in Ukrainian they are only formed from relatively few verbs. In East Slavic they may function syntactically like present active participles, especially in Russian. Elsewhere their form is that of the *l*-participle, which is the key component of compound tenses:

(182)   Rus ***priéxavšie** ne ználi o vášej svád'be*
                'the arrivals (lit. 'the having arrived ones') did not know
                about your wedding'

Present passive participles are found only in Russian, where they are morphologically derived from transitive verbs, but syntactically function mainly as adjectives:

(183)   Rus *ne-osporí-m-yj* 'incontrovertible, irrefutable'
                ne-otvratí-m-yj 'inevitable'
                dosjagáe-m-yj 'attainable'

Past passive participles are found in all eleven languages, and are syntactically the most versatile participles. Typically Slavic is the use of impersonal constructions (7.3.3) with participles, particularly the past participle passive:

(184)   Pol ***ukradziono** mi zegarek* 'my watch has been stolen'

And Slavic also has an "expanded participial attribute", as in German, where the attributive past participle passive may include in pre-nominal sequences whole sections of structure which English would rephrase as an apposition or a relative clause:

(185)   Rus *èti eščë ne vsémi avtoritétami nášego universitéta*
                ***príznannye** predložénija*
                lit. 'these not yet by all authorities of our university recognized
                suggestions'

7.3.6   Gerundial constructions

Slavic gerunds, unlike English gerunds, can refer only to the subject of the main clause (though Sorbian is a special case: 5.5.5.11). Compare

(186a) Rus *vxodjá*   *v*   *dóm,*   *já*   *uvídel*   *egó*
                enter-PresGer into house I-Nom see-MascSgPast he-Acc
                'Going into the house, I caught sight of him'
(186b) Rus *já uvídel egó, kak ón vxodíl v dóm*
                'I caught sight of him (as he was) going into the house'

Except in short sentences, the Slavic gerund-clause usually precedes the main clause, which helps to prevent another noun phrase from occurring between the gerund clause and the subject. Czech gerunds agree in gender and number with the subject of the main clause:

(187a)   Cz   **znajíce** *potřeby rostliny v růžných obdobích jejího života,*
můžeme řídit její růst
'knowing [MascPl] the requirements of the plant at various stages of its life, we can control its growth'

(187b)   Cz   *ani*   *nepromluviv*   *odešel*   *ven*
Neg   talk-MascSgPastGer   go_away-MascSgPast   away
'without a word (lit. 'not having spoken') he went away'

Gerunds are either imperfective or perfective, though Bulgarian and Macedonian lack a perfective (or past) gerund (5.5.5.11). And in any case gerunds, particularly the perfective, are rare in the spoken languages.

7.3.7   Ellipsis and deletion

The omission of subject pronouns is typical of certain Slavic sentences. Subject pronouns normally cannot be omitted unless person/number is explicitly marked on the verb. East Slavic has lost the auxiliary 'be' in what used to be the compound tenses. This means that the past tense of all verbs will lack person/number marking on the verb, and so the pronoun must remain, at least in the standard language. If the person is clear from the preceding or extralinguistic context it may drop in colloquial usage (188b):

(188a)   'I was reading':   Pol *czytał-em*   Rus *já čitál-ø*

(188b)   Rus   – *Pónjali?*   –   *(Dá,)*   *Pónjal.*
               understand-PlPast   (yes)   understand-MascPast
               '(Do you[Sg]) understand?'   '(Yes), I do/understand'

East Slavic also retains the pronouns in the inflected forms of the verb which do mark person/number explicitly – that is, the present and future. The omission of the pronoun is regarded as stylistically marked (e.g. letters) and/or colloquial, in spite of the redundancy of the person/number information in both the pronoun and the inflexion on the verb:

(189)   Rus   *já búdu starát'sja*   'I shall try' [Imprfv]

In West and South Slavic both the copula and the auxiliary are fully alive, and mark person/number consistently in most relevant forms of the verb. The 1 and 2 Person pronouns are omitted as a matter of course – indeed, their inclusion is stylistically marked and emphatic:

(190a)   Sorb   *smy (sće) běrny zběrali*   'we (you [Pl]) collected potatoes'

cf. (190b)   Sorb   **my** *smy* (**wy** *sće*) *běrny zběrali*

Third person pronouns, however, are not usually omitted:

(190c)   Sorb   **wón** *je běrny zběrał*   'he collected potatoes'

And it is in the 3 Person singular that the auxiliary is omitted in languages like Czech, Slovak and Polish, which throws the burden of distinctiveness back on the pronoun.

The ellipsis of the present tense of 'be' is not a matter of grammatical choice. In East Slavic the forms of the present tense of 'be' have been lost, with the exception of the 3 Person singular, and this form is used for all persons and numbers when the verb is used at all: Rus *est'*, Ukr *je*, Bel *ěsc'*. The verb 'be' is normally omitted in copulative sentences and in statements of location and time:

(191a)   Rus   *koncért – xoróšij /v teátre /v 5 časóv*
          'the concert is good/is in the theatre/is at five o'clock'

The non-zero present tense of the East Slavic 'be' is used for 'there is/are':

(191b)   Rus   *ést' sáxar v škafú*
          'there is some sugar in the cupboard'

in definitions in scientific, philosophical and technical language:

(191c)   Rus   *právda ést' krasotá*   'truth is beauty'

and in statements of possession, especially in response to a question about possession containing the word *est'/je/ěsc'*:

(191d)   Rus   *u nás ést' čtó pít'*   'we do have something to drink'

Polish may also omit the verb in several specific present tense contexts, when *to* and/or a dash replace *być* 'be', in some impersonal constructions, and with person-suffixes attached to adjectives:

1.   When *to* replaces the form of 'be'; with *to* the case following the copula is the nominative, unlike the instrumental which follows 'be':

     (192a)   Pol   *Maciek – to duży chłopak* 'Maciek is a big lad'

     This use of *to* only occurs with a following noun predicate, and not with adjectives, or with expressions of place or time.

2. When a dash replaces the copula in the written language. This usage, which is more regular in East Slavic, is used in definition-like statements, normally joining a noun subject and a noun predicate:

> (192b)   Pol   *Kanbera – stolica Australii*
>   'Canberra (is the) capital of Australia'

3. In some impersonal constructions, particularly those containing a "category of state" word, the present tense of 'be' may be omitted:

> (192c)   Pol   *gorąco*   *mi*   (*jest*)
>   hot-NeutSg   I-Cl-DatSg   be-3Sg
>   'I feel hot'

4. The person/number marker derived from the verb 'be', and used as an auxiliary, may be attached to the first accented word in the sentence as a suffix – like the true enclitic it is. This usage is colloquial:

> (192d)   Pol   *pijan-i-śmy*   or   *jesteśmy*   *pijan-i*
>   drunk-MascPl-1Pl   be-1Pl   drunk-MascPl
>   'we are drunk'

7.4   Word order

In Slavic word order variations are more common, and show a greater range of grammatical types and stylistic effects, than is found in English. Three principal grammatical factors influence variability in Slavic word order: the marking of grammatical relations by means other than word order; constituent structure; and conventional word order (7.4.1). Word-order effects are also closely linked to Functional Sentence Perspective (7.5).

7.4.1   Marking grammatical functions and relations

Word order is potentially more variable if a word or construction marks its grammatical role in the sentence by means of affixes (concord, agreement or government: 6.2). Conversely, word order is more fixed when it is the word order itself which marks grammatical relations. In (193a) *v ponedél'nik* 'on Monday' can either modify the noun *poézdka* 'trip', or can modify the whole sentence; the reading of 'a Monday trip' is not available in (193b), where *v ponedél'nik* is in sentence-initial position, and can only act as a sentence-adverbial:

(193a)   Rus   *oní predložíli poézdku v ponedéľnik*
            'they suggested a trip on Monday'
            (ambiguous: either the suggestion occurred on Monday, as in
            (193b), or the trip was destined for Monday)

(193b)   Rus   *v ponedéľnik oní predložíli poézdku*
            'on Monday they suggested a trip'

A second means of marking grammatical relations is the argument structure of predicates in selecting the types and sub-types of their subjects, objects and so on:

(194a)   Cz   *Honza trpí socialismus* [SVO]   'Honza tolerates socialism'

(194b)   Cz   *socialismus trpí Honza* [OVS]   'Honza tolerates socialism'

In (194a–b) the verb carries 3 Person singular agreement, which could potentially allow either *Honza* or *socialismus* to be the subject, as in *Socialism tolerates no opposition*. But the Czech verb *trpět* 'to tolerate' does not normally accept an inanimate abstract subject like *socialismus* with an animate object like *Honza*, and this fact determines the syntactic relations between the three words in the sentence. Both (194a) and (194b) are therefore acceptable, with *Honza* as the subject in both instances (for the difference in information management, see 7.5).

7.4.2   Constituent structure

Clearly signalled grammatical relations, however, cannot explain why the constituents of the verb phrase should be more mobile than the constituents of the noun phrase. Within the noun phrase most grammatical relations are clearly marked by concord. A certain amount of order variation is possible, for example in the internal ordering of modifiers:

(195)   Sorb   "these my two new suits"
    (a)   *t-ej*   *dw-aj*   *moj-ej*
          this-MascSg   two-Masc my-NomDu
          now-ej   *woblek-aj*
          new-MascImpersNomDu   suit[Masc]-NomDu
    (b)   *tej mojej dwaj nowej woblekaj*
    (c)   *tej mojej nowej dwaj woblekaj*

But noun phrases allow few external elements to intrude, and most of these are short, like clitics (7.4.3), or verbs of 'being' and 'having' with no expressed subject, as in this N + V + Adj structure:

(196a) Pol *buty*   *ma*   *ładn-e*
             shoes-Nom/AccPl have-3SgPres pretty-NonAnimNom/AccPl
             'he/she has pretty shoes'

or 'be' possessives with short subjects:

(196b) Rus *kakíe*   *ø*   *u*   *vás*   *namérenija?*
             what-NomPl (be) to you-GenPl intention-NomPl
             'what intentions do you have/what are your intentions?'

Such examples show that word order depends on the nature of the constituents of the sentence as well as on the signalling of grammatical relations. But behind both these principles of word order lies the factor of conventional order, which has a historical basis.

7.4.3   Conventional word order

Many aspects of conventional word order have already been illustrated in this chapter, reflecting the neutral order of elements in the sentence. There are three areas of conventional order which show some grammatically controlled variation within Slavic: subjects, verbs and objects; modifiers; and clitics.

7.4.3.1   *Subjects, verbs and objects*
Slavic, like English, has a dominant SVO (Subject–Verb–Object) order. The importance of this neutral word order can be appreciated from the way in which examples like (197a–b) are interpreted:

(197a) Rus *mát'*   *ljúbi-t*   *dóč'*
             mother-Nom/AccSg love-3SgPres daughter-Nom/AccSg
             'the mother loves the daughter'

(197b) Pol *byt*   *określa*   *świadomość*
             being-Nom/AccSg determine-3SgPres consciousness-
                                                               Nom/AccSg

        'being determines consciousness'

In the absence of other markers of syntactic relations, such sentences are normally interpreted as SVO: the first noun phrase is taken as the subject, although the order OVS is also consistent with the inflexions and the argument structures of the verbs. It is just possible to force an OVS reading with appropriate contexts and intonation, but this reading is stylistically marked and artificial.

The position of the object in the sentence depends on whether the object is a noun or a pronoun. A single object pronoun precedes the verb in almost 50 percent of instances in Russian (Svedstedt, 1976), and this figure agrees with what is known about object-placement in all three East Slavic languages. (198a–b) are equally natural:

(198a) Rus *mój zját'   eë   vȳgnal íz   domu*
              my   son-in-law her eject   from house
              'my son-in-law threw her out of the house'

(198b) Rus *mój zját' vȳgnal eë   íz domu*
              (. . .)   eject her (. . .)
              'my son-in-law threw her out of the house'

With two objects the pronominal object usually precedes the nominal object irrespective of case, as in English:

(199a) Rus *já dál   emú   knígu*
              I   give-MascSgPast   he-DatSg book[Fem]-AccSg
              'I gave him a book'

(199b) Rus *já dál   eë   Ivánu*
              I   give-MascSgPast   it-FemAccSg Ivan-DatSg
              'I gave it [Fem] to Ivan'

A pronominal object may even precede the verb, especially if there are two pronominal objects:

(199c) Rus *já emú   dál   knígu/eë*
              I   him-DatSg   give-MascSgPast   book-AccSg/it-FemSgAcc
              'I gave him the book/it'

Verbs in personal constructions, but lacking an expressed subject, preserve the unmarked VO order:

(199d) Rus *ótdali   egó*
              give-away-PlPast   it-Masc/NeutAccSg
              'they gave it away'

In West and South Slavic, object pronouns are clitic and occur after verbal clitics in the first unaccented syntactic position in the sentence (7.4.3.3):

(200) Cz *viděl   jsem   ho   v Praze*
           saw-MascSgPast Aux-1Sg he-Cl-Acc in Prague
           'I saw him in Prague'

In Bulgarian and Macedonian object pronouns can also be proclitic, and are used with object nouns. Having lost most of their case forms (5.4.2, 6.2.4), nouns in these languages would appear to have less freedom to invert subject and object. Macedonian, however, has overcome this difficulty by using proclitic personal pronouns, which have maintained their case forms, to signal non-nominative cases. The proclitic object pronoun can precede the first accented constituent of the sentence. This construction is used even with SVO order:

(201a) Mac *fatete   ja   mačkata*
             catch-2PlImper it-Procl-FemAcc cat-Fem-Def
             'catch the cat!'

(201b) Mac *me   najde   brat   mi*
             I-Procl-Acc find-3SgAor brother I-Encl-Dat
             'my brother found me'

In Macedonian this usage involves not only proclitic pronouns supporting nouns, but also enclitic pronouns supporting non-clitic pronouns, especially when (as in the accusative and dative) case-marking is better preserved than in the full-form non-clitic pronouns:

(201c) Mac *mene   mi   reče*
             I-Dat I-Encl-Dat say-3SgAor
             'he told me'

This extra-pronoun construction must be used in Bulgarian in OVS constructions when the morphology does not otherwise mark the grammatical roles. In (202a) it is necessary to mark the object *májkata*; in (202b) the reduplicated pronoun is required to mark the complement in sentence-initial position of a negative impersonal construction. But the reduplicated pronoun is optional in constructions like (202c), where the morphology does mark the grammatical roles adequately (Scatton, 1984: 373):

(202a) Blg *májkata   ja   gléda   detéto*
             mother-Def she-Encl-Acc look-after-3SgPres child-Def
             'the child looks after the mother'

(202b) Blg *Iván   go   njáma*
             Ivan   he-Encl-Acc   Neg-be/have
             'Ivan's not (here)'

(202c) Blg *Iván   (go)   víždam*
             Ivan   (he-Encl-Acc) see-1SgPres
             'I see Ivan'

In this way the typical flexibility of Slavic word order is maintained without a loss of clarity of the marking of grammatical relations.

The relative order of the main constituents may also vary in sentences consisting of a subject and a verb. Sentences with intransitive verbs do not show a uniform SV order. The subject usually precedes the verb if it is an agent or a "performer" of an action, and the verb is semantically "strong" (i.e. not a copula or semi-copula, inchoative, etc.):

(203a) Ukr *divčáta spivájut'*   'the girls are singing'

(203b) Ukr *vín dóbre maljúje*   'he paints well'

though even here we can find differences between the unmarked order for similar expressions in different languages:

(204a) B/C/S *sûnce se ròdilo*   'the sun has risen'

(204b) Ukr *zijšló sónce*   'the sun has risen'

But there are expressions where the subject is not an agent, and the verb is semantically "weak" (that is, it expresses the onset, continuation or unmarked natural activity of the subject). Such expressions, with their reduced concept of agency, often involve phenomena of nature, and usually occur in the VS order:

(205a) Ukr *synije nébo*   'the sky is blue' (*syníty* 'to be blue')

(205b) Rus *nastupíla vesná* 'spring has come'

(205c) Pol *wieje wiatr*   'the wind is blowing'

This apparently inverted order is simply explained by reference to the pragmatics of information structure in the sentence (7.5): the semantically and informationally heavy constituent comes last.

Impersonal constructions contain no grammatical subject, and follow the VO or Verb + Complement order:

(206a) Rus *ne slýšno slóv* [GenPl]   'no words can be heard' (lit. 'not (are) audible words')

(206b)   Pol   *zdecydowano wbudować nową szkołę*
          'it has been decided to build a new school'

But impersonal constructions with logical subjects, most commonly as the "dative of the experiencer", prefer the Dative–Verb order:

(207a)   Cz   *nám*   *už*   *se*   *chce*   *domů*
                to_us   already   ReflCl   want-3Sg   to_home
                'we already feel like (going) home'

(207b)   Rus   *nám*   *ø*   *nužná*   *sekretárš-a*
                 to_us   (be)   necessary-FemSg   secretary-NomSg
                 'we need a secretary'

(207c)   Rus   *nám*   *ø*   *núžno*   *sekretárš-u*
                 to_us   (be)   necessary-Neut = Impers   secretary-AccSg
                 'we need a secretary'

Neutral VS order may also occur with existential and predicative constructions. Positive existentials are personal constructions, while negative existentials are impersonal. Both types place the 'be' first in the neutral order:

(208a)   Rus   ***ést' gdé sidét'***   'there is somewhere to sit'

(208b)   B/C/S   ***nije*** ['not is'] *brăšna*   'there is no flour'

But a locative expression usually precedes the existential 'be':

(208c)   Sorb   *w* ***konsumje*** *njeje była butra*   'there was no butter **in the shop**'

The same word order applies with existential verbs other than 'be':

(208d)   B/C/S   *od tèbe* ***ne*** *òstalo trâga*   'there was no trace of you left'

Predicatives are more variable. Predicative adjectives regularly follow the copulative verb in neutral order, whatever the form of the adjective (long/short, nominative/instrumental, definite/indefinite):

(209a)   Slk   *dolina je* ***úzka*** [Short]   'the valley is narrow'

(209b)   Slk   *ťažký život je* ***hoden*** [Short] *viac než nic*
                 'A hard life is better (lit. 'worth more') than nothing'

(209c)   Rus   *ón býl togdá* ***molodým*** [Long: Instr]   'he was young then'

(209d)   B/C/S   *ôn je* ***dòbar***   [Indef Short]   'he is good'

(209e)   B/C/S   *ôn je* ***môj stârý*** [Def Long] *prìjatelj*   'he is my old friend'

Predicative nominals usually follow the copula, especially when in the nominative case. If there is no case-marking of the predicate, like that provided by the instrumental case, the subject is identified by the word order Subject–Copula–Predicate:

(210a) Sorb *Jan je wučer* 'Jan is a teacher'

(210b) Rus *Moskvá – stolíca Rossíi* 'Moscow (is) the capital of Russia'

If the predicate occurs in the instrumental, however, it may precede the copula, especially if the subject is long and/or syntactically complex:

(210c) Rus *pričín-oj* *vzrýv-a* *býl*
             cause-InstrSg explosion-GenSg was-MascSg
             nedostátok *vodý,* *kotór-aja ...*
             lack[Masc]-NomSg water[Fem]-GenSg which-NomFemSg
             'the cause of the explosion was the lack of water, which ...'

7.4.3.2 *Modifiers*

The order of modifiers and heads depends mainly on the syntactic type of the modifier and on its internal composition. Sentence modifiers like sentence adverbs ('probably', 'perhaps'), and place and time adverbs ('here', 'today') show the greatest mobility, occurring in sentence-initial and sentence-final position as well as within the verb phrase. But modifiers of individual constituents are more restricted in their movement, and tend to be located next to their head constituents. Modifiers consisting of a whole sentence, like relative clauses, follow their heads:

(211a) Blg *Smírnenski e poét, čiéto tvórčestvo šte óstane zavínagi*
             v zlátnija fónd na nášata literatúra
             'Smirnenski is a poet whose work will remain forever
             in the golden treasury of our literature'

Modifiers consisting of noun phrases and prepositional phrases also follow their heads:

(211b) Sorb *člowjek* *z rozumom* 'a man of [with] intelligence'

(211c) Sorb *rozumny* *člowjek* 'an intelligent man'

unless they themselves modify an adjective, usually an attributive, or a participle in an expanded participial construction. In these instances the modifier(s) may precede:

(212a) Pol *jego ze wszystkich względów udana symfonia*
             lit. 'his from all points of view successful symphony'

(212b)   Rus   *vsé èti **nám neizvéstnye** fákty*
         lit. 'all these to us unknown facts'

(212c)   Rus   *vsé èti **neizvéstnye nám** fákty*
         lit. 'all these unknown to us facts'

(212d)   Rus   *vsé èti **nášimi kollégami výbrannye** akadémiki*
         lit. 'all these by our colleagues chosen academicians'

Among adjectives and degree modifiers we find that single constituent adjective modifiers and degree modifiers tend to precede the head (213a, c), while complex adjective modifiers and degree modifiers, and other modifiers, tend to follow the head (213b, d):

(213a)   Rus   *tepér-eš-njaja*   *Moskvá*
                now-Adj-FemNomSg   Moscow[Fem]-NomSg

(213b)   Rus   *Moskvá*   *tepér'*
                Moscow[Fem]-NomSg   now[Adv]
                'contemporary Moscow'

(213c)   Cz   *černovlask-á*   *holk-a*
                black-haired-FemNomSg   girl-NomSg

(213d)   Cz   *holk-a*   *s*   *čern-ými*   *vlas-y*
                girl-NomSg   with   black-InstrPl   hair-InstrPl
                'black-haired girl, girl with black hair'

Attributive adjectives provide an example of fixed ordering which differs significantly among the Slavic languages. In all the languages except Polish, single modifiers usually precede (Adjective + Noun, as in (214a–b)), except in some fixed phrases (Noun + Adjective, as in (215a)), and in some terminological, technical and fixed combinations of nouns and adjectives, which have often been calqued (9.6.2) from Latin or Greek (215b–c):

(214a)   Sorb   *słónčny dźeń*, *módre njebjo*   'sunny day, blue sky'

(214b)   Cz   *dobrý den*, *český lid*   'good day, Czech people'

(215a)   Sorb   *Wótče Naš*   'Our Father'
                Maćica Serbska   'Sorbian Maćica'

(215b)   Rus   *Pëtr Velíkij*/*Pérvyj*   'Peter the Great/First'
                ímja prilagáteľnoe   'adjective' (Lat *nomen **adjectivum***)

(215c)   Cz   *Ústav pro jazyk český*   'Institute of the Czech language'

Polish is a special case, since some adjectives regularly follow the noun, while others precede:

(216a) Pol *czerwony plastyk syntetyczny* 'red synthetic plastic'

cf. (216b) Rus *krásnaja sintetíčeskaja plastmássa*

(217a) Pol *nowa gramatyka opisowa* 'a new descriptive grammar'

cf. (217b) Rus *nóvaja opisátel'naja grammátika*

The adjective that follows the noun in Polish is the one which occurs latest before the noun in the English and Russian equivalents. In general, qualitative adjectives (6.1.2.1) will precede the noun, except in a few fixed expressions or in emphatic constructions:

(218) Pol *dzień dobry*, cf. Cz *dobrý den*, Rus *dóbryj dén'* 'good day'

Relative adjectives in Polish follow the noun. If there are two relative adjectives, the adjective closer to the noun in the corresponding sentence in a pre-modifying language will be the adjective to follow the noun in Polish (219a–b); if there are more than two adjectives, one will remain after the noun, and the others will stack before the noun (219c):

(219a) Pol *pompa elektryczna*   'an electric pump'

(219b) Pol *elektryczna pompa wodna*   'an electric water-pump'

(219c) Pol *dobry polski słownik etymologiczny*
              'a good Polish etymological dictionary'

Polish is therefore a language with selectively post-modifying attributive adjectives, and is an intermediate stage between pre-modifying languages like the other ten modern Slavic languages and English, and a predominantly post-modifying language like French.

Slavic adjectives, except in fixed expressions, usually invert around their noun head for the purposes of emphasis. What is emphasized depends on the position of the noun phrase in the sentence. An inversion which places a noun or adjective in sentence-initial or sentence-final position will focus or emphasize that noun or adjective. The same effect can be achieved phonetically or lexico-grammatically by emphasizing individual constituents in otherwise regular word orders. Inversions are particularly common in poetry, and in rhetorical or artistic prose:

(220a) Rus *Brožú*   *li* *já* *vdól'* *úlic*   *šumnyx* (Pushkin)
              wander-1Sg Q   I   along   streets   noisy
              'If I'm wandering down noisy streets'

(220b)   Rus   *godú*   *v*   *týsjača*   *devjat'sót*   *sórok*   *devjátom*
              year-LocSg in   thousand   nine hundred   forty   ninth
              napáli   *mý*   *s*   *druz'jámi*   *na primečátel'nuju*
              came upon   we   with friends   on remarkable
              zamétku v   *žurnále*   <*Priróda*>   *Akadémii*   *Naúk*
              notice   in journal   <Nature>   of the Academy of Sciences

'about 1949 my friends and I came across a remarkable notice
in the journal *Nature* of the Academy of Sciences.'
(A. I. Solzhenitsyn, *Gulag archipelago*, p. 1)

7.4.3.3   Clitics

Slavic languages show considerable differences in their repertoires of clitics
(6.1.2.4). Enclitics are usually associated with the first ("Wackernagel") unaccented
position in the sentence (usually second position). Enclitics attach themselves to the
preceding stressed constituent, and so do not themselves bear any stress. The
constituent to which they are attached is often called the "host" (Zwicky, 1977).
Proclitics, for instance prepositions, attach to a following host. But there are major
difficulties in distinguishing between enclitics and proclitics in sentence-second
position. In particular, phonological hosts may not coincide with grammatical
hosts for a given clitic (van Riemsdijk, 1999: 15). For this reason we use 'clitic' in
the following examples except where proclitics and enclitics are explicitly discussed
(and for Slavic clitics see Dimitrova-Vulchanova, 1999):

(221a)   B/C/S   *dèca*   *bi*   *nam*   *se*   *smèjala*
                 children   CondCl   us-Cl-Dat   ReflCl   laughed
                 'the children would laugh at us'

(221b)   Blg   *včéra*   *săm*   *go*   *nabljudával*
               yesterday   AuxCl-1Sg   he-Cl-Acc   watched
               'yesterday I watched him'

(221c)   Slk   *nesmial*   *by*   *som*   *sa*   *mu*
               not-laugh   CondCl   AuxCl-1Sg   ReflCl   he-Cl-Dat
               'I wouldn't laugh at him' (*smiat' sa* 'to laugh')

(221d)   Sln   *tí*   *si*   *si*   *ju*   *kúpil*
               you   AuxCl-2Sg   ReflCl-Dat   it-Cl-Acc   bought
               'you bought it for yourself'

(221e)   Cz   *a-bych*   *nevěděl*
              in-order-that-AuxCl-1Sg   not-know
              'so that I should not know'

But in some emphatic constructions, and commonly in B/C/S, the "host" is interpreted more narrowly to mean the first non-clitic constituent within the first major constituent of the sentence. This means that clitics may occur between an attributive adjective and its head noun (222a) or even between a forename name and a surname (222b) (Browne, 1974):

(222a) B/C/S   *u   slòvēnskom   se*   *jèziku*   *gòvor* [. . .]
                 in   Slovenian   ReflCl-Acc   language   say [. . .]
                 'In Slovenian they say [. . .]'

(222b) B/C/S   *Làv   bi   te*   *se*   *Tòlstoj*
                 Lev   CondCl   you-Cl-Dat   ReflCl-Acc   Tolstoj
                 sìgūrno   ùplašio
                 certainly   feared
                 'Lev Tolstoj would certainly be afraid of you'

Sentence enclitics occur in the first unaccented position in the sentence, and semantically can focus their host. Word order can then be used to place in sentence-initial position the constituent which is to be focused:

(223a) Rus   *Iván   li   znál   ob   ètom?*
                Ivan   QEncl   knew   about   this
                'was it Ivan who knew about this?'

(223b) Rus   *ob   ètom   li   znál   Iván?*
                about   this   QEncl   knew   Ivan
                'was it about this that Ivan knew?'

But to some extent in Czech, and particularly in Polish, we find that the clitic verbal auxiliaries are now closer to being mobile verbal affixes, and may also occur within the sentence in a number of non-Wackernagel positions. They may attach to constituents like the object (224a) as well as to the verb (224b–c):

(224a) Pol   *ksiąźkę-ś*   *wziął*   *w   bibliotece?*
                book[Fem]AccSg-Cl-2Sg   took-MascSgPast   in   library
                'did you borrow a book from the library?'

(224b) Pol   *ksiąźkę wziął-eś w bibliotece?*

(224c) Pol   *ksiąźkę w bibliotece wziął-eś?*

Conversely, 'be' auxiliaries and 'be' copulae can attach to adjectives and other constituents as well:

(225) Pol   *ja-m   Peruwianką*   *jest*
                I-Cl-1Sg   Peruvian[Fem]-InstrSg   be-3Sg
                'I am a Peruvian woman'

– though the standard prefers (*ja*) *jestem*. Other Slavic languages show a similar, though less extreme, vacillation with the conditional *by*, particularly if it is invariant, and with verbal auxiliaries. If the clitic does not occur in the Wackernagel position, it usually follows the verb:

(226a)   Rus   *Sáša priéxal by pósle obéda*
               'Sasha [Masc] would have come after dinner'
         B/C/S *òvē gŏdinē tâj pĕsnīk napísao mi je knjĩgu* [PronCl] [AuxCl]
               'this year that poet wrote me a book' (Browne, 1994: 41)

There is little variation of this basic pattern within the languages, except for syntactic (not stylistic) reasons. In Polish, for example, a subordinate sentence containing a reflexive infinitive may "promote" the reflexive clitic (i.e. move it leftwards) in the main clause; consider the positions of the reflexive *się* in (140–141). In Bulgarian a negative may attract the verbal auxiliary to it:

(227)   Blg   *ne*   *si*   *li*   *go*   *vĭždal?*
              Neg   Aux-Cl-2Sg   Q-Encl   him-Cl   saw-MascSgPastPart
              'didn't you see him?'

while in Slovenian the negative may carry the conditional particle to the rightmost end of the string of clitics:

(228)   Sln   *Maríja*   *jo*   *ne*   *bi*   *vídela*
              Maria   her-Cl   NegCl   CondCl   saw-FemSgPastPart
              'Maria would not see her'

The status of some clitics can be affected by the behavior of the host: in Slovenian a preceding subordinate sentence counts as a first accented constituent, and the clitics in the main sentence are sentence-initial (de Bray, 1980b: 395):

(229)   Sln   *kò je Lávdon oblēgal Béograd,*
              Véga pŕvič odlikovàl v vójski
              se   *je*
              ReflCl-Acc   Aux-Cl-3Sg
              'when Lavdon was besieging Belgrade, Vega first
              distinguished himself in the war'

Alternatively, as happens in Sorbian, verbal auxiliary clitics and even pronoun clitics may occur sentence-initially. This is particularly true of pronouns:

(230a) Sorb *mi*   *so*   *dźije*
              I-Cl-Dat   ReflCl-Acc   dream-3SgPres
              'I dream'

(230b) Sorb *mi   je   so   dźało*
        I-ClDat Aux-Cl-3Sg Refl-Cl-Acc dream-NeutSgPast
        'I dreamed'

7.5 Syntactic pragmatics: Functional Sentence Perspective

Functional Sentence Perspective is very much a product of the Czech grammatical tradition (Cz *aktuální členění větné*, Rus *aktuáľnoe členénie predložénija* (Mathesius, 1929)). It describes the organization of information in the sentence in grammatical terms (Huddleston and Pullum, 2002: ch. 16). Here we give only a broad-scale description of how Slavic handles information with special reference to word order and grammatical markers.

The "topic" or "theme" is the part of the sentence about which something is said, and broadly corresponds to the "old" or "given" information from the physical context of utterance, or from the preceding discourse or text. The new information presented about the topic is termed the "comment" or "rheme". As a matter of conversational and communicative strategy, the old information usually comes first, and is the less informative part of the sentence. The new information, the more informative part, then follows:

(231a) Rus *stároe dérevo* [NeutSg]   *stoít v boľšóm sadú* [MascSg]
             <TOPIC>   <COMMENT>
             'the old tree   stands in a big garden'

The next sentence may make another comment about the same topic:

(231b) Rus *onó* [NeutSg] *(ø) gorázdo výše nášej škóly* [FemSg]
             <TOPIC>   <COMMENT>
             'it (the tree) is much higher than our school'

or it may take information from the previous comment, which now counts as known information, and supply some new information concerning it:

(231c) Rus *ón* [MascSg]   *prinadležít nášej škóle*
             <TOPIC>   <COMMENT>
             'it (the garden) belongs to our school'

The topic in these sentences is expressed by the grammatical subject. But the object, or a prepositional phrase, or other syntactic elements of the sentence, may also be the topic, as is clear if we read (231d) or (231e) as following (231a):

(231d) Rus *èto dérevo*   *mý vídeli v pérvyj ráz …*
              <TOPIC>   <COMMENT>
              'this tree   we saw for the first time …'

(231e) Rus *v ètom déreve* *žávoronki strójat gnezdó kážŭyj gód*
              <TOPIC>   <COMMENT>
              'in this tree   the larks build their nest every year'

There is a tendency for heavier constituents – those with more complex structure, or more lexical material, or both – to constitute the comment and to come late in the sentence.

Some sentences may consist entirely of a comment, especially if the sentence is impersonal or apersonal (personal with no expressed subject):

(232a) Rus *býlo*   *proxládno*
                        <COMMENT>
              be-3SgNeutPast   chilly-NeutSg
              'it was chilly'

(232b) Rus *pojút*   *grómko*   *na*   *úlicax*
                        <COMMENT>
              sing-3PlPres loudly   on   street-LocPl
              'people are singing loudly in the streets'

By marking given information as it does, word order is also able to compensate for the lack of a morphological category of article in all the Slavic languages except Bulgarian and Macedonian (7.1.1). The topic normally precedes the comment; the topic, being known information, is definite, and this is, in fact, one of the principal means of marking definiteness in Slavic by non-lexical means. Conversely, noun phrases in the comment will tend to be indefinite and so will be translated in English by the indefinite article:

(233a) Pol *dziewczynka*   *dała*   *mi*   *bukiet*
              girl[Fem]-NomSg give-FemSgPast I-Dat bouquet-AccPl
              kwiatów
              flowers-GenPl
              '**the** girl gave me a bouquet of flowers'

The versatility of this device is shown by the ability of the reverse word order to assign the reverse markings for definiteness:

(233b) Pol *bukiet kwiatów dała mi dziewczynka*
              'the bouquet of flowers was given to me by **a** girl'
              'it was **a** girl who gave me the bouquet of flowers'

Indeed, the OVS order in Slavic is one of the commonest ways of expressing what in English would be a passive, since one of its most useful pragmatic functions is to reverse the topic–comment structure of the arguments of a sentence.

The possibilities of word-order variation, both for emphasis and for information focusing, particularly in the spoken languages (11.2–11.3), are strongly facilitated by the ability of Slavic to provide explicit grammatical marking of syntactic roles in the sentence. In analysing the topic–comment structure of the sentence, we have four sets of factors to handle simultaneously: the identification and delimitation of the topic and comment; the grammatical division of the sentence into subject and predicate; neutral versus inverted word order; and neutral versus emphatic stress. There are many possible permutations of these four sets of variables, especially since emphasis can extend over different sections of a sentence (Švedova, 1970: 597–599). Marked intonation or word order (especially involving the movement of heavy constituents) is used to focus specific parts of the sentence.

In impersonal or apersonal (7.3.3) sentences the neutral order with non-contrastive intonation places the predicate first: compare the neutral (234a) with the marked (234b); focused elements are bolded:

(234a)   Rus   neutral: *xóčetsja pít'*   'one feels (I feel) like a drink'
                              ne slýšno slóv   'no words can be heard'

But

(234b)   Rus   marked: **pít'** *xóčetsja*
                             'I feel like a **drink**' (not a meal)
                             slóv *ne slýšno*
                             'the **words** can't be heard' (but the singing can)'

In sentences articulated into Topic + Comment the stylistically neutral order is Subject–Predicate. The reverse order, with stress on the subject/subordinate element, also reverses the Topic–Comment structure. Examples include most transitive- and intransitive-verb sentences:

(235a)   B/C/S   neutral: *òtac pèvā*   'father is singing'

(235b)   B/C/S   marked: *pèvā òtac*   'it is **father** who is singing'

These stylistically expressive versions have contrastive stress focusing specific constituents:

(235c)   B/C/S   *pèvā òtac*   'father is **singing**'

(235d)   B/C/S   *òtac pèvā*   'it is **father** who is singing'

Note how further refinement of the interaction of word order with information structuring is required to handle the placement of objects:

(236a)   Sln   *stríc je darovál knjígo*   'uncle gave a book' (neutral)
(236b)   Sln   *knjígo je darovál **stríc***   'the book was given by **uncle**'
(236c)   Sln   ***knjígo** je darovál stríc*   'it was a **book** that uncle gave'
(236d)   Sln   ***stríc** je darovál knjígo*   'it was **uncle** who gave the book'

8

Word formation

8.1 Types of word formation

Slavic stands between Germanic and Romance in its utilization of word formation. It does not share the long compound nouns found especially in German technical vocabulary, or to some extent in phrasal expressions like 'post-hostage resolution crisis' in some English professional styles. On the other hand, Slavic as a whole does not follow the analytic tendencies of the Romance languages, which prefer coding compound nouns as phrases.

In Slavic there are rich resources of word formation. For example, the root *pis-* 'write' forms prefixed (Slk *podpis* 'signature', *pod* 'under') and suffixed derivatives (Slk *písmeno* 'letter (of the alphabet)', *písomný* 'written, writing' [Adj]). There are productive patterns of root-combination in nouns (Slk *zem* 'earth', *zemepis* 'geography'). Word formation is both a key component of the exploitation of roots in different parts of speech, and a major source of lexical renewal and development (chapter 9).

The scope of word formation includes prefixation, root combination and suffixation other than inflexional suffixation (endings: chapter 5). Word formation overlaps with morphophonology (chapter 4), since the form of roots and affixes may be affected by the combinatorics of derivation. It overlaps with inflexional morphology (chapter 5), since it is concerned with the combination of roots and affixes, an area where the formation of verbal aspect spans both inflexion and word formation. It overlaps with syntax (chapter 7), since word combinations, and particularly the combinations of word-roots, share with syntax major patterns like Modifier + Head (Marchand, 1969; Selkirk, 1982). And it overlaps with lexis and lexicology (chapter 9), one branch of which has to do with lexical productivity and innovation.

For the purposes of this chapter we concentrate on "word formation" as the combination of pieces of morphological material in the construction of lexical words, excluding inflexion.

Word formation plays a key role in language use, expression and creativity in Slavic: for instance, in the formation of compound nominal concepts (8.1.3) and in the characteristic use of diminutives in conversation (8.2.2). Furthermore, in the drive to adapt the languages to new social, economic, political, cultural and technological demands, word formation has been a key resource which the Slavic languages have exploited for lexical enrichment. Many word-formed neologisms originated in governmental and social structures in the USSR, which is why Russian has so often served as a model. Since the end of Euro-Communism, Western models have been more active in the realignment of the Slavic vocabularies to meet the new demands.

A fuller idea of the extent of word-formation processes in modern Slavic can be gained from root-dictionaries and "grammatical dictionaries" (e.g. Worth, Kozak and Johnson, 1970; Tixonov, 1985), where roots are listed with their arrays of prefixes, attached roots and suffixes; and from reverse-order dictionaries (e.g. *Obratnyj Slovar'*, 1974; Zaliznjak, 1977), where words are sorted alphabetically from the right-hand end, so grouping together words with common endings.

The overall morphological and morphotactic structure of the Slavic word for parts of speech other than verbs is as in (1a), and for verbs as in (1b):

(1a)   MORPHOTACTIC STRUCTURE OF THE WORD: NON-VERBS
Stem, consisting of
  zero or more ordered prefixes
  one or more roots, with or without a link-vowel
  zero or more word-forming suffixes
  zero or more affective suffixes
Inflexion
Zero or one reflexive or definite/deictic marker, depending on the language

(1b)   MORPHOTACTIC STRUCTURE OF THE WORD: VERBS
Stem, consisting of
  zero or more ordered prefixes
  one or more roots, with or without a link-vowel
  zero or one word-forming suffix
  zero or one stem expanding suffix or thematic vowel
Inflexion
Zero or one reflexive marker, depending on the language

In (1a–b) the stem and inflexion are the obligatory components of the inflecting word. 'Word-forming suffixes' determine the part of speech and add information like 'abstract action nominal'. The last word-forming suffix usually determines the part of speech, which is confirmed by the type of inflexion which follows: see (5) below.

The Russian adjectival root *star-* 'old', for instance, forms a number of derived words, including:

(2) Russian lexeme *star* 'old':

    (2a) *stár-yj*   'old'
          old-AdjMascSgNom

    (2b) *star-é-t'*   'to grow old' [Imprfv]
          old-Verb_suffix-Inf

    (2c) *u-star-é-t'*   'to grow old' [Prfv]
          Prefix-old-Verb_suffix-Inf

    (2d) *u-star-é-l-yj*   (i) 'having grown old' [PastActPart]
                        (ii) 'old, aged' [lexicalized adjective]
          Prefix-old-Verb_suffix-Past-Adj_suffix-AdjMascNomSg

    (2e) *u-star-é-l-ost'-ø* 'old age'
          Prefix-old-Verb_suffix-Past-Abstract-NounFemNomSg

    (2f) *stár-en'k-ij*   'old' [Dim]
          old-Dim-AdjMascNomSg

    (2g) *star-úšk-a*   'old woman'
          old-Dim_Aff-NounFemNomSg

    (2h) *star-o-svét-sk-ij* 'old fashioned'
          old-Link_vowel-world-Adj_suffix-AdjMascNomSg

Not all the elements listed in (1) are available for all parts of speech or for all the Slavic languages. Verbs, for example, do not have articulated systems of diminutives in the manner of nouns, adjectives and derived adverbs, and have only a limited means for encoding such semantic concepts: e.g. B/C/S *pȇvati* 'to sing', *pevùckati* 'to hum' (Browne, 1993: 343). Only Polish includes the reflexive marker (Pol *się*) in derived abstract action nominals from verbs with the reflexive, written as a separate word:

(3)   'to put on make-up'   'putting on make-up' [Noun]
      Pol *malować się*   *malowanie się*
  cf. Rus *grimirovát'sja*   *grimiróvka*

Suffixed definite markers are found only in Bulgarian and Macedonian, and suffixed deictics only in Macedonian (5.5.1), though suffixed "definite" adjectives occur in B/C/S and more marginally in Slovenian (5.4.3):

(4)   'an old man'   'the old man'
        Blg   *stár čovék*   *stárăt čovék*
        B/C/S *stăr čòvek*   *stârī čòvek*
cf.   Cz   *starý člověk*   *starý člověk*

The selection of which affix to combine with a specific root or stem is not a simple matter. Some prefixes, especially additive semantic prefixes like *kontra-*, occur with noun and adjective roots with regular semantic and morphological results. Some suffixes tend to occur with roots of a certain grammatical category: *-tel'/-tel* occurs with action verbal roots to form agent nouns which are masculine or epicene: Sln *písati* 'to write', *pisátelj* 'writer'. The derived part of speech is normally marked by the suffixes, particularly those for forms like agent nouns, abstract nouns, derived verbs, adjectives and adverbs. The inflexion is an additional marker of word-class:

(5)   Cz root *uč-* 'to teach'
       (5a)   *uč-i-t*   'to teach'
              teach-Verb_suffix-Inf

       (5b)   *uč-i-tel-ø*   'teacher' (male)
              teach-Verb_suffix-MascAgent-NomSg

       (5c)   *uč-i-tel-k-a*   'teacher' (female)
              teach-Verb_suffix-MascAgent-NounFem-NomSg

       (5d)   *uč-i-tel-ova-t*   'to play the role of the teacher'
              teach-Verb_suffix-MascAgent-verb_formant-Inf

       (5e)   *uč-i-tel-sk-ý*   'pedagogical'
              teach-Verb_suffix-MascAgent-Adj-MascNomSg

       (5f)   *uč-i-tel-stv-í*   'teaching, teaching career, teaching staff'
              teach-Verb_suffix-MascAgent-Abstract-NomSg

(6)   Cz root *rychl-* 'quick':
       (6a)   *rychl-ý*   'quick'
              quick-MascNomSg

       (6b)   *rychl-e*   'quickly'
              quick-Adv

Slavic word formation lends itself well to the type of constituent analysis familiar from studies like Marchand (1969), particularly since Slavic languages show relatively little discontinuity of morphemes. Constituent analysis is useful not only in analysing the structure of multiple prefixes, but also in identifying the structure of complex words:

(7) Blg *varjá*   'boil' [Prfv]   [*varjá*]v
     dovarjá   'finish boiling' [Prfv]   [*do* [*varjá*]v]v
     nedovarjá 'leave half-boiled' [Prfv] [*ne* [*do* [*varjá*]v]v]v

The four main structural types of word formation in Slavic are all productive, though to differing degrees. We describe them in turn: prefixation (8.1.1); suffixation (8.1.2); root combination (8.1.3); and combined types (8.1.4). We then briefly cover the morphophonological (8.1.5) aspects of word-formation before concentrating on individual word-classes: nouns (8.2), verbs (8.3), adjectives (8.4), adverbs (8.5) and other word-classes (8.6). The special cases of acronyms and stump compounds are discussed in chapter 9. Our approach owes a great deal to Townsend (1968/1975), who established word formation as a key component of Russian language syllabuses.

There is striking uniformity in the functional load of word formation across the Slavic languages. All the languages possess similar types of word-forming operations – prefixation, suffixation, root-combination and so on – and similar types of grammatical processes – like the formation of agent and abstract action nominals and diminutives; the derivation of verbs and the formation of verbal aspect; or the derivation of adjectives and adverbs. The differences arise rather in the use made of different pieces of morphological material. An agent nominal with a cognate verb stem, for instance, may require different suffixes in different languages, as with Rus *pisátel'*, B/C/S *pisac*, Pol *pisarz* 'writer' (8.2). Or a given suffix may have different semantic and stylistic properties, either absolutely, or in combination with different stems, in the various languages. In Russian *málen'kij* 'small', now the unmarked form of the positive grade, includes the diminutive suffix *-en'k-*, but in the other languages this suffix has hypocoristic force, so that Cz *malinký* means 'dear little', contrasting with the positive grade *malý* 'small'.

8.1.1   Prefixation

Prefixation involves the addition of a bound morpheme to a root. Prefixes may occur in sequences of three as the normal maximum, though four are possible: B/C/S *u-pre-po-dò-biti se* 'to put on an innocent face' (Lekov, 1958: 14). Prefixation can be divided into two main types: general semantic prefixation; and specifically verbal prefixation, where the prefix can have a grammatical function as well. We discuss the mixed 'prefixation + suffixation' type in 8.1.4.

Semantic prefixation involves adding a prefix with the combinatorial semantic effect of combining the meanings of the prefix and root or stem:

(8) B/C/S *ultra-:*   *ŭltrazvūčan*   'ultrasonic'
            kontra-: *kŏntrarevolúcija* 'counter-revolution'

Most of the foreign-language prefixes of Slavic occur in this pattern, often but by no means exclusively with foreign roots, as can be seen from B/C/S *ŭltrazvūčan* above (B/C/S *zvûk* 'sound'). Furthermore, not all the prefixes in semantic prefixation are of foreign origin: Blg *svrăxzvúkov* 'ultrasonic' adds a native prefix *svrăx* 'above, supra, ultra' to a native root *zvuk* 'sound', forming a calque (chapter 9) from 'ultrasonic'. There are approximately thirty word-forming prefixes in each of the Slavic languages. These patterns are of limited productivity, except when words are borrowed from non-Slavic languages as in (8). Prefixed nouns, adjectives and adverbs usually have suffixes as well, being typically derived from prefixed verbs: 'felon' Pol *prze-stęp-ca*, Rus *pre-stúp-nik*, Blg *pre-stăp-nik*. Examples like Pol *na-pis* 'inscription', Rus *vý-xod*, Blg *íz-xod* 'exit', apparently suffix-less, are also derived from verbal roots: Pol *na-pis-ać*, Rus *vy-xod-ít'*, Blg *iz-xód-ja*, and will be regarded here as having a 'zero' suffix (8.2).

A more regular and productive pattern of prefixation in Bulgarian and Macedonian concerns the comparative adjectives and adverbs (8.4.2): Mac *áren* 'good', *pó-áren* 'better', *náj-áren* 'best' (both prefix and stem are stressed). Even more widely based is the productive use of the negative prefix *ne-/nie-* in combinations with adjectives and derived nouns:

(9) Slk   *neopatrný*   'careless'
     nefajčiar   'non-smoker'
     nemluvňa   'infant' (lit. 'non-speaker')
Ukr   *neljubóv*   'dislike' (*ljubóv* 'love')
Rus   *nepogóda*   'bad weather' (*pogóda* 'weather')

This pattern is not productive with verbs (the Czech, Slovak and Sorbian ortho-graphic convention of writing the negative prefix together with the verb, as in Cz *dělá* 'he does', *nedělá* 'he doesn't do', is a separate issue).

In verbal prefixation (8.3.1) the prefixes are often related to spatial prepositions like Cz *do* 'to, up to, until' (Cz *končit* 'to finish', *do-končit* 'complete') and *pod* 'under, below' (Cz *stavit* 'to place', *pod-stavit* 'to place under'). Verb prefixation is bound up with the formation of verbal aspect. The prefix may perfectivize the verb (Cz *vařit* 'to boil, cook' [Imprfv], *u-vařit* 'to boil, cook' [Prfv]). Or it may perfectivize the stem and simultaneously modify the meaning in a number of ways: for instance, by specifying the beginning or end of an action (Rus *plákat'* 'to weep' [Imprfv], *za-plákat'* 'to begin to weep, to burst out crying' [Prfv]); or may bring about more radical semantic changes, as in Cz *pod-stavit* (above). Verbal prefixation and aspect formation interact closely with verbal suffixation. We take up these questions in 8.3.1–8.3.2.

8.1.2 Suffixation

Suffixation in Slavic covers the larger part of word formation. Suffixal word formation has two major roles.

In the first, suffixation causes the transfer of a word into another word-class, or another sub-class of the same word-class:

(10)   Cz   *hor-a* 'mountain'   *hor-n-ý* 'mountainous'
        Cz   *rychl-ý* 'quick'   *rychl-e* 'quickly'
        Cz   *prádl-o* 'linen'   *prádel-na* 'laundry'
        Cz   *šťasten-ø* 'happy' [Short]   *šťastn-ý* 'happy' [Long]

There are many word-forming suffixes: Russian, for instance, has over forty different suffixes for forming masculine agent nouns, and a smaller number of other suffixes for deriving feminine agent nouns.

In the second role, suffixation is involved in the semantic and/or stylistic elaboration of individual word-classes. These processes include the formation of verbal aspect, for instance in deriving imperfective verbs from perfective stems; diminutives; gradation; and definite/indefinite formation. These processes cover more than one word-class, and often interact with prefixation as well.

For instance, diminutives and augmentatives are typical of Slavic word formation, and occur in several word-classes: nouns, adjectives, adverbs and even verbs. Diminutives express either overtones of emotion, or perceptions of size, or both. Depending on the context, and the tone of voice, Russian *kníž-ečk-a* may mean 'booklet', 'dear little book', or 'rotten little pamphlet' – for instance, as a means of belittling a colleague's latest scholarly book (from Rus *kníga* 'book'). Diminutives and augmentatives are characteristic of the spoken more than of the written language. Proper names in particular have many different diminutive forms:

(11)   Pol   *Bogumił-a* (woman's name)   *Bog-a*   *Bog-n-a*
            Bog-un-ia   *Bog-uńc-ia*   *Bog-us-ia*   *Bog-usieńk-a*

Augmentative forms mark an increase or excess of size, often with pejorative overtones: Sorb *pos* 'dog'; *psy-č-idło* 'great big horrible hound' [Aug, Pej]. The use of diminutives is endemic in certain contexts, particularly in the family and in intimate personal relationships. Using non-diminutive forms to small children can be a sign of displeasure or authority.

Diminutive and augmentative suffixes may occur in an ordered series: Ukr *hólos* 'voice', *holos-ók, holos-óč-ek* [Dim]. With adjectives and adverbs the motivation and usage of diminutives are similar to that of nouns, but the varieties of word formation are more restricted (8.4–8.6).

8.1.3   Root combination

Roots may be simplex, as in (2a–g) above, or complex, as in (2h). Combinations of more than two roots are unusual outside stump compounds (chapter 9), and are not common with verbs: Rus *velik-o-dúš-niča-t'* 'to play at being generous' (*velík-ij* 'great', *duš-á* 'soul', via *velikodúšn-yj* 'magnanimous'). Examples like (12) involve the combination of roots or full words. They may be combined in three main ways: by direct combination with hyphens (12a), less commonly by direct combination without hyphens (12b), and commonly with a "link-vowel" (12c):

(12a)   Rus   *górod–gerój* (hyphenated)   'hero city'
                    city-hero

(12b)   Rus   *Lenin-grád*   'Leningrad'
                    Lenin-city (ChSl form, cf. (12a) and see 9.3.1)

(12c)   Blg   *slab-o-úm-en-ø*   'weak-minded'
                    weak-Link_vowel-mind-Adj-MascSg

Hyphenated compounds, and direct word combinations, have limited participation in further word formation, though both parts may inflect (8.2). The pattern with a link-vowel to join the two roots is common and productive. The choice of link-vowel between /o/ and /e/ differs across the languages, and to some extent with phonological factors (8.1.5, 8.2). The link-vowel pattern is able to link roots from the major parts of speech: Slk *chleb-o-dar-ca* 'employer' (lit. 'bread-giver') consists of *chleb* 'bread', the root *dar* 'give', and the agent suffix *-ca*, with the roots joined by the link-vowel *o*. The compound words derived by this pattern are predominantly nouns and adjectives. This type of complex word can participate in further word-formation processes: Blg *slab-o-úm-en* yields the adverb *slab-o-úm-n-o* 'weak-mindedly', and there is also a parallel abstract noun *slab-o-úm-ie* 'weak-mindedness'.

Word- and root-combinations may show various internal grammatical structures, of the familiar types identified in work by Marchand (1969), Selkirk (1982) and others. Most such formations are nouns and adjectives:

(13a)   modifier + head:
             Ukr   *lže-svíd-č-yj*   'false witness' [Adj]
                        falsely-witness-Adj-MascNomSg

(13b)   head + head:

  Pol   *żelaz-o-beton-ø*   'ferro-concrete' [Noun]
       iron-LinkVowel-concrete-NomSg

  Rus   *cár'-púšk-a* (hyphenated)   'Tsar-cannon' [Noun]
       tsar-cannon-NomSg

(13c)   governed (e.g. object) + governing:

  Blg   *čovek-o-nenávist-en*   'misanthropic' [Adj]
       man-LinkVowel-hatred-AdjMascSg

  Rus   *sam-o-krítik-a*   'self-criticism' [Noun]
       self-LinkVowel-criticism-NomSg

8.1.4   Mixed types: prefixation + suffixation

The combined 'prefixation + suffixation' pattern is common and productive. As we have seen, verbs are the word-class which dominates straight prefixation (8.1.2). In word-classes other than verbs prefixation tends to be accompanied by suffixation: e.g. Sorb *bjezstrašny* 'fearless' (*bjez-* 'without' + *strach* 'fear' + *-n-* [Adj] + *-y* [Adj: MascNomSg]) and *bjezstrašnosć* 'fearlessness' (*bjezstrašn-* + *-osć* [Noun]). Even with verbs the prolific patterns of derivation often involve both prefixation and suffixation: Slk *prepracovanie* 'reworking' = *pre-* 're-' + *pracova-t'* 'to work' + *-ni(j)-(e)* [Abstract Action suffix]. We take up these types of derivation in more detail below.

A distinction must be made between "purely synchronic" derivation and "diachronic" or "etymological" derivation: the former may disregard etymological information, that is, the historical derivational process itself, and rely entirely on surface facts. Thus, Slk *prepracovanie* may be seen as prefixation in relation to *pracovanie* 'work', or as suffixation in relation to *prepracovat'* 'to work', but only the latter is the etymological process (and semantically the more natural).

Similarly, Sorb *bjezstrašny* may be seen as a prefixed form of *strašny* or as a suffixed form of the nominalized phrase *bjez strach-a*, only the latter being "natural". Other examples of this are:

(14a)   Rus   *za Vólg-oj*   'on the other side of the Volga'
             zavólž-'e   'land beyond the Volga'
             zavólž-sk-ij [Adj]

(14b)   Ukr   *miž hor-ámi*   'between the mountains'
             mižhír-'ja   'area between the mountains'
             mižhír-n-yj [Adj]

In such cases, our preferred analytical approach will be the "etymological" (or semantically more natural) one.

8.1.5   Morphophonological aspects of word formation

Morphophonological adaptations, which are sometimes signalled explicitly in the orthography (especially in the more recently codified languages: appendix B), occur frequently between prefixes and roots. Prefixes may undergo regressive assimilation of voice before stems beginning with a voiceless consonant, though the orthography marks this regularly only in Belarusian, B/C/S and Macedonian, for instance in the prefix *ot-/od-* 'from': B/C/S *ot-kúpiti*, Pol *od-kupywać* [ɔtk-] 'redeem'. Prefixes may also undergo some assimilation of place of articulation, particularly in allegro speech, though the intervening morpheme boundary may retard such assimilation in comparison with comparable sequences of sounds within a morpheme (3.4.2, 4.3): Rus *bes-čéstnyj* = {bez} + {čest'} = /(be)sč(es)/ = [-ʃtʃ-] 'dishonourable'.

Prefixes may have alternative forms to preserve phonotactic requirements. Prefixes ending in a consonant may insert a vowel before a root beginning with a consonant or consonant cluster which would otherwise result in an unacceptable cluster: Blg *píša* 'write', *v-píša* 'interpolate, enter' but *vleká* 'drag', *vă-vleká* 'drag into'. In Belarusian the restriction of [v] to pre-vocalic position results in a change of *v-* to *u-* before roots not starting with a vowel: Bel *vaz'mú* 'I shall take' [Prfv] has the infinitive *uzjác'*, cf. Rus *voz'mú, vzjat'*.

With the exception of stress-shifts, which between the stem and the suffix can bring about changes in vowel quality in East Slavic and Bulgarian, roots are phonologically otherwise unaffected by the presence of a prefix. Belarusian marks such shifts, which affect vowel quality, in the orthography: Bel *sóx-nuc'* 'to dry out' [Imprfv], *vý-sax-nuc'* 'to dry out' [Prfv].

Roots undergo important mutations in their interaction with suffixes. These types of mutation are discussed in chapters 4 and 5 in connexion with inflexional paradigms. They include palatalization (mutation and additive palatalization); vowel ~ zero and vowel grade alternations; *-nu* loss or gain; and suppletion.

Suffixes interact with stems most obviously with additive palatalization and mutation, only the latter being always visible:

(15)   Rus   *žurnál-ø* 'magazine', *žurnal-íst-ø* 'journalist' (palatalized /l'/)
        B/C/S *strâh-ø* 'terror',   *stráš-an-ø* 'terrible'

However, there are other stem-modifying processes brought about by suffixes, including the behavior of zero-grade vowels (4.2.1):

(16)   Rus   *son-ø* 'sleep' [NomSg], *sn-a* [GenSg], *són-liv-yj* 'sleepy'

      Cz   *den-ø* 'day' [NomSg], *dn-e* [GenSg], *den-n-í* 'daily'

cf. Rus   *den'-ø, dn-ja, dn-evn-ój*

In addition, phonotactic constraints across the morpheme boundary between roots and suffixes can lead to assimilation or simplification of clusters of consonants (e.g. Blg *pariž-ski* (/ž/ > [š]), Mac *radost* but *rados-en* via **radost-n-*). What may be a feature of the spoken language or allegro speech in one language can be part of the standard language elsewhere (e.g. Rus *rádost-nyj* = [-sn-] in all but very careful speech).

8.2   Word formation and nouns

8.2.1   Prefixation

There are only restricted numbers of nouns in Slavic which consist of a prefix and an unsuffixed stem, and many of these (as with adjectives: 8.4) are foreign borrowings or calques. In other words, prefixed forms without word-forming suffixes are much less common than suffixed forms with or without prefixes.

Slavic languages have about thirty prefixes each for the purposes of noun formation (17a–c). Many prefixed nouns of this sort are, in fact, not cases of pure prefixation, but are actually zero-suffixed nouns derived from prefixed verbs (17d) (see discussion above, 8.1.4):

(17a)   Prefixed noun: 'disorder'

      ne- [Neg]:   Slk *ne-poriadok*; Pol *nie-porządek*

      bez-/bes- 'without':   Blg *bes-porédak*

(17b)   Calque (9.6.2): 'influence'

      v- 'in':   Rus, Blg *v-lij-áni-e*, Cz *v-liv-ø*, Pol *w-plyw-ø*

(17c)   Borrowed prefix + (borrowed) noun

      ober-:   Rus *òber-kondúktor* 'senior conductor'

      super-:   Blg *superfósfat* 'superphosphate'

(17d)   Prefix in a noun derived from a prefixed verb:

      roz-/raz-:   Sorb *roz-sah-ø*, Rus, Blg *raz-mér-ø* 'measure, size'

      (Sorb *roz-sah-áć*, Rus *raz-mér-it'*, Blg *raz-mér-ja* 'to measure')

8.2.2   Suffixation

Suffixed nouns are derived from verbs, adjectives and other nouns. They may express both concrete and abstract notions, and are highly productive. Gender is built into suffixes, but in the case of underlying nouns is usually based on the gender of the noun. The normal way of indicating gender in suffix citation is to add the nominative singular ending, since its relationship with gender is typical (consonant = Masc, -*a* = Fem, -*o*/-*e* = Neut (5.4.4)), so that normally nouns with -*nik* are masculine, with -*nica* feminine and with -*je* neuter.

Cognate roots may take different suffixes in different languages:

(18)   'alarm clock' (root *bud*- 'to wake up'):

-*l(')nik*:	East:	Bel	*budz-íl'nik*	Ukr	*bud-ýl'nik*	Rus	*bud-il'nik*
	South:	Sln	1. *bud-ílnik*	B/C/S	*bùd-īlnīk*		
		Mac	*bud-ilnik*	Blg	*bud-ílnik*		
-*ik*:	West:	Pol	*budz-ik*	Cz	1. *bud-ík*	Slk	*bud-ík*
-*ič(e)k*:		Cz	2. *bud-íček*				
-*ilka*:		Sln	2. *bud-ílka*				
-*ilica*:		Cr	*bud-ilica*				
-*(')ak*:		Sorb	*budź-ak*				

This variation does not necessarily mean that the parallel suffixes are not present in the language, but it does often indicate that the suffixes have different meanings or connotations: in Russian *pis-éc* 'clerk, scribe' is now archaic, and Rus *pís-ar'* is derogatory, meaning 'scribbler' – cf. the cognate Pol *pis-arz* 'writer'.

It is useful to break the types of suffixal noun formation into semantic-grammatical groups, broadly following Townsend (1968/1975), into abstracts, persons, animals, objects, places, collectives and diminutives.

8.2.2.1   *Abstracts*

Deverbal abstract action nominals in -*e*/-*je* are very productive, mainly in conjunction with -*n*- or -*t*- from the past participle passive. Imperfective verbal stems generate nouns referring to the processes, while perfectives generate nouns referring to completed actions and/or their results: Rus *izda-vá-nie* (< [Imprfv]) 'publishing', *izdá-nie* (< [Prfv]) 'edition'. Examples are legion: in (19) note the Ukrainian gemination of stem-final consonants before the suffix (infinitive in brackets):

(19a)   'carrying':   Pol   *nies-ienie* (*nieś-ć*)
                      Mac   *nos-enje* (*nos-i*)
                      Ukr   *nos-ínnja* (*nos-ýty*)

(19b)   'closing':   Pol   *zamknię-cie* (*zamknǫ-ć*)
                      Rus   *zakrý-tie* (*zakrý-t'*)
                      Ukr   *zakry-ttjá* (*zakrý-ty*)
                      Blg   *zakrí-tie* (*zakrí-ja*)

Derived abstract action nominals, especially those with a zero suffix, may form new homophonous lexical items.

(20)   Rus   *vxod* 'entering' and 'entrance', *výxod* 'exiting' and 'exit'
        (= *v*(*y*)*xod-ø-ø*: verb stem + zero suffix ([Action]/[Obj]) +
        zero ending ([NomSg])

Verbs may also derive nominals of action or result by the use of various other, non-zero, suffixes:

(21)   -(')*ba*   Blg, B/C/S, Sln *bor-ba*, Rus *bor-'bá* 'battle' (*bor-* 'to fight')
        -*tva*:   Blg *klé-tva*, B/C/S *klê-tva* (Sln *klé-tev*), Rus *kljá-tva*
                   (Slk *kla-tba*) 'oath'
                   (PSl **klen-t-* > *klę-t-* 'swear', cf. infinitives B/C/S *kléti*,
                   Rus *kljá-st'sja*, Slk *kln-út'*, Blg *kăln-á*)

Other, non-verbal, abstracts are formed mostly from adjectives and nouns. The feminine suffix *-ost'/-ost* is highly productive, similar to English formations in *-ness*, and to some extent in *-tion*. The words for 'happiness, joy' are commonly formed from *rad* 'glad (at something)'. All languages etymologically have the same suffix:

(22)   'happiness, joy'

Bel	*rád-asc'*	Ukr	*rád-ist'*	Rus	*rád-ost'*	
Sorb	*rad-ość*	Pol	*rad-ość*	Cz		*rad-ost* Slk *rad-ost'*
Sln	*rád-óst*	B/C/S	*răd-ōst*	Blg, Mac	*rád-ost*	

Somewhat less productive, but still strongly active, is the neuter suffix *-stvo/-ství*, which is added to the adjective stem. Note that while Belarusian does have the *-stvo* suffix (e.g. Bel *várvar-stva* 'barbarity'), it is not used with the root in (23). We list the source adjectives as well:

(23)   Adjective base PSl *bog-at-* 'rich':

Bel	*bahát-y*	Ukr	*bohát-yj*	Rus	*bogát-yj*	
	(*bahác-ce*)		*bohát-stvo*		*bogát-stvo*	
Sorb	*bohat-y*	Pol	*bogat-y*	Cz	*bohat-ý*	Slk *bohat-ý*
	bohat-stwo,		*bogat-stwo*		*bohat-ství*	*bohat-stvo*
	bohat-ość					
Sln	*bogàt*	B/C/S	*bògat*	Mac	*bogat*	Blg *bogát*
	bogá-stvo		*bògat-stvo*		*bogat-stvo*	*bogát-stvo*

8.2.2.2   *Persons*

Nouns denoting persons and agents are derived from nouns, verbs and adjectives. Masculines commonly use *-tel'/-tel* and *-ec/-ac*, and less commonly *-ar'/-ar*,

among a large repertoire of suffixes for deverbal agents. We give the source verbs
first:

(24)   'write(r)':

Bel	*pis-ác'*	Ukr	*pys-áty*	Rus	*pis-át'*		
	pis'-ménnik		*pys'-ménnyk*		*pis-átel'*		
Pol	*pis-ać*	Sorb	*pis-ać*	Cz	*p-sát*	Slk	*pís-at'/s-pis-ovat'*
	pis-arz		*s-pis-aćel*		*pis-atel*		*s-pis-ovatel'*
Sln	*pis-áti*	B/C/S	*pís-ati*	Mac	*piš-e*	Blg	*píš-a*
	pis-átelj		*pis-ac*		*pis-atel*		*pis-átel*

Among the many other agent suffixes are *-ač* (Ukr *or-áč* 'ploughman' < *o-ráty* 'to
plough') and *-nik* (from *-ik* via Adj in *-n-*) (Rus, Blg *uče-ník* 'pupil' (*uč-* 'teach,
learn'). The suffix *-ist(a)* occurs almost exclusively with foreign roots (Rus *žurnal-
íst* 'journalist' < *žurnál* 'magazine', *marks-íst* 'Marxist'). But Pol *czołg* 'tank',
czołg-ista 'tank driver' derives from *czołgać się* 'to crawl', where the foreign affix
is added to a Slavic stem. (Two of the few such examples in Russian are *slav-íst*
'Slavist' and *rus-íst* 'Russianist'!)

Suffixed nominals not arising from verbs include deadjectivals of bearers
of properties, by means of suffixes like *-ak* and *-ec/-ac*: Blg, Rus, Ukr *prost-ák*,
Bel *prasc-ják*, Pol *prost-ak* 'simpleton' (< *prost-*, Bel *prast-* 'simple'); B/C/S *stăr-ac*,
Sln *stár-ec*, Slk *star-ec*, Rus *stár-ec* 'elder, prefect', Pol *starz-ec* 'old man' (< *star-* 'old').
Deadjectival nouns can also always be formed by nominalization for all three
genders, as appropriate: Rus *bol'-n-ój* 'sick, ill [MascNomSg]' can also mean 'a
sick person'. Such formations can be lexicalized, so that *bol'nój* also means 'an
invalid'. Where specific suffixed forms like *-ak* or *-nik* exist, however, there is a
preference for the suffixed form over the adjective nominalization.

Denominal masculines can also be formed from the names of countries or ethnic
roots to designate bearers of nationality. The *-(an)in* suffix (5.1.1) has interesting
properties in inflexional paradigms. Other suffixes used in this way are *-ø* and *-ec*,
attached to the *root*: 'Bulgarian' = Blg *bắlgar-in*, B/C/S *Bŭgar-in*, Rus *bolgár-in*,
Cz *Bulhar*, cf. Blg *Bălgár-ija*, B/C/S *Bŭgar-skā*, Rus *Bolgár-ija*, Cz *Bulhar-sko*
'Bulgaria'; 'Ukrainian' = Ukr *ukrajín-ec'*, Rus, Blg *ukraín-ec*, B/C/S *Ukrajín-ac*,
Cz *Ukrajin-ec*.

There are also suffixed forms of kinship terms (chapter 9), based on the core
names of family members. For instance, the suffix *-ix/-ih* derives 'fiancé' or 'bride-
groom' from the root for 'wife': Blg, Rus *žen-íx*, Bel *žan-íx*, Pol *żen-ich* 'fiancé'
< *žen-a* (Bel *žan-á*, Pol *żona*) 'woman, wife' (cf. also B/C/S *žènīk*, SLn *žénin*).

The East Slavs use a historically complex suffix to derive patronymics: *-ov-ič*
[Masc] and *-ov-n-a* [Fem] are each based on the possessive suffix *-ov* (8.4.3.3) and are

attached to the stem of the father's name: Rus *Iván-ovič* 'son of Ivan', *Iván-ovn-a* 'daughter of Ivan'. The masculine form of this suffix is used in parts of South and West Slavic as a family name marker, most often attached to a male name: B/C/S *Miloš-ević* lit. 'son of Miloš', * Jován-ović* lit. 'son of John' (cf. English *John-son*). See further below on female patronymics and surnames.

The most common means of forming feminine agents is to add to or modify the masculine agent suffix, most commonly, but by no means only, with *-ka* or *-ca*. Following the order of the masculine agent suffixes above, we find for the feminines:

(25) adding:

-tel'	+ nic-a	Rus	učítel'-nica	'teacher'
	+ k-a	Blg	učítel-ka	'teacher'
-ak	+ k-a	Ukr	slovák ~ slováč-ka	'(a) Slovak'
-ač	+ k-a	Mac	prodavač-ka	'salesman/-woman'
-ist	+ k-a	Rus	žurnalíst-ka	'journalist'
-ø	+ k-a	Cz	Bulhar-ka	'(a) Bulgarian'

altering:

-nik	> nic-a	B/C/S	učeník ~ učenica	'pupil' [Fem]

substituting:

-ec	> k-a	Sln	prodaját-ec ~ prodaját-ka	'salesman/-woman'
-(an)in	> (an)k-a	Blg	bălgar-in ~ bălgar-ka	'(a) Bulgarian'
		Rus	anglič-ánin ~ anglič-ánka	'Englishman/-woman'

A special set of suffixes relates to female proper names. As noted above, the East Slavs build female patronymics from the father's first name by the addition of suffixes like *-ovna*. All Slavs have feminine forms of surnames, which may be feminine forms of the homonymous adjective if the name ends in an adjective desinence (Rus *Stanisláv-sk-ij*, *Stanisláv-sk-aja*, Pol *Wiśniew-sk-i*, *Wiśniew-sk-a*, Blg *Mixajlóv-sk-i*, *Mixajlóv-sk-a*); or derived feminine forms from non-adjectival surnames (in /ov-a/: Pol *Michniewicz-owa* 'wife of Michniewicz'). In Polish unmarried women have a special form of the surname in /uvn-a/: Pol *Michniewicz-ówn-a* 'daughter of Michniewicz'.

8.2.2.3   Objects

Nouns and verbs, much more than adjectives or adverbs, can derive common inanimate nouns.

Masculines in *-(n)ik* can refer to objects: Rus *pámjat-nik*, Blg *pámet-nik*, Cz *pamat-nik/pom-nik* 'monument' (< *pam-/pom-* 'remember'). There are feminines in *-ka* and expanded suffixes including it (B/C/S *pìsāl-jka*, Blg *pisá-lka* 'pen'

(< *pis-* 'write'); Rus *vint-óvka*, Ukr *hvynt-ívka*, Bel *vint-óŭka* 'rifle' < Rus, Bel *vint*, Ukr *hvynt* 'screw'). And there are neuters in -(*d*)*lo* (Sln *mí-lo*, Rus *mý-lo*, Pol *my-dło*, Cz *my-dlo* 'soap' [< *mi-/my-* 'wash']) and -*to* (Blg, Sln, Rus, Ukr *sí-to*, B/C/S *sȉto*, Cz *sí-to* 'sieve' ([*sej-* 'sift, sow']).

All these formations are of low productivity in the modern languages.

8.2.2.4   Animals

The females of animals are formed with suffixes like -*ica*, though this is by no means universal, particularly when the female of the species is also the generic name for the species (when -*ka* is more common):

<blockquote>

female = generic:

(26a)   'cat':   Rus *kóška*,   Cz *koška*,   Slk *mačka*,
             Sln *máčka*,   Blg *kótka*

male = generic:

(26b)   'wolf':   Rus *volk*   Blg *vălk*   B/C/S *vȗk* Cz *vlk* Pol *wilk*
             'she-wolf':   *volč-íca*   *vălč-íca*   *vȕč-ica* *vlč-ice* *wilcz-yca*

</blockquote>

Immature animals, especially domesticated animals, usually retain the older -(ʹ)*e* (< PSl -*ę* and *consonant*(-*nt*)-declension) in South and West Slavic. Russian uses the suffix -*ën*(*o*)*k* in the singular, and Ukrainian and Belarusian use -*en*, at least for wild animals. All have plurals in -*at-a* (5.5.1.6):

<blockquote>

(27a)   'calf':   Rus *tel-ën*(*ok*)   (Cz, Blg, Mac, B/C/S, Sln *tel-e*, Pol *ciel-ę*,
             Ukr *tel-já*, Bel *cal-já*); Rus [Pl stem] *tel-ját-*

(27b)   'wolf-cub':   Rus *volč-ón*(*o*)*k*   (Ukr *vovč-enjá/vov-čá*, Bel *vaŭč-anjá*);
             Rus [Pl stem] *volč-át-*, Ukr *vovč-enját-*)

</blockquote>

8.2.2.5   "Places" and "containers"

The names of locations and containers are derived mainly from nouns meaning people or objects with suffixes like the masculine -*inec*: Cz *host-inec* 'inn' (< *host* 'guest') and feminine -*nica*: Rus *gost-ínica* 'inn, hotel' (< *gost'* 'guest', via the possessive adjective *gost-in-yj*); B/C/S *žȉtnica*, Sln, Rus *žít-nica*, Ukr *žýt-nycja*, Bel *žýt-nica* 'granary' (< *žit-/žyt-* 'grain, rye'). We have described above the formation of neuter place names from prepositional phrases of the type represented by Rus *primór'e* (*pri* 'by, near' + *mór-e* 'sea' + suffix -*j*(*e*): 8.1.4).

8.2.2.6   Collectives

Collectives are built mainly with -(ʹ)*j-e* and -*stv-o* (-*stv-í* in Czech). They are non-countable, and express groups of entities as a single unit. However, the stem need not refer to countable nouns itself: Rus *bel-'ë* 'linen' is derived from the adjective *bel-* 'white', Sln *mlád-je* 'youth' from *mlád-* 'young'. The suffix $-('\ )j$-e/-i also derives uncountable mass nouns for products like vegetables, which are also often *singularia tantum* if attached to underived nouns (roots): Blg *zél-e*, Bel *zél-le*, Cz *zel-í* 'cabbage', Pol *ziel-e* 'herbs', B/C/S *zêl-je* 'vegetables', Sln *zél-je* 'cabbage' (all < *zel-*/*ziel-* 'green').

The *-stv-o* suffix is used more of collections of professionals: Rus *učítel'* 'teacher', *učítel'-stvo* 'teachers; the teaching profession', Czech *učitel/učitel-ství*, Pol *nauczyciel/nauczyciel-stwo*, Blg *učítel/učítel-stvo*.

8.2.2.7   *Diminutives and augmentatives*

Diminutive and augmentative forms (8.1.2) are productive in nouns, especially in the spoken languages. Other than with abstracts and collectives, they are common with most categories of nouns. Augmentatives are much less common than diminutives.

Diminutives express overtones of either size, or emotion, or both. Diminutives form first- and second-degree suffixes (Townsend, 1968/1975: 198), where the use of both suffixes, in the order second–first, makes the derived word strongly emotional. The use of just the first-degree suffix can add implications of size, or emotion, or both (e.g. Rus *kníg-a* 'book', *kníž-k-a* 'small book', *kníž-eč-k-a* 'booklet, nice little book' < PSl *-ьk-ьk-a*). While the first diminutive suffix may supply overtones relating to either size or endearment, further suffixes relate to increased levels of endearment: Blg *glav-á* 'head', *glav-íc-a* 'head [Dim]', *glav-íčk-a* 'dear (little) head' (< PSl -*ik-ьk-a*). Diminutives may be inherently pejorative, like Rus *gorod-íšk-o* 'nasty little hole of a town' (< Rus *górod* 'town, city'), or either endearing or pejorative, according to context, and include the rich diminutive suffix systems for personal names (8.1.2).

Where the base lexical form has a different gender in the different languages, it will naturally select different suffixes. With the words for 'flower', Russian, Ukrainian, Belarusian and Sorbian have standard diminutives based on the root meaning 'colour', and the unsuffixed form is either not used (Ukrainian, Belarusian, Sorbian), or semantically different (Russian). Only in Russian is the masculine gender retained in the suffixed form:

(28)   'flower'
       Masculine:

Rus	*cvet-(ó)k-ó* (*cvet* 'colour, blossom')						
Pol	*kwiat*	Cz	*květ*	Slk	*kvet*		
Sln	*cvet*	B/C/S	*cvêt*	Blg	*cvét-e* [Neut]	Mac	*cvet*

Feminine:

Ukr   *kvít-k-a*   Bel   *kvét-k-a*   Sorb   *kwět-k-a*

In the list of common suffixes in (29), the unsuffixed (non-diminutive) forms are given in parentheses where they exist, otherwise a dash is given in brackets. For lexical diminutives – that is, words where the addition of suffixes modifies the meaning in predictable ways as described above – the base meaning is not given. We indicate where the unsuffixed form has a different meaning, which implies that the diminutive form has become an autonomous lexical item.

(29)   Diminutives
       Masculine:

-ac/-ec	Slk	*dom-(e)c*	'house'	(*dom*)
	B/C/S	*grád-(a)c*	'town'	(*grad*)
-ok/-ek	Sln	*gúmb-(e)k*	'button'	(*gumb*)
	Ukr	*holos-(ó)k, holos-óč(e)k*	'voice'	(*hólos*)
-ič	Sln	*grád-ič*	'castle'	(*grád*)
-ić	B/C/S	*bròd-īć*	'ship'	(*bròd*)
-on(o)k	Rus	*volč-ón(o)k*	'wolf-cub'	(*volk*)

       Feminine:

-k-a	Blg, Rus	*lód-k-a*	'boat'	(–)
	Ukr	*knýž-ka*		(–)
	Rus	*kníž-ka*	'book'	(*kníg-a*)
-ičk-a/-ečk-a	Cz	*nož-ičk-a*	'leg'	(*noha, nož-k-a*)
	Cz	*chvil-ečk-a*	'moment'	(*chvíl-e*)
-ic-a	B/C/S	*glàv-ica*	'head'	(*gláv-a*)

       Neuter:

-c-e	Rus	*bolót-c-e*	'bog'	(*bolót-o*)
-ic-e	Blg	*jajč-icé*	'egg'	(*jajc-é*)
-č-e	Blg	*cvet-čé*	'flower'	(*cvét-e*)
	B/C/S	*gùš-če*	'gosling'	(*gùsk-a*)
-k-o	Slk	*dievčat-k-o*	'girl'	(*dievča-t-*)
-išk-o	Rus	*zërn-yšk-o*	'grain'	(*zern-ó*)

(30)   Augmentatives
       Masculine:

-ak	Cz	*chlap-ak*	'lad'	(*chlap*)
-och	Pol	*śpi-och*	'sleepy-head'	(–)
-ac	Cz	*hlav-ac*	'big-head'	(*hlava* 'head')
-uk	Cz	*ps-uk*	'dog'	(*p(e)s*)

Feminine:

-in-a	Rus	dom-ín-a	'house'	(dóm-ø)
-ur-a	B/C/S	glàv-ur-a	'head'	(glàv-a)
-(')ug-a	Ukr	sobac-júg-a	'dog'	(sobák-a)

Neuter:

-išt-e	Blg	žen-išt-e	'woman'	(žen-á)
-išč-e	Rus	dom-íšč-e [Masc]	'house'	(dóm-ø)
-sk-o	Pol	bab-sk-o	'woman'	(bab-a)
-isk-o	Pol	bab-isk-o	'woman'	(bab-a)
	Ukr	dom-ýs'k-o	'house'	(dóm-ø)

What is a diminutive in one language may be the non-diminutive form in another language. We have seen this with 'flower' above. Similarly, the following all represent the neutral terms, but the second set in each meaning is formally diminutive: Rus reká, but Ukr ríč-ka 'river'; Pol ptak 'bird', but Rus, Blg pt-íca; Rus kníga, Cz kniha, 'book', but Ukr knýž-ka, Pol ksiąž-ka. When a diminutive has become the standard form in the language, the original unmodified form is often kept in high style, or in an augmentative sense: Pol książ-ka 'book', księg-a 'tome'.

As a rule the diminutive suffix preserves the gender of the root, as with Ukr hólos above. Sometimes, however, the suffix switches the new stem into another declension: Rus dom 'house' has the augmentative dom-íšč-e, which declines like a neuter noun but remains masculine, as can be seen from concord and agreement: Rus krasív-yj [Masc] dom-íšč-e 'beautiful big house'. The same is true of the Russian augmentative dom-ín-a and pejorative dom-íšk-o. But Pol dom-isk-o 'great big house' is neuter, though Pol dom 'house' is masculine: Pol piękn-e [Neut] domisk-o 'beautiful great big house', cf. Pol piękn-y [Masc] dom 'beautiful house'.

8.2.3   Combination, coordination and subordination

Nouns can be formed from the combination of (rarely more than) two roots, which may themselves be nouns, adjectives, verbs or other parts of speech. The derived nouns refer mainly to abstracts, persons, objects and places: Rus slovár'– správočnik 'reference dictionary' (slovár'-ø 'dictionary' + správočnik-ø 'reference-book'). The least integrated of these compounds are linked by a hyphen. If both parts are nouns, each is regularly inflected as if in syntactic apposition. However, differences can arise with the role of the constituent lexemes. In Bulgarian (Scatton, 1984: 267 ff.) articles and plural inflexions attach to the head if it is second: so the Noun–Noun structure of Modifier + Head in Blg zaméstnik– minístăr 'deputy minister' takes the plural zaméstnik–minístr-i and the definite *zaméstnik–minístăr-ăt*. But the Noun–Noun structure of Head + Modifier in Blg *studént–otlíčnik* 'outstanding student' has the plural for both nouns, treating them as in apposition (*studént-i–otlíčnic-i*) and the definite article suffix is attached to the first constituent, as in a standard noun phrase (*studént-ăt–otlíčnik*).

It is not always immediately obvious, indeed, which component is head and which is modifier. In Rus *žénščina–kosmonávt* 'female astronaut' (lit. "woman-cosmonaut"), the compound could, in principle, describe either a female cosmonaut or an astronautical woman. Although the first is semantically more plausible, agreement is feminine to agree with *žénščina*, which morphosyntactically gives a Head–Modifier structure. A similar pattern holds for Rus *górod–geró j* 'hero city' and *mát'–geroínja* 'mother-heroine' – though here the nouns for 'hero(ine)' agree in gender with the Head. Both components inflect in these Russian examples, though the trend is toward non-declension of the first part regardless of Head–Modifier status (Gorbačevič, 1978a: 182–184).

A closer type of combination involves joining with a link-vowel (*o* or *e*) rather than a hyphen. Only the second component inflects, and determines the word-class of the compound (31a–b). Sometimes the compound is completed with an agent suffix (31c):

(31a) Blg   *vzaimopómošt* 'mutual aid' [Adj + Noun]
             (*vzaím(e)n* 'mutual' + *pomóšt* 'aid, help')

(31b) Pol   *długopis* 'ball-point pen' [Adv + Verb]
             (*dług-i* 'long' + *pis-* 'write')

(31c) B/C/S *basnopísac* 'fabulist'
             (*băsn-a* 'fable' + *pís-* 'write' + *ac* 'Agent')

Some nouns are joined by straight conjunction of roots ('direct compounding'). Here only the second component inflects, but compare the Adj + Noun inflexion for 'Novi Sad': B/C/S *u Nòv-ōm Sâd-u* 'in Novi Sad' *vs u Beò-grad-u* 'in Beograd/ Belgrade'):

(32a) B/C/S *Beògrad* 'Belgrade' [Adj + Noun]
             (*bèo* 'white' + *grâd-ø* 'city')

(32b) Cz   *zemĕpis-ø* 'geography' [Noun + Verb]
             (*zemĕ* 'earth' + *pis-* 'write' + *ø* [Abstract nominal suffix])

8.2.4   Prefixation + suffixation

The 'prefix + suffix' pattern (8.1.4) accounts for most of the prefixal formation of nouns in Slavic. The most common type involves the addition of a word-forming suffix to a stem consisting of a prefix and a root, as in (14) above and (33) below. A large number, probably the majority, of prefixed–suffixed nouns are derived from a prepositional phrase, with the preposition becoming the prefix in the derived form:

(33a)   Rus   *bezrabótica* 'unemployment'
              (*bez-* 'without' + *rabót-* 'work' + *-ica* [Abstract suffix])

(33b)   Cz   *přímoří* 'maritime district'
              (*pri-/při-* 'near, by' + *moř-e* 'sea' + *-í* [Place suffix])

8.2.5 Nominalized adjectives

Any Slavic adjective can be used as a noun to mean 'the Adj one': Slk *chorý človek* 'ill man', *chorý* 'ill one, invalid'. However, a number of adjectives have become nominalized and now form independent nouns. Here we find not only proper names in *-ov, -ev* and *-in* as well as *-ski*, but also common nouns like Blg *živótn-o*, Rus *živótn-oe* 'insect', Blg *mlekopitáešt-e*, Rus *mlekopitájušč-ee* 'mammal' (lit. 'milk-feeding'), as well as agent nouns derived from Adjective + Noun phrases by deletion of the noun: Rus *portn-ój* 'tailor', *obvinjáem-yj* 'accused' ([PresPassPart]: 'he who is being accused'), *trudjášč-ie-sja* 'workers' ([PresActPart]: 'those who are labouring').

8.3   Word formation and verbs

Verbs provide the most complex, and the most controversial, area of word formation in Slavic. We discuss verbal roots and stems in chapters 4–5. However, that provides only the basic derivational structure to enable us to study the inflexional patterns of Slavic verbs, and to establish a stem to which inflexional suffixes could be added to form the paradigms (5.5.5).

In this section we take up the wider picture of the formation of the various derived verb forms. There is inevitably some overlap with our treatment of inflexion, a feature of the status of aspect in Slavic (6.3). We favor no position on whether aspect is a matter of inflexion or derivation. The principal discussion of aspect formation is located in this chapter because it allows us to achieve a better perspective on word formation in Slavic as a whole.

Typical verb forms which fall within word-formation are:

(34a)   Rus   *bi-t'*   'to beat, hit'   [Imprfv]
               po-bí-t'   'to beat, hit'   [Prfv]

(34b)   Rus   *u-bí-t'*   'to kill'   [Prfv]
               u-bi-vá-t'   'to kill'   [Imprfv]

The unaffixed form *bit'* forms a perfective with the addition of a prefix. Adding a different prefix, however, both makes a perfective and creates a new lexical form, from which a new imperfective has to be derived by the addition of a suffix. This pattern is enormously productive. However, some verbs do not perfectivize when prefixed, while some are perfectivized by suffixation. A few verbs are perfective without being affixed. The semantic changes brought about by prefixation vary from neutral perfectivization to "sublexical" modification in the so-called "Aktionsarten" (or "procedurals", 8.3.1.3), and genuine lexical modification as happens with *ubít'* above. And the choice of "neutral" prefix may differ for a given verb between languages.

Stems and aspect   As a starting-point, it is useful to consider some default cases. As Brecht shows (1985: 12), simplex verbs like *bit'* are usually atelic – that is, they do not indicate any clear termination-point – and imperfective. So are prefixed-suffixed verbs, like *ubivát'*. Prefixed, non-suffixed verbs like *ubít'* are usually telic and perfective. There are only a few simplex (unaffixed) perfectives, which tend to be among the common verbs:

(35a)   'give':   Rus *da-t'*,   Ukr *dá-ty*,   B/C/S *dȁ-ti*,   Cz *dá-t*
        'buy':   Rus *kup-ít'*, Bel *kup-íc'*, Cz *koup-it*, Blg *kúp-ja*, Sln *kup-íti*
                (cf. B/C/S *kúp-iti* is [Imprfv], the [Prfv] being prefixed *s-kúpiti*)

Other verbs of this sort are telic:

(35b)   'sit down': Rus *ses-t'*, Ukr *sís-ty*, B/C/S *sȅs-ti* (all = root *sed-*)

Some apparently unaffixed perfective verbs are in fact etymologically prefixed, e.g. Rus *skazát'* 'say' (*s-kaz-*), *vzjat'* 'take' (*vz-ja-*), *udárit'* 'strike' (*u-dar-*). They not infrequently have suppletive related imperfectives (e.g. Rus *govorít'* 'say', *brat'* 'take').

Adding prefixes to unaffixed perfective verbs results in semantic changes consistent with the properties of the prefix, and the resulting verb is also perfective (e.g. Rus *ot-dát'* 'give back'). Imperfectives are derived from such verbs either by suffixation (the norm), typically *-(i)va-* or *-ja-*, e.g. B/C/S *o-dá-va-ti* 'betray, give away', *u-bí-ja-ti* 'kill', or are provided by the suppletive verb.

As we have seen in chapter 5, there are only relatively few completely unsuffixed imperfective verb stems (i.e. lacking even a thematic vowel) like PSl *nes-ti* 'to carry'. Most verbs have either a thematic vowel which is added to the root to form the verb stem, as in PSl *pis-a-ti* 'to write'; or they have a suffix which creates a verb, often from a non-verbal root, as in Rus *úžin-a-t'*, 'to have dinner/supper' (< noun *úžin*). Such verbs are usually inherently imperfective, and form their perfective by the addition of either a prefix or a suffix. In addition to the few unaffixed perfect-ives noted above (35), there are, however, two other cases where the verb stem does not follow this pattern: bi-aspectual verbs; and verbs of indeterminate motion.

In bi-aspectual verbs the same form can be either imperfective or perfective. A few of these are of older Slavic origin, like Rus *dar-ová-t'* 'to present (a gift)' and *žen-ít'-sja* 'to get married', Pol *kaz-ać* 'to order', Sln *rod-íti* 'to give birth'. But there are also considerable numbers of borrowings, like Rus *organizovát'* 'to organize', Blg *treníram* 'train', Cz *informovat* 'to inform'. This aspectual indeterminacy is unusual in Slavic, and seems to sit ill with the dynamics of verb use. As a result, two diverging tendencies are appearing. Some of the bi-aspectual verbs have derived new imperfectives with *-iva(j)-*, e.g. Rus *arestóv-yva-t'* 'arrest' and non-standard *organizóv-yva-t'*, which may push the non-derived verbs toward perfective special-ization, as has happened in the case of *arestovát'*. A second tendency is for such verbs to form new perfectives, e.g. Rus *s-organizovát'*, Pol *za-awansować* 'to advance', Ukr *za-areštuváty* 'to arrest' (and even additional imperfectives: Ukr *za-areštóv-uva-ty*).

Verbs of motion can occur in indeterminate ~ determinate pairs, like Rus *xodít'* ~ *idtí* 'to go/walk', *nosít'* ~ *nestí* 'to carry', in which the first member is indeterminate in respect of direction or time, and the second determinate. Here the alternation is most often centred on ablaut in the root, but with additional con-jugational differences. Prefixes with verbs of motion have more predictable seman-tic (physical) effects than with non-motion verbs, and adding a prefix to the indeterminate member of the verb pair creates a derived imperfective. The parallel perfective is formed with the same prefix added to the corresponding determinate verb form. East and West Slavic and Slovenian have such paired verbs of motion and conveying (see 9.4.2). Both can be prefixed, but only the prefixed determinate forms are perfective:

(36)	Rus	Imperfective		Perfective
		nosít'	'to carry' [Indet]	–
		nestí	'to carry' [Det]	*po-nestí*
		pri-nosít'	'to bring'	*pri-nestí*
		ot-nosít'	'to take away'	*ot-nestí*
		vy-nosít'	'to take out'	*vý-nesti*
		v-nosít'	'to take in'	*v-nesti*

In Czech, Slovak and Sorbian the determinate verb with the prefix *po-* provides the future of both aspects, while in other languages this form is perfective only (these same three languages also have a set of verbs which are not perfectivized by the prefix *po-*):

(37) Cz *letím*   'I am flying' [ImprfvDet]
          po-letím   'I shall fly' [Imprfv] = *budu letět*
          (cf. Rus *po-lečú* 'I shall fly' [Prfv])

With these exceptions – bi-aspectual verbs, verbs of indeterminate ~ determinate motion, and the inherently perfective stems – most Slavic verbs engage in prefixation or suffixation for the formation of the verbal aspects.

For the purposes of discussion, we divide verbal word formation into three groups: prefixation (8.3.1), suffixation (8.3.2) and "other issues", including suppletion (8.3.3). Within prefixation and suffixation we distinguish grammatical and semantic processes, following common practice. Overall both prefixation and suffixation are intertwined with both semantic and grammatical factors. The division of prefixation and suffixation into grammatical and semantic sub-classes is not absolute, and we shall indicate the overlaps where they occur.

8.3.1 Prefixation

Verbal prefixation splits into two classes: grammatical prefixation (concerning neutral perfectivizing prefixes); and semantic prefixation (concerning non-neutral perfectives and Aktionsarten ("procedurals")).

8.3.1.1 *Grammatical prefixation*

In the following discussion we leave aside the negative prefixed verbs in Czech, Slovak and Sorbian. Here the orthographic convention attaches the negative to the verb and reflects the pronunciation, since the prefixed *n(j)e-* attracts the stress to itself:

(38) Slk *chceme spievat'*   'we wish to sing'
          nechceme [ˈɲɛ-] *spievat'*   'we do not wish to sing'

The proclitic behavior of the negative certainly resembles prefixation. But the negative comes first, whether attached to the verb or not. We discuss it in more detail under clitics (6.1.2.4, 7.4.3.3).

"Grammatical" (or "non-semantic") prefixation for verbs, in the sense proposed by Townsend (1968/1975: 117), covers the formation of perfectives by the addition of a "neutral" (or "empty") prefix to the imperfective form of the verb. Most verbs have one, and usually only one, such "neutral" prefix:

(39a) 'write' (*pis-*): all languages have *na-*
          Ukr *pysáty ~ na-pysáty*   Bel *pisác' ~ na-pisác'*
          Cz   *psát ~ na-psat*   Pol *pisać ~ na-pisać*
          Mac *piše ~ na-piše*   B/C/S *písati ~ na-písati*

(39b) 'do, work' (*děl-, rab-, rad-*): most have *s-/z-*, some *u-*

Rus	*délat' ~ s-délat'*	Bel	*rabíc' ~ z-rabíc'*
Cz	*dělat ~ u-dělat*	Sorb	*dźěłać ~ z-dźěłać*
Sln	*délati ~ z-délati*	B/C/S	*ráditi ~ u-ráditi*

Even if one contests the notion of "neutral" prefix, there is nonetheless a sense in which such prefixes add less information to the derived perfective than non-neutral prefixes: compare Rus *na-písát'* 'write' with *pere-pisát'* 'rewrite, transcribe'. In addition, the perfectives formed with neutral prefixes do not form new derived imperfectives with suffixes like *-iva-* (Rus *pere-pís-yvat'*, but not **napisyvat'*, see further below) – though this is not, unfortunately, a wholly reliable criterion for identifying the neutral prefix.

Different verbs select different neutral prefixes for the grammatical formation of perfectives. In principle the semantic content of the prefix has "fused" with that of the verb, but the subjectivity of this process in abstract extensions has allowed the neutral prefix to differ between languages for given cognate stems:

(40) 'kill':

West Slavic and Bel	*za-*:	Cz	*za-bit*	Slk	*za-bit'*
		Bel	*za-bíc'*	Pol, Sorb	*za-bić*
East and South Slavic	*u-*:	Rus	*u-bít'*	Ukr	*u-býty*
		Sln	*u-bíti*	B/C/S	*ù-biti*
		Blg	*u-bívam*	Mac	*u-biva*

There may even be more than one prefix acting as neutral on a given root within one language:

(41) Rus *mázat'* 'smear': [Prfv] *vý-mazat', na-mázat', po-mázat'*

It is nonetheless possible to identify an approximate default – or at least most common – neutral prefix in both statistical and semantic terms for each language: for instance, *po-* for Russian (with almost 28 percent of [common] verbs: Cubberley, 1982), and *z-* for Polish and Czech (Short, 1993a: 493; Rothstein, 1993: 722). If the notion of semantic fusion between prefix and root is valid, then the semantic load of *po-* – 'area or period of limitation of an action' (cf. the preposition *po* with this meaning) – makes it a likely default for bearing the meaning of perfective, which is precisely the specifying of a limit to the action.

8.3.1.2 *Semantic prefixation*
The use of a non-neutral prefix will add to the verb root not only the perfective meaning, but also extra information:

(42)   Sln   *pisáti*   'to write'   *na-pisáti* [Prfv]
            o-pisáti   'to describe'
            pod-pisáti 'to sign'
            pre-pisáti 'to copy'
            v-pisáti   'to inscribe'

(Svane, 1958: 85–86 offers a list of twelve prefixed forms for this root). Most of the prefixes are related to prepositions, but the meanings of the prepositions are only loosely tied to the meanings of the corresponding prefixed verbs (having undergone abstract extension), as happens in comparable cases in English verbs like *look up*, e.g.: Sln *v* 'in', *v-pisáti* '**in**scribe'; *pod* 'under', *pod-pisáti* 'to sign', cf. English **under-write**. The semantic correspondence of prefixes and prepositions is best seen in verbs of motion and conveying: when the prefix is related to a preposition of spatial reference, the derived verb is usually semantically predictable (see also examples in (36) of prefixed forms of Rus *nestí*):

(43)   Rus   *stáv-it'*   'to put (stand)' *po-stávit'* [Prfv]
            v-stávit'   'to insert'
            pere-stávit'   'to shift position, transpose'
            pred-stávit'   'to present' (lit. 'place before')
            pod-stávit'   'to place under'

Such formations are often called "lexical", because they form new semantic units. Since they are inherently perfective, they have to derive new imperfectives, which is accomplished by suffixation (Rus *pred-stav-ljá-t'* etc.) (see 8.3.2).

8.3.1.3   *"Aktionsarten"/"procedurals"*

A special case of prefixal perfective formation involves the "Aktionsarten". The German term "Aktionsarten", or "types of action", has not been bettered in spite of attempts by Anglophone and Anglophile neologists, but a suitable English term is "procedurals". Procedurals cover derived verb forms which are not as semantically elaborated as the aspectual formations described in 8.3.1. Instead, the meanings contributed by the prefixes under procedurals relate more to the action's beginning, continued process and termination. Procedurals therefore sit between semantically loaded aspect formation with prefixes, on the one hand, and perfectivization with neutral prefixes, on the other hand, and tend to overlap with both. They are sometimes described as "sublexical" (Townsend, 1968/1975: 118), since the pre-fixed forms do not constitute new lexical items, but lexical elaborations of the meaning of the stem verb. The verbs which typically form such perfectives are roots which are atelic, or inherently imperfective, mainly with inbuilt process, e.g. 'talk', 'work', 'cry', with prefixes marking the onset, or the limitation or specification of time:

(44)   Rus   *rabótat'* 'to work'   *govorít'* 'to talk'
        'to start VERBing':   *za-rabótat'*   *za-govorít'*
        'to VERB for a short time':   *po-rabótat'*   *po-govorít'*
        'to VERB for a specified time' (e.g. 'for an hour', 'all day'):
                                                   pro-rabótat'   *pro-govorít'*

They also tend not to form new derived imperfectives, for instance in -(*i*)*va*-, although this also is not a reliable criterion of their status as procedurals. Where apparent derived imperfectives exist, we are dealing with different semantic items (usually abstract extensions), for instance Rus *zagovorít'* can also mean 'to put a spell on' and *zarabótat'* 'to earn', with – in these meanings – the appropriate derived imperfectives *zagovár-iva-t'*, *zarabát-yva-t'*.

Other sorts of procedurals – such as "iterative" and "semelfactive" action – are marked by suffixation (e.g. -(*i*)*va*- for the former, -*nu*- for the latter) (see below, 8.3.2.3).

8.3.2   Suffixation

8.3.2.1   *Grammatical suffixation*
In English verbs are regularly formed from other parts of speech without affixation, by using – say – a noun as a verb (*oil* – *to oil* ("conversion")); or there is addition of a suffix like -*ize*. Only the second of these patterns occurs in Slavic:

(45a) 'whip'[Noun]:   Rus *knut*,   Cz *bič*
        'to whip':   Rus *bit' knut-óm* (lit. 'to beat with a whip')
                              cf. Cz   *bič-ova-t*
(45b) Sorb   *wolij* 'oil', *wolij-owa-ć* 'to oil'

Almost all derived verbs are formed from nouns and adjectives. Once again, cognate roots need not have cognate suffixes. Principal suffix types include:

(46)   -*i*-   Cz   *mraz-i-t* 'to be frosty'   (*mráz* 'frost')
                    Ukr   *suš-ý-ty* 'to dry'   (*sux-ýj* 'dry')
        -*e*-   Cz   *bel-e-t* 'to be white'   (*bílý* 'white')
        -*a*-   Ukr   *obíd-a-ty* 'to dine'   (*obíd* 'dinner')
        -(*iz*)(*ir*)*ova*- Rus   *internacional-izírova-t'* 'to internationalize'
                    Sorb   *noc-owa-ć* 'to spend the night'   (*noc* 'night');
                    cf. Rus *noč-evá-t'*

A few verbs are formed from interjections and vowel sounds (47a), pronouns (47b) and numerals (47c):

(47a)   Pol   *och-a-ć* 'to say "oh", to groan'
(47b)   Rus   *tý-ka-t'*, Cz *ty-ka-t* 'to say "ty"', Fr *tutoyer*
(47c)   B/C/S   *u-dvòj-i-ti* 'to double' (< *dvòj-e* 'two'[Coll])

A different kind of grammatical suffixation involves reflexives. In East Slavic the reflexive is written as a suffix (Ukr *mýty-sja* 'to wash oneself'). In West and South Slavic it is an enclitic particle (Pol *myć się*, B/C/S *mȉti se*).

We can set aside here verbs which have only reflexive forms, like Rus *boját'sja* 'to be afraid, fear', and where no particular function or meaning can be ascribed to the reflexive component. Some verbs, however, use the reflexive to intransitivize transitive stems, creating a form not unlike the Greek Middle Voice in function and meaning:

(48)   'to begin':   Rus   *načinát'* [Trans]   *načinát'-sja* [Intrans]
       'to open':   Rus   *otkryvát'* [Trans]   *otkryvát'-sja* [Intrans]

Such constructions are less often accompanied by an expression of the agent than the conventional passive (7.1.5), or the Object–Verb–Subject order which often corresponds to English *by*-agent passives (7.4.3.1).

Other examples of grammatical suffixation involve the rich systems of stem formation. One kind of stem formation relates to the formation of imperfectives, which we have discussed above. Some verbs mark their perfectives by a different thematic vowel, or by an *-n-* suffix; the perfectives may be shorter by a syllable:

(49)   Imperfective   Perfective
       Bel   *max-á-c'*   'to wave'   *max-nú-c'*
       Rus   *način-á-t'*   'to begin' *nač-á-t'* (*nač-n-ú* ...)
       Slk   *kop-a-t'*   'to dig'   *kop-nu-t'*

Still other verbs show an *-a-* vowel in the imperfective, often preceded by mutation or ablaut. This corresponds to other (often *-i-* or *-e-*) vowels in the perfective:

(50)   Perfective   Imperfective
       Sln   *blagoslov-í-ti* 'to bless'   *blagoslavl-já-ti*
       B/C/S   *pùst-i-ti*   'to let'   *púšt-a-ti*
       Bel   *výmus-i-c'*   'to compel' *vymuš-á-c'*
       Rus   *umer-é-t'*   'to die'   *umir-á-t'*
       Rus   *rod-í-t'*   'to give birth' *rož-á-t'/rožd-á-t'*

8.3.2.2 *Derived secondary imperfectives*

The strength of the pattern of producing imperfectives by suffixation of prefixed perfectives has often been extended to the production of such derived forms in competition to the basic, unaffixed, form:

(51)   Bel   *vý-pic'* 'to drink' [Prfv]: [Imprfv] *pic'* and *vy-piváć*

8.3.2.3 *Semantic suffixation*

Semantic suffixation involves a range of derived imperfectives. Some suffixes are simply thematic vowels or formants added to roots to form verb stems, and thus no longer have a word-formational role (e.g. Rus *pis-á-t'*). Others are associated with grammatical or lexical meaning in various ways, which makes them more than just grammatical in function:

(52)   Semantic suffixation
change of state: *-nu* (Class II), *-ej* (Class III)

'to go blind':	B/C/S	*slép-e-ti*	Rus	*slép-nu-t'*	Slk	*slep-nú-t'*
'to turn white':	B/C/S	*bél-e-ti*	Rus	*bel-é-t'*	Slk	*bel-ie-t'*

factitives: *-i* (Class IV)

'to whiten'	B/C/S	*bél-i-ti*	Rus	*bel-í-t'*	Slk	*biel-i-t'*
'to paint, to adorn'	B/C/S	*krás-i-ti*	Rus	*kras-í-t'*	Sorb	*krasn-i-ć*

statives: *-e* (Class IV), (Pal +)-*a*, *-ej* (Class III)

'to be sitting'	B/C/S	*sèd-e-ti*	Rus	*sid-é-t'*	Slk	*sed-ie-t'*
'to be/show white'	B/C/S	*bél-e-ti*	Rus	*bel-é-t'*	Slk	*bel-ie-t' sa*

Other areas of semantic verbal suffixation involve semelfactives, iteratives and reflexives.

Semelfactive suffixes designate an action performed once. They use the suffix *-nu-*:

(53)   Semelfactives

Rus	*krič-á-t'* 'to shout' [Imprfv]	*krík-nu-t'* 'to (give a) shout'
Cz	*pad-a-t* 'to fall' [Imprfv]	*pad-nou-t* 'to fall down'
Blg	*pád-a-m* 'I fall' [Imprfv]	*pád-n-a* 'I fall down'

Some unprefixed imperfective verbs may form iterative, or frequentative, forms – 'to do something again/several times' – by adding a suffix, usually *-(a/i/y)va-*, the suffix widely used to make the imperfective of prefixed perfective verbs (e.g. 51):

(54)   Iteratives

(54a)   B/C/S *bȉ-ti* 'to be' *bȉ-va-ti* 'to be occasionally' and by lengthening a stem vowel:

(54b)   Slk *hl'ada-t'* 'to look'   *hl'adá-va-t'* 'to look repeatedly'

Czech and Slovak are able to form a second (frequentative) imperfective by extra suffixation:

(54c)   Cz *chod-it* 'to go' [Indet]   *chod-ívat, chod-ív-ávat* 'to go often'

Reflexive suffixed forms designate genuinely reflexive actions which return to the subject of the sentence, either concretely or metaphorically:

(55)   'to wash (oneself)': Rus *mýt'-sja*   Pol *myć się*   B/C/S *m̃ti se*

Alternatively, reflexives may designate reciprocal actions, where A does to B what B does to A at the same time:

(56)   'to meet, see one another (regularly)':
         Rus   *vstrečát'-sja* (meet), *vídet'-sja* (see)   Cz   *setkávat se, vidět se*
         Pol   *spotkać się*   Sln   *sréčati se*
         'to correspond (in writing)':
         Rus   *perepísyvat'-sja* (write)   Cz   *dopisovat se*
         Blg   *korespondíram si*   Bel   *perapísvac-ca*

The passive and intransitive functions of the reflexive are noted above and the reflexive in general also in 5.4.8 and 7.1.5. Reflexives are often omitted from the word-formation properties of verbs, on account of the status of the reflexive particle as a clitic in West and South Slavic.

A minor area of semantic suffixal verb formation concerns diminutives. This area of word formation is very limited in contrast to the diminutive formations of nouns (8.2), adjectives (8.4) and adverbs (8.5), and is unevenly spread across the languages. The meaning of the verb is attenuated, somewhat as with procedurals, with which verbal diminutives have some important points of contact:

(57)   B/C/S   *pȇv-a-ti* 'to sing'   *pev-ùck-a-ti* 'to hum'
         Mac   *kop-a* 'he digs'   *kop-k-a* 'he digs lightly'

8.3.3   Other issues

Some common verbs show suppletive aspectual pairs:

(58)   'take':   Imperfective   Perfective
                        Rus   *brat'*   *vzjat'*
                        Bel   *brac'*   *uzjác'*

	Pol	*brać*	*wziąć*
	Sorb	*brać*	*wzać*
'come':	B/C/S	*dòlaziti*	*dóći*
'say':	Rus	*govorít'*	*skazát'*
	Slk	*hovorit'*	*povedat'*

Etymologically, the perfective verbs are all originally prefixed, and should not strictly have a further prefix added, though they sometimes do, with a semantic distinction: Rus *pred-skazát'* 'to foretell' [Prfv], Slk *od-povedat'* 'to answer' [Imprfv]. A prefix added to the imperfective verbs will produce a semantically distinct perfective verb: Rus *vý-brat'* 'to choose', *u-govorít'* 'to persuade'.

8.4 Word formation and adjectives

The word formation of adjectives is productive, but not as varied as word formation with nouns. Adjective-to-adjective formation is accomplished by some prefixes and by hypocoristics. Adjectives are productively formed from other word-classes, especially nouns, by suffixation.

It is common to divide adjectives into two types: qualitative and relative (or "relational"). Qualitative adjectives are like Rus *slábyj* 'weak' in (59). They are gradable into degrees of comparison, may have hypocoristics, form derived nouns and adverbs, and have short forms where the language allows (and where usage retains them: 5.5.2) as well as the regular long forms:

(59) Rus *sláb-yj*   'weak'
            óčen' slábyj   'very weak'
            sláb-en'k-ij (hypocoristic)   'weakish, poorly'
            slab-ée   'weaker'
            sláb-ost'   'weakness'
            slab-ø   'weak' [Short]
            sláb-o   'weakly' [Adv]

Relative adjectives, which are all derived, have none of the above properties of qualitative adjectives, with the minor exception of negative prefixes, which can be prefixed productively with the meaning of 'non-'. However, relative adjectives can be metaphorized, which makes them able to form degrees of comparison, as well as derived nominals and adverbials (60b):

(60a) Relative
       Rus *dérev-o* 'wood' > *derev-jánn-yj* 'wooden, made of wood'
            ne-derevjánnyj 'non-wooden' (e.g. furniture)

(60b)   Relative-become-qualitative
Rus   *derevjánn-yj* 'wooden, as if made of wood'
derevjánn-o 'woodenly', *derevjánn-ost'* 'woodenness'
(e.g. of a performance in the theatre)

Relative adjectives are formed productively from nouns, including neologisms, and they are much more numerous than qualitative adjectives. Townsend (1968/ 1975) estimates the number of non-derived qualitative adjectives in Russian at about 200–300, a figure which matches the information available for the other languages.

8.4.1   Prefixation

There are numerous prefixed adjectives, but only small numbers which consist of a prefix and a non-derived stem. In addition, the structure of most prefixed adjectives shows the prefix and root forming an expanded stem which is then suffixed (8.1.4). Only negative prefixes can productively be added to existing adjectives to form new adjectives: Blg *logíčen* 'logical', *ne-logíčen* 'illogical'.

Prefixed adjectives show transparent semantics. A few prefixes with gradable adjectives can express excess or degree, though the orthography may make the prefix look like a separate word:

(61)   'too':   Pol *za duży* 'too big'; Rus *pere-naselënnyj* 'over-populated'
'very':   Rus *pre-múdryj* 'very wise', Rus *raz-vesëlyj* 'very merry'
'ultra': Sorb *ultra-krotki* 'ultra-short'; Blg *svrăx-čuvstvítelen*
'ultra-sensitive'

Other prefixes have more varied semantic effects. A few function as pure prefixes, but such prefixes are often foreign in origin, or the construction is a calque of a foreign prefixed adjective (including originally Old Church Slavonic derivations from Greek):

(62)   'contra': Blg *protivo-zakónen*, Ukr *proty-zakónnyj* 'unlawful'
'co-':   Rus *so-vinóvnyj*, Ukr *spiv-výnnyj* 'co-guilty'
'pre-':   Slk *pred-posledný*, Pol *przed-ostatni*, Ukr *pèred-ostánnij*
'penultimate'

However, most prefixed adjectives involve a prefix and an adjective-forming suffix (below).

A characteristic use of the negative *ne-/nie-* is found with antonymous adjective pairs, where prefixing *ne-/nie-* to one of the extremes takes the meaning more than halfway back to the other extreme: Ukr *starýj* 'old', *molodýj* 'young', *ne-molodýj* 'middle-aged, oldish'. However, it is not obvious what rules govern the choice of which member of the antonymous pair will receive this prefix. A negativizing effect is also achieved by the prefix *bez-* 'without, -less': B/C/S *smr̀tan* 'mortal', *bè(z)-smrtan* 'immortal', Rus *grámotnyj* 'literate', *bez-grámotnyj* 'illiterate'.

8.4.2 Prefixation + suffixation

Adjectives may show combined prefixation and suffixation, similar to the pattern found with nouns (8.2). The most common pattern is for a prepositional phrase to be adjectivalized, the preposition becoming a prefix and the new stem acquiring an adjectivalizing suffix, usually *-n-*:

(63) Blg *bezdóm-(e)n-ø* 'homeless': *bez* 'without' + *dom* 'house' + *-n-*
 Pol *współczes-n-y* 'contemporary': *w-* 'in' + *spól-* 'common' + *czes* (< *czas*) 'time' + *-n-*

8.4.3 Suffixation

The relation between semantic types of adjectives and their suffixes is not as obvious as with the nouns. Depending on the semantic type of the source noun, adjectives may express possession, composition, relation, location and many other notions. It cannot be assumed that a cognate root will take the same suffix in the various languages, with either native or foreign roots. In (64) adjectives are shown with the suffix and the MascNomSg ending (note that the surface form of a suffix, like that of an ending, may be *zero*, as in (64b); see 8.2):

(64a) Adjectives formed from *zim-a* 'winter'
 B/C/S *zîm-sk-ī/zîm-nj-ī* Mac *zim-(e)n-ø*
 Bel *zim-óv-y/zím-n-i* Rus *zím-n-ij*
 Sorb *zym-sk-i* Pol *zim-ow-y* Cz *zim-n-í*

(64b) Adjectives formed from *zlat-/zolot-* 'gold'
 Sln *zlát-(ø)-ø* B/C/S *zlát-(a)n-ø* Blg, Mac *zlát-(e)n-ø*
 Bel *zalat-(ø)-ý* Ukr *zolot-(ø)-ýj*
 Pol, Sorb *złot-(ø)-y* Cz, Slk *zlat-(ø)-ý*

(64c) 'philological'
 Sln *filolóš-k-i* B/C/S *filòloš-k-ī* Blg *filolog-íčesk-i/*
 Ukr *filoloh-íčn-yj* Rus *filolog-íčesk-ij* *filolóž-k-i*
 Sorb *filolog-isk-i* Pol *filolog-iczn-y* Cz, Slk *filolog-ick-ý*

Extending Townsend's (1968/1975) approach from Russian to the other languages, we divide adjective derivation patterns into seven topics:

- short and long forms
- adjectives in -*n*-
- suffixes building relative adjectives
- suffixes building qualitative adjectives
- de-participial adjectives
- diminutives and augmentatives
- derived adjectives with more complex syntactic origins

8.4.3.1   *Short and long forms*

Proto-Slavic had about thirty suffixes for adjective formation, and in addition formed both short ("indefinite") and long ("definite") adjectives. In modern Slavic only B/C/S, and marginally Slovenian, retain the long form as a definiteness marker, and then only with qualitative adjectives (5.4.3, 5.5.2.1). In the other languages adjectives with both forms will use the short form after "be" predicates and the long form elsewhere. However, the short form is on the decline in this function, and is paradigmatically compromised (5.5.2.1). The more common pattern is for derived adjectives to have either a short form or a long form, depending on whether the suffix is inherently long or short. Possessives in -*in*- and -*ov*- are short-form adjectives, but are not productive in East Slavic, where most adjectives are long, and where the main function of possessives is to provide proper names. It is only in South Slavic that there are reasonable numbers of non-possessive short forms. Forms in -*sk*- are long, as are most suffixes forming relative adjectives. Some typical examples also show variation in the selection of suffixes:

(65)   Adjectives formed from *neb(es)*- 'sky' (on the syllable -*es*- see 5.5.1.6)
B/C/S   *nèb-es(a)n-ø*/*nèb-esk-ī*   Blg   *neb-és(e)n-ø*
Rus, Ukr *neb-ésn-yj*   Bel   *njab-ésn-y*   Cz, Slk *neb-esk-ý*
Pol   *nieb-iesk-i* (also 'blue')   Sorb *njebj-esk-i*

Vowel ~ zero alternations (4.2.1) may occur in the stem when the short-form masculine singular (nominative) has a zero ending (Blg *nebésen*).

8.4.3.2   *Adjective suffixation: -n-*

The -*n*- suffix (Proto-Slavic -*ьn*-) is productive in all the languages. It builds both qualitative and relative adjectives, and is the only major adjective-forming suffix to fulfil both these roles. The noun bases are usually inanimate. Velars and some consonants like /c/ at the end of the preceding stem undergo mutation, and some stem-final paired consonants soften (additive palatalization), subject to standard phonological constraints and with some variation across the languages:

(66)

	Blg	B/C/S	Ukr	Cz
'river' [Noun]:	*rek-á*	*rék-a*	*ríčk-a*	*řek-a*
'river' [Adj]	*réč-(e)n-ø*	*rêč-n-ī*	*ríčk-ov-yj*	*řeč-n-ý*
'science'	*naúk-a*	*náuk-a*	*naúk-a*	*nauk-a*
'scientific'	*naúč(e)n-ø*	*nàuč-(a)n-ø,-nī*	*nauk-óv-yj*	*nauk-ov-ý*

The suffix *-n-* is also involved in some extended suffixes like *-ičn-, -enn-, -ovn-*. There are some doublets with the suffixes *-ičn-* and *-ičesk-*, e.g. Rus *èkonomíčnyj/ èkonomíčeskij*, with effects like that of English *economical/economic*, French *économe/économique*. The adjective in *-n-* is either ambiguous as to qualitative/ relative, or is qualitative (here in the meaning of 'money-wise, thrifty'), and the adjective in *-ičesk-* has the relative meaning 'related to the science of economics'. Similarly Slk *hospodársky/ekonomický* 'economic' *vs hospodárny* 'economical'.

8.4.3.3 *Suffixes building relative adjectives*
The equivalent of 'linguistic' in the Slavic languages gives a useful illustration of the variation of suffix selection and use in relative adjectives.

(67)   'linguistic'
   B/C/S *lingvìst-ičk-ī*   Sln   *lingvist-íč(e)n-ø, jezikoslóv-(e)n-ø*
   Blg   *lingvist-íč(e)n-ø, lingvist-íčesk-i, ezikovéd-sk-i*
   Rus   *lingvist-íčesk-ij, jazykovéd-česk-ij*
   Ukr   *linhvist-ýčn-yj, movoznáv-č-yj*
   Cz   *lingvist-ick-ý/jazykověd-n-ý*   Pol   *językoznaw-cz-y*
   Sorb   *linguist-isk-i*

We give only a brief overview of some typical processes of adjective-formation here, focusing especially on two types: (1) the *-sk-* suffix, which represents the derivation pattern of a large number of suffixes which build adjectives, some with limited range and zero productivity; and (2) possessive adjectives.

The suffix *-sk-* is productive and widespread in Slavic, for both animates and inanimates, as well as personal proper names and the names of nationalities:

(68)

	Blg	B/C/S	Ukr	Cz
'sea' [Noun]:	*mor-é*	*mȍr-e*	*mór-e*	*moř-e*
'sea, naval' [Adj]:	*mór-sk-i*	*mòr-sk-ī*	*mor-sʹk-ýj*	*mor-sk-ý*
'town' [Noun]:	*grad*	*grȃd*	*místo*	*město*
'town' [Adj]:	*grád-sk-i*	*gràd-sk-ī*	*mís(t-s)ʹk-yj*	*měst-sk-ý*

There are also many proper (family) names in *-sk-*, like Rus *Stravínskij* (conventionally 'Stravinsky'), *Dostoévskij* (Dostoevsky), *Stanislávskij* (Stanislavsky), *Čajkóvskij* (Tchaikovsky); Pol *Wiśniewski, Dąbrowski*; Mac *Todorovski, Dimitrovski*.

Note that the preceding syllable in almost all of these is *-ov-/-ev-* or *-in-*, which represent the other type of common suffixal adjective formation, that of possessive adjectives, a type also found in possessive pronouns in some languages. The suffixes used are *-ov-, -in-* and *-j-*. The group in *-j-* mainly derives possessives from names of animals and a few other select nouns. In stem-final position consonants undergo mutation, and paired consonants may soften. In the east the masculine nominative singular has the fill vowel /i/; the form is short even where the long form is well established (East Slavic and Czech); (Polish has few possessive adjectives; and for Slovak and Sorbian, see 5.5.2):

(69)		Blg	B/C/S	Ukr	Cz
'fish' [Noun]:		ríb-a	rȉb-a	rýb-a	ryb-a
'fish' [Adj]		ríb-i	rȉblj-ī	rýb-'jač-yj	ryb-í
'God' [Noun]		Bog	Bȏg	Bog	Bůh
'God's' [Adj]		bóž-í	bȍž-jī	bóž-yj	bož-í
'wolf' [Noun]		vằlk	vûk	vovk	vlk
'wolf' [Adj]		vằlč-i	vȕč-jī	vóvč-yj	vlč-í

The second group of possessive adjectives takes the suffix *-ov-* with masculine bases (*o/jo*-declension), and *-in-* with bases in *-a* (*a*-declension), most of which are feminine. This group also shows the short form. Their declension patterns may show mixed paradigms (5.5.2) and there are often modern replacements or variants adding *-sk-* to form a normal long-form adjective:

(70)		Blg	B/C/S	Ukr	Cz
'uncle' [Noun]:		číč-o	ùjāk-ø	djád'k-o	strýc-ø
'uncle's' [Adj]		číč-ov-ø	ùjāk-ov-ø	djád'k-iv-ø	strýc-ovsk-ý
'nut' [Noun]:		órex-ø	òrah-ø	horíx-ø	ořech-ø
'nut's' [Adj]		órex-ov-ø	òrah-ov-ø	horíx-ov-yj	ořech-ovsk-ý

(For kinship terms, see 9.2.1.) This group includes many proper names, including the patronymics formed from proper names, as well as many nominalized adjectives that now make surnames: Rus *Iván-óv* (*Iván*), *Pop-óv* (*pop* '[Orthodox] priest'), *Púškin* (Pushkin) (*púšk-a* 'cannon'), *Sáxar-ov* (*sáxar* 'sugar'), *Gorbač-ëv* (Gorbachev) (*gorbáč* 'hunchback'), *Xrušč-ëv* (Khrushchev) (*xrušč* 'May-beetle'). Here too belong surnames like *Lén-in* (the River *Léna* in Siberia) and *Stál-in* (*stal'* 'steel').

In East Slavic and Polish, these possessive adjectives are literary or have given way to the genitive, and remain mainly in fossilized phrases: Rus *mám-in synók* 'mother's son' (i.e. namby-pamby); Rus *súk-a* 'bitch', *súk-in syn* 'son of a bitch'; Rus *adám-ov-o jábloko* 'Adam's apple'. The genitive is well maintained in the rest of West Slavic.

For syntactic aspects of "possession", see 6.1.2.2 and 7.1.7.

8.4.3.4   *Suffixes building qualitative adjectives*

Only a few suffixes build qualitative adjectives, usually from existing qualitative adjectives with an attenuating sense. They include *-ovat-* and *-av-*: 'white': Rus *bél-yj*, Pol *bial-y*; 'whitish': Rus *bel-ovát-yj*, Pol *bial-aw-y*. There can be doublets with relational pairs as a result of the metaphorization of some relative adjectives into qualitative adjectives: see Rus * èkonomíčnyj/èkonomíčeskij* above. While it is the *-ičn-* suffix of such doublets which metaphorizes, this suffix is only secondarily a formant of qualitative adjectives.

8.4.3.5   *De-participial adjectives*

Participles are a rich and productive source of adjectives. Starting from a base of morphology shared with adjectives, participles may lose their tense and aspect information, and become genuine adjectives. This process can result in homonyms, where one form relates to the verb, and the other to the new adjectivalized form:

(71a) Adjectives from the present active participle ('-ing')
   Slk   *ved-iet'* 'to know'   *vse-vedia-c-i* 'omniscient' ("all-knowing")
   Blg   *gor-já* 'to burn'   *gor-ést-ø* 'very hot'
   Russian makes use of the Old Russian suffix *-č-* in the adjectival sense *vs* the regular RusChSl participial suffix *-šč-*:
   Rus   *gor-ét'* 'to burn'   *gor-jášč-ij* 'burning'   *gor-jáč-ij* 'hot'

(71b) Adjectives from past active participles (or aorist *l*-participle)
   Blg   *zréj-a* 'to mature'   *zrja-l-ø* 'mature'
   Rus   *ustá-t'* 'to get tired'   *ustá-l-yj* 'tired'

(71c) Adjectives from the present passive participle
   Rus   *ljub-ít'* 'to love'   *ljub-ímyj*   'favorite'
      ispráv-it' 'to correct'   *ne-isprav-ím-yj* 'incorrigible'

(71d) Adjectives from the past passive participle
   B/C/S   *znà-ti* 'to know'   *znâ-n-ø*   'known, familiar'
   Blg   *razséj-a* 'to distract'   *razséj-an-ø* 'absent-minded'

Russian may use a single *-n-* for the adjective in place of the usual participial *-nn-*:

Rus   *žár-iť*   'to roast, fry' *žár-enn-yj* 'roasted'

žár-en-yj 'roast, fried'   (Neut *žár-en-oe* 'roast meat')

There are other, less regular, deverbal adjective formations:

(72a)   B/C/S   *zaùzim-ati* 'to occupy'   *zauzìm-ljiv-ø* 'enterprising, solicitous'

(72b)   Slk   *tvor-iť*   'to create'   *tvor-iv-ý*   'creative'

8.4.3.6   *Diminutives and augmentatives*

Diminutives and augmentatives do not change the part of speech, and they usually do not change other properties like gender either. Only qualitative adjectives regularly form diminutives and augmentatives, which is semantically consistent with their ability to form the degrees of comparison (8.4.1). Diminutive adjectives are less common in South Slavic than in the other languages. The use of diminutives with adjectives mirrors that with nouns (8.2.2). Diminutive suffixes used with adjectives include:

(73)   'small'   'very small, fine, tiny'

-*en'k*-   Ukr *mal-ýj*   *mal-én'k-yj*

-*jusen'k*-   Rus *málen'k-ij*   *mal-júsen'k-ij*

-*ičk*-   Slk *mal-ý*   *mal-ičk-ý*

-*ulink*-   Slk *drobn-ý*   *drobn-ulink-ý*

In a noun phrase both adjectives and nouns may carry a diminutive suffix: Rus *xúd-en'k-ij maľ čí-šk-a* 'a skinny little boy'.

As with nouns, adjectives may show a diminutive form in one language which is, in fact, the standard form: Ukr *malýj*, Cz *malý* 'small', Rus *mál-en'k-ij*. The original Rus *mályj* still exists, but only in fossilized phrases: *bez mál-ogo* 'almost' [lit. 'without a little'], abstract meaning: *mályj bíznes* 'small business', or as the predicative short form: *šápk-a mne mal-á* 'the hat is (too) small for me'.

Augmentatives (mainly East Slavic) include:

(74)   -*ušč*-   Rus   *tólst-yj*   'fat'   *tolst-úšč-ij*   'very fat'

-*enn*-   Bel   *zdaróv-y* 'healthy'   *zdarav-énn-y*   'robust'

-*ezn*-   Ukr   *star-ýj*   'old'   *star-ézn-y*   'very old'

8.4.3.7   *Combination, coordination and subordination*

Derived adjectives with more complex syntactic origins are mainly adjectivalized compound nouns, but may also derive from adjectival phrases (we use the IPA stress style in (75–76) to avoid confusion with other diacritics):

(75)		'north-east'	'north-eastern'
	B/C/S	ˌseveroìstok	ˌseveroìstoč-(a)n-ø
	Blg	ˌseveroiz'tok	ˌseveroiz'toč-(e)n-ø
	Rus	ˌsevero-vos'tok	ˌsevero-vos'toč-n-yj
	Ukr	piv'ničnyj' sxid	pivˌnično-'sxid-n-yj
	Slk	'severoˌvýchod	'severoˌvýchod-n-ý
	Pol	pół'nocny' wschód,	półˌnoco-' wschód półˌnocno'wschod-n-i

Non-derived adjectives may also be compounded, normally with a link vowel (dash [–] = orthographic hyphen):

(76)		'dark-red'		
	B/C/S	ˌtámn-o-cřven	Blg	ˌtămn-o-čer'ven
	Rus	ˌtëmn-o-'krasnyj	Ukr	ˌtemn-o–čer'vonyj
	Pol	ˌciemn-o-czer'wony	Cz	'tmav-o-ˌčervený

8.4.4 Gradation of adjectives

The comparative and superlative forms occur with qualitative adjectives, and with adverbs derived from them. There are four types of gradation formation: prefixation; analytic forms; synthetic forms (prefixation and suffixation); and suppletion.

8.4.4.1 *Prefixation*

Bulgarian and Macedonian use simple prefixes (always stressed, in addition to the stress on the adjective, hyphenated in Bulgarian, not in Macedonian):

(77)			Positive	Comparative	Superlative
	a.	'good'			
		Blg	dobắr	pó–dobắr	náj–dobắr
		Mac	úren	pó–áren	náj–árcn
	b.	'quick'			
		Blg	bắrz	pó–bắrz	náj–bắrz
		Mac	brz	pó-bŕz	náj-bŕz

Most other languages use *naj-/nej-* for the superlative, prefixed to the (suffixed) comparative:

(78)	'new'			
		Positive	Comparative	Superlative
	B/C/S	nȍv-(ī)	nȍv-ijī	nâj-nov-ijī
	Bel	nóv-y	nav-éjš-y	naj-nav-éjš-y
	Slk	nov-ý	nov-š-í	naj-nov-š-í

In Russian *nai-* is restricted to either high or journalistic style, or it has the meaning of the absolute superlative:

(79)   Rus   *blíz-k-ij* 'near'   *nai-bliž-ájš-ij* 'nearest' (high)
                 interésn-yj 'interesting'   *nai-interésn-ejš-ij* 'most interesting'

8.4.4.2   *Analytic forms*

Many languages have both analytic and synthetic gradation: all of East Slavic, all West Slavic except Czech, and Slovenian. B/C/S and Czech have only synthetic forms, Bulgarian and Macedonian only prefixation (77).

In analytic gradation a comparative/superlative (indeclinable) adverb is used with the positive adjective or adverb, like English 'more/most'. In the comparative we have: Sln *bòlj*, Bel *bol'š*, Ukr *bíľš(e)*, Rus *bólee*, USorb *bóle*, LSorb *wěcej*, Slk *viac/väčšmi*, Pol *bardziej*, plus the positive grade of the adjective. In the superlative the corresponding superlative adverb is formed by adding the prefix *naj-* to these forms, in all but Russian:

(80)   'new'

	Positive	Comparative	Superlative
Ukr	*nóv-yj*	*bíľ š(e) nóv-yj*	*najbíľ š(e) nóv-yj*
Pol	*now-y*	*bardziej now-y*	*najbardziej now-y*
Slk	*nov-ý*	*viac/väčšmi nov-ý*	*najviac/najväčšmi nov-ý*
(U)Sorb	*now-y*	*bóle now-y*	*najbóle now-y*

Russian (and Belarusian optionally) uses the declinable adjective *sám-yj*, Bel *sám-y* with the positive: Rus *sám-yj nóv-yj* 'the newest'. Where suffixed (synthetic) comparative/superlative adjectival forms exist (e.g. Rus *lúčš-ij* 'better' – see below), *sám-yj* may (optionally) be used to specify the superlative: *sám-yj lúčš-ij*.

8.4.4.3   *Synthetic forms*

In synthetic gradation we find both prefixation and suffixation. A suffix, parallel to English *-er/-est*, is added to the adjective stem. This is the most common type of gradation in Slavic. The analytic formation may be preferred for derived words (like those in *-sk-*) and borrowed words. In languages with both analytic and synthetic forms, the analytic form tends to occur as a modifier in noun phrases, and either the synthetic or the analytic form may appear in predicates, more often the former:

(81)   Rus   *bólee dešëv-aja mašín-a*   'a cheaper car'
            Rus   *èt-a mašín-a dešévl-e/bólee dešëv-aja*   'this car is cheaper'

The comparative is formed by adding a suffix to the positive adjective's stem. The choice between them is sometimes purely lexical (unpredictable from the form of the word), and is sometimes dependent on phonological factors like the number or nature of consonants at the end of the root. In Proto-Slavic the comparative/ superlative suffix was *-ějš-*, and this is still the most common:

(82)

	Positive	Comparative
'clean'		
Sln	*čist*	*čistéjši*
Pol	*czyst-*	*czyśc-iejsz-y*
Slk	*čist-ý*	*čist-ejš-í*
'clever'		
Bel	*xítr-y*	*xitr-èjš-y*
Cz	*chytr-ý*	*chytr-ejš-í*
Sorb	*mudr-y*	*mudr-iš-i*

However, in Proto-Slavic, this suffix was missing in the nominative singular masculine and neuter, and the suffixless form was that used later for the comparative adverb or adjective inflexion *-(e)je*. The *-(ej)š-* suffix is absent from B/C/S, which has comparative *-(i)jī*, superlative *naj- + -(i)jī*:

(83) B/C/S *stằr-ø* 'old' *stằr-ijī* 'older'
       naj-stằr-ijī 'oldest'
      B/C/S *tĩh-ø* 'quiet' *tĩšī* (*h > š* = mutation) 'quieter'

In Russian the *-(ej)š-* suffix has the meaning of the superlative (above), except in a few irregular cases, usually suppletives (below).
    Other forms of the suffix used for this purpose are:

(84a) *-š-*, with prepalatalization, and the loss of 'vowel + *k*' in roots:

	Positive	Comparative
Sln	*sláb-ø* 'weak'	*sláb-š-i*
Ukr	*star-ýj* 'old'	*stár-š-yj*
Slk	*nov-ý* 'new'	*nov-š-í*
	bliz-k-ý 'near'	*bliz-š-í*

(84b) *-iš-*, often after stems in clusters:
      Ukr *molod-ýj* 'young' *molod-íš-yj*
      Sorb *spěšn-y* 'quick' *spěšn-iš-i*

(84c) *-č-*, with the adjectives retaining the *-k-* (i.e. *č* is mutated *k*):
      Ukr *vuz'-k-ýj* *vúž-č-yj*

Rus   *lëg-k-ij* 'light'   *lég-č-e*
Cz   *ten-k-ý* 'thin'   *ten-č-í*

In Russian the forms in *-e* and *-ee* are indeclinable comparatives, and occur only in predicates. The former causes mutation:

(85)   Positive   Comparative
      Rus   *níz-k-ij* 'low'   *níž-e*
      Rus   *krasív-yj* 'beautiful'   *krasív-ee*

8.4.4.4   Suppletion

A few common adjectives, as in English, show different roots in the comparative and superlative, as distinct from the positive degree:

(86)   'bad'
	Positive	Comparative	Superlative
Ukr	*zl-yj*	*hír-š-yj*	*naj-hír-š-yj*
Rus	*plox-ój*	*xúd-š-ij/xúž-e*	*xúd-š-ij*
Cz	*špatn-ý*	*hor-š-í*	*nej-hor-š-í*
Pol	*zł-y*	*gor-sz-y*	*naj-gor-sz-y*

8.5   Word formation and adverbs

Adverbs show only restricted prefixation, especially involving negatives and indefinites (cf. 8.6.2). Most other types of prefixed adverbs involve suffixation as well, especially with the remains of prepositions and cases:

(87)   *po-*: Rus   *rússk-ij*   [Adj]   'Russian'
                    po–rússk-i   [Adv]   'in Russian, in a Russian manner'
                    e.g. *govorít' po–rússki*   'to speak (in) Russian'
       na-: Slk   *na-pred* 'forwards'   (former Acc in *-ø*)
       v-:   Slk   *v-predu* 'in front'   (former Loc in *-u*)
       z-:   Slk   *z-vrchu* 'from above'   (former Gen in *-u*)

Outside prefixation, adverbs are formed principally from nouns, prepositional phrases and qualitative adjectives. Only the last of these three types is still productive. Adverbs formed from nouns, or from Adjective + Noun phrases, show fossilized case-forms:

(88)   B/C/S   *zîm-*   *i*   'in winter'
               winter-   [LocSg]
               gòr-   *e*   'up, higher'
               mountain- [(Former)LocSg]

Bel	*bjáh-*	*om*	'at a run'
	run-	[InstSg]	
Rus	*s-egó-*	*dnj-a*	'today'
	this (arch.) [GenSg] – day [GenSg]		
Cz	*celk-*	*em*	'in general, quite'
	whole-	[InstrSg]	

But most derived adverbs are manner adverbs, and are formed from adjectives by replacing the adjectival inflexion, usually with *-o* or *-e*. Hard adjective stems are followed by *-o* (89a); soft and formerly soft stems, and West Slavic non-velars, generally take *-e*, with prepalatalization where appropriate (89b). Some instances of *-e* continue Proto-Slavic *-ě*, and so may appear on a hard stem (89c). Adjectives in *-sk-* take *-i* (or *-y*) (89d):

(89) DERIVATION OF ADVERBS FROM ADJECTIVES

(89a) *-o*: 'quiet'   *tix-*
'quietly': B/C/S *tȋh-o*, Rus, Blg *tíx-o*, Ukr *týx-o*,
Cz, Slk *tich-o*, Pol *cich-o*

(89b) *-e*: 'extreme'   *kraj-n′-*
'extremely':   Rus, Bel *krájn-e* (cf. from *-ě*: Cz *krajn-ě*)

(89c) *-e* (< *ě*): 'good'   *dobr-*
'well':   Blg *dobr-é*, Ukr *dóbr-e*, Pol *dobrz-e*, Cz *dobř-e*
(cf. B/C/S *dòbro*, Sln *dóbro*, Mac *dobr-o*)

(89d) *-i/-y*: Blg   *vráž-esk-i* [Adj and Adv] 'enemy, inimical, inimically'
B/C/S *ljȗd-skȋ-* 'human', *ljȗd-sk-i* 'humanly'
Rus   *drúž-esk-ij* 'friendly', *drúž-esk-i* 'in friendly manner'
Cz   *ru-(s)ský* 'Russian', *rus-(s)ky* 'in Russian'
e.g. *mluvit rusky* 'to speak Russian'

Adverbs derived from qualitative adjectives may show the same diminutive suffixes as the adjectives: Pol *cich-y* 'quiet', *cich-o* 'quietly', *cich-uteńk-o* [Dim].

A small number of adverbs derive from gerunds: Rus *mólč-a* 'silently' (<*molč-át′* 'to be silent'), and a few from numerals: Rus *trí-ždy* 'thrice' (<*tri* '3'). These formations are not productive.

8.5.1 Gradation of adverbs

Graded adverbs belong mainly to the category of adverbs of manner. They are formed from the corresponding adjectives by the four methods described for adjectives in 8.4.1: prefixation, analytic forms, synthetic forms and suppletion. The patterns and selection of forms are close to those of adjectives.

Prefixation operates as for adjectives, and is standard in Bulgarian and Macedonian: Blg *glúpavo* 'stupidly', *pó–glúpavo* 'more stupidly', *náj–glúpavo* 'most stupidly'. Prefixation also forms superlatives from synthetic comparatives – see below.

As compared to the choice of analytic *vs* synthetic formation in the adjectives (above), some languages have a lesser choice in the adverb: Slovak, Sorbian and Slovenian form the adverb only synthetically (in addition to Czech and B/C/S).

The analytic forms use the appropriate form of 'more, most' with the positive degree of the adverb: Rus *bólee krasívo* 'more beautifully'. In this case Russian too uses the prefix *naj-* (in the form *nai-*) to make the superlative: *naibólee krasívo*. The analytic forms are alternatives to the synthetic forms, where they exist.

In synthetic forms of the degrees of comparison a suffix is added to the stem, and may prepalatalize or mutate the stem at the same time. The suffix is the same as for the adjectives, namely a reflex of either PSl -*(ě)je* (the NomSgNeut of the comparative adjective) (90a) or -*(ě)jš-e* (from other forms) (90b). The superlative is formed by prefixing *naj-* to the comparative form:

(90a)

		Positive	Comparative	Superlative
'wisely'				
B/C/S	*mûdr-o*	*mùdr-ije*	*nâj-mudr-ije*
'near'				
Bel	*blízk-a*	*bliž-èj*	*naj-bliž-èj*
Sorb	*blis-k-o*	*bliž-e*	*naj-bliž-e*
'weakly'				
USorb	*słab-je*	*słab-je*	*naj-słab-je*
LSorb	*słab-je*	*słab-jej*	*nej-słab-jej*
'silently'				
Cz	*tich-o*	*tiš-e*	*nej-tiš-e*

(90b)

		Positive	Comparative	Superlative
'beautifully'				
Slk	*pekn-e*	*pekn-ejš-ie*	*naj-pekn-ejš-ie*
'strongly'				
USorb	*syln-o*	*syln-iš-o*	*naj-syln-iš-o*

Suppletion occurs in a few cases of mostly high-frequency items, where the corresponding adjective also shows suppletion between the positive degree, on the one hand, and the comparative and superlative, on the other, e.g. Ukr *baháto* 'much', *bíľš(e)* 'more' (see above).

8.6   Word formation and other parts of speech

Word formation in other parts of speech is not productive, with the partial exception of compound prepositions. Some of these are formed from the adjunction of two prepositions, which may be hyphenated. They are semantically compositional:

(91)		'from'	'under'	'(out) from under'
	Blg	iz	pod	is-pod
	Rus	iz	pod	iz–pod

Others are lexicalized from prepositional phrases, like Blg *v rezultát* 'as a result of'.

We discuss below two areas where word-formation processes are active, if not productive, in the modern languages: numerals (8.6.1); and pronouns, determiners and pro-adverbs (8.6.2).

8.6.1   Numerals

Five topics in Slavic numeral systems belong with word formation: cardinals, ordinals, collectives, distributives and de-numeral adverbs.

8.6.1.1   *Cardinal numerals*

The formation of non-simplex cardinal numerals is sometimes handled within lexicology. But it is also a conventionalized word-formation process in the terms used here, since whole words are combined into uninterruptible wholes in compound numbers, since numbers inflect, and since affixes, like the ordinal suffix, are added either to the whole number, or to various component parts of the number.

The general pattern of cardinal-number composition follows the familiar Indo-European decimal orientation (avoiding the twenties-counting ("vigesimal") system of languages like Danish and French). Numbers from 11 to 19 contain a "teen" element derived from the number 10, while the "-ty" numbers like 20, 30 . . . contain a different reflex of "ten" (see 5.5.4 for Proto-Slavic forms and further details of the modern ones):

(92)		'three'	'ten'	'thirteen'	'thirty'	'thirty-three'
	Blg	tri	desét	tri-na-déset	tri-déset	tridéset i trí
	Rus	tri	désjat'	tri-ná-dcat'	trí-dcat'	trídcat' trí
	Pol	trzy	dziesięć	trzy-na-ście	trzy-dzieści	trzydzieści trzy

Some of the "-ty" numbers are inflexionally impoverished, with strong case syncretism (5.5.4). Some are lexically irregular, like East Slavic *sórok* (Rus, Ukr)/*sórak* (Bel) '40' and *devjanósto* (Rus, Ukr)/*dzevjanósta* (Bel) '90'.

Compound numbers (with more than one lexeme) above '21' are formed by
adjunction, with the largest numbers to the left and the digits to the right.
(Bulgarian and Macedonian insert *i* 'and' before the last digit: "twenty and
one".) In Sorbian the hundreds–tens–digits pattern is replaced by a form like
the archaic English "two-and-twenty", resulting from constant contact with the
same pattern in German. Czech, Slovak and Slovenian have both this pattern as
well as the more regular "twenty-two" order, which is archaic and rare in
Slovenian, but may be preferred in Czech and Slovak, where only the final "ten"
need then be declined:

(93)   'thirty-three'   'three-and-thirty'
    Sln   (*trî-deset trî*)   *trî-in-trîdeset* [Fem, Neut]
    Sorb   –   *tři-a-třiceći* [Masc Impers, Fem, Neut]
    Cz   *tři-cet tři*   *tři-a-třicet*
    Slk   *tri-dsat' tri*   *tri-a-tridsat'*

(Sln *in*, Sorb, Cz, Slk *a* 'and'). The words for 'thousand' and 'million' behave like
lexical nouns.

There is a current instability in the declension of cardinal numbers, especially
compound numbers. While normative grammars may specify that each component
of a number should be inflected, there is a strong tendency in Slavic, and especially
in the spoken languages, to make complex numbers indeclinable. It is already
standard in B/C/S to decline only the numbers 1–4, 100, 1,000 and 1,000,000. As
an alternative, speakers will avoid constructions where numbers are in any case
other than the nominative or accusative; or they will simply place the number
phrase in apposition, which – at least subjectively – partly isolates it from the case-
agreement requirements. While this does not affect the word-formation composition of the number system, it does have an important effect on the word-class
status of compound nouns and their function in morpho-syntax (see also 5.5.4.1
and 6.1.2.3).

8.6.1.2   *Ordinal numerals*
Ordinal numerals – except for '1' and '2' (5.5.4.2) – are derived from the cardinals
by the addition of adjectival suffixes. Depending on the number and on the
language, there is some variation with compound numbers as to whether it is
only the last element which receives the adjectival suffix and inflexion, as with the
English *-th*, or the last element as well as other elements. East and South Slavic
follow the former pattern, in West Slavic Czech suffixes and declines all elements,
while Slovak and Polish suffix and decline only the last two, and Sorbian only the
last element:

(94) 'three hundred and thirty-third' [MascNomSg] Ordinal suffix on:

SouthSl: Blg: *trí-sta trí-deset i tré-t-i* last

B/C/S: *trȉ-sta trí-deset (i) trȅćī* last

Sln: *trí-sto trí-in-trí-deset tré-tj-i* last

EastSl: Rus: *trí-sta trí-dcat' tré-t-ij* last

WestSl: Cz: *tří-st-ý tři-cát-ý tře-t-í* all

Pol: *trzy-sta trzy-dziest-y trze-c-i* last two

Sorb: *tři sta tři-ceć-i tře-ć-i* last

8.6.1.3 Collective numerals

A not too systematic, but typologically noteworthy, area of Slavic involves collective numerals expressing a group of entities specified by number, like English *pair* (5.5.4.3), and other suffixed numeral forms expressing groups and approximations.

B/C/S, Slovenian, and all of East and West Slavic, share a collective numeral suffix in *-oj(e)* (for 2–3), *-er(o)/-or(o)* (for 4 +). This form is used not only for collective groups, but also to quantify *pluralia tantum* nouns:

(95) B/C/S *dvȍj-e čàrap-e* 'two pairs of stockings'

Sln *deset-ér-o ljud-í* '(a group of) ten people'

Rus *íx* *bý-l-o* *dvó-e*

they-Gen be-PastNeutSg two-CollNom

'there were two of them'

Slk *pät-or-o det-í* 'five children'

Bulgarian and Macedonian have *-(i)n-a* and *-m-a* to express groups and approximate number: Blg *petnadeset-ín-a* 'about fifteen, a group of about fifteen'. These languages also use a *-(t)in-* suffix for 400–900: '400': Blg *čétiri-sto-tin*, Mac *četiri-stó-tini* (cf. B/C/S *čètiri-stō* or *čètiri stȍ-tine*, Rus *četýre-sta*). The concept of "approximate number" has various means of expression, not only by prepositions like 'about', but also by Noun–Numeral order in Russian: *pját' karandašéj* 'five pencils', *karandašéj pját'* 'about five pencils' and by particles like Slovak *zo: zo dvadsat'* 'about 20'.

Lexicalization from collectives can result in new substantives: B/C/S *trȍj-ic-a*, Rus *tró-ic-a* 'group of three, Trinity', Rus *trój-k-a* 'troika, three-horse sleigh, group of three people (e.g. a three-person junta, etc.)'.

8.6.1.4 Distributive numeral expressions

Slavic uses the preposition *po* to express the idea of 'x each'. *Po* most often here takes the accusative, but in Czech and Sorbian it takes the locative; in Ukrainian and Belarusian 'one' takes the locative and other numerals the accusative; and in Russian 'one' takes the dative, '2–4' the accusative (= nominative form), and other numerals may take either case. The construction does not allow constituents between *po* and the numeral, and so constitutes a case of virtual prefixation, in spite of the orthographic convention of writing the two elements as separate words (further, in Russian *po* is stressed before 'two' and 'three'):

(96)   Rus   *dáli*   *ím*   *pó*   *dv-á*   *jáblok-a*
             gave-Pl   they-Dat   Prep   two-Acc   apple-GenSg
             'they gave them two apples each'

8.6.1.5   *De-numeral adverbs*

A small, marginal and unproductive group of de-numeral words expresses 'how many times': Cz *dva-krát*, Rus *dvá-ždy*, Mac *dva-pati* 'twice'. Sorbian has two such forms: *dwaj-króć* and *dwój-ce* 'twice'.

8.6.2   Pronouns, determiners and pro-adverbs

Pronouns and determiners, and some adverbs, undergo special types of word formation involving semantic modification with prefixes or suffixes. The word-categories involved are interrogatives, relatives, negatives, and specifics and indefinites. None of the patterns is productive.

The prefix-pronoun nexus may be interrupted by prepositions, if they occur, so making these formations an unusual kind of word:

(97)   'no-one'   NomSg   InstrSg   Prep + InstrSg ('with no-one')
       B/C/S   *nȉ-(t)ko*   *nȉ-kīm*   *nȉ s kīm*
       Bel   *ni-xtó*   *ni-kím*   *ni z kím*

8.6.2.1   *Interrogative*

The formation of the interrogative forms, like English w H -words of the *who? when?* type, is usually regarded as part of either etymology or lexicology. But it is useful to present them here to see how the various systems interrelate. The interrogatives are identical or similar to the corresponding relative forms, and mostly show a *j-*, or *k-/č-* (the last by palatalization), where the definite/demonstrative has *t-*:

(98a)   'so, thus', 'how'
        B/C/S   *tàko/kàko*   Sln   *takó/kakó*   Mac *taka/kako*
        Blg   *taká/kak*   Bel, Ukr   *tak/jak*   Rus *tak/kak*
        Pol, Cz *tak/jak*   Sorb   *tak/kak*   Slk *tak/ako*

(98b) 'such a kind', 'of what kind?'

B/C/S	*tàk-av-ø/kàk-av-ø*			Blg	*takǎv-ø/kakǎv-ø*
Sln	*ták(-š(e)n)-ø/kák(-š(e)n)-ø*			Mac	*kak-ov-ø/tak-ov-ø*
Bel	*tak-í/jak-í*	Ukr	*tak-ýj/jak-ýj*	Rus	*tak-ój/kak-ój*
Sorb	*tajk-i/kajk-i*	Pol	*tak-i/jak-i*	Slk	*tak-ý/ak-ý*

The words for *who?* and *what?* are less regular. Their definite partners are the personal pronouns (5.5.2.3), or the neuter singular of 'this' or 'that' (5.5.2):

(99) 'who?/what?'

B/C/S (Serb)	*kȍ/štȁ*	B/C/S (Cr)	*tkȍ/štȍ*	Sln	*kdó/káj*
Mac	*koj/što*	Blg	*koj/kakvó = što*		
Bel	*xto/čto*	Ukr	*xto/ščo*	Rus	*kto/čto*
USorb	*štó/šta*	LSorb	*chto/co*	Pol	*kto/co*
Cz	*kdo/co*	Slk	*kto/čo*		

8.6.2.2 *Relative*

As in English, the relative pronouns are close to the interrogatives, with a few important exceptions, like the addition of the enclitic *-ž* in Czech and Sorbian, *-r* in Slovenian and *-to* in Bulgarian. The Czech *jenž* formation, however, is now high or formal style, and is giving way to *který*. Most of these forms are inflexionally adjectival (for agreement, see 6.2.2), but there is often a non-agreeing variant, usually the interrogative pronoun:

(100) 'who' (declined unless marked invariable – [Inv])

B/C/S *kòj-ī* Sln *katér-i, kdó-r* Mac *koj-ø, koj-što* Blg *kój-to*

Bel *jak-í, što* [Inv] Ukr *jak-ýj, što* [Inv] Rus *kotór-yj, kto*

Sorb *kotr-y-ž/kotar-y-ž, štó-ž/chto-ž* + USorb *kiž*, LSorb *kenž* [Inv]

Pol *któr-y, co* [Inv] Cz *ktēr ý/jen ž* Slk *ktor ý, čo* [Inv]/[Colloq]

English grammars tend to regard the non-interrogative *when* (etc.) as adverbs, in sentences like 'I know when he rang'. Slavic grammars sometimes classify these as relatives, which is justified on both morphological and syntactic (7.2.2.3) grounds.

8.6.2.3 *Negative*

Negative pronouns and adverbs are broadly formed by prefixing *ni-* to the interrogative (not *ne-*, see below). For adjectival 'no' a different root *žadn-* is used in West Slavic and Ukrainian, and *nobe(d)n-* in Slovenian:

(101a) 'no-one'

B/C/S *nȉ-ko* Sln *ní-kdo* Blg, Mac *ní-koj*

Bel, Ukr *ni-xtó*   Rus *ni-któ*   Sorb *ni-chto*
Pol   *ni-kt*   Cz *ni-kdo*   Slk *ni-k, ni-kto*

(101b)   'no, none'
B/C/S *nĩ-kak(a)v-ø*   Sln *nobêd(e)n-ø*   Blg *ni-kak(á̃)v-ø*
Mac   *ni-kak(o)v-ø*   Bel *ni-jak-í*   Ukr *žódn-yj*
Rus   *ni-kak-ój*   Sorb *žad(y)n-ø, ni-jak-i*   Pol *žad(e)n-ø*
Cz   *žadn-ý*   Slk *žiadn-y, ni-jaký*

(101c)   'never' (< 'when')
B/C/S *nĩ-kad(ā)*   Sln *ni-kdàr*   Blg, Mac *ní-koga*
Bel   *ni-kóli*   Ukr *ni-kóly*   Rus   *ni-kogdá*
Sorb   *ni-hdy*   Pol *ni-gdy*   Cz, Slk   *ni-kdy*

Slavic negatives are like those of French, and require both the negative forms listed above and a negative particle (7.1.3).

8.6.2.4   *Specifics and indefinites*

Interrogative pronouns and adverbs can be converted into specifics or indefinites by the addition of preposed and postposed elements. Specifics correspond roughly to English *some-: somewhere, someone*, etc. Indefinites are approximately like English *any-*. In Slavic, however, the specifics and indefinites form a more complex series than in English. Some descriptions claim that there are three levels of specificity/indefiniteness:

a   any-at-all   (most indefinite)
b   any/some   (intermediate)
c   some   (most specific)

The (b) category, which falls between the indefinite and specific extremes, is difficult to characterize exactly. It is supposed to express a "stronger" *any*, or a "weaker" *some*, and to correspond to "any, within a specified or implied group":

(102)   Rus   *ésli **któ-nibud'** iz vás zaxóčet pomóč'*
              'if any/some of you want to help'

However, most descriptions are satisfied with the basic two, the 'some' type – used when existence is not questioned, only identity, and the 'any' type – where even existence is in doubt or only potential, and these can usually be signalled in English by the choice of either *some* or *any* in translation. In Slavic there are often several affix-formants for each of the semantic types. (103) shows the main prefixes and suffixes which can be attached to the interrogative words ('who', 'what', etc.), with the semantic results as listed in (103a) and (103b). Some are typically found in colloquial usage rather than written:

(103a)   'any (at all)', 'ever' (hyphen = morpheme marker only; dash (–) = orthographic hyphen, # = separate word, orthographic space)

B/C/S ĩ-, *bílo#*   Sln -(*r*)*kóli*   Blg #*da e*   Mac #*bilo*, #*da e*

Rus *–nibud'*, *–libo*   Ukr *–nébud'*, *bud'-*, *abý-*   Bel *–nébudz'*, *aby–*

Pol *-kolwiek*, #*bądź*   Sorb *-žkuli*   Cz *-koli*, *-si*   Slk *-kol'vek*, *hoc*(*i*)-

(103b)   'some (or other)' (brackets = 'many a', 'one or two')

B/C/S *nĕ-*, (*kojè-*)   Sln, Mac *ne-*   Blg *njá-*, *ne-*

Rus   *né-*, *–to*, (*kóe–*)   Ukr   *dé–*, *–to*, *-s'*   Bel *né-*, *-s'ci*

Pol   *-ś*   Sorb   *nĕ-*, (*-žkuli*)   Cz *nĕ-*, *-si*   Slk *nie-*

9

Lexis

9.1   Patterns of lexis

'From the point of view of lexis, all the [Slavic] languages are very like each other' (Skalička, 1966: 23). It is true that the lexicons of the Slavic languages differ less systematically than their phonology or morphology, which are responsible for some of the most widespread differentiating features in the Slavic lexicons, like pleophony in East Slavic (Rus *molokó* 'milk'; cf. Cz *mléko*, Blg *mléko*; 3.2.1.7) or differing word-formation patterns (chapter 8). Nonetheless, there are major patterns in the Slavic lexicons which show different compositions and histories, and which affect the degree to which the languages are mutually comprehensible. Slavic is also much less overlaid by foreign lexical borrowing than is English, where some estimates of non-indigenous lexis 'are well over 80%' (Stockwell and Minkova, 2001: 2).

   Lexicology is well developed as a named field of descriptive Slavic linguistics, and the lexicons of the Slavic languages have been intensively studied and described over the last two centuries. Much of the research has been related, directly or indirectly, to the question of the definition and delimitation of national languages, together with their formation and culture (chapter 2), including lexical enrichment and purification: the Slavs' prescriptive approach to the regulation of their national languages is shown in their approach to the lexicon (together with grammar, orthoepy and orthography) in language planning and policy (11.2.3). Lexicographical work on individual Slavic languages has resulted in dictionaries of the standard languages, phraseologisms, collocations and borrowings; dialect dictionaries (chapter 10); multilingual dictionaries, especially with Russian and major West European languages like English, French and German; word-frequency lists, root dictionaries and reverse-order dictionaries; in 'grammatical' dictionaries; and in specialized dictionaries, notably in technological areas. Before the fall of Communism there was, however, relatively less work on non-standard lexis in areas like socially defined slang, (e.g. student slangs) or professional technolects (as opposed to terminology, which is better documented). The Slavic linguistic regulatory and printing bodies were prudish about printing non-standard language, though there has been more freedom since decentralization and deregulation following the fall of Communism. Significantly, before 1990 all of the dictionaries of Russian slang, vulgar language and obscenities were published in the West. And under Communism there was a general ideological constraint on research related to class-based sociolinguistic lexical research (chapter 11).

With the exception of etymologically and historically oriented research, contrastive Slavic lexicology is less developed. We shall concentrate on a series of typical issues where the lexis of the Slavic languages is most characteristically displayed, without attempting to combine them under a unified descriptive approach. The material in this chapter overlaps to some extent with word formation (chapter 8), and with the historical evolution of Slavic (chapter 2).

9.2   Lexical composition and sources in the modern Slavic languages

The standard approach to specifying the lexical profile and content of the Slavic languages echoes the diachronic record, and simultaneously provides a layered categorization from the oldest to the most recent lexical developments. Oldest of all are the words showing Indo-European origins; then those from the Common Slavic period; then those reflecting the tripartite division into East, West and South Slavic; then those reflecting subdivisions within these groups, where appropriate (e.g. Czech-Slovak; Bulgarian-Macedonian; B/C/S and Slovenian); and, finally, words specific to individual languages, especially those derived from local dialect sources and subsequently standardized. It is then possible to take alternative "horizontal" views of the lexicons from the point of view of geography (the origins of lexical borrowings), semantic fields and so on. Taken together, these views provide a characterization of the lexical composition of each language, including a cultural history of the languages, since they document borrowings between individual Slavic languages and from outside Slavic.

9.2.1   Indo-European and general Slavic

A contrastive analysis of some basic lexical items (essentially those in the relevant sections of Comrie and Corbett, 1993) gives the following:

1.   of 15 basic body parts, 10 are Indo-European, 14 are shared by all 11 languages and 1 is missing in 1 language (Sorbian does not have *$sr'd$-ьce* 'heart');

2. of 9 basic colour terms, 6 are Indo-European, 5 are shared by all languages, 3 are missing in one language each (*sin-* 'blue' and *siv-* 'grey' in Sorbian, and *ser-* 'grey' in Bulgarian), and 1 is missing in three languages (*modr-* 'blue' in East Slavic);

3. of 12 basic kinship terms, 11 are Indo-European, 10 are shared by all languages, 1 is missing in 2 languages (*stryj-* 'paternal uncle' in Russian and Sorbian) and 1 is missing in 3 languages (*otьc-* 'father' in Belarusian, Ukrainian and Bulgarian).

Although these numbers are small, they show the strength of the Indo-European base in Slavic and the common Slavic nature of the basic vocabulary.

Kopečný (1981) lists 1,990 words of common Slavic origin. Of these, 1,170 remain in all languages, and 875 of these are structurally identical. This figure of around 2,000 items is the one most often taken as reliable, though other much larger ones have been proposed, e.g. 9,000 by Sławski and 20,000 by Trubačev (from Ondrus, 1976: 299). Lekov (1955: 102) considers that about two-thirds of the original word-stock has been retained in the modern languages, as measured by modern dictionaries.

9.2.2   The lexis of the individual Slavic languages

Glottometric analyses (for example by Kotova and Janakiev, 1973, and Suprun, 1983) suggest that the closest pairs of languages are: Belarusian/Ukrainian, Russian/Ukrainian, Polish/Ukrainian, Bulgarian/Macedonian, and Czech/Slovak (Kotova and Janakiev, reported in Mel'ničuk, 1986). Beyond the expected pairings reflecting historical (and to a lesser extent geographical) proximity, Bulgarian and Russian are notably close.

A different view of the group is gained by pursuing the extent to which individual languages retain Proto-Slavic lexemes or are missing a common Slavic lexeme (as above for colour terms, etc.). Kopečný (1981: 53) claims that Czech and Slovak have retained the highest proportion of Proto-Slavic lexemes, and Macedonian the lowest. A different count by Suprun (1983: 18, of one sample letter (B) in Trubačev's *Slavic Etymological Dictionary*) puts not only Czech and Slovak, but also B/C/S and Slovenian, at the top of the retention list, but Belarusian and Sorbian at the bottom. And a count of 300 high-frequency lexemes (Ondrus, 1976: 300) places Slovak at the top, and then, in order, Czech, Ukrainian, Russian and Polish. From Kopečný's list Mel'ničuk (1986: 198) grades the languages by the number of missing common lexemes (from most to least): Macedonian, Bulgarian, Belarusian, Ukrainian, B/C/S, Russian, Slovenian, Polish, Slovak and Czech (Sorbian missing); and by pairs of languages both missing the same lexeme and sharing a common replacement: Bulgarian/ Macedonian, Belarusian/Ukrainian, B/C/S/Macedonian, Russian/Belarusian, Polish/Belarusian, Russian/Ukrainian and B/C/S/Slovenian. In each case we note that Bulgarian and Macedonian are at the "outer" extreme, and Czech and Slovak at the "inner". In the second case, B/C/S is closer to Macedonian than to Slovenian, which may reflect the closer cultural history of the former two as against the closer linguistic shapes of B/C/S and Slovenian in other respects.

In summary, Czech and Slovak appear to have best retained the Proto-Slavic lexis, Macedonian and Bulgarian least, and the measures of lexical proximity between languages reflect largely what one would expect from the linguistic and other history of the group, sometimes overriding geography.

9.2.3 Slavic and non-Slavic elements

This interaction, and sometimes tension, between Slavic and non-Slavic lexis, and between indigenous Slavic and loans from other Slavic languages, has been a major force in the development of the Slavic languages, and in their current directions. A well-known example of the parallel existence of Slavic and non-Slavic lexical systems in different languages concerns the names of the months. Seven Slavic languages adopted the month names of the Julian calendar: all of South Slavic, together with Slovak (but not Czech), Russian (but not Ukrainian or Belarusian) and Sorbian. Croatian has both the Julian and the Slavic names. Table 9.1 shows the Russian (Julian) names of the months for comparison with the five Slavic versions (exceptional Julian names within non-Julian systems are shown in bold).

Table 9.1. *Names of the months*

	Rus	Bel	Ukr	Pol	Cz	Cr
January	*janvár'*	*stúdzen'*	*síčen'*	*styczeń*	*leden*	*sìječanj*
February	*fevrál'*	*ljúty*	*ljútyj*	*luty*	*únor*	*vèljača*
March	*mart*	*sakavík*	*bérezen'*	**marzec**	*březen*	*ožujak*
April	*aprél'*	*krasavík*	*kviten'*	*kwiecień*	*duben*	*trâvanj*
May	*maj*	**maj**	*tráven'*	**maj**	*květen*	*svîbanj*
June	*ijún'*	*čérven'*	*čérven'*	*czerwiec*	*červen*	*lîpanj*
July	*ijúl'*	*lípen'*	*lýpen'*	*lipiec*	*červenec*	*sřpanj*
August	*ávgust*	*žníven'*	*sérpen'*	*sierpień*	*srpen*	*kõlovoz*
September	*sentjábr'*	*vérasen'*	*véresen'*	*wrzeszień*	*zářrí*	*rûjan*
October	*oktjábr'*	*kastrýčnik*	*žóvten'*	*październik*	*říjen*	*Îistopād*
November	*nojábr'*	*listapád*	*lystopád*	*listopad*	*listopad*	*stùdenī*
December	*dekábr'*	*snéžan*	*hrúden'*	*grudzień*	*prosinec*	*pròsinac*

As can be seen, the Julian term for 'May' has intruded into Belarusian and Polish, and Polish *marzec* 'March' is also Julian in origin. The other Slavic names show etymologies (not all fully established, and only established ones are noted below) reflecting various aspects of flora, fauna, climate and activity:

'January'	cold (Bel); cutting (wind) (Ukr, Cr); icy (Cz)
'February'	bitter (Bel, Ukr, Pol);
'March'	birch-tree (Ukr, Cz); juice (Bel); revival (Cr)
'April'	flower (Bel, Ukr, Pol); oak-tree (Cz); grass (Cr)
'May'	grass (Ukr); flower (Cz); dogwood (Cr)
'June'	red (-flower) (Bel, Ukr, Cz); worm (Pol); linden-tree (Cr)
	(Note that the roots of 'red' and 'worm' are the same: *červ-*)
'July'	linden-tree (Bel, Ukr, Pol); (second) red-flower (Cz); sickle (Cr)
'August'	sickle (Ukr, Pol, Cz); reaping (Bel); hay-dance (Cr)
'September'	heather (Bel, Ukr, Pol); shining (or rutting) (Cz); red/yellow (Cr)
'October'	flax (Bel, Pol); yellow (Ukr); hunting (or rutting) (Cz); leaf-falling (Cr)
'November'	leaf-falling (Bel, Ukr, Pol, Cz); cold (Cr)
'December'	snowy (Bel); hard earth (Ukr, Pol); grey (Cz, Cr)

9.2.4   Slavization and vernacularization

The Czechs and Croats in particular seek to preserve Slavic roots and words – Lencek's (1982) "Slavization" and "vernacularization" – in the face of competing lexis from other countries: German (and to some extent Polish) in the case of the Czechs, and Serbian/Serbo-Croatian, as well as German and Hungarian, in the case of the Croats.

Consider the word for 'music': Czech, Slovak, Sorbian, Slovenian and B/C/S have both the Greek/Latin root *muzik-* and a local one, which is preferred:

(1)   'music'

Rus, Bel, Ukr, Pol	*múzyka*	Blg, Mac	*múzika*
Cz, Slk	*hudba + muzika*	Sorb	*hudźba + muzika*
B/C/S	*glázba + mùzika*	Sln	*glásba + múzika*

The Slavicizing tendency is also found in country and city/town onomastics, with more local instead of international names. This tendency is particularly evident in Czech, but is also common in West Slavic and B/C/S:

(2)   Austria: Cz *Rakousko*   Slk *Rakúsko*
        Egypt: B/C/S *Mìsīr*

Regensburg: Cz *Řezno*

Venice: B/C/S *Mlèci*

Vienna: Cz *Vídeň*   Slk *Viedeň*   B/C/S *Bêč*

                 Ukr *Víden'*

There is an interaction here with the category of number. Polish tends to favor *pluralia tantum* for the names of countries more than other Slavic languages do. This no doubt reflects the older system of referring to countries by the plural ethnonym, i.e. 'the land of the Xs', e.g. in the Old Russian Chronicle *ide v ǫgry* 'he went to the (land of the) Ugry/Ugrians'. In Polish these plural names are related usually to the plural form of the inhabitants, without the palatalization:

(3a)   'Hungary': Pol *Węgry* [Pl] (*Węgier* 'a Hungarian', Pl *Węgrzy*)
                    Blg, Mac *Ungárija*   Rus *Véngrija*   Ukr *Uhórščyna*
                    Bel *Véngryja*   B/C/S *Màdjarskā* and *Ũgarskā*
                    Sln *Madžarska*   Cz, Slk *Maď arsko* [Neut]
                    USorb *Madžarska*   LSorb *Madjarska* and *Hungorska*

(3b)   'Bohemia (and Moravia)'
                    Blg, Mac, Rus, Ukr *Céxija*   Bel *Cèxija*   Sorb *Česka*
                    Cz Slk *Čechy*   Pol *Czechy* (and *Morawy*)   Sorb *Čechi*

9.3   Coexistent lexical strata

Languages may have multiple lexical layers, either Slavic and non-Slavic, or two different Slavic layers. Examples of the first are B/C/S (9.3.2) and Bulgarian (9.3.3), and of the second East Slavic, and particularly Russian, which shows clear influence from South Slavic in lexis borrowed from and through the Orthodox Church, parallel to native Russian words (9.3.1).

9.3.1   Russian: Church Slavonic and Russian

Russian is an archetypal example of the coexistence of two lexical layers in certain areas of the vocabulary. The historical development of Russian parallel to Church Slavonic (2.3.1) resulted in both a partial Russianization of Church Slavonic, and the importation into Russian of significant numbers of words, particularly in the spheres of religion and abstract concepts. These terms were not naturalized, as in Ukrainian or Belarusian, but tended to remain in their original phonological form. As a result, there are numerous words which phonologically, morphologically or lexically bear a non-native Russian imprint in the modern language.

Typical indications of Church Slavonic origins include the *št*/*žd* reflexes of
Proto-Slavic *tj*/*dj* (4a) or the South Slavic *CraC* shape in place of East Slavic
pleophony (4b) (see 1.3.1.7, 3.2). Where two terms exist side by side the South
Slavic, Church-related term will be higher in stylistic register, and usually more
abstract (the contrasting features are bolded):

> (4a) Rus *prosvetít'* (1) 'to illuminate' (2) 'to enlighten'
>
> 1Sg: (1) *prosvečú* (2) *prosveščú*

> (4b) Rus 'town': neutral: *górod* high, poetic: **grad**
>
> 'milk': neutral: *molokó* calque: *mlekopitájuščee* 'mammal'
>
> Rus *róvnyj* 'even, level' *rávnyj* 'equal'

In other cases, Church Slavonic forms have become neutral, at least in Russian:
present participles now all have the Church Slavonic suffix shape -*šč*- in place of
the Old Russian (= Common East Slavic) shape -*č*-, still seen in adjectives:
Rus *gorjáščij* 'burning' *vs gorjáčij* 'hot', cf. *gorét'* 'to burn' (8.4.3). Or the man's
name *Vladímir* (with non-pleophonic shape) has the hypocoristic pleophonic form
Volódja. The Ukrainian and Belarusian forms of the full name have the East Slavic
shape: Ukr *Volodýmyr*.

Such Church Slavonic forms are uncommon in Ukrainian, and even more so in
Belarusian:

> (5) Ukr Pres Part: *kipljáčyj* 'boiling' (Rus *kipjáščij*)
>
> Ukr *prosvitýty* 'to enlighten' [Prfv]: [Imprfv] *prosviščáty*
>
> 'to illuminate': [Imprfv] *prosvíčuvaty*

9.3.2   B/C/S: Slavic and non-Slavic

B/C/S is in the unique situation of having a fairly homogeneous phonology, morphology and syntax, certainly to the level of mutual comprehensibility between its three
variants. But it also shows some diametrically opposed lexical differences which reflect
underlying cultural, religious and intellectual attitudes. The actual volume of lexis
affected is not large, and speakers of each variant are usually aware of the existence,
and nature, of alternative forms in the other standard variants of the language.

In broad terms, Serbian follows the pattern of the religiously Orthodox languages,
and borrows openly from Greek, other Slavic, Turkish and European sources.
Croatian, like Slovenian and Czech and to a lesser extent Slovak, often prefers to use
indigenous lexical material where possible, and so tends less to favour direct borrowing. Similar sentiments were expressed during the "Slavophiles *vs* Westernizers" controversy in the history of Russian (2.3.1). There the Westernizers' view prevailed in

this context, whereas in Croatian the Slavicizers have established a pattern of lexical maintenance and renewal which depends less on borrowing.

There is a series of concepts represented by different words in the three variants:

(6)		Croatian (Slavic root)	Bosnian and Serbian
	factory	*tvórnica* (make; also Bos)	*fàbrika*
	library	*knjȋžnica* (book)	*bibliotéka*
	music	*glàzba* (voice)	*mùzika*
	railway station	*kȍlodvōr* (track + yard)	*stȁnica* (stand)
	telegram	*bȑzojāv* (fast + inform)	*telègram*
	university	*sveùčilīšte* (all + learn)	*univerzìtēt*

Now that Bosnian is emerging as a language separate from both Croatian and Serbian, distinct lexical items like the following are candidates to become a formal part of the new standard Bosnian language. The data show Bosnian positioned lexically between Croatian and Serbian, though the links to Serbian are somewhat closer:

(7)		Croatian	Bosnian	Serbian
	'bread'	*krȕh*	*krȕh (hl(j)ȅb)*	*hlȅb*
	'train'	*vlâk*	*vôz*	*vôz*
	'window'	*prózor*	*prózor (pêndžer)*	*prózor*
	'town'	*grâd*	*grâd/vároš*	*vároš*
	'corner'	*kût*	*ȕgao/ćòšak*	*ćòšak*

There are also some words which have different primary meanings in the two older variants. The number is restricted, but the semantic discrepancies can be striking. The B/C/S data are based on Frančić (1963: 22–23). Bulgarian and Slovenian examples are also supplied as an indication of the north-western *vs* south-eastern nature of many of these variants:

(8)

B/C/S	Sln	Cr	Bos	Serb	Blg
gȕša	–	goiter; craw	–	throat	throat
kòvčeg	trunk; suitcase	trunk; suitcase	trunk; suitcase	coffin	coffin
krìvica	injustice	injustice	injustice; offence	crime	*krivda* = injustice
kȓst	christening	christening	cross	cross	cross
nàučnīk	–	apprentice	scientist	scientist	–
ùnùtrašnjōst	interior	interior	interior	province(s)	interior; provinces
ȍbjava	advertisement; announcement	advertisement; announcement	advertisement; announcement	announcement	advertisement; announcement
porúčiti	inform	inform	inform; order	order	inform; order
prȃvdānje	quarrel	quarrel	apology	explanation	–

In general, Croatian is closer to Slovenian, and Serbian to Bulgarian.

9.3.3   Bulgarian: Russian and Turkish

Something like the reverse situation obtains with modern Bulgarian, which, as a result of influence from Moscow (still seen as the 'Third Rome' after the fall of the Ottoman empire), shows a layer of lexis derived from Russian, some in fact a reimportation of Church Slavonic forms, e.g. *verojáten* 'probable', *starája se* 'to try'. But there are also many internationalisms via Russian Church Slavonic, e.g. *gramátika* 'grammar', other Russian forms of the Soviet period, e.g. *petilétka* 'five-year plan', and now globalizing English and other European influences as well.

The long period of Ottoman Turkish rule inevitably saw a high number of borrowings, but the late nineteenth-century revival in turn saw the mass replacement of these forms, either by neologisms or borrowings from more 'acceptable' sources, in the first place Russian. The survivors include many (some 800 in the three-volume dictionary of 1955–1959) basic everyday items like *čórap* 'sock' and *čánta* 'purse'. A somewhat larger number are listed as non-standard, alongside preferred native synonyms, e.g. *kjutúk* vs native *pắn* 'tree-stump'. Scatton (1993: 241) reports that in analyses of this dictionary, Turkish, with 1,900 items in all, constitutes 13.5 percent of borrowed words, behind Latin (25.5 percent), Greek (23 percent) and French (15 percent), and ahead of Russian (10 percent). However, these figures underestimate the Russian influence, since Bulgarian phonological patterns tend to mask the Russian or Russian Church Slavonic origin of words like Blg *veléna*, Rus *vselénnaja* 'universe'.

Since 1990 globalizing influences have begun to oblige Bulgarian language legislators to cope with a flood of imports, especially English, with the introduction of Western consumer culture, technology and capitalistic structures.

9.4   Root implementation and exploitation

9.4.1   Extending word formation

In English, root exploitation is counterbalanced by borrowing (Hughes, 2000), and the results of word formation and combination tend to lexicalize more readily, and form semi-autonomous new units. We tend to think of *Longfellow*, for instance, as the name of a poet, and only secondarily as 'long' + 'fellow'. In contrast, Slavic roots are often widely exploited: Tolstoy (*Tolstój*) is more readily perceived as deriving from *tólstyj* 'fat'; Pushkin (*Púškin*) from *púška* 'cannon'; and Lenin from *Léna* 'the River Lena'.

In chapter 8 we demonstrated the productivity of affixes in word formation. It is also useful to survey the productivity of roots. Some common roots like *bel-* 'white' can form more than a hundred affixed and root-combined words in a single language, and in all the four major parts of speech. The relatively greater vitality of the root *bel-* is evident from the cases where English does not use *white-*, but borrows from Greek, Latin and other sources:

(9) Rus *bel-* 'white'

abstracts (*belizná* 'whiteness')

politics (*belogvardéec* 'White Guardsman', *bélye* 'the Whites')

medicine (*béli* [*plurale tantum*] 'leucorrhoea', *belkovína* 'albumen'),

animals (*belúga* 'white sturgeon, beluga', *belúxa* 'white whale', *belják* 'white hare')

objects (*belók* 'egg white', *beljánka* 'white mushroom', *belíla* 'white-out fluid')

adjectives (*belovátyj* 'whitish')

verbs (*belét'* 'to be white', *belít'* 'to whiten, cause to be white').

We show elsewhere (chapter 8), how prefixes, particularly verb prefixes (8.3.1), form families of derived stems. In contrastive lexicology it is useful to consider the lexical properties of a single root. We take *pis-* 'write' (see 8.3.1.2) in B/C/S, Russian, Polish and Czech, following Herman (1975: 337–342):

1. All four languages have an unprefixed verb meaning 'write', though in some of the languages it can also mean 'paint' (its earlier meaning, cf. the PSl root *pis-* from IE *pik'-*, from which come Latin and English (etc.) *pict-*):

    (10a) B/C/S *písati* Rus *pisát'* Pol *pisać* Cz *psát*

2. The derived noun in *-mo* is present in all the languages:

    (10b) B/C/S *písmo* Rus *pis'mó* Pol *pismo* Cz *písmo*

    But it differs somewhat in meaning. It can mean 'writing-system, script' in all four languages (having earlier meant a single 'letter (of the alphabet)' in OCS, cf. the early work on the alphabet known as 'O pismenĕxъ' – 'On the letters/alphabet'). But in Russian and Czech it can also mean 'the ability to write'. In all but Russian it can designate 'handwriting', or the manner of writing. And while in all four languages this word can refer to what is written, it does so in different ways: 'letter' (Rus, B/C/S; Pol also *list*), cf. Cz *dopis*, B/C/S *dópis*; 'written matter' (Pol, Cz); 'magazine, periodical' (Pol); and in Polish and Czech it may also designate 'printer's type'.

3.   Other affixed forms cover abstract meanings like 'scripture' (Rus *pisánie*),
     the process of 'writing' (Rus, Pol *pisánie*, B/C/S *písānje* 'writing'; Pol
     pisanina 'pen-pushing'), with various media (Rus *zapisát'*, Pol
     zapisać, Cz *zapisovat*, B/C/S *zapísati* 'to record') and the results (Rus
     zápis', Pol *zapis*, Cz, B/C/S *zápis* 'recording'), agents (Rus *pisátel'*, Pol
     pisarz, Cz *pisatel*, B/C/S *písac* 'writer'; Rus *piséc*, Cz *písař*, B/C/S *pìsār*
     'scribe'; Rus *pisáka*, Cz *pisálek* 'scribbler') and objects (Cz *pisátko* 'slate-
     pencil', B/C/S *pìsāljka* 'pencil'). (For the many verbal prefixed forms,
     see 8.3.1.) The meaning 'paint' is seen in Rus *íkonopis'* 'icon-painting'.

9.4.2   Lexical specialization and verbs of motion

Lexical specialization presents a number of interesting phenomena. Some of these
are of restricted generality: for instance, Russian has no generic word for 'blue', but
two more specialized terms, *sínij* 'dark blue' and *golubój* 'light blue'. More widespread examples of specialization through types of subject concern verbs like 'die',
where one term relates to people and another to animals: using the animals' term to
refer to people denigrates both the deceased and the manner of dying: Ukr *umyráty*
'to die [of people]', *zdyxáty* 'to die [of animals]'. This example parallels German
essen 'eat [of people]' and *fressen* 'eat [of animals]'.

More typologically relevant is the rich Slavic lexical system of common verbs of
motion. There are two special vectors. The first involves "natural" *vs* "assisted"
motion: on foot, say, as opposed to movement by vehicle, boat, horse and so on,
similar to German *gehen* "natural motion" vs *fahren* "assisted motion": Rus *vestí*,
Sorb *wjesć* 'to bring, lead', Rus *veztí*, Sorb *wjezć* 'to convey'.

The second dimension involves the old (Indo-European) feature of 'determinate ~
indeterminate' (8.3), which survives in West and East Slavic. All the languages
retain between 9 (Polish, Slovak) and 20 (Ukrainian) pairs like Rus *nestí* [Det] ~
nosít' [Indet] 'to carry'. Of the South Slavic languages, only Slovenian retains a
trace of this distinction, including Sln *nésti ~ nosíti*, but some of the small number
of pairs are actually lexically distinct forms, e.g. Sln *peljáti* [Det] ~ *vozíti* [Indet] 'to
convey'. Determinate motion has a goal or end-point, as when one 'goes' to the
shop. Indeterminate motion concentrates on the activity rather than achieving a
goal, or 'walking about':

(11)   'go' Russian
                                Natural   Assisted
         Determinate   *idtí*   *éxat'*
         Indeterminate   *xodít'*   *ézdit'*

This pattern for "natural/assisted" motion covers only the unmarked 'go' and 'lead, convey' verbs, and not uniformly in all languages at that. But the "determinate/ indeterminate" motion criterion applies to a range of verbs – 'run, fly, carry, swim, climb, crawl, drag, drive, chase, roll, wander' – again with some lexical gaps in individual languages.

These verbs have a special interaction with aspect (6.3, 8.3). Since perfective aspect favors telic action with an end-point and a goal, the determinate form is the unmarked perfective. Prefixes reflect their spatial meanings more closely than in general prefixal perfectivization. Imperfectives are normally derived by prefixing the parallel indeterminate verbs (8.3).

9.5 Lexical innovation: indigenous lexical resources

Lexical innovation gives rise to a genuine neologism only relatively infrequently, for example in patented products. Elsewhere new realia or concepts are reflected in lexis through reallocation of existing words: by the creation of new words from within by the novel use of existing lexical and morphological material, for instance by compounding; or by abbreviation of one sort or another (stump compounding, clipping or *univerbácija*, acronyms or initialisms). The importation of new words (borrowing) and the morphological nativization of foreign lexis and calquing are covered in 9.6.

9.5.1 Semantic change

Extending or changing the semantic (denotative) range of existing words occurs commonly through metaphor or technological advance: on the launch of the first Soviet satellite in 1957 Russian *spútnik* 'human companion; natural satellite' acquired a new "man-made satellite" reading, and in the process became one of the important Russian contributions – lexical as well as technological – to globalized communication. Words may also "determinologize", losing their specialist senses as they widen their sphere of use and reference (e.g. Rus *dén'gi*, (30)).

A major internal semantic change in connotations occurred with the Communist revolutions between 1917 and 1948. Here the ideological switch to a totalitarian atheist regime realigned the connotative value of religious and ethical lexis, or marginalized it, and supplied a new range of favored lexis. Some of the changes, however, had been accumulating from around 1900, and the Revolution was lexically less abrupt than was earlier thought. The pre-Revolutionary institutions and social roles became of historical interest, and some vocabulary like the word for 'secretary' assumed new importance with its role in the Communist hierarchy. More important were compounds and abbreviated forms.

9.5.2   Compounding

"Straight" compounding – often hyphenated, and with or without a link-vowel – is a common phenomenon in Slavic, producing such "new" objects as Rus *diván–krovát'*, Pol *kanapa–łóżko* 'bed-settee', Rus *vagón–restorán*, B/C/S *vàgōn – restòrān* 'restaurant-car', which may be phrases in some languages (Pol *wagon* [Noun] *restauracyjny* [Adj], Cz *jídelní* [Adj] *vůz* [Noun] 'restaurant-car'); Cz *železobeton* (lit. 'iron+*o*+concrete'), cf. B/C/S *àrmīrānī bètōn* 'reinforced concrete' (8.2.3 for details).

9.5.3   Abbreviated words

Single words and especially compounds are reduced in various ways: by using only stumps of their parts ("stump compounding", 9.5.3.1); by abbreviating and fusing the elements of phrases by retaining only one element, and normally supplying a suffix (*univerbacija*, 9.5.3.2); or by using initials or a combination of syllables and initials (acronyms and initialisms, 9.5.3.3).

9.5.3.1   *Stump compounds*

Stump compounds are words which are formed from two or more words by taking syllables, usually the first syllable of each word, and creating a new word. Russian, as the originator of the bulk of these terms in the early years of Communism, has the largest inventory, and has provided models for the other languages. In English there are relatively few stump compounds like the former airline *PanAm*. In English linguistics the nearest equivalents are "clipping" (*demo* for *demonstration*) and blends (*brunch* for *breakfast + lunch*), neither quite like the syllable-based stump compound. Like acronyms and initialisms (9.5.3.3), stump compounds are mostly nouns, or nouns providing a derivational basis for the formation of adjectives. The most common source is a phrase consisting of an adjective and a noun. In Russian the stress of the new word generally falls on the stump of the head noun in the original phrase – normally in last position, even if that syllable was not originally stressed in the full noun (12a), though sometimes the second word may be retained in full (12b):

(12a) Rus *kolxóz* 'collective farm' < *kollektívnoe xozjájstvo*
       Rus *specfák* 'special faculty' < *speciál'nyj fakul'tét*
(12b) Rus *fizkul'túra* 'physical education' < *fizíčeskaja kul'túra*
       Rus *specodéžda* 'special clothing' < *speciál'naja odéžda*

Stump compounds formed from more than two words take the first syllable of each (not necessarily in the same order as the phrase):

(13)   Rus   *Učpedgíz* 'state educational pedagogical printing house'
            < *gosudárstvennoe* (state) *učébno-pedagogíčeskoe izdátel'stvo*
      Cz   *Čedok* 'Czech Travel Agency' < *Česká dopravní kancelář*

Some stump compounds derive from a phrase consisting of Noun + Noun, with the first noun as the head of the phrase, and the second noun in an oblique case (14a), while others combine the Adjective + Noun and Noun + Noun types (14b):

(14a) Rus   *kòmbát* 'commander of a battalion' < *komandír batal'óna*

(14b) Rus   *Komsomól* 'Communist Union of Youth'
            < *Kommunistíčeskij sojúz molodëži* [Gen]

Even the order of the underlying phrase can be rearranged (cf. (13)):

(15)   Rus   *sòcdogovór* 'pact on socialist competition'
            < *dogovór o socialistíčeskom sorevnovánii*

Key words, even head nouns, can be omitted from the underlying phrase:

(16)   Rus   *šírpotréb* 'wide demand goods'
            < *továry šírókogo potreblénija* 'goods of wide demand'
      Rus   *ròslesxóz* 'Russian federal forestry service'
            < *federál'naja slúžba lesnógo xozjájstva Rossíi*

It often happens that Russian stump compounds are borrowed *in toto*, with appropriate phonological adjustments, into other Slavic languages:

(17)   Rus   *kònármija* 'cavalry' < *kónnaja ármija* (lit. 'horse army')
      Ukr   *kinármija* < *kínna ármija*

In other instances the underlying phrase is wholly or partly calqued into the target language, and a stump compound formed from it:

(18)   Rus   *kòmjačéjka* 'Communist cell'
            < *kommunistíčeskaja jačéjka*
            (or *jačéjka kommunistíčeskoj pártii*)
      Ukr   *komoserédok* < *komunistýčnyj oserédok*

The stump compound has proved to be a very convenient device, especially in East Slavic and Bulgarian. It is shorter than the original phrase. It is usually transparent, since unfamiliar compounds can often be recovered by analogy from existing known compounds: stump compounds containing Rus *sov-* usually refer to *sovétskij* 'Soviet', as in *sovxóz* 'Soviet farm' < *sovétskoe xozjájstvo*, or to *sovét* 'council', as in *sovnarxóz* 'council for the national economy', and *nar-* is usually *naródnyj* 'people's'. Confusion does occasionally arise, however, as with *kom-*, which may mean *komitét* 'committee', *komissár* 'commissar', *komíssija* 'commission', *komandír* 'commander' and *kommunistíčeskij* 'Communist', among other less common meanings. A significant number of the components of stump compounds stem from "internationalisms" – words borrowed from international technical vocabulary, or derived from the writings of Marx and Engels translated into Russian.

Guessing the underlying phrase of unfamiliar stump compounds is something of a verbal game in these languages. The form of the abbreviated syllable is sometimes varied to avoid confusion. *Komsomól* itself forms a derived stump compound *komsórg* 'Komsomol organizer' < **komsomól'skij organizátor**, in which the stump form *kom-* would otherwise lead back to *komitét* 'committee' or *kommunistíčeskij* 'communist', etc. rather than to *Komsomol*. The decodability of stump compounds stems from the limited collocation possibilities of most of the component syllables, and to a certain regularization of the vocabulary used in them.

The currency of stump compounds varies widely among the Slavic languages. They are strongest in East Slavic, and to a lesser extent in Bulgarian, which has a strong tradition of lexical borrowing from Russian since the language revival of the nineteenth century. Bulgarian has borrowed many Russian stump compounds as words (the parts not being equivalent forms, e.g. 'youth' in Bulgarian has the root *mlad-*, not *mol*(*od*)-):

(19)   Rus, Blg   *komsomól*

Rus, Blg   *komsomólec* '(male) member of the Komsomol'

Rus, Blg   *komsomólka* '(female) member of the Komsomol'

In other cases Bulgarian can have partial stump compounds parallel to the full stump compounds in Russian:

(20a)   Rus   *politrúk* 'political leader' < **politíčeskij rukovodítel'**

Blg   *politrăkovodítel* < **politíčeski răkovodítel**

(20b)   Blg   *glavsék* 'senior secretary' < **gláven sekretár**

Blg   *litrabótnik* < **literatúren rabótnik** 'literary worker'

Blg   *specsrédstvo* 'special measure' < **speciálno srédstvo**

though since Bulgarian is virtually caseless, straight compounds like *zaméstnik-diréktor* 'deputy + director' are probably more accessible to direct compounding processes, that is without abbreviation.

In West Slavic, and other South Slavic languages, the tendency is still toward phrases and calques rather than full stump compounds. Russian stump compounds provide a concept which is often translated as a phrase

(21)	Rus	Cz	B/C/S
agitkollektív 'agitation group'	*agitační kolektiv*	*kòlektiv agìtātōrā*
agitpúnkt 'agitation centre'	*agitační středisko*	*propàgāndnī cèntar*
narkóm 'people's commissar'	*lidový komisar*	*národnī komèsār*
profsojúz 'trade union'	*odborový svaz*	*sindìkāt*

The total number of stump compounds in recent lists of neologisms in languages outside East Slavic and Bulgarian, like that of Smółkowa for Polish (1976), is relatively small. Bulgarian has shown a much greater readiness to adopt and borrow words from Russian than these other languages have. In addition, the structures of society, economics and administration which were adopted in these countries after the Second World War were less like the Russian models than those in Ukraine or Belarus. The stump compounds in widest use across the Slavic world were the names of economic and political institutions: organizations like Comintern, Cominform, Komsomol, and these are borrowings from Russian and now part of the past.

9.5.3.2 *Clipping and* univerbacija

One indication of recent developments, especially in Russian and languages (Ukrainian, Belarusian) more closely in its sphere of influence, is *univerbácija*, the Russian term for making a new single word from a phrase, usually a noun phrase, and usually by the removal of the head noun (earlier terms included *sraščénie* 'splicing' (Švedova, 1980: vol. 1:256) and *vključénie* 'incorporation' (e.g. Gorbačevič, 1971: 135). Šanskij (1975: 224) called it *leksiko-sintaksičeskij sposob slovoobrazovanija* 'lexico-syntactic method of word formation'). *Univerbacija* is to be distinguished, on the one hand, from regular nominalization from adjectives and participles, where "thing" can be supplied for a neuter, and "person, people" for other genders and numbers: Rus *glávnoe* 'the main thing', *bol'nój* 'a patient' < 'ill'; and, on the other hand, from anaphora, where adjectives and participles can refer to "the ADJECTIVE one(s)": Pol *wolę niebieskie* 'I prefer the blue (ones)'.

Univerbacija usually involves an adjective stem. The inflexion and preceding word-forming elements are removed, and a suffix, sometimes zero, is added. The noun deleted, unlike the nominalization cases (above), is not predictable from the adjective itself. The Russian pattern often involves the suffix -*ka*:

(22) Rus *налíčnye* < ***naлíčnye** dén'gi* 'ready (money), readies'
        èlektríčka < ***èlektríčeskij** póezd* 'electric train'

Léninka < *Bibliotéka ímeni Lénina* 'Lenin Library'
amerikánka < *amerikánskij restorán* 'American (= fast-food)
restaurant'

This tendency is continuing vigorously: a 'mobile/cell phone' in Russian is either *mobílka* (< *mobíl'nyj* 'mobile') or *sótka* (< *sótovyj* 'cellular'), each with the loss of *telefón*, cf. similarly Pol *komórka* (< *komórkowy* 'cellular' *telefon*).

9.5.3.3   Acronyms and initialisms

The modern Slavic languages have a large number of abbreviated forms in current usage. In Western countries we find new abbreviations mainly originating in the commercial and technical area, in the names of companies, manufacturers or products (EMI, MG, SAAB, BMW, etc.), and occasionally in the names of government instrumentalities: agencies like NASA have contributed to the development of shortened words in English. Readers of Anthony Burgess's novel *A Clockwork Orange* (1963) will remember how unnatural these structures sounded in English. In the Eastern Bloc such terms stem more from social, economic and administrative structures. After the 1917 Revolution the new leaders of the Soviet Union wanted to break sharply with pre-revolutionary Russia. They consequently changed, and/or renamed, the basic social and administrative structures of the country. And with the Communist take-overs in the other countries of the Eastern Bloc, aspects of the Russian model were adopted for both administration and language. The Russian experiment with the new forms of language was very much in the spirit of Futurist poets like Mayakovsky during the first decades of the century. Many abbreviations of the early Soviet period have vanished, together with the objects or entities which they designated, and many other terms have not been adopted by non-Russian Slavs. Furthermore, the conservatism and normative approach of Slavic lexicographers has kept many such abbreviations out of the dictionaries, which makes it difficult to establish the vitality of abbreviations in each Slavic language. Certainly, many abbreviations have been ephemeral. But they also constitute one of the major means of adapting modern Slavic lexicons to the demands of changing social and technological factors in the modern world.

Like stump compounds (9.5.3.1), acronyms and initialisms are mostly nouns. But, unlike stump compounds, they are not semantically transparent, and are established purely by convention. We again use Russian examples, since Russian is the main source of this tendency in Slavic.

Acronyms are pronounced as words, and have a conventional syllable structure:

(23)   Rus   *vuz* 'higher education institution' < *výsšee učébnoe zavedénie*
              GUM 'state universal/department store'

< *gosudárstvennyj universál'nyj magazín*
TASS 'Telegraphic Agency of the Soviet Union'
< *Telegráfnoe Agéntstvo Sovétskogo Sojúza*

Initialisms are pronounced as a series of letters:

(24)   Rus   *SSSR* [ɛsɛsɛ'sɛr] 'Union of Soviet Socialist Republics'
                < *Sojúz Sovétskix Socialistíčeskix Respublik*
                MGU [emgɛ'u] 'Moscow State University'
                < *Moskóvskij Gosudárstvennyj Universitét*
                KGB [kagɛ'bɛ] 'Committee of State Security'
                < *Komitét Gosudárstvennoj Bezopásnosti*

There are also some mixed types, part pronounced and part "spelt" (25a), and some involving remodelling (25b):

(25a)   Rus   *AzSSR* [azɛsɛ'sɛr] 'Azerbaizhan Soviet Socialist Republic'
                < *Azerbajdžánskaja Sovétskaja Socialistíčeskaja Respúblika*

(25b)   Rus   *Detgiz* [dʲet'giz] 'Children's State Publishing House'
                < *Gosudárstvennoe Izdátel'stvo Détskoj Literatury*
                (note the re-ordering of the component parts, cf. (13))

Acronyms may be assimilated into the inflexional patterns of the language if their terminations correspond to regular inflexional requirements: *-a/-ja* for feminines, and so on (this termination assigns the acronym to a gender and a declensional class), and if they have ceased to refer to a unique entity, like *vuz* (23), they can be pluralized:

(26)   Rus   *vuz* [NomSg], *vúza* [GenSg], *vúzu* [DatSg] ...
                vúzy [NomPl], *vúzov* [GenPl] , ...

Initialisms, on the other hand, remain lexically and grammatically less integrated by case. They can show gender, officially that of the head noun, e.g. Rus *KGB* is masculine (*komitét*), as are *SSSR* (*sojúz*) and *MGU* (*universitét*) (24). With less well-known initials, speakers are likely to make a guess based on the termination, which usually means masculine from a final consonant, e.g. Rus *ÈVM* 'computer' might be thus treated, though its head word is *mašína* 'machine' [Fem]. The same principle and problem arises with acronyms: the Soviet news agency *TASS* (23) was neuter, its head word being *agéntstvo*, but it was often treated as masculine by shape (and sound).

    Purists often flinch at the aesthetic clumsiness of stump compounds and acronyms. It is true that the number of such words is larger in East Slavic, with Russian feeding Ukrainian and Belarusian, than in West or South Slavic. Names of countries are a notable exception, and even in speech Slavs in the Communist era often referred to other countries by their initials or acronyms. This practice is now declining as 'socialist' and 'people's' are removed from the country name. The former Socialist names included:

(27)   Blg   *PNR* 'Polish People's Republic'
             < *Pólska Naródna Repúblika*
             GDR 'German Democratic Republic'
             < *Germánska Demokratíčna Repúblika*

Some acronyms are ephemeral, either because they denote ephemeral realia, or because they are maladroit, grammatically unstable, or simply ugly:

(28)   Rus   *ÈOASSPTR* 'Expedition section of air-rescue,
             vessel-raising and underwater-technical works'
             < *Èkspediciónnyj otrjád avarìjno-spasítel'nyx,*
             sudopod"ëmnyx i podvòdnotexníčeskix rabót

Acronyms perform a valuable function in providing short words for complex entities, and their use is increasing as technology advances, in the Slavic world as elsewhere.

9.6   Lexical innovation: external influence

The Slavs have millennia of continuous experience of close contact with other languages, resulting in bilingualism, code-switching, language interference and borrowing. Coexistence is one context in which borrowing occurs; the two other principal contexts are a culturally dominant language, or a politico-militarily dominant one. External influences have been moderated by linguistic purism and language management (11.2), and the avoidance of the wholesale importation of foreign lexis has resulted in a substantial use of calques (9.6.2).

9.6.1   Borrowing

The Slavic languages have tended to be lexical recipients rather than donors, especially when compared to major international lexical donors like Greek, Latin, French and English. The main exception, with Slavic in the donor role, have involved Bulgarian–Macedonian, in the early centuries of Orthodoxy; Czech on Polish, and then Polish on Ukrainian, Belarusian and Russian; but most of all Russian.

The role of Moscow, Russia and Russian has several phases: first as the Third Rome and defender of Orthodox religion; and later as the primary vehicle of Marxist–Leninist ideology and its vocabulary, and the political rhetoric and styles which it engendered. Though this theory is still awaiting empirical proof, one can discern an inner circle, Russian-centered and covering the old Soviet Union, with the oldest and strongest effect of Communist lexis and stylistics; then Bulgarian, which maintained fairly close ties with Moscow under Communism; then former Czechoslovakia and Sorbia; then Poland; and, finally, former Yugoslavia, which was least under Moscow's direct influence, and where Slovenia was arguably the most Westernized of the Slavic lands.

The ideological components of these Russian-based linguistic models were often not welcomed by the receiving languages and cultures, where they were often regarded as unnatural and unlovely, and have now been vigorously and promptly discarded in the aftermath of the fall of Communism (9.7). Since 1990 the already lively tendency to adopt covert borrowings from the West has become a flood. The language academies have been largely helpless to stem the tide. And, most typically, viable Slavic words are now being overlooked or bypassed by Western-oriented borrowings. In joining the mainstream of international consumer and technical culture, the Slavic languages are making themselves less Slavic, but at the same time also more international.

Excluding local language contact – e.g. Macedonian with Greek – the external lexical influences on Slavic form several layers. Direct Greek loans are fundamental to the Orthodox-based languages from the earliest years of literacy, as Latin borrowings are to the Catholic Slavs. Latin was also a medium for transmission of Greek lexis to Catholic Slavs:

(29)   Rus   *tetrád'* 'exercise-book' < Gk *tetradi(on)* 'quarter-page'

Turkic loans persist in East Slavic as a legacy of the Golden Horde (thirteenth–fifteenth centuries, see 2.3.1), for instance in vocabulary relating to equine matters, some domestic words and jewellery:

(30)   Rus   *dén'gi* 'money' < Tatar *täŋkä* 'silver coin' (via *den'gá* 'half-kopeck')

More substantial are Turkic elements in South Slavic, especially Serbian, Macedonian and Bulgarian, from the five hundred years of the Ottoman empire:

(31)   Blg *čorbá*, B/C/S *čórba* 'broth' < Turk *çorba*

Bulgarian has conducted a de-Turkification lexical policy since 1878, though around 13 percent of foreign words in Bulgarian are still Turkish, including 800 common household terms (Scatton, 1993: 241).

German has been a source of numerous loans, especially in the countries of the former Austro-Hungarian Empire (as has been Hungarian, to a lesser degree). But there are important traces in East Slavic and especially Russian as well, from the time when Peter the Great (r. 1682–1725) imported German advisers, technologists and military experts to modernize Russia:

(32)   Rus *buxgálter* 'accountant' < Germ *Buchhalter*

French, with centuries of cultural leadership in Europe, has left a major mark on Slavic:

(33)   Cz, Slk   *menu, klišé, bordó*
        Pol   *menu, cliché, bordo*

Recently English has achieved a dominant position as lexical donor to all Slavic languages (9.7–9.8).

Slavs as a whole are more sensitive than are English speakers to lexical imports. Borrowings can either continue to look and function as borrowed words, and may even be orthographically unassimilated, as is found in the burgeoning use of Roman-script English words and phrases in Cyrillic texts on the Internet (9.8). Unassimilated loans may show non-native spelling and/or phonology, as with the Slavic adoption of forms like *jazz* and (its initial) /dž/, and may lack normal inflexions. Or they can undergo integration into the patterns of the receiving language. Phonological adaptations involve the replacement of foreign sounds: if written 'i' or 'e' do not prepalatalize when they can in East Slavic, the word is still phonologically foreign: Rus *kafé* [-'fɛ]. But different phonological properties may be copied with unfamiliar sounds: Fr *bureau*, Rus *bjuró*, but Cz *byro*, B/C/S *bìrō* (ignoring the feature [Round]). On the other hand, some foreign words can enter into word-formation processes while still being unassimilated in terms of phonology and inflexion: Russian *šossé* 'roadway' ([-'sɛ]) does not decline, but does have a derived adjective *šosséjnyj*. Some foreign words may be morphophonologically acceptable but still not decline (at least in standard usage, see 11.3.1), like Russian *pal'tó* 'overcoat' (< Fr *paletot*), *bjuró* 'office' and *metró* 'metro', all of which could, in principle, decline like regular Russian neuter nouns, as does, for example, *vinó* 'wine'. With *metró*, however, Russian phonology has at least replaced the [mɛ-] with [mʲɪ-], making it phonologically normal. In 5.5.1 and 6.2 we discuss gender and borrowing: Czech, Slovak and mostly Polish adapt anything ending in -a/-o/-e, e.g. *radio* 'radio' is declinable in all three, and so is *kakao* 'cocoa', only as a variant in Polish.

9.6.2   Calques

Calques, also called "loan-translations", involve the translation of source-language words morpheme-by-morpheme:

(34a) 'manuscript'

OCS *rǫkopisanie* < *rǫk-* 'hand' + *pis-* 'write' Lat *man-* + *scrib-*

Blg *răkopís* Rus *rúkopis'* Pol *rękopis* Cz *rukopis*

(34b) 'blink of an eye, moment'

Cz *okamžik* < *oka* 'eyes' + *mžikat* 'to wink'

Slk *okamih* < *oka* 'eyes' + *mihat'* 'to wink'

< Ger *Augenblick*

Such calque patterns have also involved syntactic calques – with appropriate adjustments to word order:

(35a) 'to like' Cz *mít rád* < Ger *gern haben*

(35b) 'to perish (of people)' Cz *přijít o život* < Ger *ums Leben kommen*

The advantage of the calque is that it uses native lexical material. If there is no available homeland word to cover a new idea, whether by metaphor or some other kind of semantic adaptation, then a calque is often preferable to lexical borrowings, which can fill the language with partially integrated, and nationalistically and aesthetically irritating, vocabulary. A successful calque requires that the donor and recipient language have comparable processes of word formation and root combination, for instance a Head–Head or Modifier–Head order in both languages:

(36) Rus *vodoród* 'hydrogen' (*vod-* 'water' + *o* + *rod-* 'birth')

< Gk *hydr-* + *o* + *gen-*)

Cz *zeměpis* 'geography' (*zem-* 'land' + *e* + *pis-* 'write')

< Gk *ge-* + *o* + *graph-*)

French, which tends to phrasal innovation, is therefore a less suitable donor language for calques. This process does not always coincide with the source of the realia concerned: the Russian system of *zaóčnoe obučénie* 'distance education/ learning', where the root means 'out of sight', when borrowed into Czechoslovakia after the Second World War, was represented in Czech by a calque from German, *dálkové studium* ('distance learning', Ger *Fernstudium*).

Calquing also occurs between Slavic languages: Rus *udárnik* 'shock worker', Cz *úderník*. And, as Unbegaun remarks (1932), many words of Polish origin in Ukrainian should be analysed as calques rather than as loans:

(37) 'Renaissance': Pol *odrodzenie* Ukr *vidródžennja*

'translation': Pol *przekład* Ukr *peréklad*

Isačenko (1976: 387) observes that

> ... loan translation among the Slavic languages has, in our days, come
> into widespread use. But this seems to be the rule whenever one Slavic
> literary language is strongly influenced by another Slavic literary
> language.

A sub-variety of calques involves mixed calques, where part of the word is loan-translated, but some of the morphological material, like a word-forming suffix, is indigenous to the target language, and does not accurately translate a morpheme in the source language. An example of mixed calquing as a lexical policy is Czech (Isačenko, 1968). Here the purist movements of the nineteenth century left a permanent dislike for words or expressions which reflect German influences. Former calques like Cz *rychlovlak* 'express train' (Ger *Schnellzug*) have now given way to mixed calques like Cz *rychlík*, which uses a native word-forming element *-ík*, and so is also an example of *univerbacija* (9.5.3.2). Czech shows numerous other examples, for instance:

(38)   Cz   *nádraží* 'railway station', Ger *Bahnhof*
       < Cz *dráha* 'way, road' = Ger *Bahn*
       and *na-* + *-í* 'place': cf. Cz *náměstí* 'town square' (< *město*)

9.7   Lexis after Communism

Under Communism there was a certain homogenizing effect on the lexicons of the public use of the Slavic languages, caused by the ideological, political, economic and, to some sense, cultural pressure from Russian. But even before the fall of Communism there was an unofficial alternative model from the capitalist West, for instance in popular and technical culture, and especially in the relatively more liberal regimes of former Yugoslavia, Poland and (to a lesser extent) Czechoslovakia. After 1990 the pace of change was very rapid (11.4.2). The Russian influence, which had been generally resented and in some areas (notably in the intelligentsia and youth culture) actively despised, disappeared in an astonishingly short time, to be replaced by the Western models-in-waiting. The Russians themselves were not slow to clear away many of the lexical reminders of Communism.

The lexicon was where the effects of the change were most immediately obvious, and they have been dramatic. While still more centrist and regulatory than the policy-makers of English – such as they are – the Slavs now have a much more permissive, flexible, pluralistic and fundamentally democratic approach to language development amounting to a substantial *de facto* deregulation of the languages (11.4.2). Former ideologically prohibited subjects are now freely discussed in print and in public, together with the forbidden lexicons, which have switched affective values: 'red' is now often pejorative, as is 'Communist'. This process is sometimes described by the Russian terms *aktualizácija/passivizácija*, whereby formerly backgrounded lexical fields like religion, ethics and non-socialist economics are brought into active use, while the lexicon of socialism is "passivized", or demoted from active to more passive use.

From the lexical point of view, with the Russian ideological influence gone, the Slavic lexicons are now showing some convergence as a result of wholesale borrowings from the West, and especially from English. While this will not affect the core vocabularies – the Indo-European, Proto-Slavic and specifically modern Slavic lexical bases – it is likely that youth and technical jargon, and the language of advertising and business, will have a longer-lasting radical effect on the language of everyday life. On the other hand, the conservative effect of the national language academies and the education systems are likely to act as a brake, or at least a moderating influence. A growing political disillusionment is already making itself felt in a revival of voter support for the representatives of the old order. With this comes a heightened suspicion of the merits of the Western way. When combined with nationalism, these forces may well reinforce a movement back from a wider Westernization and internationalization of the lexicons. A striking feature of the modern Slavic lexicons is a growing pluralism, which has replaced the former top-down monolithic model of language regulation under Communism.

Ryazanova-Clarke and Wade (1999) present a detailed summary of the categories of lexical realignment and change in Russian. Their overall profile is applicable broadly to other Slavic languages, though Russian – together with Ukrainian and Belarusian – had been longest under Communism, and so had more to reform. For Ukrainian and Belarusian there was the additional process of de-Russification. Eastern Europe, and to a lesser extent Bulgaria, had not been lexically so closely in the Moscow ambit, and Yugoslavia still less.

The list of lexical changes offered by Ryazanova-Clarke and Wade includes:

- revitalization and reorientation of formerly marginalized pre-1917 vocabulary, including religious (e.g. words in *blágo-*), culture (*gimnázija* 'high school'), economic (*ákcija* 'share', *rýnok* 'market'), workplace (*zabastóvka* 'strike') and related vocabulary;
- restoring older forms of address, e.g. *továrišč* 'comrade' has been replaced by *gospodín* 'Mr' and *gospožá* 'Mrs';

- some continuations of Soviet patterns of lexical enrichment, e.g. initialisms like *NDR = Naš Dom Rossíja* 'Our Home (is) Russia', the name of a new political party in the 1990s;
- restoring institutions like the *Duma* (parliament) and functions like *mèr* 'mayor';
- reinstating positive connotations in words like *kapitál* 'capital' and shifting formerly positively valued words like *sovétskij* 'soviet' into negative evaluation. *Solidárnost'* 'solidarity' – the political use of the term derived from the French social philosopher Proudhon – had already earned a new place in the post-Communist pantheon by its association with the Polish trade union *Solidarność*;
- words like *máfija* 'mafia', formerly used of foreign entities, could now refer to Russian ones;
- increasing use of vulgar language, argot, criminal and street slang in everyday usage, including the media and written language;
- extensive borrowing, mainly from or via English, in areas like economics (*audít* 'audit'), technology (*péjdžer* 'pager'), lifestyle (*karaóke* 'karaoke'), realia (*transseksuál* 'trans-sexual'), media (*remíks* 'remix'), fashion (*léginsy* 'leggings'), food (*kórnfleks* 'cornflakes'), sports (*fítness* 'fitness') and music (*džèm-séšn* 'jam-session'). Many of the trendier borrowings have unstable spelling, and may not survive; others are superfluous but trendy, like *šop* 'shop';
- massive reversal of the names of towns, cities, streets, squares and monuments to pre-Communist times: *Leningrád* reverted to *Sankt Peterbúrg*, and *Gór'kij* to *Nížnyj Nóvgorod*. Names involving Communist hallowed words like 'October' (Rus *oktjábr'*) and 'Communist' (Rus *kommuníst*) were changed virtually across the board.

And, more generally, there was a de-cliché-ization of public language, so that the worn journalistic phrases quickly fell out of use. New capitalist clichés are taking their place.

Such changes are paralleled, though to a lesser degree, outside the old Soviet Union, where, for instance, place-naming had not been ideologized to anything like the same extent, and where there was more continuity with pre-Communist patterns. There were also people alive who could remember what it had been like before Communism. Scholar-publicists like Solzhenitsyn have been active in promoting a more "Slavizing" approach, and there have been debates about the integrity and direction of the languages, for instance in the new Russian Academy journal *Rusistika segodnja* 'Russian Studies Today', and in bodies like the Russian Language Council, established in 1995.

9.8 Slavic on the Internet

The Internet has been enthusiastically welcomed in the Slavic countries, though its degree of penetration is stronger in urban areas and wealthier countries, and is limited by physical networks and the cost and speed of hardware and connectivity. The commercial and interpersonal communication potential of the Internet was quickly taken up as Slavic Internet use increased with breakneck speed from a low starting-point. The Internet brought overseas language, styles, commerce, communication and news directly into the personal experience of the Slavs, and has made their world culturally and linguistically radically more pluralistic and international. The Internet has also contributed to the loosening of the language norms, because it encourages rapid, semi-edited interaction which may break the formal rules of orthography, grammar and lexis, together with linguistic experimentation and idiosyncrasy, non-standard forms (e.g. ignoring diacritics on the Internet and in SMS communications) and abbreviations.

As a result, the Internet shows a celebration of non-standard language which is very similar to what one finds in France or Germany, where imported English-language models jostle for position with indigenous ones. Similar trends are found in paper media like magazines, but not to the same rampant extent. The influence of English in particular is dominant in borrowings. A search for *cool* or *kool* (to [partially] accommodate orthography) on the Internet on language domains for the Slavic languages listed on Google in October 2003 showed:

Russian: 96,400   Polish: 78,600   Czech: 38,600   Slovak: 15,800
Serbian: 8,860   Slovenian. 7,770

(comparable figures for French are 335,000, and for German 871,000: one would need to check total Internet users to compare the numbers proportionately against population and Internet access).

Code-switching into English is endemic (11.4.2) – including Cyrillic ∼ Roman alphabet-switching – especially in "excited" discourses like MTV, chat rooms and advertising, and in SMS messages. Using *cool* again (and *hot*) we find both attributive and predicative use:

(39)   Cz (from an advertisement for rubber body-suits)
       ***Cool** materiál, **hot** pocit.*
       'Cool material, hot sensation.'

>   *Jsem kluk, který má rád latex, gumu, igelit, PVC a jiné COOL*
>   *materiály ve kterých je skvěle HOT.*
>   'I am a man who likes latex, rubber, polythene, PVC and other
>   COOL materials in which he is sensationally HOT.'

An Internet Russian example is possibly linguistically even more outrageous:

(40)   Rus   (from an advertisement for a mobile/cell phone)
            Súper ákcija! Mobíla ot rússkogo sájta!
            'Super sale! A mobile from a Russian site!'
            Na sájte predstávlen rezul'tát ob″ektívnogo i nezavísimogo
            isslédovanija spónsorov, platjáščix reál'nye $$$ Rossíjskim web
            masterám. ('$$$' and 'web' are in Roman script)
            'On the site is presented the result of an objective and inde-
            pendent examination by sponsors who are paying real $$$ to
            Russian web masters.'

Here *web masterám* shows a new tendency (in addition to alphabet-switching): to take an Adjective + Noun sequence from English, treat the modifier as indeclinable, and decline only the head. *Cool sajt* 'cool site' is found in Bosnian, Croatian and Polish sites, and in Polish we find the plural *cool sajty*, just as we also find *top modelki* 'top models'. But the Adjective + Noun construction can sometimes be treated with a post-posed invariant modifier: a Russian site has *igrá cool* 'cool game' with the order Noun + Adjective (5.5.2).

10

Dialects

10.1 Overview

After national languages, the most intensively studied area of Slavic sociolinguistics is dialectology. Investigations into the dialectology of the major Slavic languages were begun over a century ago, and all the modern Slavic languages are now provided with dialect descriptions, sometimes based on extensive surveys. The material gathered has concentrated on variation in phonetics, morphology and vocabulary. Work on dialectology has tended to be biased toward the national languages, so that dialects have usually been seen as regional variants of individual languages, as dialect clusters related centripetally to national standard variants, rather than as part of a total continuous trans-national dialect map of Slavic.

The Slavic languages in Europe – in other words, excluding non-European Russia – show the densely packed dialect map familiar in European languages. After the settlement of the Slavs in their present homelands, which was substantially completed by about the sixth century AD, the settled, agricultural lifestyle of the Slavs tended to discourage geographical mobility. The effects of military and cultural activity and dominance were felt more by the urban classes than by the rural population. It was only in the twentieth century that rural populations began to achieve significant geographical mobility. The two World Wars, and the aftermath of the Russian Revolution, played an important role in this social change, both directly and indirectly, as whole areas of the rural population in the USSR perished or were relocated. A second important factor has been the expansion of Russia into Asia from the eighteenth century, and the settlement and development of the new lands. Russian has come into contact with new languages, ethnic groups and contexts, resulting in the emergence of some local variations like Siberian Russian. Such recent regional variants, however, differ most obviously in lexis, and have had little effect on the standard language.

A more profound influence on the Slavic dialect map has been the social and economic changes brought about by the 1917 Revolution. Increased social mobility has broken down the traditional labourer–small farmer composition of the rural areas, making it possible for people whose families had hitherto remained geographically and socially immobile to achieve both social and geographical movement. The economic changes of the Revolution – apart from virtually wiping out certain social levels of the intelligentsia and rural landowners – also accelerated existing trends of migration from the country to the towns, and the disintegration of the traditional Slavic extended family, together with the social and linguistic stability and rigidity which it represented (Friedrich, 1966, 1972). Policy in the Soviet Union, especially during the Stalin years, was also directed expressly toward the dilution of regionalism and local nationalism by the planned relocation of individuals, families and even whole populations. The net effect of such upheavals in the USSR was to promote both Great Russian nationalism and the culture of standard Russian – since there was less motivation to learn a new local language or variant in a new environment, when the economic incentives are in favor of the national standard. There has also been the effect of universal education and the mass media, particularly film, radio and television. Military service also brought young males into contact with the national standard in some form, on an educational as well as a social and professional level.

Since 1917 an important factor has been the increasingly less permeable nature of Slavic geopolitical boundaries. Neighboring dialects communicated more freely across national boundaries until the twentieth century. But the political and ideological necessities of preserving the Revolution, and the desire of the early Soviet governments to insulate their populations from outside influence, meant that it became more difficult for Slavs to communicate easily with adjacent dialects across the new national boundaries. This meant a lessening of dialectal interchange across political borders, for instance between Ukrainian and Belarusian in the east, on the one hand, and Polish and Slovak in the west. And after 1945–1948, when the Communist take-overs in Eastern Europe were finally complete, even borders like that between Poland and Czechoslovakia were more strictly controlled than before. Similarly, the former internal Yugoslav borders between Slovenia and Croatia, Serbia and Croatia, and Serbia and Macedonia are now national borders. Such factors, together with the strong emphasis on the national language and the promotion of Russian as a supra-national language in the Soviet Union, have served to alter the patterns of dialectal interaction, and the relation of the dialects to each other and to the national language: regional variants are increasingly oriented toward the national standard language of their political–geographical area.

Overall, Slavic dialects have suffered a certain decline and dilution over the last fifty years. The constant trend, irrespective of ideology, has been in the direction of convergence on the national standard language. The younger generation of today is more aware of the national language, and less loyal to local variants, than their parents. In spite of strong regional loyalties which have their roots in customs and folklore as well as in language and geography, there is evidence of a decline in the vitality, local prestige and general viability of many smaller local variants. Revivals of regional folklore, which is generally well maintained through most of the native Slavic-speaking areas, have not achieved a revival of local language styles to the same extent. And dialect maintenance has been hindered by the fact that there must by now be few speakers of Slavic languages who are monolingual dialectal speakers. Universal education and the high level of literacy in the Slavic lands mean that almost all speakers are now diglossic, with strong exposure to the national standard through education and the media. While dialects are generally conservative, in the case of Sorbian, Czech and Slovenian the heightened conservatism of the national language has actually increased the distance between the dialects and the national standard (2.2.5, 2.4.2, 2.4.5).

We have selected features which illustrate each major dialect, together with the links between dialects and neighbouring dialects, and between dialects and neighbouring standard languages. We shall concentrate on general phenomena allowing comparison across dialects, rather than on atypical local features, whatever their inherent interest. We treat the dialects from two perspectives: from within the context of each national language, following our conventional ordering from west to east, and from north to south; and across geopolitical language borders, in order to preserve as far as possible the continuity of the dialect chains. This will lead to some redundancy, but also to a better understanding of the chains themselves.

Using the national languages as a point of reference, however, can create difficulties. The national languages are often not based squarely on the dialect of the area where the capital is now located, but have been constructed out of dialectal elements from various parts of the nation. The establishment of a capital and the siting of the national language in it has a centripetal effect, selectively drawing elements from different parts of the country into a culturally cohesive linguistic whole. Rather than working solely from the national languages to the dialects, therefore, we need also to consider the dialects in their own right if we are to achieve a clear view of the nature and extent of Slavic dialects. Some dialects, sometimes for historical, cultural or other reasons, exhibit similarities with dialects in other areas which are not related by genetic or areal contiguity: some North Russian dialects, for instance, have post-posed articles like those of Bulgarian and Macedonian. The Slavic dialect map is not always linear, and it is not always continuous.

The majority of the features which we shall select for the description and determination of the Slavic dialects are phonological and morphological, following the central trends of Slavic dialect research over the last century. The list of features is representative rather than comprehensive, and is designed to provide a broad-scale picture of the Slavic dialects.

Following the discussion, the main dialectal features of each language are summarized in a table, with the standard language forms listed in the left-hand column for comparison. "CS-" designates the contemporary standard form of each language. The final 'Summary' section (10.5) offers a diagrammatic view of the connections across the whole area (figure 10.1, p. 542).

10.2   Dialects of South Slavic

South Slavic has been separated from East and West Slavic by non-Slavs (Hungarians, Austrians, Romanians) for a thousand years. As a result, we lack the gradual dialectal transitions to East and West Slavic, although there are some significant similarities between dialects of Slovenian and Croatian, the northern-most South Slavic languages, and Slovak, the southernmost of the West Slavic languages, especially in Central Slovak dialects. Within the South Slavic group, however, there is a rich and continuous dialectal chain leading from Slovenian in the north-west to Macedonian and Bulgarian in the south-east. Comprehensibility between dialects is strongly related to geographical and topographical distance. Reasonable levels of comprehension can be achieved between Slovenian and Croatian, and good levels between Croatian and Serbian, and Macedonian and Bulgarian. However, the complexity and diversity of Slovenian dialects sets them somewhat apart, even within Slovenia. This situation contrasts with the higher level of commonality between Bulgarian and Macedonian. The Serbian Torlak dialects serve as a transition between Serbian, on the one hand, and Bulgarian and Macedonian, on the other.

10.2.1   Dialects of Slovenian

Slovenia borders on Italy to the west, Austria to the north, Hungary to the east, and Croatia to the east and south. The Slovenian-speaking area overlaps with Italian around the city of Trieste, and there are substantial numbers of Slovenian speakers in south-eastern Austria. There are also areas where Slovenian and Croatian overlap.

Slovenian, as a result of its mountainous terrain and difficult communications, has the densest dialect map of all the Slavic languages, and is notorious for the difficulties of inter-comprehension posed by some of the dialects. Some dialect-ologists of Slovenian have estimated that there are fifty dialects (Logar and Rigler,

1986). Sławski (1962) has nine, Priestly (1993) eight and Lencek (1982) seven.
Particularly important are Carinthia (Sln *Koroško*, Ger *Kärnten*) (abbreviated as
Koroš) in the north and north-west; the Littoral (Sln *Primorsko*) dialects (**Prim**) on
the Adriatic; the Rovte (Sln *Rovtarsko*) dialects (**Rovt**) between the Littoral and
Upper Carniola (Sln *Gorenjsko*) (**Gor**), with Inner Carniola (Sln *Notranjsko*) (**Notr**)
to its south, bordering on Croatian (and the Adriatic); the two key central dialects
of Upper and Lower Carniola (Sln *Dolenjsko*) (**Dol**); the Styrian (Sln *Štajersko*)
dialects (**Štaj**) to the east of Carniola; and the Pannonian (Sln *Panonsko*) dialects
(**Pan**) to the east of Styrian, reaching into Hungary.

Although standard Slovenian is based on the Carniolan dialects around the area
of the capital Ljubljana, it was designed to reflect models of the Slovenian literary
language of the seventeenth century (2.2.5). For these reasons, there is a significant
gap between modern written and spoken Slovenian. In addition, migration from
rural to urban centres has created mixed dialect models, especially in Ljubljana,
which is situated in the south of the Upper Carniola area and adjacent to Lower
Carniola. Apart from the suggestive but restricted set of parallelisms with Central
Slovak dialects (10.4.4), the dialect allegiances all run south and east from Slovenia,
anchoring it firmly in South Slavic.

The only adjacent Slavic language area to Slovenian is Croatian to the east and
south. The most important transitional dialects to Croatian are those of Notranjsko,
Štajersko and Panonsko. Although geographically contiguous, many of these dialects remained remarkably stable until 1945 (Lencek, 1982: ch. 4), when modern
communications and media, as well as geographical mobility and the migration of
rural populations to urban areas, began to blur distinctions which had held fairly
stable for centuries, thanks in part to the mountainous nature of much of the Balkans.

Lencek (1982) identifies fourteen features, based on the modern reflexes of
various aspects of Proto-Slavic phonology, as a means of defining the modern
dialect areas. We shall make eclectic use of these, together with some morphological criteria, in the analysis below.

10.2.1.1 *Phonology*
Standard Slovenian has two variants: a tonal variant (3.5.3), though tone is less
well maintained than in B/C/S; and a non-tonal variant, where stress and length are
the distinctive phonological features (Lencek, 1982: 163–166; Priestly 1993:
390–394). Tone and length are maintained in the conservative central dialects on
a north–south axis (Koroš, Gor, Dol). Stress is the only prosodic phonemic feature
in the other dialects.

Three other features are considered criterial in classifying Slovenian dialects: the
modern reflexes of the nasals / ę ǫ / (*pét* 'five', *zób* 'tooth'), of *jat'*/ě/ (*lép* 'fine'), and

of the *jers* (*pès* 'dog', *dán* 'day', *sèn* 'sleep'). The nasals yield low [ɔ], and *jat'* yields [ɛ], in the north-western dialects of Koroško and Primorsko. Elsewhere we find the higher vowel articulation of [e o] for the nasals and [e] for *jat'*. On the other hand, the *jers* when lengthened yield /e/ in the north and east (in Koroš, Štaj and Pan), and /a/ elsewhere (as in Croatian).

Less systematic are features like the variation in the number of vowel phonemes, diphthongization of vowels, and the degree and nature of vowel reduction in unstressed or tonally non-prominent syllables. Some nasal vowels are retained in parts of Koroško. Some northern dialects also spirantize /g/ to [ɣ] or [h], change velarized /l/ to [w], and maintain the Proto-Slavic sequences /tl/ and /dl/, as in West Slavic (CS-Sln *krílo* 'wing': Koroš *kridwo*; CS-Sln *pála* 'fall' [PartFem]: Gor *padwa*).

10.2.1.2   *Morphology*

Slovenian dialects show broad evidence of morphological simplification, with the partial (and in one dialect the total [Stankiewicz, 1965]) absorption of the neuter gender into the masculine and the feminine, and the decline of the dual number and the supine. Standard Slovenian maintains these categories, in increasing distance from the dialects, by conscious conservatism and language management and legislation.

In the summary of features in table 10.1 we omit the Rovtarsko dialects, which are a transition between the Primorsko and Carniolan dialects.

10.2.2   Dialects of B/C/S

The total area of Bosnian, Croatian and Serbian has common borders with Slovenia in the north, Hungary in the north-east, Bulgaria in the east, FYR Macedonia in the south and Albania in the south-west. This rich and continuous dialect area has two focal points in terms of standards: Zagreb for Croatian; and Belgrade for Serbian. The Bosnian standard is gradually emerging as a distinct third variant. Although Belgrade (B/C/S *Beògrad*), the former national Yugoslav capital, is situated in the area of the Serbian variant, it shows the expected dialect mixture of modern capital cities.

The concept of "dialect" is more closely involved with the concept of "national language" in B/C/S than in any other Slavic language. We describe in 2.2.4 the process by which an East Hercegovinian dialect of Serbian was accepted as a national language in the nineteenth century. Serbo-Croatian was the only modern Slavic language which had two standard variants, unless one accepts that Upper

Table 10.1. *Dialects of Slovenian*

NW to SE	CS-Sln	Koroš	Prim	Notr	Gor + Dol	Štaj + Pan
Phonology						
Vowels						
PSl ь	a/ə	e	a	a	a	e
PSl ъ	a/ə	e	a	a	a	e
PSl ę	e	ɛ	ɛ	= CS	= CS	= CS
PSl ǫ	o/ɔ	ɔ	ɔ	o	o	o
PSl ě	e/ɛ	ɛ	ɛ	e	e	e
phonemic stress	+ / −	−	+	+	−	+
phonemic pitch	+ / −	+	−	−	+	−
phonemic length	+	+	−	−	+	−
Consonants						
PSl g	g	ɣ	ɣ	= CS	= CS	= CS
PSl l	l	w	w	= CS	Gor: w	= CS
PSl tl, dl	l	l	tl dl	= CS	= CS	= CS
Morphology						
Neuter lost	−	= CS	= CS	= CS	Gor: +	= CS
NomSgNeut Adj	o	= CS	= CS	= CS	Dol: e	= CS
Inf in -ti/-t	ti	t	= CS	= CS	= CS	= CS

Notes:
The broad IPA values correspond to written Slovenian as follows (tonal/non-tonal systems):
[e] = 'ẹ/é'   [ɛ] = 'e (or ẹ)/ê-è'   [o] = 'ọ/ó'   [ɔ] = 'o (or ọ)/ô-ò'
The Štajersko, Dolenjsko and Panonsko dialects in particular form a transition to the *kaj*
dialects of Croatian (10.2.2). (See further details in figure 10.1.)

and Lower Sorbian are two variants of a single language (10.4.1, 11.3.3). These two
standard variants of Serbo-Croatian not only had historical dialectal roots, but
also had a *de iure* status in the constitution and the language policies of Yugoslavia.
For this reason the boundary between "standard", "dialect" and "variant" was
particularly complex in Serbo-Croatian. In this book we have consistently treated
B/C/S as a language on the grounds that the major variants are still formally and
functionally close enough to constitute a single entity. This approach, however,
does not touch the political or ethnic issues of the variants – which are becoming
three as Bosnia asserts its own independence and linguistic credentials. For the
purposes of dialectology, however, the difference is less crucial: we are dealing with
variants within geographical space.

The underlying dialect structure of the B/C/S language area conventionally
involves three groups, named after the word for 'what'. Moving from north to
south, the Kajkavian (*kaj* 'what') dialects (**Kajk**) are spoken around Zagreb and up

to the Slovenian border, and form a transition from Croatian to Slovenian. The Čakavian dialects (ča 'what') (Čak) are spoken in an area centered on Northern Dalmatia and several islands in the Adriatic. The core of the modern literary languages, and the major dialect area, is Štokavian (što 'what') (Štok), which covers the rest of the area where B/C/S is spoken.

Within the Čakavian and Štokavian dialect areas there is a further sub-division based on the modern reflexes of Proto-Slavic /ě/ (Kajk, like Slovenian, shows /e/ from /ě/). "Ikavian" (Ik), with /i/ from /ě/, is spoken in Dalmatia and the west of Bosnia and Hercegovina, but is now no longer used as a written language. In the east and south are the "ekavian" (Ek) dialects (/ě/ > /e/), covering Serbia and the Vojvodina, as well as modern literary Serbian. The "jekavian" (Jek) dialects, with /je/ as a short and /ije/ as a long reflex of /ě/, are found in Croatia, Bosnia and Montenegro, and were also the variant found in older Serbian literature and in the work of Vuk Karadžić (2.2.4), who promoted them as the basis for Serbo-Croatian. Modern B/C/S is regularly written in ekavian in Cyrillic, and in jekavian in Roman. However, linguists most often use the ekavian version in Roman, and this is the convention used in this book. We discuss the ikavian–ekavian–jekavian phenomenon in 2.2.4 and 3.3.2.1.

Mutual comprehensibility is high except when north-western speakers try to communicate with south-eastern speakers. Communication with Slovenian is easiest for speakers of Kajkavian dialects of Croatian in the north, and with Bulgarian and Macedonian for speakers of the fourth group of so-called Torlak (mainly Prizren-Timok) dialects (B/C/S torlački) (Torlak), in the south-east of Serbia, which show the most transitional "Balkan" features to Bulgarian and Macedonian, as well as stronger Turkish influence.

10.2.2.1   Phonology
Leaving aside the reflexes of /ě/, which have more to do with the definition of the standard variants than with dialects (2.2.4, 3.2.1.3), the three main dialect areas of B/C/S, plus the Torlak dialects, show a wide range of features:

Vowels

- *jers* (*dân* 'day', *sàn* 'sleep'): Kajk has /e/, like the eastern Slovenian dialects (10.2.1), and some Torlak dialects have [ə], like Bulgarian.
- *nasals* (*zûb* 'tooth'): Kajk has /o/ from the back nasal, like Slovenian.

Consonants

- *tj, dj* (*svéća*, 'candle', *mèdja* 'border'): Kajk has /č/ from *tj*, like Slovenian, and from *dj* it has either /j/, like Slovenian, or /dž/; some Čakavian dialects have palatal stop /t'/.

- *final /l/* (*dȁo* 'give' [PastMasc]): Kajk retains /l/ in syllable-final position (unlike any adjacent dialect group), as do some Torlak dialects (like Bulgarian and Macedonian).
- *devoicing* (*sûd* 'court'): Kajk devoices final obstruents, like Slovenian.

Suprasegmental features Čak preserves the neo-acute pitch (3.2.4.3), and did not undergo the stress retraction which happened throughout the Štokavian territory (with the exception of some areas in the south). Slavonia in the north-west has a three-tone system similar to that of Čak and Slovenian, with a tonal opposition only on long syllables. Many areas have a quantity opposition only on stressed vowels (Vojvodina in the north-east and Smederevo and Zeta in the south).

10.2.2.2 *Morphology*

Kajk and Čak remain conservative, preserving the distinct forms of the dative, instrumental and locative in the plural of the nominal declensions – unlike Štokavian, where these forms have coalesced (in the old dual forms *-ma*, 5.4.1). Of the last group, the Slavonian area also retains all plural case forms.

The Torlak dialects show "Balkan" features: loss of the infinitive, and the use of periphrastic devices to replace Verb + Infinitive constructions; the decline of the cases to a maximum of three (nominative and non-nominative/oblique, plus, in some, dative) though with retention of the vocative; doubled objects with the additional object pronoun; retention of the aorist and imperfect; and post-positive articles – all features shared with Bulgarian and Macedonian.

The Zeta sub-group (Štok/Jek), in Montenegro, has an intermediate plural nominal case system, with syncretization of dative/instrumental and genitive/locative.

Table 10.2 shows the expected transition between Kajk, and to a lesser extent Čak, and Slovenian, and between south-east Štok (Torlak) and Bulgarian and Macedonian. The column 'B/C/S' here means "standard" in all three areas.

10.2.3 Dialects of Macedonian

FYR Macedonia is bordered by Albania in the west, Serbia in the north, Bulgaria in the east and Greece in the south. Varieties of Macedonian are spoken across the border in all of these countries, though the extent of this dialectal spread and vitality is not easy to determine. In Albania there could be between 5,000 and

Table 10.2. *Dialects of B/C/S*

	B/C/S	Kajk	Čak	Štok	Torlak
Phonology					
pitch	+	−	= CS	= CS	= CS
length	+	= CS	= CS	= CS	−
jers	a	e	= CS	= CS	ə
ǫ	u	o	= CS	= CS	= CS
ě	e/(i)je	e	e/i	e/je/i	e
tj	ć	č	č/t'	= CS	= CS
dj	dž (dj/đ)	j/dž	j	= CS	= CS
final /l/	o	l	= CS	= CS	a/l
final voice	+	−	= CS	= CS	= CS
Morphology					
cases in plural	4	6	6	= CS	3
Vocative	+	−	−	= CS	= CS
Infinitive	+	= CS	= CS	= CS	−
Aorist/Imperfect	(+)	−	−	+	+
Syntax					
doubled object	−	= CS	= CS	= CS	+

150,000 Macedonians, but the census data are equivocal. In Serbia there is a transitional dialect chain leading north, notably through the Torlak dialects (10.2.2). In Bulgaria there may be as many as 250,000 Macedonian speakers, but the Bulgarians regard these Pirin dialects, together with the language varieties spoken in FYR Macedonia, Albania and Greece, merely as south-western dialects of Bulgarian. For their part, the Greeks reject a country called "Macedonia", since they consider the name to have been Greek since the times of Alexander the Great of Macedon (fourth century BC), and have been culturally unsympathetic to the Vardar Macedonian dialects spoken in Northern Greece, which have been subjected to vigorous hellenization.

The dialects of Macedonia are divided conventionally into an eastern (**E-Mac**) and a western (**W-Mac**) group, the boundary roughly following a SSW–NNE line along the Rivers Vardar and Crna. There are about half a million speakers in each area, with somewhat over 300,000 in the dialectally mixed capital, Skopje. The national language, which was formally established only in 1944–1945, reflects central western dialects (**WC-Mac**) in the area of Bitola, rather than those of Ohrid in the south-west. Some analyses also propose a northern dialect, situated between Skopje and the border, as a transition to Serbian (**NE-Mac**).

10.2.3.1 Phonology

Vowels Proto-Slavic /ě/ gave /e/ except in eastern dialects after hard /c/ (where it gave /a/): CS-Mac and other dialects with *cel* 'whole' contrast with E-Mac *cal*.

Friedman (1993: 301) gives the data for the reflexes of Proto-Slavic /ъ̩br̩ḷǫ/. This offers a particularly clear illustration of dialect chains between two neighbouring standards: in (1) and (2) we have added standard Serbian and Bulgarian equivalents for contrast. The data are in two blocks: from Serbian to the northern dialect (1); and from Debar in the west of Macedonia to Seres-Nevrokop and Bulgarian in the east (2). Of particular interest are remnants of nasality in the southwest, where /ǫ/ may be 'vowel + nasal consonant' (e.g. PSl *zǫbъ* > *zamb, zəmb*).

As we move southwards from Serbian through the northern transitional dialect of Macedonian, syllabic /r̩/ is maintained, the *jers* yield schwa and /ǫ/ yields /u/:

(1)		Serbian	NE-Mac	CS-Mac	
	PSl ъ	*săn*	*sən*	*son*	'dream'
	PSl ь	*dân*	*dən*	*den*	'day'
	PSl r̩	*kȓv*	*krv*	*krv*	'blood'
		pȓvi	*prv*	*prv*	'first'
	PSl ḷ	*vûk*	*vuk*	*volk*	'wolf'
	PSl ǫ	*pût*	*put*	*pat*	'road'

From west to east the picture is more complex:

(2)		W-Mac	WC-Mac	E-Mac	Blg	
	PSl ъ	*son*	*son*	*sən*	*sən*	'dream'
	PSl ь	*den*	*den*	*den*	*den*	'day'
	PSl r̩	*korv*	*krv*	*kərv*	*krəv*	'blood'
		perv	*prv*	*pərv*	*prəv*	'first'
	PSl ḷ	*volk/vlk*	*vək*	*vəlk*	*vəlk*	'wolf'
	PSl ǫ	*pot*	*pat*	*pət*	*pət*	'road'

Stress Word-stress is fixed in the western dialects, on the antepenult in FYR Macedonia itself (and in CS-Mac) and on the penult in Greece and Albania. Eastern dialects share non-fixed stress with Bulgarian, and have reduction of quality in unstressed vowels.

Consonants Western dialects, like CS-Mac, have lost /x/: E-Mac has *xleb* 'bread', Blg *xljab*, for CS-Mac and other dialects' *leb*.

Western dialects have also lost intervocalic /v/: *glava* 'head' becomes *glā*; eastern dialects and the standard language retain the /v/.

Prothetic /j/ in the western dialects before Proto-Slavic initial ǫ corresponds to prothetic /v/ in the east:

(3)   PSl *ǫže* 'rope' W-Mac, CS-Mac *jaže* E-Mac *važe* (cf. Blg *vắžé*)

Western and standard Macedonian /k̂ ĝ/, mainly from PSl /tj dj/, result in various biphonemic combinations – /št šč žd ždž/ – in the eastern dialects, which links up with western Bulgarian dialects (10.2.4).

10.2.3.2   *Morphology*

Western dialects generally show a more synthetic pattern and similarities to Serbian, whereas eastern dialects share some of the analytic features of Bulgarian.

In nominal morphology the eastern dialects, like Bulgarian, do not have the deictic suffixal articles in *-on* and *-ov* (5.4.3) of CS-Mac and W-Mac. Pronominal case forms are also less evident in the eastern dialects: for instance the dative plural of the 1 Person pronoun is *nam* in W-Mac and CS-Mac, but *na nas* in E-Mac, as in Bulgarian.

In verbal morphology the 3 Singular present of verbs ends in *-t* in W-Mac, and in *-ø* in E-Mac and CS-Mac (*odi* 'he goes') (as also in Bulgarian). In W-Mac too, the aorist and imperfect are obsolete (as in B/C/S).

Table 10.3 summarizes the phonological and morphological features of the Macedonian dialects.

10.2.4   Dialects of Bulgarian

Bulgaria has Slavic borders with Serbia in the west and with FYR Macedonia in the south-west. Non-Slavic borders are with Romania to the north, and with Greece and Turkey to the south. There are no clear dialect boundaries with Serbia or FYR Macedonia, or with Greece.

Bulgarian dialects are conventionally divided by the north–south so-called "*jat'*-line", named after the reflexes of PSl /ě/. This line runs south from Nikopol through Pleven to Etropole and Pazardžik, and then moves west and then south in an arc. The west–east divide follows approximately a horizontal line across Bulgaria through Pazardžik. The four unequal quadrants are therefore: (1) the Pirin dialects in the south-west, which are transitional to Macedonian (**SW-Blg**); (2) the north-western dialects, transitional to the Torlak dialects of Serbian (**NW-Blg**); (3) the north-eastern dialects, including the historically important centre of Veliko Tărnovo, which have contributed much to the contemporary literary language (2.2.2) (**NE-Blg**); and (4) the south-eastern dialects, which are the most conservative, and have transitional phenomena to the Slavic spoken in north-eastern Greece (**SE-Blg**). Although the capital, Sofia (Blg *Sófija*), lies in the

Table 10.3. *Dialects of Macedonian*

	CS-Mac	W-Mac	E-Mac
Phonology			
Vowels			
ě	e	= CS	e, a after /c/
ъ	o	= CS	ə
ь	e	= CS	= CS
ǫ	a	a (some VN)	ə
r̥	r̥	= CS	ər
l̥	ol	= CS	əl
stress	fixed: antepenult/penult	fixed: penult	free
Consonants			
/x/	−	−	+
/VvV/	V:	VvV	VvV
Morphology			
Nominal			
suffixed deictics	+	= CS	−
1PlDat 'we'	*nam*	= CS	*na nas*
oblique of pers N	+	= CS	−
quantified plural	±	−	+
Verbal			
3 SgPres	-ø	-t	= CS

central-western part of Bulgaria, these dialects have contributed unevenly to the modern literary standard language. In this century urbanization and mass communications have supported the spread of the hybrid Sofia standard. Most educated speakers show variable elements from their own local dialects mixed with elements of the standard (Scatton, 1993: 190).

Many of the other features pattern less neatly than the *jat'*-line in terms of typological classifications of the dialects.

10.2.4.1 *Phonology*

Vowels

- Proto-Slavic *jat'* (*ě*) gives /e/ in western dialects, as in Serbian and Macedonian, while in eastern dialects it gives /ja/:

  (4a)   W-Blg *mléko* 'milk'   CS-Blg, E-Blg *mljáko*
          cf. CS-Mac *mleko*, Serbian *mléko*

  In NE-Blg, however, the modern /ja/ reflex of PSl /ě/ occurs only under stress and before a hard consonant, as in CS-Blg:

(4b)   CS-Blg, NE-Blg   *mljáko* [Noun]

mléčen [Adj] 'milk'   *mlekár* 'milkman'

In SE-Blg PSl /ě/ becomes *ja* in all positions:

(4c)   SE-Blg *mljáko* [Noun]   *mljáčen* [Adj] 'milk'   *mljakár* 'milkman'

- In the western dialects, as in Serbian and Macedonian, the quality of unstressed vowels is maintained. But in eastern, and especially north-eastern, dialects, unstressed vowels show narrowing: unstressed /o/ > [ʊ]; unstressed /e/ > [ɪ]; and unstressed /a/ > [ə]. The last of these is found, and then not strongly, also in western dialects: CS-Blg *červéno víno* 'red wine', NE-Blg *č*[ɪ]*rvén*[ʊ] *vín*[ʊ].

- The reflexes of the *jers* (ъ ь) and nasals (ǫ ę) are also criterial in the classification of Bulgarian dialects. In the south-eastern dialects both *jers* and both nasals become [ə], often with softening of the consonant before former front vowels; the north-east also has soft consonants before current front vowels:

(5)   PSl *zętь*   'son-in-law' > CS-Blg *zet*

SE-Blg [zʲətʲ]   NE-Blg [zʲetʲ]

In NW-Blg both *jers* develop into [ə] (as in SE-Serb/Torlak), while CS-Blg observes the distinction between /e/ and /ə/:

(6)   CS-Blg *den* [dɛn]   NW-Blg *dən*   SE-Serb *dən*   Serb *dân* 'day'

CS-Blg *săn*   NW-Blg *sən*   SE-Serb *sən*   Serb *săn* 'sleep'

- Proto-Slavic syllabic sonorants behave differently in different dialects: in general the west has syllabic /r̥/, like B/C/S and Macedonian, and syllabic /l̥/, like East Macedonian; the east has *rə/ər* etc. as in the standard (*prăv/părva* 'first' Masc/Fem]).

Consonants

- In the eastern dialects consonants may soften before /i/ and /e/, and even before /ə/ from former front vowels (see (5)).

- Proto-Slavic *tj dj kt*, which give *št* and *žd* in eastern and standard Bulgarian (*svešt, meždá*), give in western Bulgarian a series of 2-phoneme combinations closer to the situation in eastern Macedonian dialects: /tj kt/ > /čk, šč/, and /dj/ > /džg, ždž/.

Table 10.4. *Dialects of Bulgarian*

West-to-East:	CS-Blg	(N/S)W-Blg	NE-Blg	SE-Blg
Phonology				
Vowels				
PSl *ě*	e	= CS	e, a[†]	a
PSl *a* after Pal	a	= CS	e	e
PSl *ǫ*	a/ə	= CS	ə	ə
PSl *ę*	e	= CS	= CS	ə
PSl *ь*	e	= CS	= CS	ə
unstressed V reduction	low	= CS	high	low
syllabic liquids	Rə/əR	r̥/l̥	= CS	= CS
Consonants				
PSl *tj kt*	št	(č, ḱ, šč)	= CS	= CS
PSl *dj*	žd	(dž, ǵ, ždž)	= CS	= CS
C > C' before front vowels	limited	limited	+	+
Morphology				
Case forms	–	–	–	+
1pSg Pres	-ă/-m	-m	= CS	= CS
1pPl Pres	-m/-me	-me	= CS	= CS

Note: † = only before a hard consonant

- Some changes, like the increasing loss of palatalization of consonants before front vowels, date from 1945, and show the growing influence of Sofia norms (Hill, 1986: 30).

10.2.4.2 *Morphology*

SE-Blg (in the Rhodope mountains, the "end of the Slavic line") are the most conservative, with numerous remains of the former case-system. They also show the suffixal deictics, as in Macedonian (but with /s/ instead of /v/ for proximates, see 5.4.3, 5.5.1). In NE-Blg the 1 Person plural of all verbs has the suffix *-me*, rather than the standard Bulgarian *-m/-me*: CS-Blg *xódim*, W-Blg *xódime* 'we go'.

Table 10.4 summarizes the key phonological and morphological features of the Bulgarian dialects.

Transitional dialects occur in south-west Bulgarian to eastern Macedonian (with considerable overlap) and in north-west Bulgarian to the Torlak dialects of Serbian (figure 10.1).

10.3 Dialects of East Slavic

East Slavic constitutes a coherent geographical area with rich continuous dialect chains in Belarus, Ukraine and European Russia. To the east, over the vast spaces to the Pacific, Russian has been transported to new environments. While some local features, especially lexical features, are characteristic of these dialects, the principal dialect patterns are those of European Russia.

There is a good level of comprehensibility between East Slavic languages and dialects, particularly in the spoken medium: the phonetic bias of Belarusian spelling makes it harder to read than to listen to for a Russian or Ukrainian. There are significant transitional dialectal features from Ukrainian and Belarusian to Slovak and Polish in the west. These links to West Slavic, however, antedate the closing of the Soviet borders in the early twenties, when the centuries-old continuous contact between the East and West Slavs was physically interrupted. This separation was not absolute, however, since many speakers were trapped outside their home-lands by the territorial treaties of 1917–1918, a situation rectified to some extent after 1945. While speakers of western Belarusian and Ukrainian dialects have a good level of understanding of eastern Polish and Slovak dialects, speakers of standard East Slavic languages will not be so readily able to understand these West Slavic dialects.

10.3.1   Dialects of Belarusian

Seen in the context of East Slavic, Belarusian is closest to Ukrainian, and slightly less close to Russian (reflecting their history, see 2.3). There are clear transitional features to Ukrainian dialects in the south, and to Russian dialects in the east. Features linking Belarusian to West Slavic are less prominent. Standard Belarusian shares *akan'e* with standard Russian and with south Russian dialects, but shares more of its phonology and morphology with Ukrainian.

Belarusian has two main dialects, in the south-west (**SW-Bel**) and the north-east (**NE-Bel**). SW-Bel, which includes the capital Minsk, is the basis for modern literary Belarusian. This dialect shares some phonetic and morphological features with northern Ukrainian dialects, although lexically it shows significant influence from Polish, resulting from centuries of contact with dominant Polish cultural models (2.4.1). NE-Bel is closer to Russian. Some Soviet dialectologists, following Avanesov's (1964) research based on the 1963 dialect atlas of Belarusian (*Dyjalektalahičny atlas belaruskaj movy*), also identified a central band of dialects between the South-West and North-East and located around Minsk, and this has now become the standard approach (Mayo, 1993: 942). However, this is a transitional area rather than a separate dialect, since it exhibits various mixes of phenomena from the two main dialect areas rather than a set of special features of its own.

Belarusian dialects appear to be less threatened than the standard Belarusian language, which was being eroded by the dominant presence of Russian in public life (Wexler, 1974) until the collapse of the USSR. There is now a good chance that their continuation will be helped by the new national support for standard Belarusian from the capital in Minsk. However, the recent economic "pact" (2003) between Belarus and Russia, as well as the personal inclination of President Lukašenka to encourage the use of Russian, may work in the opposite direction.

10.3.1.1 *Phonology*

Pretonic unstressed vowels If a stressed syllable contains the vowel /a/, the first pretonic syllable's vowel is weakened in different ways. In NE-Bel pretonic /o e a/ merge into /a/ before a stressed syllable whose vowel is *not* /a/. When the stressed syllable does contain /a/, pretonic /o e a/ after hard consonants become [ɨ] or [ʌ], while pretonic /e/ after a palatalized consonant, as in Russian, becomes [ɪ]. This is called "weak" or "dissimilative *akan'e/jakan'e*", since the phonetic realizations of the unstressed vowel are distinct from the vowel of the stressed syllable (3.3.2.6).

Non-dissimilative *akan'e* is found in CS-Bel and SW-Bel. In this type the realizations of an unstressed vowel fall together as /a/ (or [ɪ], [ɨ], [ʌ]) whatever the stressed syllable's vowel. In standard Belarusian – in contrast to Russian – the quality of /a/ is always [a], including after soft consonants ("strong *akan'e/jakan'e*"). In Russian the results are [ə/ʌ] after hard and [ɪ] after soft, the latter called *ikan'e* (3.3.2.6).

Ekan'e, or the failure to reduce unstressed /e/ to [ɪ], is the main feature specific to the central dialects (though one does not find the expected equivalent *okan'e* after hard consonants). Both of these are features of north Russian (10.3.3).

Stressed vowels In a way which recalls both standard and dialectal Slovak as well as Ukrainian dialects and Sorbian, in SW-Bel stressed /o/ and /u/ become either diphthongs or raised versions of the vowel, in the direction of the first element of the diphthong:

(7)   CS-Bel *xleb* 'bread'   SW-Bel *xlieb*,   *xl*[*e*]*b*
       CS-Bel *žónka* 'wife'   SW-Bel *žuónka*, *ž*[*o*]*nka*

This feature is also found in N-Ukr dialects (10.3.2) and N-Rus dialects (10.3.3), as well as in Slovak (10.4.1) and Sorbian (10.4.4) to the west. CS-Bel and NE-Bel preserve the monophthongs.

Vowels after labials After labials the phoneme /y/ is pronounced as [u], rather than the [ɨ] of standard Russian and Belarusian:

(8)   'ox': CS-Bel, Rus, Ukr *byk* [bɨk]   SW-Bel [buk]
       'was' [MascSg]: Rus *byl* [bɨł]   CS-Bel *byŭ* [bɨu̯] SW-Bel [buu̯]
       (cf. Ukr *buv* [buu̯], but here by analogy with the future stem)

Prothetic consonants   Standard Belarusian and NE-Bel regularly show prothetic /v/ before initial /o/ and sometimes also before initial /u/. CS-Bel shows common prothetic /v/ before initial stressed /o/ and /u/ (3.2.1.4). NE-Bel shows an extension of prothetic /v/ to other words: CS-Bel *ósen'* 'autumn', NE-Belv *ósen'* (Ukr *ósin'*, Rus *ósen'*). SW-Bel has prothetic [ɣ] before initial /i/ /a/ /o/ /u/: [ɣ]*ósen'* 'autumn'.

Cokan'e   Some NE-Bel dialects, like some N-Rus dialects (10.3.3), have /c/ where standard Belarusian and Russian have /č/ (known as *cokan'e*): CS-Bel: *čort* 'devil', NE-Bel: [tsɔrt] (Rus *čërt*).

Status of soft consonants   As in standard Belarusian and N-Ukr dialects, soft /r'/ hardens in SW-Bel, but the NE-Bel dialects around Vicebsk and Mahilëŭ preserve soft /r'/, as in standard and dialectal Russian (10.3.3). Some NE-Bel dialects also show soft /č'/, as in standard Russian and in contrast to standard Belarusian, where /č/ is hard, and Ukrainian, where /č/ may be either hard or soft.

10.3.1.2   *Morphology*

Nouns   Various inflexional phenomena deviate from the Belarusian standard, often showing evidence of other dialects and standard Slavic languages.

- Certain masculine nouns have a nominative plural in stressed *-e* in SW-Bel: CS-Bel *hórad* 'town', [NomPl] *haradý*, SW-Bel [NomPl] *haradè*, cf. Rus *górod, gorodá*.
- Feminine nouns in SW-Bel show the old full instrumental singular in *-oju*:

  (9)   *pčalá* 'bee'
  [InstrSg]: CS-Bel, NE-Bel *pčalój/pčalóju*   SW-Bel *pčalóju*.

- Neuters in SW-Bel show a nominative plural in *-a*, like Russian and Ukrainian but unlike standard Belarusian:

  (10)   *vóblaka* 'cloud': [NomPl]: CS-Bel *vóblaki*   NE-Bel *vóblaka*.

- Neuters and feminines in SW-Bel also show an old dual with '2': CS-Bel *dzve halavý* 'two heads', SW-Bel *dzve halavé*.
- Masculine nouns in SW-Bel show a dative plural in *-óm* and locative plural in *-óx*, which recall standard Slovak (5.5.1) as well as Eastern Slovak dialects (10.4.4):

  (11)   *hórad* 'town': [DatPl]: CS-Bel *haradám*   SW-Bel *haradóm*.

- In NE-Bel feminines (as in CS-Rus) do not show the standard's 2nd Palatalization of Velars in the locative singular:

  (12)   *nahá* 'foot': [LocSg]:   CS-Bel *nazé*   NE-Bel *nahé.*

Adjectives

- SW-Bel is like standard and SW-Ukrainian in contracting 'vowel + *j* + vowel' to a single vowel: CS-Bel *darahája* [NomSgFem] 'dear', SW-Bel *darahá.*
- On the other hand, NE-Bel retains /j/ in masculine adjective inflexions: CS-Bel *dóbry* 'good' [NomSgMasc], NE-Bel (Rus, Ukr) *dóbryj.*

Numerals

- In SW-Bel – as in Slovak – the neuter form of the numeral '2' is *dzve,* which is usually only feminine in East Slavic: CS-Bel *dva sjalý* '2 villages', SW-Bel *dzve sjalý.*

Verbs

- NE-Bel shows a transition to Russian in the consonantal ending for the 3 Person singular non-past in both main conjugations: CS-Bel *čytáe* 'he reads', NE-Bel *čytáec'* (CS-Rus *čitáet*).
- In contrast, in SW-Bel the *-c'* ending is lost in the *i*-conjugation (when stem-stressed), so making it like the *e*-conjugation: CS-Bel *mólic'* 'he prays', SW-Bel *móli.*
- Ukrainian-type features of SW-Bel include a 1 Person plural imperative in *-ma* rather than *-m*: SW-Bel *kín'ma* 'let us throw', CS-Bel *kiném* (CS-Ukr *kýn'mo*).
- The 3 Person present of the verb *byc'* 'be' is SW-Bel *esc'* rather than *ësc'.*
- SW-Bel has the option of an analytic form of the future, parallel to the more regular synthetic form: CS-Bel *búdu čytáty* 'I shall read', SW-Bel also *čytác'mu.*
- NE-Bel never has final *-i* in the infinitive: CS-Bel *klásci* 'put', NE-Bel *klasc'* (CS-Rus *klast'*).

Setting aside features where the dialects all agree with the standard language, the key features of the individual dialects are summarized in table 10.5.

10.3.2   Dialects of Ukrainian

Ukrainian is closest to Belarusian, though it shares some important transitional features with southern Russian dialects as well. The basis of modern literary

Table 10.5. *Dialects of Belarusian*

	CS Bel	NE-Bel	SW-Bel
Phonology			
akarn'e	strong	dissimilative	= CS
stressed /o/ /u/	monophthongs	= CS	diphthongs/high V
prothetic consonants	v-	= CS	γ-
consonant + j	C′C′	= CS	C′
cokarn'e	–	some	= CS
soft /r′/	–	some	+
Morphology			
Noun morphology:			
Fem InstrSg	-oj/-ej	= CS	-oju/-aju
Neut NomPl	-y	-a/ja	-a
Masc Dat/LocPl	-am/-ax	= CS	-′om/-′ox
Masc NomPl	-y	-a-	-e
Adjective desinence	Short (-y, -a)	Long (-yj, -aja)	= CS
Verb morphology:			
3SgNon-past I–III	-ø	-c′	= CS
3SgNon-past IV	-c′	= CS	-ø
Inf	-sci	-s′c′	= CS
1PlImper	-em	-ma	= CS

Ukrainian is the central and south-eastern dialects, with historical lexical contributions from the Polish-influenced western dialects. The principal transition features are to Belarusian in the north-west, to Russian in the north-east and east, and to Polish in the west, with less extensive transitions to Slovak.

Classifications of Ukrainian dialects differ in the number and location of dialects. In general terms, there are: (a) a northern dialect (**N-Ukr**) to the north of a line running from Luc′k (NW) through the capital Kiev (Ukr *Kýjiv*) to Sumy (NE), showing some transitional features to Russian, particularly in the border regions; (b) the south-western dialects (**SW-Ukr**), west of a line running from Xvastiv to Balta, which form a transition to Polish. These dialects have contributed a significant proportion of the modern Ukrainian lexis, through Polonisms or internationalisms borrowed through Polish. In other respects, however, the south-western dialects have not been so influential on the modern standard, which is based on the south-eastern, less Polish-like, dialects; (c) the south-eastern dialects (**SE-Ukr**), which lie to the east of the Xvastiv–Balta line, and have provided much of the phonological and morphological basis of modern standard

Ukrainian. For these reasons they show fewer dialectal features distinct from the national standard.

10.3.2.1 *Phonology*

Vowels

- Ukrainian /i/ derived from Proto-Slavic /o e ě/ occurs in both accented and unaccented positions in standard Ukrainian, but in N-Ukr it is found only in accented syllables: CS-Ukr, N-Ukr *bílyj* 'white' (CS-Rus *bélyj*), where standard Ukrainian has /i/ in unaccented syllables as well: CS-Ukr *stárist'* 'old age', N-Ukr (CS-Rus) *stárost'*.

Even in accented syllables Proto-Slavic /o e ě/ may not result in standard Ukrainian /i/, but in diphthongs with [i̯] or [u̯] as the first element, a feature also found in SW-Bel (and Slovak):

(13)   'grave': CS-Ukr *hrib* [hrʲib]   N-Ukr [fìru̯ɔb]   (CS-Rus *grob*)
       'hay':   CS-Ukr *síno* ['sʲinɔ]   N-Ukr ['si̯ɛnɔ]   (CS-Rus *séno*)

Also as in Russian and Belarusian, in SW-Ukr /i/ from Proto-Slavic /i/ can palatalize the preceding consonant, that is, the distinction between /i/ and /y/ is retained, unlike standard Ukrainian: CS-Ukr *odýn* [ɔ'dɨn] 'one', N-Ukr [ɔ'dʲin] (CS-Rus *odín* [ʌ'dʲin]).

Consonants

- N-Ukr /r/ is hard as in Belarusian, and not followed by the /j/ of standard Ukrainian. Some SE-Ukr dialects have soft /rʲ/, like Russian:

(14)   'clerk' [NomSg ~ GenSg]:
       N-Ukr *pýsar* ~ *pýsara*   CS-Ukr *pýsar* ~ *pýsarja* [-rja]
       SE-Ukr *pýsarʲ* ~ *pýsa*[rʲa]   CS-Rus *písarʲ* ~ *písarja* [-rʲa]

- Proto-Slavic '/rl/ +*jer*' is represented in SW-Ukr by /er el ir il/, presumably via a stage of syllabic /r̥l̥/:

(15)   'tear' [Noun]: CS-Ukr *sl'ozá*   SW-Ukr *selzá* (CS-Rus *slezá*)
       'bloody':   CS-Ukr *kryvávyj* SW-Ukr *kirvávyj*
                                         (CS-Rus *krovávyj*)

This represents a transition to the syllabic /r̥/ l̥ / of Slovak.

- In SW-Ukr there is devoicing of final voiced obstruents, in common with Russian and Belarusian and unlike standard Ukrainian:

(16) 'oak':   CS-Ukr *dub* [dub] SW-Ukr [dup] (CS-Rus *dub* [dup])
      'knife': CS-Ukr *niž* [nʲiʒ] SW-Ukr [nʲiʃ] (CS-Rus *nož* [nɔʃ])

- Some SW-Ukr dialects show alveolo-palatalization of palatalized dentals, as in Polish: /sʲ zʲ cʲ/ > /ś ź ć/ (*sja* [Refl]: CS-Ukr [sʲa], SW-Ukr [ɕa], Pol *się* [ɕɛ̃]).

10.3.2.2   *Morphology*
Nouns

a.   In N-Ukr
- Neuters favor -*e* over -*ja* in the characteristic formation following a doubled soft consonant, which contrasts with the single consonant in SW-Ukr (see below): CS-Ukr *žyttjá* 'existence', N-Ukr *žytté* (CS-Rus *žit'ë* [-tʲɔ]).
- In the dative singular of masculine *o*-/*u*-declension nouns the inflexion in -*u* is preferred to the CS-Ukr ending -*ovi*. SW-Ukr has here -*ovy*:

(17) 'brother' [DatSg]:   CS-Ukr *brátovi*   N-Ukr *brátu*
                            SW-Ukr *brátóvy*   (CS-Rus *brátu*).

b.   In SW-Ukr
- The dative-locative singular of soft-stem feminine nouns is represented not by -*i* but by -*y*, with a further hardening of the stem-final consonant: CS-Ukr *na zemlí* [-'lʲi] 'on the earth', SW-Ukr *na zemlý* [-'lɨ].
- The feminine genitive plural has not -*ej* but -*ij*/*yj*: CS-Ukr *nočéj* 'nights' [GenPl], SW-Ukr *nočýj*.
- There is an instrumental singular feminine of nouns and adjectives in -*ou̯* or -*om*: CS-Ukr *rukóju* 'hand' [InstrSg], SW-Ukr *rukóu̯, rukóm*.

c.   In SE-Ukr
- Archaic forms of the dative plural and locative plural of soft-stem nouns in -*im*/-*ix*, mostly found in the Dnepopetrovsk region: CS-Ukr *kónjam* 'horse' [DatPl], SE-Ukr *kónim*.

Adjectives
- In N-Ukr, adjectives in the feminine and neuter nominative and accusative have 'vowel + *j* + vowel' as in Russian, rather than the

single vowel termination of standard Ukrainian: CS-Ukr *dóbra žínka*
'good woman', N-Ukr *dóbraja žínka* (CS-Rus *dóbraja žénščina*).

Pronouns

- A West Slavic feature occurring in SW-Ukr is the existence of clitic
  forms of the personal pronouns /m'a, t'a, s'a, my, ty, sy, ju, n'u/,
  parallel to the regular forms *mené, tebé, sebé, mení, tobí, sobí, jijí*.
  The reflexive particle *-sja* is able to function as it does in Polish, as a
  separable word- and sentence-enclitic, and not just as a verbal suffix as
  it does in the standard East Slavic languages: CS-Ukr *vin b'jét'sja* 'he
  beats himself', SW-Ukr *vin b'jé sja/vin sja b'jé*.

Verbs

- Many SW-Ukr dialects show infinitives in *-čy* after the velars /k g x/:
  CS-Ukr *mohtý* 'to be able', SW-Ukr *mohčý, moučý* (cf. CS-Bel *mahčý*).
- SW-Ukr also shows a remnant of the former compound past tense
  (5.5.5.6), very much as in Polish, where the auxiliary has been reduced
  to a suffix:

  (18) 'I was going': CS-Ukr *xodýv* [xɔˈdiṷ]
         SW-Ukr *xodívjem*   (< *xodilъ jesmь*)
         (cf. Pol *chodziłem*)

- A SE-Ukr tendency – among the eastern steppe dialects – is to show an
  unstressed *-e* in the 3 Person singular of Class IV verbs: CS-Ukr *xódyt'*
  'he/she goes', SE-Ukr *xóde*.

The key features of the individual dialects are shown in table 10.6.

10.3.3   Dialects of Russian

Russian is closer to Belarusian than to any other Slavic language, though it also
shares some features with Ukrainian dialects. Russian covers an enormous dialect
area, from the western boundary of the Russian Federation to the Pacific Ocean.
However, its dialectal base is in European Russia, and contains three main dialect
areas: northern (**N-Rus**), southern (**S-Rus**) and a central area (**Cen-Rus**) extending
in a narrow belt from Pskov through Moscow (Rus *Moskvá*) to the Perm'-Saratov
area in the east. Contemporary standard Russian is based on the Moscow dialect,
and broadly speaking has N-Rus consonants and S-Rus vowels. The language of
the Russians in the Asian provinces of the Russian Federation shows some local

Table 10.6. *Dialects of Ukrainian*

	CS-Ukr	N-Ukr	SE-Ukr	SW-Ukr
Phonology:				
PSl o/e/ĕ stressed	i	diphthongs	= CS	= CS
PSl o/e/ĕ unstressed	i	o/e	= CS	= CS
unstressed /o/	o/u	= CS	= CS	u
/r′/	rj	r	r′	= CS
PSl 'liquid (R) + *jer*'	RV	= CS	= CS	VR
word-final voice	+	= CS	−	= CS
Morphology:				
Nouns:				
NomSgNeut < Cje	C′C′a	C′C′e	= CS	C′e
DatSgMasc	-ovi	-u	-u/-ovi	-ovy
Dat/LocSgFem	-i	= CS	= CS	-y
InstSgFem	-oju	= CS	= CS	-oʉ/-om
GenPlFem	-ej	= CS	= CS	-ij
Dat/LocPl soft	-jam/-jax	= CS	-im/ix	= CS
Adj NomSg Masc/Neut	-a/-e	-aja/-oje	= CS	= CS
clitic pronouns	−	= CS	= CS	+
Verbs:				
Inf velar stems	-ty	= CS	= CS	-čy
Past with Aux	−	= CS	= CS	+
3SgPres IV	-yt′	= CS	-e	-it′

lexical interference, and some regional regularities, but cannot be described as dialects in the same terms as the dialects of European Russia.

10.3.3.1   *Phonology*

Vowels

- The most commonly noted phonological feature of N-Rus is the vocalic feature of *okan′e*: unstressed /o/ is distinguished from unstressed /a/,
in contrast to the standard language, which reduces unstressed /o/ to [ə]
or [ʌ], depending on its position in the word (3.3.2.6). Standard
Belarusian, which shows strong *akan′e*, has [a] (10.3.1.1). *Okan′e* is
also a feature of standard Ukrainian:

  (19)   *molokó* 'milk':
          CS-Rus, Cen-Rus   [məlʌˈkɔ]
          N-Rus (and CS-Ukr)   [mɔlɔˈkɔ]
          S-Rus (and CS-Bel)   [malaˈkɔ]

Parallel to *akan'e* (after hard consonants) in S-Rus is *jakan'e* after soft consonants. CS-Rus has unstressed /a/ and /e/ coalescing as [ı] after soft consonants (*ikan'e*); *jakan'e* dialects, however, coalesce unstressed /a/ and /e/ as [a]:

(20) Rus *bedá* 'misfortune':
CS-Rus [bʲıˈda]   S-Rus (and CS-Bel) [bʲaˈda]
Rus *pjatí* 'five [GenSg]':
CS-Rus [pʲıˈtʲi]   S-Rus [pʲaˈtʲi]   (CS-Bel [pʲaˈt͡sʲi]).

- Some N-Rus dialects (like SW-Bel and N-Ukr) have the diphthongs [u̯ɔ], [i̯ɛ] or else high mid [o], [e], from various sources, including the neo-acute (3.2.4.3) and *jat'*, as well as continuing the Old Russian distinction of original /o e/ (which became high) from new (low) /o e/ from the *jers* (3.2.1):

(21) Rus *stol* 'table':
CS-Rus [stɔɫ]   N-Rus [stu̯ɔɫ], [stoɫ]
Rus *méra* 'measure'
CS-Rus [ˈmʲɛrə]   N-Rus [ˈmi̯ɛra], [ˈmʲera].

- *cokan'e* (lit. 'saying [t͡s]'), brings the standard Russian phonemes /c/ and /č/ together as hard [t͡s] or soft [t͡sʲ], mainly the latter and mainly in N-Rus.

(22) *čúdo* 'miracle':
CS-Rus, Cen-Rus [ˈt͡ʃʲudə]   N-Rus [ˈt͡sudɔ], [ˈt͡sʲudɔ]
car' 'tsar':
CS-Rus, Cen-Rus [ˈt͡sarʲ]   N-Rus [ˈt͡sʲarʲ]

In some dialects the result of the fusion is /č'/.
- /g/: occlusive or fricative. In its consonant system S-Rus clearly shows features transitional to Ukrainian, and distinct from both Cen-Rus and N-Rus, as well as from CS-Rus. Most prominent is the fricative pronunciation of /g/ ([ɣ]), also found in standard Belarusian; Ukrainian, Czech and Slovak /h/ parallels this feature. In S-Rus /g/ is phonetically either [ɦ], like Ukrainian, or [ɣ], like Belarusian:

(23) Rus *gorá* 'mountain' [NomSg]:
CS-Rus [ɡʌˈra]   N-Rus [ɡɔˈra]   S-Rus [ɣaˈra]
cf.Bel *hará*   Ukr *horá*   Cz, Sorb *hora*   Pol *góra*   B/C/S *gòra*

- In all three areas, progressive assimilation, otherwise uncommon in Slavic, is found in the softening of /k/ and /g/ after soft consonants:

  (24)   Rus *trójka* 'troika': CS-Rus ['trɔjkə]   Rus-dial ['trɔjkʲa]
         Rus *Ól'ga* 'Olga':   CS-Rus ['ɔlʲgə]   Rus-dial ['ɔlʲgʲa]

- The marginal status of /f/ in Slavic (3.2.2.4) is seen in the replacement of /f/ in S-Rus by [x] or [xv]. This occurs in areas where /v/ is a sonorant, so that /f/ is not its phonological partner: CS-Rus *funt* [funt] 'pound', S-Rus [xvunt];

- Final /v/ and /l/, as in Ukrainian and Belarusian, are pronounced [u̯]: CS-Rus *byl* [bɨl] 'he was', S-Rus (and Bel) *byŭ* [bɨu̯] (Ukr *buv* [buu̯]). On the pronunciation of final /v/ and /l/ elsewhere in Slavic, see 3.2.2.4–5.

- Contraction of 'vowel +*j*+ vowel' sequences occurs in N-Rus, with results varying between double vowels in hiatus (cf. also Macedonian), long vowels (cf. also Czech, B/C/S) and single vowels (cf. also Ukrainian and Macedonian adjectives, and Bulgarian):

  (25)   Rus *znáet* 'he knows':
         CS-Rus ['znajɪt] N-Rus ['znaat], [znaːt], [znat] (Cz *zná*, B/C/S *znâ*)
         Rus *stáraja* 'old' [FemSgNom]:
         CS-Rus: ['starəjə] N-Rus ['stara], ['staraa]
         (Cz *stará*, Ukr *stará*, Blg *stará*, Mac *stára*)

10.3.3.2   *Morphology and morphophonology*

- An outstanding feature of N-Rus is a post-posed definite article, parallel to that of Bulgarian and Macedonian (5.5.1, 8.1.1):

  (26)   CS-Rus *kníga* '(a/the) book'   *ta kníga* 'that book'
         N-Rus *kníga* '(a) book'   *knígata* 'the book'

- Simplification of gender: southern dialects show some break-down in the nominal gender system, with the neuter gender transferring words to the masculine or the feminine. This tendency has also been noted by Schupbach (1984) for varieties of standard Russian:

  (27)   CS-Rus *sálo* [Neut] 'fat, lard'   *bélogo sála* [GenSg]
         S-Rus *sála* [Fem]   *béloj sály* [GenSg] 'of white lard'

  The basic cause of this change is probably phonological, namely the lost distinction between unstressed /a/ and /o/, which gives identically sounding feminine and neuter nominative singular forms.

- In S-Rus there are many instances of the locative singular of masculine and neuter nouns in /-u/. This tendency, restricted to some masculine monosyllables in Russian, is more common in Ukrainian and Belarusian, and is very common in West Slavic, and to some extent in Slovenian and B/C/S (5.5.1):

(28)   CS-Rus, S-Rus *póle* [NomSg] 'field'
        CS-Rus *v póle* [LocSg] 'in the field'   S-Rus *v pólju*

- In N-Rus, the instrumental plural of adjectives, and also nouns, may acquire the dative plural ending: CS-Rus *s nóvymi domámi* 'with new houses', N-Rus *s nóvym domám*;
- The 1–2 Person personal pronouns, and the reflexive pronoun, form their accusative in /-e/, rather than CS-Rus /-ja/:

(29)   'me':   CS-Rus *menjá* [mʲɪˈnʲa]   S-Rus *mené* [mʲaˈnʲɛ]
        (similarly: Rus *tebjá* 'you' [Sg], *sebjá* 'self')

- In its verbal morphophonology S-Rus shows some clear parallels with standard Ukrainian. There is the softening of final /t/ to /tʲ/ in the 3 Person plural non-past (cf. Belarusian's softened affricate): CS-Rus *idút* 'they go', S-Rus (and Ukr) *idútʲ* (Bel *idúcʲ*);
- Stressed /e/ is preserved in some verb forms, which regularly mutate to *ë* [ʲɔ] before original hard consonants in standard Russian:

(30)   CS-Rus *vedët* [vʲɪˈdʲɔt] 'he/she leads'   S-Rus [vʲaˈdʲɛtʲ]
        (Ukr *vedé* [-ˈdɛ]   Bel *vjadzé* [-ˈdzʲɛ])

In this case the retention of soft /tʲ/ in the system would have contributed to the retention of /e/ in S-Rus, while Ukrainian and Belarusian had more restricted contexts for the change of /e/ > /o/ (see 3.2.1.5).

10.3.3.3 *Syntax*
- The use of the nominative for the direct object after an infinitive, expressing purpose, is a feature of some north-eastern dialects:

(31)   'we must buy a boat':
        CS-Rus *nádo lódku* [Acc] *kupítʲ*   N-Rus ... *lódka* [Nom] ...

- A more general northern feature is the impersonal passive, using the neuter form of the passive participle and the logical object in the nominative:

Table 10.7. *Dialects of Russian*

	CS-Rus	N-Rus	Cen-Rus	S-Rus
Phonology				
akan'e	non-dissim	*okan'e*	= CS	strong
jakan'e	ikan'e	ekan'e	= CS	strong
[u͜ɔ] [i͜ɛ] [o] [e]	–	+	= CS	= CS
VjV > V(V)	–	+	= CS	= CS
/c č/	both	one only	= CS	= CS
/g/	occlusive	= CS	= CS	fricative
final /v/	v	= CS	= CS	u̯
/f/	f	= CS	= CS	x/xv
final /l/	l [ɫ]	= CS	= CS	u̯
Morphology				
Def. article	–	+	= CS	= CS
Fem = Neut	–	= CS	= CS	+
Loc = DatSg	–	= CS	= CS	+
Instr = DatPl	–	+	= CS	= CS
3PlPres	-t	= CS	= CS	-t'

(32)   'a soldier is buried here':

CS-Rus   *zdés'*   *poxorónen*   *soldát*
      here   buried [Masc]   soldier [Nom]

N-Rus   *odín*   *soldát*   *poxoróneno*   *zdés'*
      one [NomMasc]   soldier [Nom]   buried [Neut]   here

- A western feature appearing in all three groups, though mainly the northern, is the use of the past gerund as a main verb:

(33)   'he has gone out': CS-Rus *ón výšel*   N(W)-Rus *ón výšedši*

The key phonological and morphological features of the individual dialects are shown in table 10.7.

10.4   Dialects of West Slavic

West Slavic covers a coherent geographical area which borders on East Slavic (Belarusian and Ukrainian) in the east, on Baltic in the north-east, on German in the west and south and on Hungarian in the south-east. The westernmost area of West Slavic, Lusatia, where Sorbian is spoken, contains a majority population of Germans, which places Sorbian in some jeopardy, in both its standard and dialectal forms. West Slavic contains all the Slavic languages which have died out over the last two hundred years.

High levels of inter-comprehension are achieved between Czech and Slovak, with Slovaks understanding Czech more readily than the Czechs Slovak, for cultural and historical reasons. Comprehension between Sorbian and Polish, Sorbian and Czech or Slovak, and Polish and Czech or Slovak, is less reliable. And Kashubian (10.4.2.3) is not so readily understood by other speakers of Polish. The West Slavic dialect area has not always been continuously Slavic, with former German settlements between Poland and former Czechoslovakia, and between Lusatia and Poland over many centuries, and Lusatia and Czechoslovakia, lessening the graded continuity of transitional dialects.

10.4.1   Dialects of Sorbian

Sorbian is surrounded by, and interspersed with, German. Although its eastern and southern borders touch Poland and the Czech Republic, respectively, the Ore Mountains form a natural barrier, and one cannot speak of transitional dialects in the same sense as we can between, say, Czech and Slovak or Serbian and Croatian. The most important dialect groups are internal to Sorbian. Some scholars, like Šewc (1968), divide Sorbian into two dialect groups, based on Upper and Lower Sorbian. Stone (1993a), however, following the work of the *Sorbischer Sprachatlas* (1965–1996), has two groups of dialects with a transitional zone between Upper and Lower Sorbian.

The question of whether Lower Sorbian is a language, a co-variant of Sorbian together and on a par with Upper Sorbian, like the situation of Croatian and Serbian in Serbo-Croatian, or a dialect of Sorbian where Upper Sorbian is the major variant, is resolved differently depending on the criteria used. There is, however, consensus that Lower Sorbian is not merely a dialect of Upper Sorbian. It is formally differentiated from Upper Sorbian to a degree which would support some argument for language-hood, rather like Kashubian vis-à-vis Polish. It has standardized forms, and adequate historicity. But it is lacking in vitality and prestige.

Since we treat Upper and Lower Sorbian in this book as co-variants of a single language with two standard forms (2.4.2), and not as dialects, the main dialectal interest lies in variation within each of these two standards, and the transitional dialect area between them. In other words, we do not regard the distinction between Upper and Lower Sorbian as a matter of dialectology, and we have devoted separate attention to both variants in the appropriate chapters on the formal properties of Slavic.

The small number of speakers of Sorbian, however, and the distance between the written and spoken standards, have not helped the maintenance of the dialects, nor has the level of German influence in grammar and lexis. Nonetheless, Sorbian shares with Slovenian the distinction of having the most varied and tightly packed dialect map on a dialects/population basis. Variation is highest in the transitional areas (**Trans-Sb**), and lowest in Lower Sorbian (**LSb-Dial**). The Upper Sorbian group (**USb-Dial**) is intermediate. A great deal of attention is paid in the *Sorbischer Sprachatlas* to determining the isoglosses between Upper and Lower Sorbian. The transitional dialects run horizontally across the Sorbian speech area between Spremberg in the north and Hoyeswerda in the south, with western and eastern sub-groups (**W-Trans-Sb**, **E-Trans-Sb**), and it is in this area that many of the isoglosses fall. On balance, the transitional dialects are closer to Lower Sorbian, and especially E-Trans-Sb.

10.4.1.1   *Phonology*

The vowel systems are the same throughout the area. In the consonant system, on the major feature of the quality of /g-h/, W-Trans-Sb has /h/ like Upper Sorbian, while E-Trans-Sb has /g/ like Lower Sorbian. Original /č/ has become /c/ in E-Trans-Sb and Lower Sorbian. But the reflexes of soft /t′ d′/ are /ć dź/ in all Trans-Sb, as in Upper Sorbian, and /ś ź/ only in Lower Sorbian ('to work': USorb, Trans-Sb *dźěłać*, LSorb *źěłaś*).

10.4.1.2   *Morphology*

Upper Sorbian and W-Trans-Sb have the ending *-aj* in the nominative dual masculine against *-a* in Lower Sorbian and E-Trans-Sb. The secondary gender category of Masculine Personal exists only in Upper Sorbian, not in Lower Sorbian or Trans-Sb. And in the verbal system, too, the aorist and imperfect have been lost in Lower Sorbian and all Trans-Sb, but are retained in Upper Sorbian.

There are some lexical isoglosses matching Upper Sorbian with Trans-Sb, and others matching Upper Sorbian with W-Trans-Sb and Lower Sorbian with E-Trans-Sb. These are shown in the summary table 10.8.

10.4.2   Dialects of Polish

Poland has borders with Germany to the west, Lithuania and Belarus to the east, the Slovak Republic to the south-east and the Czech Republic to the south-west. The dialect area of contemporary Poland is more coherently Polish than it has been for centuries, even though it is not historically the same Poland that existed before 1945. There are large areas of territory in the west and south-west, and in the far north-east, which were formerly inhabited by Germans (referred to in dialect maps as "new mixed dialects"). After the end of the Second World War

Table 10.8. *Dialects of Sorbian*
(' = CS' here means the same as either Upper Sorbian or Lower Sorbian as appropriate)

	CS-USb	USb-Dial	Trans-Sb	LSb-Dial	CS-LSb
Phonology					
/g/	h	=CS	W-: h; E-: g	=CS	g
/č c/	both	=CS	W-: č; E-: c	=CS	c
/t' d'/	ć/dź	=CS	ć/dź	=CS	ś/ź
Morphology					
Supine	–	=CS	–	+(North)	–
Verbal Noun	-enjo	-enjo/-enje	-enjo/-enje	=CS	-enjo
Dual Number	+	–(South)	+	=CS	+
Nom/AccDuMasc	-aj	=CS	W-: -aj; E-: -a	=CS	-a
MascPers	+	=CS	–	=CS	–
Aor/Imperf	+	=CS	–	=CS	–
Lexical					
'yes'	haj	haj/ju/jow	W-: haj; E-: jo	=CS	jo
'who'	štó	štu	do	chto/ko	chto
'say'	prajić	prajić/rjec	prajić	=CS	groniś

these Germans were resettled in parts of Germany, and Poles were re-established in the newly vacated zones. The Polish inhabitants of these areas are not dialectally homogeneous, having come from different parts of the country, a situation mirrored in similarly resettled areas of the Czech and Slovak Republics. These factors limit the numbers of transitional dialects, particularly to Czech and Slovak in the south, since Polish has not had the same long-standing direct dialectal contact with Czech and Slovak. However, there are transitions to Kashubian in the north, and historically to Belorusian and Ukrainian in the east.

The traditional dialects of Polish are four – five, if Kashubian (Pol *Kaszuby, kaszubski*) (**Kash**) is also counted as a dialect. As noted in 2.4.3, Kashubian is both less than a language and more than a dialect of standard Polish, hence its appearance in this chapter under 'Polish dialects' but with a subset of its own dialects (10.4.2.3). The four areas are: (a) Great Poland (Pol *Wielkopolska*) (**Wielk**) in the west, centred on the cities of Poznań and Gniezno. These dialects are generally held to have been the basis for the formation of literary Polish. As a result, they show fewer features which distinguish them from modern standard Polish; (b) Little Poland (Pol *Małopolska*) (**Mał**) in the south-east, centered on Cracow (Pol *Kraków*), an important second influence on the development of the modern standard language; (c) Mazovia (Pol *Mazowsze*) (**Maz**), the area around the capital Warsaw

(Pol *Warszawa*) and to its east and north-east; and (d) Silesia (Pol *Śląsk*) **(Sil)** in the south-west, around the mining city of Katowice.

The Polish dialects are traditionally divided by Mazovianism (Pol *mazurzenie*), which is found in Mazovia, Małopolska and northern Silesia. Mazovianism involves the collapse of the dentals and post-alveolars /š ž č dž/ into a single series of dentals /s z c dz/, similar to the *cokan'e* of Belarusian and north Russian dialects:

(34)   CS-Pol *czapka*   ['t͡ʃapka]   'hat'   Maz ['t͡sapka]
        CS-Pol *żaba*   ['ʒaba]   'frog'   Maz ['zaba]

10.4.2.1   *Phonology*

- Features distinguishing Polish dialects include the many realizations of the nasal vowels (/ą ę/): in Mał both may appear as denasalized [a] or [ɔ] (East Mał) or nasal [ã] (South Mał); the back nasal may be [ɔm], the front nasal [ɛ̃] (West Mał); this last is also the result in West Maz, while Central Maz has [ã] for /ę/ and [ũ] for /a/. Only in Sil are the nasal vowels and distinct quality retained. Wielk shows the realization typical of the colloquial standard (3.3.2.3).

- Prothetic /v w/ before /o/ are common in Wielk (and Kash): CS-Pol *oko* 'eye', Wielk [vɔkɔ], Kash [wɔkɔ].

- Apart from Mazovianism, the most widely used characteristic distinguishing the dialects is regressive assimilation of voice across word-boundaries (see 3.4.3.4). In Maz (and in Kash) final voiceless consonants are not voiced before a word beginning with a vowel or a sonorant; in Wielk, Mał and Sil such consonants are voiced:

(35)   *brat idzie* 'the brother is going'
        CS-Pol, Maz ['brat 'idʑɛ]   Wielk, Mał, Sil   ['brad 'idʑɛ]
        brat robi 'the brother is doing'
        CS-Pol, Maz ['brat 'rɔbʲi]   Wielk, Mał, Sil   ['brad 'rɔbʲi]

- In Wielk, and also in Kash, the progressive assimilation of /v/ to [f] does not take place: CS-Pol *twój* 'your [SgMasc]' [tfuj], Wielk, Kash [tvuj].

- Maz shows an instability in the palatalization of the velars /k g/ before /ę/: standard Polish hard velars can be softened: CS-Pol *mogę* ['mɔgɛ̃] 'I can', Maz ['mɔgʲɛ̃]; and soft velars (before /e/) can be hardened: CS-Pol *kiedy* 'when' [kʲɛ-], Maz [kʲɛ-] or [kɛ-]

- In Mał final /-x/ may be realized as [k]: CS-Pol *na nogach* 'on one's feet' [-ax], Mał [-ak].

- In Sil there is a reflex of /r′/ as [r͡ʒ], perhaps a transition to the Czech /ř/, which is pronounced as a simultaneous [r] and [ʒ]:

(36) 'river' [NomSg]: CS-Pol *rzeka* ['ʒɛka] Sil ['r͡ʒɛka] (Cz *řeka*)

- The velarization of /n/ to [ŋ] before velars, common to all of West Slavic, but not East Slavic, does not occur in Maz: CS-Pol *bank* 'bank' [baŋk], Maz (and ESl) [bank].

10.4.2.2 *Morphology*

- Some Mał and Sil dialects have a 1 Person plural of verbs in [-va], and a 2 Person plural in -*ta* (the old dual forms):

(37) 'we are sitting':   CS-Pol *siedzimy*   Mał *siedzi*[*va*]
'you [Pl] are sitting': CS-Pol *siedzicie* Mał *siedzi*[*ta*]

- Some Maz dialects have -*m* in the 1 Person plural – a transition to East Slavic. Some Sil dialects have 1 Pl -*me*, and Kash has -*më* [mə] or -*ma* and 2 Pl -*ta*.
- In Mał and Sil there are non-standard inflexions for *ja*-stem nouns, with an accusative singular in -*ǫ* (CS-Pol -*ę*) (that is, the effect of lengthening) and a genitive singular in -*e* (CS-Pol -*i*) (that is, a reflex of *ě*), the latter also optional in Kash:

(38) 'earth' [AccSg, GenSg]:
CS-Pol *ziemię, ziemi* Mał, Sil *ziemiǫ* Mał, Sil, Kash *ziemie*

The summary table (table 10.9) follows and incorporates the discussion of Kashubian.

10.4.2.3 *Kashubian and its dialects*

Kashubian, according to Ethnologue, is spoken by about 3,000 people in northern Poland. Poles tend to regard Kashubian as a dialect of Polish, prompted by the lack of ethnic or linguistic cohesion of the Kashubians. On the other hand, Kashubian is more distinct from other Polish variants than is any single Polish dialect. But it lacks the status of a full literary language (2.4.3), and is very much under the domination of Polish in official, cultural and educational life. Seen in this light, Kashubian is a transitional dialect to the former West Baltic Slavic languages Polabian and Slovincian (2.4.3–4).

Among the features which differentiate Kashubian as a whole from Polish, whether as a language or a dialect, of interest are the following.

Table 10.9. *Dialects of Polish and Kashubian*

	CS-Pol	Wielk	Maz	Mał	Sil	Kash.
Phonology						
mazurzenie	– (s š ś)	= CS	+ (s)	+ (s)	N: +; S: –	– (s š)
voice sandhi	N: –; S: +	+	–	+	+	–
/v/ after *s t k*	f	v	= CS	= CS	= CS	v
denasalize /ą ę/	–	+ / –	= CS	E: +	= CS	–
prothetic /v/ before o-	+	–	–	–	–	+
unstable velars	–	= CS	+	+	+	č dž
final /-x/ = [-k]	–	= CS	= CS	+	= CS	–
/n/ before velar	ŋ	= CS	n	= CS	= CS	ŋ
stress	penult	= CS	= CS	S: initial	= CS	S: initial
				N: penult		N: free
Morphology						
AccSg *ja-* (< ǫ)	-ę	= CS	= CS	-ą	-ą	-ę
GenSg *ja-* (< ę. i)	-i	= CS	= CS	-e	-e	-i/-ë
1SgPres *-aj-*	-am	= CS	= CS	= CS	= CS	N: -ają
						S: -óm
1PlPres	-my	= CS	-m	-va	-my/-me/-va	-mə/-ma
2PlPres	-cie	= CS	= CS	-ta	= CS	-ta

Vowels

- the merging of /i/ and /y/ into /i/;
- short /i/ > /ə/ (written *ë*) ('quiet': *cëchi* ['tsəxi], Pol *cichy* ['tɕixɪ]).

Consonants

- the loss of the hard ~ soft opposition;
- loss of the alveolo-palatals (ś ź ć dź), which become /s z c dz/ (similar to *mazurzenie* and known in Polish as *kaszubienie*) (cf. *cëchi* above).

Internally, Kashubian itself has two well-defined dialect areas. In the southern Kashubian dialect (**S-Kash**) stress is initial, as in Sorbian to the west, and like Czech and Slovak to the south of Polish, and in some of the southernmost dialects of Małopolska (and in the literary language of the sixteenth century). In contrast, northern Kashubian dialects (**N-Kash**) have free and mobile stress, as in East Slavic and Bulgarian. North-eastern Kashubian also collapses /l/ and /ł/ into a single /l/, and changes /x/ before a front vowel into /š/ (an extension of the PV2 alternation): CS-Pol *muchy* 'flies' [NomPl], N-Kash *muši*.

In addition, some verbs in *-aj-* with a 1SgPres in *-am* in CS-Pol show *- aję* in N-Kash, *-óm* in S-Kash: CS-Pol *szukam* 'I seek', N-Kash *szukaję*, S-Kash *szukóm*.

Table 10.9 summarizes the key features of both Polish and Kashubian.

10.4.3   Dialects of Czech

The Czech Republic consists of two main areas, Bohemia and Moravia. The Czech Republic borders on Germany in the west and south-west; on Poland in the north; on Slovakia in the east; and on Austria in the south.

Czech dialects are commonly divided into three (Stieber, 1965) or four (Horálek, 1962; Short, 1993a) major groups. The three basic dialects are Bohemian (or Czech proper, Cz *český*) (**Boh**), Central Moravian (Hanák, Cz *hanácký*) (**Han**) and Lach (or Silesian, Cz *lašský*) (**Lach**). Short adds Moravian-Slovak, called also Eastern Moravian (Cz *slovácký*) (**E-Mor**), and others (e.g. de Bray, 1980c: 45) additionally divide the Bohemian region into three sub-regions (Central – around Prague (Cz *Praha*), North-East, and South-West). We shall follow the intermediate position of Short (1993a).

It is also important to remember that in Czech there is a significant gap between the phonology of the national written standard language (*spisovná čeština*), standard spoken Czech (*hovorová čeština*) and colloquial Czech (*obecná čeština*) (2.4.5, 11.3.2). The distance from standard Czech becomes progressively greater as one moves eastwards from Bohemia through the Hanák dialects to the Lach dialects and Eastern Moravian.

10.4.3.1   *Phonology*
- Treatment of the long vowels: in the Bohemian dialects, which cover the western part of the Czech Republic and the cities of Prague, Plzeň and Liberec, there are several important classes of diphthongs from long vowels:

    (38a)   /ý/ > [ei̯]: *mlýn* 'mill' Boh [mlei̯n]

    (38b)   /í/ > [ei̯] after /s z c/ (i.e. after hard):
    vozík 'little wagon' Boh [ˈvɔzei̯k]

    (38c)   /ú/ > [ɔu̯]: *ústav* 'institute':   CS-Cz [uː]   Boh [ɔu̯]

- The Hanák dialects, centered on the city of Brno, collapse Czech /u ú/ (from PSl *u, ǫ*) into /o ó/:

    (39a)   'torment': CS-Cz *muka*   Han *moka*
              'flour':   CS-Cz *mouka*   Han *móka*

    They also collapse Czech /ý í ej] into /é/:

(39b)   'good' [MascNomSg]:   CS-Cz *dobrý*   Han *dobré*
         'best':   CS-Cz *nejlepší* Han *nélepší*

In Lach there are no long vowels, as in Polish: *muka, dobry, nejlepši.*

- Prothetic /v-/: in Boh and colloquial Czech there is a prothetic [v-], also common in certain contexts in Sorbian, Belarusian and Ukrainian: CS-Cz *okno* 'window'; Boh, Colloq-Cz *vokno.*

  In Han the prothetic [v-] of Boh has been extended to a prothetic [h-], more like Sorbian: CS-Cz *úterý* 'Tuesday', Han *hóterek.*

- Stress is initial as in standard Czech, except in Lach, which has penultimate stress, confirming its transitional role to Polish.

- Lach has, also like Polish, lost phonemic quantity (see (1)). Han and E-Mor retain it, but vowels are often short where CS-Cz vowels are long (like Slovak): CS-Cz *vrána* 'crow', Han, E-Mor (and Slk) *vrana.*

- Czech *přehláska* (3.2.1.5): all except Boh have limitations on realizations of *přehláska*: Lach: a > e, root-internally only; Han: a > e, u > i, root-internally only; E-Mor: never:

(40)   'to be lying':   CS-Cz, Lach, Han *ležet* E-Mor *ležat*
        'soul' NomSg: CS-Cz *duše*   Lach, Han, E-Mor *duša*
        'foreign':   CS-Cz, Han *cizí*   Lach, E-Mor *cuzí*
        'I drink':   CS-Cz *piji* Han *piju/pijo* Lach, E-Mor *piju.*

- In E-Mor, as in Slovak, Czech /ě/ becomes [ɛ] after labials: CS-Cz *věra* 'faith' [vjɛra], E-Mor (and Slk) [vɛra].

- Vocalic liquids: in Lach vocalic liquids, from whatever Proto-Slavic source, as in Sorbian, Polish and East Slavic, are usually replaced by 'vowel + liquid', while in E-Mor vocalic /l/ has become /u/ (/r̥/ is retained):

(41)   'full':   CS-Cz *plný*   Lach *pylny*   E-Mor *puný*
        'neck':   CS-Cz, EMor *krk* Lach *kryk/kyrk*

E-Mor (like Slovak) even has vocalic /r̥/ in more cases than CS-Cz: CS-Cz *žerď* 'mast', E-Mor *žrd* (Slk *žrď*).

- /v/: in E-Mor, as a further part of the transition to Slovak, /v/ becomes [u̯] finally and before consonants (as also happens in Belarusian and Ukrainian): CS-Cz *pravda* 'truth' [-vd-], E-Mor (and Slk) [-u̯d-].

- Palatalization: in a reverse of Mazovianism, Lach, like Polish, converts /s z t d/ to /ś ź ć dź/ before front vowels and /j/: CS-Cz *zima* 'winter' [zi-], Lach (and Pol) [ź]*ima.*
- Also in Lach, /t d n/ automatically become palatal [c ɟ ɲ] before /e/, as in Slovak: CS-Cz *ten* 'that' [tɛn], Lach (and Slk) [cɛn].
- Voice sandhi: the voicing of final consonants across word boundaries in Lach and Han follows the pattern of Slovak and South Polish, namely, obstruents are voiced even before initial vowels or sonorants:

(42)   *k mostu* 'towards the bridge':
        CS-Cz [kˈmɔstu]   Lach, Han (and Slk) [gˈmɔstu]

10.4.3.2   *Morphology*

- In Boh the instrumental plural of nouns has [-ma] (the old dual) for CS-Cz [-mi]: CS-Cz *knihami* 'books' [InstrPl], Boh *knihama.*
- In Lach and E-Mor the accusative plural of animate nouns takes the form of the genitive plural, whereas in CS-Cz it has the form of an inanimate nominative plural:

(43)   'sons' [AccPl]:   CS-Cz *syny*   Lach *syn* [*uv*] (see below)

- In E-Mor the dative/locative singular masculine has -*oj*, not -*ovi* as in CS-Cz; and the dative/locative plural masculine and neuter have -*om* (= Pol Masc/Neut and Slk Masc) and -*och* (= Slk Masc): CS-Cz *chlapům, chlapech* 'fellow' [Dat/LocPl], E-Mor (and Slk) *chlapom, chlapoch.*
- Lach has the genitive plural masculine in [-uv] (cf. Pol -*ów*): CS-Cz *sousedů* 'neighbors' [GenPl], Lach *suśeduv* (Pol *sąsiadów*).
- In verbs of the *aj* and *i* classes, the 3 Person plural present/non-past has a non-standard ending in Boh (-*aj, -ej*) and Han (-*ijó*):

(44)   'they do':   CS-Cz, Han *dělají*   Boh *dělaj*
        'they walk':   CS-Cz *chodí*   Boh *chod'ej*   Han *chodijó*

The key features of the individual dialects are shown in table 10.10.

10.4.4   Dialects of Slovak

Slovakia is bounded by the Czech Republic in the west and north-west; by Poland in the north and east; and by Ukraine in the east. The southern borders with

Table 10.10. Dialects of Czech

	CS-Cz	Boh	Han	Lach	E-Mor
Phonology					
Vowels					
	ý, í	ej	é	y, i	= CS
	é	í	i/í	e	= CS
	ú/ou	ou	ó	ou	ú
fusion of *i/y*	+	= CS	= CS	–	= CS
přehláska: a > e	+	= CS	+ internal	+ internal	–
přehláska: u > i	+	= CS	+ internal	–	–
syllabic /r̥/	+	= CS	= CS	Vr/rV	= CS
syllabic /l̥/	+	= CS	= CS	Vl/lV	u
vowel length	+	= CS	= CS	–	= CS
stress	initial	= CS	= CS	penult	= CS
Consonants					
prothetic C	–	v	v/h	= CS	= CS
t d n soft before /e/	–	= CS	= CS	+	= CS
s z c dz > ś ź ć dź	–	= CS	= CS	+	= CS
voice sandhi	–	= CS	+	+	= CS
Morphology					
InstrPl	mi	ma	= CS	= CS	= CS
DatPl Masc/Neut	ům	= CS	= CS	um	om
LocPl Masc/Neut	ech	= CS	= CS	= CS	och
GenPl Masc	ů	= CS	= CS	uv	= CS
3PlPres *-aj-*	ají	aj	= CS	ají	= CS
3PlPres *-i-*	í	ej	ijó	i	= CS

Austria and Hungary are also important in the map of Slovak dialects. Slovak and Czech dialects show good levels of mutual comprehension.

The Central Slovak dialects (**Cen-Slk**), based on the town of Martin close to the geographical centre of Slovakia, were promoted by Štúr (2.4.6) in the nineteenth century as the basis for modern literary Slovak. But Bratislava, the capital of Slovakia, is situated at the south-western boundary and close to the border with Austria, on the outer edge of the Western Slovak dialect area (**W-Slk**).

In the west the dialects merge with Eastern Moravian Czech, though with some fairly clear isoglosses for specific features. In the east the dialects (**E-Slk**) show features which are transitional to Polish, though Slovak and Polish were separated by German settlements until 1945. To a lesser extent there are transitional dialects to the Carpathian (south-west) dialects of Ukrainian. Central Slovak dialects show some properties, sometimes known as "Yugoslavisms", which reflect South Slavic elements, and so stand out from the continuous chain between the western and eastern dialects.

10.4.4.1   *Phonology*

  a. A series of features opposes the central dialects and standard Slovak to the western and eastern dialects:

- Proto-Slavic initial *orC- olC-* with non-rising pitch: Cen-Slk has only *raC- laC-*, and CS-Slk most often has the same, while W-Slk (like Czech) and E-Slk (like Polish) have *roC- loC-* (3.2.1.7):

    (45) 'willow': CS-Slk, Cen-Slk *rakyta* W-Slk, E-Slk *rokita*
            'elbow': CS-Slk, Cen-Slk *laket'* W-Slk *lokec*
                        E-Slk *loket'*

    raC-/laC- is also the South Slavic result.

- Proto-Slavic *jers*: the *jers* give predominantly /e/ in W-Slk and E-Slk, but a larger range of outcomes – including /o/ and /a/ (the result in B/C/S and dialectal Slovenian) as well as /e/ – is found in Cen-Slk and CS-Slk:

    (46) 'rye': CS-Slk, Cen-Slk *raž* W-Slk, E-Slk *rež*
            'oats': CS-Slk, Cen-Slk *ovos* W-Slk, E-Slk *oves*

- Proto-Slavic *ę*: the result of /ä/ for Proto-Slavic short /ę/ after labials is limited to CS-Slk and Cen-Slk, while W-Slk has /a/ and E-Slk /e/:

    (47) 'meat': CS-Slk, Cen-Slk *mäso* W-Slk *maso* E-Slk *meso*

- Slovak diphthongs: the characteristic Slovak diphthongs *ie* and *uo* (orth. *ô*) are replaced by monophthongs in both W-Slk and E-Slk. In the east this links with Polish and in the west with Czech:

    (48) 'measure': CS-Slk, Cen-Slk *miera* W-Slk *méra/míra*
                      E-Slk *mera/mira*
            'horse': CS-Slk, Cen-Slk *kôň* W-Slk *kóň/kúň*
                      E-Slk *koň/kuň*

- Proto-Slavic *stj/skj/zdj/zgj*: the resulting sequences are *št'/žd'* in Cen-Slk and CS-Slk, *šč/ždž* inW-Slk and E-Slk:

    (49) 'still': CS-Slk, Cen-Slk *ešt'e* W-Slk, E-Slk *ešče*

- /v/: final /v/ becomes [u̯] in CS-Slk and Cen-Slk, but [f] or [v] in W-Slk and E-Slk:

(50)   *bratov* 'brothers' [GenPl]:
CS-Slk, Cen-Slk [-ɔu̯]   W-Slk [-ɔf]/[-ɔv]   E-Slk [-ɔf]

b.   Several features are distinctive of individual dialects.
  1. Western
      - The boundary with Eastern-Moravian Czech is most clearly marked by the isogloss of Cz /ř/ ~ Slk /r/, as in Cz *řeka*, Slk *rieka* 'river' (3.4.1).
      - Vowel length is contrastive, as in CS-Slk and CS-Cz, but the Slovak Rhythmic Law (3.5.2) is not operative.
      - The Proto-Slavic back *jer* (ъ) is realized as /e/ after a hard consonant, in contrast to CS-Slk /o/:

        (51)   PSl *sъnъ* 'sleep':CS-Slk (ESl) *son* W-Slk (Cz, Pol) *sen*

      - The two /l/ phonemes are reduced to one (with the loss of the soft one): CS-Slk *l'ud* 'people', W-Slk *lud*.
      - The palatal stops /t'/ and /d'/ of the standard become hard dental affricates /c/, /dz/: CS-Slk *deti* 'children' [ˈɟeci], W-Slk *dzeci* [ˈd͡zɛtsi].
      - Gemination of consonants is common: CS-Slk *mäso* 'meat', W-Slk *masso*.
  2. Central
      Although situated geographically between W-Slk and E-Slk, Cen-Slk shows some similarities (in bold) with South Slavic (Slovenian and Čakavian Croatian):

      (52)

PSl		Cen-Slk	W-Slk	E-Slk	SouthSl
ъ, ь		*e/o/a*	*e*	*e*	Čak *a*
					(Kajk, Sln *e*)
'rye'	CS-Slk *raž*	**raž**	*rež*	*rež*	Čak,
					B/C/S *râž*
ôRC		*RaC*	*RoC*	*RoC*	*RaC*
'elbow'	CS-Slk *laket'*	**laket'**	*lokec*	*loket'*	Sln *láket*,
					B/C/S *lâkat*

      Although it is the basis for modern literary Slovak, Cen-Slk also shows some features not found in the literary language:
      - Proto-Slavic *tl/dl* are preserved in E-Slk and W-Slk, and in CS-Slk, but are simplified to /l/ in Cen-Slk, as in B/C/S and Slovenian (and East Slavic) (see also below under Morphology): CS-Slk *šidlo* 'awl', Cen-Slk *šilo*, B/C/S *šîlo*.

- The vowel /ä/ may occur also after velars: CS-Slk *kameň* 'stone', Cen-Slk *kämeň*.
- Final /l/ in *l*-participles becomes [u̯], a feature only colloquial in the standard: CS-Slk *dal* 'gave' [-al], Cen-Slk [-au̯].

3. Eastern
- Stress is penultimate, as in Polish, and phonemic quantity is lost, as in Polish and East Slavic. With the loss of quantity goes the loss of the Slovak Rhythmic Law.
- Vocalic /l̥/ and /r̥/, which can be both short and long in standard Slovak, are not found in E-Slk, as in Polish and East Slavic. In their place are 'vowel + liquid' (more rarely 'liquid + vowel') sequences:

  (53) CS-Slk *vlk* [vl̥k] 'wolf' E-Slk *vil'k/vel'k* (Pol *wilk*)
  CS-Slk *vrch* [vr̥x] 'top' E-Slk *verch* (Pol *wierzch*, Ukr *verx*).

- Proto-Slavic *ę*, when short, becomes /e/, as in South Slavic: CS-Slk *mäso* 'meat', E-Slk *meso* (Sln *mesó*, B/C/S *mêso*).
- The palatal stops /t'/ and /d'/ of the standard become hard dental affricates /c/, /dz/ as in W-Slk (above), though here we may see a transition to Belarusian's affrication (3.2.2.1, 10.3.1). Some areas have instead post-alveolar /č dž/, closer to Polish (ć dź).
- /s/ and /z/ are palatalized before front vowels, as in Polish: CS-Slk *seno* 'hay', E-Slk *śeno*; CS-Slk *zima* 'winter', E-Slk *źima*.

10.4.4.2 *Morphology and morphophonology*
1. Western
Nouns
- Hard nominative singular neuter nouns have *-o* against CS-Slk *-e*: CS-Slk *vajce* 'egg', W-Slk *vajco*.
- Soft nominative singular neuter nouns have *-é/-í* against CS-Slk *-ie*: CS-Slk *zbožie* 'corn, grain', W-Slk *zbožé/zboží*.
- Nominative plural masculine animate nouns have *-é/-ie/-ié* against CS-Slk *-ia*: CS-Slk *l'udia* 'people', W-Slk *ludé/lud'ie/ lud'ié*.
- Genitive singular masculine *a*-stems have *-i* against CS-Slk *-u*: CS-Slk *gazdu* 'farmer' [GenSg], W-Slk *gazdi*.
Nominal
- The instrumental singular feminine has *-u/-ú* against CS-Slk *-ou*: CS-Slk *s tou dobrou ženou* 'with that good woman', W-Slk *s tú dobrú ženú*.

Adjectives

- The soft type have 'hard' endings, in *-ého* etc., against CS-Slk *-ieho* etc.: CS-Slk *cudzieho* 'foreign' [GenSg], W-Slk *cudzého*.
- The locative singular masculine/neuter has *-ém* against CS-Slk *-om*: CS-Slk *dobrom* 'good', W-Slk *dobrém*.

Verbs

- The infinitive has hard *-t* against CS-Slk *-t'*. CS-Slk *vedet'* 'to know', W-Slk *vediet*.
- The present/infinitive theme has short *-e-* against CS-Slk *-ie*: CS-Slk *nesiem* 'I carry', W-Slk *nesem*.
- 'Not to be' is *neni som*, etc. against CS-Slk *nie som* . . .

2. Central

Adjectives

- The nominative singular neuter has *-uo* (*ô*)/*-o* against CS-Slk *-é*: CS-Slk *dobré* 'good', W-Slk *dobruo/dobro*.

Verbs

'They are' is *sa* against CS-Slk *sú*.

3. Eastern

Nouns

- Genitive singular masculine *a*-stems have *-i* against CS-Slk *-u*, as in W-Slk (above).
- Also like W-Slk, hard nominative singular neuter nouns have *-o* against CS-Slk *-e* (above).
- The instrumental singular masculine/neuter has *-om* against CS-Slk *-em*: CS-Slk *bratem* 'brother' [InstrSg], E-Slk *bratom*.
- The genitive/locative plural of all genders has *-och* against CS-Slk *-ov/-ø*, *-och/ách*:

  (54)   'brother', 'town' [Gen/LocPl]:
         CS-Slk *bratov* [GenPl], *bratoch* [LocPl]
            E-Slk *bratoch* [Gen = LocPl]
         CS-Slk *miest* [GenPl], *mestách* [LocPl]
            E-Slk *mestoch* [Gen = LocPl]

- The dative plural of all genders has *-om* against CS-Slk Masc only:

  (55)   'woman', 'town' [DatPl]:
         CS-Slk *ženám, mestám*   E-Slk *ženom, mestom*

Table 10.11. *Dialects of Slovak*

	CS-Slk	Cen-Slk	W-Slk	E-Slk
Phonology				
Vowels				
PSl *jers*	e, a, o	= CS	e	e
PSl ę	ä, a, ia	= CS	a	e
vocalic liquids	+	= CS	= CS	–
diphthongs	ie, uo	= CS	í/é, ú/ó	i, u
PSl *ôrC-, ôlC-*	raC-, laC-	= CS	roC-, loC-	roC-, loC-
Consonants				
PSl *tl dl*	tl, dl	l	= CS	= CS
/t' d'/	t', d'	= CS	= CS	c, dz
/s z/ before front V	s, z	= CS	= CS	ś, ź
PSl *stj* etc.	šť	= CS	šč	šč
/l/ and /l'/	+	= CS	–	= CS
final /v/	u̯	= CS	f	f
gemination	–	= CS	+	= CS
Suprasegmentals				
stress	initial	= CS	= CS	penult
phonemic quantity	+	= CS	= CS	–
Rhythmic Law	+	= CS	–	–
Morphology				
Nouns				
NomSg Neut	e	= CS	o	o
NomSg Neut -*j*	ie	= CS	é/í	e
NomPl MascAnim	ia	= CS	é/ie/ié	i/e/ove
GenSg Masc *a*-stems	u	= CS	i	i
InstrSg Masc/Neut	em	= CS	= CS	om
GenPl all	M ov, N ø	= CS	= CS	och
LocPl all	M och, N ách	= CS	= CS	och
DatPl all	M om, N ám	= CS	= CS	om
Adjectives				
Soft type	ie-ho	é/ie/í-ho	é-ho	e-ho
NomSg Neut	é	o/ó/uo	é	e
NomPl Poss	Anim i, Inan e	= CS	= CS	o
LocSg Masc/Neut	om	= CS	ém	im
Nouns, adjectives and pronouns				
InstrSgFem	ou	= CS	u/ú	u
Verbs				
Inf	t'	= CS	t	= CS
1Pl Pres	m	= CS	= CS	me
Pres/Inf theme	ie	= CS	e	e
'be' *l*-participle	*bol-*	= CS	= CS	*bul-*
'they are'	*sú*	*sa*	= CS	*sa/su*
'not to be'	*nie som* ...	= CS	*neni som* ...	*ňe som* ...

NW ———————————————————————————————————— NE

							(Est)	C-Rus	N-Rus
				(Lith)	(Lith)	(Lith)	(Latv)	C-Rus	C-Rus
Polab	(G)	P-New	N-Kash	Maz	SW-Bel	C-Bel	NE Bel	S-Rus	C-Rus
(Germ)		P-New	S-Kash	Maz	SW-Bel	C-Bel		S-Rus	
LSorb	(G)	P-New	Wielk	Maz	SW-Bel	C-Bel		S-Rus	
USorb	(G)	P-New	Sil	Mał	N-Ukr	N-Ukr		S-Rus	
(Germ)		P-New	Sil	Mał	SW-Ukr	SE-Ukr		S-Rus	
Cz-New		Boh/Cz-new	Lach	W-/Cen-/E-Slk	SW-Ukr	SE-Ukr		S-Rus	
	Boh	C-Mor	E-Mor	W-/Cen-/E-Slk	SW-Ukr	SE-Ukr		S-Rus	
(Germ)		(Austr)	(Austr)	(Austr/Hung)	(Hung)	(Rom)		(Rom)	
		(Austr:	Koroš)	Štaj	Pan	(Hung)			
(Ital)		Prim	Gor	Štaj	Kajk	E-Herc	Šum-V	(Rom)	
(Ital)		Prim	Rovt	Dol	Kajk	E-Herc	Šum-V		
		Notr	Notr	Dol	Čak	E-Herc	Šum-V		
		Notr	Notr		Kajk/Čak	E-Herc	Kos-R	W-Blg	E-Blg
			Ik	Ik	E-Herc	Kos-Res	Torlak	W-Blg	E-Blg
						Zeta	Kos-Res	W-Blg	E-Blg
						(Alb)	Torlak	W-Blg	SE-Blg
						(Alb)	W-Mac	E-Mac	SE-Blg
							C-Mac	E-Mac	W-Blg
							(Gr)	(Gr)	(Gr)

SW ———————————————————————————————————— SE

Figure 10.1 Slavic dialects: contacts in diagrammatic form Geographical layout: Columns = north to south; Rows = west to east N = north; S = south; E = east; W = west; C = central; others as in text or Appendix A. 'New' = areas of new mixed dialects since 1945; brackets = adjacent countries (G = Germ). Single underline: transitions across languages within major groups (vertically or horizontally). Double underline: transitions across major groups (")

Adjectives

- The locative singular masculine/neuter has -im against CS-Slk -om (and W-Slk -ém, above): CS-Slk dobrom 'good', E-Slk dobrim.
- The nominative plural of possessive pronouns and adjectives of all genders has -o against CS-Slk -i/-e: CS-Slk vaši deti 'your children', E-Slk vašo dzeci.

Verbs

- The 1 Person plural present has -me against CS-Slk -m: CS-Slk nesiem 'we carry', E-Slk ňeśeme.

- 'Not to be' is *ňe som* ... against CS-Slk *nie som* ... (/e/ for /ie/).
- 'They are' is both *sa* and *su* against CS-Slk *sú*.
- The 'be' *l*-participle has the stem *bul-* against CS-Slk *bol-* (cf. Ukr *bul-*).

10.4.4.3   *Lexical*

'What?' is *co* (the common West Slavic form) in E-Slk, against CS-Slk, Cen-Slk and W-Slk *čo* (cf. Čak *ča*).

In summary, key features of the dialects are shown in table 10.11.

10.5   **Dialects: summary**

The interconnections and transitions between the languages and dialects are shown diagrammatically in figure 10.1.

11

Sociolinguistic issues

11.1 The sociolinguistics of the Slavic languages

With the exception of language standardization and regional variants (chapter 10), the sociolinguistics of the Slavic languages has been under-researched. Much remains to be done in the area of sociolects, for instance, except in so far as they overlap with questions of the national language, language planning, language in education, corpus planning and what the Russians call *kul'túra réči* – the 'culture of (good) speech'. Raskin (1978) regarded this deficiency under Communism as mainly ideological: a classless society is difficult to reconcile with sociolectal variation, and attempts to work out a genuinely Marxist–Leninist philosophy of language have so far failed to solve this question – though investigations like the Soviet Russian *Russkij jazyk i sovetskoe obščestvo* (Panov, 1968; Krysin, 1974; 11.3.1) provided a strong empirical platform for socially correlated studies of language variation. The after-effects of these problems of ideology and scholarship help to explain the uneven state of sociolinguistics in the modern Slavic languages (Brang, Züllig and Brang, 1981). Since the decline of Communism this field has become a major growth area of research (Cooper, 1989) in fields like colloquial language (Patton, 1988), political correctness (Short, 1996), culture-marginal slangs (Skachinsky, 1972), graffiti (Bushnell, 1990) and gay language (Kozlovskij, 1986), which were areas of scholarship not encouraged at the official level under Communism. It is still too early to evaluate how lasting is the linguistic effect of Communism, but we can begin to appreciate how the modern languages are reinventing themselves in their new globalized context.

11.2 Language definition and autonomy

11.2.1 Status and criteria

A variety of socio-cultural criteria complement the diachronic analysis of the emergence of the Slavic national languages (chapter 2, especially 2.5). Picchio

(1984) identifies two central factors in determining language-hood: *dignitas* and *norma*. These criteria correspond approximately to "status" and "standardization". A language needs to be valued, especially by its speakers but also by outsiders. It needs a description which defines it as distinct from others (Kloss's *abstand*), and to capture its internal consistency (Garvin, 1959; Issatschenko, 1975). It should also cover the required social and functional roles (Kloss's *ausbau* [1952]), and should be stable enough to constitute a defined and constant core around which its identity is defined and maintained. But, at the same time, it should exhibit "flexible stability" (Cz *pružná stabilita*), a concept developed by linguists of the Prague School (Havránek and Weingart, 1932; Havránek, 1936, 1963; Mathesius, 1947), allowing it to adapt to changing circumstances, social needs and communicative demands. We can augment the criteria presented in Stewart (1968) to arrive at the following characteristics.

1. **Standardization.** A standardized language is formally unified, and culturally unifying. The lack of a standardized variant has prevented Kashubian from qualifying as a separate language. Standardization needs to be exemplified in grammars, dictionaries, style and usage guides, and orthoepy, and it needs to be realized in written and spoken usage, and in policy, the media and education.

2. **Autonomy (*abstand*).** Languages need to assert their formal autonomy (distinctiveness) and cultural autonomy (independence). The autonomy of two modern Slavic languages is under some threat: Belarusian (2.3.3), which feels the cultural pressure of Russian; and, to a lesser degree, Macedonian (2.2.3), though here internal loyalty to the language counterbalances the Bulgarian perception that Macedonian is a western dialect of Bulgarian. Of the rest, Bosnian (2.2.4.3) is still establishing and defining its autonomy; Croatian (2.2.4.2) is distancing itself from Serbian; and Ukrainian (2.3.2), about which there were some fears under Russian-dominated practices in the USSR, is looking increasingly secure, though not necessarily stable or homogeneous (Pugh and Press, 1999: introduction).

   Among the means of maintaining, safeguarding and promoting autonomy are Lencek's (1982) criteria of "Slavization" and "vernacularization" (9.2.4). Lexical purification is one of the most obvious signs of this policy, particularly since it lends itself to direct management more than other aspects of language planning and policy.

3. **Historicity.** Historicity is concerned with early linguistic monuments and continuous cultural development. Authentic historicity is an

advantage to a language-culture, for instance in the Classical languages. Languages lacking historicity may try to establish claims to historicity in order to avoid the appearance of an upstart culture-come-lately. Competing claims for historicity can cause tension: between Bulgarian and Macedonian over Old Church Slavonic culture; and between Russian, Ukrainian and Belarusian for old East Slavic culture. Lencek's (1982) criterion of "archaization", the conscious and directed evocation of historical models, is an expression of historicity. It is seen in the revival of the Czech, Sorbian and Slovenian literary languages during the Romantic era. It also describes, in a rather different way, the strong continuing presence of Church Slavonic elements in modern Russian. A recent re-analysis of the history of Slovak (Lifanov, 2001) aims to establish a deeper historicity vis-à-vis Czech than has hitherto been accepted.

4. *Ausbau* is the way in which a language develops to fulfil society's functional, cultural and social roles. Languages which lack a full range of communicative roles are thereby restricted. A common restriction is liturgical, a role filled by Latin or Church Slavonic for most of the history of the Slavic literary languages. Another was political: in the former Czechoslovakia, for instance, German occupied many public roles until 1918. Belarusian is currently constrained by the parallel use of Russian in some public roles, including administration and intellectual life. Kashubian has little presence at the intellectual, journalistic or administrative level, and so is functioning more as a language of local solidarity, folklore and literature. The establishment of a full range of styles in Macedonian after 1944 replaced functions which had been fulfilled by Bulgarian, Serbian or Serbo-Croatian. A similar task now faces Bosnian vis-à-vis Croatian and Serbian.

5. **Vitality**. A vital language has sufficient numbers of speakers to defend itself against cultural invasion or dilution. A vital language is used in all contexts and walks of life, and has first claim for all relevant language roles. Sorbian shows a genuine lack of vitality, since its numbers are declining and the dominating German culture fulfils many language roles, especially in non-spoken contexts. And Belarusian has long been lacking in vitality in its interaction with the Russian language.

6. **Prestige**. Prestige may be based on an awareness of a standardized norm, autonomy, historicity or vitality. It may also involve loyalty and pride, and a cultural self-awareness. Prestige is of fundamental importance to the survival of languages in émigré communities. It has

also played a vital part in the survival of the less populous Slavic languages – especially Sorbian, Macedonian and Slovenian – and in the maintenance of larger languages like Bulgarian, Polish, Czech and Ukrainian through periods of foreign invasion and domination. Prestige can also be enhanced by status planning and institutionalization, the use of the language in public life (including administrative functions, for instance in the chancery language of the East Slavs).

7. **Monocentricity *vs* pluricentricity**. Most Slavic languages are typically monocentric, with a single, well-defined monolithic standard. But languages like English, French and German (Clyne, 1991a,b; Clyne ed., 1991) have multiple standards, depending on their geographical dispersion. Within Slavic, B/C/S (Brozović, 1991) is a stereotypical case of a pluricentric language, and moreover one established by political agreement (2.2.4.1). A contrasting example is that of Macedonian (Tomić, 1991), where the failure to establish a pluricentric language in collaboration with Bulgarian contributed to the *abstand* formation of a new Macedonian literary language. A similar set of circumstances contributed to the emergence of Slovak vis-à-vis Czech.

The notion of pluricentricity also offers possibilities for the study of other Slavic literary languages, particularly those where there have been competing centres and standards during the emergence and establishment of the national language. Here we find the Kiev ∼ Moscow, and later Moscow ∼ St. Petersburg dichotomy in Russian; western ∼ eastern tensions in Ukrainian; the Great Poland and Little Poland elements in Polish, as well as the Kashubian ∼ Polish dichotomy; Upper and Lower Carniolan variants in Slovenian; and western ∼ eastern tensions in Bulgarian recensions of Church Slavonic and in the dialectal input between Tărnovo and Sofia in the emergence of Contemporary Standard Bulgarian. The dichotomy between Upper and Lower Sorbian also lends itself to pluricentric interpretation. Whereas Lower Sorbian may have enough typological properties to warrant status as a separate language, the sociolinguistics of its current position allow us to interpret Upper and Lower Sorbian as the two foci of a single pluricentric language.

11.2.2 Standardization

In contrast to Schleicher's view of languages as organic organisms (*organische Naturkörper*) (Robins, 1967: 196, n. 73), which should be left to develop according to their own dynamics, the Slavs overtly manage their languages through legislation and standardization. Without such language engineering the contemporary languages would look very different. Arguably, some might not have survived to modern times.

In the Slavic countries education and the media are highly centralized, and there are Language Institutes of the Academies of Science in each country, one for each language, with printing houses and journals whose specific concern is the culture, promotion and defence of the native tongue. Even before the political disintegrations of 1991–1992, there were two such academies in Czechoslovakia: one in Prague for Czech; and one in Bratislava for Slovak. In Yugoslavia there were four: in Ljubljana for Slovenian; in Zagreb for the Croatian variant of Serbo-Croatian; in Belgrade for the Serbian variant; and in Skopje for Macedonian. In the German Democratic Republic, in spite of the numerical domination of German, the Academy in Berlin included an 'Institut für sorbische Volksforschung', and a new Sorbian Institute ('Serbski Institut') opened in Bautzen in 1992. These language institutes continue in the new autonomous states. They make policy, and publicize, implement and monitor decisions about the national language. In this way they can bring about a degree of uniformity and top-down direction which is impossible for contemporary English. Historically speaking, the convention of language legislation in orthography, grammar and lexis (through either church, or state, or both) influenced the formation and standardization of all the Slavic literary languages. In some cases, it was precisely the official legislating institutions, together with institutions devoted to the promotion of the national language and culture, which were among the most effective influences in promoting the new literary languages, for instance the various nineteenth-century Matice (language and culture institutes, often with strong nationalist missions grounded in ethnology and folklore (Herrity, 1973)).

The acceptance of a language as part of a constitution or national language policy is a powerful way of reinforcing its standing, defending it against the language of military or cultural invaders, and providing it with a *de iure* basis in the legal and educational structures of a country. Serbo-Croatian could never have been established as a national language without both legislation and agreement (2.2.4). And Slovak in Czechoslovakia was recognized as a separate language only after the Second World War, and officially established as such in one of the few solid results of the Prague Spring of 1968 (Ďurovič, 1980).

It is also true that centralized control allows language to become an instrument of political power. The rhetoric of Communism, for instance as it is illustrated in Soviet journalistic style, was powerfully reinforced by the ability of a central body to legislate on the language. The definition of the language itself was subject to centralized top-down definition, which excluded non-standard forms. And it allowed politically motivated manipulation: under Communism the academies were able to provide dictionaries with authoritative definitions of evaluative ideological words like *capitalist, bourgeois* and *Western*. Dissident and émigré writers like Solzhenitsyn were often officially marginalized in print before about 1990, and so had to publish through *samizdát*, the Russian term for underground publication. As a result, their work was not able to take an official place in descriptions of the language. Indeed, the boundary between description and prescription, as well as proscription, was often blurred. The current partial Westernization of the Slavic lexicons (chapter 9) is placing new responsibilities on the academies and on the language-regulating bodies.

All living Slavic languages now have contemporary reference grammars of substantial size and quality. Multi-volume dictionaries of the national language have also been a feature of the larger Slavic languages: the seventeen-volume Soviet dictionary of Russian was first published in 1957–1961. But official monolingual dictionaries of Belarusian and Slovenian have appeared only in the last few years. Before this the most extensive sources for Belarusian were Belarusian–Russian bilingual dictionaries. The national official dictionaries of both Bulgarian and Macedonian are still incomplete, and there is no official, modern monolingual dictionary of Sorbian, though there are, significantly, several large Sorbian–German dictionaries for both variants of Sorbian, and one substantial Upper Sorbian–English dictionary (Stone, 2002). A similar bilingual situation currently prevails for Bosnian (Uzicanin, 1995). The dictionaries of B/C/S have the expected emphases toward Serbian or Croatian, together with the name of the language ('Serbo-Croatian' or 'Croato-Serbian') and the use of either Roman or Cyrillic script. More even-handed dictionaries have been published outside former Yugoslavia (Benson, 1990a,b; Tolstoj, 1970), and even here there are difficulties: Tolstoj, for instance, while giving only the ekavian versions of words like B/C/S *réka* 'river', gives both Serb *bibliotéka* and Cr *knjížnica* for 'library', though with no indication as to which word belongs to which variant of Serbo-Croatian. In one sense this may no longer matter: with the political disintegration of Yugoslavia, the continuation of Serbo-Croatian itself is anachronistic. However, the approach of the Bosnian government, mirrored in Benson's (1998) dictionary of English with Bosnian, Croatian and Serbian, suggests that a parallel, pluricentric approach may be workable, at least for Bosnian.

Reference grammars and dictionaries show official language institutions consecrating and consolidating the status of the national language. These institutions can also be instruments of ethnic separatism. After 1945 a decade of solidaristic sentiment led to the Novi Sad Agreement (*Novosadski dogovor*) of 1954 for

Serbo-Croatian, which validated both alphabets and both the Serbian and Croatian norms of Serbo-Croatian (2.2.4). A prescriptive orthography (*Pravopis*) common to both major variants was published in 1960. However, in 1967 a group of leading Croatian writers and intellectuals published a "Declaration on the name of the Croatian literary language". This was prompted by a mixture of nomenclature (the label "language" has profound symbolic significance among the Slavs), linguistic *abstand* (11.2.1), ethnic values and identity. After 1967 the Serbs became identified both politically and linguistically with the centralist movement, and were more in favor of Serbo-Croatian, while the Croats pressed for independent status of Croatia and Croatian. The fragmentation of Yugoslavia has brought Serbo-Croatian to an end as a geocultural entity, at least in its pre-1990 form.

Nationalism throughout Eastern Europe is one of the key factors which has brought about the end of Communism (Suny, 1994). It is also helping to re-form the language ecologies of Central and Southern Europe.

11.2.3   Purism and the culture of language

Purism has been a continuing theme in Slavic languages since the nineteenth-century language revivals, and particularly so in the twentieth century. The larger languages like Russian have sought to protect themselves from foreign influences – pathologically so during the xenophobic years of the reign of Stalin. The other languages have tried to rid themselves of both non-Slavic and non-indigenous Slavic elements, especially in the languages of the old Austro-Hungarian empire (Czech, Slovak, Croatian and Slovenian). Bulgarian has been operating a policy of de-Turkification for a century, and since 1990 Ukrainian and Belarusian have instituted a policy of de-Russification (see chapter 9).

Purism has both a positive aspect (national sentiment and pride) and a negative-normative one (xenophobia). It is often more proscriptive than prescriptive, and where it can it works top-down through national authoritative agencies, education, the media and political pressure. It can be militant and destructive, as happened between the World Wars. It has been used not only to vilify foreign elements, however useful or relevant they might be, but also to reinforce national standards at the expense of regional and social variants, for instance as a lever against the growth of regional sentiment. Significantly, there were no studies of Russian "sub-standard language" (whether socially or regionally "sub-standard") between 1932 and the end of the Stalin era (Perelmuter, 1976: 95).

A more moderate approach to language regulation and growth is the "culture of language" (Cz *kultura jazyka*, Rus *kul'túra jazyká/réči*, Ger *Sprachpflege*). This set of attitudes was apparently first nurtured in the pre-Revolutionary Moscow

Linguistic Circle (Rothstein, 1976), and was widely supported in the 1920s, particularly in Czechoslovakia, where anti-German attitudes were expressed in the journal *Naše Řeč*. There is no satisfactory equivalent – or activity – in English for this concept. Among the Czechs it was combined with the functionalist approach of the Prague Linguistic Circle, and referred to the development, oversight and enrichment of the language (Havránek and Weingart, 1932). This theme was echoed in Russia by Vinokur (1929).

11.3 Standard written and spoken variants

The degree of regulation and the explicit fostering of "pure" language have tended to distance the formal canons of the modern Slavic written languages from the spoken standards and from the dialects more than is the case in contemporary English, where a generally lower level of regulation, and a more relaxed attitude to acceptable variation in the many standard forms of English, have helped the spoken language to penetrate more easily into the written media. On the other hand, written Slavic languages on the Internet are almost as chaotic, creative and undisciplined as their English counterparts, and Slavic languages have become more flexible and open to innovation since the fall of Communism.

All Slavic languages show lively spoken variants which are distinct from dialects. The nature of these spoken variants vis-à-vis the national standard depends on two principal factors: the degree of archaicity of the national standard; and the geographical distance between the capital and the dialect area on which the national standard is based. Slovak, Serbo-Croatian and Bulgarian have felt the effect of geographical distance between the capital and the dialect focus of the national standard. In the case of Slovak (Ďurovič, 1980), this serves to limit the impact of Bratislava Slovak on the national standard. Before its separation Serbo-Croatian was pluricentric, with two linguistic capitals, two standard variants and a geographical dialect base corresponding to neither of the capitals (2.2.4, 10.2.2).

The question of an archaic national standard poses different problems. Four of the modern Slavic languages – Czech, Slovenian, Sorbian and, to some extent, Russian – include in their national standards elements of older standards which were deliberately made part of the modern written medium.

If Sorbian is analysed as two languages, then it looks more like Serbo-Croatian, with two major variants distinguished by features of phonology, grammar and lexis (2.4.2). Unlike Serbo-Croatian, however, written Sorbian has a direct line of inheritance from established seventeenth-century models. The status of standard Sorbian is influenced by two major issues: the relative status of Upper and Lower

Sorbian as variants of a single language, or as independent languages; and the relation of both to the presence of German.

There are intriguing issues of the Sorbian spoken language in its contact with the numerically dominant Germans. Upper Sorbian, for instance, shows the influence of German in its use of the deictic *tón* 'that' as a definite article, and *jedyn* 'one' as an indefinite article, although the syntactic functions are not wholly identical with the syntax of the German articles. This contrasts with the post-posed articles of Bulgarian, Macedonian (5.5.1) and northern Russian dialects (10.3.3), though it mirrors a growing phenomenon in spoken Czech (Townsend, 1990: 101–102) and Polish. Other features of the modern Sorbian spoken standard include a preference for the nominative in complements of *być* 'be' rather than a choice between the nominative or the instrumental. More striking still is the use of the auxiliary USorb *wordować* (LSorb *wordowaś*) + Passive Participle, on the model of German *werden*, to form passives (1a). The written Sorbian standard would use a reflexive ((1b); and see 7.3.2; examples from Stone, 1986: 101):

> (1)   USorb   'the flight departure will be prepared'
>   a.   spoken: *wulět worduje přihotowany*
>   b.   written: *wulět so přihotuje*

Other extensive areas of German interference are to be found in Sorbian dialects (10.4.1). The Sorbs have made efforts to purify their language from Germanisms, but the dominant presence of German in the Sorbian area is such that major German penetration of the language is unavoidable.

We shall select two examples to give a more detailed illustration of the differences and tensions between the written and spoken standards: Russian and Czech.

11.3.1   Russian

In the 1960s the Russian Language Institute of the Soviet Academy of Sciences undertook an original and ideologically potentially challenging investigation of contemporary Russian, which was published under the title *Russkij jazyk i sovet-skoe obščestvo* ('The Russian language and Soviet society': Panov, 1968; Krysin, 1974). It involved a wide-ranging study of non-dialectal variation in modern Russian, including ideologically sensitive social factors like membership of the intelligentsia. This study, which was thoroughly assessed in Comrie and Stone (1978), confirms that the Revolution democratized, rather than removed, the pre-Revolutionary standard language. Many features of what used to be sub-standard Russian have become acceptable colloquial, and many features formerly colloquial have become part of the standard, particularly in pronunciation, while features of the former standard have become archaic.

The questionnaire for the study on Russian and Soviet society was distributed only to native-speaker informants who had completed secondary education and were living in urban areas. As expected, the language of writers and journalists was closest to the standard, and blue-collar workers furthest, with other "intellectuals" and white-collar workers in between. The survey also confirmed that:

> The spread of education [after the Revolution] led to the adoption of standard features into the speech of those who had previously used non-standard varieties of the language. Over all [*sic*], the latter has been the more powerful factor: except perhaps for the immediate post-Revolutionary years, there has been no trend to reject the traditional standard as a whole in favour of a norm closer to the actual usage of the working class.
> (Comrie and Stone, 1978: 21)

The Soviet Academy's study, however, also showed that there was more variation in standard Russian than had previously been suspected, and that some of this variation had social correlates. The survey also confirmed a number of important distinctions between the written standard, the spoken standard and other spoken variants of Russian. Even before the Revolution, as Comrie and Stone (1978) observe, Russian was both socially and dialectally less diverse than many European languages. It was also stylistically more sensitized to non-standard forms, partly through the stratified nature of Russian society and the conventions of correct and polite usage at the higher levels. This sensitivity to stylistic appropriateness remains today, and can be seen in the large set of descriptors which Russian dictionaries, normative grammars (Ickovič, 1968) and stylistic manuals use to describe not only the functional styles of Russian but also the precise stylistic quality of constructions and particularly lexical items. These include some descriptors which are not easily paralleled in English, like *prostoréčie* 'popular speech' (Marszk, 1988). This is not the same as *razgovórnaja reč'*, which refers to colloquial usage which may or may not be part of the standard (Patton, 1988). *Prostoréčie*, on the other hand, is more pejorative, and refers to popular usage, especially non-standard urban popular usage.

Russians have traditionally been sensitive about propriety, as well as prescription, of linguistic usage. We can see this clearly in the synchronic variation found between some forms of Russian which reflect changes which have taken place since the Revolution (for vocabulary, see chapter 9, and for patterns of address, see 11.4.1). One of these parameters of variation concerns pronunciation. At the turn of the century spoken Russian had an accepted standard pronunciation known as the 'Old Moscow Norm', even though the capital was in St. Petersburg (later Petrograd, then Leningrad, now St. Petersburg again). There was linguistic rivalry between Moscow and St. Petersburg, including issues like the pronunciation of the sound represented by the letter щ /šč/ and by sequences like сч 'sč' and зч 'zč': Moscow favored a long palatalized fricative [ʃʲ:] while St. Petersburg preferred [ʃʲtʃʲ]. In contemporary Russian the long palatalized fricative [ʃʲ:] is dominant except across transparent morpheme boundaries like Preposition + Noun, or Prefix + Root, as in *rasčiščát'* 'to clear (an account)' [rəʃʲtʃʲɪʲʃʲ(t)ʃʲætʲ]. Comrie and Stone (1978: ch. 1) ascribe this to a tendency to spelling pronunciation, which marks a social effect of literacy on the national standard. The move toward spelling pronunciation turns out to be even more widespread than this: there is a move away from the old ecclesiastical pronunciation of *r/g/* as [ɣ] or [ɦ] in favor of [g], so that compounds beginning with *blago-*, like *blagosklónnyj* 'favorable', are now pronounced [blag-]. Spelling effects are also evident in the move from the [-əj] pronunciation for adjectival endings in *-kij, -gij* and *-xij*, as in *tíxij* 'quiet', in favor of [-ɪj]. This pronunciation has continued to spread rapidly and is now well established (Comrie, Stone and Polinsky, 1996: 46–49).

The domain of word- and phrase-stress (Krysin, 1974: 223–241) is also undergoing change, largely in the direction of the removal of variation and exceptions. This tendency mirrors the more progressive southern dialects of Russian, while in the north traditional stress patterns (like the morphological paradigms) are better maintained. The tendency to regularization results in fewer stress alternations of the type *golová* [NomSg] 'head', *gólovu* [AccSg], *gólovy* [NomPl], *golovám* [DatPl], in both singular and plural, so that alternation within a singular or plural paradigm is reduced:

(2)   Rus   'water'

	NomSg	NomPl	DatPl
Formerly:	*vodá*	*vódy*	*vodám*
Now:	*vodá*	*vódy*	*vódam*

The stressed preposition in some Preposition + Noun phrases is declining, except in conventionalized combinations like *zá gorod* 'out of town' (accusative = motion/ direction). And monosyllabic-root prefixed verbs like *ot-dát'* 'to give up', which used to stress the prefix in the masculine singular past, are tending toward root stress: *ótdal* 'he gave up' > *otdál*. A similar movement of stress toward the root is found with the stressed reflexive suffix *-sjá*, which used to be found in a few verbs. This stress pattern now tends to be replaced by more regular stem-stress (*rodilsjá* 'he was born' > *rodílsja*).

Within morphology two broad tendencies are asserting themselves: a more analytic approach at the expense of some traditional synthetic forms (Comrie and Stone, 1978: chs. 3–4), and again a tendency to regularization and the reduction of variation. Regularization can be found in the lessening vacillation of gender in nouns which used to be seen as either masculine or feminine (*fil'm* 'film' is now masculine, while *duèl'* 'duel' is feminine); Schupbach (1984) notes an even greater regularization offered by the decline of the neuter gender and nouns of the third (feminine, *i*-) declension. The partitive genitive in *-u* (with masculine nouns of the *o*/*jo*-declension) is giving way to the genitive in *-a*, though there are a few nouns which still cannot take a partitive genitive in *-a* (*dájte čajkú*/ **čajká*, 'give [me] some tea'). Numerals, especially complex numerals, are losing their case forms in oblique case contexts, as has already happened in some other Slavic languages (5.5.4). On the other hand, there is a growing number of nominative plural forms of masculine nouns in stressed *-á*, which have been gaining ground since the turn of the century (*proféssory* 'professors' [NomPl] > *professorá*, with the resulting concomitant stressing of all the plural inflexions).

The tendency to a more analytic approach in morphology and syntax can be found in the increasing quantities of indeclinable nouns, both regular and borrowed, as well as those resulting from abbreviating processes like stump compounds and acronyms (9.5.3). Nouns in apposition are also showing an increasing tendency not to inflect:

(3a) Rus *reká* [NomSg] *Vólga* [NomSg] 'the River Volga'

(3b) Rus *na reké* [LocSg] *Vólga* [NomSg] 'on the River Volga'

In such cases the syntactic function of the noun can be determined only from the grammatical context. There is also some levelling of case usage: the genitive direct object after transitive verbs is giving way to the accusative (6.2.3). And semantic factors are exerting a strong influence on grammatical ones, as when verbs of "directing" and "controlling" like *rukovodít'* 'to direct' tend to abandon a governed accusative in favor of the instrumental. There is also a growing tendency for semantic agreement to win over syntactic agreement (Corbett, 1983: 30–39), an issue which has become more acute in the post-Communist era as western notions of political correctness have become more evident in the Slavic languages:

(4) Rus 'the doctor came'

        vrač   *prišël*

        doctor [Male referent]   come-PastMascSg

        vrač   *prišël*/*prišlá*

        doctor [Female referent]   come-PastMascSg/PastFemSg

Here a grammatically conservative tradition of gender-maintenance is coming into conflict with social and political agendas of issues like gender equality.

Spoken colloquial Russian (*rússkaja razgovórnaja reč'*) is even more richly varied. It shows a series of features typical among the Slavic colloquial variants vis-à-vis the national standard: heightened creativity, looser norms, ellipsis and the productive violation of the rules of the standard language for the purposes of expressive communication. Most of the following examples are taken from Zemskaja (1973). Phonetically, we find the predictable features of allegro speech: simplification of consonant clusters and syllable structure and the dropping of unstressed syllables:

(5)   *sejčás* 'immediately'   CS-Rus [sʲɪ'tʃʲas]   Colloq-Rus [ʃʲ ʃʲas]

as well as a much higher frequency of conversation-oriented particles like *déskat'* and *-to*:

(6a)   Rus   *on,   déskat',   prostudílsja*
             'he   they say has fallen ill'

(6b)   Rus   *u   neë   èkzámeny-to   sdaný   užé?*
             at   her   exams-Particle   sat   already
             'has she sat her exams already?'

More interesting, however, are the ways in which the language is restructured in the colloquial variants. Notable among the grammatical features of Spoken Colloquial Russian is the use of the vocative for kinship terms and diminutive forms of people's forenames in *-a*. The standard language has only two instances of the vocative left, both referring to the Deity (7a). The colloquial vocative of forenames and kinship terms is formed by removing the final *-a*, leaving either a soft or hard stem (7b):

(7a)		Nom		Voc	
	CS-Rus	*Bog*	'God'	*Bóže!*	'O Lord!'
		Gospód'	'Lord'	*Góspodi!*	'Goodness!'
(7b)	Colloq-Rus	*djádja*	'uncle'	*djad'!* [dʲætʲ]	'uncle!'
		Sáša	'Sasha'	*Saš!*	'Sasha!'

Not unexpectedly, some of the more esoteric morphology of the standard language, like exceptions to case-formation rules, often fail. The Soviet Russian author Zoshchenko, in a celebrated short story called 'The bath-house', has the central character, a man of very modest education, decline the indeclinable noun *pal'tó* 'overcoat' as an instrumental singular: *idú za pal'tóm* 'I'm going to get my coat' (instead of the indeclinable form *pal'tó*).

Spoken Colloquial Russian also has enclitic pronouns, which are unknown in the standard East Slavic languages, this being one of the features which distinguishes them clearly from West and South Slavic. Russian already knows about the "second grammatical position" or "Wackernagel position" in the sentence, as can be seen from the syntax of particles like *li* (Question) (7.1.2.4) and *by* (Conditional) (5.5.5.7). Spoken Colloquial Russian can apply this syntax to unstressed personal pronouns, particularly accusatives (Shapiro, 1968: 25):

(8)   'I see you'

     Colloq-Rus   *já t'ə*   *vížu (*já vížu t'ə)*

                 I you-Acc-Encl see

     CS-Rus   *já tebjá*   *vížu / já   vížu   tebjá*

                 I you-Acc   see / I   see   you-Acc

A typical example of the relaxation of grammatical rules is in the omission of the complementizer *čto* 'that', which is obligatory in the standard language, but optional in colloquial speech:

(9)   Rus   *Vánja znáet, (čto) oná nezdoróvitsja*

               'Vanja knows (that) she is unwell'

Of the various complementizers, *čto* 'what' and *kak* 'how' are omissible in most colloquial contexts; *kogdá* 'when', *gde* 'where', *kudá* 'whither' and *otkúda* 'whence' are omissible only in more transparent contexts (Zemskaja, 1973: 356–357). More unexpected is the omission of relative pronouns, accompanied by frequent perturbations in the normal word order:

(10)   Colloq-Rus *Ljúda,   tý   kní-ž-ku   já dal-á   pročl-á?*

                Ljuda   you   book-Dim-Acc I gave-Fem read-Fem?

       CS-Rus   *Ljúda,   tý   pročl-á   knígu,   kotóruju   já*

                Ljuda   you   read-Fem   book   which   I

                       tebé   dal-á?

                       you-Dat   gave-Fem?

                       'Ljuda, have you read the book (which) I gave you?'

Word order in the colloquial language is freer, with modifiers and heads being moved from their standard locations in the sentence, and particularly from their standard adjacent locations, in the interests of information management, emphasis and expressiveness:

(11)   'my yellowish pen'

     Colloq-Rus *žëlt(en'k)aja   mojá   rúčka*

                yellow(ish)   my   pen

       CS-Rus   *mojá   žëlt(en'k)aja   rúčka*

Conjunctions may appear after the conjuncts (Zemskaja, 1973: 394):

(12)   'it will be unpleasant if it rains'
  Colloq-Rus   *neprijátno   dóžd'   pojdët   ésli*
               unpleasant-NeutSg rain   [will go] if
  CS-Rus   *neprijátno, ésli pojdët dóžd'*

Major constituents of embedded clauses can appear outside their clause and before the conjunction:

(13)   'are you satisfied when visitors come to (see) dad?'
  Colloq-Rus   *dovól'na   tý   gósti   kogdá   prixódjat   k   pápe?*
               pleased   you   visitors   when   they come   to dad?
  CS-Rus   *tý dovól'na, kogdá gósti prixódjat k pápe?*

Lexically the colloquial standard shows a heightened use of diminutive, augmentative and pejorative suffixes on adjectives and especially nouns, as well as vigorous neologisms and creative patterns with existing word-forming lexical material and morphology. Very common is the tendency to transform Adjective + Noun phrases into a nominal based on the modifier or adjective root and the nominal suffix *-k(a)* or *-lk(a)*. The gender of the underlying noun is sometimes retained, and sometimes not ("univerbacija", see 9.5.3.2):

(14)   Rus   *Večérnjaja gazéta* [Fem] 'evening newspaper' > *Večërka* [Fem]
             komissiónnyj magazín [Masc] 'second-hand shop' >
             komissiónka [Fem]

This pattern is also used for well known places:

(15)   Rus   *Bibliotéka ímeni Lénina* 'the Lenin library' > *Léninka*
             (via **Léninskaja bibliotéka*)

(The name of the library has now been changed to *Rússkaja Gosudárstvennaja Bibliotéka* 'Russian State Library', but it is still known as *Léninka*.) A given form in *-k(a)* can, depending on the context, have a number of different possible referents:

(16)   Rus   *akademíčka*
       a. hospital of the Academy
       b. dining room of the Academy
       c. library of the Academy

Many such forms are expected in the colloquial language: it is unusual to use *èlektríčeskij póezd* or even *èlektropóezd* 'electric train' instead of *èlektríčka*.

There is a similar preference for the suffixed form in *-nik* for people: *serdéčnik* 'heart patient', 'heart specialist'.

11.3.2   Czech

Czech shows a particularly complex elaboration of codes between the written and the spoken languages. The deliberate attempt in the late eighteenth century to reform the literary language on the basis of the models of the sixteenth–seventeenth centuries, in a conscious evocation of the historicity of the language, contributed to the institutionalization of a considerable gap between the educated written and spoken standards. There is a significant difference between *spisovná čeština* 'Written Czech', which is the formal written standard; *obecná čeština* 'Common Czech', the general spoken language of most of the people living in Bohemia and Moravia, and existing in two somewhat differentiated versions which show evidence of influence from the dialects; *hovorová čeština* 'Spoken (Literary) Czech', the spoken form of the literary language which is sometimes claimed by purists to be a spoken realization of the written language, and sometimes seen (e.g. Micklesen, 1978: 438) as resulting from the 'tension between the literary language and the common language' (2.4.5); and the local dialects. In his study of spoken Prague Czech Townsend (1990) deals with the Common Czech of Prague, which he calls "Spoken Prague Czech", a version of Common Czech which has achieved wider acceptance because of the cultural pre-eminence of Prague. We shall keep to the three terms listed above: Written Czech, Common Czech and Spoken Literary Czech, bearing in mind that Common Czech in particular has many variants.

The underlying situation is diglossic (Ferguson, 1959; and see 11.5 below). Diglossia is endemic in modern Slavic, and has been a major factor in the formation of the modern languages (2.5). But the situation in Czech is more complex than this. Common Czech, with a strong base in Bohemian dialects, is spoken as a *lingua communis*, with some local variation, throughout the Czech-speaking areas. Stieber (1965: 86–87), Micklesen (1978: 446–449) and Townsend (1990) treat a number of features which separate Written Czech from Common Czech:

(17)   Written Czech   Common Czech

       a.   Phonological

           ý: *velký* 'big' [MascNomSg]   *ej*:   *velkej*

                mlýn 'mill' [NomSg]   *mlejn*

          é: *dobrého mléko* 'good milk'   *í*:   *dobrího mlíko*

                [NeutGenSg]

#*ú*:	*úřad* 'institution' [NomSg]	*ou*:	*ouřad*
#*o*-:	*on* 'he' [NomSg]	#*vo*-:	*von*
	oko 'eye' [NomSg]		*voko*

b.   Morphological

instrumental plural of nouns, adjectives and pronouns:

-*ami*/-*emi*	-*ama*/-*ema*:
ženami 'woman' [InstPl]	*ženama*
námi '(by) us' [InstPl]	*náma*

1 SgPres forms:

-*i*: *kupuji* 'buy'	-*u*: *kupuju*

2 SgPres of the verb *byt* 'be':

jsi	*seš*

adjectives and participles in predicates:

short form	long form
bud' tak laskav 'be so kind'	*bud' tak laskavej*

c.   Syntactic (tendencies rather than across the board):

genitive > accusative in negated direct objects

nemít peněz [GenPl]	*nemít peníze* [AccPl]
'to have no money'	

genitive > accusative in verbal government (e.g. with partitives)

nabrat vody [Gen] 'fill with water'	*nabrat vodu* [Acc]

dative > accusative

učím se češtině [Dat]/*češtinu* [Acc]	*učím se češtinu*
'I study Czech'	

instrumental case with prepositions

píšu tužkou [InstrSg]	*píšu s tužkou*
'I write with a pencil'	

predicative instrumental	predicative nominative
chtěl být dobrým vojákem [Instr]	*chtěl bejt dobrej voják*
'he wanted to be a good soldier'	

possessive adjective	possessive genitive
Petrova žena 'Peter's wife'	*žena Petra* [GenSg]

pronoun-drop	include pronoun subjects
vím 'I know"	*já vím*

definiteness

syntactic (7.1.1)	article from *ten* 'this, that'
vzal jsi knihu	*vzal seš tu knihu*
'did you take the book?'	

d. Lexical

'match':	*zápalka*	*sirka*
'girl':	*dívka*	*holka*
'very':	*velmi*	*moc*
'now':	*nyní*	*ted'*

Common Czech coexists with the dialects, which are used locally. The written language and its spoken form are a kind of diglossic 'H' superstructure (11.5), with clearly defined roles. Two issues have exercised Czech linguists in particular: the status of the various spoken forms of Czech relative to each other, especially the status of Common Czech, as a *de facto* standard; and that of Spoken Literary Czech, which is theoretically the spoken form of the written language, but in practice shows elements from Common Czech.

In the early 1960s the issue of Spoken Literary Czech was hotly debated. Kučera (1958) and Sgall (1960) had observed that Written and Common Czech can be blended in a variety of communicative situations. This blending is not entirely stable, though it does show some regularities, specifically (a) that phonological elements of Written Czech can combine with morphological elements of Common Czech, but not the other way round; and (b) that Written Czech stems may take Spoken Czech inflexions, but not the other way round. Purists like Bělič (Bělič, Havránek, Jedlička and Trávníček 1961) objected that the Written standard was autonomous from Common Czech, and that Spoken Literary Czech was closely bound to Written Czech. The key problem is therefore the status of Spoken Literary Czech.

Spoken Literary Czech is not just a vocalized version of Written Czech. The features of Spoken Literary Czech which do not accord with Written Czech are clearly accommodations in the direction of Common Czech. Spoken Literary Czech, then, occupies an intermediate position, showing morphological penetration from Common Czech, with some two-way lexical penetration. Spoken Literary Czech, however, is not yet stable enough to constitute a self-standing variant of Czech proper. Spoken Literary Czech – if indeed it does exist – matches Ferguson's description of variants intermediate between the "high" and "low" varieties of the classic diglossic situation. Townsend (1990), however, would not accept that Common Czech is in any sense "low" and, with Sgall and Hronek (1992), argues that Spoken Literary Czech is little more than a conservative fiction.

Micklesen (1978: 454) suggests that Spoken Literary Czech will eventually become the single spoken Czech standard. However, it is also plausible that increasing adjustments will occur between Written Czech and Common Czech. How this will affect the formal written standard is less predictable, and will depend to some extent on the importance which Czech language legislators place on the historicity of the written standard, and on the need to maintain a direct link with the great Czech literary monuments of the sixteenth–seventeenth centuries.

The situation in contemporary Slovenian shows a development in one sense parallel to Czech. Lencek (1982: ch. 6) observes that, in spite of the notably archaic character of standard written Slovenian, there is emerging a spoken variant which is less rigid than the written medium, and which is starting to form what he calls an "interdialect" within the highly varied dialect map of Slovenia. This interdialect is similar in its sociolinguistic properties to Spoken Literary Czech. Lencek believes that the Slovenian interdialect will become a new *lingua communis* in Slovenia.

11.3.3   Toward a more analytic Slavic?

The data from Russian and Czech suggest that some aspects of their spoken variants at least are moving toward a more analytic model of language, like that which is already in place in Bulgarian and Macedonian, particularly in nominal morphology. The evidence often coincides with phenomena in other standard and non-standard Slavic languages, and so allows us to ask to what extent the relatively conservative nature of Slavic morphology in particular is being modified under pressure from the spoken variants.

The general direction of many of the changes involves morphological simplification, the regularization of irregular forms, and the reduction of the number of morphological paradigms. This is not of itself a sufficient condition for an analytic restructuring, but it does tend to weaken the morphological articulation of the languages. More specifically analytic is the lexicalization of formerly grammaticized relations (e.g. the use of Preposition + Case form instead of a case form by itself), a tendency to favor lexicalized options where the language offers both lexicalized and grammaticized possibilities, and a tendency to leave grammatical relations implicit and contextual rather than explicit and morphosyntactically marked. Comrie and Stone (1978) identify the growing analyticity of Russian in phenomena like indeclinable nouns, the use of the nominative (citation) form with nouns in apposition ((3a) above), the declining use of oblique case forms of numerals, and the increasing use of verbs with preposition objects rather than case-marked objects alone.

Townsend's (1990) evidence from Spoken Prague Czech, as cited above (11.3.2), broadly supports a more analytic interpretation. There is some paradigmatic levelling, for instance in the loss of short-form adjectives and participles in predicative position. The case system is under attack: the genitive and dative are giving ground to the accusative, and the instrumental now tends to be used with prepositions, and to give way to the nominative in predicative position. On the other hand, possessive adjectives are often replaced by nouns in the genitive. Pronoun drop is often inoperative. And definiteness may be lexicalized with an article derived from *ten* 'this, that'.

The tendency toward analyticity in Slavic is not universally accepted. Dunn (1988), for instance, argues that the evidence from the indeclinability of nouns does not necessarily lead to a more analytic structuring of Russian, since other grammatical information in the sentence, in word order and constructions, maintains intelligibility. What is lost is some of the redundancy otherwise present in the Russian sentence, whereby morphology and syntax, as well as grammatical and lexical semantics, can over-determine grammatical information.

In addition, some pieces of the evidence from the colloquial variants do not favor the analytic interpretation. While spoken Russian is showing more use of the predicative instrumental (Comrie and Stone 1978: 117–120), Spoken Czech is going in the opposite direction (Townsend 1990: 105). Some of the data from Russian *prostorécie* (11.3.1; Patton 1988) also favor morphological diversification rather than reduction: the growth of the *-á* masculine plural of nouns (Rus *oficér* 'officer" [NomSg] – *oficerá* [NomPl]) on the model of Rus *proféssor – professorá*; extension of the locative in *-ú* in nouns like Rus *pljaž* 'beach', *na pljažú* 'on the beach'; or declension of indeclinables like Rus *metró* 'metro', as in *na metré* 'on the metro'.

Both linguistically and sociolinguistically, the prospects for this more analytic tendency, especially in the written languages, depend centrally on the policies of the language-governing bodies in the Slavic countries. As we have seen (11.2), these academies play a conservative and directive role in regulating the written languages. If they conduct a rearguard policy against analytic changes in the spoken languages, there will be more situations like that in Czech, Sorbian and Slovenian, where the written standard is some distance from the spoken standard. This distance could grow even wider. On the other hand, if some of the analytic changes are sanctioned, the languages may begin to converge on a position in some respects more like that of contemporary Bulgarian and Macedonian.

11.4 Sociolectal variation

The sociolinguistic effect of the Proletarian Revolution in the Slavic countries was neither consistently proletarian nor revolutionary. The most obvious change was some rapprochement between the social extremes. The nobility and/or upper classes of most of the Slavic nations were, at some time in the past, linguistically far removed from their more lowly subjects, sometimes to the extent of speaking another language – as happened with Slovenian, Sorbian and Czech (where the upper classes spoke German), Croatian and Slovak (German and Hungarian), Russian (French), Ukrainian and Belarusian (Russian and Polish). By the twentieth century, however, most members of the Slavic language-cultures were speaking their own languages. But it has taken the restructuring of society by the Communist regimes, and the destruction of a significant part of the aristocracy and intelligentsia during the Stalinist terrors, to remove some of the linguistic barriers which still existed. While regional varieties have been largely maintained, there has been some reduction of sociolectal diversity, although still far short of a linguistically classless society. These developments can be partly explained by the weakening of traditional social structures. More important, however, are increased social and geographical mobility, increased urbanization, equal rights for women and universal education.

Enhanced vertical social mobility, and the elevation of proletarian labor to prestige status, did much in the heyday of Communism to erase the old linguistic association between social class and occupation. The removal of the hereditary upper classes tended to spread the educated variant more widely over a range of socio-economic and professional groups. Instead of assimilating the old upper classes to lower class speech, the Communist Revolution tended to make the language of the proletarians less proletarian. In the history of the Slavic languages, education has been one of the keys to national and linguistic self-establishment. With universal education, the educated norm has spread socially downwards. Literacy has also made enormous advances: before the turn of the twentieth century less than 21 percent of the inhabitants of the Russian empire were able to read, let alone write, and the figure for women was close to half that for men.

Against this we must set three factors: conservatism, specialization and voluntary de-standardization. The influence of Communist language policy was more uniform among the urban proletariat. But the rural peasant element, which is traditionally a strong and conservative component of Slavic communities, showed less of the standardizing effect of national language policies. This represents a source of sociolectal variety, though a declining one. A different type of sociolectal stratification, and one which is clearly on the increase, is the growth of specialized jargons for various professions. The differences are mainly lexical, and can generally be treated as technolects which are substantially international in character. They contrast with more homeland-based restricted codes like prison-camp jargon, which was found principally in Russian, and which became more widely known through the work of writers like Solzhenitsyn.

We select pronominal and nominal address as a typical case providing important insights into a key area of the social dimension of Slavic. In 11.4.2 we outline some key social and linguistic features of the transition from the Communist to the post-Communist Slavic world.

11.4.1 Address systems

Slavic languages share with Romance and Germanic languages a well-established system of polite and familiar address in pronouns and titles, though not as elaborate as the honorifics of languages like Japanese (Shibatani, 1990: 374–380). The sociolinguistic factors underlying these usages were discussed by Brown and Gilman (1960), who identified the parameters of power and solidarity as having the crucial roles in the selection of forms of pronominal address. In Slavic the most broadly based model is that of the T/V opposition, with the familiar T pronouns like French *tu*, German *du*, Russian and Polish *ty*, Bulgarian *ti* contrasting with the V pronouns like French *vous*, Russian *vy*, Polish *wy* (with some significant qualifications) and Bulgarian *vie* (Stone, 1977). The T series is used only for singular address, where it has the overtones of familiarity and emotional solidarity. The V series, though morphologically plural, can be used for either plural, or polite singular, address. In addition to pronominal address, however, there is an elaborate system of nominal address, using both names and titles. In terms of power and solidarity, the T/T pattern, where T is both given and received, is mutual and solidaristic; V/V is mutual and non-solidaristic, since it lacks the element of greater emotional or personal closeness expressed by T; and T/V is power-oriented and non-solidaristic, since it implies a hierarchical distinction between the interlocutors. The causes of the hierarchical dislocation can be inherent factors like age, gender or acquired factors like social or professional status. Typically, the superior can choose the mode of address, while the inferior is restricted to respectful forms of pronouns and titles.

11.4.1.1 *Pronominal address*

The history of the T/V system in Slavic shows that before about the eighteenth century the address system in the pronouns was semantically based: one said T to singular addressees, and V to plural addressees. Politeness was expressed by address in the third person, using titles like 'Excellency'. During the eighteenth century French influence encouraged Slavic imitation of the French conventions for the use of *tu* and *vous*, with the result that the address systems of Slavic underwent a significant reanalysis (Friedrich, 1966). The parameters controlling the selection of the T and V forms of nineteenth-century Russian, for instance, reflect the structure of interpersonal communication in a society very conscious of social position and relative social distance:

(18)   topic of discourse   kinship

topic of discourse	kinship
context of the speech event	dialect
age	group membership
generation	relative authority
sex	emotional solidarity

The relative significance of these factors varies between contexts of usage. Polovina (1984), on the basis of a sample of 258 speakers of Serbo-Croatian, was able to report a ranking which she described, in order of descending importance, in terms of age > distance > respect > social status > educational level > and custom.

Asymmetrical T/V systems, where the senior person would give T and receive V, were common. Husbands would give T and receive V from their wives. Adults would give T and receive V from their children or pupils.

During the Soviet era, and beginning with East Slavic, the egalitarian ethos of Communism resulted in a strong movement away from "power"-oriented (= asymmetrical T/V) address, where T and V are not simultaneously given and received. Indeed, strikes in Russia in 1912 were partly to do with demands for the management to address the workers with V. After 1917, Party usage also promoted the introduction of symmetrical T between Party members. Of these two changes, the first has had a more widespread effect, so that in modern Russian asymmetrical T/V usage has theoretically become more restricted, especially to adult–child contexts; it also persists in some South Russian dialect areas (Jachnow, 1973). The attempt to propagate the use of T, however, sat relatively ill with two centuries of respect for strangers and superiors. The result is that strangers will give and receive V until they agree to switch to T: a premature transition to T, especially in socially or sexually asymmetrical contexts, can give offence or may be rejected by the other party. In a number of institutions, including the Soviet army, legislation was introduced to enforce symmetrical V. The evidence of Nakhimovsky (1976), however, suggests that practice in the Soviet army could be at odds with official regulations.

There is, nonetheless, significant variation within and between the languages in the use of T and V. Ukrainian uses *ty* less, and in fewer contexts, than Russian does (Stone, 1977), so that Russian speakers find that Ukrainian tends to sound more formal and studied. In Russian the use of *ty* to strangers is very much a matter of age and shared context. Kindergarten children will use *ty* to each other and some-times to the teacher, but they learn at the same time to use forename + patronymic to the teacher for more formal communication. University students, even students of opposite sexes, may exchange *ty* if they clearly belong to the same class or institution, but will exchange polite *vy* in more formal settings outside their shared context. Some West Slavic cultures imitate the German habit of drinking to *Bruderschaft*, linking arms and downing a glass of vodka to cement the agreement to exchange *ty*. Slavic languages have verbs for "*ty*-saying", like Rus *týkat'* (alongside more formal phrases like Rus *govorít' na 'ty'* 'speak using *ty*'), parallel to French *tutoyer*, Ger *duzen*.

The question of agreement with the semantically singular but morphologically plural "V" gives rise to some differences between the Slavic languages. Polish has strictly plural agreement, though the usual masculine personal gender, whatever the actual gender of the addressee, can vary in usage (Stone, 1977):

(19) Pol *Aniu,*   *czy* *wyście*   *to*   *napisali?*
          Ania-Voc   Q   you-Aux2Pl   Dem   wrote-PlMascPers
          'Ania, did you write that?'

Czech and Bulgarian do the converse, with singular agreement:

(20a) Cz   *napisal*   *jste*   *to?*
            wrote-MascSg   Aux2Pl   Dem
            'Did you [Sg] write that?'

(20b) Blg *víe*   *ste*   *razséjan*
            you   be-2PlPres   absent-minded-MascSg
            'you [SgPolite] are absent-minded'

Russian takes an intermediate position, with plural agreement for verbs and short-form adjectives, but singular (semantic) agreement for nouns and long-form adjectives:

(21a) Rus *vý*   *napisáli*   *èto?*
            you   wrote-Pl   Dem
            'did you [SgPolite] write this?'

(21b) Rus *vý*   *ø*   *bogáty*
            you   (are)   rich-Pl (Short-form adjective)
            'you are rich'

(21c) Rus *vý-*   *bogátyj*
            you   (are)   rich-NomSgMasc (Long-form adjective)
            'you are rich/a rich man'

(21d) Rus *vý-*   *bogáč*
            you   (are)   rich man-NomSg (Noun)
            'you are a rich man'

V in Polish is a special case. Although promoted by the Party after the Communist take-over in 1945, nominally in the name of Party solidarity, it did not achieve wide popularity, and is now mainly found in rural dialects. Its functions have been taken over by *pan* (see below).

A third type, which Stone (1977: 499) calls "O" because of its use of 3 person plural pronouns, expressed or implied, is found to some extent in Polish, Czech, Slovak and Slovenian (Cz *onikání* 'saying *oni*'). There were remains of it in Russian at the turn of the twentieth century (Comrie and Stone, 1978: 178). The 3 Person plural can be used for formal address:

> (22)   Cz   *jak*   *se*   *máš/máte/mají*
>   how   self-Cl   have-2Sg/2Pl/3Pl
>   'how are you?'

The "O" type was found only in asymmetrical address, and is generally thought to originate in German (*Sie*) or Hungarian (*maga/ön*; both are singular). In Sorbian, however, the Slavic language with the greatest degree of exposure to German, it is unknown (Stone, 1977: 499).

11.4.1.2   *Nominal address*

The tradition of nominal address (for English, see Brown and Ford, 1961) involves three related phenomena in Slavic: the Polish use of the Noun + 3 Person Verb structure for second person address; the use of forenames, in various forms, for expressing solidarity or intimacy – or, in the appropriate contexts, their converses; and the use of titles in respectful or more formal address. These three phenomena can also be combined to form complex modes of address.

Polish has taken the habit of 3 Person address further than the other Slavic languages. A transitional stage between pronominal address and the use of titles (see below) is the standard use of *pan* 'man' and *pani* 'woman' for respectful 2 Person address. There are also forms for the plural: *panowie* 'men' and *panie* 'women', as well as the neuter collective *państwo* for addressing sexually mixed groups:

> (23)   CS-Pol   *czy*   *państwo*   *wiedzą,*   *że* . . .
>   Q   people-Sg   know-3Pl   that . . .
>   'do you [Pl] know that . . .'

The function of 2 person address has resulted in a colloquial and non-standard use of 2 Person verbal inflexions with *pan* (etc.):

> (24)   Colloq-Pol   *czy*   *pan*   *wiesz?*
>   Q   man   know-2Sg
>   'do you know?'

In Polish it is also common to use certain terms, including religious kinship terms, for 2 Person polite address: *ksiądz* 'priest', *kolega* 'colleague' and *siostra* 'sister [nun]', as well as *tata* 'daddy', *mama* 'mummy', *ciocia* 'aunt', *babcia* 'grandma' and a small number of related words:

(25) Pol *czy ciocia   by   chciała   kawy?*
      Q   aunt Cond like-Fem coffee
      'would you [i.e. aunt] like some coffee?'

These forms are certainly used in other Slavic languages, but less commonly for 2 Person address. Using *ciocia* in this way is less formal than *pani*, and more respectful than *ty*.

The Catholic and Protestant Slavs have Christian names and surnames, with one or more additional names often relating to saints' days. Orthodox Slavs have names formed from a forename (which in the Russian empire was originally chosen from a list specified by the church); in East Slavic a patronymic formed from the father's name with the addition of a suffix; and a surname. If the father's name is *Iván*, for instance, a male child will have the patronymic *Ivánovič*, normally abbreviated in pronunciation to [iˈvanɨtʃ], and a daughter will have the patronymic *Ivánovna*, abbreviated to [iˈvanːə]. The hereditary surname, which became common usage from the time of Peter the Great, is also often formed from a forename, e.g. *Ivánóv* (variant stress). It may also be derived from place names (the River Lena in Siberia gave its name to *Lénin*, whose surname was actually the more prosaic *Ul'jánov*), or from common nouns (Rus *gorb* 'hunch, hump', *Gorbačëv*). *Stálin* originally had the surname *Džugášvili*, but he changed it to a name derived from Rus *stal'* 'steel' (Unbegaun, 1972; Benson, 1992).

The prototypes of titles were the nobility, and hierarchies of the civil service, institutionalized in Russia by Peter the Great into the Table of Ranks, with fourteen levels, and appropriate forms of address in five layers. The Bolsheviks abolished these ranks in 1919, together with Rus *gospodín* 'Mr.' and *gospožá* 'Mrs.'. They introduced Rus *továrišč* 'comrade', and Rus *graždanín* [Masc], *graždánka* [Fem] 'citizen', a pattern which was promoted in other Slavic languages as they were communized.

Some Slavic languages share the German tendency to address people by title, or to include professional designations in modes of address: for instance, *Herr Ober!* 'Head Waiter!' has been translated literally into Czech as *Pane Vrchní!* The question of combining titles, forenames and pronouns is complex and delicate. As Stone observes,

> There are few, if any, combinations of nominal and pronominal address forms which can be regarded as totally impossible. Indeed,

the fact that T/V and T/P [i.e. *pan*, etc. – RS, PC] systems are complemented by, but not strictly correlated with, systems of nominal
address makes possible a greater degree of subtlety in the reflection
of social relationships than would otherwise be so.   (Stone, 1977: 503)

In addition, there is an isogloss – perhaps an isonym – between the languages with
patronymics, the languages without patronymics excluding Polish, and Polish.

With patronymic languages, of which Russian is a prime example, it is possible
to have any of the three names alone, though solitary patronymics are now somewhat dated: Lenin was sometimes called *Il'íč* (the patronymic from *Il'já*). The main
combinations involve either 'forename + patronymic', or 'forename + surname',
or all three, but not usually 'patronymic + surname', or 'short forename + surname',
on its own (Comrie and Stone, 1978: 181). Under Communism Rus *továrišč* was
more neutral than Rus *graždanín/graždánka*, the latter being associated with
policemen addressing possibly wayward citizens. *Továrišč* was nonetheless clearly
associated with Party membership and Party solidarity. It was widely used in
official contexts, and in the army:

(26)   Rus [Soldier to officer]
        Továrišč   kapitán,   móžno . . .
        'Comrade   captain,   can (I) . . .'

This usage is still alive in the armed forces. The plural *továrišči!* became a
more neutral inclusive form of address to groups of people of either sex, not unlike
Eng *guys!* (now *rebjáta* lit. 'children'). Contemporary Russian usage is still uncertain: *továrišč* and *graždanín*, and also (previously already impolite) *mužčína*
'man' and *žénščina* 'woman', are no longer acceptable, while *molodój čelovék*
'young man' and *dévuška* 'girl, young lady, miss' have survived for younger
addressees.

Addressing an unknown person in Russian requires *izviníte* . . . 'excuse me . . .'
and the use of the polite *vy*, avoiding other address forms altogether. On the other
hand, the formula 'forename + patronymic + *vy*' (e.g. Rus *Iván Petróvič*, . . . *vy*)
covers formal public occasions as well as contexts of more intimate contact with
elders and seniors, and is very widely used because of this neutrality. It is less formal
to exchange 'forename + *vy*', and still less formal to use forename, with or without
diminutive suffixes, and *ty*. Nakhimovsky (1976: 90) cross-correlates these three
levels with age and generation: it is harder for older generations to reach the level of
formality of the 'forename + *ty*' pattern of the younger generation.

Non-patronymic languages other than Polish superimposed in public life a
Russian-like Soviet pattern of address on native address formulae. Cz *soudruh*,

Slk *súdruh*, Blg *drugár*, Mac *drúgar* 'comrade' were used in many contexts in parallel to Rus *továrišč*, particularly in combination with titles of positions in organizations:

    (27)   Slk   *súdruh akademik*!
                    'Comrade Academician!'

In Polish, on the other hand, some of the functions of the patronymic are paralleled by *pan* (etc.), so that where Russian has 'forename + patronymic', Polish may have '*pan* + forename':

    (28a)   Rus   *Iván Ivánovič, gdé vý*?
                    'Ivan Ivanovich, where are you?'
    (28b)   Pol   *Panie Janie, gdzie pan jest*?
                    'Mr. Jan, where are you?'

Pol *pan* also overlaps with Rus *továrišč* when combined with titles and designations of social office. Pol *towarzysz* was relatively infrequent under Communism, and the rhetoric of Party solidarity was consequently less intrusive in Polish. *Towarzysz* is now largely defunct:

    (29a)   Rus   *Továrišč Prezidént, já* ...
                    '(Comrade) President, I ...'
    (29b)   Pol   *Panie Prezydencie, ja* ...
                    'Mr. President, I ...'

The rules for the use of forenames in Polish, with or without *ty*, are approximately as in the other languages.

11.4.2   After Communism

The post-Communist social profile of the Slavic languages is multi-faceted, unstable and hard to grasp. In their public use the languages have radically altered to become more Western-like. There is less adherence to centralized norms, and a wider range of styles, including the extremely colloquial and the extremely vulgar, with neologisms and extensive borrowing, especially from English. Journalism is much more flamboyant and idiosyncratic. And the range of publicly discussed topics is much larger. Recent issues of the online Polish women's journal *Polki.pl* (http://polki.wp.pl), which is published through the web site Wirtualna Polska, cover the same range of material as is found in parallel Western publications, including sexuality, homosexuality and abortion, topics which did not find a place in comparable publications under Communism. The vocabulary has expanded correspondingly:

(30a)   Rus   *Besplátnyj kommérčeskij **xósting**, **čáty** i konferéncii*
'Free and commercial hosting, chats and conferences'

(30b)   Pol   *Tatu – zmierzch **homomarketingu***
'Tatu [Russian pop group] – the twilight of homo(sexual) marketing'

Western patterns are also evident in marketing, which was commercially subdued under Communism. Advertising is not only Western in visual presentation and design but often also in language, where there is frequent borrowing from and code-switching with English. We find mixed codes especially in popular culture like MTV, and most of all in Internet styles (email, chat rooms, web sites), where the osmosis with Western patterns is especially unobstructed. English lexis is often used with little restraint: Pol *cool sajt* 'cool site', which incidentally violates the order of nominal heads and modifiers (7.5, see also 9.8), or Pol *fan cluby* 'fan clubs', which also violates Polish orthography, since there is already an accepted word *klub* 'club'. Still more extravagant are teenage argots.

Code-switching has been a feature of Slavic for centuries – Tolstoy, at the start of *War and Peace*, has a famous episode where aristocratic Russian women are having trouble in finding Russian vocabulary as they code-switch between Russian and French. Code-switching into Western lexis, and especially English, was increasingly common in youth culture during the last two decades of Communism. Direct contact with Western lexis, values and practices, partly through capitalism and marketing, partly through the media, and now in accelerated form via the Internet, places all the Slavic languages in a dynamic and unstable situation of vocabulary and stylistic evolution.

Purists deplore this commercialization, internationalization and globalization of Slavic. The conservative agencies like the language academies and educational bodies are tracking the new developments, and in many cases trying to apply cautious and conservative delays to their approval. There are major debates about the integrity and directions of the national languages in the face of this new global challenge.

11.5   Bilingualism and diglossia

For centuries foreign political and cultural pressures have forced the Slavs to be linguistically aware of their neighbors, and of each other, resulting in extensive diglossia and bi- or multilingualism. Diglossia has been a major factor not only in the general sociolinguistics of Slavic, but also in the formation of the standard languages and in their relation to the prestigious religious languages, especially Church Slavonic (2.2.1).

The classic formulation of diglossia is Ferguson's:

> Diglossia is a relatively stable linguistic situation in which, in addition to the primary dialects of the language (which may include a standard or regional standards), there is a very divergent, highly codified (often grammatically more complex) superposed variety, the vehicle of a large and respected body of literature, either of an earlier period or in another speech community, which is learned largely by formal education and is used for most written and formal spoken purposes but is not used by any sector of the community for ordinary conversation. (Ferguson, 1959: 336)

In some of the languages there are very significant differences between the standard language and the local variants. Two literary languages – Czech and, to a lesser degree, Slovenian – have been deliberately modelled on much older literary monuments, which has created a diglossic gap between them and the various spoken forms of the language. Czech (11.3.2) is probably the most extreme example of Slavic diglossia. Polish, Sorbian, Slovenian and Russian all show a conservatism in the written language, which can become increasingly distant from the contemporary spoken language with the passage of time. The strong influence of normative grammars, and the authority of the political and educational structures supporting that national language, have the effect of insulating the written language from rapid change, or even from responding quickly to innovations in the spoken language.

Because of their dialect structure (chapter 10), all Slavic languages present a potentially diglossic situation between the national standard and a regional variant. Some dialects are relatively close to the standard literary language. This is particularly clear with the recently evolved literary languages like Macedonian and Belarusian, which were based specifically on selected regional dialects. But the richness of the Slavic dialect map, combined with (officially) universal literacy based on the national standard, create and institutionalize a typical diglossic situation. This pattern has not been fundamentally altered by a certain reduction in the vitality of regional variants, and some dialect levelling. For some Slavs, particularly those living close to the geographical centre of the national language's regional base, the gap between the local variant and the national standard can be relatively slight. But for others the adjustments are very considerable. Eastern Slovak, for instance, has penultimate stress like Polish, while standard Slovak has initial stress. North Russian pronounces unstressed /o/ as [ɔ], in contrast to [ə] and [ʌ] in Contemporary Standard Russian. And in the Polish regional variant called "mazurzenie" (10.4.2) the pronunciation of fricatives and affricates differs radically from that of standard Polish.

The situation in former Yugoslavia was more complex still. There the standard pronunciation – and to some extent the grammar and lexis – of Serbo-Croatian were significantly different from major dialect areas in Croatia and Serbia, especially at the geographical extremes in western Croatia and south-eastern Serbia. There was the additional factor of multilingualism, not only for émigré minorities, like the groups of Albanians and Romanians, but also for the Slovenes and Macedonians. Serbo-Croatian, as the language of inter-cultural communication, was taught universally in the school system, and as a foreign language for the Slovenes and Macedonians. A similar situation is found with the Kashubians in Northern Poland, who have to learn Polish; and for the Sorbs, who live in a German-dominated society.

A very different example of diglossia is described by Magner (1978) in the language of the inhabitants of Split in Croatia. Even in Zagreb the local kajkavian ekavian dialect (10.2.2) is in a diglossic relation to Croatian, let alone the former Serbian variant. In Split, however, historical as well as ethnic factors conspire to present a sociolinguistic situation of particular interest. Italian was the official language of this part of Dalmatia from the fifteenth century until the formation of the Yugoslav state in 1918, and the Split dialect contains a large number of words and phrases of Italian origin. In contemporary Split, however, the diglossic focus is on the distribution of sociolinguistic functions between what Magner calls "textbook Croatian" (the former official Croatian variant of Serbo-Croatian), the various versions of spoken (even educated spoken) Croatian, and the local dialect. Inhabitants of Split have to learn the relation not only between the "H" (high) and "L" (low) varieties but also the differing degrees of "H" which are countenanced. In Split, for instance, as in most Croatian dialects, /h/ is not pronounced, though it is meant to be in official "textbook" Croatian (Brabec, Hraste and Živković 1968: 31). In some contexts /h/ is realized as zero: Cr *hladno*, Split *ladno* 'cold'. After back vowels the Split dialect realizes /h/ as [v], as in Cr *kruh*, Split *kruv* 'bread'; but after front vowels the Split dialect realizes /h/ as [j]: Cr *ih*, Split *ij* 'them' (similar to the selection of prothetic consonants in languages like Sorbian: 3.2.1.4). The contrasts are even more pronounced in the tonal system, since Split has only a contrast of length in the vowels (Magner, 1978: 409):

(31) ekavian (Serbian)   ikavian (e.g. Split)   jekavian (Croatian)
      mèsto 'place'   *mȋsto*   *mjèsto*
      mléko 'milk'   *mlȋko*   *mlijèko*
      sêno 'hay'   *sȋno*   *sȉjeno*
      lêp 'beautiful'   *lȋp*   *ȓijep*
      lépa [Fem]   *lȋpa*   *lijèpa*
         'beautiful'

These details will give some idea of the complexity of the issues which face language communities where there are not only local dialects, but also conflicting variants of the official standard. Magner and Matejka (1971) have shown that the tone and length features of standard Serbo-Croatian were better preserved in rural areas than in the towns, where mixing of variants tended to make tone, and particularly post-tonic length, unstable.

All these examples of diglossia and bilingualism apply to languages in the home-land, where the contemporary language situation is the result of long and steady cultural development and interaction. The situation with external multilingualism has different historical roots. The important factor here is not the difference between standard and non-standard varieties of the same language, but the gap between two different languages – either on the same soil (German in the West Slav lands and Slovenia, Turkish in the Balkans, Russian in Ukraine and Belarus), or as the imitation of foreign models. All the Slavic languages, irrespective of size, have a long and continuous educational and cultural tradition of multilingualism. In the twentieth century the incentive to master other languages was directed to two main foci: Russian; and Western European languages, especially English and German.

Before the fall of Euro-Communism Russian was taught at primary and secondary schools; within the Soviet Union it was made compulsory by decree in 1938. It was also an obligatory component of many university courses in the Eastern Bloc. At least a passive knowledge of Russian was considered necessary for public and intellectual life, especially within the USSR. Russian literature and culture were promoted, in translation and in the original, through the media and education. Russian was an administrative *lingua franca* of the USSR, but its status is now declining in favour of English, German and French. Russian is still one of the official languages of the United Nations, UNESCO, the World Health Organization and other international bodies.

Russian was resented as the language of the dominant political-economic culture. Education policy, indeed, presented Russian as more of a second native language than a *lingua franca* (Kreindler, 1982). In spite of the official standing of Russian in the secondary and tertiary curriculum throughout Eastern Europe and the USSR, Russian was neither popular as a subject nor educationally very effective. After what was often ten years of compulsory instruction, many students had only a perfunctory knowledge of the language. Within the Soviet Union there were also special problems of national languages. The official guidelines had been Lenin's theories of nationality, language-culture autonomy, and the supra-national nature of the USSR itself. These ideas, which were written into the Constitution of the USSR, stated that language-cultures must be able to pursue culture and education in their own tongues. There was much debate over the interpretation and implementation of this policy in the history of education in the USSR. In Stalin's time many national minorities were subjected to a brutal policy of forced Russification. This took several forms. The least subtle method was by ethnic dilution. Native speakers were moved elsewhere, and Russians were moved in – for example in the Baltic states (Estonia, Latvia, Lithuania – though here the situation is now reversed, with ethnic Russians required to acculturate to the local national language). Russian schools were provided for the new resident Russian minorities. The superior employment opportunities for proficient Russian speakers then attracted non-Russian speakers to the Russian-language schools, in which there were often as many Russian as non-Russian children. People who had been moved outside their ethnic homeland would send their children to Russian-language schools rather than to a school using the local language. In an era of militant official anti-nationalism, it was easy to label ethnic spirit as "bourgeois nationalism" or "national provincialism", while Russian was associated with the supra-national spirit, especially in its role of the language for popularizing Communism:

> Though theoretically elective, Russian is widely studied in all types of schools as a required second native tongue and as a language of international communication and "socialist culture".   (Kreusler, 1963: 75)

This notion was explicitly pursued in the journal *Russkij jazyk v nacional'noj škole* ('Russian in the Ethnic School'), which discusses and proposes policy, materials and methods for the teaching of Russian in non-Russian schools. The promotion of Russian abroad is also the responsibility of the Pushkin Institute in Moscow, which functions like the Alliance Française or the Goethe Institut.

Within the Soviet Union, Russian was an indispensable language for universal communication. Geographical mobility inside the USSR required a knowledge of Russian. Publication in intellectual fields was principally in Russian, and writers or scholars anxious for general recognition tended to write in Russian. Russian was consequently the dominant language of publishing, for national reasons as well as by virtue of being the most populous single language in the Soviet Union. Ukrainian and Belarusian received less publishing space than was warranted by their population status within the USSR, and many smaller languages fared much worse.

11.6   The Slavic languages abroad

(In this section we do not provide indications for stress, length or tone in migrant Slavic data, since reports of most of the data do not include this information, which is among the most error-prone areas of émigré Slavic.)

The Slavs do not rank with the world's great navigating nations. Unlike the far-ranging Dutch, Portuguese, Spanish, French and, especially, British, the Slavs were not responsible for global exploration by sea. Indeed, by the time the Russian merchant marine and navy were properly organized by Peter the Great – no other Slavic nation has had serious maritime pretensions – the imperial seaborne land-grab was virtually over. The Slavs, it is true, did make important expansions by land – like Bulgaria, Bohemia and Poland-Lithuania, in their respective periods of glory, and Russia in its long maintained push toward the Pacific. With the exception of the Russian imperialist expansion to the east, however, these movements had no major lasting linguistic effects on the conquered territories. This means that, apart from the case of Russian in Imperial Russia and later the USSR, the Slavs have no counterpart to the European languages which were established officially in the colonial and post-colonial empires: Spanish and Portuguese in South America; English and French in Africa, South East Asia and through much of the Pacific; Dutch in South Africa and the Indies; and English in the Americas, Africa, Asia, Australasia and the Pacific. Nevertheless, when we consider the current distribution of the world's languages, we find very substantial numbers of Slavs outside the geographical and ethnic homelands, in North America, Australasia, in other European countries and, to a lesser degree, in South America and Africa. These modern Slavic émigré populations date from the nineteenth century, particularly from its second half, when economic conditions in Eastern Europe and Russia forced the mass migration of Slavs, especially to North America; and from the twentieth century as a result of political pressures.

Economic necessity was one major motive. The other was political necessity. Political exile was nothing new for the Slavs. Scholars like Comenius, or exiles of conscience like Herzen, are a few eloquent examples of people driven abroad by their beliefs. For others the motive was semi-voluntary cultural exile. Many of the best nineteenth-century Polish writers, and many Russians like Turgenev, spent more time in Paris than they did at home. These three forces – money, belief and art – contributed to the systematic and widespread dispersal of the Slavs over Europe and North America and in the latter part of the nineteenth century.

The political and military upheavals of the twentieth century did even more to accelerate the emigration of the Slavs from their homelands. The immediate cause was the First World War and its aftermath in the Russian Civil War. This disaster had a profoundly unsettling effect on the Slavs. Millions perished. After 1918 many Slavs found themselves still homeless in one or more of several categories: political refugees from the Communist Revolution; economic refugees from hardship and homelessness; or ethnic misfits in the redrawn political boundaries of Central Europe, in which millions of Belarusians and Ukrainians, among others, were delivered into "foreign" domination. These factors all promoted a further wave of emigration, which was exacerbated by the Depression. The rise of Nazism and anti-Semitism, and the horrors of the Second World War, repeated the social effects of the First World War in heightened form – this time the West and South Slavs were involved as well, and many left Europe to escape repatriation under the Yalta Agreement. With the end of the Second World War, however, Slavic emigration dwindled. The installation of the new Communist regimes in Eastern Europe and the Balkans was accompanied by rigorous restrictions on personal mobility, particularly in the 1950s. It was difficult to leave the Eastern Bloc countries without exceptional family or other circumstances. Yugoslavia, which remained politically outside the Eastern Bloc, continued to permit migration, especially to North America and Australasia. There were also large numbers of Yugoslav guest workers, especially in West Germany. There was also something of a controlled thaw in the policies governing the emigration of Jewish Slavs over the 1980s. Nevertheless, the non-Yugoslav Slavic émigré communities were being replenished largely from within, and emigration from the ethnic homeland continued to be numerically of small import-ance. The end of Euro-Communism and the opening of the borders of Eastern Europe, however, will substantially remove the category of "political refugee", and will cause major changes in patterns of emigration and remigration to the homeland.

The largest groups of émigré Slavs are found in the U.S.A., which also has the longest history of accepting Slavic migrants. Canada, Britain and France have substantial Slavic minorities, as does Australasia. Greece has a large number of ethnic Macedonians within its borders, while Hungary and Romania have certain admixtures of longer resident Slavs. Smaller Slavic communities are found in other European countries, in South America (mainly Brazil and Argentina) and Africa (mainly South Africa). Hard figures are difficult to come by. The multicultural basis of the Canadian Census of 1971 yielded rich material on the Slavs and other émigré communities. But many countries, including the former German Democratic Republic and Poland, have not given ethnic minorities an appropriate place in their official census figures. There is a wide variation in the methods of census-compilation, the definitions of ethnic identity, and the relation of ethno-centric activities to the overall activity of the community.

In these communities language is a central factor of ethnicity in its social, communicative and differentiating functions. Migrant languages present several perspectives: the language in its own right, or with reference to interaction with the language of the host country and the homeland country, as well as in comparison to other migrant languages. In the total context of émigré language groups, the Slavs overall show a higher-than-average degree of language retention. They have a strong, almost proprietary concern for the preservation of their languages, which reflects the very normative bias of language education in the Slavic countries. Nevertheless, there is considerable interference from host languages, especially English, particularly in the areas of lexis, phonetics and inflexional morphology. Since the fall of Euro-Communism this influence is now paralleled in the Slavic homelands (chapter 9) as Westernization and globalization exert a new influence, especially through the Internet.

Lexical interference is the most obvious, and most far-reaching, area of interference from the host language. Speakers with a native command of the phonology and grammar of their language will still use host-language words, and often with alarming frequency. Interference often begins with new realia: the flora, fauna, weights, mea-sures and customs of the new homeland may have no direct parallels in Slavic, and a neologism or calque is much less readily intelligible than a borrowed word widely known to the local émigré community. But other processes, including the internal degeneration of the émigré Slavic lexical and grammatical systems, means that we have to be more precise about the kinds of interference which we are dealing with.

Haugen (1953) presents a useful classification of lexical interference: transfers, which are direct borrowings; extensions, where the meanings of a word are extended, usually under the influence of the host-country language; loan translations (calques), where individual parts of words or phrases are translated piece-by-piece; and hybrids, involving mixtures of the three methods. To the Haugen classification we must add shifts or code-switching, where whole sequences of one language are imported unchanged into another. Émigré Slavic languages provide an abundance of examples of all these types of interference: the following examples are taken principally from Benson's (1960) data from American Russian, Albijanić's data from Californian Croatian (1982) and Rappaport's (1990) data from American Polish:

(32a)　Transfers
　　　　American-Rus　　*koll-gérl* 'call-girl'
　　　　CS-Rus　　　　　*prostitútka, prixodjáščaja po výzovu*

        American-Rus   *stéjšn végn* 'station wagon'

        CS-Rus   *mnogoméstnyj avtomobíl' furgónnogo típa*

(32b)   Extensions

        rénta: CS-Rus 'annuity, pension'

                American-Rus also 'rent'

(32c)   Loan Translations

        American-Rus   *losjón krasotý* 'beauty lotion'

        CS-Rus   *žídkoe kosmetíčeskoe srédstvo*

        American-Rus   *ogón' tráfika* 'traffic light'

        CS-Rus   *svetofór*

(32d)   Hybrids

        Australian-Rus   *délat' dén'gi* 'to make money'

        CS-Rus   *zarabátyvat' dén'gi*

(32e)   Shifts/code-switching

        American-Serbian/Croatian   *ja sam rabotala ovde for nothing*

                                'I worked here for nothing'

It is not always easy to distinguish borrowing from the host language – here English – from words which are in any case being borrowed into the homeland language. The influence of English on all modern homeland Slavic languages is widespread and growing (Filipović, 1982, 1990), and many words which are being accepted in the homeland are also being borrowed at the same time, but in the different context of an émigré language, by émigré Slavic languages. It is also not easy for émigré communities to distinguish dialectal forms, brought from the homeland, from the forms of the national literary standard. Rappaport's Texas Silesian informants use the dialectal word *rządzić*, which means 'to rule' in standard Polish, to mean 'speaking Silesian dialect'; they use the regular Pol *mówić* 'to speak' in other contexts:

(33)   Texas-Pol   *wy mówicie, a my rządzimy*

                      'you speak (proper) Polish, but we talk Silesian dialect'

Borrowings of novel flora and fauna are less serious than the replacement of viable Slavic words by host-language synonyms. Nouns are the most productive class of lexical interference, probably because they can most easily be assimilated into the native Slavic inflexional paradigms. Non-Slavic adjectives lack the characteristic adjective suffixes like *-n-* and *-sk-*, and are less frequently borrowed, though it is not uncommon to borrow roots and add these suffixes – see below. Non-Slavic verbs, which are inflexionally even less like Slavic verbs, are the least frequent borrowings in the major word-classes. Émigré Slavic languages follow and extend homeland language practices in adapting adjectives (sometimes) and verbs (always) to Slavic word formation and inflexional patterns, resulting in hybrids like Rus *komfortábel'ny* 'comfortable' (also listed in the Ožegov and Oxford dictionaries) or *drájvovat'* 'to drive'. Alternatively, again as in the homeland language, the borrowed word may simply be treated as non-inflecting, which is syntactically feasible for nouns and adjectives (Albijanić 1982; Jutronić-Tihomirović 1985), but impossible for verbs.

This external incursion into lexical systems is paralleled by internal decline. Alternative words representing individual concepts tend to be progressively reduced in the direction of a single base unit or form. Rappaport's (1990) Texas Silesian Poles of Panna Maria have blurred the distinction between Pol *chodzić* 'to go [Habitual, Iterative]' and Pol *iść* 'to go [Punctual]', so that they say (34a) rather than (34b):

(34a) American-Pol *dzieci szły do szkoły*
'the children went [daily] to school'

(34b) CS-Pol *dzieci chodziły do szkoły*
'the children went [daily] to school'

There is also a reduction in alternative forms of individual words. This is why the array of diminutive forms in Slavic nouns (8.2.2) can reduce to one or a few forms, a base form and one or two diminutives. It is not uncommon for émigré Slavs, especially from the second generation, to believe that the diminutive form is indeed the base form, since the diminutive is the form which they will hear most often – sometimes to the exclusion of the non-diminutive root. Second-generation Polish teenagers use words like CS-Pol *piesek* 'dog, doggie' in otherwise formal contexts. In addition to this de-structuring, émigré languages tend to lose their inherent lexical creativity. The corresponding patterns and conventions in the host language and the homeland language are unacceptable for ethnic and ideological reasons, respectively, and forces of émigré conservatism can often lead to an emphasis on pre-migration models which are unable to match the vitality required by poetry or, for that matter, the expressive requirements of dynamic prestige teenage registers like that of young America.

Parallel to the decline in variety of roots and word-structures is a decline in the range and use of inflexional morphology, as a result of contact with languages like English which possess a less elaborate inflexional system. Marginal case forms, complex verb paradigms and low-frequency irregular forms are among the first to disappear from use. Among the forms which do survive, there tends to be a confusion or levelling of distinctions between inflexional paradigms: for instance, the genitive singular in *-u* or *-a* of masculine nouns is commonly misused (5.5.1). And distinctions of gender, particularly secondary gender, can collapse into a single undifferentiated category, as when masculine personal forms in the plurals of nouns, adjectives and determiners are swallowed up in a single plural inflexion. A substantial study of case-loss has been carried out by Ďurovič (1983) and his colleagues at Lund University (*Language in diaspora*). They have found that the pattern of case-loss is consistent with the analysis of Jakobson in his 1936 studies of case-markedness. The Russian second genitive and second locative, together with the instrumental, are the cases most at risk. In other émigré Slavic languages there are also examples of interference in preposition and case usage, notably from English. Benson (1960) notes American-Rus *na rádio* 'on the radio' instead of CS-Rus *po rádio*, and American-Rus *po televízion* 'on television' instead of CS-Rus *po televídeniju*. Meyerstein (1969) has even more far-reaching data from American Slovak. Here not only are the prepositions becoming confused, but the cases which they govern are undergoing wholesale reduction, sometimes to the point of there being only a nominative and a non-nominative case left, and their usage may correspond not at all to the conventions of the standard language. Henzl (1982) reports a parallel phenomenon from Czech, where some speakers have collapsed all cases into the nominative:

(35a)   'the girl has a little dog'

	CS-Cz	*slečna*	*má*	*psíčka/pejsečka*
		girl-Nom	have-3Sg	dog-Dim-Acc = Gen
				(alternative diminutives)

(35b)   American-Cz   *slečna má pejseček* [Acc = Nom]

She also suggests that it is possible to use inflexional morphology as a direct metric for estimating the degree of language loss.

Typologically speaking, a decline in a language's case-system will tend to be accompanied either by the development of particles to mark grammatical relations, or by a growing rigidity of word order, which then becomes one of the principal means of marking subjects and objects. This is what happens in émigré Slavic in contact with English. The OVS order (7.4.3), which is so expressive and common in homeland Slavic, becomes progressively rarer in second- and third-generation émigré Slavic speakers exposed to a SVO language like English. So, too, do expressive inversions of modifiers and heads (7.4), or the separation of modifiers and heads, and the topicalization of modifiers for emphasis:

(36)   Rus   *krasívuju*   *tý*   *sebé*   *našël*
              beautiful-FemAccSg you   self-Dat   found-MascSgPast
              dévušku!
              girl-FemAccSg
              'you have found yourself a beautiful girl!'

Subordinate clauses decay before coordinate ones, and speakers unsure of their linguistic control will rephrase sentences as sequences of 'and' clauses rather than risk subordinate structures. Overall, there is a trend from synthetic case-structures toward analytic uses of prepositions in the syntactic structure of the sentence.

Among the most obvious features of émigré Slavic languages is their phonetic decline. It is here that we find direct evidence of influence and interference from the host language. The articulatory settings of the host language are copied into the Slavic languages: even the trilled [r] can be replaced by an English-like [ɹ] within five years of arrival in English-speaking countries; dentals become alveolars, and unaspirated initial stops are aspirated:

(37)   CS-Rus *tam* 'there' [tam]; Australian-Rus [tʰam]

In addition, articulatory distinctions which are a proper part of the Slavic languages start to degrade. Palatal consonant series are particularly open to degradation, like the [č] ~ [ć] (post-alveolar ~ alveolo-palatal) contrast of Polish and B/C/S: they normalize on a sound close to the English [č], thereby obliterating an underlying phonemic contrast in the standard languages. Stress and tone also suffer radically, and in poor speakers can be virtually ignored, or treated randomly.

First-generation speakers, however, are still sufficiently in control of the native phonology for them to resist pure lexical shifts, in Haugen's sense (above), and to Slavicize borrowed words from the host language. So *freeway* is pronounced ['frivej], and *whale boat* ['vɛlbɔt]. However, when words are adopted and adapted into émigré Slavic languages, their pronunciation is unstable, varying from host language-like approximations, to spelling pronunciations seen from the point of view of Slavic orthoepy, to phonetic adaptations. Over time, and with declining linguistic competence, the kinds of phonetic patterns found in these imported words begin to appear in the native Slavic lexis. Within three generations, according to Saint-Jacques (1979), there may be little left of the émigré language other than some ceremonial phrases for feasts like Easter and Christmas.

Before the fall of Euro-Communism in 1989 the diasporic Slavic communities were in an ambivalent position. From one point of view they were involuntary émigrés, in the sense that those who wanted to return would have found it difficult, and potentially dangerous, to re-establish a lifestyle in the homeland. The community organizations – church, political groups, media and especially newspapers, ethnic schools, social clubs and other organizations – projected and protected the ethos of a culture in exile, one which stood for the true continuation of the values (cultural, linguistic and other) which had allegedly been traduced by the advent of Communism. This was particularly true for Russians, Ukrainians and Belarusians who had left the homeland or failed to return after the Russian

Revolution; or for other Slavs who had left or not returned after the Yalta Agreement at the end of the Second World War. Many of these émigré Slavs were strongly anti-Communist and conservative, and they resisted the kinds of changes which were taking place in the homeland. There was strong pressure in favor of endogamy, and the larger communities provided a wide range of social structures which could effectively support existing and new émigrés throughout a lifetime of work, worship and leisure. Language and its maintenance was central to this system of values, and tended to resist change. Older Russian émigrés, for instance, preserved the use of the letter *jat'* (appendix B) decades after it had been very properly removed from use in the Soviet Union. And the notion of cultural integrity was valued, so that the use of Anglicisms in English-country Slavic communities, for instance, was widely criticized. In this context the maintenance of core values of language and culture (Smolicz, 1979) ranked high in the life of the community.

After 1989, however, this legitimacy no longer held. The removal of the Communist regimes, and their political and military threat to the West, meant that many émigré Slavs could now return to the homeland. Many did in increasing numbers over the following decade – some to take up senior political, management and other leadership roles. These returning Slavs included many who had grown up in émigré communities. In addition, homeland Slavs were now equally able to travel abroad and, in some cases, to emigrate. In one sense this two-way traffic has weakened the *raison d'être* of the émigré communities, which are no longer insulated by their claim to be the exclusive true inheritors of homeland values. On the other hand, the influx of new speakers has enriched and re-charged the linguistic and cultural life of the communities. And unrestricted two-way communications, and access to cable and satellite television, have made possible not only the globalization of the lives of the homeland Slavs, but also the updating of the lives of Slavs in what is no longer a diaspora in exile.

This reunification – the word is apposite not only of Germany – of the Slavic communities has had a further important consequence for the maintenance of languages outside the homeland, and one which is most strongly evident in Slav communities in the English-speaking countries. The homeland languages, as a result of globalization and the radical de-Communization of public language, have become more Western and, in particular, more like English. It is difficult for émigrés to keep pace with the changes in the homeland language, changes for which there are now only aesthetic, rather than ideological, objections. As a result, the émigré Slavic communities are having to re-invent their sense of identity, and to refocus their orientation to the homeland.

In the midst of this change, however, the Slavs' allegiance to their languages is not at risk. The Slavs remain one of the modern world's biggest ethnic groups of émigrés. They have also, as a result of their history, come to associate language very closely with ethnic identity and self-respect. Slavic parents abroad have consecrated an enormous amount of effort to continuing their language traditions, as the dearest and the closest part of the heritage which they can pass on to their children. The millions of émigré Slavs who continue to preserve their language – perhaps not wholly pure or intact, but preserved – would approve of a remark of Samuel Johnson:

> I am always sorry when any language is lost, because languages are the pedigrees of nations.   (Boswell's *Life of Johnson*, 1776)

APPENDIX A: ABBREVIATIONS

A.1   Language names

B/C/S	Bosnian/Croatian/Serbian (see 0.3)
Bel	Belarusian
Boh	Bohemia(n) (Cz)
Bos	Bosnian
Čak	Čakavian (B/C/S)
Cen	Central (C in figure 10.1)
ChSl	Church Slavonic
Cr	Croatian
CS	Contemporary Standard
Cz	Czech
Dol	Dolenjsko (Sln)
E	East
Ek	Ekavian (B/C/S)
Eng	English
ESl	East Slavic
Fr	French
Ger	German
Gk	Greek
Gor	Gorenjsko (Sln)
Han	Hanák (Cz)
Herc	Hercegovina (-ian) (B/C/S)
Ik	Ikavian (B/C/S)
Jek	Jekavian (B/C/S)
Kajk	Kajkavian (B/C/S)
Kash	Kashubia(n) (Pol)
Koroš	Koroško (Sln)
Kos-Res	Kosovo-Resava (B/C/S)
Lach	Lach(ian) (Cz)
Lat	Latin

Lith	Lithuanian
LS	Lower Sorbian (in tables)
LSorb	Lower Sorbian
Mac	Macedonian
Mał	Małopolska (Pol)
Maz	Mazovia(n) (Pol)
Mor	Moravia(n) (Cz)
N	North
Notr	Notranjsko (Sln)
O	Old (in combination with names of languages)
OCS	Old Church Slavonic
Pan	Panonsko (Sln)
PIE	Proto-Indo-European
Pol	Polish
Polab	Polabian
Prim	Primorsko (Sln)
PSl	Proto-Slavic
Rovt	Rovtarsko (Sln)
Rus	Russian
S	South
Sb	Sorbian (dialects in Ch. 10)
Serb	Serbian
Sil	Silesia(n) (Pol)
Slk	Slovak
Sln	Slovenian
Sorb	Sorbian
SSl	South Slavic
Štaj	Štajersko (Sln)
Štok	Štokavian (B/C/S)
Šum-V	Šumadija-Vojvodina (B/C/S)
Trans	Transitional (dialect)
Ukr	Ukrainian
US	Upper Sorbian (in tables)
USorb	Upper Sorbian
W	West
Wielk	Wielkopolska(n) (Pol)
WSl	West Slavic

A.2   Linguistic terms

Act	active
Adj	adjective

Adv	adverb
Aff	affix, affective
Aor	aorist
Aug	augmentative
Aux	auxiliary
B	back (vowel)
C	consonant
Cl	clitic
Coll	collective
Colloq	colloquial
Compar	comparative
Cond	conditional
Conj	conjunction
Dat	dative
Def	definite
Dem	demonstrative
Dent	dental
Det	determinate
Dial	dialectal
Dim	diminutive
Dir	direct
Du	dual
Encl	enclitic
F	front (vowel)
Fem	feminine
Fut	future
Gen	genitive
Ger	gerund
Imper	imperative
Imperf	imperfect
Impers	impersonal
Imprfv	imperfective
Inan	inanimate
Indef	indefinite
Indet	indeterminate
Indir	indirect
Inf	infinitive
Instr	instrumental
Intrans	intransitive
Inv	invariant
Lab	labial
Loc	locative

Masc	masculine
N	nasal (vowel)
Neg	negative
Neut	neuter
Nom	nominative
O, Obj	object
Obl	oblique
Pal	palatal
Part	participle
Pass	passive
Pej	pejorative
Perf	perfect
Pers	person, personal
Pl	plural
Poss	possessive
PPP	past passive participle
Pred	predicate
Pref	prefix
Prep	preposition
Prepnl	prepositional
Prfv	perfective
Pro	pronominal
Procl	proclitic
Pron	pronoun
PV1	First Palatalization of Velars
PV2	Second Palatalization of Velars
PV3	Third Palatalization of Velars
Q	question
Refl	reflexive
Rel	relative
S	subject
Sg	singular
Sup	supine
Trans	transitive
V	verb; vowel
Vel	velar
Voc	vocative

APPENDIX B: ORTHOGRAPHY
AND TRANSLITERATION

B.1 **Diacritics and symbols**

B.1.1 Diacritics

Note

1. Where orthographic use is noted ('orth.'), details may be found in section II).
2. 'Spec. orth.' means orthographic only in special contexts, mainly lexicographic and pedagogical.
3. 'Translit.' means transliteration from Cyrillic.

'(vertical prime)
    phonetic (before a syllable):   primary stress in IPA, or abnormal stress in fixed-stress languages

,(subscript prime)
    phonetic (before a syllable):   secondary stress in IPA or in fixed-stress languages

'(italic prime)
    phonemic (after a consonant)   palatalized consonant (see B.2 below)
    translit. (after a consonant):   Cyrillic ь ("soft sign")
"(double italic prime)
    translit. (after a consonant):   Russian Cyrillic ъ ("hard sign")
'(acute)
    orth. (over a consonant):   (alveolo-)palatal: Pol, Sorb *ś ź ć ń*, Mac *ǵ ǵ*
    orth. (over a vowel):   quality: Pol *ó* = [u], Sorb *ó* = ['uɔ] or [o]
    orth. (over a vowel):   long vowel in Czech and Slovak
    phonemic (over a vowel):   Proto-Slavic rising (acute) pitch
    spec. orth. (over a vowel):   long rising tone in B/C/S; in Slovenian either the same or (in the non-tonal variant) high quality of long /e/ and /o/; stress in East Slavic and Bulgarian

'(apostrophe)
    orth. (after *t, d, l*):   palatal: Cz, Slk *t'* = [c], *d'* = [ɟ], *l'* = [ʎ]

phonemic (after a consonant): `(grave)	palatal consonant, e.g. /k'/
spec. orth. (over a vowel):	short rising tone in B/C/S; short falling tone or short vowel in Slovenian
translit. (over *e*): ˝(double grave)	*è* in Russian and Belarusian = Cyrillic э
spec. orth. (over a vowel): ^(circumflex)	short falling tone in B/C/S
orth. (over *o*): ˇ(caron)	Slk *ô* = diphthong [u̯ɔ]
orth. (over *e*):	Cz, PSl *ě* = /j + e/ or /e/ with palatalization of the preceding consonant
orth. (over a consonant):	Czech, Slovak, B/C/S, Slovenian palatal (post-alveolar) consonant, e.g. *č š ž ň*
˘(breve) phonemic (over a vowel):	short vowel in Indo-European and Proto-Slavic
translit. (over a vowel):	Blg *ă* = Cyrillic ъ, phonetic schwa [ə] Bel *ŭ* = Cyrillic ў, phonemic /w/ or u̯/ ([w])
̑(inverted breve) phonemic (over a vowel):	Proto-Slavic non-rising (circumflex) pitch
spec. orth. (over a vowel):	long falling tone in B/C/S; in Slovenian either the same or (in the non-tonal variant) low quality of long /e/ and /o/
̯(subscript inverted breve) phonemic/phonetic (under *i, u*):	semivowel or glide (/i̯, u̯/)
˙(dot) orth. (over *z*):	Pol *ż* = /ž/ ([ʒ])
¨(diaeresis) orth. (over *a*):	Slk *ä* = [æ]
orth. (over *e*):	Bel *ë* = /jo/ or 'soft consonant + /o/'
spec. orth. (over *e*):	Rus *ë* = /jo/ or 'soft consonant + /o/'
˛(hook, ogonek) orth. (under *a, e*):	Pol *ę ą* = nasal vowels
phonemic (under *e, o*):	PSl *ę ǫ* = nasal vowels
¯(macron) phonemic (over a vowel):	long vowel in Indo-European and Proto-Slavic
spec. orth. (over a vowel):	long post-tonic vowel in B/C/S
°(ring, circle) orth. (over *u*):	Cz *ů* = long [u:]
˳(subscript ring, circle) phonemic (under a consonant):	vocalic (syllabic) consonant, e.g. /r̥, l̥/

phonetic (under a consonant):   voiceless consonant, e.g. [r̥, l̥]
(subscript vertical line)
    phonetic (under a consonant):   vocalic (syllabic) consonant, e.g. [r̩, l̩]

superscript letters:

w phonemic/phonetic (after a consonant):   labialized consonant, e.g. k^w
h phonemic/phonetic (after a consonant):   aspirated consonant, e.g. k^h
j   phonemic/phonetic (after a consonant):   palatalized consonant, e.g. t^j
ɣ phonemic/phonetic (after a consonant):   velarized consonant, e.g. $l^ɣ$

B.1.2   Symbols

\# in examples: word boundary
-   in examples: word-internal morpheme separator for word-structure
                and glosses
— in examples: orthographical hyphen in morpheme-separated examples

B.2   Orthographical systems

B.2.1   Old Church Slavonic (table B.1)

The order of letters is by the transliterated form (col. 1) of the most commonly accepted alphabetical order, based on the numerical value of the letters, as well as the standard order in the modern Cyrillic alphabets (col. 1a). (The use of letters for numbers followed the Ancient and Medieval Greek principle, and also the Greek values up to *omega*, after which there is some uncertainty about the values of certain letters (Col. 1b).) The Glagolitic forms are given in col. 2 (both older, round, and later, Croatian "square" shapes), and col. 2a gives the numerical values, which were allotted to all letters in distinction from the Cyrillic values. Col. 3 gives the formal reflexes of the letters in the modern Cyrillic languages (as marked: no comment means that all languages have this shape and value, a dash means none have it).

B.2.2   Modern languages (tables B.2–B.12)

The order of letters is by the alphabetical order of each language. In non-Cyrillic languages diacritic forms and digraphs which represent separate phonemes but are *not* lexicographically distinguished are indented and marked as follows:

    1.   = may be initial (thus have a capital form) and are ordered separately within a lexicographic entry (this type is rare, since a capital normally implies a separate letter section);

B.1. *Old Church Slavonic*

1 Translit.	1a Cyrillic	1b Numerical	2 Glagolitic	2a Numerical	3 Modern
a	Ⰰ	1	✝ / ⰰ	1	a
b	Ⰱ	–	Ⰱ / Ⰱ	2	б
v	Ⰲ	2	Ⰲ / Ⰲ	3	в
g	Ⰳ	3	Ⰳ / Ⰳ	4	г
d	Ⰴ	4	Ⰴ / Ⰴ	5	д
e	Ⰵ	5	Ⰵ / Ⰵ	6	e
ž	Ⰶ	–	Ⰶ / Ⰶ	7	ж
dz	Ⰷ	6	Ⰷ / Ⰷ	8	Mac s
z	Ⰸ	7	Ⰸ / Ⰸ	9	з
i	Ⰻ	8	Ⰹ / Ⰹ	20	и
i	Ï, I	10	Ⰺ, Ⰹ / Ⰹ, Ⰹ	10	Bel, Ukr i
					pre–1918 Rus i
g'/j	Ꙉ	–	Ꙉ / Ꙉ	30	Serb ħ (and ђ)
k	Ⰽ	20	Ⰽ / Ⰽ	40	к
l	Ⰾ	30	Ⰾ / Ⰾ	50	л
m	Ⰿ	40	Ⰿ / Ⰿ	60	м
n	Ⱀ	50	Ⱀ / Ⱀ	70	н
o	Ⱁ	70	Ⱁ / Ⱁ	80	о
p	Ⱂ	80	Ⱂ / Ⱂ	90	п
r	Ⱃ	100	Ⱃ / Ⱃ	100	р
s	Ⱄ	200	Ⱄ / Ⱄ	200	с
t	Ⱅ	300	Ⱅ / Ⱅ	300	т
u	ОⓊ, Ⱆ	400	Ⱆ / Ⱆ	400	у
f	Ⰱ	500	Ⱇ, φ / φ	500	ф
x	Ⱈ	600	Ⱈ / Ⱈ	600	х
o	Ⱉ	800	Ⱉ / Ⱉ	700	–
c	Ⱌ	900	Ⱍ / Ⱍ	900	ц
č	Ⱍ	90	Ⱍ / Ⱍ	1000	ч
š	Ⱎ	–	Ⱎ / Ⱎ	800	ш
št	Ⱋ	–	Ⱋ / Ⱋ	–	Blg, Rus щ
ŭ(/ə (ъ))	Ⱏ	–	Ⱏ / Ⱏ	–	Blg, Rus ъ
y	Ⱏⰺ	–	Ⱏⰻ	–	Bel, Rus ы
ĭ(ь)	Ⱐ	–	Ⱐ / Ⱐ	–	Blg, ESl ь
ě (ä)	Ⱑ	–	Ⱑ / Ⱑ	–	pre–1918 Rus ѣ
					pre–1945 Blg ѣ
ju	Ю	–	Ⱓ / Ⱓ	–	ю
ja	Ꙗ	–	–	–	я
je	Ⰵ	–	–	–	Ukr є
ę	Ⱔ	900	Ⱔ	–	–
ę/ję	Ⱗ	–	Ⱗ	–	–
ǫ	Ⱘ	–	Ⱘ	–	pre–1945 Blg Ⱘ
jǫ	Ⱙ	–	Ⱙ	–	–
ks	Ѯ	60	–	–	–
ps	Ѱ	700	–	–	–
f	Ѳ, Ѳ	9	Ⱚ / Ⱚ	–	pre–1918 Rus ѳ
i/v	Ѵ, Ѵ	400	Ⰻ / Ⰻ	–	pre–1918 Rus v

2.   = may be initial (hence with capital), but are *not* ordered separately;
3.   = may not be initial, but are ordered separately;
4.   = may not be initial and are not ordered separately.

For Cyrillic languages, the order is by transliterated forms in Cyrillic order, with Cyrillic shown in col. 2.

For the phonemic "realizations" of the letters, refer to chapter 3 for the effects, the major ones being:

1.   devoicing of word-final obstruents (all except B/C/S and Ukrainian);
2.   neutralization of voice in obstruent clusters (all languages, at least to some extent);
3.   assimilation of place or mode of consonant articulation in clusters (all languages, at least to some extent);
4.   vowel quality changes related to stress position (especially Russian and Belarusian, also Bulgarian and Slovenian; orthographically reflected only in Belarusian).

Where the basic phonemic transcription differs from the graph, it is shown in slashes.

B.2. *Bulgarian*

Translit.	Cyrillic	Translit.	Cyrillic
a	А а	p	П п
b	Б б	r	Р р
v	В в	s	С с
g	Г г	t	Т т
d	Д д	u	У у
dž (2)	Дж дж	f	Ф ф
e	Е е	x	Х х
ž	Ж ж	c	Ц ц
z	З з	č	Ч ч
i	И и	š	Ш ш
j	Й й	št	Щ щ
k	К к	ă	Ъ ъ
l	Л л	' (3)	ь
m	М м	ju	Ю ю
n	Н н	ja	Я я
o	О о		

B.3. *Macedonian*

Translit.	Cyrillic	Translit.	Cyrillic
a	А а	n	Н н
b	Б б	nj	Њ њ
v	В в	o	О о
g	Г г	p	П п
d	Д д	r	Р р
ǵ	Ѓ ѓ	s	С с
e	Е е	t	Т т
ž	Ж ж	ḱ	Ќ ќ
z	З з	u	У у
dz	Ѕ ѕ	f	Ф ф
i	И и	x (h)	Х х
j	Ј ј	c	Ц ц
k	К к	č	Ч ч
l	Л л	dž	Џ џ
lj	Љ љ	š	Ш ш
m	М м	'	'

B.4. *B/C/S*

(Order is of the Roman (Croatian) alphabet; Cyrillic order matches others, especially Macedonian)

Roman	Cyrillic	Roman	Cyrillic
a A	А а	l L	Л л
b B	Б б	lj Lj	Љ љ
c C	Ц ц	m M	М м
č Č	Ч ч	n N	Н н
ć Ć	Ћ ћ	nj Nj	Њ њ
d D	Д д	o O	О о
dž Dž	Џ џ	p P	П п
dj Dj (đ Đ)	Ђ ђ	r R	Р р
e E	Е е	s S	С с
f F	Ф ф	š Š	Ш ш
g G	Г г	t T	Т т
h H	Х х /x/	u U	У у
i I	И и	v V	В в
j J	Ј ј	z Z	З з
k K	К к	ž Ž	Ж ж

B.5. *Slovenian*

a A	lj Lj
b B	m M
c C	n N
č Č	nj Nj
d D	o O
dž Dž	p P
e E	r R
f F	s S
g G	š Š
h H /x/	t T
i I	u U
j J	v V
k K	z Z
l L	ž Ž

B.6. *Russian*

Translit.	Cyrillic	Translit.	Cyrillic
a	А а	r	Р р
b	Б б	s	С с
v	В в	t	Т т
g	Г г	u	У у
d	Д д	f	Ф ф
e	Е е	x	Х х
ë (2)	Ё ë /o/	c	Ц ц
ž	Ж ж	č	Ч ч
z	З з	š	Ш ш
i	И и	šč	Щ щ
j	Й й	″(3)	ъ
k	К к	y	Ы ы
l	Л л	′(3)	ь
m	М м	è	Э э
n	Н н	ju	Ю ю
o	О о	ja	Я я
p	П п		

B.7. *Ukrainian*

Translit.	Cyrillic	Translit.	Cyrillic
a	A a	m	М м
b	Б б	n	Н н
v	В в	o	О о
h	Г г	p	П п
(g	Ґ г)	r	Р р
d	Д д	s	С с
dz (2)	Дз дз	t	Т т
dž (2)	Дж дж	u	У у
e	Е е	f	Ф ф
je	Є є	x	Х х
ž	Ж ж	c	Ц ц
z	З з	č	Ч ч
y	И и	š	Ш ш
i	I i	šč	Щ щ
ji	Ï ï	ju	Ю ю
j	Й й	ja	Я я
k	К к	'(3)	ь
l	Л л	'(4)	'

B.8. *Belarusian*

Translit.	Cyrillic	Translit.	Cyrillic
a	A a	o	О о
b	Б б	p	П п
v	В в	r	Р р
h	Г г	s	С с
d	Д д	t	Т т
dž (2)	Дж дж	u	У у
dz (2)	Дз дз	ŭ	Ў ў
		f	Ф ф
e	Е е	x	Х х
ë	Ё ё /o/	c	Ц ц
ž	Ж ж	č	Ч ч
z	З з	š	Ш ш
i	I i	y	Ы ы
j	Й й	'(3)	ь
k	К к	'(4)	'
l	Л л	è	Э э
m	М м	ju	Ю ю
n	Н н	ja	Я я

B.9. *Polish*

a A			ł Ł	/w/
ą (3)			m M	
b B			n N	
c C			ń (3)	
ch Ch (2)	/x/		o O	
cz Cz (2)	/č/		ó (3)	/u/
ć Ć			p P	
d D			r R	
dz, Dz (2)			rz Rz (2)	/ž/
dź Dź (1)			s S	
dż Dż (1)	/dž/		sz Sz (2)	/š/
e E			ś Ś	
ę (3)			t T	
f F			u U	
g G			w W	/v/
(h H)	/x/		y Y	
i I			z Z	
j J			ź Ź	
k K			ż Ż	/ž/
l L				

B.10. *Sorbian*

a A			o O	
b B			ó (4) (not LSorb)	/uo/
c C			p P	
č Č			r R	
d D			ř (3) (not LSorb)	/ś/
dź Dź			LSorb: ŕ (4)	/r'/
e E			s S	
ě (3)	/ie/		š Š	
f F			LSorb: ś Ś	
g G			t T	
h H			ć Ć	
ch Ch (not LSorb)	/x/		u U	
i I			w W	
j J			y (4)	
k K			z Z	
ł Ł	/w/		ž Ž	
l L			LSorb: ź Ź	
m M				
n N				
ń (4)				

B.11. *Czech*

a A		i I		s S	
á Á (2)		í (4)	/ī/	š Š	
b B		j J		t T	
c C		k K		t' Ť (2)	
č Č		l L		u U	
d D		m M		ů (4)	/ū/
d' Ď (2)		n N		ú Ú (2)	/ū/
e E		ň (4)		v V	
é É (2)	/ē/	o O		(w W)	
ě (4)		ó Ó (2)	/ō/	(x X)	
f F		p P		y Y	/i/
g G		(q Q)		ý (4)	/ī/
h H		r R		z Z	
ch Ch	/x/	ř Ř		ž Ž	

B.12. *Slovak*

a A		i I		r R	
á Á (2)	/ā/	í Í (2)	/ī/	r (4)	/r̩/
ä (3)		j J		ŕ (4)	/r̩̄/
b B		k K		s S	
c C		l L		š Š	
č Č		l (4)	/l̩/	t T	
d D		lĹ (2)		t' Ť (2)	
d' Ď(2)		ĺ (4)	/l̩̄/	u U	
dz (4)		m M		ú Ú (2)	/ū/
dž Dž (2)		n N		v V	
e E		ň Ň		(w W)	
é É	/ē/	o O		(x X)	
f F		ó Ó	/ō/	y Y	/i/
g G		ô Ô (2)	/uo/	ý (4)	/ī/
h H		p P		z Z	
ch Ch	/x/	(q Q)		ž Ž	

APPENDIX C: SLAVIC LINGUISTICS: RESOURCES

C.1 Overview

The literature on Slavic linguistics is very large (see *Introduction*), and covers around 25 percent of the world's linguistics output. The most up-to-date bibliographical information available is held on Internet- or CD-ROM-based databases like *LLBA* (*Linguistics and language behavior abstracts*), *MLA* (*Modern Language Association of America*), *ERIC*, or ISI's *Current contents connect* and *Arts and humanities citation index*. Printed bibliographies like *New contents slavistics* and *Bibliographie linguistique de l'année*, and the commented overview *The year's work in modern language studies*, provide annual listings of the year's research, although they can appear with a delay of about two years. Annual bibliographies of the year's work on individual languages are usually published by the official national language journal (see below).

Slavic language and linguistic studies are published in four main sources: journals; proceedings of conferences; monographs; and increasingly on the Internet.

C.2 Journals

The journals fall into two main classes: journals concerned with a single language, usually published in the country of the language, often by the language institute of the country's Academy of Sciences; and general Slavic journals. Authoritative national language journals of each Slavic language include:

Belarusian	*Belaruskaja linhvistyka*
Bulgarian	*Bălgarski ezik*
Croatian	*Jezik*
Czech	*Naše Řeč*
Macedonian	*Makedonski jazik*
Polish	*Język polski*
Russian	*Rusistika segodnja*
Serbian	*Zbornik Matice srbske za filologiju i lingvistiku, Naš jezik*
Slovak	*Slovenská reč*
Slovene	*Slovenski jezik*

| Sorbian | *Lĕtopis* |
| Ukrainian | *Movoznavstvo* |

Journals concerned especially with Russian are also published in a number of non-Russian countries: e.g. *Język rosyjski, La revue russe, Ruský jazyk, Russisch, Russian Language Journal* and *Russian Linguistics*. Slavic linguistic research – as opposed to single-language research – is published in a wide variety of worldwide Slavistics journals, and journals of linguistics published in the Slavic homelands. A guide to journals and other resources on Slavic languages and linguistics can be found at: http://www.bl.uk/collections/wider/subguides/slavguide.html.

C.3   Conferences

Important events are the (usually annual) conferences of national associations for Slavic studies, and especially the five-yearly International Congress of Slavists, whose papers are published by the Slavists' association of each participating country. These papers often give the clearest overview of the current state of Slavic linguistics. More targeted conferences include the meetings of FASL (Formal Approaches to Slavic Linguistics). Conference announcements are regularly made via national Slavists' associations and through the Internet. Professional associations like AATSEEL (American Association of Teachers of Slavic and East European Languages) and BASEES (British Association for Slavonic and East European Studies) and many other national associations are a vital part of the network of Slavic linguistics.

C.4   Monographs

The leading non-Slavic-country-based monograph publisher is Slavica Publishers (http://slavica.com/). Publishing houses in the Slavic countries are increasingly publishing materials in English (also French and German), sometimes in parallel to homeland languages. Major library holdings in Slavic allow convenient bibliographic searching, for instance:

British Library	http://blpc.bl.uk
Library of Congress	http://www.loc.org
Harvard University	http://lib.harvard.edu/

University of London, School of Slavonic and East European Studies: http://library.ucl.ac.uk/ALEPH?750643313

Major Slavic homeland libraries, especially in Russia, Poland and the Czech Republic, are coming on-line too, but the digital coverage is still incomplete, though some of the collections, especially that at the Russian State Library in Moscow, are very large.

C.5   **Electronic networks and resources**

Internet sources and resources for Slavic have grown very rapidly since the widespread introduction of electronic communications in the Slav lands. While some private sources are unstable, there are a number of valuable portals. For general Slav material:

British Library: http://www.bl.uk/collections/easteuropean/slavonicindex.html

and for Slavic languages:

http://www.seelrc.org/
http://www.library.uiuc.edu/absees/
http://www.ssees.ac.uk/dirctory.htm

There is also the SEELANGS-L email discussion list:

http://www.linguistlist.org/subscribing/sub-seelangs.html

and more generally the LINGUIST-L list:

http://listserv.ilstu.edu/cgi-bin/wa?SUBED1=linguist-l&A=1

Dictionaries (a small selection, some with translation facilities):

http://www.yourdictionary.com/
http://slovari.net/
http://www.ims.uni-stuttgart.de/euralex/resources/Dictionaries.html

On-line grammars of B/C/S, Czech, Macedonian, Polish and Russian from
   SEELRC:

http://www.seelrc.org/projects/grammars.ptml

On-line newspapers and magazines:

http://www.princeton.edu/~nshapiro/slavicpapers.shtml

The list of language lists: http://www.evertype.com/langlist.html

Internet resources: http://www.bl.uk/collections/easteuropean/slavonicinternet.html

Corpora are developing rapidly, and can be located via the British Library list (above), and via searches on the Internet with the keywords 'language AND corpus AND (Slavic or Slavonic or specific language) AND machine AND online'.   •

Selected journals from major publishing houses in Western Europe and North America are available on-line in major research libraries from consortia like JSTOR ("Journal Storage"), Oxford Journals, Cambridge University Press Online Journals, Kluwer Online, Swetswise, Ingenta Select and others.

BIBLIOGRAPHY

The following bibliography includes the direct references from the text, as well as a representative but also personal selection of items from the bibliography on Slavic languages and linguistics which have influenced our thinking.

Albijanić, A. 1982. 'San Pedro revisited: language maintenance in the San Pedro Yugoslav community'. In Sussex (ed.): 11–22

Albin, A. 1970. 'The creation of the Slaveno-Serbski literary language'. *Slavonic and East European Review* **48**: 483–491

Andrejčin, L. [1942] 1978. *Osnovna bălgarska gramatika*. 2nd edn. Sofia: Nauka i izkustvo

Andrejčin, L., Popov, K. and Stojanov, S. 1977. *Gramatika na bălgarskija ezik*. Sofia: Nauka i izkustvo

Apresjan, Ju. D. 1992. *Lexical semantics: user's guide to contemporary Russian vocabulary*. Ann Arbor, MI: Karoma

Ararx, J. S. 1984. *Slovoobrazovanie i formoobrazovanie suščestvitel'nyx v istorii russkogo jazyka*. Moscow: Nauka

Armstrong, J. A. 1962. *Ideology, politics, and government in the Soviet Union*. New York: Praeger

Aronson, H. I. 1968. *Bulgarian inflexional morphology*. The Hague: Mouton
1985. 'Form, function and the "perfective" in Bulgarian'. In Flier and Timberlake (eds.): 274–285

Arumaa, P. 1964–1976. *Urslavische Grammatik. Einführung in das vergleichende Studium der slavischen Sprachen*. Bd. I: *Einleitung, Lautlehre, Vokalismus*. Bd. 2: *Konsonantismus*. Heidelberg: Carl Winter Verlag

Asher, R. E. (editor-in-chief) 1994. *The encyclopedia of language and linguistics*. Oxford: Pergamon Press

Atlas gwar polskich. 1998–2002. Ed. K. Dejna, Warsaw: Upowszechnianie Nauki

Atlas slovenského jazyka. 1968–1984. Vols. 1–4. Bratislava: SAV

Atlas ukrajins'koji movy. 1984–1988. Akademija nauk Ukrajins'koji RSR, Instytut movoznavstva im. O. O. Potebny, Instytut suspil'nyx nauk. 2 vols. Kiev: Naukova Dumka

Auty, Robert 1953. 'The evolution of literary Slovak'. *Transactions of the Philological Society*. 143–160
1961. 'Dialect, koine and tradition in the formation of literary Slovak'. *Slavonic and East European Review* **39**: 339–345
1963. 'The formation of the Slovene literary language against the background of the Slavonic national revival'. *Slavonic and East European Review* **41**: 391–402
1972. 'Sources and methods of lexical enrichment in the Slavonic language-revivals of the early nineteenth century'. In Worth (ed.). 41–56

1973. 'The role of purism in the development of the Slavonic literary languages'. *Slavonic and East European Review* **51**: 335–343

1977. 'The Russian language'. In Auty and Obolensky (eds.): 1–40

1980. 'Czech'. In Schenker and Stankiewicz (eds.): 163–182

Auty, Robert and Obolensky, Dmitri (eds.) 1977. *The companion to Russian studies. 2: An introduction to Russian language and literature.* Cambridge: Cambridge University Press

Avanesov, R. I. 1964. *Narysy pa belaruskaj dyjalektalohii.* Minsk: Navuka i tèxnika

(ed.) 1964. *Voprosy dialektologii vostočnoslavjanskix jazykov.* Moscow: Nauka

1968. *Russkoe literaturnoe proiznošenie.* Moscow: Prosveščenie

1974. *Russkaja literaturnaja i dialektnaja fonetika.* Moscow: Prosveščenie

Avanesov, R. I. and Bromlej, S. V. (eds.) 1986. *Dialektologičeskij atlas russkogo jazyka.* Moscow: Glav. upr. geodezii i kartografii pri Sovete Ministrov SSSR

Avanesov, R. I. and Kotkov, S. I. (eds.) 1962. *Voprosy obrazovanija vostočno-slavjanskix nacionaľnyx jazykov.* Moscow: AN SSSR

Babby, Leonard H. 1980. *Existential sentences and negation in Russian.* Ann Arbor: Karoma

Babić, S. 1998. *Sročnost u hrvatskome književnome jeziku.* Zagreb: Matica hrvatska

Bahmut, A. J. (ed.) 1977. *Typolohija intonaciji movlennja.* Kiev: Naukova dumka

Bednarczuk, L. 1968–1988. *Języki indoeuropejskie.* Warsaw: PWN

Baláž, G. *et al.* 1989. *Sovremennyj russkij jazyk v sopostavlenii so slovackim. Morfologija.* Bratislava: SPN

Baláž, Peter *et al.* 1976. *Slovak for Slavicists.* Bratislava: SPN

Bălgarska Akademija na Naukite/Bulgarian Academy of Sciences. 1980. *The unity of the Bulgarian language in the past and today.* Sofia: BAN

Balhar, J. and Jančák, P. 1992–. *Český jazykový atlas.* Prague: Academia

Banac, Ivo 1984. 'Main trends in the Croat language question'. In Picchio and Goldblatt (eds.), vol. I: 189–259

Barnet, Vladimir 1985. 'Toward a sociolinguistic interpretation of the origins of the Slavonic literary languages'. In Stone and Worth (eds.): 13–20

Bartoš, J. and Gagnaire, J. 1972. *Grammaire de la langue slovaque.* Paris: Institut d'Etudes Slaves and Bratislava: Matica Slovenská

Barxudarova, E. L. 1999. *Russkij konsonantizm: tipologičeskij i strukturnyj analiz.* Moscow: IMU

Bělič, J., Havránek, B., Jedlička, A. and Trávníček, F. 1961. 'K voprosu ob "obixodnorazgovornom" češskom jazyke i ego otnošenie k literaturnomu češskomu jazyku'. *Voprosy jazykoznanija* **10**(1): 44–51

Bělič, J., Jedlička, A., Jóna, E., Ružička, J., Štolc, J. and Pauliny, E. 1972. *Slovenština.* 4th edn. Prague: SPN

Benacchio, Rosanna 2002. 'Konkurencija vidov, vežlivosť i ètiket v russkom imperative'. *Russian Linguistics* **26**: 149–178

Ben-Iakov, B. 1982. *Slovar' argo GULaga.* Frankfurt am Main: Possev

Bennett, D. 1987. 'Word-order change in progress: the case of Slovenian and Serbo-Croat and its relevance for Germanic'. *Journal of Linguistics* **23**: 269–286

Benson, Morton 1960. 'American Russian speech'. *American Speech* **35**: 163–174

1990a. *Serbo-Croatian English dictionary.* Cambridge: Cambridge University Press

1990b. *English Serbo-Croatian dictionary.* Cambridge: Cambridge University Press

1992. *Dictionary of Russian personal names: with a revised guide to stress and morphology.* Cambridge, New York: Cambridge University Press

1998. *Standard English–SerboCroatian, SerboCroatian–English dictionary: a dictionary of Bosnian, Croatian and Serbian standards.* Cambridge and New York: Cambridge University Press

Bernštejn, S. B. 1961. *Očerk sravnitel'noj grammatiki slavjanskix jazykov*. Moscow: Izd-vo AN
SSSR
1974. *Očerk sravnitel'noj grammatiki slavjanskix jazykov: Čeredovanija: imennye osnovy*.
Moscow: Nauka
(ed.) 1978. *Nacional'noe vozroždenie i formirovanie slavjanskix literaturnyx jazykov*.
Moscow: Nauka
Bethin, C. Y. 1984. 'Local markedness in Russian genitive plurals'. *Lingua* **62**(4): 319–323
1998. *Slavic prosody: language change and phonological theory*. Cambridge, New York:
Cambridge University Press
Bibliographie linguistique de l'année (1939–). Utrecht: Spectrum
Bidwell, Charles E. 1963. *Slavic historical phonology in tabular form*. The Hague: Mouton
1969. *A morpho-syntactic characterization of the modern Slavic languages*. Pittsburgh:
University Center for International Studies, University of Pittsburgh
1970. *The Slavic languages – their external history*. Pittsburgh: University of Pittsburgh
Center for International Studies
Bielec, Dana 1998. *Polish: an essential grammar*. London and New York: Routledge
Bilodid, I. (ed.) 1969a. *Sučasna ukrajins'ka literaturna mova. Vstup, fonetika*. Kiev: Naukova
dumka
(ed.) 1969b. *Sučasna ukrajins'ka literaturna mova. Morfolohija*. Kiev: Naukova dumka
(ed.) 1972. *Sučasna ukrajins'ka literaturna mova. Syntaksys*. Kiev: Naukova dumka
(ed.) 1973a. *Sučasna ukrajins'ka literaturna mova. Leksyka i frazeolohija*. Kiev: Naukova
dumka
(ed.) 1973b. *Sučasna ukrajins'ka literaturna mova. Stylistyka*. Kiev: Naukova dumka
Birnbaum, H., 1966. 'The dialects of Common Slavic'. In H. Birnbaum and J. Puhvel
(eds.), *Ancient Indo-European dialects*. Berkeley, CA: University of California Press,
153–197
[1975] 1979. *Common Slavic. Progress and problems in its reconstruction*. Columbus,
OH: Slavica
1985. 'The Slavonic language community as a genetic and typological class'. In Stone and
Worth (eds.): 21–28
Birnbaum, Henrik and Merrill, Peter T. 1983. *Advances in the reconstruction of Common
Slavic (1971–1982)*. Columbus, OH: Slavica
Biryla, M. V. and Šuba, P. 1985–1986. *Belaruskaja hramatyka. 1. Fanalohija. Arfaèpija.
Marfalohija. Slovaŭtvarènne. Nacisk*. (1985). *2. Sintaksis*. (1986). Minsk: Instytut
movaznaŭstva AN BSSR
Bloomfield, Leonard 1933. *Language*. New York: Holt, Rinehart and Winston
Bogusławski, A. and Karolak, S. 1973. *Gramatyka rosyjska w ujęciu funkcjonalnym*. Warsaw:
Wiedza Powszechna
Brabec, Ivan, Hraste, Mate and Živković, Sreten [1952] 1968. *Gramatika hrvatskosrpskoga
jezika*. 8th edn. Zagreb: Školska knjiga
Bradley, J. F. N. 1971. *Czechoslovakia: a short history*. Edinburgh: Edinburgh University Press
Brang, Peter, Züllig, Monika and Brang, Karin 1981. *Kommentierte Bibliographie zur
slavischen Soziolinguistik*. Berne: Peter Lang Verlag
Bräuer, Herbert 1961–1969. *Slavische Sprachwissenschaft. I: Einleitung, Lautlehre.
II/III: Formenlehre*. Berlin: Walter de Gruyter
Braun, M. 1947. *Grundzüge der slawischen Sprachen*. Göttingen: Bendenhoeck and Ruprecht
Brecht, Richard D. 1985. 'The form and function of aspect in Russian'. In Flier and Brecht
(eds.): 9–34
Brecht, Richard D. and Chvany, Catherine V. (eds.) 1974. *Slavic transformational syntax*.
Ann Arbor: Michigan Slavic Publications

Brecht, Richard D. and Levine, James S. (eds.) 1986. *Case in Slavic*. Columbus, OH: Slavica

Brezinski, Stefan S. 2000. *Bălgarski sintaksis*. 2nd edn. Sofia: UI "Sv. Kliment Oxridski"

Bright, William O. (ed.) 1991. *International encyclopedia of linguistics*. New York: Oxford University Press

Brown, R. and Ford, M. 1961. 'Address in American English'. *Journal of Abnormal and Social Psychology* **62**: 373–385. Reprinted in John Laver and Sandy Hutcheson (eds.) 1972. *Communication in face to face interaction*. Harmondsworth: Penguin: 128–145

Brown, R. and Gilman, A. 1960. 'The pronouns of power and solidarity'. In T. A. Sebeok (ed.), *Style in language*, Cambridge, MA: Technology Press of M.I.T.: 253–276. Reprinted in Giglioli, Pier Paolo (ed.) 1972. *Language and social context*. Harmondsworth: Penguin: 252–282

Browne, E. Wayles. 1974. 'On the problem of enclitic placement in Serbo-Croatian'. In Brecht and Chvany (eds.): 36–52

1993. 'Serbo-Croat'. In Comrie and Corbett (eds.): 306–387

Browne, E. Wayles and Alt, Teresa (n.d.) *A handbook of Bosnian, Serbian and Croatian*. Retrieved (22 August 2004) from: http://www.seelrc.org:8080/grammar/mainframe. jsp?nLanguageID = 1

Browne, E. Wayles and McCawley, James D. 1973. 'Serbo-Croatian accent'. In E. D. Fudge (ed.), *Phonology: selected readings*. Harmondsworth: Penguin: 330–335

Brozović, D. 1970. *Standardni jezik*. Zagreb: Matica hrvatska

1991. 'Serbo-Croatian as a pluricentric language'. In Clyne (ed.): 347–380

Brozović, D. and Ivić, P. 1988. *Jezik srpskohrvatski/hrvatskosrpski, hrvatski ili srpski*. Izvadak iz II izdanija Enciklopedije Jugoslavije. Zagreb: Jugoslavenski leksikografski zavod

Bruchis, M. 1982. *One step back, two steps forward: on the language policy of the Communist Party of the Soviet Union in the national republics*. Boulder, CO: East European Monographs. Distributed by Columbia University Press

Brugmann, Karl 1886–1900. *Grundriß der vergleichenden Grammatik der indogermanischen Sprachen*. 5 vols. Strassburg: K. J. Trübner

Bugarski, Ranko and Hawkesworth, Celia 1992. *Language planning in Yugoslavia*. Columbus, OH: Slavica

Bulaxov (= Bulaxaŭ), M. G., Žovtobrjux, M. A. and Koduxov, V. I. 1987. *Vostočnoslavjanskie jazyki*. Moscow: Prosveščenie

Bushnell, John 1990. *Moscow graffiti. Language and subculture*. London and Boston: Unwin Hyman

Carlton, Terence R. 1990. *Introduction to the phonological history of the Slavic languages*. Columbus, OH: Slavica

Carpovich, Eugene and Carpovich, Vera V. 1976. *Solzhenitsyn's peculiar vocabulary: Russian–English glossary*. Mt Vernon, ME: Technical Dictionaries Company

Čedić, Ibrahim 2001. *Osnovi gramatike bosanskog jezika*. Sarajevo: Institut za jezik

Channon, Robert 1980. 'On PLACE advancements in English and Russian'. In Chvany and Brecht (eds.): 114–137

Chloupek, Jan and Nekvapil, Jiří (eds.) 1987. *Reader in Czech sociolinguistics*. Amsterdam: John Benjamins

Chvany, Catherine V. 1988. 'Distance, deixis and discreteness in Bulgarian and English verb morphology'. In Alexander M. Schenker (ed.) *American Contributions to the Tenth International Congress of Slavists (Sofia)*. *Linguistics*. Columbus, OH: Slavica: 69–90

Chvany, Catherine V. and Brecht, Richard D. (eds.) 1980. *Morphosyntax in Slavic*. Columbus, OH: Slavica

Clyne, Michael G. 1967. *Transference and triggering*. The Hague: Martinus Nijhoff (ed.) 1991. *Pluricentric languages. Differing norms in different nations*. Berlin and New York: Mouton de Gruyter

1991a. 'Introduction'. In Clyne (ed.): 1–9

1991b. 'Epilogue'. In Clyne (ed.): 455–465

Čolakova, K. (ed.) 1977–. *Rečnik na bălgarskija ezik*. Sofia: BAN

Comrie, Bernard 1975. 'Polite plurals and predicate agreement'. *Language* **51**: 406–418

1976. *Aspect: an introduction to the study of verbal aspect and related problems*. Cambridge: Cambridge University Press

1978. 'Genitive-accusatives in Slavic: the rules and their motivation'. *International Review of Slavic Linguistics* **3**: 27–42

1981. *The languages of the Soviet Union*. Cambridge: Cambridge University Press

1985. *Tense*. Cambridge: Cambridge University Press

(ed.) 1987. *The world's major languages*. London and Sydney: Croom Helm

Comrie, Bernard and Corbett, Greville G. (eds.) 1993. *The Slavonic languages*. London: Routledge and Kegan Paul

Comrie, Bernard and Stone, Gerald 1978. *The Russian language since the Revolution*. Oxford: The Clarendon Press

Comrie, Bernard, Stone, Gerald and Polinsky, Maria 1996. *The Russian language in the twentieth century*. Oxford: The Clarendon Press (2nd rev. edn. of Comrie and Stone 1978)

Cooper, Brian 1989. 'Russian underworld slang and its passage into the standard language'. *Australian Slavonic and East European Studies* **3**(2): 61–89

Corbett, Greville G. 1979. *Predicate agreement in Russian*. Birmingham: Dept. of Russian, University of Birmingham

1980. 'Animacy in Russian and other Slavic languages: where syntax and semantics fail to match'. In Chvany and Brecht (eds.): 43–61

1983. *Hierarchies, targets and controllers. Agreement patterns in Slavic*. London and Canberra: Croom Helm

1987. 'Serbo-Croat'. In Comrie (ed.): 391–409

1991. *Gender*. Cambridge: Cambridge University Press

Cubberley, Paul 1982. 'On the "empty" prefixes in Russian'. *Russian Language Journal* **36**, 123–124: 12–30

1987. 'Syllabic [r̩] in the Slavonic languages: a computer-based investigation'. *International Journal of Slavic Linguistics and Poetics* **35/36**: 7–28

1994. *Handbook of Russian affixes*. Columbus, OH: Slavica

2002. *Russian: a linguistic introduction*. Cambridge: Cambridge University Press

Dalewska-Greń, Hanna 1997. *Języki słowiańskie*. Warsaw: PWN

Darnell, R. (ed.) 1971. *Linguistic diversity in Canadian society*. Edmonton and Champaign: Linguistic Research, Inc

de Bray, R. G. A. 1980a. *Guide to the East Slavonic languages*. Columbus, OH: Slavica

1980b. *Guide to the South Slavonic languages*. Columbus, OH: Slavica

1980c. *Guide to the West Slavonic languages*. Columbus, OH: Slavica

Dejna, Karol 1998. *Atlas gwar polskich*. Warsaw: Upowszechnianie Nauki-Oświata "UN-O"

Derbyshire, William W. 1993. *A basic reference grammar of Slovene*. Columbus, OH: Slavica

Dimitrova-Vulchanova, M. 1999. 'Clitics in the Slavic languages'. In van Riemsdijk (ed.): 83–122

Dobrovsky, J. (Dobrovský) 1822. *Institutiones lingua slavicae dialecti veteris*. 2nd edn. Vienna: Schmid

Doroszewski, W. 1938. *Język polski w Stanach Zjednoczonych Ameryki*. Warsaw: Prace Towarzystwa Naukowego Warszawskiego, Wydział 1, Nr. 15

Dunn, J. A. 1988. 'Is there a tendency towards analyticity in Russian?' *Slavonic and East European Journal* **66**: 169–183

Ďurovič, Ľ. 1980. 'Slovak'. In Schenker and Stankiewicz (eds.): 211–228

1983. 'The case systems in the language of diaspora children'. In 'Lingua in diaspora: studies in the language of the second generation of Yugoslav immigrant children in Sweden.' *Slavica Lundensia* **9**: 21–94

Dyer, Donald L. 1992. *Word order in the simple Bulgarian sentence: a study in grammar, semantics and pragmatics.* Amsterdam, Atlanta, GA: Rodopi

Eckert, Eva (ed.) 1993. *Varieties of Czech: studies in Czech sociolinguistics.* Amsterdam, Atlanta: Rodopi

Elson, Mark J. 1976. 'The definite article in Bulgarian and Macedonian'. *Slavic and East European Journal* **20**: 273–279

1989. *Macedonian verb morphology. A structural analysis.* Columbus, OH: Slavica

Entwistle, W. J. and Morison, W. A. 1964. *Russian and the Slavonic languages.* 2nd edn. London: Faber and Faber

Fasske, H. and Michalk, S. 1981. *Grammatik der obersorbischen Schriftsprache der Gegenwart. Morphologie.* Bautzen: Domowina

Feldstein, Ronald F. (n.d.) *A concise Polish grammar.* Retrieved (22 August 2004) from: http://www.seelrc.org:8080/grammar/mainframe.jsp?nLanguageID=4

Ferguson, C. 1959. 'Diglossia'. *Word* **15**: 325–340

Feuillet, Jack 1996. *Grammaire synchronique du bulgare.* Paris: Institut d' études slaves

Fielder, Grace E. 1993. *The semantics and pragmatics of verbal categories in Bulgarian.* Lewiston: Edwin Mellen

Filin, F. P. (ed.) 1979. *Russkij jazyk. Ènciklopedija.* Moscow: Sovetskaja Ènciklopedija

Filipović, R. (ed.) 1982. *The English element in European languages.* Vol. 2. Zagreb: Institute of Linguistics, University of Zagreb

1990. *Anglicizmi u hrvatskom ili srpskom jeziku: poreklo – razvoj – značenje.* Zagreb: Jugoslavenska akademija znanosti i umjetnosti, Razred za filološke znanosti, knj. 70

Flier, Michael S. and Brecht, Richard D. (eds.) 1985. *Issues in Russian morphosyntax.* Los Angeles: *UCLA Slavic Studies* 10. Distributed by Slavica

Flier, Michael S. and Timberlake, Alan (eds.) 1984. *The scope of Slavic aspect.* Columbus, OH: Slavica

Frančić, Vilim 1963. *Gramatyka opisowa języka serbo-chorwackiego.* Warsaw: PWN

Franks, Steven 1995. *Parameters of Slavic morphosyntax.* New York: Oxford University Press

Franolic, Branko 1984. *An historical survey of literary Croatian.* Paris: Nouvelles Editions Latines

1988. *Language policy in Yugoslavia (with special reference to Croatian).* Paris: Nouvelles Editions Latines

Friedman, Victor A. 1977. *The grammatical categories of the Macedonian infinitive.* Columbus, OH: Slavica

1993. 'Macedonian'. In Comrie and Corbett (eds.): 249–305

2002. *Macedonian.* Munich: Lincom

(n.d.) *Macedonian.* Retrieved (22 August 2004) from: http://www.seelrc.org:8080/grammar/mainframe.jsp?nLanguageID=6

Friedrich, Paul 1966. 'Structural implications of Russian pronominal usage'. In William O. Bright (ed.), *Sociolinguistics.* The Hague: Mouton: 214–259

1972. 'Social context and semantic feature: the Russian pronominal usage'. In J. J. Gumperz and D. Hymes (eds.), *Directions in sociolinguistics,* New York: Holt, Rinehart and Winston: 270–300

Fryščák, M. 1978. 'The two official languages of Czechoslovakia'. In Schmalstieg and Magner (eds.): 343–352

Gajda, Stanisław *et al.* (eds.) 2002. *Język w przestrzeni społecznej.* Opole: Uniw. Opolski

Galler, M. 1972. *Soviet prison camp speech: a survivor's glossary.* Madison, WI: University of Wisconsin Press

Gamkrelidze, T. V. and Ivanov, V. V. 1991. *Indo-European and the Indo-Europeans.* Berlin: Mouton de Gruyter

Garde, Paul 1976. *Histoire de l'accentuation slave.* Paris: Institut d'Etudes Slaves. 2 vols.

Garvin, P. L. 1959. 'The standard language problem: concepts and methods'. *Anthropological Linguistics* 1: 28–31

Georgiev, V. V. 1981. *Introduction to the history of the Indo-European languages.* 3rd edn. Sofia: BAN

Georgieva, Elena *et al.* (eds.) 1989. *Istorija na novobălgarskija knižoven ezik.* Sofia: BAN

Gołąb, Z. 1992. *The origins of the Slavs – a linguist's view.* Columbus, OH: Slavica

Golub', I. B. 1976. *Stilistika sovremennogo russkogo literaturnogo jazyka. Leksika. Fonetika.* Moscow: Vysšaja škola

Gorbačevič, K. S. 1971. *Izmenenie norm russkogo literaturnogo jazyka.* Leningrad: Prosveščenie

1978a. *Normy sovremennogo russkogo literaturnogo jazyka.* Moscow: Prosveščenie

1978b. *Variantnost' slova i jazykovaja norma. Na materiale sovremennogo russkogo jazyka.* Leningrad: Nauka

Gray, Russell D. 2003. 'Language-tree divergence times support the Anatolian theory of Indo-European origin'. *Nature* **426**, 27 January 2003: 435–439

Greenberg, J. H. 1969. 'Some methods of dynamic comparison in linguistics'. In Jaan Puhvel (ed.), *Substance and structure of language.* Berkeley, CA: University of California Press: 147–203

(eds.) 1978. *Universals of human language.* 4 vols. Stanford: Stanford University Press

Greenberg, Marc 2000. *A historical phonology of the Slovene language.* Heidelberg: Winter

Grenoble, Lenora A. 2003. *Language policy in the Soviet Union.* Dordrecht etc.: Kluwer

Gvozdanović, J. 1980. *Tone and accent in standard Serbo-Croatian (with a synopsis of Serbo-Croatian phonology).* Vienna: Österreichische Akademie der Wissenschaften

Gyllin, Roger 1991. *The genesis of the modern Bulgarian literary language.* Uppsala: Acta Universitatis Upsaliensis, *Studia Slavica Upsaliensia* 30

Halle, M. 1959. *The sound pattern of Russian.* The Hague: Mouton

1971. 'Remarks on Slavic accentology'. *Linguistic Inquiry* 1: 1–19

Haugen, E. 1953. *The Norwegian language in America.* Philadelphia: University of Pennsylvania Press

Havránek, B. 1936. 'Vývoj spisovného jazyka českého'. *Československá vlastivěda III, 2: Spisovný jazyk český a slovenský.* Prague: Sfinx: 1–144

1963. 'Funkce spisovného jazyka. Vliv funkce spisovného jazyk na fonologickou a gramatickou strukturu spisovné češtiny. Úkoly spisovného jazyka a jeho kultura. K funkčnímu rozvrstvení spisovného jazyka'. *Studie o spisovném jazyce.* Prague: ČSAV: 11–68

Havránek, B. and Jedlička, A. 1986. *Česká mluvnice.* 5th edn. Prague: SPN

Havránek, B. and Weingart, M. (eds.) 1932. *Spisovná čeština a jazyková kultura.* Prague: Melantrich

Henzl, V. M. 1982. 'American Czech: a comparative study of linguistic modifications in immigrant and young children speech'. In Sussex (ed.): 33–46

Herman, Louis Jay 1975. *A dictionary of Slavic word families.* New York: Columbia University Press

Herrity, P. 1973. 'The role of the Matica and similar societies in the development of the
    Slavonic literary languages'. *Slavonic and East European Review* **51**: 368–386
1985. 'France Prešeren and the Slovene Literary Language'. In Stone and Worth (eds.):
    147–159
2000. *Slovene: a comprehensive grammar*. London and New York: Routledge
Hill, Peter 1982. 'Different codifications of a language'. In W. Girke (ed.), *Slavistische
    Linguistik* 1981. Referate des VII Konstanzer Slavistischen Arbeitstreffens (*Slavistische
    Beiträge* 160). Munich: Sagner: 48–63
1986. 'Das Bulgarische'. In Rehder (ed.): 20–32
Hill, Peter and Lehmann, Volkmar (eds.) 1988. *Standard language in the Slavic world*. Munich:
    Verlag Otto Sagner (*Slavistische Beiträge* 235)
Hingley, Ronald 1972. *A concise history of Russia*. London: Thames and Hudson
Horálek, K. [1955] 1962. *Úvod do studia slovanských jazyků*. 2nd edn. Prague: ČSAV
1992. *An introduction to the study of the Slavonic languages*. Translated from the Czech
    [Horálek 1962] and amended by Peter Herrity. Nottingham: Astra Press
Huddleston, Rodney and Pullum, Geoffrey K. 2002. *The Cambridge grammar of the English
    language*. Cambridge: Cambridge University Press
Hughes, Geoffrey 2000. *A history of English words*. Oxford and Malden, MA.: Blackwell
Huntley, David 1993. 'Old Church Slavonic'. In Comrie and Corbett (eds.): 125–187
Hüttl-Worth, G. 1978. 'Diglossija v drevnej Rusi'. *Wiener Slavistisches Jahrbuch* **24**:
    103–123
Ickovič, V. A. 1968. *Jazykovaja norma*. Moscow: Prosveščenie
Illič-Svityč, V. M. 1971–1976. *Opyt sravnenija nostratičeskix jazykov: semitoxamitskij,
    kartvel'skij, indoevropejskij, ural'skii, dravidijskij, altajskij*. [Ed. V. A. Dybo]. Moscow:
    Nauka
Illich-Svitych, V. M. [1963] 1979. *Nominal accentuation in Baltic and Slavic*. Translated by
    Richard L. Leed and Ronald F. Feldstein. Cambridge, MA: MIT Press
Iovine, Micaela S. 1984. 'The "Illyrian" language'. In Picchio and Goldblatt (eds.):
    101–156
Isačenko. See also Issatschenko
Isačenko, A. V. 1958. 'Kakova specifika literaturnogo dvujazyčija v istorii slavjanskix
    narodov?' *Voprosy jazykoznanija* **9**(3): 42–45
1968. *Die russische Sprache der Gegenwart. Teil I: Formenlehre*. Halle (Saale): Max
    Niemeyer Verlag
1976. *Opera selecta. Russische Gegenwartssprache, russische Sprachgeschichte, Probleme der
    slavischen Sprachwissenschaft*. Munich: Fink Verlag (*Forum Slavicum* 45)
Issatschenko, see also Isačenko
Issatschenko, A. V. 1975. *Mythen und Tatsachen über die Entwicklung der russischen
    Literatursprache*. Vienna: Sitzungsberichte (Österreichische Akademie der
    Wissenschaften. Philosophisch-Historische Klasse, 298. Bd., Abh. 5)
1980. 'Russian'. In Schenker and Stankiewicz (eds.): 119–142
1980–1983. *Geschichte der russischen Sprache*. 2 vols. Heidelberg: Carl Winter Verlag
Ivić, Pavle 1985. *Dijalektologija srpskohrvatskog jezika: uvod u štokavsko narečje*. 2nd edn.
    Beograd: Matica Srpska
1986. 'Funkcionalna nosivost prozodijskih sistema u kajkavskim govorima'. *Filologija*
    14: 129–144
1991a. *O slovenskim jezicima i dijalektima*. Niš: Prosveta
[1958] 1991b. *Srpskohrvatski dijalekti: njihova struktura i razvoj*. Sremski Karlovci: Izd.
    Knjiž. Zorana Stojanovića
1998. *Pregled istorije srpskog jezika*. Sremski Karlovci, Novi Sad: Z. Stojanović

Jachnow, Helmut 1973. 'Zur sozialen Implikation des Gebrauches von Anredepronomen (mit besonderer Berücksichtigung des Russischen)'. *Zeitschrift für slavische Philologie* **37**: 343–355

1978. *Wortbildung und ihre Modellierung: Anhand des Serbokroatischen Verbalbereiches.* Wiesbaden: Harrassowitz

(ed.) 1984. *Handbuch des Russisten.* Wiesbaden: Otto Harrassowitz

Jahić, Dževad *et al.* 2000. *Gramatika bosanskoga jezika.* Zenica: Dom Štampe

Jakobson, Roman 1929. *Remarques sur l'évolution phonologique du russe comparée à celle des autres langues slaves.* Prague: TCLP (Klaus Reprint 1968)

1936. 'Beitrag zur allgemeinen Kasuslehre. Gesamtbedeutungen der russischen Kasus'. *Travaux du Cercle Linguistique de Prague 6.* Reprinted in translation as: 'Contribution to the general theory of case: general meanings of the Russian cases', in Jakobson 1984: 59–103

1948. 'Russian conjugation'. *Word* **4**: 155–167. Also in Roman Jakobson, *Russian and Slavic grammar. Studies 1931–1981.* Berlin: Mouton, 1984: 15–26

1955. *Slavic languages. A condensed survey.* Columbia University, New York: King's Crown Press

1984. *Russian and Slavic grammar: Studies 1931–1981.* Berlin, New York: Mouton. Edited by Linda R. Waugh and Morris Halle

Janda, Laura A. and Townsend, Charles E. 2000. *Czech.* Munich: Lincom Europa

(n.d.) *Czech.* Retrieved (22 August 2004) from: http://www.seelrc.org:8080/grammar/mainframe.jsp?nLanguageID = 2

Janko-Trinickaja, N. A. 2001. *Slovoobrazovanie v sovremennom russkom jazyke.* Moscow: Indrik

Jassem, W. 1964. *Fonetyka języka angielskiego.* Warsaw: PAN

Joseph, Brian 1983. *The synchrony and diachrony of the Balkan infinitive.* Cambridge: Cambridge University Press

Jutronić-Tihomirović, D. 1985. *Hrvatski jezik u SAD.* Split: Logos

Kalogjera, D. 1985. 'Attitudes toward Serbo-Croatian language varieties'. *International Journal of the Sociology of Language* **52**: 93–109

Karolak, Stanisław 2002. *Podstawowe struktury składniowe języka polskiego.* Warsaw: Slawistyczny Ośrodek Wydawniczy

Karskij, E. F. 1955. *Belorusy. Jazyk belorusskogo naroda.* Moscow: AN SSSR. Originally published in Warsaw, 1908–1912. Belarusian version 1992

Katičić, R. 1984. 'The making of standard Serbo-Croat'. In Picchio and Goldblatt (eds.), vol. I: 261–295

Keipert, H. 1985. 'Old and new problems of the Russian literary language (arguments for a new kind of Russian linguistic history)'. In Stone and Worth (eds.): 215–224

Kiparsky, V. 1963–1975. *Russische historische Grammatik. Band I: Die Entwicklung des Lautsystems (1963); Band II: Die Entwicklung des Formensystems (1967); Band III: Entwicklung des Wortschatzes (1975).* Heidelberg: Carl Winter Verlag. (Translation of Band I by J. I. Press: *Russian Historical Grammar*, Ann Arbor: Ardis, 1979.)

Kirkwood, M. (ed.) 1989. *Language planning in the Soviet Union.* London: Macmillan and School of Slavonic and East European Studies, University of London

Klemensiewicz, Z., Lehr-Spławiński, T. and Urbańczyk, S. 1981. *Gramatyka historyczna języka polskiego.* 4th edn Warsaw: PAN. (1st edn. 1955)

Kloss, H. 1952. *Entwicklung neuer Germanischer Kultursprachen.* Munich: Pohl

1967.' "Abstand languages" and "ausbau languages" '. *Anthropological Linguistics* **9**: 29–41

Klymenko, N. F. 1998. *Slovotvirna morfemika sučasnoji ukrains'koji literaturnoji movy.* Kiev: Inst. movoznavstva NAN

Kočev, I. (ed.) 2001. *Bălgarski dialekten atlas.* 3 vols. Sofia: BAN; KK "Trud"

Kolesov, V. V. 1998. *Russkaja reč': včera, segodnja, zavtra.* St. Petersburg: Iuna

Koneski, B. [1961–1966] 1967–1981. *Gramatika na makenskiot literaturen jazik. So srpskohrvatski tolkuvanja.* 2nd edn. Skopje: Kultura

1968. *The Macedonian language in the development of the Slavonic literary languages.* Translated by I. Kovilovska-Poposka and G. W. Reid. Skopje: Kultura

1980. 'Macedonian'. In Schenker and Stankiewicz (eds.): 53–63

1983. *A historical phonology of the Macedonian language. With a survey of the Macedonian dialects and a map by B. Vidoeski.* Translated by Victor A. Friedman. Heidelberg: Carl Winter

Kopečný, F. [1964/1976] 1981. *Základní všeslovanská slovní zásoba.* Brno: ČSAV

Kordić, Snježana 1997. *Serbo-Croatian.* Munich: Lincom

Koschmieder, Erwin 1977. *Phonationslehre des Polnischen.* Munich: Fink

1987. *Aspektologie des Polnischen.* Neuried: Hieronymus

Kotova, N. V. and Janakiev, M. 1973. 'Glottometričeskij podxod k voprosu o blizosti slavjanskix jazykov'. *Slavjanskaja filologija* vyp. **9**: 238–260

Kožina, M. N. 1977. *Stilistika russkogo jazyka.* Moscow: Prosveščenie

Kozlovskij, V. 1986. *Argo russkoj gomoseksual'noj subkul'tury. Materialy k izučeniju.* Benson, VT: Chalidze Publications

Krámský, Jiří 1969. *The word as a linguistic unit.* The Hague: Mouton

Kreindler, I. (ed.) 1982. *The changing status of Russian in the Soviet Union.* The Hague etc.: Mouton

1985. 'The non-Russian languages and the challenge of Russian: the eastern versus the western tradition'. In Kreindler (ed.) 1985: 345–367

(ed.) 1985. *Sociolinguistic perspectives on Soviet national languages: their past, present and future.* Berlin: Mouton de Gruyter

Kreusler, A. 1963. *The teaching of modern foreign languages in the Soviet Union.* Leiden: Brill

Krysin, L. P. (ed.) 1974. *Russkij jazyk po dannym massovogo obsledovanija.* Moscow: Nauka

Kučera, H. 1958. 'Inquiry into coexistent phonemic systems in Slavic languages'. In *American contributions to the Fourth International Congress of Slavists (Moscow).* The Hague: Mouton: 169–189

1961. *The phonology of Czech.* The Hague: Mouton

1984. 'Aspect in negative imperatives'. In Flier and Timberlake (eds.): 118–128

Kuraszkiewicz, W. 1963. *Zarys dialektologii wschodniosłowiańskiej.* 2nd edn. Warsaw: PAN

Kuryłowicz, J. 1964. *The inflectional categories of Indo-European.* Heidelberg: Carl Winter

L'Hermitte, René 1987. *Science et perversion idéologique: Marr, marrisme, marristes.* Paris: Institut du monde soviétique et de l'Europe Centrale et Orientale, Cultures et sociétés de l'est, 8

Lehiste, I. and Ivić, P. 1963. *Accent in Serbo-Croatian: an experimental study.* Ann Arbor, MI: University of Michigan

Lehiste, Ilse and Ivić, Pavle 1986. *Word and sentence prosody in Serbocroatian.* Cambridge, MA: MIT Press

Lekov, Ivan 1955. *Edinstvo i nacionalno svoeobrazie na slavjanskite ezici v texnija osnoven rečnikov fond.* Sofia: BAN

1958. *Slovoobrazovatelni sklonnosti na slavianskite ezici.* Sofia: BAN

Lencek, Rado L. 1982. *The structure and history of the Slovene language.* Columbus, OH: Slavica

1984. 'The modern Slovene language question: an essay in sociolinguistic interpretation'. In Picchio and Goldblatt (eds.), vol. I: 297–317

1985. 'On sociolinguistic determinants in the evolution of Slavic literary languages'. In Stone and Worth (eds.): 39–52

Lencek, Rado L. and Magner, T. F. (eds.) 1976. *The dilemma of the melting pot.* Philadelphia, PA: Pennsylvania University Press. (*General Linguistics* 16: 2–3)

Levinson, S. 1983. *Pragmatics*. Cambridge: Cambridge University Press
Lifanov, K. V. 2001. 'Metod rekonstrukcii i problema vozniknovenija slovackogo
    literaturnogo jazyka'. *Australian Slavonic and East European Studies* **15**: 5–19
Lingua in Diaspora. 1983. *Studies in the Language of the Second Generation of Yugoslav
    Immigrant Children in Sweden*. (*Slavica Lundensia* 9)
Lipson, Alexander 1968. *A Russian Course*. Cambridge, MA: Slavica
Logar, Tine and Rigler, Jakob 1986. *Karta slovenskih narečij*. Ljubljana: Geodetski zavod SRS
Lorentz, F. A. 1919. *Kaschubische Grammatik*. Danzig: Gedania (repr. 1971)
    1958–1962. *Gramatyka pomorska*. 2 vols. Wrocław: Ossolineum
Lötsch, R. 1963. 'Das Problem der obersorbisch-niedersorbischen Sprachgrenze'. *Zeitschrift
    für Slawistik* **8**: 172–183
Lunt, Horace G. 1952. *Grammar of the Macedonian literary language*. Skopje: Državno
    Knigoizdatelstvo na NR Makedonija
    [1955] 2001. *Old Church Slavonic grammar*. 7th rev. edn. Berlin, New York: Mouton de
    Gruyter
McMillin, Arnold 1980. 'Belorussian'. In Schenker and Stankiewicz (eds.): 105–117
Magner, Thomas F. (ed.) 1976a. *Slavic linguistics and language teaching*. Columbus,
    OH: Slavica
    1976b. *A Zagreb kajkavian dialect*. University Park, PA: Pennsylvania State Studies 18
    1978. 'Diglossia in Split'. In Schmalstieg and Magner (eds.) 400–436
    1991. *Introduction to the Croatian and Serbian language*. Rev. edn. University Park:
    Pennsylvania State University Press (1st edn. 1956)
Magner, Thomas F. and Matejka, Ladislav 1971. *Word-accent in modern Serbo-Croatian*.
    University Park, Pennsylvania and London: Pennsylvania State University Press
Magocsi, Paul R. 1984. 'The language question among the Subcarpathian Rusyns'. In Picchio
    and Goldblatt (eds.), vol. II: 65–86
    1992. 'The birth of a new nation, or the return of an old problem? The Rusyns of East
    Central Europe'. *Canadian Slavonic Papers* **34**(3): 199–233
Maksimov, V. I. *et al.* 1992. *Slovar' perestroiki*. St. Petersburg: Zlatoust
Maldžieva, Vjara 1995. *Non-inflected parts of speech in the Slavonic languages: syntactic
    characteristics*. Warsaw: Wyd. Energeia
Mallory, J. P. 1989. *In search of the Indo-Europeans: language, archaeology and myth*. New
    York: Thames & Hudson
Mańczak, Witold 2002. *O pochodzeniu i dialekcie Kaszubów*. Gdańsk: Oficyna Czec
Marchand, Hans 1969. *The categories and types of present-day English word-formation;
    a synchronic-diachronic approach*. Munich: C. H. Becksche Verlagsbuchhandlung
Marder, Stephen 1992. *A supplementary Russian–English dictionary*. Columbus, OH: Slavica
Marszk, Doris 1988. 'On the linguistic character of the Russian *prostorečie*'. In Hill and
    Lehmann (eds.): 58–79
Marvan, J. 1979. *Prehistoric Slavic contraction*. (trans W. Gray). University Park, PA, and
    London: Pennsylvania State University Press
Mathesius, V. [1929] 1964. 'Functional linguistics'. In J. Vachek (ed.) *A Prague school reader
    in linguistics*. Bloomington, IN: Indiana University Press: 121–142
    1947. *Čeština a obecný jazykozpyt*. Prague: Melantrich
Mathiesen, Robert 1984. 'The Church Slavonic language question: an overview (IX–XX
    centuries)'. In Picchio and Goldblatt (eds.), vol. I: 45–65
Mayo, P. J. 1982. 'The Byelorussian language: its rise and fall and rise and ...'. In
    F. E. Knowles and J. I. Press (eds.), *Papers in Slavonic Linguistics*, vol. I. Birmingham:
    University of Aston in Birmingham: 163–184
    1993. 'Belorussian'. In Comrie and Corbett (eds.): 887–946

Mečkovskaja, N. B. 2003. *Belorusskij jazyk: sociolingvističeskie očerki.* Munich: Sagner
Meillet, A. 1934. *Le slave commun.* 2nd edn. Paris: Champion
   1967. *The Indo-European dialects.* (trans. by S. N. Rosenberg of *Les dialectes indo-européens,* 1908). University of Alabama: University of Alabama Press
Mel'ničuk, A. S. (ed.) 1966. *Vstup do porivnjal'no-istoryčnoho vyvčennja slov'jans'kyx mov.* Kiev: Naukova dumka
   1986. *Istoričeskaja tipologija slavjanskix jazykov.* Kiev: Naukova dumka
Mencken, H. L. [1919] 1936. *The American language.* 4th edn. New York: Alfred A. Knopf
Meyerstein, G. P. 1969. 'Interference in prepositional phrases: immigrant Slovak in America'. *Lingua* **22**: 63–80
Micklesen, Lew R. 1978. 'Czech sociolinguistic problems'. In Schmalstieg and Magner (eds.): 437–455
Miklosich, F. 1875–1883. *Vergleichende Grammatik der slavischen Sprachen.* 2nd edn. Vienna: W. Braumüller
Miodunka, W. (ed.) 1990. *Język polski w świecie.* Cracow: PAN
Mistrík, J. 1976. *Retrográdny slovník slovenčiny.* Bratislava: UK
   1985. 'The modernisation of contemporary Slovak'. In Stone and Worth (eds.): 71–76
Mluvnice češtiny 1986–1987. 1: Fonetika, fonologie, morfonologie a morfemika, tvoření slov. Ed. M. Dokulil, K. Horálek, J. Hůrková, M. Knappová and J. Petr. 2: Tvarosloví. Ed. M. Komárek, J. Kořenský, J. Petr and J. Veselková (1986). 3: Skladba. Ed. F. Daneš, M. Grepl and Z. Hlavsa (1987). Praha: Academia
Moguš, Milan 1995. *A history of the Croatian language: toward a common standard.* Zagreb: Globus (translation of 1993 original)
Mološnaja, T. N. 2001. *Grammatičeskie kategorii glagola v sovremennyx slavjanskix literaturnyx jazykax.* Moscow: Inst. slavjanovedenija RAN
Moszyński, L. 1984. *Wstęp do filologii słowiańskiej.* Warsaw: PWN
Mucke, Karl Ernst [1891] 1965. *Historische und vergleichende Laut- und Formenlehre der niedersorbischen (niederlausizisch-wendischen) Sprache: mit besonderer Berucksichtigung der Grenzdialekte und des Obersorbischen.* Leipzig: Zentral-Antiquariat der Deutschen Demokratischen Republik
Nakhimovsky, A. D. 1976. 'Social distribution of forms of address in contemporary Russian'. *International Review of Slavic Linguistics* **1**(1): 79–118
Naylor, Kenneth E. 1980. 'Serbo-Croatian'. In Schenker and Stankiewicz (eds.): 65–83
Neidle, Carol 1988. *The role of case in Russian syntax.* Dordrecht, Boston: Kluwer
Neščimenko, G. P. 1999. *Ètničeskij jazyk: opyt funkcional'noj differenciacii: na materiale sopostavitel'nogo izučenija slavjanskix jazykov.* Munich: Sagner
Nikol'skij, L. B. 1976. *Sinxronnaja sociolingvistika.* Moscow: Nauka
Nikolaeva, T. M. [1969] 1977. *Frazovaja intonacija slavjanskix jazykov.* Moscow: Nauka
Norman, Jerry 1988. *Chinese.* Cambridge: Cambridge University Press
Obratnyj slovar' russkogo jazyka. 1974. Moscow: "Sovetskaja Ènciklopedija"
Obščeslavjanskij lingvisticeskij atlas: materialy i issledovanija 1985–1987. Sbornik naučnyx trudov. Ed. V. V. Ivanov. Moscow: Nauka. 1989
Ondrus, P. 1976. 'Praslovanský základ slovenčiny v slovnej zásobe'. *Studia academica Slovaca* **5**: 295–316
Ostaszewska, Danuta and Tambor, Jolanta 2000. *Fonetyka i fonologia współczesnego języka polskiego.* Warsaw: PWN
Otwinowska-Kasztelanic, Agnieszka 2000. *A study of the lexico-semantic and grammatical influence of English on the Polish of the younger generation of Poles (19–35 years of age).* Warsaw: Dialog
Panov, M. V. (ed.) 1968. *Russkoe jazyk i sovetskoe obščestvo.* Moscow: Nauka

Panzer, B. 1967. *Der slavische Konditional. Form, Gebrauch, Funktion*. Munich: Fink
1975. *Strukturen des Russischen*. Munich: Fink
1991a. *Die slavischen Sprachen in Gegenwart und Geschichte: Sprachstrukturen und Verwandtschaft*. Frankfurt an Main: Peter Lang
1991b. *Handbuch des serbokroatischen Verbs: Derivation*. Heidelberg: Winter
Patton, Frederick R. 1988. 'Colloquial Russian and urban substandard speech: an overview'. *Russian Language Journal* **42**: 133–144
Pauliny, E., Ružička, J. and Štolc, J. 1968. *Slovenská gramatika*. 5th rev. edn. Bratislava: SPN
Perelmuter, Joanna 1976. 'Substandard usage: Russian and Polish lexicographical attitudes'. In Magner (ed.): 94–111
Picchio, Riccardo 1984. 'Guidelines for a comparative study of the language question among the Slavs'. In Picchio and Goldblatt (eds.), vol. I: 1–42
Picchio, Riccardo and Goldblatt, Harvey (eds.) 1984. *Aspects of the Slavic language question*. 2 vols. New Haven, Conn.: Yale Concilium on International and Area Studies. (Yale Russian and East European Publications, distributed by Slavica Publishers)
Pinto, Vivian 1980. 'Bulgarian'. In Schenker and Stankiewicz (eds.): 37–51
Pljušč, N. P. (ed.) 2000. *Sučasna ukrajins'ka literaturna mova*. 2nd ed. Kiev: Vyšča škola
2002. *Sučasna ukrajins'ka literaturna mova: fonetyka*. Kiev: Kyjivs'kyj VPCS
Polański, K. 1980. 'Sorbian (Lusatian)'. In Schenker and Stankiewicz (eds.): 229–245
1993. 'Polabian'. In Comrie and Corbett (eds.): 795–824
Polovina, Vesna 1984. 'Upotreba jednine i množine ličnih zamenica u obraćanju sagovorniku u savremenom srpskohrvatskom jeziku'. *Naučni sastanak slavista u Vukove dane* **13**: 185–195
Požarickaja, S. K. 1997. *Russkaja dialektologija*. Moscow: MGU
Priestly, T. M. S. 1983. 'On "drift" in Indo-European gender systems'. *Journal of Indo-European Studies* **11**: 339–363
1993. 'Slovenian'. In Comrie and Corbett (eds.): 388–451
Pugh, Stefan M. and Press, Ian 1999. *Ukrainian: a comprehensive grammar*. London, New York: Routledge
Rappaport, Gilbert 1990. 'Sytuacja językowa Amerykanów polskiego pochodzenia w Texasie'. In Miodunka (ed.): 159–178
Raskin, V. 1978. 'Structuralism and after: notes on the current Soviet linguistic scene'. *Slavica Hierosolymitana* **2**: 257–283
Rehder, P. (ed.) 1986. *Einführung in die slavischen Sprachen*. Darmstadt: Wissenschaftliche Buchgesellschaft
Robins, R. H. 1967. *A short history of linguistics*. London: Longmans
Romanski, Stojan (ed.). 1954–1959. *Rečnik na săvremennija bălgarski knižoven ezik*. Sofia: BAN
Rothstein, R. 1976. '*Kultura języka* in twentieth century Poland and her neighbours' In Magner (ed): 58–81
Rothstein, Robert A. 1980. 'Gender and reference in Polish and Russian'. In Chvany and Brecht (eds.): 79–97
1993. 'Polish'. In Comrie and Corbett (eds.): 686–758
Rubach, J. 1993. *The lexical phonology of Slovak*. Oxford, New York: Oxford University Press
Ružička, J. 1970. *Spisovná slovenčina v Československu*. Bratislava: SAV
Ryazanova-Clarke, Larissa and Wade, Terence 1999. *The Russian language today*. London, New York: Routledge
Šadyko, Stanislav 2000. *Abbreviatury v russkom jazyke (v sopostavlenii s polskim)*. Moscow: RGPU
Saint-Jacques, B. 1979. 'The languages of immigrants: sociolinguistic aspects of immigration in Canada'. In J. K. Chambers (ed.), *The languages of Canada*. Ottawa: Didier: 207–225

Samardžija, Marko (ed.) 1993. *Jezični purizam u NDH*. Zagreb: Hrvatska sveučilišna naklada
    1999. *Norme i normiranje hrvatskoga standardnoga jezika*. Zagreb: Matica hrvatska
Šanskij, see also Shanskii
Šanskij, N. M. 1975. *Russkij jazyk. Leksika. Slovoobrazovanie*. Moscow: Prosveščenie
Šaumjan, S. K. 1958. *Istorija sistemy differencial'nyx èlementov v pol'skom jazyke*. Moscow: AN SSSR
Saussure, Ferdinand de 1916. *Cours de linguistique générale*. Trans. by Roy Harris and published as *Course in general linguistics*. London: Duckworth, 1983
Scatton, Ernest A. 1984. *A reference grammar of modern Bulgarian*. Columbus, OH: Slavica
    1993. 'Bulgarian'. In Comrie and Corbett (eds.): 188–248
Schaarschmidt, Gunter 1997. *A historical phonology of the upper and lower Sorbian languages*. Heidelberg: Winter
    2002. *Upper Sorbian*. Munich: Lincom
Schenker, Alexander M. 1954. 'Polish conjugation'. *Word* **10**: 469–481
    1964. *Polish declension. A descriptive analysis*. The Hague: Mouton
    1980. 'Polish'. In Schenker and Stankiewicz (eds.): 195–210
    1993. 'Proto-Slavonic'. In Comrie and Corbett (eds.): 60–121
    1995. *The dawn of Slavic*. New Haven, London: Yale University Press.
Schenker, Alexander M. and Stankiewicz, Edward (eds.) 1980. *The Slavic literary languages: formation and development*. New Haven, Conn.: Yale Concilium on International and Area Studies. Distributed by Slavica
Schleicher, A. 1871. *Laut- und Formenlehre der polabischen Sprache*. St Petersburg: Commissionäre der Kaiserlichen Akademie der Wissenschaften, Eggers and Co. (reprint Wiesbaden, 1967)
Schmalstieg, William R. and Magner, Thomas F. (eds.) 1978. *Sociolinguistic problems in Czechoslovakia, Hungary, Romania and Yugoslavia*. Columbus, OH: Slavica
Schupbach, R. D. 1984. *Lexical specialization in Russian*. Columbus, OH: Slavica
Schuster-Šewc. See also Šewc
Schuster-Šewc, H. 1959. 'Sprache und ethnische Formation in der Entwicklung des Sorbischen'. *Zeitschrift für Slawistik* **4**: 577–595
    1996. *Grammar of the Upper Sorbian language: phonology and morphology*. Translation of Šewc, 1968 by Gary H. Toops. Munich, Newcastle: Lincom
Selkirk, Elisabeth O. 1982. *The syntax of words*. Cambridge, MA: MIT Press
Ševel'ov, Jurij (Shevelov, G.) 2002. *Istorična fonolohija ukrajins'koji movy*. Kharkov: Akta (trans. of Shevelov, 1979)
Šewc, Hinc 1968. *Gramatika hornjoserbskeje rěče. 1: fonematika a morfologija*. Bautzen: Domowina
Šewc-Schuster (Šewc), Hinc 1976. *Gramatika hornjoserbskeje rěče. 2: syntaksa*. Bautzen: Domowina
Sgall, P. 1960. 'Obixodno-razgovornyj česskij jazyk'. *Voprosy jazykoznanija* **9**(2): 11–20
Sgall, P. and Hronek, J. 1992. *Čeština bez příkras*. Prague: H & H
Sgall, P., Hronek, J., Stich, A. and Horecký, J. 1992. *Variation in language: code switching in Czech as a challenge for sociolinguistics*. Amsterdam, Philadelphia: J. Benjamins.
Shanskii, N. M. 1969. *Russian lexicology*. Trans. by B. S. Johnson and ed. by J. E. S. Cooper Oxford, New York: Pergamon Press
Shapiro, Michael 1968. *Russian phonetic variants and phonostylistics*. Berkeley, Los Angeles: University of California Press
Shevelov, see also Ševel'ov

Shevelov, George Y. 1964. *A prehistory of Slavic*. Morningside Heights, NY: Columbia University Press

(Šerex, Ju.) 1979. *A historical phonology of the Ukrainian language*. Heidelberg: Carl Winter Verlag

1980. 'Ukrainian'. In Schenker and Stankiewicz (eds.): 143–160

1989. *The Ukrainian language in the first half of the 20th century (1900–1941). Its state and status*. Cambridge, MA: Harvard University Press

1993. 'Ukrainian'. In Comrie and Corbett (eds.): 947–998

Shibatani, Masayoshi 1990. *The languages of Japan*. Cambridge: Cambridge University Press

Short, David 1993a. 'Czech'. In Comrie and Corbett (eds.): 455–532

1993b. 'Slovak'. In Comrie and Corbett (eds.): 533–592

1996. 'The westernization of Czech and Estonian in commerce and advertising since the "Velvet" and "Singing" revolutions'. In D. Short, *Essays in Czech and Slovak language and literature*, London: SSEES, University of London: 193–211

Širokova, A. G. and Gudkov, V. P. (eds.) 1977. *Slavjanskie jazyki*. Moscow: Izd-vo Moskovskogo universiteta

Sjatkovskij, S. and Tixomirov, T. S. (eds.) 1997. *Problemy izučenija otnošenij èkvivalentnosti v slavjanskix jazykax*. Moscow: Dialog-MGU

Skachinsky, A. 1972. *Slovar' blatnogo zhargona v SSSR*. Wisconsin: University of Wisconsin Press

Skalička, V. 1966. 'K voprosu o tipologii'. *Voprosy jazykoznanija* **15**(4): 22–30

Sławski, F. 1962. *Zarys dialektologii południowosłowiańskiej*. Warsaw: PAN

Smirnov, L. N. (ed.) 1997. *Tendencija internacionalizacii v sovremennyx slavjanskix jazykax*. Moscow: Institut

Smó'kowa, T. 1976. *Nowe słownictwo polskie. Badanie rzeczowników*. Warsaw: Ossolineum

2001. *Neologizmy we współczesnej leksyce polskiej*. Cracow: Wyższa Szkoła Humanistyczna, w Pu'tusku

Smolicz, J. J. 1979. *Culture and education in a plural society*. Canberra: Curriculum Development Centre

Sorbischer Sprachatlas. 1965–1996. Ed. H. Fasske, H. Jentsch and S. Michalk. 15 vols. Bautzen: Domowina

Stankiewicz, E. 1965. 'Neutralizacja rodzaju nijakiego w dialektach słowieńskich'. *Studia z filologii polskiej i słowiańskiej* **5**: 179–187. Reprinted as 'The fate of the neuter in the Slovenian dialects'. In Stankiewicz, 1986: 143–152

1968a. *Declension and gradation of Russian substantives in contemporary standard Russian*. The Hague: Mouton

1968b. 'The grammatical genders of the Slavic languages'. *International Journal of Slavic Linguistics and Poetics* **11**: 27–41

(tr. and ed.) 1972. *A Baudouin de Courtenay anthology*. Bloomington, IN, and London: Indiana University Press

1979. *Studies in Slavic morphophonemics and accentology*. Ann Arbor, Michigan: University of Michigan.

1980. 'Slovenian'. In Schenker and Stankiewicz (eds.): 85–102

1986. *The Slavic languages. Unity in diversity*. Berlin, etc.: Mouton de Gruyter

1993. *The accentual patterns of the Slavic languages*. Stanford, CA: Stanford University Press

Stegherr, Marc 2003. *Das Russinische: Kulturhistorische und soziolinguistische Aspekte*. Munich: Sagner

Stewart, W. A. 1968. 'A sociolinguistic typology for describing national multilingualism'. In J. Fishman (ed.), *Readings in the sociology of language*, The Hague: Mouton: 531–545

Stieber, Z. 1930. 'Z zagadnień podziałów dialektycznych grupy zachodnio-słowiańskiej'. *Lud Słowiański* 1: 212–245

1965. *Zarys dialektologii zachodniosłowiańskiej*. 2nd edn. Warsaw: PAN

1969–1973. *Zarys gramatyki porównawczej języków słowiańskich. I. Fonologia; II. zesz. 1: Fleksja imienna; II. zesz. 2: Fleksja werbalna*. Warsaw: PWN

Stockwell, Robert and Minkova, Donka 2001. *English words. History and structure*. Cambridge: Cambridge University Press

Stolz, Benjamin A., Titunik, I. R. and Doležel, Lubomir (eds.) 1984. *Language and literary theory: in Honor of Ladislav Matejka*. Ann Arbor, MI: University of Michigan, Department of Slavic Languages and Literatures

Stone, Gerald 1972. *The smallest Slavonic nation. The Sorbs of Lusatia*. London: University of London, The Athlone Press

1977. 'Address in the Slavonic languages'. *Slavonic and East European Review* 55: 491–505

1985. 'Language planning and the Lower Sorbian literary language'. In Stone and Worth (eds.): 99–104

1986. 'Das Ober- und Niedersorbische'. In Rehder (ed.): 96–102

1993a. 'Sorbian'. In Comrie and Corbett (eds.): 593–685

1993b. 'Cassubian'. In Comrie and Corbett (eds.): 759–794

2002. *Upper Sorbian–English dictionary*. Budyšin: Domowina

Stone, Gerald and Worth, Dean S. (eds.) 1985. *The formation of the Slavonic literary languages. Proceedings of a conference held in memory of Robert Auty and Anne Pennington at Oxford, 6–11 July 1981*. Los Angeles: UCLA Slavic Studies 11. Distributed by Slavica

Suny, R. G. 1994. *The revenge of the past. Nationalism, revolution, and the collapse of the Soviet Union*. Cambridge: Cambridge University Press

Suprun, A. E. 1983. *Leksičeskaja tipologija slavjanskix jazykov*. Minsk: Izd-vo Belorusskogo universiteta

Sussex, Roland 1976. 'A new grammatical category of determiners in Polish?' *International Review of Slavic Linguistics* 1(2): 307–325

(ed.) 1982. *The Slavic languages in émigré communities*. Carbondale, Edmonton: Linguistic Research Inc.

(ed.) 1984. *The maintenance of the Slavonic languages abroad*. (*Melbourne Slavonic Studies* 18)

1994. 'On the language-hood of Sorbian'. *Australian Slavonic and East European Studies* 8(2): 59–80

Sussex, Roland and Eade, J. C. (eds.) 1985. *Culture and Nationalism in Nineteenth-Century Eastern Europe*. Columbus, OH: Slavica, and Canberra: Humanities Research Centre, Australian National University

Svane, G. O. 1958. *Grammatik der slovenischen Schriftsprache*. Copenhagen: Rosenkilde and Bagger

Švedova, N. Ju. *et al.* (eds.) 1970. *Grammatika sovremennogo russkogo literaturnogo jazyka*. Moscow: Nauka

(eds.) 1980. *Russkaja grammatika*. 2 vols. Moscow: Nauka

Svedstedt, Dag 1976. *Position of objective personal pronouns: a study of word order in modern Russian*. Stockholm: University and Almqvist & Wiksell

Šwela, Bogumił 1952. *Grammatik der niedersorbischen Sprache*. 2. Aufl., bearb. und hrsg. von Dr Frido Mětšk. Bautzen: Domowina-Verlag

Taszycki, W. 1928. 'Stanowisko języka łużyckiego'. In *Symbolae grammaticae in honorem Joannis Rozwadowski, II*. Cracow: Gebethner & Wolff: 127–138

Thelin, Nils B. (ed.) 1990. *Verbal aspect in discourse: contributions to the semantics of time and temporal perspective in Slavic and non-Slavic languages*. Amsterdam, Philadelphia: J. Benjamins

Thomas, George (ed.) 1977. *The languages and literatures of the non-Russian peoples of the Soviet Union*. Hamilton, Ontario: Interdepartmental Committee on Communist and East European Affairs, McMaster University

1989. 'The role of diglossia in the development of the Slavonic literary languages'. *Slavistična revija* **37**(1–3): 273–282

1991. *Linguistic purism*. London, New York: Longman. (*Studies in language and linguistics*)

Thomson, S. H. 1953. *Czechoslovakia in European history*. 2nd edn. Princeton: Princeton University Press

Timberlake, Alan 2003. *A reference grammar of Russian*. Cambridge: Cambridge University Press

Tixonov, A. N. 1985. *Slovoobrazovatel'nyj slovar' russkogo jazyka*. 2 vols. Moscow: Russkij jazyk

Tolstaja, S. M. 1998. *Morfonologija v strukture slavjanskix jazykov*. Moscow: Indrik

Tolstoj, I. I. (comp.) 1970. *Serbo-xorvatskij–russkij slovar'*. Moscow: Sovetskaja Ènciklopedija

Tomić, O. M. 1991. 'Macedonian as an Ausbau language'. In Clyne (ed.): 437–454

Topolińska, Zuzanna 1980. 'Kashubian'. In Schenker and Stankiewicz (eds.): 183–194

Toporišič, J. 1965–1970. *Slovenski knjižni jezik*. 4 vols. Maribor: Obzorja

1978. 'A language of a small minority in a multilingual state'. In Schmalstieg and Magner (eds.): 480–486

Townsend, Charles E. [1968] 1975. *Russian word-formation*. 2nd edn. Columbus, OH: Slavica

1981. *Czech through Russian*. Columbus, OH: Slavica

1984. 'Can aspect stand prosperity?' In Flier and Timberlake (eds.): 286–295

1990. *A description of spoken Prague Czech*. Columbus, OH: Slavica

Townsend, Charles E. and Janda, Laura A. 1996. *Common and comparative Slavic: phonology and inflection. With special attention to Russian, Czech, Serbo-Croatian, Bulgarian*. Columbus, OH: Slavica

Trautmann, R. 1923. *Balto-slavisches Wörterbuch*. Göttingen: Vandenhoeck & Ruprecht

Trudgill, Peter 1974. *Sociolinguistics*. Harmondsworth: Penguin

Unbegaun, B. O. 1932. 'Le calque dans les langues slaves littéraires'. *Revue des Etudes Slaves* **12**: 19–48

1935. *Les débuts de la language littéraire chez les serbes*. Paris: Champion

1972. *Russian surnames*. Oxford: Clarendon Press

Urbańczyk, S. *et al.* (eds.) 1978. *Encyklopedija wiedzy o języku polskim*. Wrocław, etc.: Ossolineum

Uzicanin, Nikolina S. 1995. *Bosnian–English, English–Bosnian dictionary*. New York: Hippocrene Books

Vaillant, A. 1950–1977. *Grammaire comparée des langues slaves*. Paris: IAC (Vols. 1–2), and Paris: Klincksieck (Vols. 3–5)

Vakurov, V. N. 1978. *Stilistika gazetnyx žanrov*. Moscow: Vysšaja škola

van Riemsdijk, H. 1999. 'Clitics: a state-of-the-art report'. In H. van Riemsdijk (ed.): 1–30

(ed.). 1999. *Clitics in the languages of Europe*. Berlin, New York: Mouton de Gruyter

Vasmer, Max (Fasmer) 1964–1973. *Ètimologičeskij slovar' russkogo jazyka*. 4 vols. Trans. and suppl. by O. N. Trubačev. Moscow: Progress

Videnov, Mixail 2003. *Bălgarska ezikova politika (v svetlinata na teorijata na knižovnite ezici): cikăl lekcii*. Sofia: Meždunarodno sociolingvističesko društestvo

Vinogradov, V. V. 1960. *Grammatika russkogo jazyka*. 3 vols. Moscow: IAN

Vinogradov, V. V. *et al.* (eds.) 1966. *Jazyki narodov SSSR. T.1. Indoevropejskie jazyki*. Moscow: Nauka

Vinokur, G. O. 1929. *Kul'tura jazyka*. 2nd edn. Moscow: Federacija

Wade, Terence [1992] 2000. *A comprehensive Russian grammar.* 2nd rev. edn. Oxford, Malden, MA: Blackwell

Walicki, A. 1975. *The Slavophile controversy: history of a conservative utopia in nineteenth-century Russian thought.* Trans. by H. Andrews-Rusiecka, Notre Dame, IN: University of Notre Dame Press

1982. *Philosophy and romantic nationalism: the case of Poland.* Oxford: Clarendon Press and New York: Oxford University Press

Weingart, M. 1949. *Československý typ církevnej slovančiny.* Bratislava: SAVU

Wexler, P. 1974. *Purism and language. A case study of modern Ukrainian and Belorussian nationalism (1840–1967).* Bloomington, IN: Indiana University

1979. 'The rise (and fall) of the modern Belorussian literary language'. *Slavonic and East European Review* **57**: 481–508

Wierzbicka, Anna 1980. *The case for surface case.* Ann Arbor: Karoma

Worth, Dean S. (ed.) 1972. *The Slavic word.* The Hague, Paris: Mouton

1975. 'Was there a "literary language" in Kievan Rus'?' *Russian Review* **34**(1): 1–9

Worth, Dean S., Kozak, Andrew S. and Johnson, Donald B. 1970. *Russian derivational dictionary.* New York: Elsevier

Zaliznjak, A. A. 1977. *Grammatičeskij slovar' russkogo jazyka. Slovoizmenenie.* Moscow: Russkij jazyk

Zemskaja, E. A. (ed.) 1973. *Russkaja razgovornaja reč'.* Moscow: Nauka

1996. *Russkij jazyk konca XX stoletija: 1985–1995.* Moscow: Jazyki russkoj kul'tury

Zwicky, Arnold M. 1977. *On clitics.* Bloomington, IN: Indiana University Linguistics Club

INDEX

Italic page numbers indicate presence of a table.

CPSIA information can be obtained
at www.ICGtesting.com
Printed in the USA
FSOW02n2339201216
28751FS

9 780521 294485